PARTY, STATE, AND
SOCIETY IN THE
RUSSIAN CIVIL WAR

PARTY, STATE, AND SOCIETY IN THE RUSSIAN CIVIL WAR

Explorations in Social History

EDITED BY

DIANE P. KOENKER,
WILLIAM G. ROSENBERG,
and RONALD GRIGOR SUNY

INDIANA UNIVERSITY PRESS

Bloomington and Indianapolis

This book was brought to publication with the assistance of a grant from the Andrew W. Mellon Foundation to the Russian and East European Institute, Indiana University, and the Center for Russian and East European Studies, University of Michigan.

© 1989 by Indiana University Press

Manufactured in the United States of America

Library of Congress Cataloging-in-Publication Data
Party, state, and society in the Russian Civil War : explorations in social history / edited by Diane P. Koenker, William G. Rosenberg, and Ronald Grigor Suny.
p.   cm. — (Indiana-Michigan series in Russian and East European studies)
Bibliography: p.
Includes index.
ISBN 0-253-33262-1. — ISBN 0-253-20541-7 (pbk.)
1. Soviet Union—History—Revolution, 1917–1921.   2. Soviet Union—Social conditions—1917–   3. Socialism—Soviet Union—History.
I. Koenker, Diane.   II.
Rosenberg, William G.   III. Suny,
Ronald Grigor.   IV. Series.
DK265.9.D45P37   1989
947.084′1—dc20
88-46042
CIP

1   2   3   4   5   93   92   91   90   89

CONTENTS

IV   The Bolsheviks and the Intelligentsia

V   Workers and Socialists

VI   The Legacy of the Civil War

INTRODUCTION

One of the most exciting and, as it turned out, influential collective intellectual enterprises in which scholars of Russian history and politics were engaged in recent years was the Seminar in Twentieth-Century Russian and Soviet Social History. From its first meeting in Philadelphia in 1980, the seminar, conceived initially by Moshe Lewin and Alfred Rieber of the University of Pennsylvania, brought together dozens of historians and political scientists to consider broad analytical problems that cut across the imagined dividing line of 1917. In contrast to the conference mode of scholarly gatherings, which generally invites scholars to present the results of their work, our efforts were deliberately structured to initiate new research and to allow a group of younger and older scholars to think creatively, in a small setting, about major problems of twentieth-century Russian and Soviet social history. The success of the seminar is evidenced by its duration, its popularity as a forum of scholarly discussion, and, we hope, its product, as demonstrated in this and forthcoming volumes.

The meeting on the social history of the Russian Civil War was the fourth in the series. The first raised general historiographical and conceptual issues and outlined plans for future meetings. The second explored problems of the Russian and Soviet peasantry. The third looked at the evolution of the tsarist and Soviet bureaucracies. At each meeting it became clear that many of the papers were more than works-in-progress and represented well-conceived and publishable work. Yet, the organizers were reluctant to turn the seminar into a setting for the presentation of finished work rather than a place where new ideas and tentative conclusions could be aired, challenged, reformulated, and defended. We wanted to remain open to false starts as well as significant new contributions. No one attending our sessions could doubt that freewheeling discussion contributes enormously to understanding important questions.

The editors of the present volume were the principal designers of the meeting on the Civil War, though the independence and areas of interest of the individual participants had an important effect on the ultimate shape of the project. That is why certain broad areas—such as the peasantry, the Red Army, and the party—are not represented in the essays published here. What the volume might lack in comprehensiveness is more than offset, however, by the new avenues of research taken by the authors. Not all papers presented at the conference were included, and one article by a participant that was not presented at the meeting has been added. Otherwise all the chapters in this book are considerably revised versions of the original presentations. Each reflects the important role of the commentators in shaping the final contributions. Introductions by the chairs of the sessions have been added, and the editors have attempted to sum up the discussion and comments after each section.

Reginald E. Zelnik contributed comments on the section dealing with workers and socialists.

Our goal has been to preserve the sense of exploration and revision that animated the seminar. We hope that the volume provides a sense of the spirit of intellectual inquiry that has been the core of the seminar itself, that it opens many new questions even as it attempts tentative answers to some old ones. Its success will be reflected in the further research on the Civil War that it stimulates.

We have subtitled the book "Explorations in Social History" to emphasize both the seminar's function as a forum for work in progress and its special perspective, the illumination of the history of society and not just of individuals, events, and ideas. The political and military history of the Russian Civil War has occupied historians for more than fifty years, and the political outlines of the years 1917–21 are by now well known.[1] For approximately six months after the Soviets took power in November 1917, opposition to Soviet rule largely took a political form. Bolshevik opponents hoped the long-awaited Constituent Assembly could reenfranchise them and protect their interests. When the assembly was dispersed in January 1918, political mobilization still dominated opposition activity, although officers loyal to the tsar were preparing in the south of Russia to restore the old order by force. Widespread military conflict did not begin until May 1918, when Czech troops enroute to Vladivostok took up arms against the Soviet government. Thereafter, successive armies in Siberia, Northern Russia, and South Russia waged war on the new regime. These White armies received varying amounts of aid from foreign governments concerned to protect their own interests. In the process, a Red Army was created from the nucleus of the revolutionary Red Guards and radical soldiers of the tsar, and a central state emerged to administer the simultaneous tasks of self-defense and social construction.

At times the new state came close to defeat and collapse. In the summer of 1918, with the Red Army still in embryonic form, peasant rebellions and military intervention severed the center's control of food and other resources and political oppositions attracted the support of many of those who had joined with the Bolsheviks in their attacks on the old regime. In the fall of 1919, the Volunteer army of General Denikin advanced to within 250 miles of Moscow, and in the northwest General Yudenich and his troops approached the outskirts of Petrograd. Finally, in the early spring of 1921, a population exhausted by seven years of war, scarcity, and sacrifice nearly rebelled against the military centralization of Soviet rule, forcing the Communist Party to concede a restoration of free trade, the reforms that became known as the New Economic Policy.

This ebb and flow of Soviet fortunes during the Civil War was the product partly of the nature of the war itself: lines of battle were rarely clear, both sides suffered desertions and mutinies, both responded with draconian discipline and terror. The constant tension of military emergency made the articulation of social policy extremely difficult. By 1921, the Red Armies and the Soviet system emerged victorious, but the social and political consequences of this victory, the implications of the experience of the war years themselves, remain an unresolved issue on the historians' agenda for this period. It is on this issue that social historians, those represented in this volume and others, can offer important new perspectives, review unanswered questions, and propose new hypotheses for further investigation.

Among the many themes that run through this book—the costs of survival, the creation of new institutions and structures, the social function of intellectuals and culture—one that returned repeatedly in the discussions was the question: to what extent were responses and political choices of the Civil War years the product of social and economic circumstances, to what extent the independent exercise of conscious political will? Why was there a progressive erosion of democratic practices and forms in the soviets, in the central government, in trade unions, and in the factories themselves in the post-October period?

The process that led from a radical grass-roots democracy in soviets and factory committees to a new state authority that proudly proclaimed itself a dictatorship has been chronicled many times (most notably by Leonard Schapiro and Robert V. Daniels), but explanations for the seemingly inevitable degeneration of the revolutionary democracy have usually been limited to the political level.[2] As in the earlier attempts to explain Bolshevik triumph in 1917, so in trying to illuminate the demise of democracy, there has been a tendency to overemphasize the role of ideology and personality and to avoid the more difficult reconstruction required by a full social historical explanation.[3] The works of E. H. Carr were a notable and, until recently, almost singular exception to this pattern,[4] but happily a number of Western historians and sociologists have begun to extend their analyses of the revolution into early 1918. David Mandel, Alexander Rabinowitch, Donald J. Raleigh, William G. Rosenberg, Carmen Sirianni, and Steve Smith have all been studying workers, the party, and the social milieu in which they operated in the crucial six months after the Bolsheviks came to power.[5] Books by T. H. Rigby and Robert Service have dealt with the Bolshevik state and party through the Civil War into the early NEP period.[6] Attention has been concentrated on the centers of Soviet power, Petrograd and Moscow, but interest in the provinces and the non-Russian regions has been growing as the importance of comparative studies has been recognized.[7]

Yet even as new questions are asked of new material, specific images of the Bolsheviks based on the Petrograd experience or on a selected reading of isolated threads of Bolshevik writings have dominated interpretations. Bolsheviks are frequently still seen as political manipulators, dishonest in their political practices, given to opportunism in order to exploit any possibility of coming to power.[8] The basest of motives are often routinely ascribed to Bolsheviks, while the specific contexts in which the party operated are poorly illuminated. The failure of more democratic forms to survive early Bolshevik rule, then, is usually attributed to Lenin's particular personality or to the ideology that bore his name.

The range of reinterpretation on the post-October "degeneration" is well represented in the recent works by Rigby, Service, Sirianni, and Smith. In his study of workers' control, Sirianni argues that mass labor organizations (factory committees, trade unions, and so on) were effective in organizing and managing factory production but that the Bolsheviks time and again opted for a more centralized, "bureaucratic" solution to the problem of social organization. In his view ideological blinders guided the party to prefer solutions that they believed would raise production. As admirers of Taylorism and other Western "productivist" methods, the Bolsheviks neglected considerations of social justice. In Marxist terms they were more concerned with developing the forces of production than with transforming the relations of production within industry.

Although Steve Smith shares Sirianni's appreciation of the constraints of Leninist ideology, he emphasizes the weight of "objective circumstances" that "would ultimately have conspired to drain socialism of its democratic content."[9] Robert Service, however, rejects both the view that authoritarianism was inherent in Lenin's personality and thinking and the opposing determinist view that bureaucratization was the inevitable outcome of any party's coming to power. Rather, he holds that both "the 'objective' nature of the international and domestic environment" and ideas played a role in the organizational metamorphosis.[10] Civil war created a situation in which the party's human resources were stretched to the breaking point. As Bolshevik functionaries took on more and more tasks, both in the military and political apparatuses, they resisted the kind of popular scrutiny and sanction that had characterized policymaking in 1917. Many of the rank-and-file as well as top leaders desired hierarchy and discipline. "Almost overnight it was witnessed that nearly all those dyed-in-the-wool defenders of local rights in 1917 were now ready, however reluctantly, to recognise that the military crisis called for the introduction of stern internal discipline if the party was ever to stay in power."[11]

Like Service, T. H. Rigby combines in his analysis the context of the Civil War and the particular inputs of Lenin. Concerned to explain the decline of Lenin's Sovnarkom and its replacement as the supreme authority by the Politburo, he argues that this "was not the fruit of some grand design, but was rather the cumulative effect of many decisions with far more limited objectives and of more or less spontaneous adaptation to specific circumstances."[12] Bolsheviks, at first, were not convinced that the party should become the coordinator, supervisor, and director of state policy. Some party members even suggested that the party might be abolished once there were soviets composed of Communists. But in the Civil War, with soviets themselves in a state of decline, party committees that could act speedily and authoritatively filled the political vacuum in the provinces.

While the requirements of fighting a war pushed the party into a certain kind of political practice, Lenin's personal style, Bolshevik political culture, and the particular inspirations of Marxism all contributed to the kinds of "spontaneous" choices made. Rigby suggests that "simple greed for power does not seem to have been in Lenin's character," but at the same time the Bolshevik leader was convinced that "erstwhile comrades were leading his cause astray and only his guidance could confirm it on the right path."[13]

Whether one concludes that Soviet state and social formation during the Civil War was largely a working out of ideology or a determination of circumstances (or some complex combination of factors), there is clearly no substitute for the hard empirical work on which such conclusions might be built. It is our conviction that understanding the fundamental questions of the Civil War requires an approach that combines social and political history, considers the state as well as society, culture, and ideology, circumstance as well as purpose and intention. It is our hope that the essays in this volume will contribute to a new and deeper understanding of all aspects of Russia's Civil War.

NOTES

1. Still the classic treatment of the period is William H. Chamberlin, *The Russian Revolution*, vol. 2 (New York, 1935), reissued in 1987 by Princeton University Press.

2. See, for example, Leonard Schapiro, *The Origin of the Communist Autocracy: Political Opposition in the Soviet State; First Phase, 1917–1922* (Cambridge, Mass., 1955); and Robert Vincent Daniels, *The Conscience of the Revolution: Communist Opposition in Soviet Russia* (Cambridge, Mass., 1960).

3. Ronald Grigor Suny, "Toward a Social History of the October Revolution," *American Historical Review*, February 1983, 88, 1, pp. 31–52.

4. *The Bolshevik Revolution, 1917–1923*, 3 vols. (London, 1950–53).

5. Vladimir Brovkin, "The Mensheviks' Political Comeback: The Elections to the Provincial City Soviets in Spring 1918," *The Russian Review*, January 1983, 42, 1, pp. 1–50; David Mandel, *The Petrograd Workers and the Fall of the Old Regime: From the February Revolution to the July Days, 1917; The Petrograd Workers and the Soviet Seizure of Power: From the July Days 1917 to July 1918* (London, 1984); S. A. Smith, *Red Petrograd: Revolution in the Factories, 1917–1918* (Cambridge, 1983); William G. Rosenberg, "Russian Labor and Bolshevik Power after October," *Slavic Review*, Summer 1985, 44, 2 pp. 213–56; Carmen Sirianni, *Workers Control and Socialist Democracy: The Soviet Experience* (London, 1982); and works in progress by Alexander Rabinowitch (on Petrograd) and Donald J. Raleigh (on the Volga region).

6. T. H. Rigby, *Lenin's Government: Sovnarkom 1917–1922* (Cambridge, 1979); Robert Service, *The Bolshevik Party in Revolution: A Study in Organisational Change, 1917–1923* (London, 1979).

7. For a partial sampling of the literature on non-Russian areas, see Arthur Adams, *Bolsheviks in the Ukraine: The Second Campaign, 1918–1919* (New Haven, 1963); Firuz Kazemzadeh, *The Struggle for Transcaucasia (1917–1921)* (New York, 1951); Richard Pipes, *The Formation of the Soviet Union: Communism and Nationalism, 1917–1923* (Cambridge, Mass., 1964); Ronald Grigor Suny, *The Baku Commune, 1917–1918: Class and Nationality in the Russian Revolution* (Princeton, 1972); *The Making of the Georgian Nation* (Bloomington and Stanford, 1988). Helpful works on provincial Russia include Vladimir N. Brovkin, *The Mensheviks after October: Socialist*

Opposition and the Rise of the Bolshevik Dictatorship (Ithaca, 1987); the two volumes by Peter Kenez, *Civil War in South Russia, 1918: The First Year of the Volunteer Army*; and *Civil War in South Russia, 1918–1919: The Defeat of the Whites* (Berkeley, 1971, 1977); and the relevant chapters in William G. Rosenberg, *Liberals in the Russian Revolution: The Constitutional Democratic Party, 1917–1921* (Princeton, 1974).

8. In this regard the work of John L. H. Keep is especially germane; see his *The Russian Revolution: A Study in Mass Mobilization* (New York, 1976) and the revealing introduction to his *The Debate on Soviet Power: Minutes of the All-Russian Central Executive Committee of Soviets, Second Convocation, October 1917–January 1918* (Oxford, 1979).

9. Smith, *Red Petrograd*, p. 263.
10. Service, *Bolshevik Party*, p. 205.
11. Ibid., p. 208.
12. Rigby, *Lenin's Government*, p. 178.
13. Ibid., p. 228.

I
Civil War and
Social Revolution

NEW PERSPECTIVES ON
THE CIVIL WAR

Sheila Fitzpatrick

Western historians are just beginning to tackle the social and sociopolitical history of the Civil War. The emphasis of earlier scholarship was on high politics and diplomatic and military history, and the recent shift reflects a general reorientation of Western Soviet historians away from party politics and the perspective "from above" and toward society and the perspective "from below." We have much better access to source material—including Soviet archival sources—than the previous generation of scholars, and, as this volume indicates, the first products of the new research are promising. In any new field, however, there are pitfalls as well as opportunities. In this introductory essay, I will try to survey the field of Civil War social history as a whole, noting the possibilities and potential problems for research and offering some thoughts on the research agenda for the future.

The Problem of Class

Western historians are latecomers to the social history field, but Soviet historians have already produced a large scholarly literature on the subject.[1] Many of the Soviet works are valuable and solidly researched, and they are bound to be extensively cited as Western scholarship develops. This is a welcome change, since in the past the paths of Western and Soviet scholarship rarely crossed and both sides suffered as a result. Nevertheless, there are some possible disadvantages for Western scholarship inherent in the situation. One is that we may find ourselves using the analytical framework and categories of Soviet scholarship automatically, without stopping to ask whether they are the most appropriate to our needs.

Soviet social history uses a simple Marxist framework that divides the society in three basic categories: workers, peasants, and intelligentsia. For the Civil War and NEP periods, there is also a residual "bourgeoisie" whose conflicts

3

with the new "proletarian" Soviet state are part of the revolutionary class war begun in 1917. The industrial working class is the lynchpin of the new order and thus receives much more attention from Soviet scholars than, for example, artisans or the urban petty bourgeoisie—larger social groups, but politically less significant. The intelligentsia is mainly "bourgeois," though it may also be considered as a service class in process of transition from serving the old regime (from which it derived its "bourgeois" coloration) to serving the new one. The peasantry is differentiated by class, with semibourgeois "kulaks" exploiting semiproletarian "poor peasants."

This framework rests on a set of political and ideological assumptions not necessarily shared by Western scholars. Nevertheless, the temptation to use it is strong, not only because of the bias of Soviet secondary works but also and more importantly because of the bias of sources, including social statistical data. Most contemporary statistics—including population censuses—were broken down into class categories before publication and are not available in any other form. Almost all contemporary analysis of society in the 1917–29 period focuses on class and class conflict. For historians to impose another analytical framework is often extremely difficult because that involves working against the original data and introducing categories they did not distinguish.

Some recent Western work on the revolutionary and Civil War period is written from a Marxist perspective and stays close to the Soviet framework.[2] Other studies, like Teodor Shanin's on the peasantry,[3] explicitly takes issue with it, but Shanin has the advantage of drawing on the cyclical mobility studies of the 1920s, whose implications were non-Marxist,[4] and there are no comparable data sets available for urban society. In the present volume, Daniel T. Orlovsky's article on state building emphasizes the role of the petty bourgeoisie and thus challenges a conventional Soviet interpretation without departing from Marxist class categories. Daniel R. Brower goes further in his article on Russian cities by trying to avoid Marxist categories and substituting terms like "townspeople" and "*meshchanstvo*" (an urban estate in the old Russian *soslovie* system). The difficulty here is that *meshchanstvo* has various meanings and arguably lacked clear social definition even when it was a legal tsarist estate category.

The decision whether to use, modify, or reject the Soviet Marxist framework has to be made by all historians of the Soviet period. But the Civil War poses particular problems. On the one hand, it was a period in which class was greatly emphasized. The Bolsheviks saw the war as a class conflict between the proletariat (those who had been oppressed under the old regime) and the bourgeoisie (those who had been privileged), and this view was shared by many contemporaries, including non-Marxists. On the other hand, it was a period of social mobility and flux in which the old class structure visibly disintegrated and class identification of individuals was often a subjective matter. The historian cannot ignore class, because the conflicts of the time were defined in class terms, but neither can he ignore its deficiencies as a framework for describing social reality.

According to the Bolsheviks, the proletariat was the new ruling class in the

Soviet state. Leaving aside the problems with this concept in political terms, its social implications must be perplexing even to Marxist social historians. Were industrial workers to become a new social elite, superior in status and economic position, as well as a political ruling class? Certainly the old upper classes—landowning nobility, bureaucratic officeholders, commercial and industrial bourgeoisie—had disintegrated, leaving a vacuum at the top of the social hierarchy. The professional middle class was the sole survivor of the old "feudal-bourgeois" group, and the Bolsheviks often treated this "bourgeois intelligentsia" as an elite in the pejorative sense and as the proletariat's competitor for social leadership. As for the peasantry, its internal differentiation had been leveled in the land redistribution of 1917–18, many ties with urban society had been severed, and it seemed a dark and amorphous mass from the viewpoint of the towns. Russia's old class structure had vanished or become unrecognizable. The new social structure had yet to emerge.

Meanwhile, the upheavals of war, revolution, and civil war had made the population exceptionally mobile, not just physically but also in social and occupational terms. Peasants and workers had become soldiers, classified by the Bolsheviks as "proletarian" regardless of social origin. Factory workers and miners, driven out of the towns by hunger and industrial collapse, had gone back to their native villages and resumed life as peasants. Other workers had become Red Army political commissars, factory managers, and administrators. High-ranking bureaucrats of the old regime had taken cover as accountants and teachers; members of the old nobility were surviving as street traders, selling off the family possessions. Some of this mobility was temporary, or thought to be so by those who experienced it. But many changes of occupation and social position were products of social revolution and would prove to be permanent.

Class affiliation had great importance during the Civil War, since the Bolsheviks used this criterion to distinguish social allies from enemies and introduced class-discriminatory clauses in many legislative acts and policy resolutions.[5] Given the mobility of the Civil War years, however, it was often necessary to use a double identification, taking into account an individual's class position before the revolution (which was the crucial determinant of political attitudes in Bolshevik eyes) as well as his current occupation and social position. From the Bolshevik standpoint, somebody who had been a worker or soldier in 1917 was still "proletarian" in 1920, even if he had moved into a white-collar managerial job. Conversely, somebody who had owned a factory in 1917 remained "bourgeois" even if he had since become a factory worker. To complicate matters further, class affiliation was often seen as a product of political allegiance, not just a determinant of it. Those who actively supported the revolution, regardless of social origins, were "proletarians by conviction." Those who opposed it, or opposed the Bolsheviks, were "essentially bourgeois" (or, if they came from the lower classes, "infected by petty-bourgeois attitudes").

In a society where so many people were effectively *déclassés*,[6] the emphasis on class was paradoxical. But it was not only a Bolshevik emphasis. The revolution had polarized society on lines that were commonly associated with class. Most individuals who were touched by it seem to have developed strong convictions about their own class status—and those convictions may well have been stronger in 1920, though less well founded than they had been in 1917. But the belief did not necessarily fit social reality. Some people thought they were proletarian because they worked in a factory, or used to do so. Others thought this because they were Communist Party members or Red Army volunteers, or just because they had quarreled with middle-class parents and joined the Komsomol. In addition, there were people who, seeking career advantages or security, claimed to be proletarian *without* any conviction or objective justification. Once class became a political indicator, the reliability of class data automatically diminished.

Historians of the Civil War must deal with class as an aspect of politics and social psychology. In these areas, the Bolsheviks' Marxist ideology imposes a framework that is inescapable, and the Marxist class categories in contemporary usage are the only ones that are appropriate. This does not mean, however, that historians have to use the same Marxist class categories as a basis for analyzing the society of the Civil War period. On the contrary, they would do better to avoid them. The class structure was in flux at this time, class identification was politicized, and the population's abnormally high mobility makes any kind of static analysis unsatisfactory.

Furthermore, the "class consciousness" associated with the revolution and so prized by the Bolsheviks is potentially a great pitfall for historians. In the first place, the relationship between consciousness and social reality was often ambiguous. In the second place, the class consciousness of these years focused on two specific classes, the proletariat and the bourgeoisie, whose symbolic and political significance greatly exceeded their actual social presence.

Even in 1917, as Brower's article reminds us, the industrial proletariat and capitalist bourgeoisie were relatively small groups in the urban population, not to speak of the population as a whole. By 1920, a large part of the industrial proletariat had disintegrated, and the old capitalist bourgeoisie had been expropriated and ceased to exist as a class. In effect, the great "class struggle" was being waged by a surrogate proletariat (the Red Army and the Communist Party) against a surrogate bourgeoisie (the White Armies and the urban intelligentsia). This is a fascinating topic, but social historians should bear in mind that it leaves the greater part of Russian society outside the picture. In this case, at least, to equate social history with the history of class consciousness is a reductio ad absurdum.

Social Mobility

Social mobility is neither a Marxist concept nor, in the past, a prominent theme in Soviet or Western historiography of Soviet Russia.[7] If one accepts the premise that the proletariat became the ruling class after the Bolshevik Revolution, this might theoretically be regarded as upward mobility of a whole class, comparable, for example, with the upward mobility of whole subcastes that has been observed in India.[8] Subcastes, however, can change occupations as well as cultural mores, a possibility unavailable by definition to an industrial proletariat. Nobody has in fact tried to argue that the proletariat was upwardly mobile as a class, and few Western scholars would accept the Soviet Marxist premise that it became anything like a ruling class, either politically or socially. Soviet social historians assert this, as they must, but are generally prudent enough to avoid detailed explication of the theory.

As I have argued elsewhere,[9] in practice postrevolutionary upward mobility was available to large number of individual proletarians, not to the proletariat as a class. But this in itself was a significant product of social revolution, as was the corresponding downward mobility of members of the old elite that was characteristic of the Civil War period. In the first years after the revolution, upwardly mobile proletarians (as well as other members of the lower classes) joined the new "ruling class" or sociopolitical elite by virtue of moving into traditionally elite occupations—administration, management, Army command, and so on. But they moved by revolutionary channels, not traditional ones. This was also true of the expropriated landowners and businessmen and former Tsarist *chinovniki* who were evicted from their old elite positions and forced to find a niche lower down the scale.

The social mobility that occurred as a direct consequence of the revolution is one of the most interesting aspects of Civil War social history. Of course it was not unique, for all successful revolutions have such consequences. The peculiarity of the Russian case was that the process was only obliquely acknowledged in the early years, since it did not fit into the framework of Marxist revolutionary ideology. Despite the new institutions of revolutionary "soviet democracy," and the Bolsheviks' genuine regard for them, it was clear from the beginning that "cadres" had some part to play in the organization of the revolutionary state. To the Bolsheviks, it was equally clear that the bulk of the new cadres should come from the proletariat and other lower classes that had had no stake in the old regime. Thus, large numbers of workers, soldiers, sailors and peasants (usually peasants-in-uniform) were drafted into administrative, managerial, and officer positions after the October Revolution and throughout the Civil War.

These assignments were not generally regarded as permanent during the Civil War. They were seen more as temporary service to the revolution, analogous to the familiar pattern of call-up for wartime military service to the nation. The workers who were "mobilized" as cadres went off to serve (since the assignments usually involved physical relocation) with the expectation that they would ultimately return to their previous occupations. This, at any rate, was the expectation conventionally expressed in revolutionary circles. It was known that "careerists" joined the party and became cadres for other reasons, but these were not the kind of cadres the revolution needed.

This was not, however, the whole story, even in the early days. In the first place, the boundary between revolutionary activism and making a career in public life became fuzzy as soon as the revolutionaries created permanent institutions. As we see in Alexander Rabinowitch's article, the transition from elected soviet deputy to Soviet officeholder could occur quite casually in 1917–18, and many workers made the transition almost involuntarily, on the basis of competence and responsibility rather than personal ambition. In the second place, the revolution had promised to make workers "masters" in the new Soviet state. For the workers who found themselves serving as cadres, it was only a small mental step, though a significant one, to realization that in their own case the promise had already been honored.

The process whereby workers, soldiers, and others from the lower classes moved into the Soviet managerial elite during the Civil War deserves more detailed study by historians.[10] This should be facilitated in the future by the biographical Data Bank initiated by Arch Getty and William Chase,[11] which will encourage prosopographical work on cohorts like the Civil War *vydvizhentsy* (upwardly mobile workers). The attitudinal aspect also needs investigation. It is clear that some of the new working-class cadres quickly began acting like the old bosses and that this provoked resentment (and envy?) from workers still at the factory bench. But there are also indications that working-class revolutionary bosses were preferred to those who came from the old privileged classes.

Another type of mobility that deserves close attention is the return of workers to the villages, discussed in this volume by Chase and Brower and (in connection with women) Barbara Evans Clements. This was mainly a temporary migration prompted by food shortages and industrial closures in the towns. But it sheds light on one of the major questions of revolutionary and labor history, namely, the degree to which Russian urban workers had separated from the land and the peasantry to become, in Marxist terms, a true urban proletariat.

The Bolsheviks had a vested interest in showing that Russia's industrial proletariat was a mature class, separate from the peasantry and capable of leading a socialist revolution. This probably influenced the Soviet statisticians of the 1920s and certainly left its mark on later Soviet historiography. Soviet historians do not ignore the movement of workers to the villages during the Civil War, but they tend to downplay some of its interesting features. For example, many of the workers involved were skilled and had years of industrial experience (meaning that this movement was not simply an outflow of recently arrived peasant workers), the workers returning to their native villages often received land in the general redistribution of 1917–18 (implying that they had not lost touch with their village roots and were still regarded by other peasants as members of the village community). Soviet historians also use a broad definition of "hereditary (*potomstvennye*) workers"—a key category in determining the maturity of the urban proletariat—which includes *otkhodniki* (peasants who spent part of the year working outside the village) whose fathers had also been *otkhodniki*. This surely begs the question of a group that clearly had one foot in the urban working class and the other in the peasantry. In sum, the evidence supporting the maturity of the urban proletariat is weaker than Soviet historians suggest, particularly in the light of the Civil War out-migration.

The Bolshevik leaders did not overlook the disturbing implications of the workers' departure. They were startled and dismayed since their seizure of power had been made possible by working-class support and justified in terms of proletarian maturity. This is a social dimension of Soviet political history missed by Western Sovietologists, despite its relevance to the substitution of party dictatorship for "dictatorship of the proletariat." It is true, as Sovietologists have pointed out, that Kronstadt was a symbol of proletarian alienation from the new regime, but the dramatic fall in numbers of industrial workers shown by the statistics of 1918–21 was almost as alarming to the Bolsheviks. Political opponents taunted them, with some justice, for becoming the vanguard of a nonexistent class. They could not know, in 1920–21, whether the workers would ever come back from the villages. To those who remembered the old debates between Populists and Marxists, it must have seemed possible that the Populists had been right, and Russia's urban workers (or a substantial proportion of them) were merely dispossessed peasants who had taken the first chance of returning to the land.

In a sense the question about the identity of this generation of Russian workers remains, despite the workers' practical reasons for leaving the towns and the fact that the majority returned to urban employment when industry revived in the first years of NEP. The workers who left for the villages in 1918 might have seen themselves as returning peasants who would spend the rest of their lives on the land. Some surely did, at least at that particular time when unfavorable conditions in the towns coincided with the peasants' acquisition of land and the revival of communal spirit in the villages. But the odds were against the returnees' economic survival. Although they shared in the redistribution of land, they lacked horses and other prerequisites for successful farming and seem to have fallen quickly into the "poor peasant" category in many cases. Thus, some subsequent departures for the towns might be attributable to the same motivation as the family's original departure ten, twenty, or thirty years earlier, namely failure to make a living on the land. But even this is problematic, since failure would tend to produce a psychological reorientation toward a working-class identity. There is, in fact, no simple answer to the question of whether these people were workers or peasants. They were probably both.

The impact of worker migration to the villages should be examined by historians of the peasantry as well as labor historians. Like the Marxists, though for different reasons, agrarian scholars usually find the subject of mobility between village and town uncongenial. This was so in the 1920s, when the Chayanov school emphasized the self-containment of the peasantry with the same vigor that Bolsheviks defended the thesis of the proletariat's separation from the peasantry and maturity as a class, and it tends to be true even now. The limitations of this approach can be seen particularly clearly in regard to the Civil War period.

The relationship between rural and urban populations varied considerably in different parts of the country. But in Russia's Central Industrial Region around Moscow, and also in the provinces adjacent to Petrograd, the relationship in the early twentieth century was much closer than most scholars have allowed.[12] This was a consequence of infertile soil, industrialization, and high rates of peasant *otkhod* and departure to the towns. Thus, there was considerable proletarian influence in the villages—which should make us wary of categorical statements about the separateness of urban and rural revolution in 1905 and 1917—as well as a large peasant component in the urban working class.

Most workers who left the towns during the Civil War went to villages in the Central Industrial, Northwestern, and Western Regions, though a substantial contingent of miners returned from the Donbass to villages in the Central Agricultural Region. Whatever the mix of peasant and proletarian in their class identity, these workers and miners must have brought news of the outside world back to the villages—just as the returning soldiers of the Imperial Army did in 1917 and those of the Red Army in 1921—and disseminated urban and revolutionary attitudes.

The returning workers' role as disseminators of outside ideas becomes particularly relevant when we consider the vexed question of class war in the villages and the alleged "second revolution' in the countryside that, according to Soviet historians, expropriated kulaks in 1918. Shanin disputes the existence of an internally generated "second revolution" against kulaks.[13] It is clear, nevertheless, that some kind of conflict was occurring, even if it was not the class war of poor peasants against kulaks that the Bolsheviks anticipated. One documented type of conflict involved the forceable return of Stolypin "separators" to the peasant commune. But there are also indications that conflicts arose when returned workers, struggling to make a living on the land without draught animals and adequate equipment, found themselves sinking downward into the poor-peasant group. This question, which has not yet been raised by Soviet or Western historians, needs careful investigation. It seems plausible that, in such circumstances, the returned workers might have challenged the authority of the elders of the *mir* or even initiated "expropriation" of kulak horses and inventory. In any case, an intriguing possibility is that the Bolsheviks' "class war" in the countryside was a real if not universal phenomenon, but that it occurred only after the return of workers and miners, with former urban proletarians acting as instigators in their new social role as "poor peasants."

Working-Class Mentalité

As the focus of Civil War scholarship shifts toward society, studies of *mentalité* (the attitudes, mores, and culture of social classes and groups) are likely to proliferate, taking the place that studies of political ideology had in earlier Western scholarship. This trend is already noticeable in recent work on 1917 and the revolution.[14] It is a welcome change, but the methodological problems and possible biases of *mentalité* studies should not be underestimated. Working-class *mentalité* is a particularly tricky subject in twentieth-century Russian history because of the mystique attached to the workers' movement and the revolution. Soviet and other Marxist historians are especially prone to romanticize the working class, and *mentalité* studies lend themselves to subjective treatment.

The basic problem in describing class or group attitudes is that generalizations are hard to prove or disprove, since historians make their own judgments about what is representative or typical. Individual memoirs are often cited in *mentalité* studies, but the criteria by which we decide that an individual's attitudes and experience are peculiarly representative of a class are difficult to define. The problem is compounded when the memoirs deal retrospectively with great events that have generated their own mythology. In the 1920s, the Bolsheviks encouraged working-class and other participants in the revolutionary movement and Civil War to record their experiences. This created a valuable body of source material on working-class *mentalité* for future historians, but clearly these sources have an built-in bias, since the writers knew the "judgment of history" on their life experiences and could not be unaffected by received Bolshevik interpretations of the working-class revolutionary movement.

The historian of *mentalité* deals, by definition, with clichés and conventional wisdom. But whose clichés? Did nineteenth-century Russian peasants really love the tsar, as they told officials and other outsiders, or were they expressing an expected and approved attitude for reasons of expediency?[15] Similar questions could be raised about working-class attitudes in the early twentieth century and the degree to which workers in the revolutionary movement expressed attitudes likely to please their mentors in the intelligentsia. And in the case of workers there is further complication: these mentors were deeply interested in *mentalité* ("proletarian consciousness") and passed on their own preconceived notions about it to the workers under their tutelage. To be a "conscious" worker meant, among other things, knowing what kind of *mentalité* workers were expected to have. Even Proletkult (described by Lynn Mally in this volume), run by intellectuals who believed the working class had to develop its own culture, imposed a framework of expectations about working-class *mentalité*. The Proletkultists knew a priori that collectivism was part of working-class *mentalité*, whereas "petty-bourgeois" aspirations toward individual self-betterment and advancement were not. The paradox, as Mally indicates, was that workers who preferred working-class culture tended to stay away from Proletkult's clubs and adult-education classes. Those who attended were eager to learn from the intelligentsia, hoping to better themselves culturally and no doubt socially, just like Proletkult's unwanted lower middle-class clientele.

This should serve as a warning to historians about the dangers of bringing Marxist assumptions on "proletarian consciousness" into the study of working-class *mentalité*. These assumptions lead to tautologies and circular arguments in the Soviet literature on the working class, and the same tendencies are discernible in some of the recent Western scholarship.[16] The most acute problems arise when historians take over the Bolsheviks' premise that "consciousness" went hand in hand with support for the Bolshevik Revolution and the new Soviet regime. This unverifiable assumption confuses two issues: it obscures the empirical question of which workers supported the Bolsheviks and muddies the waters on working-class *mentalité*.

The Bolsheviks derived their assumptions from a mixture of Marxist theory, observations of actual political behavior (from which the Mensheviks drew different but no less partisan conclusions), prejudice, and practical calculations about the utility of different working-class groups to the Civil War effort and future tasks of proletarian state building. From the Bolshevik standpoint, the most "conscious" workers were revolutionary before October but disciplined and responsible after the establishment of Soviet power. They tended to come from large, mechanized industrial enterprises, especially in heavy industry where the workforce was predominantly male. Their experience under capitalism had instilled collectivism, class hatred of the bourgeoisie, and the capacity to organize, but the most "conscious" workers had also acquired literacy, technical skills, and the self-confidence necessary for leadership. Where proletarian consciousness was absent, the Bolsheviks' explanation was either that "peasant" influences prevailed or—if the workers in question were urbanized and skilled, but not pro-Bolshevik—that the taint came from a "petty-bourgeois" milieu.

For historians, the problem is not only that the familiar stereotype of "conscious" workers is unsatisfactory but also that the whole approach is predicated on the idea that working-class consciousness is monolithic. Why should we assume that only one set of working-class attitudes is legitimate or typical and label the rest as deviant, degenerate, and immature? A number of working-class *mentalités* seem to have existed in Russia in the first quarter of the twentieth century, as in other times and places. There is no logical reason why historians should not accept this natural pluralism, unless they share the Marxist premises about class that exclude it.

If we admit pluralism of *mentalités*, Barbara Clements's article suggests one fruitful line of approach. As Clements points out, women's experiences of the Civil War differed significantly from those of men. The experience and attitudes of working-class women, consequently, tended to differ from those of working-class men. Moreover, women workers were likely to have different experiences from workers' wives who were not themselves workers, especially the wives whose home was in the village. Here we already have a variety of working-class *mentalités*, all conditioned by characteristically working-class circumstances. The Bolsheviks clearly thought that a particular male *mentalité*, shared by only a minority of the women workers and quite alien to the non-working wives, had superior status. This view made sense politically, since the men were potential soldiers and cadres, and the women, by and large, were not. But it is hard to justify as a basis for social analysis.

The sociological literature of the 1920s, however, accepts the male-oriented view without question. This was not because the sociologists (or the Bolsheviks) were unenlightened on women's liberation; on the contrary: their enlightenment led them to take a particularly dim view of the traditional orientation of workers' wives. The best-known study of working-class life was written by a woman, Kabo, who was clearly appalled by the wives' backwardness and, moreover, found them almost impossible to interview (in contrast to their husbands, who read newspapers and were pleased to tell her about their progressive attitudes) and disconcertingly hostile.[17] It did not occur to Kabo that the women might be showing their own form of antibourgeois class consciousness by this hostility.

As a result, Kabo and other sociologists of the 1920s had little sense of the internal dynamics of working-class families. They saw "proletarian" men whose wives had "peasant" or "petty-bourgeois" attitudes and assumed that this was a disease of the transition and a source of disappointment to the men. But they ignored the alternative hypothesis that men and women had different conventional roles, which both generally accepted. Politics, comradeship, and drink—all recognized by the Bolsheviks as typically proletarian attributes—belonged to the male sphere. Family and the domestic economy, which the Bolsheviks saw as "petty-bourgeois" concerns, belonged to the female. Thus, the "conscious" proletarian man might often be, in effect, a collaborator in his wife's lack of proletarian consciousness.

If the *mentalité* of working-class wives tends to be dismissed for nonconformity with stereotypes of proletarian consciousness, the same is true of some attitudes that were more commonly found among working-class men. One example is the aspiration toward self-betterment that led workers to attend adult-education classes, read newspapers, dress up in a good suit for Sunday outings, and perhaps even in some cases, dare it be said, join the Communist Party. Ambition and emulation of the bourgeoisie are not recognized by Marxists as legitimate proletarian characteristics. Yet it is doubtful that the Social Democratic circles at the turn of the century would have found working-class clients without them, and implausible to suggest that by 1920 the possibility of upward mobility was not part of the Communist Party's appeal to workers, even if this was not consciously acknowledged.

Another example of "deviant" working-class *mentalité* may be found at the other end of the spectrum in outbursts of antisemitism, xenophobia, anti-intellectualism (*spetseedstvo*), and mob violence against individual *burzhui* and their wives and property. According to the Bolshevik stereotype, "conscious" proletarians did not let class hatred carry them so far, though "peasant elements" in the working class might fall into excesses. Yet it was often an urban milieu that generated popular hostility against Jews, foreigners and the intelligentsia, and the Bolsheviks' "peasant" label for such attitudes was mainly a way of dissociating themselves and indicating disapproval. And their disapproval was not absolute, since the cruder forms of class intimidation and resentment sometimes served revolutionary purposes.

The concept of "proletarian consciousness" sometimes leads historians to practice a kind of internal censorship, screening out "bad" working-class attitudes (those that are unacceptable in moral or Marxist terms) and focusing exclusively on the "good" ones. Thus, in Soviet and to some extent Western scholarly literature, Russian workers are suspiciously free of acquisitiveness, materialism, competitiveness, individual ambition, and inclinations towards brutality and violence. They may be forced, on occasion during the Civil War, to sell factory products on the black market, but the trading mentality is quite alien to them (and presumably, even less plausibly, to their wives). They may accept upward mobility, but only because it is thrust on them. Their anger against the bourgeoisie is a noble and selfless class sentiment: it seems almost an error of taste to ask if class vengeance in individual instances was ever fueled by alcohol, accompanied by robbery or looting, or manifested in the rape of upper-class women or violent physical attacks on well-dressed men in dark streets. Yet there were surely workers, close to the artisan and small-trading milieu, who dreamed of setting up their own businesses; workers who wanted to be foremen and live like the bourgeoisie; and workers whose grievances against society were expressed in criminal acts and drunken violence. Their *mentalités* may be less appealing to historians than that of the upstanding proletarian collectivist celebrated in Soviet scholarship and fiction. But this is no justification for writing them out of the historical record.

Elites, Old and New

The collapse of the old upper classes—landowning and officeholding nobility, capitalist bourgeoisie—is one of the most striking social phenomena of the period 1917–21. Soviet sources identify expropriation as the cause and emigration during and immediately after the Civil War as the process that permanently removed many of these undesirable elements from Soviet society.[18] The sources are less helpful on the fate of the *byvshie* (members of the old privileged classes) who remained and the manner of their relocation in the new social order. The emergence of new elites is a difficult topic for Soviet Marxist historians, though it can be subsumed under the heading of "formation of a new intelligentsia". Indeed, it is a difficult topic for any historian of the Civil War period, since the process of elite formation was only just beginning and became much more visible after the introduction of NEP. Nevertheless, this question is worth exploring, even for the Civil War, as this was in many respects a formative period for Soviet society.

The abrupt and almost total disintegration of the old elites is sometimes taken as an axiomatic consequence of the revolution that needs no further explanation. Yet, a comparative perspective, such as is suggested by Ronald Grigor Suny's study of Georgia in this volume, raises a number of questions. If the Georgian landowning aristocracy partially survived through the Civil War period, was the quick collapse of its Russian counterpart a product of internal weakness and absenteeism, a more hostile peasantry, or the fact that

Bolshevik social policies in Russia were tougher than Menshevik policies in Georgia?

A similar comparison focused on the urban capitalist bourgeoisie might also yield illuminating results and perhaps direct our attention to the ethnic and national component of revolutionary "class struggle" that historians of Russia are liable to overlook. In Russia, the victory of Labor over Capital was achieved remarkably, and perhaps deceptively, easily. This owed in part to the historic weakness of private capital and the high degree of state involvement. But also relevant is that many of the big capitalist enterprises in Tsarist Russia were foreign owned and at least partly foreign run, and that the First World War had already led to departure of personnel and curtailment of operations. The large foreign component in the capitalist sector made it a particularly tempting target, but also particularly vulnerable and easy to defeat. Moreover, that xenophobia may have been a more typical part of Russian working-class *mentalité* than is usually acknowledged—perhaps even a part of the "proletarian consciousness" that the Bolsheviks tapped or encouraged among their supporters.

Many Russian capitalists, landowners, and others from the old elites moved into White-held territory during the Civil War and finally left the country with the defeated White Armies. But others remained, and a sizeable contingent of former tsarist bureaucrats and professionals ended up working in the Soviet state bureaucracy, often in responsible positions. This group is relatively easy to keep track of, since the Bolsheviks monitored it for political reasons and the statistical surveys of bureaucratic personnel in the 1920s identified former tsarist *chinovniki* as a special category.[19] These surveys, however, did not identify former zemstvo employees, many of whom presumably stayed on to work in similar jobs for the local soviets, so we lack the data for a complete picture of personnel continuity between pre- and postrevolutionary bureaucratic institutions.

Data on other types of relocation of members of the old privileged classes are less satisfactory. With the exception of "bourgeois specialists" (a category that included bureaucrats as well as professionals), the new regime's policy was to impose downward mobility on members of the old elite and their children. Soviet institutions were periodically purged of "class aliens," and access to higher education was restricted. This meant in practice, however, that the *byvshie* made every effort to disguise their social origins, making it difficult not only for the Bolsheviks but also for later social historians to locate them. A systematic study of city directories is the most promising approach,[20] though it can only be applied to the capitals and will not illuminate provincial processes or movement between the capitals and the provinces. My impression from sampling the directories over the two decades from 1910 to 1930 is that downward mobility was common during the Civil War; many members of the old elites took low-level white-collar jobs as office-workers, schoolteachers, accountants, and so on. By the late 1920s, however, a proportion of these people seem to have moved back into higher status occupations. The Bolsheviks' efforts to keep them down were probably frustrated, at least in part, by chronic shortages of educated and skilled personnel.

Professionals, now described as "bourgeois specialists," were considered indispensable to the new regime, despite their possible political unreliability and the resentment many rank-and-file Bolsheviks felt toward them. But there were many anomalies in their situation. As Kendall E. Bailes points out, the intelligentsia or professional middle class had had unusual weight and visibility in prerevolutionary Russian society because of the comparative weakness of other bourgeois groups. Furthermore, it was the only old-elite group to survive the revolution intact as a distinctive entity. This meant that it was often spotlighted as the symbolic representative of the old order and the "bourgeois" class enemy, even though such rhetoric was at odds with the actual policies of the new Soviet regime.

But the Russian intelligentsia had never considered itself "bourgeois" or a pillar of the old order. It had a long history of opposition to the tsarist autocracy, assuming a role as society's conscience that was by definition above narrow class interests. Moreover, the intelligentsia itself used "bourgeois" as a pejorative term, often in conjunction with "philistinism," and traditionally disdained the industrial and commercial bourgeoisie as culturally and socially inferior. This made it peculiarly difficult for the intelligentsia to accept the symbolic bourgeois role forced on it after the Bolshevik Revolution. Countless memoirs of the early Soviet period attest the intelligentsia's sense of insult and unfairness, which was exacerbated during the Civil War by arrests and material deprivation.

Some professional groups fared better than others in the Civil War years, as is demonstrated in the articles by Bailes and James C. McClelland in this volume. McClelland, writing about the professoriate, highlights the issues of autonomy and creative freedom that had been a major cause of conflict between the intelligentsia and the tsarist regime and quickly arose again after the revolution. But, as Bailes shows, other professional groups had different priorities. The natural scientists were valued and generally well treated by the Bolsheviks. The physicians, with a strong public-health orientation, often had a positive attitude to state intervention and found it relatively easy to adjust to the new order.

If we step back to consider the whole picture, it appears that for all the discomforts of the Civil War period the intelligentsia nevertheless emerged with its socially privileged position more or less intact and its status in some respects higher than it had been before the revolution. It remained an elite group, and this was reflected in lower-class (including Bolshevik lower-class) resentment of bourgeois specialists. This raises the general question of whether, even at this early stage, the outlines of a broader elite structure can be discerned and its constituent groups identified.

There are various approaches to the question. In one sense, the most striking characteristic of Civil War society was *absence* of acknowledged and clearly recognizable elites, following the collapse of the old privileged classes. From another standpoint, the distinctive process—already observable in the Civil War, though not completed until the 1930s—was transformation of part of the revolutionary proletariat into a Communist administrative elite via mobilization of workers to service as party, Soviet, Red Army, and Cheka cadres.

A third approach is to focus on groups whose economically privileged position gave them at least temporary elite status during the Civil War. Under the rationing system of the time, leading Bolshevik cadres had special privileges, as did part of the "bourgeois" intelligentsia. Also economically privileged, though without official sanction, was an entrepreneurial group profiting from operations on the black market.

These disparate groups appeared to have little in common except a slightly higher living standard than the rest of the urban population. Nevertheless, some connections developed between them, especially the first two. In the Red Army and the state bureaucracy, Bolshevik cadres and "bourgeois" specialists were often paired and had to learn to work together, however prickly the initial relationship between Reds and experts. The Bolshevik Party leaders of intelligentsia background had personal connections with members of the "bourgeois" (nonparty) intelligentsia, and by the end of the Civil War lower-class Bolsheviks were expressing fears of collusion, based on an unspoken sense of class solidarity, between the Bolshevik intelligentsia and its "bourgeois" counterpart.[21] At another level, the frequency of marriages and liaisons between Bolshevik cadres and "bourgeois" women from cultured or formerly well-off families began to arouse concern.[22]

In the long term, according to most analyses of the later Soviet elite, this emerging relationship between Communist administrators and "bourgeois" professionals had particular significance. In the short term, focusing on the first ten years of Soviet power, the possibility of developing interconnections between all three economically advantaged groups deserves some attention, since this epitomized the much-feared "Thermidorian degeneration" of the revolution that some Communists perceived in NEP. The black-market entrepreneurs of the Civil War, semilegitimized as "Nepmen" in the 1920s, typically operated with one foot in the state sector (since the state was the chief source of goods) and the other in the black or free market. Many were actually on the payrolls of state economic institutions, acting as *tolkachi* and procurements agents.[23] Nepmen therefore had contacts in the official world, and they are described as mingling with high-ranking Communists and leaders of the "bourgeois" cultural intelligentsia in Moscow's new "high society" of the 1920s.[24] This elite milieu was a NEP phenomenon. But its roots, and perhaps its first manifestations, go back to the Civil War period.

Networks and Subgroups

As our study of Civil War social history develops, broad units of analysis like class will become increasingly inadequate for many purposes. We are bound to begin looking at narrower strata, defined in terms of occupation, skills, wage levels, and so on, as well as investigating differentiation by sex, ethnic group, and age. But there is another line of approach, perhaps less familiar in Soviet studies, which focuses on social subgroups and cohorts linked by common experience or shared values. Such subgroups are particularly interesting when they are studied as networks, that is, informal associational and communication systems that reinforce a sense of common identity.

The Bolsheviks were understandably suspicious of networks developed outside a party or soviet context, because they could potentially be used for clandestine political organization by "bourgeois" class enemies. The Bolsheviks sometimes regarded the old intelligentsia as a whole as such a network, not without justification. In the nineteenth and early twentieth centuries, the Russian intelligentsia had developed a strong sense of identity and a value system that was consciously opposed to that of the tsarist autocracy and incorporated a belief in the intelligentsia's own mission to provide moral leadership and act as society's conscience. The values and sense of identity survived the revolution, and most of the intelligentsia initially opposed the Bolshevik takeover. The "bourgeois" intelligentsia and the "proletarian" Bolshevik Party were in some sense competitors for moral leadership, since each claimed a natural right and responsibility to provide guidelines for society's future.

During the Civil War, both groups were preoccupied with redefining their roles and responsibilities in a postrevolutionary setting. Although some members of the intelligentsia considered the possibility of abdicating moral leadership, the emerging group consensus· was that the old responsibilities remained; the intelligentsia must preserve its separate identity, guard the nation's cultural heritage against destruction in the revolutionary turmoil, and transmit its values intact to subsequent generations.[25] This produced conflicts with the new regime like the professoriate's struggle for university autonomy described in McClelland's article. The intelligentsia often lost the battles, but an issue that scholars will continue to debate is which side ultimately won the war. The old intelligentsia kept its identity (despite a vigorous Communist assault in the Cultural Revolution at the end of the 1920s), held on to its privileged status, and arguably had remarkable long-term success in transmitting its values, not just to society but also to the regime in the "Great-Retreat" of the 1930s. This makes the intelligentsia's reaffirmation of mission during the Civil War a subject of particular interest to social and cultural historians.

The old intelligentsia may be considered a network in the broad sense that its members could "recognize" each other and assume communality of values and tacit alliance in dealing with the new Bolshevik regime. But smaller networks, for example, those existing within particular professions, often had more practical significance. Kendall E. Bailes's study of engineers suggests the rich possibilities of research on professional networks.[26] The real pioneer in this field, however, was the OGPU during the Cultural Revolution, when the old intelligentsia was collectively under suspicion and its cultural "hegemony" challenged by Communists.

No doubt the OGPU conducted many network investigations at this time, but the one on record deals with leaders of the engineering profession holding responsible positions in various Soviet economic agencies.[27] The data came from interrogations, and some of the men interrogated later appeared as defendants in the Industrial Party trial of 1930, in which the state prosecutor laid out an elaborate and implausible scenario of conspiracy, sabotage, and covert communication with foreign intelligence. But the OGPU report, circulated to delegates at the Sixteenth Party Congress earlier in the year, bore no resemblance to the later show-trial scenario. It was essentially a sociological study of the informal associational and communication mechanisms developed after the revolution by a specific cohort of "bourgeois" specialists, designed to illuminate the general issue of relations between specialists and the Communists with whom they worked and, in particular, to investigate the hypothesis that the specialists' expertise and close relationship with Communist industrial administrators enabled them to influence policy.[28]

Although the OGPU's investigation techniques cannot be duplicated by historians, nor its motives admired, its approach to networks could be profitably applied in scholarly studies of intelligentsia subgroups during and after the Civil War. One of the OGPU's starting-points was old-boy networks: which specialists had been students together at the major prerevolutionary higher technical schools, and how did the alumni of these schools keep in touch with each other? The interrogators were also interested in cohorts of engineers who had worked together in big firms like Nobel Oil before the revolution (eliciting valuable testimony on the strong group spirit of the *nobelevtsy* and its contribution to Soviet rebuilding of the oil industry in the early 1920s). They collected data on professional organizations, clubs, publication patterns (which Soviet scientific journals the specialists regarded as "theirs"), institutional loyalties and rivalries, patronage mechanisms, lobbying channels and methods, techniques of self- and group-protection, and bureaucratic responses to outside investigation (which revealed Communists who received confidential police inquiries about their specialists often reacted protectively as well as defensively in the 1920s and sometimes even asked the specialists in question to draft their replies).

As the investigators intended, these data are particularly useful in assessing the relationship between Communist-administrative and bourgeois-professional elites, and they tend to confirm the hypothesis that firm working relationships often developed as early as the Civil War period and continued on a stable basis until the Cultural Revolution. The OGPU study, which focuses on work relationships, gives little sense of social interaction between the two elite groups. But this question should also be studied by historians. On the social relationship in an industrial and military context, some interesting retrospective testimony came from the wives of Communist administrators and engineers who joined the *obshchestvennitsa* movement of the mid-1930s.[29]

The best sources on the social dimension, however, are literary and artistic memoirs. This is the only genre of Soviet publication in which gossip is considered to have redeeming social value, and the juiciest intelligentsia gossip, particularly in the early Soviet period, often deals with the interaction of political leaders with the cultural elite. Data on Civil War Petrograd are particularly rich, because a number of the participants among the intelligentsia emigrated at the end of the Civil War and published memoirs abroad. There is, for example, an enormous amount of material on Maxim Gorkii's circle, one of the meeting-grounds for writers, scientists, and Bolsheviks. The émigré memoirs naturally stress the hostility and resentment many members of the intelligentsia felt toward the Bolshevik leaders, especially Zinoviev and his associates in Petrograd. This certainly was one characteristic of the relationship between Bolsheviks and the intelligentsia during the Civil War. But for a social historian, perhaps the most striking characteristic of the relationship is its intimacy. In some circles, at least, an interconnection of elites existed in these years.

Intelligentsia networks are not the only ones worthy of investigation. Some working-class networks are accessible to research as well: worker-alumni of the Putilov factory, for example, are an identifiable group, and the big Donbass enterprises like Yuzovka may have developed an even stronger esprit de corps among skilled workers because of the tensions associated with foreign management and personnel before the War and the workers' struggle to save the plants during the Civil War.[30]

The Bolshevik Party also deserves its sociological investigations. So much has been written about the party that it is surprising to realize that this aspect has been generally neglected. In the literature on the Civil War party, political factions provided the classic focus, and more recently analysis has included study of the relationship between center and periphery and leadership and rank and file.[31] But the Civil War party was a complex social organism as well. The cohort of returned émigrés in the leadership was sharply distinguished from the komitetchiki, who had remained in Russia after 1905 and worked in the revolutionary underground. In the party as a whole, intelligentsia Bolsheviks and worker Bolsheviks were equally distinct, and there was often tension between the two groups during the Civil War. Indeed, this class tension informed much of the party's factional fighting, and its neglect is a serious deficiency in the political histories.

Working-class Bolsheviks, in turn, had split into two subgroups by the end of the Civil War. Workers still at the factory bench constituted the first subgroup, and worker-vydvizhentsy (former workers who had become cadres after the revolution) made up the second. The vydvizhentsy rarely got involved in fights among political factions but their relations with worker Bolsheviks were often uneasy because of differences in status. There was probably cultural uneasiness in their relationship with Bolshevik cadres from the intelligentsia, although this topic has not been adequately researched. Yet the distinction between Bolshevik cadres from the intelligentsia and Bolshevik cadres from the working class clearly is relevant to the question of interconnection of elites raised earlier in this essay. The intelligentsia cadres had a common language with the "bourgeois" intelligentsia, but this was presumably not true of the vydvizhentsy.

On the basis of an impressionistic evaluation, it seems likely that the *vydvizhentsy* were belligerent and suspicious in their initial dealings with bourgeois specialists, who in turn likely treated them with veiled contempt and arrogance. But sometimes *vydvizhentsy* and bourgeois specialists later developed good working relationships, based on a division of labor in which the specialists ran the operation and their Communist bosses used proletarian clout to protect it politically. Outside working hours, the *vydvizhentsy* were less likely than the Bolshevik intellectuals to mix with the "bourgeois" intelligentsia. They may, however, have been particularly inclined to exchange an old working-class wife for a new one from the bourgeoisie after their rise in social status. Unfortunately the question of marriage patterns, which are of great significance on a wide range of social history topics, will probably remain obscure for lack of any corpus of systematic data.

One final question of Bolshevik Party sociology that deserves attention from Civil War historians is the distinction between "civilians" and "military" Bolsheviks that the Civil War itself produced. This topic will be further discussed in my concluding essay, since it relates particularly to the legacy of the Civil War. But this discussion of networks would be incomplete without reference to the Red Army, which generated the biggest and proudest network of them all, and the one most characteristic of the period. Other Bolshevik subgroups like the *vydvizhentsy* and the Bolshevik intelligentsia had a somewhat ambiguous status as networks: their members "recognized" each other, but that recognition may not have been accompanied by a strong desire for further association and communication, since the *vydvizhentsy* may have had the social insecurity of other upwardly mobile groups and the Bolshevik intelligentsia suffered from sociopolitical anxiety about not being working class. The Bolshevik "civilians," similarly, felt that they ought to be at the front and must defer to the mores of the "military" group.

But the "military" Bolsheviks knew that they were in the right place, fighting for the Revolution. They were proud of their comradeship and solidarity, and their mutual recognition was always a cause of celebration. This confidence in their own values was perhaps matched by that of the "bourgeois intelligentsia." But the old intelligentsia celebrated its Civil War meetings in a spirit of apocalyptic gloom, while the Red Army Bolsheviks celebrated heroic struggle and inevitable future victory.

NOTES

1. In the Soviet literature, two basic works are the collectively written *Izmeneniia sotsial'noi struktury sovetskogo obshchestva, oktiabr 1917–1920* (Moscow, 1976); and *Izmeneniia sotsial'noi struktury sovetskogo obshchestva, 1921–seredina 30-kh godov* (Moscow, 1979). Among the most interesting social historians of the Soviet period are V. P. Danilov (peasants), E. G. Gimpelson, and V. Z. Drobizhev (workers) and I. Ia. Trifonov (for an idiosyncratic class-war perspective on the 1920s and 1930s).

2. For example, S. A. Smith, *Red Petrograd: Revolution in the Factories 1917–1918* (Cambridge, 1983); David Mandel, *The Petrograd Workers and the Fall of the Old Regime* (New York, 1983); and Mandel, *The Petrograd Workers and the Soviet Seizure of Power* (New York, 1984).

3. Teodor Shanin, *The Awkward Class: Political Sociology of Peasantry in a Developing Society, Russia 1910–1925* (Oxford, 1972).

4. On the "dynamic studies" of peasant households conducted by the Central Statistical Administration in the 1920s, see Shanin, pp. 71–76.

5. See Elise Kimerling, "Civil Rights and Social Policy in Soviet Russia, 1918–1936," *Russian Review*, January 1982, vol. 41, no. 1, pp. 24–46.

6. For some interesting case studies illustrating the difficulties of class identification in an era of revolution, civil war, and frequent occupational changes by individuals, see data from the 1924 Purge Commission of Perm University in *Krasnaia molodezh'*, 1924, no. 2, pp. 126–27.

7. Among Soviet historians, the best work on social mobility comes from V. Z. Drobizhev (e.g., "Rol' rabochego klassa SSSR v formirovanii komandnykh kadrov sotsialisticheskoi promyshlennosti [1917–1936 gg.]," *Istoriia SSSR*, 1961, no. 4; and Iu. V. Arutiunian ("Kollektivizatsiia sel'skogo khoziaistva i vysvobozhdenie rabochei sily dlia promyshlennosti," in *Formirovanie i razvitie sovetskogo rabochego klassa [1917–1962 gg.]* [Moscow, 1964]). The topic is often discussed under the heading "Formirovanie intelligentsii," "Formirovanie rabochego klassa," and so on.

8. See, for example, William L. Rowe, "The New Cauhans: A Caste Mobility Movement in North India," in James Silverberg, ed., *Social Mobility in the Caste System in India: An Interdisciplinary Symposium* (The Hauge, 1968), pp. 66–77.

9. Sheila Fitzpatrick, *Education and Social Mobility in the Soviet Union, 1921–1934* (Cambridge, 1979), pp. 15–17.

10. For the 1920s, this topic is examined in Don Karl Rowney, "Proletarianization, Political Control and the Soviet State Administration in the 1920s: Their Impact on Upward Social Mobility," paper presented at National Seminar on the Social History of Russia in the Twentieth Century, meeting on "Bureaucracy," Philadelphia, January 1983.

11. The Soviet Data Bank project, directed by William Chase (University of Pittsburgh) and J. Arch Getty (University of California at Riverside), is currently in the process of computerizing officeholding data on party and state bureaucrats in the 1920s and 1930s contained in the city directories *Vsia Moskva* and other sources, including the biographical files of individual scholars. The project, which has been supported by grants from the National Endowment for the Humanities and the National Council for Soviet and East European Research, aims at creating a publicly available, machine-readable data bank on leading political and economic figures.

12. On this question, see the important work of Robert Eugene Johnson, *Peasant and Proletarian: The Working Class of Moscow in the Late Nineteenth Century* (New Brunswick, 1979).

13. Shanin, pp. 145–52.

14. See, for example, Diane Koenker, *Moscow Workers and the 1917 Revolution* (Princeton, 1981); and Koenker, "Urban Families, Working-Class Youth Groups, and the 1917 Revolution in Moscow," in David L. Ransel, ed., *The Family in Imperial Russia: New Lines of Historical Research* (Urbana, Ill., 1978).

15. For a stimulating discussion of this question, see Daniel Field, *Rebels in the Name of the Tsar* (Boston, 1976).

16. For example, Mark David Mandel, "The Development of Revolutionary Consciousness among the Industrial Workers of Petrograd between February and November 1917," Ph.D. diss., Columbia University, 1977. Diane Koenker makes a valiant but perhaps not wholly successful effort to deal with this problem in her *Moscow Workers*, esp. pp. 7–10 and 356–67.

17. E. O. Kabo, *Ocherki rabochego byta. Opyt monograficheskogo issledovaniia* (Moscow, 1928).

18. On emigration, see Ts. Urlanis, *Istoriia odnogo pokoleniia* (Moscow, 1968), p. 94.

19. The biggest of these surveys is Ia. Bineman and S. Kheinman, *Kadry gosudarstvennogo i kooperativnogo apparata SSSR* (Moscow, 1930).

20. The city directories *Vsia Moskva* and *Ves' Petrograd (Leningrad)* were published regularly in the prerevolutionary decade and (after a brief hiatus during the Civil War) in the 1920s, with more sporadic publication in the 1930s.

21. See, for example, *Deviataia konferentsiia RKP(b). Sentiabr' 1920 goda. Protokoly* (Moscow, 1972), pp. 144, 149, 193; *Desiatyi syezd RKP(b). Mart 1921 g. Stenograficheskii otchet* (Moscow, 1963), pp. 90, 105, 263.

22. On the 1924 discussion of this problem in the Red Army, see Mark L. von Hagen, "School of Revolution: Bolsheviks and Peasants in the Red Army, 1918–1928," Ph.D. diss., Stanford University, 1984, pp. 170–79. The "unhealthy influence" of the bourgeois wives was commonly blamed on NEP mores, but at least some of the marriages took place during the Civil War.

23. I. S. Kondurushkin, *Chastnyi kapital pered sovetskim sudom* (Moscow-Leningrad, 1927), p. 3.

24. For fictional representations of this "high society," see Mikhail Bulgakov's *Master i Margarita* (written in the 1920s, though not published until many years later) and a play by V. Kirshon and A. Uspenskii, *Konstantin Terekhin (Rzhavchina)* (Moscow, 1927).

25. This theme is explored in Boris Thomson, *Lot's Wife and the Venus of Milo: Conflicting Attitudes to the Cultural Heritage in Modern Russia* (Cambridge, 1978).

26. In his *Technology and Society under Lenin and Stalin: Origins of the Soviet Technical Intelligentsia 1917–1941* (Princeton, 1978); and, particularly, his article "The Politics of Technology: Stalin and Technocratic Thinking among Soviet Engineers," *American Historical Review*, April 1974.

27. *Material k otchetu TsKK VKP(b) XVI s"ezdu VKP(b). Sostavlennyi OGPU (k dokladu t. Ordzhonikidze)* (Moscow, 1930). This report was circulated in numbered copies to delegates at the Sixteenth Party Congress.

28. The hypothesis was Stalin's: see Sheila Fitzpatrick, "Stalin and the Making of a New Elite, 1928–1939," *Slavic Review*, September 1979, vol. 38, no. 3, p. 380.

29. This movement, encouraged by Stalin, Ordzhonikidze, and other members of the party leadership in the mid-1930s, aimed to draw the wives of top-level cadres and specialists into voluntary cultural and social work at their husbands' enterprises. It produced a journal, *Obshchestvennitsa*, published from 1935 to 1941, and several well-publicized All-Union meetings: see, for example, *Vsesoiuznoe soveshchanie zhen khoziaistvennikov i inzhenerno-tekhnicheskikh rabotnikov tiazheloi promyshlennosti. Stenograficheskii otchet* (Moscow, 1936).

30. Some data on worker networks are available in factory histories such as G. Volodin's *Po sledam istorii, Ocherki iz istorii Donetskogo ordena Lenina metallurgicheskogo zavoda im, V. I. Lenina* (Donetsk, 1967).

31. For example, Robert Service, *The Bolshevik Party in Revolution, 1917–1923: A Study in Organisational Change* (New York, 1979).

CIVIL WAR AND THE PROBLEM OF SOCIAL IDENTITIES IN EARLY TWENTIETH-CENTURY RUSSIA

Leopold H. Haimson

The most basic and difficult task in seeking to provide a historical perspective on the upheavals that Russian society experienced during the period of the Civil War is to explore the relationships that the images of self, of other actors, and of the body politic as a whole that the members of various social groups articulated or acted out during these years actually bore to the patterns of their individual or collective existence. The analytic problems that this task poses lie partly in the dramatic changes in political and social attitudes displayed during this period by various groups in national life—changes that were so strikingly reflected in the vertiginous upturns and downturns in the fortunes of the major political protagonists of the Civil War. But they also stem from the fact that this period—from the inception of the Civil War in the summer of 1918 up to the decision of the Bolshevik Party to embark on the experiment of NEP—encompassed, to a degree unprecedented since the Time of Troubles, processes of disintegration and reintegration of the very fabric of Russian society. These processes involved not only the periodic loosening and retightening of social bonds, but also repeated redefinition—both willed and unwilled, from above, but also from below—of the identities of various groups in national life, as well as of their relationship to one another and to the body politic as a whole.

To trace adequately the sources of these processes in Russia's earlier historical experience appears all the more daunting, given the fact that, especially from the Emancipation onward, the country's development had already been marked by profound and steadily growing contradictions not only in the relationships that its various constituent groups bore to each other and to the state, but also in the evolution of their respective social, psychological, and political identities. The Russia that underwent the Revolution of 1917 was a society out of joint, and the severe convulsions that beset it under the stresses of the Civil War were, at least in part, but a demonstration of this fact.

The most glaring of these contradictions in the development of post-Reform Russia, and one which became especially evident among the growing number of the individuals and groups not in state service who experienced most deeply the effects of various processes of "modernization," was that between the *sosloviia* and *sostoianiia*—the legal statuses assigned to them by the state— and the nature of the occupations in which they actually engaged. These discrepancies came to reflect not merely the degree of geographical, occupational, and social mobility that members of various social groups managed to achieve in the course of their lifetimes. Increasingly, these discrepancies tended to become hereditary, demonstrating that even to the degree that a society of classes was beginning to coalesce, especially in urban Russia, its development could no longer be contained within the institutional framework and the various legal definitions provided by the state.[1]

By the turn of the century, such discrepancies had become especially apparent in urban-commercial-industrial Russia. Consider, for example, the growing number of industrial workers born in cities who were still legally ascribed to the peasantry, even after they had lost (especially in the wake of the Stolypin land reforms) any tangible ties to the countryside and to the land; or for that matter, the steadily growing numbers of members of the free professions— another outgroup in Russia's society of *sosloviia*—who were ascribed to the *meshchanstvo* (especially if they were Jews), or in most other cases still to the nobility. As various processes of social, cultural, as well as economic modernization made their way into the countryside, especially after 1905, with no institutional framework to contain them—given the aborting of the reform projects of local administration that were intended to provide such a framework for the Stolypin land legislation—such contradictions also became increasingly characteristic of rural Russia, contributing there as well to the fragility and potential explosiveness of social relationships and to the growing confusion of social identities.

To be sure, the growing chasm between the experience of various social groups and the legal statuses still ascribed to them by the state was partially filled by the various institutions of self-administration that had emerged in Russia in the post-Emancipation period. It was in large measure these institutions of self-administration—most notably the *zemstva*—that provided the institutional foci for the emergence, already by the end of the 1870s, of the image of a civil society—an *obshchestvo*—with its principles of order and legitimacy distinct from, and potentially counterposed to, those of the state. By the same token, the crystallization of a sense of the commonweal (*obshchestvennoe delo*), and of an educated elite not only dedicated to serve it but also to infuse it with a sense of dedication to the People, contributed, by the turn of the century, to the emergence of the conception of a struggle against absolutism, led by a coalition of the liberal and radical groups of a "noncaste," "non-*soslovie*," "nonclass" intelligentsia, to conquer political freedom and civic rights for a "nation" already seen in the making, if not in actual existence.

However, the experience of 1905 would unveil, and that of 1917 amply confirm, the degree to which this notion of a civil society had failed not only to bridge the divisions between rural and urban-commercial-industrial Russia, and between the upper and lower strata of both, but even to encompass the processes of economic, social, and psychological change actually experienced by various social groups. The caste features that had remained imprinted on the institutions of self-administration of "society" since the Counter Reforms of the 1880s and the failure of Stolypin's efforts to eliminate them in the wake of the 1905 revolution obviously contributed to the sharpness of the divisions between social groups, especially in rural Russia, as well as to the acuteness of the contradictions between the processes of socioeconomic change at work among various social groups and the institutional framework in which these processes remained contained right up to the outbreak of the Revolution of 1917.

It is precisely because of their recognition of the growing contradictions in Russia's social and institutional development in the late nineteenth and early twentieth centuries that historians who have sought to scrutinize the webs of social relationships in which they were reflected have increasingly sought subtler and more fluid conceptual terms than "estate," "caste," or even "social class" to distinguish the fissures, as well as the patterns of association and shared experience, that marked the evolution of Russian society during these years. While recognizing the continued importance of the oscillations between caste and service class features in Russia's particularistic system of *sosloviia*, as well as the emergence of more fluid, more universalistic class features, especially in the development of urban Russia, many of these historians now prefer to apply such conceptual terms as "networks," "cohorts," "clusters," and the like to designate the social groups on which they focus attention, and the patterns of collective behavior, shared attitudes, and collective mentalities that they attribute to them.

What these labels suggest is that the *mentalités* and patterns of collective behavior of various groups in post-Reform Russia, and indeed their very definition, can at best be correlated with complexes—syndromes—of social characteristics. No single set of social characteristics provides any adequate objective indices for them, but they frequently assume significance as guides to collective behavior *joined with others*. Thus, while in and of themselves *sosloviia* and *sostoianiia* (the legal definitions ascribed by the state) increasingly failed to provide any adequate indices of patterns of shared experience and collective behavior, they did continue in combination with other indices— of occupation, education, as well as age, nationality, religion, and geographical location—to provide significant clues to the collective mentalities and behavior of certain social groups. While it is arguable, for example, to what degree, by the eve of the Revolution of 1917, those members of the free professions living in cities who were members of the *dvorianstvo* displayed different political and social attitudes from those who were not nobles, it can hardly be denied that their appurtenance to the hereditary nobility continued to provide an essential element of the sense of identity of the Great Russian *pomeshchiki* who still lorded over much of the countryside of the Central Agricultural Region, and, in different but equally important ways, of the sense of identity and patterns of collective behavior of the largely landless hereditary nobles with higher education who, to almost the same degree, still dominated the higher reaches of many of Russia's bureaucratic institutions.

Even with this important qualification, however, the patterns of collective action, the attitudes, indeed the very sense of identity, that various individuals and groups in national life came to display, particularly during the periods of crisis that increasingly marked Russia's experience after the turn of the century, can hardly be reduced to any set of "objective" social characteristics, however subtly defined. The problem lies not merely in the discrepancies normally to be discerned between the evolution of patterns of social existence and that of *mentalités,* attitudes, and behavior. Nor does it lie solely in the contradictions peculiar to social relationships in post-Reform Russia. More fundamentally at issue is the fact that the collective representations of themselves and of the world around them acted out by various social groups—and particularly by those in urban Russia that did not serve the state and had been affected more sharply by processes of modernization—did not magically spring out of their social characteristics or even out of the patterns of their collective existence. Just as their legal identities had been imposed on them by the state, so the alternative representations of their identities to which many of these groups were drawn—given the increasingly contradictory character of their own experience—were also formulated for them, more often than not, by others, most notably by the various political and social actors who sought to mobilize them against the state. These other actors—in particular, those members of the educated elite who had themselves assumed the collective representation of an "intelligentsia" in their efforts to divine as well as to direct the shaping of the new society that they saw in the making on Russian soil—had themselves drawn these representations not only from their own experience, but also from their interpretations of the examples provided by the experience of the West.

Here, it seems to me, one must avoid two major methodological pitfalls. The first, already suggested by the cautions I have raised, would be to seek to "reify" these representations: to reduce them to any set of objective correlatives and, by the same token, to associate automatically the strengthening or weakening of their appeal for various social groups with major changes in these groups' social characteristics, or even in their basic conditions of life and work. But the other, even more dangerous pitfall to be avoided would be to fail to recognize the crucial significance of these representations in the shaping of political and social attitudes and patterns of collective behavior, especially during those periods of acute political and social crisis when members of various social groups had to establish—indeed to decide—who they were, in order to determine how they should feel, think, and ultimately act.

Examples of the major roles that these representations played in the shaping of patterns of political behavior, and yet of their often fragile and swiftly changing qualities, abound in Russia's historical experience after the turn of the century. Consider, for example, the changing political attitudes displayed by various strata of industrial workers who at different moments in the course of the Revolution of 1905 and indeed during much of 1917 were alternatively drawn to (or indeed torn between) the representations of being "class-conscious proletarians," *trudiashchikhsia* (that is, "laboring people" just like other members of the *narod*), or members of a workers' (*rabochaia*) intelligentsia, and wavered accordingly in their political allegiances between the various factions of Russian social democracy and of the Party of Socialist Revolutionaries. Or consider the attitudes and behavior displayed by those industrialists, especially in Moscow and neighboring areas of the Central Industrial Region, who oscillated during the years after 1905 between the representation of being *kuptsy*—that is, members of a particularistic and relatively isolated interest group in Russia's society of *sosloviia*—and that of being part of a "big bourgeoisie" (*krupnaia burzhuaziia*), representative not only of the interests of their own class but also of those of Russian society as a whole. Consider also the ways in which, already in the early months of 1917, members of this group were torn between the different and clashing political definitions of their "class" interests and "class identity" proposed to them by the now divided spokesmen of the Moscow "Progressisty." Consider, as well, the evolution of the attitudes of certain of the more moderate circles of the liberal intelligentsia which, between 1905 and 1917, shifted from the representation of being part of a noncaste, non-*soslovie*, nonclass social group—or more precisely, a group transcending these social differences and barriers by virtue of its superior qualities of consciousness and conscience—to that of being members of a "middle class," destined to become the vital center of a new, more modern, nation-state. Or take the example, which I like best because it so sharply brings out the compelling power that certain of these representations could exercise, as well as their evanescent quality: The pharmacists' assistants, mostly of Jewish origin, employed in Moscow's pharmacies, who, like other members of the city's lower and higher professions and of its various trades and industrial occupations, formed a union in the late spring and summer of 1905. In order to determine what this union should do and whom it should follow (whether to join the camp of social democracy or gravitate like most other professional unions into the orbit of the Union of Unions) they had to decide whether they were themselves "workers" or members of the "intelligentsia."[2]

Even more generally, it bears recalling that the very concept of "class" and of a "class" society to which *members* of various social groups were invited to subscribe, as an alternative to the statuses assigned to them by the state for the definition of their identities and of Russian society as a whole, was offered to them by spokesmen of various circles of the educated elite, even if the appeal and staying power of these representations would ultimately hinge on their degree of correspondence with these groups' own collective experience. In examining the conditions under which these representations were adopted or discarded, as well as the changing contents with which they were infused, I would suggest that we consider not only the roles of structural factors and longer-term processes of change in the social characteristics and conditions of life and work of the groups that entertained these representations, but also those of specific political and economic conjunctures and events, as well as the effects of the *interplay* between these longer and shorter-term processes of change.

We especially need to bear in mind, in this connection, that the changes in the character and power of attraction of these representations did not always reflect, or even induce, irreversible changes in the most basic and stablest aspects of psychological orientations that we associate with the term *mentalité*. As often as not, they reflected more transient changes in the grievances and aspirations of individuals and groups and, especially in their sense of the possibility of satisfying them, induced by changing political conjunctures, as well as the effects of the translation of this sense of possibility—under the even more immediate catalytic influence of specific historical events—into patterns of collective action.

The changing attitudes and patterns of behavior displayed in this, as well as in other, periods of Russian history by the masses of the peasantry provide especially striking illustrations of the complexity of the problem. Even in the early twentieth century, the behavior of many of these peasants, and especially of those who lived in the more isolated and economically backward areas of the Central Agricultural Region (CIR) ranged from what may be described (in admittedly simplified terms) as political apathy to deferential appeals to superordinate authority (whether through petitions to the czar, or to the *gospoda*, the "gentlemen" of the State Duma), to the insistent pressing of their interests and claims through their own "peasant" deputies in the Duma, to *bunty*— "elemental" revolts which could at least momentarily assume cataclysmic proportions. It may well be argued that in earlier centuries, at least, even the most dramatic of these swings—from apathy to appeals to higher superordinate authority to "elemental" revolt—had occurred among various strata of Russian peasants without effecting any significant changes in their *mentalités*. Rather, what these swings, however dramatic, in peasant attitudes and behavior appeared to reflect were in the main changes—usually induced by changing political conjunctures and events—in these peasants' perceptions of the stability of the structures of power and authority that normally contained their lives and, therefore, in their sense of the inevitability of their condition and of the possibility of altering it through collective action.

It remains for us to establish to what degree, and in what respects, the collective actions in which Russian peasants, as well as members of other social groups, engaged in 1917 and during the years of the Civil War differed from these earlier patterns of behavior of the Russian peasantry, and reflected, or ultimately induced, irreversible changes in their collective mentalities.

II

With these methodological considerations in mind, let us investigate what the patterns of collective behavior that various groups of the Russian body politic displayed by 1917 and the eve of the Civil War may suggest about their political and social attitudes, and about the representations of their own identities, of those of other social groups, and of the body politic as a whole, in which these attitudes were cast. We should first take note of the fact that in contrast to the consensus, however fragile, expressed in the conception of an "all-nation struggle" to which the leaderships of various radical as well as liberal political groups subscribed at the beginning of the Revolution of 1905, the representations of the body politic proffered even by the most moderate socialist factions during the early and most euphoric days of the Revolution of 1917 articulated a sense of the deep divisions that separated the upper and lower strata of urban and rural Russia, and of the inevitability of their reflection in the institutional framework that would have to be pieced together to defend the country and the revolution.

This sense of the deep divisions between "census," privileged, educated "society" and the masses of the unprivileged in both city and country was clearly reflected in the conception of "Dual Power" that surfaced during the February days to represent the relationship between the Provisional Committee of the State Duma (and eventually the first provisional government) and the Petrograd Soviet, and that between the social groups from which they respectively drew their support. It was equally characteristic of the soviets and the Committees of Public Safety that sprang up in most of Russia's provincial capitals to represent respectively their lower social strata (*nizy*)—and those elements of their *verkhi*—of their "census society," including members of their professional classes—which had rallied to the cause of the revolution. Hence the great symbolic significance—especially given the recognition that neither the State Duma nor the local organs of self-administration inherited from the old regime could claim to represent the lower strata of the sharply divided body politic—that was assigned to the Constituent Assembly that would eventually devise and legitimize a new institutional framework for Russian society.

Yet, one should not discount the degree of assent, indeed of support, that the Dual Power, established to assure the transition until this Constituent Assembly was convened, originally evoked among broad strata of the population, especially in urban Russia, nor should one underestimate the degree of restraint, if not of good will, that this new definition of the repartition of political authority temporarily induced in these groups' mutual relations. Much of the importance of the work of Ziva Galili lies precisely in her emphasis on this fact, as well as in her recognition of the rapidity with which this mutual restraint eroded not only because of the strains and sufferings induced by the war, but also as a result of the loss of legitimacy that the moderate socialist parties experienced once they made the political decision (however inevitable it may have appeared in the wake of the April Crisis) to form a coalition government with the "progressive circles of the bourgeoisie."[3] Galili's study shows very clearly, it seems to me, how the very representation of such a coalition regime—notwithstanding the image of the "union of the vital forces of the nation" that Iraklii Tsereteli and his allies sought to sustain in its support—rather than plastering over the deep divisions between the *verkhi* and *nizy* of the body politic, contributed instead to the translation of these divisions into more open and uncontainable political conflicts. Galili's study, as well as William G. Rosenberg's and Diane P. Koenker's work in progress on the dynamics of labor unrest during these months, sharply bring out how these processes were reflected in the politicization as well as the radicalization of patterns of collective action among industrial workers. In particular, these studies show how the issue of workers' control over conditions in their enterprises, which assumed steadily growing urgency and weight by the spring of 1917 among Petrograd metal workers—given the temporary shutdowns and threats of closure of their enterprises by employers—was necessarily broadened and redefined in the new political context created by coalition into the goal of workers' control of the national economy and of the body politic as a whole. Hence, the increasing shift from strikes to political demonstrations in these workers' patterns of collective action (culminating in their massive participation in the June and July demonstrations calling for "All Power to the Soviets") should be viewed not only in the light of the growing economic difficulties that these workers were experiencing, or even of the Bolsheviks' ability to exploit them, but also of the changes in these workers' representation of the new political order that the formation of a "coalition" government induced.

Let us now shift our attention to the political representations suggested by the patterns of voting behavior displayed, especially in the wake of the *Kornilovshchina,* by the various constituent groups of urban Russia in municipal elections, reelections to local soviets, and eventually in the elections to the Second Congress of Soviets and to the Constituent Assembly.

The first conclusion drawn by Fedor Dan, as he sought to analyze for the Menshevik press the returns from the various districts of Petrograd in the elections to the Constituent Assembly, was that these returns prefigured and probably made inevitable the outbreak of a civil war.[4] (Dan only partially recovered from this impression as returns poured in from other parts of the country.) What Dan had immediately in mind when he labeled these voting patterns "civil war returns" was the dramatic shrinking of support by various groups of voters for the bloc of Revolutionary Defensists—Mensheviks and Socialist Revolutionaries alike—that had sought to hold together the "vital forces of the nation" in support of coalition. Dan had in view, by the same token, the polarization of the returns from the poorer and more well-to-do districts of the capital between Bolsheviks and Kadets—the two parties whose leading cadres Dan considered (quite correctly, I think) as already consciously oriented toward the *inevitability*, if not the desirability, of civil war.

Dan and most other Menshevik observers also had in mind an even more significant aspect of the polarization of the body politic suggested by these returns from Petrograd and other major cities. It was the equally sharp process of *social* polarization that they had unveiled in urban Russia between the upper, more privileged, better educated strata of "census" society (now rejoined by the overwhelming majority of members of the professional classes) and the vast masses of the *nizy* of these cities—including industrial workers, but also members of other hitherto "tributary" social groups employed in various "menial" occupations. These other strata of the *nizy* of urban Russia—laborers, house servants, shop clerks, and the like—had joined with industrial workers in casting their ballots overwhelmingly for the Bolsheviks.

Obviously, the various members of this "plebs" had voted for the Bolsheviks on the basis of a wide range of grievances and aspirations, and, indeed, entertained when they did so quite varied images of who the Bolsheviks were and of what could be expected of them. Many, indeed most, had so voted because they expected the Bolsheviks to bring them Peace and Bread; others had assigned to their act, and to the achievement of Soviet power, the wider if more imprecise promise of a "brighter future" (*svetloe budushchee*); others still—undoubtedly a much smaller number—had done so on the basis of the firmer and more explicit vision of the establishment of a proletarian dictatorship, if not of a dictatorship of workers and poor peasants. Yet however varied or imprecise the visions and the impulses that underlay them, one should not underestimate the acuteness of the sense of antagonism toward "census" society that had now been exposed by the lower orders and social strata of urban Russia. Nor should one minimize the acuteness of their feelings, in casting their ballots for the Bolsheviks, that their grievances and aspirations—however variously defined—could be satisfied only through the establishment of a political order in which the influence of "census" society would be drastically reduced, if not entirely eliminated. Indeed, whatever labels these voters of the plebs of urban Russia applied to those whom they were voting against—whether "burzhui" or "gospoda"—they reflected, to varying degrees, a revolt against the exercise, or perceived exercise, of all forms of superordinate authority, however blended or intermixed this rejection of caste relationships had now become with the content, and especially the language, of class conflict and class revolt.

As will be recalled, the signs of such a revolt against relations of superordination had appeared much earlier among industrial workers, and surfaced massively in the course of the 1905–1907 and especially the prewar strike waves, in which complaints of "rudeness" on the part of supervisors and demands for *vezhlivoe obrashchenie*—polite treatment and polite address—

had emerged as a major motif in labor unrest. By the fall of 1917, such a sense of *unizhenie i oskorblenie*—of "humiliation and insult" over the very exercise of superordinate authority—had spread to other strata of the *nizy* of urban Russia, surfacing in the grievances voiced by house servants against their masters, of sales clerks against the owners and patrons of their shops, as well as in the ballots that the members of these groups now cast for the Bolsheviks in Petrograd and other major cities with mixed populations.

Just as we need to take into account the patterns of revolt against relations of superordination that had surfaced by the fall of 1917 among the *nizy* of urban Russia, so we should not underestimate the acuteness of the fears and resentments that had spread among their *verkhi*, including the many former supporters of the moderate socialist parties among members of the free professions who now cast their ballots for the Kadets. In voting for the Kadets many of these members of the professional intelligentsia believed that they were seeking to uphold a conception of the national, if not of the state interest (*gosudarstvennyi interes*). But they were also voting, in the last resort, in defense of "order" against what they perceived to be processes of "elemental" revolt and social disintegration unleashed or at least encouraged by the Bolsheviks, which now threatened, so they believed, to destroy the very fabric of national life, including the patterns and values of their own "cultured" and "civilized" existence.

By the fall of 1917, these processes of social and cultural, as well as political polarization between the *verkhi* and *nizy* of urban Russia had thus spread very widely in the metropolitan centers and large cities of European Russia. In however varied and different forms, they had also spread to most provincial capitals, especially to those with substantial military garrisons whose soldiers had ceased to obey their officers or, indeed, to heed the orders of any existing organs of political authority, and only responded, already well before the October seizure of power in Petrograd, to the appeals of often obscure if not improvised "Bolshevik" leaderships.

We shall return to the subject of the political attitudes and behavior displayed by soldiers in the rear as well as at the front, but let us first extend our gaze to another group of the body politic, which made an equally crucial and certainly more enduring contribution to the Bolsheviks' seizure of power and especially to their ability to survive and ultimately win the Civil War: the workers of the Central Industrial Region.

The various strata of workers who lived and worked in the CIR overwhelmingly supported the Bolsheviks in the late summer and fall of 1917: workers in Moscow and other industrial centers, such as Ivanovo-Voznesensk, but also those employed in the industrial villages of the provinces of Vladimir and Kostroma, and even in the large *manufaktury* that had sprung up at the end of railroad sidelines in the middle of the countryside, especially in Moscow *guberniia*. Indeed, the workers of these outlying areas of the Central Industrial Region significantly contributed to the Bolsheviks' ascendancy at the Second Congress of Soviets, as well as to the denouement of the armed conflicts—far more bitter than those that unfolded in Petrograd—which marked the Bolshevik seizure of power in Moscow. (Their outcome was not finally decided until the arrival on the scene of workers' militias mobilized outside the city.)

The workers of the Central Industrial Region also overwhelmingly supported the Bolsheviks in the elections to the Constituent Assembly and were joined in the process by large numbers of local peasants—the only large masses of the peasantry in these elections to cast their ballots for the Bolsheviks. The phenomenon is hardly puzzling, given the close intertwining of industrial and agricultural labor that distinguished the economy of the region. This intertwining of working class and peasant life could in fact be traced back to the traditional involvement of the peasants of the Central Industrial Region in handicraft and cottage industries, which had been channeled into industrial development through the path of the domestic system, but it had also been reinforced by the patterns of recruitment into the textile *manufaktury* of the region of local ("mestnye") as well as immigrant *("prishlye")* peasants. Given these patterns of shared experience, the broadly similar patterns of voting behavior that surfaced among many of the workers and peasants of the CIR in the elections to the Constituent Assembly are not surprising. They do, however, raise some fundamental issues about the evolution of Bolshevik political culture during this period—about its ability to survive but also to be transformed by the traumatic experience of the Civil War.

Sukhanov describes himself in his *Zapiski o revoliutsii* as having been profoundly struck by the contrasts in social, cultural, as well as political types that the workers' deputies,[5] many of them from the Central Industrial Region, who supported the Bolsheviks at the Second Congress of Soviets in October 1917, presented to the workers' deputies he had encountered in June at the First Congress of Soviets, who had given, by and large, such unwavering support to the bloc of Revolutionary Defensists. The deputies to the Second Congress of Soviets appeared to Sukhanov far "greyer" (*serye*) if not darker (*chernye*) in appearance, far more dour if not "primitive" in their manners as well as their political responses, than the more highly urbanized, "cultured," "Europeanized" types with whom he was familiar from his Petrograd experience. Even while taking account of Sukhanov's journalistic license—after all, we should bear in mind that by this time, and indeed for many months, the Bolsheviks had been drawing considerable support from the highly urbanized and "cultured" workers employed in Petrograd's most advanced electrotechnical and mechanical plants—there is little doubt that the Bolshevik deputies elected to the Second Congress of Soviets from the Central Industrial Region and the workers who had elected them in fact represented quite different social and cultural types than those whom Sukhanov had previously encountered.

Indeed, it is worth recalling how tenuous a relationship the social characteristics and *mentalités* of these workers of the Central Industrial Region bore to Sukhanov's received ideas about the working class, and especially about its politically more "advanced" and "class conscious" strata. Most of these workers, as we have already noted, still maintained, or at the very least had entertained earlier in their lives, close relationships to the countryside and to the land. In fact, with the exception of the workers of the Urals, the industrial work forces employed in the CIR included, according to the data of the 1918 industrial census, the highest proportions of workers who still possessed, or whose families still possessed, land, or were recorded as being themselves engaged in agricultural work on a part-time basis. (To be sure, these statistical indices reflected a wide range of current and past life experiences, from the situations of the workers of industrial villages who regularly cultivated their household plots even while engaging full time in industrial work to the immigrant workers in cities like Moscow and Ivanovo-Voznesensk who returned to the countryside during the summer months to participate in agricultural field work.)[6]

According to other census data, these work forces of the Central Industrial Region also included—again with the sole exception of the industrial workers of the Urals—the highest proportion of hereditary workers in Russia, that is, of workers, at least one of whose parents had been employed in industry before them. (Again, this is hardly surprising when we consider that, along with the Urals, the CIR was the oldest industrial region of the Empire.)[7]

The long tradition of industrial experience of the towns and industrial villages of the CIR, which had been contained much more sharply within the traditional institutional framework and values of Russia's society of *sosloviia* than was the case of large urban centers such as Petersburg and Moscow, had made for a distinctive intermixture of "caste" and "class" characteristics in their workers' *mentalités* and behavior, including their patterns of labor unrest. Let me briefly take note of some of their most prominent features. One clearly was the degree to which, at least from the 1880s and 1890s up to the eve of the revolution, outbreaks of labor unrest among these workers repeatedly involved "defensive" strikes, in protest against infringements of a sense of moral economy still profoundly anchored in traditional values and cast in equally traditional terms by the workers who participated in these labor conflicts. The strikes that broke out over the reduction by employers, following the issuance of the labor legislation of 1897, of the number of days of rest allocated to religious holidays, were obvious examples. But so were the "defensive" strikes that broke out in the provinces of Vladimir and Kostroma in the spring and summer of 1915, partly over the failure by employers to fulfill their traditional responsibility of providing adequate food supplies to the workers of their *manufaktury*. We should also recognize the dramatic shifts and swings of attitudes, moods, and patterns of collective behavior that distinguished the dynamics of labor unrest among workers of the Central Industrial Region, from narrow economic concerns to militant support of social democracy—and indeed, as the workers of Ivanovo Voznesensk demonstrated in the course of the Revolution of 1905, from pogroms to the creation of workers' councils dominated by the Bolsheviks. Even as late as 1917, these patterns of collective attitudes and behavior among workers of certain areas of the CIR shifted from the formulation, during the early months of the revolution, of their own variations on the theme of Dual Power in their relations with employers, to stalwart support by summer and fall of full and undivided Soviet Power.

Such examples clearly suggest, it seems to me, that there were many roads to Bolshevism—and many forms of Bolshevik, as indeed of Menshevik, political culture during these years (consider, after all, the hold of Menshevik political culture on the Georgian peasantry)—and that the path followed by the workers of the industrial villages of the Central Industrial Region was no less important than that traced by Petrograd metal workers in accounting for the dynamics of the Revolution of 1917 and especially for the capacity of the Bolsheviks to survive and eventually win the Civil War. Indeed, in weighing the significance of these workers' contribution to the eventual outcome, one needs to consider not only the part that they played in the Bolshevik seizure of power in Moscow and the patterns of their votes in the elections to the Constituent Assembly, but also the ways in which the dramatic advances of the White armies in the course of the Civil War were repeatedly stopped and eventually repelled once they reached and came up against the inner redoubts of Soviet power in the industrial towns and villages of the Central Industrial Region.

I have already noted that well before the October seizure of power in Petrograd, the soldiers of most military garrisons in the rear—not only in Petrograd and Moscow but also in the provincial capitals, from Kazan to Tiflis—had ceased to obey their officers, and indeed to heed the orders of any organs of previously constituted authority—responding only to the appeals of Bolshevik leaderships, often improvised from their own ranks. Most of the soldiers who displayed these attitudes were revolting against all forms and organs of authority that stood in the way of the fulfillment of the Bolsheviks' promises of Peace and Land. Even before peace actually came, many of these peasant soldiers melted away, to return home to take part in the Black Repartition already sanctioned by the decree on land issued by the Second Congress of Soviets.

But what of the attitudes and behavior of soldiers at the front? In an article written late in 1919 to explain to Western comrades why, notwithstanding their failure to win a majority in the elections to the Constituent Assembly, the Bolsheviks had managed to stay in power and were now winning the Civil War, Lenin emphasized the massiveness of the support they had received not only from the large concentrations of industrial workers and soldiers in the two capitals, but also from the armies of the Northwestern and Western fronts, strategically located nearest to the seats of their political power.[8] What political and social dynamics underlay the patterns of these election returns and the attitudes and representations of the body politic that they reflected?

In the first volume of his magisterial social history of the Russian army in 1917,[9] Allan K. Wildman emphasizes how little the masses of peasants who had been drafted into the army and bled at the front during the years of the First World War actually shared the conception of national interest, indeed the very sense of nationhood, to which the Provisional Government sought to appeal in 1917. Wildman's study brings out very clearly, by the same token, that far from contributing to the disintegration of these soldiers' sense of military discipline and morale, the new structures of political and military authority improvised by the Executive Committee of Soviets—from the commissars delegated to the fronts to the Soviets of Soldiers' Deputies—actually played a major, indeed indispensable, role in keeping the front-line armies in being during the first months of the revolution and especially in sustaining a semblance of order and authority to fill the void created by the deterioration of the relations of superordination between officers and men on which military discipline had hitherto largely rested. Wildman's second volume shows just as dramatically, it seems to me, how in the wake of the failure of the June offensive, and especially of the *Kornilovshchina*, this new improvised structure of order, but also of mutual trust and loyalties, almost entirely broke down, opening the door, almost as widely and instantaneously at the front as it did in the rear, to a massive response on the part of the soldiers of this largely peasant army to the Bolsheviks' slogans of Peace and Land.

From Wildman's description of this process, one can also draw a dual, only superficially contradictory, set of impressions concerning the representations of the existing structure of power and authority that surfaced among these increasingly mutinous peasant soldiers as they confronted those of their officers who still sought to impose on them a modicum of military discipline, if not to induce them to keep on fighting, instead of going home to join in their fellow peasants' Black Repartition.

On the one hand, one is repeatedly struck by the volatility of the labels— the terms "burzhui" and "pomeshchik" (sometimes elaborated with the attribution to the "culprits" of estates of so many thousands of *desiatiny*) being applied arbitrarily, and seemingly interchangeably, to those officers who thus stood in the way of these soldiers' pent-up grievances and aspirations. On the other hand, one also draws from this composite picture—however chaotic— the impression that these mutinous soldiers were in fact giving voice to a generalized view of the structure of power and authority that they were now overturning, and indeed assigning to all those who sought to keep it in place the representations of an old order and an old regime. We should note that these labels were liberally and indiscriminately applied to representatives of authority from urban as well as rural Russia: to the "Junkers" drawn from the universities and professional classes of the cities who had been drafted into service and risen to officer rank, just as easily as to career officers of noble status—with or without landed estates. Hence the very volatility of the labels— the terms "burzhui" and "pomeshchik" now being interchangeably applied to representatives of the old order that was being overturned and to the structure of superordinate authority and relations on which it was perceived to rest.

A similarly dual impression is to be drawn about the representations that these soldiers now articulated of the new Soviet Power that was to take the place of the hated Old Order and old regime. On the one hand, it would be

erroneous to consider that this new Soviet power stood merely in the eyes of
these peasant soldiers for the Peace and Land promised by the Bolsheviks,
including their promise of the immediate fulfillment of their dream of a *Chernyi
peredel*. It also stood, at the very least, for the establishment of a social, if not
a political, order in which all forms of superordinate authority, all patterns of
superordinate relations—whether those traditionally imposed in the countryside, or those more recently introduced from urban, commercial, industrial
Russia—would be entirely erased, leaving in place only social relationships
rooted in the peasant community itself. On the other hand, it is evident from
these remarks that these peasant soldiers' notion of Soviet Power—even though
most of them now probably viewed this power as their very own, rather than
as a superordinate authority, however benevolent, hovering over them—did
not encompass any conception of the relationships between themselves, their
village communities, or even the peasantry as a whole *and other social groups*—
let alone any generalized view of the Russian body politic.

By the same token, once this army dissolved, and its peasant soldiers had
gone home to their native villages, most of them—including those who had
voted most enthusiastically for the Bolsheviks—while originally contributing
to the radicalization and especially the mobilization of the peasant masses, did
so, by and large, in ways that the peasants of their native villages themselves
wanted to take. After the Black Repartitions in which these processes culminated and eventually subsided, most of them were reabsorbed very quickly
into the peasant communities, now more homogeneous than ever before, which
emerged in the wake of this *Chernyi peredel*.

In the analysis for Western comrades that I already cited, Lenin readily
conceded that the vast majority of Russian peasants (aside from those of the
Central Industrial Region) had *not* supported the Bolsheviks in the elections
of the Constituent Assembly and in fact voted overwhelmingly for the Party
of Socialist Revolutionaries (PSR). Indeed, the whole purpose of the exercise
had been to explain how and why, notwithstanding this fact, the Bolsheviks
had managed to stay in power and were now winning the Civil War.

To be sure, the meaning of the returns from the countryside in the elections
to the Constituent Assembly had been obscured, and their political effect ultimately blunted, by the profound political divisions among the various factions
of the PSR, which had already culminated in the split of the Left Socialist
Revolutionaries from the other factions of the party and in their coalition with
the Bolsheviks in support of the October seizure of power. Nor should we
forget that the degree of support that the Left Socialist Revolutionaries actually
enjoyed among the peasantry had undoubtedly been underestimated in the
returns by the procedures under which the elections to the Constituent Assembly had been conducted. (In most regions of the country the candidates of the
Left SRs had appeared on the same electoral lists, usually in lower positions,
with those of other factions of the Party of Socialist Revolutionaries and had

thus been disfavored under the system of proportionate representation adopted for the allocation of seats to the assembly.)[10]

Given this vexing fact (to which Lenin obviously did not draw attention in his 1919 article, in view of the break between the Left Socialist Revolutionaries and the Bolsheviks by the summer of 1918), as well as the even more serious problem that no real study of how these elections actually unfolded in the countryside has been conducted to date, it is hardly possible to draw any sense of how the differences between the Left Socialist Revolutionaries and other factions of the party were actually perceived at the grass-roots level. Yet these difficulties, however frustrating, should not deter us from hazarding certain generalizations about the nature of peasant political attitudes at this moment, transcending the range of peasant responses to the various factions of the PSR. This is not to suggest that the coalition of the Left Socialist Revolutionaries with the Bolsheviks up to the summer of 1918 did not substantially contribute to the Bolsheviks' ability to neutralize, if not to win the support of, the peasantry during these crucial months. Unquestionably it did. But the glimpses that we are able to draw of the evolution of peasants' political attitudes and behavior during these months also amply suggest, it seems to me, the limits of the peasantry's support during this period for *all* the national political parties and factions which claimed and sought to represent them—including the candidates of the various factions of the Party of Socialist Revolutionaries for which they had voted in such overwhelming numbers.

To bring out the nature of these political attitudes, let me draw on an illustration, already cited in my earlier study of the politics of rural Russia, from the one-day proceedings of the Constituent Assembly in January 1918. Well into this almost interminable session, at a moment when the Left Socialist Revolutionaries, just like the Bolsheviks, were already maneuvering to find the propitious issue over which to walk out, the peasant deputy selected by the Left Socialist Revolutionaries to be their official spokesman came up to the podium to deliver their statement. But after reading off the belligerent text of this official declaration, this peasant "spokesman" of the Left Socialist Revolutionaries, Sorokin, expressed the wish to deliver a "few words" of his own to his fellow peasant deputies—of all parties and factions—assembled in the hall. Let me cite these "few words" in full, since they bring out so sharply the nature of the political attitudes and representations which proved so important, it seems to me, in accounting for peasants' patterns of political behavior at this moment and in the subsequent unfolding of the Civil War:

> I will say a few words of my own. Many millions of peasants have sent us here. We are under the obligation to work for these peasants without laying down our hands. We must give this deprived, forgotten, hungry, cold peasantry Land and Freedom [*Zemlia i Volia*]. *All of us came here with the order and instructions not to return to the countryside without this.*
>
> *Therefore, comrade peasants, I am appealing to all of you, without exception,*

whatever faction you belong to: we will obtain this Land and Freedom, and only then, freely, with a clear conscience, return to the countryside. [Applause]. And then the peasantry will greet us with open arms. If we fail to do so, the peasantry will be entitled to hold us in contempt and to hate us. [Voices: "Correct!"] [Applause in the *center* and *right* of the hall]. I hope comrade peasants, that we shall fulfill our mission to the end. [Noise from the Left: "Sabotage!"]

In this respect, there are no differences among us peasants. [Extended applause in center and right of the hall]. *We are all alike here, rights and lefts.* ["Correct!" Prolonged applause in center and right]. *My last request to you, peasants, is that we fulfill precisely these commands and requests.* [Applause].[11]

Two psychological features starkly stand out in the extraordinary impromptu statement of this peasant deputy—who had been selected, it bears repeating, to read the official statement of the Left Socialist Revolutionaries, and yet was greeted (as the official transcript indicates) by such a storm of applause from their political opponents assembled in the center and right of the hall, and by cries of betrayal on the left. Both features need to be emphasized, for *both* appear to me equally characteristic of most peasants' political attitudes at this moment.

The first, of course, was the extraordinary particularism of the statement, in both content and form. Transcending all other political considerations, even at this critical moment in the confrontation between the Left Socialist Revolutionaries and their Bolshevik allies and the majority of the deputies assembled—transcending, by the same token, the basic issue involved in this confrontation of the kind of political order and political structure that was now to be established (or at least legitimized by the assembled delegates)— Sorokin was reminding the other peasant deputies that they had been sent to the assembly by their fellow peasants, first and foremost, to obtain Land and Freedom, or more precisely to secure the legal sanctioning of their Black Repartition. By the same token, regardless of their ostensible particular political affiliations and of the political stakes invested in the assembly's ongoing scenario by their respective parties and factions, these peasant deputies should now stay put, join hands in pressing for the passage of this land legislation, and not dare go home to their native villages and face their peasant constituents without it.

The other equally notable feature of both the substance and form of Sorokin's statement was the total absence of any appeal in the pressing of this particularistic interest of any shade of deference, *real or sham*, for any superordinate authority. (This was a far cry from the deferential behavior of peasant deputies toward the *gospoda* of the First State Duma, not to mention the inventions of superordinate authority involved in the phenomenon of "pretendership" in the major peasant uprisings of the seventeenth and eighteenth centuries—the masquerading of a Sten'ka Razin as Tsar Alexis, or of Pugachev and his entourage as Peter III and the members of his court.) But neither—the point should be emphasized—did the statement really reflect any explicit or even implicit recognition of a broader, transcendent, societal interest and principle of legitimacy and, by the same token, of any form of its political or institutional expression. Sorokin was appealing neither to the Left SRs and their Bolshevik allies, nor to the Party of Socialist Revolutionaries as a whole—indeed, not even to the Constituent Assembly as the institutional expression of the will of the nation, or even of the People, the *narod—but only to his fellow peasant deputies, regardless of party or faction*, to obtain for the peasantry what he believed it wanted most: Land and Freedom—or more precisely, freedom *from others*.

Both of these features, I believe, were profoundly characteristic of peasant political attitudes at this moment, and continued to be, with profound implications for the unfolding of the Civil War. One—particularism—reflected a continuity in the *mentalité* of Russian peasants stretching back to the very inception of the Russian state and would only gradually erode under Soviet rule, until it was shattered, along with the traditional peasant community, by the experience of collectivization of the 1930s. The other—the refusal to recognize, let alone defer to any superordinate authority, *real or sham*—reflected, I believe, a major change in the peasantry's deepest, underlying, political orientation, although this change had been prefigured, even if less sharply and nakedly, in the conduct of peasant deputies to the soviets in 1917, and indeed of peasant deputies to the Second State Duma. *Both* of these dimensions, old and new, of these peasants' *mentalité* surfaced in the behavior that they displayed in the course of the Civil War toward all major political actors—including the rival factions of the Party of Socialist Revolutionaries—who sought to enlist them to support actively the claims of a broader "societal," "national," or "state" interest. But before elaborating on this point, let us consider however briefly, how these two dimensions of the *mentalité* of the Russian peasantry were acted out in the Black Repartition, which Sorokin had so insistently called on his fellow peasant deputies at the Constituent Assembly to sanction before they dispersed.

A large body of documentary evidence has by now been assembled and analyzed in both Russia and the West about the processes of this Black Repartition, which had effectively begun by the summer and fall of 1917, although they were vastly accelerated after the Second Congress of Soviets issued its decree on land, and the terms of this decree were eventually spelled out. Notwithstanding the very different angles of vision that have been imposed on this body of evidence (I am thinking in particular of the contributions by Pershin and Keep), one can, I think, extrapolate from it two, only superficially contradictory, impressions:

The first is that of the extraordinarily spontaneous, "elemental," character that these processes assumed—the inception, the pace, but even the shaping of the repartitions displaying the character of initiatives from below, by the peasants themselves, only superficially contained and channelized by local and central authorities, both before and after the imposition of Soviet rule. Indeed, these processes occasionally assumed a truly chaotic character, as neighboring peasant communes laid conflicting claims to—and sometimes fought over—the land, the cattle, and the chattels to be seized and parceled out. (Similar phenomena had occurred, especially in the Central Agricultural Region, during the agrarian disorders of 1905–1907.)

The other, no less forceful, impression to be drawn is that of the sharpness of the sense of moral economy—of moral order, rather than disorder—that guided the peasants who were involved in them. This sense of moral economy, and the calculus in which it was reflected, were most sharply etched in the patterns of repartition that the peasants adopted. Even when these patterns reflected, as they usually did, the application of "consumption" norms—the land and the chattels being redistributed among peasant families according to the number of mouths to be fed rather than their numbers of "labor hands"— the application of these norms nevertheless sought to give weight to the other principles of equity that the village commune had traditionally sought to uphold (the principles of *pravo truda* and *pravo na trud*—that is, of the rights *of* and *to* labor). Thus, in the implicit time scale that they calculated of the labor that would be invested by peasant households in the allotments to be parceled out, the "consumption" norms usually applied assigned greater weight for the numbers of adult males than they did for those of adolescents, for adolescents than they did for children, and for children than they did for infants.[12]

In however convulsive a fashion, these conceptions of peasant morality and peasant justice—indeed, of peasant rationality—were also acted out in the scenes of seemingly "senseless" violence and destruction that marked, especially at the outset, the processes of this Black Repartition: the occasional murders of *pomeshchiki*, the considerably more frequent destruction or burning of their manors, their furniture, their books, and the cutting down of their poplar trees. For what the peasants sought to accomplish by these acts of violence was not only to drive all *pomeshchiki* away, but also to erase the traces—the very memory—of their presence. In a usually less dramatic fashion, the peasant communes also reabsorbed all of the peasants who had separated and consolidated their plots before and during the Stolypin land reforms. Once these processes had been completed and consecrated by the various decrees and laws issued from the center, and the peasant communities had emerged as a result more homogeneous and more self-contained than ever before in the memories of their members, all that the vast majority of the peasantry really sought and wanted from the world at large was what it would not grant them: that it should leave them to themselves to live out their own lives.

III

Many of the studies that have appeared in the West over the past two decades concerning the character and dynamics of the October Revolution have laid considerable emphasis on the modest number of participants who were actively involved, on both sides, in the events—and especially the armed conflicts— that marked the Bolshevik seizure of power in October 1917. The point is obviously well taken with respect to the events that punctuated the Bolshevik takeover in the capital. It may even be the case that underlying the scenes of the October days in Petrograd was a considerable degree of *attentisme* among workers of the capital—itself a product of the combination of confusion, fears, and hopes reflected in the widely shared yearning for the formation of the All-Socialist government, which Vikzhel (the Executive Committee of the All-Russian Union of Railwaymen) sought to mobilize in its last minute efforts to impose such a political settlement.

Yet, however valid the observation, the inferences often drawn from it about the character of the Bolshevik seizure of power—let alone about the underlying dynamics of the October Revolution—ignore the unfolding of events outside the capital: the much more bitter and drawn-out conflicts that marked the Bolshevik takeover in Moscow, and especially the gradual, almost inperceptible, way in which, in other areas of urban and industrial Russia, the actual "shift," if not the formal transfer, of power actually occurred even before the seizure of power in Petrograd. In the last analysis, the breadth if not the depth of popular support for the Bolsheviks in the fall of 1917 can be gauged more accurately by the various elections that took place in the late summer and fall, including the patterns of the returns in the elections to the Constituent Assembly that I have sought, however briefly, to bring out.

I shall not seek to discuss how and to what degree this support actually eroded between the fall of 1917 and the summer of 1918 (except to note that I find little to question in Alexander Rabinowitch's and William G. Rosenberg's ongoing discussions of the evolution of political attitudes among Petrograd workers during these months). Let me note, however, that the emphasis laid in Western historiography on the modest number of participants involved in the armed confrontation between the Bolsheviks and their opponents during the October seizure of power assumes much greater significance and weight with respect to the opening chapters, in the summer of 1918, of the Civil War. I have in mind in this connection, not only the modest size of the military forces that actually clashed in the early phases of the conflicts between the Red and White armies, but also, and indeed especially, the extraordinarily small numbers of men involved in the skirmishes and pitched battles that marked, and eventually decided, the confrontations between the Bolsheviks and the forces led by the Right Mensheviks and Socialist Revolutionaries in the Iaroslavl' uprising, between Bolsheviks and SRs in the establishment of the Socialist Revolutionary Directory in East European Russia, and in the eventual overthrow of SR rule in Eastern European Russia and Siberia by the military forces under Aleksandr Kolchak. The military forces deployed in these opening chapters of the Civil War, especially in Eastern Russia and Siberia, were not only usually minuscule, but almost entirely drawn from these regions' urban and industrial settlements. Even the "independent-minded" peasants of Siberia, who had voted so massively for the Socialist Revolutionaries in the elections to the Constituent Assembly, failed to display any more tangible support for them than did the peasants of European Russia against the eventual restoration of White, let alone "Red" rule.

But even more significant for our concerns than the scale of the forces that actually fought out the opening battles of the Civil War, or even than their social composition, was the degree to which the political programs, political values, indeed the political cadres of both the Red and White regimes were originally drawn almost exclusively from the political cultures of urban-commercial-industrial Russia, to the exclusion of the countryside. The point is obvious with regard to the Bolsheviks, but just as notable was the contribution made to the political leadership of the Whites, especially during these early months of the Civil War, by the Kadet party and elements of the liberal intelligentsia of the cities from which this party had traditionally drawn its support. The concept of a Great, Independent, and Indivisible Russia (*Velikaia, nezavisimaia, nedelimaia Rossiia*) to which Denikin and his followers originally rallied, and the political programs in which it was articulated, owed little in fact to the ideas and values of the old regime. They reflected in the main the representation of a nation-state and the conception of national interest that had already surfaced among the Right Kadets and Progressisty by the eve of the First World War, and which the Kadet party and its supporters, largely among the professional classes of the cities, acted out with such increasing conviction, if with a growing sense of despair, during the years of the First World War and the Revolution of 1917.

By 1919, the situation began to change, as both sides drafted millions of peasants, and the political behavior, if not the political programs, acted out by the Whites, increasingly reflected the interests and orientations of holdovers from the old regime. But the major imprint laid by the Kadets on the ideas and values originally propounded by the Whites should not, for this reason, be forgotten. For it reflected the basic fact that—on both sides—only the divided strata of urban Russia proved capable at this moment of articulating and acting out representations of a political order encompassing all, or at least most, of the body politic, and claiming the allegiances of most of its constituent groups in both city and country.

Neither the *nizy* of rural Russia, nor the survivors of its former *verkhi* could, or indeed seriously sought, to contribute to this process. The point is obvious with respect to the former *pomeshchiki* of rural Russia, who proved by and large capable only of acting out the particularistic interests and values that they had so stubbornly sought to defend during the last days of the old regime—to seek to recover their landed estates and to reimpose on their peasants the old "patriarchal" relations of superordination, the very memory of which these peasants had so recently sought to erase. But in different ways, this was also the case of the peasantry itself.

In his triumphalist article of 1919, Lenin recognized that the masses of the peasantry had not supported the Bolsheviks at the time of their seizure of power, but that the experience of the Civil War had taught the peasants that they would have to choose between Reds and Whites—between Soviet rule and the rule of the *pomeshchiki*. This was an overstatement, given the degree of peasant support that peasant movements such as the Antonovshchina managed to mobilize, even in the waning days of the Civil War. But the statement had a kernel of truth. For while the peasants did display an occasional willingness to fight and die to defend their own interests and way of life, they did not, by and large, articulate any conception of a political and social order encompassing other groups of the body politic, nor indeed any aspirations to rule it. What they did act out was a profound urge to be left alone.

This was what other political actors would not let them do, in a historical drama whose unfolding thus reflected—more sharply than had ever before been the case in modern Russian historical experience—the differences between the interests, the values, and even more fundamentally, the political cultures of urban and rural Russia, as well as the divisions that still survived, or were reintroduced, in however disguised a form, between the ruling groups and the *nizy* of both.

The sharpness of the divisions that were now exposed in national life clearly suggest, by the same token, the formidable problems that both Reds and Whites had to address in their efforts to win the Civil War and to impose their rule: to create, or recreate, an institutional framework to transcend these divisions, especially those between urban and rural Russia; to create a new state, indeed a new body politic, if not a new nation; and, necessarily, in order to do so, to seek to win the support—and if not the support, the assent, or at least, the neutrality—of other major groups in national life.

The Bolsheviks ultimately proved more successful in meeting these challenges than did the Whites. Indeed, they proved in the end more successful than did the Whites in securing the assent of significant numbers of members of the professional and technical intelligentsia of the cities who had voted so over-whelmingly against them in 1917, but who also eventually had to choose between Reds and Whites, and notwithstanding their earlier opposition to the Bolsheviks, opted, however passively, for Soviet rule, as meeting more nearly, among the options they had to face, their own sense of national, state, or popular interest. In the processes of state building, even more than fighting and terror, that this experience involved, the Bolsheviks eventually won the Civil War, but, as subsequent developments demonstrated, they too emerged from this convulsive and harrowing experience transfigured, if not entirely transformed.

In the longer-term perspective of the evolution of the Soviet regime—whose original social impulses and ideological aims were, after all, directed at the very abolition of the state—one may draw a sense of historical irony about the character that these processes of state building increasingly assumed under Soviet rule. For the sense of *gosudarstvennost'* and *gosudarstvennyi interes*—the primacy assigned to the role and interest of the state—that these processes reintroduced among both rulers and ruled increasingly involved, at least from the 1930s onward, a restoration of the traditional image of the state as a superordinate authority, transcending the particular interests of various social groups, even while the party continued to act out, however precariously, the role of representing the interests and aspirations of these groups.

The full effects of these processes would only surface in the wake of the new series of convulsions that beset Russian society in the course of the 1930s. The convulsions that attended processes such as collectivization and the Great Purges contributed, on an even wider scale than the convulsions of the Civil War, to the disintegration, if not the extinction, of existing social groups—including the old revolutionary elite and the traditional peasant community—and to the reintegration of their surviving members into the body politic on the basis of new definitions imposed by the party and state.

Once again, the statuses and roles of various social groups would tend to be defined, in large measure, on the basis of the duties they performed for the state. Once again, these new definitions while immensely reinforcing, in the shorter term, the power and reach of the party and state over the lives of individuals and groups would reintroduce, in the longer term, oscillations between service class and caste features in the evolution of the ruling groups of Russian society, and thus contribute to the partial congealment of the body politic.

These dynamics in the subsequent development of the Soviet state and society lie well beyond the chronological scope of our discussion. Yet one can hardly avoid raising the question whether, how, and to what degree, certain of the root causes of these longer-term political and social processes should not in fact be sought in the convulsive historical experience that Russia underwent during the period of the Civil War.

NOTES

This chapter was originally published as "The Problem of Social Identities in Early Twentieth Century Russia," *Slavic Review*, vol. 47, no. 1, spring 1988, reprinted here by permission.

1. For an exhaustive recent treatment of the subject, with somewhat different emphases, see Gregory L. Freeze, "The Soslovie (Estate) Paradigm and Russian Social History," *American Historical Review*, February 1986, 91, pp. 11–36.

2. See Jonathan Sanders, "Drugs and Revolution: Moscow Pharmacists in the First Russian Revolution," *Russian Review* 1985, 44, pp. 351–77; and Laura Engelstein, *Moscow, 1905: Working-Class Organization and Political Conflict* (Stanford, 1982), pp. 120–21.

3. Ziva Galili, *The Menshevik Leaders in the Russian Revolution: Social Realities and Political Statistics* (Princeton, 1989).

4. F. D. [Fedor Dan], "Nekotorye itogi," *Rabochaia Gazeta*, November 16, 1917, no. 214.

5. Nikolai Sukhanov, *Zapiski o revoliutsii* (Berlin-Peterburg-Moscow, 1923), 7:197.

6. "Vserossiiskaia promyshlennaia i professional'naia perepis' 1918-g," see *Trudy Tsentral'nogo statisticheskogo upravleniia* (Moscow, 1926), tom XXVI, vyp. 2, tables 25 and 26, pp. 18–133.

7. For data of the industrial census of 1908, see I. M. Kozmynnykh-Lanin, *Ukhod na polevye raboty fabrichno-zavodskikh rabochikh Moskovskoi gubernii* (Moscow, 1912), tables 1, 6; and *Semeinyi sostav fabrichno-zavodskikh rabochikh Moskovskoi gubernii* (Moscow, 1914), p. 116. For data of the 1897 census, see Tsentral'ny i statistichekhii komitet, *Chislennost' i sostav rabochikh na osnovanii dannykh pervoi vseobshchei perepisi naseleniia Rossiiskoi Imperii* (St. Petersburg, 1897), 1:xiii–xv and I. M. Kozmynnykh-Lanin, *Fabrichno-zavodskie rabochie Vladimirskoi gubernii (1897)* (Vladimir, 1912), p. 32. For more fragmentary data, see also L. M. Ivanov, "Preemstvennost' fabrichno-zavodskogo truda i formirovanie proletariata v Rossii," in *ANSSR*, Institut istorii, *Rabochii klass i rabochee dvizhenie v Rossii (1861–1917)* (Moscow, 1966).

8. This article, "Vybory v Uchreditel'noe Sobranie i diktatura proletariata," was published in December 1919 in the journal *Kommunisticheskii Internatsional*, nos. 7–8. It is reprinted in Lenin's *Polnoe sobranie sochinenii*, 5th ed. (Moscow, 1963), 40:1–24.

9. Allan K. Wildman, *The End of the Russian Imperial Army: The Old Army and the Soldiers' Revolt (March–April 1917)* (Princeton, 1980).

10. See Oliver H. Radkey, *The Elections to the Constituent Assembly of 1917* (Cambridge, Mass., 1950).

11. *Uchreditel'noe sobranie. Stenograficheskii otchet* (Petrograd, 1918), pp. 56–57 (all emphases mine).

12. See P. N. Pershin, *Agrarnaia revoliutsiia v Rossii* (Moscow, 1966), 2:255–57, and 261–63; and John L. H. Keep, *The Russian Revolution: A Study in Mass Mobilization* (New York, 1976), pp. 405–406.

II

The Social and Demographic
Impact of the Civil War

INTRODUCTION
SOCIAL AND DEMOGRAPHIC CHANGE IN THE CIVIL WAR

Diane P. Koenker

The relationship between social composition and political attitudes and behavior is critical for students of Russian social history in this period. Russian
revolutionaries, particularly Bolsheviks, were especially conscious of the sociology of the revolutionary movement: to Bolsheviks, worker-peasants with
minimal industrial experience and workers in small factories or in service occupations were assumed to be less capable of attaining revolutionary consciousness than skilled workers in large technologically advanced plants.

However valid these observations were for 1917 (and much recent research
has helped expand our understanding of these relationships in Russian society
in the early twentieth century),[1] the Bolshevik Party and especially its chief
theoretician, V. I. Lenin, firmly believed in the primacy of social position as
a determinant of political attitudes. Hence, Bolshevik leaders explained away
their lack of worker support in the early months of the February 1917 revolution by citing the change in working-class composition that had occurred
from 1914 to 1917. Workers by 1917 had become dominated by petty-
bourgeois elements, they said. In early 1921, it was said that the Kronstadt
sailors who mutinied were different individuals than those who had helped
conquer Soviet power in October 1917: the mutineers were peasant recruits,
not the hardened revolutionaries of the past. Throughout the Civil War, when
Bolshevik party leaders saw support slipping away, they blamed the physical
disappearance of their supporters rather than changes in attitudes.[2]

But this sociological imperative becomes a fallacy when sociology is deduced
from attitudes rather than vice versa. The loss of the Bolsheviks' social base
may have eroded the party's political support, but it was not necessarily true
that because the party lost support, its social base must have disappeared. Such
iron logic leaves no room for the interplay of social relations, economics, and

consciousness. Therefore, any study of the social history of the Civil War period must confront anew the sociological imperative by carefully investigating the objective evidence of social and demographic change. Only then can the tenuous links between social change and political change be fairly examined.

In any discussion of social and demographic change, certain terms and concepts—birth, death, age, marital status—require little explanation, but many others present greater problems for the scholar. What were the relevant "social groups" in revolutionary and Civil War Russia? The answer of course depends on the issues to be addressed, but while a number of groups appear regularly in the essays that follow, it is important to heed the advice Sheila Fitzpatrick offers in her contribution, that in periods of great social turmoil, such as 1918–21, individuals often possessed multiple social identities.

To start with an important example, any overall assessment of social change in this period must deal with distinctions between rural and urban populations. But these distinctions, fuzzy enough even before 1917, became even more blurred under the troubled conditions of the Civil War. As cities contracted during these years, did the differences between urban and rural dwellers become more pronounced? Daniel R. Brower suggests that contrary to Rudzutak's pronouncements, city populations were purged first of their transient rural elements and took on an even more urban character than they had in the years of expansion before 1917. But what of the countryside? With streams of urban transients now returning to native villages,[3] the social structure of the village was bound to be altered by the influx of migrants who established some tenuous place in both urban and rural worlds.

Conflict between town and country centered on the item of greatest scarcity: food. "Power may belong to you, the workers," said peasants in early 1918, when they drove off a band of foragers from a nearby factory settlement, "but the potatoes are ours. To reap a harvest, you have to know how to plant, and this is something the 'workers' power' still does not know how to do."[4] Perhaps such hostility was modified when the same workers' wives and children returned to the village to escape the hardships of industrial collapse or when demobilized soldiers came home with new sets of political attitudes. But first the description of the rural and urban populations must be established as thoroughly as possible.

Definitions of class and occupation (*professiia*) similarly pose complex problems for any assessment of social change. The bourgeoisie was disenfranchised and many fled Russia during the Civil War years, but as Brower points out, trade, commerce, and manufacturing continued. Who were the traders? They must have included the old "petty bourgeoisie" of the cities, the *meshchanstvo*, but many workers and family members of workers engaged in trade as well. If everybody trades, what happens to old identities based on the primary distinctions between those who have property to sell and those who have only their labor?[5] This was a period that also saw tremendous mobility within the industrial labor force: workers of 1917 became party and Soviet officials, soldiers, political commissars. How should they be defined? What social category is appropriate for a skilled metal worker who spent half his work-time manufacturing goods to sell on the black market to keep his family alive? Of course, social and occupational distinctions were not meaningless, and Fitzpatrick reminds us that even the worker who had left for the commissariat may still have defined himself primarily as a worker. But strict definitions must be approached with great caution.

Demographic indicators appear to be more straightforward: birth, death, and marriage are fairly well-defined terms. But despite the abundance of statistical material collected during the Civil War producing data on disease, on marriage rates, on birth and death rates, the conditions under which these statistics were collected must be kept in mind. Surely there is a story to be told about the arithmeticians (many of them Menshevik and SR intellectuals) who collected their numbers and added up columns of figures in dark and unheated Moscow offices.[6] The formation and organization of the Central Statistical Administration during these disorganized years is nothing less than amazing, but important gaps remain in the statistical record. Consequently, the construction of certain statistical series has become almost impossible.[7]

The three essays in this section begin to address some of the issues of social and demographic change during the Civil War. Daniel Brower takes as his focus the fate of the urban population of Russia during the period. Diane Koenker addresses this theme with particular reference to the alleged disappearance of the working class in Moscow, discussing the implications this has for understanding the working-class base of Soviet power. Barbara Evans Clements concentrates on the impact of the Civil War on the position of women in the twentieth-century Russian family. All continue to develop themes that have already been studied for other and longer periods in the history of Russia,[8] and all raise issues for further investigation. All three employ a sensitive approach to statistical indicators of demographic change; Brower and Koenker in particular make resourceful use of census data from 1918 and 1920. As Clements points out with respect to changes in the rate of marriages, these indicators cannot be accepted in isolation, but they do provide benchmarks and a framework for further analysis using both quantitative and qualitative sources.

The essays also raise the important issue of stability versus disorder. Significantly, all three find that once we look beyond the perception that cities and family life were disintegrating, a picture emerges of remarkable persistence of both urban and family institutions. This is an important observation, one that will surely be tested by further research. It is important because it raises one critical question in interpreting the Civil War: to what extent did the Civil War cause a major rupture in the continuities of Russian social life? In terms of shaping political outlooks, there is much to be said for interpreting the Civil War (rather than the 1917 revolution) as the major watershed of twentieth-century Russia. The crisis of civil war, even more than of international war or revolution, fostered a mentality of encirclement, of militarization, of arbitrary violence and civilian disruption, of rule by fiat.[9] But within social institutions of family and urban community, the Civil War was only the final segment of a longer crisis beginning in 1914; moreover, even these seven years of war, revolution, and war again must also be considered as an epiphenomenon in a more durable and secular process of social change. As Barbara Clements points out, the Russian urban family had already evolved toward the form of the modern nuclear family; parallel changes in the countryside would no doubt have continued to occur with or without the disruption of the Civil War. As for the cities, the structural characteristics of population concentrations—the need for markets, traders, administration and law enforcement—also produced their own logic for social development. Therefore, the will to survive of the *meshchanstvo* (and probably most other urban groups) transcends the immediate disruption of revolution and civil war.

Thus, despite a natural tendency to view the Civil War as a distinct and unique period, when the world was turned upside down, we risk distorting our interpretation if we do not simultaneously look for elements of continuity and persistence, elements perhaps most likely to be found by examining the social and demographic structure of Russian society.

These three essays and other work under way and recently published, represent an important step toward an understanding of the period. But as the authors themselves point out, much is left to explore. Changes within the peasant community and family, touched on in the Clements paper, is a fertile area for further study.[10] If the countryside were as well documented as the cities, perhaps more would be known about the impact of the descent on the village of demobilized soldiers and deurbanized workers, women, and children. The evocative picture of rural social relationships contributed by novelists such as Mikhail Sholokhov and Fedor Gladkov must be augmented by ethnographic, statistical, and documentary study of the rural community during these years.

Similarly, non-Russian areas have received scant attention. When confronted with the vastness and diversity of the Russian Empire, historians often focus resolutely on ethnic Russia, or throw up their hands at the hopelessness of integrating the experience of so many diverse populations. The study of the "ethnic borderlands" must be brought into the mainstream of the social history of this period, both for their own sake and for the sake of comparison with Russian society, to test arguments about long- and short-term social and demographic change.[11]

Finally, a plea must be made for the relevance of comparison with other societies torn as Russia was by revolution and civil war. Russian social historians, particularly those of the family and urbanization, have already benefited from tapping the methodological and conceptual resources of historians of other places. All social historians of this period need to continue to pay attention to similarities with societies outside the USSR, as with the ethnic regions, to evaluate better the differences between short-term disruptions and long-term processes of social change. The Weimar Republic during the years of hyperinflation, the United States—particularly the South—during its Civil War, China during the Cultural Revolution, and many countries in Africa,

Latin America, and the Middle East all provide examples of societies rent by social and political turmoil at least as disruptive as that of the Russian Civil War. But everywhere institutions remained—kinship systems, urban and rural structures, technology—to provide an element of stability in what seemed to contemporaries to be a shipwrecked world.[12]

NOTES

1. Robert E. Johnson, *Peasant and Proletarian: The Working Class of Moscow in the Late Nineteenth Century* (New Brunswick, N.J., 1979); Laura Engelstein, *Moscow, 1905: Working-Class Organization and Political Conflict* (Stanford, 1982); Victoria E. Bonnell, *Roots of Rebellion: Workers' Politics and Organizations in St. Petersburg and Moscow, 1900–1914* (Berkeley, 1983); Henry Reichman, *Railwaymen and Revolution: Russia, 1905* (Berkeley, 1987), Heather Hogan, Ph.D. dissertation, "Labor and Management in Conflict: The St. Petersburg Metal-Working Industry" (University of Michigan, 1981) and Gerald Suhr, "Petersburg Workers in 1905: Strikes, Workplace, Democracy, and the Revolution" (Ph.D. dissertation, University of California, Berkeley, 1979); Leopold H. Haimson and Ronald Petrusha, "Two Strike Waves in Imperial Russia (1905–1907, 1912–14): A Quantitative Analysis," in Leopold H. Haimson, Michelle Perrot, Charles Tilly, eds., *Patterns in the Evolution of Industrial Labor Conflicts in the Late Nineteenth and Early Twentieth Centuries* (Cambridge and Paris, forthcoming); S. A. Smith, *Red Petrograd: Revolution in the Factories, 1917–1918* (Cambridge, 1983); David Mandel, *The Petrograd Workers and the Fall of the Old Regime* (London, 1983), and *The Petrograd Workers and the Soviet Seizure of Power* (London, 1984); Diane Koenker, *Moscow Workers and the 1917 Revolution* (Princeton, 1981).

2. See the words of Bukharin, Rudzutak, and Lenin, cited in Diane P. Koenker, "Urbanization and Deurbanization in the Russian Revolution and Civil War," in this volume.

3. Or perhaps they were returning to nonnative provincial towns, a phenomenon that has not been considered in any of the literature. Donald J. Raleigh's current research on the Civil War in Saratov and Saratov province will fill an important gap.

4. Eduard Dune, "Zapiski krasnogvardeitsa," manuscript in the Nicolaevsky Collection, Hoover Institution Archives, p. 99 (my translation).

5. An American visitor to Moscow in 1918 could barely leave the Sukharevka market with the loaf of bread he had just bought, since it was assumed that he had bought it only to resell it. Indeed, he entered into a shouting match with a trading woman who demanded, "How much? How much?" (Oliver M. Sayler, *Russia, White or Red* [Boston, 1919], p. 48).

6. Ample material would seem to be available for a study of early Soviet statistical work in journals (*Biulleten' Tsentral'nogo statisticheskogo upravleniia, Vestnik statistiki, Narodnoe khoziaistvo, Statisticheskoe obozrenie* [from 1926], *Uchenye zapiski po istorii statistiki*) and in newspapers (*Ekonomicheskaia zhizn', Torgovo-promyshlennaia gazeta*). Some work has been done on the early history of Soviet planning statistics: V. E. Varzar, *Ocherki osnov promyshlennoi statistiki* (Moscow, 1925); V. Z. Drobizhev, *Glavnyi shtab sotsialisticheskoi promyshlennosti: Ocherki, istorii VSNKh 1917–1932 gg.* (Moscow, 1966); A. Gurovich, "Vysshii sovet narodnogo khoziaistva: Iz vpechatlenii goda sluzhby," *Arkhiv russkoi revoliutsii* (Berlin), 1922, vol. 6; S. G. Wheatcroft, "The Reliability of Russian Pre-War Grain Output Statistics," *Soviet Studies*, April

1974, no. 2, pp. 157–80; Thomas F. Remington, *Building Socialism in Bolshevik Russia: Ideology and Industrial Organization, 1917–1921* (Pittsburgh, 1984), especially chap. 4; See also S. G. Wheatcroft and R. W. Davies, eds., *Materials for a Balance of the Soviet National Economy 1928–1930* (Cambridge, 1985), pp. 34–37; and E. H. Carr, *The Bolshevik Revolution 1917–1923* (Harmondsworth, Eng., 1966), vol. 2, chap. 20. Much less attention appears to have been paid to collectors of social and demographic statistics, the province of the Central Statistical Administration (TsSU) and not Gosplan. I am indebted to S. G. Wheatcroft, who has called my attention to many of these sources.

7. One example relates to the discussion in Barbara Clements's and Diane Koenker's essays about the rise in marriage rates beginning in 1918. If the great leap owed to couples "catching up" on marriages postponed because of the war, we might find that the average age of brides would rise during these years of high marriage rates. The Moscow city government published this information in its monthly statistical bulletin, *Ezhemesiachnyi statisticheskii biulleten' goroda Moskvy* (1912–17), but this publication was suspended between 1917 and 1924, precisely the years necessary to answer this question. (I am grateful to J. Harvey Smith for suggesting this approach.)

8. On Russian cities and urbanization, see Gilbert Rozman, *Urban Networks in Russia, 1750–1800, and Premodern Periodization* (Princeton, 1976); Michael F. Hamm, ed., *The City in Russian History* (Lexington, Ky., 1976); Michael F. Hamm, ed., *The City in Late Imperial Russia* (Bloomington, Ind., 1986); James H. Bater, *St. Petersburg: Industrialization and Change* (London, 1976); P. G. Ryndziunskii, *Gorodskoe grazhdanstvo doreformennoi Rossii* (Moscow, 1958); P. G. Ryndziunskii, *Krest'iane i gorod v kapitalisticheskoi Rossii vtoroi poloviny XIX veka* (Moscow, 1983); Daniel Brower, "Urban Russia on the Eve of World War One: A Social Profile," *Journal of Social History*, 1980, vol. 13, no. 3, pp. 424–36; Joseph Bradley, *Muzhik and Muscovite: Urbanization in Late Imperial Russia* (Berkeley, 1985); William Chase, *Workers, Society, and the Soviet State: Labor and Life in Moscow, 1918–1929* (Urbana, Ill., 1987). On women and the family, a great deal of research is now under way. See, for example, Dorothy Atkinson, Gail Lapidus, and Alexander Dallin, eds., *Women in Russia* (Stanford, 1978); Richard Stites, *The Women's Liberation Movement in Russia, 1860–1930* (Princeton, 1978); Rose Glickman, *Russian Factory Women: Workplace and Society 1880–1914* (Berkeley, 1984); Barbara Alpern Engel, *Mothers and Daughters: Women of the Intelligentsia in Nineteenth-Century Russia* (Cambridge, 1983); David L. Ransel, ed., *The Family in Imperial Russia: New Lines of Historical Research* (Urbana, Ill., 1978); H. Kent Geiger, *The Family in Soviet Russia* (Cambridge, Mass., 1968). On demography, see Ralph S. Clem, ed., *Research Guide to the Russian and Soviet Censuses* (Ithaca, N.Y., 1986); Barbara Anderson and Brian Silver, "Demographic Analysis and Population Catastrophes in the USSR," *Slavic Review*, 1985, no. 3, summarizing the current debate about censuses of the 1930s; Barbara A. Anderson, *Internal Migration during Modernization in Late Nineteenth-Century Russia* (Princeton, 1980); Ansley Coale, Barbara Anderson, and Erna Harm, *Human Fertility in Russia since the Nineteenth Century* (Princeton, 1979); A. G. Rashin, *Naselenie Rossii za sto let* (Moscow, 1956).

9. See the discussions of the generational effect of the Civil War in Sheila Fitzpatrick, "The Civil War as a Formative Experience," in Abbott Gleason, Peter Kenez, and Richard Stites, eds., *Bolshevik Culture: Experiment and Order in the Russian Revolution* (Bloomington, Ind., 1985); Robert C. Tucker, "Stalinism as Revolution from Above," in Robert C. Tucker, ed., *Stalinism* (New York, 1977), pp. 91–92; Stephen F. Cohen, "Bolshevism and Stalinism," in ibid., pp. 3–29; Remington, *Building Socialism in Bolshevik Russia*; compare with Robert C. Wohl, *The Generation of 1914* (Cambridge, Mass., 1979).

10. Dorothy Atkinson, in *The End of the Russian Land Commune* (Stanford, 1983), deals mainly with institutional aspects of the rural community during the Civil War.

Orlando Figes of Cambridge University is engaged in research, using local archives, into peasant activity along the Volga during the Civil War.

11. Ronald Grigor Suny's essay in this collection, and his valuable contributions on the revolutionary years in the Transcaucasus, are important and significant exceptions: for example, his *The Baku Commune, 1917–1918: Class and Nationality in the Russian Revolution* (Princeton, 1972).

12. The reference is to Countess Kleinmichel, *Memories of a Shipwrecked World* (New York, 1923).

"THE CITY IN DANGER"
THE CIVIL WAR AND THE RUSSIAN URBAN POPULATION

Daniel R. Brower

The Russian Civil War, profoundly undermining the complex human relations of urban life, at the same time endowed the concept of the city with special ideological significance. The Communists and their allies viewed the city as the symbol and dynamic force of social revolution. To the syndicalist Victor Serge, he and his Communist comrades were "building the City of the future." It was a daring gamble, for he found on arriving in Russia in 1918 the urban revolutionary forces so feeble that he proclaimed "the city is in danger."[1] He gave to this term the abstract meaning befitting his vision of the future, similar to that of the Proletkult movement. In a contrary spirit but on an equally lofty symbolic level, Evgenyi Zamiatin projected onto the city of his novel *We* the characteristics, in Edward Brown's words, of a "monster of mechanical efficiency."[2] Zamiatin's fear of the dehumanizing impersonality of social engineering revealed itself in an urban antiutopia as far removed from contemporary conditions as Serge's utopian "City of the future."

This connotative manner of understanding the Russian city in the Civil War has, in less vivid terms, colored historical treatment of urban conditions in those years. Placed within the larger context of the end of the imperial era or the beginning of the Soviet age, the Civil War history of Russian cities appears primarily a grim story of the destruction of past achievements or an indicator of the challenging task of revolutionary reconstruction confronting the Communists. As Diane Koenker points out in her essay on Moscow workers and deurbanization, Soviet historians, repeating Lenin's judgment, sought to explain the collapse of working-class support for the Communist regime by arguing that the Civil War cities had reverted to an earlier social structure dominated by peasants and petty bourgeois.[3] From their perspective, the urban history of that period is only a prologue to NEP and the great social transformation of the 1930s. Many Western historians, inclined to treat the Civil War as tragic epilogue to decades of social development, stress on the other hand the collapse of recognizable urban life as Russia, in Paul Avrich's words, "reverted to the primitive agrarian society from which it had only recently begun to emerge."[4] In both cases, the cities of those years constitute an arena of political struggle and economic turmoil. The typical grand narrative of war, revolution, and civil war pays little attention to the affairs of those townspeople caught in the midst of that conflict.[5]

This essay adopts a very different point of view. It assigns to the urban population of those years a separate and important role in the historical process of revolutionary change. The supposed "deurbanization" of Moscow and St. Petersburg emphasizes the demographic movement of population out of the cities, and secondarily the structural changes referred to above.[6] But the city, even in the cruel conditions of the Civil War, ought in my opinion to be understood in terms of the townspeoples' practices, that is, their predominant "ways of operating" within the urban environment.[7] Although these practices changed dramatically, I will argue that they assured the survival of urban life and ultimately contributed to the Communists' reluctant legalization of private trade and artisanry in the so-called NEP reforms. This manner of posing the issues of urban history presents a substantially broader perspective on the Civil War city than those few studies that have explored the experience of the working class in Civil War cities.[8] It assumes that the turnover of inhabitants and the acute problems of survival in the cities gave a new meaning to urban life among the remaining inhabitants. It also emphasizes the commonality of the Civil War urban experience, defined not by numbers of townspeople, but by similarity of economic and social pressures shaped by war and revolution.

The focus here is on the struggle of townspeople to cope with the extraordinary conditions of shortages and other hardships in urban area throughout the country (particularly those under Soviet control). In this sense, it is the story of the "survivors" (my loose translation of *obyvateli*), a group dismissed by Victor Serge for their refusal to share in the Communists' dream of the "City of the future." The attitude of the typical survivor, as parodied by one Communist railroad official in 1919, was summed up in one phrase: "To hell with all [the parties]—whoever gives me bread will suit me fine."[9] So widespread was this "struggle to survive" (*obyvatel'shchina*) that it transformed cities into the kingdom of petty traders, the *meshochniki*.[10] The remainder of this essay will explore the dynamics and characteristics of this remarkable new pattern of urban relations.

I. The Survivors

Although the general configuration of the social crisis confronting Russia's urban population is well known, a brief review of it will set the context for this study of the survivors. In the first place, the campaigns of the Civil War had only a passing effect on urban life, since most fighting took place outside the cities. The war did, however, have a devastating impact on it indirectly, through the destruction of the means of communication and transportation (especially the railroads), the diversion of resources to war, the disruption of basic public services, and the spread of infectious diseases. Second, the Communists' hasty implementation of their radical reforms threw the previous social and economic practices of the urban population into turmoil. Although the process itself is still poorly understood, its effects are easily discerned. The war and revolutionary conflict together placed unprecedented strains on the fabric of Russian urban life.

The decay of the rail and water networks proceeded with extraordinary rapidity. By 1920 the total tonnage of goods carried by rail amounted to only one-fifth of the 1913 amount.[11] Shipments by waterway probably declined as much. This trend undermined the market relations on which cities and towns had depended for their development during the previous half-century. Migration into the cities ceased, thereby cutting back the availability of temporary labor and creating by 1920 an urban labor shortage.

The most serious consequence of the transportation crisis was the increasingly difficult movement of agricultural produce to urban areas, especially those in the northern regions dependent on food imports from distant provinces. It compounded and aggravated the worsening terms of trade in agricultural produce, a result of the disorder of the Civil War, of the disappearance of consumer goods, and of the confiscatory procurement policies of the Soviet regime. The shortage of food in the northern towns in 1918 suddenly became a major problem for the Soviet regime, which it attempted to resolve by instituting the food dictatorship. This response to the crisis measure began a period of confiscatory expeditions into the countryside to obtain food from the peasantry both for the army and for the urban population.[12] Similar conditions spread to the south in the winter of 1919–20. They had a devastating effect on urban life. Although harvests in those years provided adequate food supplies for the rural population, after the revolution hunger became increasingly prevalent in cities throughout the country.

A third factor that drastically constrained and altered urban conditions was insufficient fuel. First oil, the newest energy source, virtually disappeared. Then coal supplies dwindled as production from the mines of the Ukraine and Urals fell and as transportation failed. Wood became the major source of fuel, both to power machinery and to heat residences. In this respect the north, despite its abundant forests, suffered more than the south. The cold of winter penetrated homes, slowed the rhythm of life, and weakened the resistance of the population to the spread of infectious diseases.

Epidemics devastated urban centers in the Civil War years. Communicable diseases that had not disrupted urban life for generations reappeared as the turmoil of war spread and as health care declined and public sanitation ceased to operate. Epidemics swept through urban areas, carried (in the words of one observer) "with geometrical precision" along the rail lines from one town to the next by traders, refugees, and soldiers.[13] In 1919 the northern population suffered particularly from typhus, but this was only one among many natural scourges of a virtually defenseless population.

Under these conditions, the relative permanence of urban classes and stability of urban inhabitants were no longer insured. Deaths far outnumbered births; enterprises ceased operations and dismissed workers and employees. Migrants abandoned their temporary urban residence to return to the countryside. Men left to serve in the armies of Reds and Whites, and middle- and upper-class families fled to foreign lands. To the historian the question arises whether the towns of the Civil War bore any resemblance at all to those of the prewar years. One cannot assume continuity in development of urban demography and economic activity. It is important therefore to determine who remained within town boundaries and how they dealt with their elementary needs of food and shelter.

The simplest indicators of change in the urban environment over the three Civil War years are the census figures on the urban population of the country. Yearly records of the total population of cities and towns were kept by local authorities until the revolution; despite great difficulties, the Central Statistical Administration undertook in August 1920 a comprehensive urban census. The results, while of dubious precision, are indicative of population movement during the Civil War years.[14]

Using the Petrograd figures, historians have painted a lurid picture of flight from the cities. In 1918 alone the former capital lost 850,000 people and was by itself responsible for one-half of the total urban population decline of the Civil War years.[15] If one sets aside aggregate figures to determine the trend characteristic of most cities, however, the experience of Petrograd appears exceptional. Only a handful of cities (including Pskov and Nizhny-Novgorod, as well as Petrograd) lost half or more of their population between 1917 and 1920, and even Moscow, which declined by over 40 percent, was not typical of most towns in the northern, food-importing areas. A study of all cities (so identified in the 1897 census) found that the average decline in the north (167 towns in all, excluding the capital cities) amounted to 24 percent between 1917 and 1920.[16] Among the towns in the food-producing areas in the southern and eastern regions of the Russian Republic (a total of 128), the average decline came to only 14 percent. These regional variations are sufficiently great to suggest abandoning the image of overall catastrophic urban decline.

The most revealing figures are those that reflect population movement according to city size. Small towns (below 10,000) lost in the period 1917–21 on average only 10 percent of their inhabitants; those of between 10,000 and 50,000 fell by 17 percent; Russia's major cities (those, numbering 23, of over 50,000 population in 1917) declined by 25 percent.[17] The evolution of these large urban centers, though relatively few in number, provides the most meaningful indicator of the fate of the urban population. Centers of administrative activity, commercial development, and popular literate culture in previous decades, their expansion had played a key role in the development of Russian society. They embodied the dynamism of modernity and for that reason had a symbolic importance for believers in Russian progress (including Lenin) that transcended their actual significance in the social development of the country. Their loss on average of one in four of their 1917 inhabitants during the three years of Civil War provides the clearest quantitative measure of the demographic decline of urban Russia in that period.

Did this decline constitute the "deurbanization" of Russia? What happened to the missing population—killed by famine or epidemic, fled to safer regions, called up in the manpower mobilization of War Communism, returned to family in the countryside? Who remained behind? Answers to questions on the sudden movement of millions of people can come only from a scattering of clues drawn from isolated examples, from our understanding of the characteristics of the population before the revolution, and from certain revealing entries in the 1920 census.

The records of urban mortality rates provide vivid evidence of the fate of one part of the towns' population. Although a variety of circumstances explain this tragic story, the sudden spread of disease furnishes the most important clue to the rising mortality curve. Unsanitary conditions within a population weakened by hunger and cold and lacking essential health care produced periodic devastating epidemics, whose effects are cruelly apparent in the yearly mortality record of Petrograd. Until 1918, the figure remained close to the low prewar level (22 per thousand); that year it doubled, and in 1919 almost doubled again, rising to the astounding rate of 80 per thousand (owing principally to the typhus epidemic).[18] Other urban centers may not have reached this level, yet the general trend was the same. Data on the towns of Iaroslavl' province indicate that the mortality rate doubled between 1913 and 1919, when it reached a peak of 60 deaths per thousand. Even in that hard-hit province, the rural population suffered less; its death rate rose to 43 per thousand that year.[19] Only the end of the fighting and the slow economic recovery of NEP brought the urban mortality rate down to a level approaching that of prewar times.

The most striking demographic characteristic of the remaining townspeople was the high proportion of women. Before the war the country's expanding urban centers, poles of attraction for millions of peasant migrants, appeared to be in demographic terms predominantly a "man's world" (in these urban centers males constituted on average 55 percent of the population). During the Civil War years the balance swung the other way. By 1920 only 45 percent of the inhabitants in large towns were male; the proportion held true in port cities such as Rostov, textile centers like Ivanovo-Voznesensk, and administrative capitals such as Kiev.

Where had the men gone? The simplest and probably most important explanation lay in the massive tsarist conscription, repeated by the Soviets after a brief period of demobilization. The age group subject to conscription contained the lowest proportion of urban males, both in the Ukrainian and Russian republics—37 and 39 percent in the two republics for the ages 20 to 29, 34 and 33 percent for age 19.[20] Koenker's findings for Moscow bear out this general observation.[21] Some of these men would never return, casualties of long, bloody war. Another form of service took party activists, trade union leaders, and workers for work as civilian and military cadres of the new regime. These figures reveal clearly the human price of years of revolution and war.

Another important factor in the decline of male townspeople lay in the structural changes produced in the urban economy by the Civil War. The economic decline that began in 1917 reversed the trend of urban migration from the rural hinterland. Unemployment affected all sectors of the economic life, from domestic work to factory labor. As in previous years of recession, these migrants took the road back to their rural homes. Among the unemployed who left Petrograd in the summer of 1918, three-fifths intended to go to some village, according to figures collected (undoubtedly in a haphazard manner) by the city statistical bureau; the remainder were headed for other towns.[22]

The pressures on the rural migrants to leave the cities grew greater as the industrial and commercial depression spread. In many towns urban factory production soon came to a complete halt. Even when the factories continued to operate, the hardship of urban living pushed workers to leave their positions to seek food and shelter among relatives in rural areas. A report from the Briansk metallurgical factory in 1920 stated flatly that "all the workers with ties with villages prefer to abandon the factory to settle there."[23] We may assume that similar considerations determined the action of laborers in other sectors, such as transportation and construction, that had previously attracted many peasant workers.

The movement of large numbers of recent or temporary migrants back to their villages resulted as well from important developments in the countryside. For those facing unemployment with some claim to communal land the villages appeared a much more attractive refuge during the Civil War than in earlier times. To the pressure of urban hardship was added the pull of land repartition resulting from the seizure of landed estates and revival of the repartitional commune. Were women of village origin as likely as men to return? It seems likely that they were not, for among them were many (such as widows) who had lost all ties with their rural community. Thus, despite the absence of census data on place of birth of urban dwellers in 1920, one can reliably surmise that a high proportion of the missing townsmen were peasants who had returned to their birth places in the countryside. To this extent, the demographic upheaval in the cities strengthened the presence of the urban-born among townspeople, increasingly divided by vital interests and outlook from the Russian peasant masses.

For urban dwellers another direction of flight was open. By 1918 chances of survival depended above all on access to food. The breakdown of transportation deprived the northern towns of their usual supply lines from the southern and eastern food surplus areas; potentially, it made more food available to towns in the southern and eastern regions. The departure for other urban centers of two-fifths of those Petrograd unemployed, noted in the 1918 survey cited above, was presumably due largely to the need to find better living conditions in any town closer to the peasants' surplus food supplies. The census of 1920 revealed that between 1917 and 1920 this compensatory factor had kept the average population loss of the towns in food-producing lands of the RSFSR at a level half that of cities in the food-importing areas. In fact, among the towns in food surplus regions one-fourth had actually gained in population.[24] Survival depended on direct access to food supplies; just how this food could be obtained became the daily preoccupation of townspeople throughout the land.

Until late 1919 Ukrainian cities had attracted large numbers of northerners. Food was abundant there. In addition, the economic policies of the German, Ukrainian, and White Russian forces successively occupying the area protected property and trade. To cities such as Kiev and Odessa came middle-class refugees, bringing with them as much of their previous wealth as possible and creating in Kiev what one observer termed "a period of speculative fever and *griunderstvo*."[25] Konstantin Paustovskii, one of the northern migrants, found in Odessa "speculators pouring in from the north [who] overwhelmed their local counterparts with bold and ruthless trading. They flashed diamonds . . . they handled brand-new pound sterling notes."[26] For a few months, they could continue to pretend that the October Revolution had not occurred. They represented the extreme in the trend of townspeople becoming traders for their own survival.

The evidence of the demographic impact of the Civil War on the urban centers points to a process one might call social "homogenization." The migrants from the villages had departed. The diverse groups that had emerged in recent decades to fill professional and business positions had contracted drastically in size, many of their numbers fleeing to foreign lands. Factories shut down or operated at a reduced level. Men left for the army; those committed to the Communist cause went off at the call of the party to defend the revolution.

How can we best characterize the remaining townspeople? Two answers appear plausible, one relying on earlier historical conditions, the other suggested by Civil War economic pressures. To the extent that social identity retained any meaning in those years, the single largest group remaining in the cities probably had its roots in the tsarist estate of the *meshchanstvo*. Once consisting largely of petty traders, artisans, and laborers, it had become a diverse group united only by that distinctive official estate notation. In the less dynamic urban centers, the *meschanstvo* probably preserved the older traits of dependence on small-scale commercial and manufacturing activities, relative geographical stability with the attendant habits of strong family and neighborhood ties, and indifference to political affairs. Its characteristics fit very well the stereotypical "survivor" as defined by Communist activists.

The polemical nature of these social labels warns against undue reliance on such facile generalizations. Without rejecting entirely this approach, one ought to take account also of the dynamic changes under way in the previous decades in the major urban centers, as well as the special conditions of the Civil War years. By the early century social identity bore little resemblance to the official estate hierarchy, for occupational opportunities and new cultural values were reshaping urban relations. The Civil War acted as a powerful corrosive agent, weakening or destroying class divisions and forcing the townspeople to concentrate their energy and activities on the struggle to survive. Those townspeople with no refuge in the countryside had little choice but to eke out a paltry existence, by means that bore little relation to previous social station and economic skills.

The predominance of the "survivors" was attested to by eyewitnesses and by census figures. The proportion of working population grew as dependents left (and as children and old people, more susceptible to disease, died in the epidemics). In Moscow, two-thirds of the men and over one-half of the women in 1920 declared themselves self-supporting.[27] Two years before, Victor Serge had noted that the "survivors," whom he characterized as a "gray crowd of thousands of people who are neither workers nor rich nor poor nor revolutionaries nor absolutely ignorant nor truly educated," were "ten times more numerous than the Communist proletariat."[28] These urban masses needed whatever skills and guile they possessed in those harsh conditions. Their efforts to survive is the subject of the remainder of this essay.

II. The Struggle to Survive

In the Communist-controlled areas of the country, townspeople found that privileged and menial ranks had suddenly reversed standing in a deadly serious transformation of social position. The policies of rationing and priority allocation of resources favored factory workers—whose numbers were drastically shrinking—and employees, for whom demand had greatly increased as a result of sweeping nationalization and state controls. The party slogan "he who does not work neither shall he eat" set the new official criteria of status according to the simplest and most easily understood measure—access to food. By these standards the old marks of education, birth, and property lost all standing in the community. Landlords, manufacturers, and merchants were singled out for punitive assessments, expropriation of housing, and humiliating work assignments such as removal of filth from public places. Once-honored intellectuals found themselves in the third category of rationing and obligated to undertake the menial labor earlier provided by servants.

Under these conditions, townspeople needed any kind of work in the new Soviet administration. Thrust into a world of nascent petty officialdom in the midst of hunger and war, these new bureaucrats were liable to consider their experience either pure fantasy or a means to personal survival. Konstantin Paustovskii recalled much later the fantastic atmosphere surrounding his work in Soviet-controlled Kiev in a "strange organization" that had something to do with calico cloth. All the rooms and corridors in its offices were filled with bales of cloth. It was never given out to anyone, under any circumstances, but it was always being brought in or shipped back to warehouses and then brought back to the office and piled up again in the corridors. . . . [29]

Its public utility mattered little to Paustovsky; what he sought was a class-2 ration card.

A more somber, and probably more realistic, appreciation of the concerns of the new army of employees came from a Cheka investigation in late 1919 of the state enterprises in charge of preparing and distributing military uniforms for the Red Army. It uncovered a variety of profiteering techniques devised by workers and employees intent on "the sale of goods privately at speculative prices and the use of materials."[30] To zealous Communists, such sale constituted blatant theft of the people's property. To those engaged in these new practices, the principal consideration was finding the material means to trade on the black market.

These practical goals most easily explain the incentives of those who swelled the ranks of white-collar workers in all sectors of the (official) urban economy. Among Petrograd's ten metal-working factories, where the number of blue-collar workers steadily declined, the number of employees increased, constituting 25 percent of the total work force by 1920.[31] In Moscow, employees represented the single largest occupational group among the employed—47 percent. Although manufacturing had diminished there at the lowest rate among Russia's towns, workers constituted only 41 percent of the labor force.[32] The evil force of "bureaucratism" appeared to Soviet leaders to be attacking their new socialist institutions; to the urban population, it provided a chance to survive.

There remained a tiny legal private sector within the urban economy. Even at the end of War Communism, nationalization still did not encompass all small shops and enterprises. The 1920 census of manufacturing enterprises in the Russian Republic revealed that 280,000 remained in private hands, most with no hired workers.[33] These small-scale enterprises provided a meager source of livelihood. In Moscow, the private sector gave work to only 6 percent of the labor force. Yet it became a particular target for Communist zealots. The militant spirit of War Communism reached its zenith late that year. Certain soviets set out to liquidate all private trade and artisanal activity. Conditions varied from city to city, and state policy itself did not provide clear guidelines. The Petrograd Soviet's executive committee saw its July order closing all private stores annulled by the Supreme Economic Council in September.[34] Still, as late as March 1921 the Don Soviet ordered the liquidation of all private stores and cafes, the arrest of all shopkeepers, and the confiscation of their goods.[35]

These draconian measures cannot be explained by the actual importance of the legal private sector, an insignificant part of urban commerce and manufacturing. Their intent appears symbolic, for their extremist spirit suggests the anger and frustration of local Soviet leaders. Although virtually all private trade and manufacturing were banned, a vast illegal commercial network had come into existence. In Russia's cities and towns, the decrees of War Communism proved weaker than the will to survive. In the words of one popular saying, "we live by decrees and survive by our wits."[36]

The acute need for food provided the primary impetus for private trading. The crisis had become acute in the spring of 1918. Petrograd had received 1,300 freight cars of grain in March, but the arrivals fell to 500 in April and 386 in May. Moscow received only 188 cars (500 carloads would have been needed that month to assure the inhabitants 1/4 pound of bread per day). Food distribution centers in Petrograd replaced the flour they previously sold with potatoes in mid-May, then with nothing at all.[37] At the same time, telegrams reaching the Food Commissariat from smaller towns revealed a disastrous situation. Kazan announced that the local food agency had "ceased distributing the meager ration, having exhausted its reserves." Briansk, center of a major metallurgical enterprise, proclaimed at the end of the month that the food agency in the city was "besieged by crowds of workers, peasants, and townspeople." The mood of the crowds was ugly, producing in some towns riots directed against the authorities.[38] The crisis of that "hungry spring" threatened the regime itself.

The intent of the food dictatorship was to overcome this crisis by draconian means strictly controlled by the state. In general terms, it set the legal guidelines for food procurement and distribution to the end of the Civil War, reinforcing the legal and administrative power of the state to permit the requisitioning of grain (as well as sugar and salt at that time; other commodities such as potatoes were added in 1919). The critical situation of the late spring and summer led Petrograd workers to request the right to form groups to seek out grain in the countryside and to bring it back to their factories. Lenin approved and expanded the operation, authorizing this "Food Army" to mobilize under the control directly of the Food Commissariat and also of the trade unions. These "detachments" numbered, according to a Soviet historian, 72,000 men by the end of the year.[39] They appear to have had little difficulty finding recruits from factory workers (the Soviet claim) and other townspeople in the northern towns and cities. Hunger spurred them on; food for their families and comrades was the goal.

The powers of the Soviet regime extended into the urban trade network as well. The decreases of May 1918, that instituted the food dictatorship included measures placing trade in "essential items," including basic food commodities, under "supervision of local food authorities"; in November the food monopoly ended legal private trade in key foods and placed the distribution of these items in state and cooperative food stores. That summer, the simple rationing system inherited from the Provisional Government expanded to become a "class ration system," creating a preferential ranking of the urban population according to food needs as determined by the state. Not surprisingly, people employed every means to obtain the ration card in the highest category. Among the 1.4 million cardholders in Petrograd that fall, 54 percent belonged to the first category,

39 percent to the second, only 7 percent to the third—and none to the fourth.[40] In theory, the Soviet state had developed a new system of forcible requisitioning and priority allocation of scarce resources to insure the survival of the urban population as well as the supplying of the army.

At the very start of the implementation of the new policies the state had to allow large-scale deviations from the strict rules of the food dictatorship. Two months after its introduction, it proved so inadequate a source of urban supplies that the Soviet leaders authorized the legal purchase by every urban "worker and laborer" or their representatives of peasant produce totaling approximately 50 pounds per person (1 1/2 *pud*, hence labeled by its critics *poltorapudni-chestvo*). They thus gave their stamp of approval to a resurgence of small-scale trade, an action one Soviet historian claims "legalized petty trade [*meshoch-nichestvo*] in the whole country." By the end of September, Saratov alone attracted the emissaries of 126 organizations representing 300,000 workers from northern areas, and more continued to arrive that fall.[41]

At that point, the state ended its official toleration of private food trade. For the next year the food monopoly remained strictly in force until, in the summer of 1919, in the words of one Soviet historian, "conditions once again forced the Soviet state to repeat roughly the same measures (*dvukhpudni-chestvo*)."[42] The legal norm remained state requisitioning and distribution, with severe punishments for those engaged in private food trade. When the Ukraine finally came under Soviet control in the winter of 1919–20, its food network was placed under the same restrictions. In theory, the survival of the urban population was the responsibility of the state.

It was a responsibility the Soviet regime could not meet. The total population dependent on state supplies (townspeople of various categories, Red Army, and so on) grew rapidly, from 13 million in 1918–19 to 30 million in 1920–21. New demands kept placing more and more needy groups high on the list for priority distribution—children received a special ration, workers in military industry obtained a "guaranteed ration," and so on. For the average towns-person, the best to be hoped for was access to the soup kitchens and cafeterias set up largely in industrial centers. The Petrocommune cafeterias of Petrograd served some food or other to "over 600,000 people" in 1919; in Moscow, 2,000 "food centers" served over 800,000 people.[43]

It was apparent then, and subsequently proven by Soviet studies, that the supplies available through all the state sources could not possibly keep the population alive. The statistics compiled by various Soviet historians, though differing in detail, tell a uniform tale of gross insufficiency of even bread supplies. In March 1919, Iaroslavl' workers in the highest ration category were receiving only one-half a pound of bread per day; in June, deliveries almost stopped. Compounding the shortages was the state demand that the region provide from its own meager crops supplies of potatoes and cabbage for the Red Army. By February 1920, rations to Iarosiavl' workers for the entire month had fallen to four pounds; other townspeople received nothing.[44] The Ukrainian cities and industrial centers were not spared; in the first half of 1920, miners in the critically important Donets basin received only one-half of their bread norm. In the first two months of that year, they received no meat at all.[45]

This urgent need for food provided the driving force behind private trading. The Food Commissariat estimated in the spring of 1919 that townspeople obtained between 50 percent (the average in the food-producing regions) and 60 percent (in northern areas) of their bread through illegal exchange.[46] Dependence on this network for meat, vegetables, and dairy products was much greater; the government's surveys, producing figures too precise to be believable, indicated that 70 to 80 percent came through the market. The outlines of this dual food-supply network had first emerged in the spring of 1917 when the Provisional Government proclaimed the food monopoly. It grew increasingly important throughout the period of War Communism, whose official network could not by 1919 furnish sufficient food even for the priority groups.[47] These conditions placed on the urban population a burden unlike anything encountered since Muscovite times. Their lives depended, despite Soviet efforts, largely on their own efforts. The struggle for food became their overriding concern.

While the state increased its legal controls over the urban economy, a second economy kept the population alive. When they arrived in 1921, the ARA administrators were baffled by the survival of apparently poverty-stricken towns, noting wherever they went closed shops and abandoned factories along with active markets. One official commented that in the towns on the upper Dnepr river "trade is now restricted almost entirely to foodstuff in the market and there is an almost complete absence of shops or stores."[48] What they discovered then were the vestiges of the bankrupt urban supply system of War Communism. The effects of the introduction of the Soviet trade monopoly in Kiev in 1919–20 led one resident to conclude that "the nationalization of trade means that the whole nation trades."[49]

It meant also that markets exist everywhere. They operated with the tolerance or in defiance of the local police, on the fringes of legality or extralegally. The large Moscow open-air market, Sukharevka, remained in operation throughout the Civil War years; a survey in May 1919, reported that the market brought together that month over three thousand traders with a turnover of over five million rubles.[50] Consumer goods reached Petrograd inhabitants in the same manner. An official report in 1921 emphasized that

> private trade in Petrograd has existed for the past years despite the prohibitive measures against it. [Legal] markets were banned, their salespeople thrown out into the streets, but nonetheless in many places in Petrograd appeared free markets where it was possible to purchase necessary food supplies and consumer goods.[51]

Along the railroad lines markets functioned at every station. Fedor Dan, on his way in 1920 to Ekaterinburg from Moscow, noted in his memoirs that "guards defending that year's economic policy and traders violating this policy

somehow peacefully settled their affairs and got along with one another."
Cheka detachments occasionally raided the markets, seizing goods and sending
traders off for a short period of compulsory labor. For a few days trading
slowed and prices climbed; then the market resumed operations.[52] Throughout
Russia essential trading activities turned increasingly to direct buyer-seller relations in markets where prices were free to soar to the levels set by "speculation," that is, by supply and demand as determined by the shortcomings of
the state supply network, the readiness of traders to risk arrest, and the ability
of the needy to pay for the goods they sought.

Traders showed remarkable ingenuity and enterprise in obtaining supplies
and transporting them to urban markets. Easiest to arrange were their relations
with peasant producers. Prerevolutionary experience with urban demand for
rural products had taught villagers the essential practices of the market. If
Soviet procurement agencies failed to respect these rules, other outlets were
available. Villagers in regions close to the northern cities found eager buyers
for their produce. The Kursk area acquired by 1918 the reputation of being
the "empire of the private traders," estimated by the provincial soviet to number 150,000.[53] Such numbers assured an abundance of goods for trade. The
provincial food commissariat admitted that summer that "exchange with the
private traders is extremely profitable for the peasants . . . ; goods have been
brought in [to the countryside] in such quantities that there exist no shortages
here."[54] In nearby Orel province, the food procurement officials complained
in May that "private traders have arrived with bags filled with the best and,
one might say, the most luxurious products, much better than ours."[55] The
introduction of forced requisitioning and the organization of procurement bri-
gades by the state authorities made these private purchasing operations more
difficult in the following years. There is no indication that the rural network
ceased to flourish, however, until in 1920–21 draconian procurements combined with bad weather in the eastern regions to reduce drastically the food
surplus in the countryside.

From the meager information available, it would appear that even the transportation of produce from countryside to town did not present insuperable
problems. The labor-intensive scale of operations represented in this respect a
great advantage over the movement of bulk shipments by the Food Commissariat. Any available form of transportation under any conditions attracted
crowds of traders carrying their goods, either to or from the countryside. River
boats and barges, passenger and freight trains, all had their contingent of
traders, some accompanied by bodyguards to protect their precious goods. A
survey (yet another!) of travelers on a main line through the grain-producing
area of Voronezh in January 1921, found that the five daily trains carried on
an average some 20,000 traders transporting an estimated 160,000 *pud* (5.5
million pounds) of various supplies.[56] When one extrapolates from such figures
the probable movement of goods between countryside and towns across the
country, the scale of private trading dwarfs state shipments.

These traders struggled in their own way—and with as much or greater success than the Food Commissariat—with the transportation crisis. Reports from railroad officials in early 1919 revealed cases of such crowding of trains that the locomotives could not progress, even cases of commandeering of trains by traders who threatened the lives of the trainmen to reach their destination.[57] Eyewitness accounts told of "traders filling the interiors and the outsides of trains—on the roof, the couplings, etc."[58] One can only conclude that whatever means of transportation was available must have been exploited to the greatest possible degree by these industrious petty capitalists.

Who were these shadowy figures moving about with their bags of goods? The term by which they were known at the time—"bagmen"—masked their identity in the nondescript colors of their cloth bags. A comprehensive Soviet study emphasizes on the one hand the role of the prerevolutionary petty shop-keepers, supposedly "transformed into market speculators by economic dif-ficulties," and on the other the "petty-bourgeois, anarchistic force (*stikhiia*) of millions of individual peasant and worker households from whose midst emerged speculators, petty traders organizing . . . throughout the country a significant commercial exchange."[59] Translated into non-Leninist language, this description suggests that class distinctions were meaningless in character-izing the social groups engaged in trade. Motivated by their own desire to survive and—for some—to profit by the shortages of the townspeople, those who engaged in private trade appear to have come from all walks of life and to have included, to a greater or lesser degree, most urban dwellers. Still, in these new extralegal commercial exchanges, peasant farmers, their "city re-lations," and traders from tsarist times (a sizeable proportion of the earlier urban population) held the upper hand over townsfolk inexperienced in com-mercial practices.

These conditions placed extraordinary pressure on the urban population to find some means of tapping this subterranean river of goods. Prices on essential items rose to levels far beyond the means to pay through ordinary work. One Moscow doctor noted that even with several meager incomes from his house-hold he could feed his family with the necessary foods (including milk for their infant) for one week in a month.[60] The resulting decline of monetary exchange, praised by utopians such as Bukharin, signaled not the devalorization of money per se but the diminished value of monetized market relations. From this fact resulted several important changes in urban practices of labor and trade. A quick inventory of the new conditions would include the prevalence of barter, the use of personal belongings for exchange and the enhanced importance of women in fixing the terms of trade, the severe shortage of skilled factory labor and the low productivity of labor, the great rise in the theft of state property, and the development of a handicraft economy in part staffed by former workers who put their skills to use turning out items in immediate demand. The com-plexities of this barter economy of survival, of which we have only a vague understanding, defy comprehensive description. Some people could not make the transition; intellectuals never trained to such skills suffered particularly. Yet the ingenuity of most was remarkable and was responsible for the survival of urban centers throughout the country.[61]

The acquisition of goods with which to enter the private market became the principal concern of most townspeople. It took precedence over other aspects of daily life. With such possessions individuals and families avoided starvation; some found in trading the sole occupation to keep themselves alive. Households searched among their belongings for any item, such as linen or skirts, to the taste of peasant traders. Wives whose husbands had left to fight in the war became "grass widows," many of whom had to survive through the private market. Their desperate need provides at least a partial explanation why the Petrograd Soviet found in May 1918, "no less than 30,000 people for whom private trading provided their sole means of livelihood." Their actual number was in the opinion of a Soviet historian "undoubtedly greater."[62]

Access to state supplies provided many opportunities for trading or personal consumption. Workers developed a proprietary attitude toward workshop and factory items that had nothing in common with Marxist principles. Their demand for a "living wage" led managers increasingly to make payments in kind sufficient in quantity not only for personal needs but also for bartering. The practice, begun extensively in 1919, followed the simple principle: "Feed us first, then we'll work." Thus a Moscow soap factory began that year to pay its 10,000 workers two dozen pieces of soap each month.[63] The policy merely acknowledged that the workers would take whatever they needed.

When ARA officials began supervising the distribution of their food supplies in the winter of 1921–22, they quickly made their peace with what had become by then a well-established practice. Striking dockworkers at Rybinsk explained to the American there that a supervisor "would not let the men steal what they considered their legitimate share of the supplies; what they could take away, they pointed out, would after all be a small amount." They won their protest and went back to work.[64]

Far more serious for the nationalized economy was the move away from factory work to participate in the barter economy. Often the closure of an enterprise left workers no other choice than to turn to handicrafts. Fedor Gladkov, in his novel Cement, described the "natural economy" of the workers who had turned by the winter of 1920–21 to making cigarette lighters with materials stolen from their derelict factory, raising geese and pigs, and traveling with bags on their shoulders over the hills to the villages.[65] The picture was true to life, though oversimplified. The barter economy had penetrated operating factories as well. Reports from such enterprises sounded by 1920 a dismal note. At the Briansk metallurgical factory a Pravda correspondent painted an almost folkloric picture describing how "daily 500 metal workers go off to the villages carrying with them 500 axes to trade for grain for themselves. . . . Iron, glass, paints, everything available is taken for barter."[66]

The operations of the railroads felt the impact of the food crisis directly. According to another report, railroad repair workers, on whose labors depended the desperately needed locomotives and freight cars, were instead "working on sleighs, pipes for samovars, and axes, and all this with state materials; in the meantime the presses remain still and, of course, the repair of engines and cars is forgotten." The irate reporter accused the workers of "manufacturing goods to speculate [on the private market]." He did note their "excuse: 'we are earning our living, it's very hard to survive.' "[67] In the winter of 1918–19, the Transportation Commissariat's paper reported that "there are few locomotives, repairs are poor, and workers are fleeing to search for bread."[68] The recovery of the Ukrainian railroads in 1920 was impeded by the absence of many repair workers—50 percent in the Kiev yards—and the unwillingness of the remainder to work with any enthusiasm. The cause for this reluctance presented no mystery to one observer, who noted that these workers "often receive no money despite their demands" and could not obtain "everything that is necessary" for basic rations.[69] One might well suppose that the introduction of proletarian dictatorship encouraged a more relaxed pace of work. Still, hunger by itself explains most easily the decline in productivity. Fewer trains meant fewer food shipments to cities, in turn curtailing the workers' ability to work, which in its turn held back the availability of trains for food shipments. This vicious circle could not be resolved by simple actions such as militarization of the railroads.

The evidence collected from worker budget surveys made in 1919 and 1920 indicates that most factory workers, as other townspeople, found their livelihood as much or even more through trading as through their regular work. One Soviet official observed that "there are some enterprises, some important branches of our economy, where the percent of workers [who have] become primarily petty traders is extremely great." Earnings from private trade provided Moscow and Petrograd workers in 1919 with "not less than 50 percent of their income." Railroad workers, with ready access to transportation, obtained two-thirds of their consumer goods from trade.[70] Similar figures characterize the consumption strategy of workers in other branches of the urban economy. Unable to furnish the basic necessities, factory work had depreciated, often to the level of an occasional occupation. Such a process represented, not a "transformation" or "disintegration" of the working class,"[71] rather, its assimilation into the mass of trading townspeople.

Factory employ became so unrewarding that many workers preferred to set up their own small shops. In Petrograd, at least 15,000 former qualified factory workers made this move by 1920.[72] The extent of the massive shift of workers to the barter economy can best be measured by the acute shortage of skilled workers felt by 1920. With an industrial economy reduced to a shadow of its former self, war factories still lacked 30,000 workers in the winter of 1919–20. The Tver textile factory was reduced to "beating the bushes" in surrounding villages to mobilize missing skilled workers needed to keep the factory operating.[73] Soviet leaders preferred to attribute this trend to peasant and petty-bourgeois elements among the workers and wrote them off as *déclassés* proletarians. Yet urban workers continued to use their skills and remained, to the extent they retained physical strength and good health, as industrious as before. It would thus be incorrect to judge the spread of private trading a return to a "primitive" economy; it represented in fact a complex and massive adaptation of the urban population to the critical needs created by economic collapse.[74]

The key to survival for the majority of townspeople was thus self-sufficiency in work and trade. The intricate scaffolding of interregional and rural-urban exchange had fallen away. The downward spiral reached what probably was its lowest point by 1920; the countryside experienced its own disaster the following year. Until than, the urban population had good reason to believe itself abandoned by the more fortunate villagers. The desperate search for any means to barter for food on the terms set by traders, largely peasants, represented one aspect of the rural economic dominance.

Shortage of labor was another. No longer did seasonal laborers arrive to work for low wages in construction and other low skill occupations. The Moscow provincial authorities estimated that in the summer of 1920 its urban areas lacked 250,000 construction workers and 20,000 day laborers.[75] The "exceptional measures" taken throughout the country to meet this shortage consisted primarily of labor conscription, to which the entire urban population was in theory subject. It provided the manpower to seek wood for fuel, to unload barges and freight cars, even to shovel snow. The work was done poorly, by people debilitated by lack of nourishment and preoccupied with their own needs. As one Muscovite remarked, of what importance were poorly shoveled streets resembling "something like frozen ocean waves, on which it was worse traveling than an amusement ride?" More revealing was his comment that "we went on foot; only the commissars rode."[76] In better times an abundance of rural migrants had been available to execute these tasks. The conditions created by the Civil War abruptly ended the attraction of urban labor, while placing increased value on the peasants' own production—to the extent they could protect it from the requisitioning parties. Economic rewards were found in the villages. Urban society was forced to rely on its own skills and labor for even the most menial jobs.

Next to food shortages, the most intractable hardship confronting townspeople was inadequate shelter. In prewar years, the greatest problem facing those seeking lodgings was the shortage and poor quality of cheap rentals. The well-to-do, on the other hand, enjoyed a wide choice of luxurious houses and apartments.

The Soviet regime undertook a sweeping reform of urban housing within its first year in power. In August 1918, a decree ended private ownership of urban real estate in towns of over 10,000 population and empowered local soviets to take over buildings at their discretion to rehouse the poor, to provide rooms for officials, and to quarter troops. The slogan was: "Palaces for the workers, cellars for the bourgeois."[77] Neither palaces nor cellars could serve their inhabitants, however, when the buildings themselves could no longer offer real shelter and basic comforts. The critical shortage of heating fuel, discussed above, left all urban dwellers without adequate heat for winter. Inhabitants of the vast number of small wooden houses and cottages, typical still of "one-story Russia," had simple needs since they lacked indoor plumbing and running water. Apartment dwellers of the major cities had to make far more painful adjustments when deprived of such conveniences. Whatever the circumstances, survival dictated a reduction of comforts to the absolute minimum.

One visible result consisted of a physical contraction of urban living space. The decline of the urban population produced a reserve of abandoned buildings, a convenient source of wood for neighbors desperate in wintertime for fuel. Other buildings became shells of their former selves as sanitary conditions worsened and as the remaining occupants seized what material they could for heating. As a result, the number of lodgings considered "suitable for occupancy" by normal health standards fell sharply; in Moscow, the municipality in 1921 judged three-fifths of 1914 lodgings unfit for residence (130,000 of the prewar total of 231,000).[78]

In apartment buildings and houses alike families abandoned all but the most necessary rooms, where they slept, cooked, and passed the long winter evenings in virtual darkness. They lived, as the Kharkov ARA administrator found in late 1921, "four, five, even six and seven in a room without electric lights, without running water, and without adequate fuel."[79] Overcrowding did at least generate warmth. Heat came from tiny stoves, the "burzhuiki," constructed with the means at hand (including rainpipe for chimneys) and set in whichever room was needed. After fires had indicated mistakes in construction, the stoves provided, with little fuel, heat sufficient for cooking and brief hours of warmth.[80] This grim picture appears characteristic of all large towns, particularly in the northern regions, where the urban crisis was most acute.

The contraction of living space forced on Russia's urban population as a result of war conditions provides an appropriate image of the overall conditions of life in the towns. Public services dwindled or disappeared; elementary schooling ceased; refuse gathered in streets and courtyards. Factories struggled to maintain a minimal level of production or kept only maintenance staff; stores offered a meager selection of products or closed. Immediate needs of townspeople took precedence over future goals; private concerns mattered more than public interests for all save a small minority. "Everyone lived for the present," one Muscovite remembered thinking back on his last winter there in 1919–20.[81] The same attitude characterized the outlook surely of many living in White-occupied areas.

The adaptation forced on the population by the revolution and civil war had dramatically altered living conditions, as the economic crisis had changed through death and migration the composition of the population itself. The stark contrast between utopian visions of the "City of the future" and social reality refuted long before 1921 the capacity of War Communism to impose a collectivist pattern of behavior on the urban population. The obstacles confronting the townspeople in the northern regions were most severe and the "struggle to survive" most intense, yet the southern cities followed at a slower pace the trends of the north. Contraction of urban life did not signify complete

"deurbanization"; townspeople did survive by their wits. Reduced to bare
essentials, urban relations and activities still retained the minimal, one might
say skeletal, contours of public life.

To outsiders, the social and economic crisis appeared to have destroyed the
foundations of civilized life in Russian towns. Cut off from ready access to
the food in the villages and subject to devastating epidemics, towns of Russia
altered radically in substance and appearance. Americans arriving shortly after
the Civil War concluded on first sight that some cities had virtually died.
Feodosia, once a bustling southern seaport, reminded one ARA administrator
of

> a deserted western mining town. Doors and windows were barred and shuttered
> and very few persons were stirring about. Not a single ship or store of any kind
> was open and one marveled how the population managed to secure the barest
> necessities with which to sustain life . . . At night the town was in total dark-
> ness.[82]

This image of night descending on cities fits well the prevailing view of Russian
urban life in Western historiography, cited at the beginning of this article. Yet
substantial evidence points to the conclusion that the appearance of death hid
vigorous and, in their own terms, effective urban practices capable of sustaining
basic functions. While the physical environment resembled a ghost town, the
nexus of human relations sustained a diminished urban society.

Through those years there emerged in response to this crisis a second
economy operating beyond the control of the Soviet commissariats. The "profiteering" and "speculation" that so offended the authorities—and undoubtedly
many of the townspeople themselves—had their origins in prerevolutionary
times. What the Soviet leaders would not recognize, however, was that their
own failures made inevitable the entry into that market of the great majority
of townspeople and destroyed the very class distinctions on which they relied
for working-class support.

The impact on the towns of War Communism was thus to strengthen, not
weaken, the operations of a petty capitalist economy. The level of trade was
pathetically small, and the supplies reaching the cities by this path were so
meager that famine and hunger were widespread. Even so, the major towns
were able to retain three-fourths of their 1917 population to the end of the
war. The inhabitants' manner of dealing with the crisis drew on the experience
of nineteenth-century townspeople. Self-sufficiency became a vital survival
strategy; workers shifted to artisanry; gardens spread about the towns in sum-
mertime; households had to rely on their own skills and devices to sustain life.
The qualities of urban life characteristic of prewar years had disappeared. Yet
there remained an urban population with generations of experience in city life,
engaged in intense trading and exchange among themselves and with rural
traders, sustaining themselves and keeping the urban centers alive. From this
perspective, the legalization of small trade and artisanry included in the early

NEP reforms represented the triumph of these urban practices over the revolutionary zealotry of the Communist authorities. We should not be surprised at the vitality of the NEP trading economy, for it represented a direct extension of the urban second economy of the Civil War years.

The issue raised at the beginning of this essay of the disintegration of urban society would appear poorly stated. The problem confronting historians is not disintegration. Too much evidence points to the continuation of urban social life. Attention should instead focus on the level of urban relations, social and economic, as well as on the impact of the traumatic experiences of those years on families, individuals, and social groups. Adaptation suggests heroic struggle in the face of apparently daunting obstacles. Utopian visions of the future were meaningless when set next to the pressures of daily life. The Russian city survived, but the countryside appeared until 1921 the source of life.

Among the psychological effects of the Civil War one might include a heightened sense of identity among townspeople differentiating them from villagers. The two groups emerged from the war more segregated than in many generations and deeply divided by access to vital commodities. Peasants possessed essential food and shelter; many urban dwellers did not. The latter may well have built up a deep and abiding hostility toward the villagers. One Soviet historian hinted at such a reaction. Citing a survey conducted in 1919 of Kostroma townspeople, he reported feelings of anger and resentment at their powerlessness "to defend their interest in trade of goods for food in the countryside" and a strong desire that the Soviets "call a halt to, end, and straighten out this looting by village kulaks."[83] Many townspeople shared with Communist militants a similar view of a common enemy. In this sense the social experience of the Civil War prepared the urban population for the Stalin Revolution. Some among them had acquired a taste of war on the peasantry as participants in the requisitioning parties. The introduction of NEP left unresolved the conflict between countryside and city, with the peasantry still controlling the food resources. Collectivization ended that fragile alliance. Many townspeople may well have welcomed the defeat of private farming as their own victory.

NOTES

1. Victor Serge, "La ville en danger," *L'an I de la révolution* (Paris, 1971), p. 119.

2. Edward Brown, *Brave New World, 1984, and We: An Essay on Anti-Utopia* (Ann Arbor, Mich., 1976), p. 22.

3. See below, Diane Koenker, "Urbanization and Deurbanization in the Russian Revolution and Civil War."

4. Paul Avrich, *Kronstadt 1921* (Princeton, 1970), p. 25.

5. Characteristic of this approach is E. H. Carr's *History of Soviet Russia,* (New York, 1953) the first three volumes of which, devoted to the Civil War years, subsume urban conditions under economic and political topics.

6. Koenker, "Urbanization and Deurbanization."

7. This concept of the autonomy of the city as a human environment is derived from Michel de Certeau, *The Practice of Everyday Life,* trans. Steven Rendall (Berkeley, 1984), esp. pt. 3.

8. For example, William Chase, *Workers, Society, and the Soviet State: Labor and Life in Moscow, 1918–1929* (Urbana, Ill., 1987).

9. V. Ivanchikov, "Obyvatel' i nashe voennoe polozhenie," *Krasnyi put' zheleznodorozhnika,* June 12, 1919, p. 2. This weekly paper, published by the Commissariat of Transportation until Trotskii closed it in the spring of 1920, reported on economic problems throughout the vast railroad network and thus provides valuable information on social conditions and economic policy in those years (the title of the paper remained that of the prerevolutionary publication, *Vestnik putei soobshcheniia,* until the spring of 1919, when it became *Krasnyi put' zheleznodorozhnika*).

10. The derogatory implications of the generic term *meshochnichestvo,* incorporated in contemporary Communist attacks on the practice of private trading and preserved by most Soviet historians, have been retained by the literal English translation of "bagmen." I have chosen to employ the more prosaic and less accusatory terms "petty trade" and "petty traders."

11. Sidney Brooks, "Russian Railroads in the National Crisis," *ARA Bulletin,* November 1923, series 2, no. 42, p. 22. These records of the American Relief Administration (kept at the Hoover Institution of Stanford University) contain the eyewitness accounts of the American relief workers who arrived in 1921–22 to organize famine assistance and also include documents, collected by these workers, prepared by Russians on social and economic conditions in their country. They are gathered together in *ARA Russian Operations: Documents* and *ARA Bulletin* (series 2).

12. Lars Lih, "Bolshevik *Razverstka* and War Communism," *Slavic Review,* 1986, vol. 45, pp. 674–75.

13. *Vestnik putei soobshchenii,* 1919, no. 12, p. 6.

14. These data are found in "Predvaritel'nye itogi perepisi naseleniia 28 avgusta 1920 g. Naselenie 25 gubernii Evropeiskoi Rossii," in *Trudy Tsentral'nogo statisticheskogo upravleniia* (abbreviated Ts. S. U.), 1920, vol. 1, nos. 1–4 (Moscow). The figures are presented in Koenker's essay, "Urbanization and Deurbanization," table 1. The census data, though subject to cautious interpretation, provide an invaluable indication of demographic trends during the Civil War. The Central Statistical Bureau published in its periodical publications a wide array of census reports and analyses, including the 1920 urban census noted above. Its two major publications are *Trudy Ts. S. U.* and *Biulleten' Ts. S. U.*

15. O. Kvitkin, "Naselenie gorodov Evropeiskoi chasti RSFSR po perepisiam 1897, 1917, 1920, 1923 gg.," *Biulleten' Ts. S. U.,* 1923, no. 77, p. 13.

16. Ibid.

17. "Sbornik statistichiskikh svedenii po Soiuzy S.S.R.," *Trudy Ts.S.U.,* 1924, vol. 18, pp. 18–29.

18. D. A. Baevskii, *Rabochii klass v pervye gody Sovetskoi vlasti* (Moscow, 1974), p. 216.

19. G. I. Kurochkin, "Dvizhenie naseleniia v Iaroslavskoi gubernii za poslednye gody," *Sbornik: Proizvoditel'nye sily Iaroslavskoi gubernii* (Iaroslavl', 1928), p. 331; figures on the increase in death rates for other towns, so vague they are merely suggestive, are found in E. G. Gimpel'son, *Sovetskii rabochii klass, 1918–1920* (Moscow, 1974), p. 289.

20. E. G. Gimpel'son, *Sovety v gody inostrannoi interventsii i grazhdanskoi voiny* (Moscow, 1968), pp. 101, 104.

21. Koenker, "Urbanization and Deurbanization."

22. V. I. Nosach, "Sostav i sotsial'nyi oblik rabochikh Petrograda (1918–1920)." *Istoricheskie zapiski,* 1977, vol. 98, pp. 69–70.

23. Gimpel'son. *Sovetskii rabochii klass,* p. 113.

24. Kvitkin, pp. 13–14.

25. A. A. Gol'denveizer, "Iz Kievskikh vospominanii," *Arkhiv russkoi revoliutsii,* 1922, vol. 6 p. 219.

26. K. Paustovsky, *The Story of a Life,* trans. Joseph Barnes (New York, 1964), p. 647.

27. V. Mikhailovskii, "Naselenie Moskvy," *Biulleten' Ts.S.U.,* 1923, no. 77, p. 29.

28. Serge, "La ville en danger," pp. 118–19.

29. Paustovsky, p. 600.

30. Cited in V. P. Dmitrenko, "Nekotorye itogi obobshchestvleniia tovarooborota v 1917–1920 gg.." *Istoricheskie zapiski,* 1967, vol. 79, p. 233.

31. Gimpel'son, *Sovetskii rabochii klass,* pp. 121–22.

32. Mikhailovskii, "Naselenie Moskvy," p. 29.

33. Gimpel'son, *Sovetskii rabochii klass,* p. 108.

34. Gimpel'son, *Sovety v gody grazhdanskoi voiny,* p. 359.

35. Iu. A. Poliakov, *Perekhod k nepu i sovetskoe krest'ianstvo* (Moscow, 1967), p. 220, n.42.

36. Ibid., p. 151 (loose translation of *imeem po dekretu, zhivem po sekretu*).

37. Davydov, *Bor'ba za khleb* (Moscow, 1971), p. 73; I. S. Kulyshev, *Bor'ba za khleb* (Leningrad, 1972), p. 47.

38. N. Orlov, *Deviat' mesiatsev prodovol'stvennoi raboty Sovetskoi vlasti* (Moscow, 1918), pp. 46–47.

39. Davydov, *Bor'ba,* pp. 77–93, 99–104.

40. Ibid., pp. 170–171, 184–85.

41. S. A. Sokolov, *Revoliutsiia i khleb* (Saratov, 1967), p. 76.

42. Davydov, *Bor'ba,* pp. 97–99.

43. Gimpel'son, *Sovetskii rabochii klass,* p. 265.

44. L. B. Genkin, *Iaroslavskie rabochie v gody grazhdanskoi voiny* (Iaroslavl', 1958), pp. 229, 252.

45. Gimpel'son, *Sovetskii rabochii klass,* p. 260.

46. Davydov, *Bor'ba,* pp. 199–200.

47. Dmitrenko, "Nekotorye itogi," pp. 236–37.

48. "Conditions in the Kharkov District," *ARA Bulletin,* February 1923, series 2, no. 33, pp. 28–29.

49. Gol'denveizer, p. 286.

50. Cited in Dmitrenko, "Nekotoryi itogi," p. 232.

51. Cited in ibid., p. 238.

52. F. Dan, *Dva goda skitanii* (Berlin, 1921), pp. 30, 35.

53. M. Feigel'son, "Meshochnichestvo i bor'ba s nimi," *Istorik-Marksist,* 1940, no. 9, p. 77.

54. M. I. Davydov, "Gosudarstvennyi tovaroobmen mezhdu gorodom i derevnei v 1918–1921 gg.," *Istoricheskie zapiski,* 1982, vol. 108 p. 41.

55. Feigel'son, p. 74.

56. Dmitrenko, "Nekotoryi itogi," p. 236.

57. Cited in Feigel'son, p. 79, n.1.

58. *Krasnyi put' zheleznodorozhnikov,* 1919, no. 21, p. 4.

59. Dmitrenko, "Nekotorye itogi," pp. 231, 239.

60. R. Donskii (pseud.), "Ot Moskvy do Berlina v 1920 g.," *Arkhiv russkoi revoliutsii,* 1922, vol. 1, p. 212.

61. This ability of townspeople to survive through their own efforts produced its own black humor. When one official in Kiev's transportation agency was asked by a friend why the cabbies had not been nationalized along with the rest of urban transportation, he explained that "we tried, but a major difficulty arose. When people are not fed, they somehow continue living. But when horses are not fed,

they inevitably die. Therefore we have not nationalized the cabbies." Gol'denveizer, p. 288.

62. Feigel'son, p. 78.

63. Gimpel'son, *Sovetskii rabochii klass*, pp. 184, 263.

64. Sidney Brooks, "The Russian Railroads," *ARA Bulletin*, November 1923, series 2, no. 42, p. 76.

65. Fedor Gladkov, *Tsement* (Moscow, 1982), esp. pp. 58–60.

66. *Krasnyi put'*, 1920, nos. 9–10, p. 3.

67. *Vestnik putei soobshcheniia*, 1919, nos. 6–8, p. 2.

68. *Krasnyi put'*, 1920, nos. 12–13, p. 18.

69. Cited in Gimpel'son, *Sovetskii rabochii klass*, p. 185.

70. Dmitrenko, "Nekotorye itogi," pp. 240–41.

71. Chase, p. 33.

72. Gimpel'son, *Sovetskii rebochii klass*, p. 115.

73. Ibid., pp. 140, 143.

74. In this sense I would agree with Koenker, in her essay in this volume, that a "core" of the working class retained "its own brand of urban culture" ("Urbanization and Deurbanization"), though I would place more emphasis on the peculiar urban practices associated with the trading culture.

75. Gimpel'son, *Sovety*, p. 351.

76. Donskii, p. 208.

77. Gimpel'son, *Sovetskii rabochii klass*, pp. 273–74, 276.

78. Dr. Henry Beeuwkes, "American Medical and Sanitary Relief in the Russian Famine," *ARA Bulletin*, April 1926, series 2, no. 45 p. 10.

79. George Harrington, "Report on the Kharkov District," *ARA Russian Operations: Documents*, vol. 8, p. 155.

80. Donskii, pp. 210–11.

81. Ibid., p. 211.

82. J. Brown, "Theodosia," *ARA Russian Operations: Documents*, vol. 5, p. 179.

83. Cited in Dmitrenko, "Nekotorye itogi," p. 231.

URBANIZATION AND DEURBANIZATION IN THE RUSSIAN REVOLUTION AND CIVIL WAR

Diane P. Koenker

Urban Russia in 1917 was the crucible of revolution. The collapse of the tsarist government began first in the capital city of Petrograd; the appeal of the Bolshevik party among the urban populations of Petrograd, Moscow, and other cities (along with its influence among troops at the front) was critical in ensuring the successful seizure of power by the Soviets in October 1917. Indeed, the city, and especially its urban work force, had long been central to Marxist theorists, who opposed their vision of a proletarian revolution centered in the city to that of the populists, who believed that rural peasants would provide the spark of revolution in Russia.[1]

It was not only a historical irony, then, but a critical threat to the future course of the revolution, that from the very moment of Bolshevik success in late 1917, thousands and thousands of urban residents, workers and non-workers, were abandoning the cities for the relative security of provincial towns and rural hamlets. Between May 1917 and April 1918, the city of Moscow lost 300,000 of its 2 million inhabitants. From 1918 to 1920, the city lost another 700,000 people. Moscow's population toward the end of the Civil War was thus half of what it had been in the midst of the 1917 revolution. An even more catastrophic fall occurred in Petrograd: its population plummeted from 2.5 million in 1917 to 700,000 in 1920.[2]

Between 1917 and 1920, nearly every city in the former Russian Empire had suffered similar population losses. Of the ten largest cities in 1910, the decline in Kiev came closest to Moscow's and Petrograd's: Kiev's population dropped by 28 percent in the years spanning the revolution and Civil War. Only a handful of cities gained in population between 1910 and 1920: two,

Baku and Tiflis, were politically independent after 1917, and as such were havens for refugees from the destitution and conflict of revolutionary Russia. The other cities that grew were all located on the periphery of European Russia, close to sources of grain but also at one time or another centers of White army activity as well. Samara and Tsaritsyn on the Volga, Perm in Western Siberia, and Rostov-on-Don all recorded marked increases in population at a time when cities everywhere were contracting (see Table 1).[3]

Bolshevik leaders feared they were losing their working-class base of support, that the proletariat that demonstrated such revolutionary class consciousness in 1917 was becoming "declassed" as a result of the economic pressures and dislocations of the Civil War. Menshevik leaders used this same fear to argue that since the social base of Bolshevik legitimacy had withered away, the Bolsheviks themselves should reconsider the assumptions on which they based their right to rule.[4]

Nikolai Bukharin spoke in March 1918 of the disintegration of the proletariat; Ian Rudzutak reported to the Second All-Russian Congress of Trade Unions in January 1919: "We observe in a large number of industrial centers that the workers, thanks to the contraction of production in the factories, are being absorbed in the peasant mass, and instead of a population of workers we are getting a half-peasant or sometimes a purely peasant population."[5] And

TABLE 1

Change in Population of Major Russian Cities from 1910 to 1920

City	1910	1920
St. Petersburg	1,962,000	722,000
Moscow	1,533,000	1,028,000
Odessa	506,000	435,000
Kiev	505,000	366,000
Khar'kov	236,000	284,000
Saratov	206,000	190,000
Ekaterinoslav	196,000	164,000
Tiflis	188,000	327,000
Kazan	188,000	146,000
Baku	167,000	256,000
Astrakhan	150,000	123,000
Rostov-on-Don	121,000	177,000
Nizhnyi Novgorod	109,000	70,000
Ufa	103,000	93,000
Minsk	101,000	104,000
Samara	96,000	177,000
Tsaritsyn	78,000	81,000
Perm	50,000	74,000

Sources: For 1910, B. R. Mitchell, *Abstract of European Historical Statistics*, abridged ed. (New York, 1975), pp. 12–15; Baedeker, *Russia* (1914; New York, 1970). For 1920, Tsentral'noe statisticheskoe upravlenie, *Trudy*, vol. 8, vyp. 1, part 1, table 3; and Mitchell.

Lenin reiterated this theme at the Tenth Party Congress in March 1921: "People have run away from hunger; workers have simply abandoned their factories, they set up housekeeping in the countryside and have stopped being workers."[6]

Western scholars, too, citing the contemporary record, describe the "withering away of the proletariat." John L. H. Keep writes: "The men who made the October revolution, in so far as they were civilians and not soldiers, were soon dissipated to the four winds. . . . their place would eventually be filled by men who came straight from the village and were cast in a different mold."[7]

In this light, it becomes extremely important to examine the reality of this postulated decline of the working class and to ask how the demographic and social changes that took place between 1917 and 1921 affected the set of factors that had propelled the Bolshevik Party to power in the first place.

It is one thing, however, to examine concrete indices of economic and social change, particularly demographic data, and quite another to link such changes to more elusive concepts that usually go under the name of "revolutionary" or "class" consciousness. For example, it can be argued that there existed, among Bolshevik supporters in late 1917, a "revolutionary consciousness," a common sense of purpose and commitment to replacing the old regime with something new and more socially just. Some of the elements of this revolutionary consciousness have been identified in recent studies of the revolution and working class by S. A. Smith, David Mandel, and Rex A. Wade, among others.[8] It was a consciousness shaped by short-term factors, most notably the specific economic and political experience of 1917, and by long-term factors as well. These include the ideology of Marxism itself, which fostered a tendency among workers to interpret their experience in terms of social class and class conflict. Another long-term factor was the workplace and the relations it engendered: an autocrat-subject relationship between management and labor and solidarity among workers who labored and suffered together in such close proximity. Still other factors have to do with social attributes of workers—education, skill, maleness, and youth—which predisposed them first to develop a sense of politics and then to respond in a calculated, conscious manner, rather than in a visceral way, to the visions of revolution posed by the Marxist parties and by events leading up to 1917. Finally, the location of workers in cities also helped to shape revolutionary consciousness, in ways that will be detailed below. Suffice it here to say that urban working-class culture reflected several important attributes of the urban milieu, such as individual autonomy, utilization of a wide array of cultural and educational opportunities, and a social heterogeneity that enriched the perceptions and experience of urban residents.

All of these factors helped shape a specific kind of revolutionary consciousness pertinent to the specific conditions of 1917. It was a consciousness strongly influenced by ideas of class and of socialism. It does not follow, however, that these attitudes or this revolutionary consciousness, were necessarily permanent and unchangeable. If some elements influencing this consciousness were changed, it is completely plausible that different attitudes might emerge. Kin, neighborhood, or possession of skill, for example, might be placed above class as the immediate source of a worker's identity. In such a case, the party whose popularity was based on its appeal to class interests, the Bolsheviks, might not command the same loyalty they had enjoyed under earlier conditions.

Of course, conditions did change after 1917. Of the factors important in shaping the consciousness of 1917, perhaps the only constant was Marxist ideology, which remained a powerful mediator of experience and whose appeal cannot be dismissed. But factory relations were dramatically transformed, the political and economic context of public life was also fundamentally different from what it had been before the revolution, and the cities, instead of representing the attractions of modernity and culture, became after 1917 places from which to flee.

There were many signs, by early 1918, that the Bolshevik Party did not command the same allegiance that had brought it to power. Although the Bolsheviks had not completely lost their mandate to rule, there were uncomfortable signs of an independent factory movement in Petrograd in early 1918 and a string of Menshevik successes in local Soviet elections in the summer of 1918.[9] By 1921, amidst discontent and strikes among Petrograd workers and a growing Workers' Opposition movement within the Communist Party, sailors at the Kronstadt naval fortress rebelled, demanding soviet reelections without Communist participation. The revolt was crushed by loyal Red Army troops, but the alienation it reflected prompted the party to search for a new economic policy to placate frustrated workers and peasants alike.

The party assessment of this debacle depended on its interpretation of the social composition of its former supporters. The old Kronstadt revolutionary sailor had left the fortress, and his place was occupied by peasants and other unrevolutionary elements. The "true" working class had been driven away from the cities by hunger, to be replaced, presumably, by new workers from cottage industry, agriculture, and white-collar jobs eliminated by the revolution.[10] (This was the same argument used to explain the Bolsheviks' lack of success among workers in the early months of 1917—that the cadres of conscious proletarians were diluted by nonproletarian elements.) In addition, Bolshevik ideology assumed that large factories were an essential component of proletarian consciousness; with the shrinking of the work force in these plants, with the decision by skilled workers to manufacture cigarette lighters that could be more easily exchanged for grain than machine tools, party officials believed that Russian workers were losing their class consciousness: this could only be restored by the resumption of production in large-scale plants.[11]

The questions of support and of working-class consciousness are critical in interpreting this period and in understanding the sources of the Soviet political and social system, and they deserve a prominent place on the research agenda. This article will investigate just one aspect of changing social relations during the Civil War, the problem of social composition in the former urban strongholds of the Bolshevik Party. Given the obvious social dislocations indicated by the drastic decline of Russia's urban population, the question of who stayed and who departed becomes important in identifying the nature of the available constituency for Soviet power during its early period of rule. In particular, this article will address the question of the nature of the deurbanization of Russia and the relationship between this deurbanization, the "declassing" of the proletariat lamented by the Communist Party, and the formation of a new and possibly different set of attitudes among workers—working-class consciousness—during these years.

Urbanization and Revolution

A discussion of Russian urbanization is inevitably a tale of two cities, St. Petersburg (after 1914, Petrograd) and Moscow. In large part, this is because of their political prominence and relative magnitude. St. Petersburg, with 2 million residents in 1910, and Moscow, with 1.5 million, were four and three times the size of their nearest competitors.[12]

Other Russian cities had grown as well since the early 1860s, when Russia's emancipation of its serfs loosened the bonds that restricted economic growth. But urban growth did not necessarily produce urbanization, in the sense of the adoption by the society of values associated with cities and with urbanism. Proportionally, Russia's urban population was dwarfed by the countryside. In 1860, cities accounted for 11.3 percent of the total population; this share had not quite doubled by 1917, to 21.6 percent. St. Petersburg and Moscow provinces, however, were the two most urban in the empire: in 1915, 75 percent of Petrograd province's population lived in cities and 53 percent of Moscow's did.[13] By contrast, Riazan province, an agricultural region that sent many migrants to Moscow, could claim an urban population of only 7 percent of its total in 1915.[14]

The social composition of Russian urban dwellers defies the strict definitions of census categories. Although urban growth was fueled largely by migration, the passage to the city was not one way, and an inhabitant did not acquire all the facility and characteristics of urban residence as soon as he or she passed the city barriers. The research of R. E. Johnson has shown that migrants themselves traveled back and forth many times during their years in the city; their families also tended to be distributed between city and village. It was not unusual for a working-class wife to bear her children in the city and then send them back to the country to live with relatives until they were old enough to work. Even more common, married male migrants lived and worked in the city while their wives and children remained home in the country.[15]

Such characteristics suggest that there existed a number of types of workers in Russian cities on the eve of revolution and that workers responded in different ways to the opportunities and pressures of 1917 and the years that followed. To clarify the following discussion, it is useful to rank these urban types in terms of a hypothetical "level of urbanization," in which urbanization is defined as the complete adoption of urban values, culture, and experience:

Type A: most urbanized, parents permanent city residents, children born and raised in city;
Type B: parents in city, children move back and forth (consecutively as much as all together);
Type C: father in city, mother in country, children (especially boys) move back and forth;
Type D: father in city, mother and children in country;
Type E: sons and daughters come to city as first-generation migrants, parents remain in country.

The working-class memoir literature provides examples of all five types, although it is impossible to assign numerical weights to each category.[16] Families of Type A, however, were clearly in the minority, although growing in numbers; barely 10 percent of the Moscow working class in 1912 had been born in the city, although the percentage of workers whose parents had also been workers (Types A through D) was greater. For all of Moscow province in a 1908 study, about 40 percent of workers had parents who were workers, a figure that rose to 45 percent for workers aged fifteen to twenty-five years.[17]

In assessing the impact of the urban crisis on urbanized workers after 1917, two questions arise. First, it is important to inquire whether and in what ways the city acted on its inhabitants, especially those of the working class, to produce a particular cast of mind (*oblik* is the Russian term), a set of characteristics and values that can be labeled as "urban working-class culture." The second question concerns the link between such culture and propensities to revolutionary activism.

Among the city's special contributions toward the creation of a working-class culture were the ways in which city life encouraged workers to act together, such as in food supply and dining cooperatives and in sick funds. The necessities of communal living developed the practice of cooperation, and of course, as the Marxists argued, the experience of working in large mechanized factories also taught cooperation. On the other hand, the diversity of the urban work force also provided opportunities for individual mobility and encouraged separatism as well as cooperation; typesetters, highly skilled urban workers, were notorious for setting themselves apart from other workers and often rejected participation in a wider labor movement in favor of helping themselves.[18]

In addition to these competing values of cooperation and individualism, the city offered its working-class residents cultural opportunities that in turn encouraged workers to value culture and education. Evening schools, public schools, neighborhood clubs and libraries, theater, and an active publishing industry offered workers a wide range of opportunities for self-improvement. Many workers used their reading ability to familiarize themselves with basic political issues, which were far more accessible in the cities than anywhere else, thanks to the concentration there of publishers and political activists.[19]

Among the ways in which these urban values were transmitted, three deserve special mention. The first of these is family. The typology offered above might suggest that the nuclear family was a rare phenomenon in urban Russia. Yet the children who grew up in such families quickly absorbed the values of their parents and used these values to define for themselves a distinct subculture of their own. The attributes of an urban youth culture are complex and have been discussed at greater length elsewhere;[20] moreover, there is surely room for further investigation into the entire problem of urban culture, both of the young and the old. There did exist, however, an urban youth subculture based on substantial personal autonomy deriving from the absence at home of working parents, from the less restrictive control by heads of urban families, from the availability of culture, recreation, and work away the family's strict tutelage. Youths in the city were thus relatively free to gravitate toward associations of their teenage peers, which reinforced a special sense of local identity. The favorite activities of such groups—literary discussions, drama, politics— also helped forge an identity that was seen to be distinctly modern and distinctly urban.[21] Further, perceptions and experiences of social relations interpreted in the light of Marxist class ideology were surely an important lesson imparted by working-class fathers.[22] Thus the urban working-class family was perhaps weaker as an institution than the archetypical patriarchal peasant family, but this weakness gave members of urban families a flexibility and freedom not easily found in the countryside.

A second important urban medium for transmitting new values was the city's concentration of workplaces and the proximity of plants in different industries, of different sizes, and representing different types of work. In contrast to laborers in single-industry towns such as Ivanovo-Voznesensk or the mining communities of the Urals, city workers could share a variety of experiences, among family members employed in different places, or in local taverns and dining halls, or in the activities of youth groups. The political and social attitudes that developed among urban workers who assimilated diverse experiences reflected the interaction of workers of different types.

The exemplary working-class neighborhoods of the two capital cities were Vyborg in Petrograd and Zamoskvorech'e in Moscow. Both districts were dominated occupationally by highly skilled metalworkers, but they also housed workers of other industries, especially women in textiles and food processing. The two districts shared a physical isolation from the upper-class and political culture of their cities, but were not so homogeneous that residents never came into contact with nonworkers or with workers of different social backgrounds. In 1917, both districts were far more politically active than other working-class neighborhoods of more homogeneous industrial composition.[23]

A third means by which the city fostered a special working-class culture was the concentration of political power and activity. Newspapers ranging from government gazettes to sensationalist tabloids were printed in the cities, and they were read avidly by urban workers.[24] The world of politics easily became the stuff of conversation in working-class neighborhoods, and urban workers had much better access to political information than workers scattered in provincial factory and mining towns. Furthermore, as political centers, both cities (although St. Petersburg more than Moscow) attracted opposition and underground activists. Socialists naturally sought to organize among workers, and their participation as evening-school teachers as well as professional political activists helped give a socialist cast to ideas of political opposition. The city's particular advantage was to make available to workers a mixture of theory and a variety of experience that made a revolutionary socialist world view seem especially valid.

But how did this urban working-class culture contribute to the outcome of the two revolutions of 1917? It is indeed difficult to prove that working-class supporters of Soviet power were somehow more "urban" in attitudes than those who supported other parties or none at all. Recent research by Heather J. Hogan, Victoria E. Bonnell, and others[25] has demonstrated that organized workers—those active in trade unions, factory committees, soviets—tended to be urban, skilled, and predominantly male. Craft unions were especially successful in organizing in the first few weeks after February 1917, as they had been after 1905. Although the attribute of skill rather than urban experience may have been more important in facilitating such organization, the union ideology reflected values fostered by urban working-class life: socialism, collectivism, organization, and culture.[26] It is also true that maleness was a more important factor in organization than urban experience per se; women did not organize themselves effectively either in 1917 or before, even though the proportion of urban-born women in the work force was generally higher than that of urban-born men.[27] The contributions of urban women to the development of working-class culture, as wives, mothers, and workers, are largely uncharted, in part because they did not participate in the unions that provide much of the published record of working-class life before and during 1917, but their role deserves further study.

The future of the urban working class was represented by its youth, the children chiefly of families of Type A and to a lesser extent of Types B and C. These youths espoused urban and socialist values: education and culture, collectivism and comradeship, sobriety, sexual equality (apparently on a level higher than that of their parents), class pride and solidarity.[28] In 1917, working-class youth and others organized for the first time on a large scale; fragmentary biographical information suggests the leaders of their youth groups came from urban rather than from migrant families.[29] By October, and even earlier, many working-class youth groups were enthusiastic if undisciplined supporters of the Bolshevik Party. By contrast, young workers who had come recently from the countryside, as a young Moscow metalworker recalled,

> were still weakly developed, and after the February revolution wavered among the Mensheviks, Socialist Revolutionaries, and Bolsheviks. The other and large

part of the youth—products of worker families—already had experienced hard factory labor, had received the tempering of a worker. This worker youth after the February revolution very quickly organized around Bolshevik party cells, joined in protest meetings against the policies of the Provisional Government, fought for the eight-hour working day.[30]

Although youth organizations as such played only a supporting role in the actual seizure of power, the energy and commitment of youth were tapped by the revolution in other ways. Armed worker militias and Red Guards recruited members predominantly from among young and unmarried workers between the ages of seventeen and twenty-four.[31] Moreover, Bolshevik Party electoral candidates, in Moscow at any rate, tended to be substantially younger than those of the other two socialist parties. Alexander Rabinowitch also suggests indirectly that Petrograd Bolsheviks were attractive to and perhaps composed of young workers, particularly those under thirty years old. Although he does not dwell on the social composition of the party rank and file, he indicates that the Bolsheviks in Petrograd were a highly autonomous group of activist workers (a characteristic also of the Red Guards), who shaped the policy of the leadership, sometimes against Lenin's wishes.[32] Their political independence and self-confidence reflected the advantages of urban culture: education and individualism, underscored by the strong sense of class separateness and consciousness that characterized the Bolshevik program in 1917. But although the revolutionary activists were dominated by skilled young male urban workers, more recent migrants were also brought into the revolutionary arena in Moscow and Petrograd precisely because of their location in the urban centers: here the urban working class gave its special stamp to the revolutionary outlook of the nonurban elements it was able to mobilize.

The evidence is only circumstantial that young workers of urban families supported the radical Bolsheviks more than other parties, and that their radicalism was conditioned by prior attitudes shaped by urban life. But there is little evidence for the contrary argument that urban radicalism in 1917 was fueled by the rawest and least politically experienced elements of urban society. As for the Bolsheviks themselves, they had no doubts about the social composition of their supporters; they read the results of the elections to the Constituent Assembly in November 1917, when they received 36.5 percent of the urban vote to 24 percent overall (and 47 percent in Petrograd and Moscow).[33] And even though the army gave nearly half its votes to the Bolsheviks, the army would soon be demobilized. Thus their urban supporters were all important, and the Bolshevik reaction to the urban depopulation following the revolution suggests they feared that the loss of their urban proletarian cadres would seriously undermine their legitimacy, if not their ability to govern. "Without such an economic base," argued Lenin in March 1921, in advocating the New Economic Policy, "there can be no lasting political power for the working class."[34]

Indeed, when the cities collapsed after 1917, among those who departed were the same urban and skilled young male workers who had fought for Soviet power in October, now leaving to fight in the Civil War. Bolshevik hegemony was threatened in two ways: by the loss of these supporters and others like them who rusticated themselves outside the cities, and by changing social and economic conditions that might have served to alter the components of urban culture that had produced such firm Bolshevik support in October. Bolsheviks thus feared "declassing" in two senses, both in changes in social composition and in changing attitudes.

Deurbanization in Moscow: Demographic Changes

Given the tremendous transformation that occurred in Russia between 1910 and 1920, it is not surprising that statistical sources can only hint at the dimensions of that transformation. Nonetheless, published census results permit us to trace the movement of the overall population of Moscow by size, age, sex, and precinct from its peak in 1917 through 1918, and up to 1920. Specific divisions by occupation were reported only in the 1918 and 1920 censuses, so a detailed study of changes in population by employment categories can be made only for the shorter period.

Over the entire period from February 1917 to August 1920, Moscow's population dropped by almost one million, a loss of 520,000 males, and 470,000 females. During the same period, there were roughly 110,000 births and 200,000 deaths, a natural decrease of 90,000.[35] Thus, about 900,000 people must have left the city by the summer of 1920. Further, William Chase estimates from the 1926 census that about 160,000 people moved into Moscow during the Civil War,[36] so the task becomes to account for one million lost Muscovites. Who were they? The sober, urban, most class-conscious workers? Or the politically marginal recent recruits from the Russian countryside? The answer to this question should provide a new appreciation of the nature of the social base underlying the political decisions made during these years, decisions that were to have a critical formative influence on the subsequent shape of the Soviet state and society.

To develop a profile of the changing social composition of Moscow, ideal indices would be place of birth, length of residence in the city, occupation, length of time in that occupation, education, parents' occupation, and so forth. Most of these are unavailable, so it is necessary to estimate changes in social composition using age, sex, and occupational indices only.

Because occupational data were published only in the 1918 and 1920 census reports, it is difficult to determine who were the first 300,000 people to leave Moscow. The actual outflow did not begin until after May 1917, since a population count made for electoral purposes showed a slightly higher population in May than in February. By September, there were 195,000 fewer inhabitants in the city; about 163,000 of these were aged fifteen or over. Yet over the same period, the number of registered voters in the city—adults over twenty—increased slightly. It is unlikely that fifteen- to nineteen-year-olds (of whom there were 250,000 in September[37]) would have left in such disproportionate numbers. Therefore, the adults who had left by the autumn of 1917 may have been so marginal to the urban community that they had not bothered to participate in the electoral process in 1917. Most of those who departed were men (103,000 to 60,000 women); the evidence is suggestive that these were men and women most closely connected to the countryside, abandoning the city to make sure they would share in the expected redivision of land.

From September 1917 to April 1918, another 120,000 people left, 83,000 of them adults, 42,000 of them adult males. (Men and women over sixty did not participate in this exodus; their numbers actually increased from February 1917 to April 1918, a phenomenon that raises intriguing questions about the position of the aged in Russian society during this period.) By early 1918, Moscow had lost a considerable number of adults, especially adult males. Men left in the greatest numbers from the industrial suburbs to the east of the city center and from the southern Zamoskvorech'e. Some of these losses may have been because of relocation, as the city soviet commandeered large private houses and reassigned them to workers' families.[38] But the decline in the female population was uniform throughout the city, and this reaffirms the suggestion that the men who left the factory districts were the marginal and single men, those of Type D, who had only recently come to the city from the countryside.[39]

Where exactly did the refugees go? Scattered evidence suggests that they returned to the countryside, both in the north and in the grain-producing districts far beyond Moscow. Already in April 1918, four trainloads of women and children, accompanied by extra cars of food for the journey, were en route to Syzran on the Volga, an evacuation sponsored by the local trade union council.[40] A comparison of the rural population between 1917 and 1919 indicates that the farming population of agriculturally nonproductive Moscow province declined from 72,000 in 1917 to 64,000 in 1919, echoing the urban pattern. Moscow city workers with ties to nearby regions may have preferred to trust their chances in the city rather than to return home, even if home were nearby. On the other hand, the agrarian population of more fertile Riazan province, the source of many Moscow migrants, increased from 175,000 in 1917 to 192,000 in 1919.[41] The northernmost regions of Russia around Arkhangel, Vologda, and Tver also increased in population during the Civil War, and surely substantial population gains went unrecorded in the southern regions beyond the limit of the twenty-two provinces of the Russian Soviet Federative Socialist Republic. Once again, as in the Time of Troubles in the early seventeenth century, town-dwelling Russians escaped to the forest and to the steppe. What is most curious about the changes in rural population is that the overall rural growth of about 8 percent was accounted for entirely by men; the female rural population remained constant, so the destination of the female out-migrants from Moscow remains something of a mystery.[42]

Between 1918 and 1920, Moscow's net loss was about 690,000 people.[43] Of these 690,000 missing persons, only 190,000 were economically self-supporting; the remaining 490,000 or so were dependents. Thus 70 percent of the missing Muscovites were children, nonworking women (and men, about 34,000 of them) between the ages of twenty and fifty-nine and those too old to work. Little else is known about these refugees, neither whom they depended on nor whether the women were workers' wives, factory workers themselves made redundant by the return of their husbands from the front, grandes dames of society, or shopkeepers' spinster daughters. But by and large, for a whole series of cultural reasons, nonworking women had not played a significant role in political activity in 1917,[44] and their absence after 1918 probably had little affect on the political and social consciousness of the Muscovite supporters of Soviet power. The children who left, on the other hand (especially some 100,000 teenagers), were now removed from a formative urban experience. But their absence, too, would little affect current political life in the city. If the city was "declassed," in other words, it was not because of the departure of women and children.

To evaluate the impact of Moscow's depopulation on its political life, it is important to know which *self-supporting* individuals left the city. The net loss of 194,000 economically independent residents can be accounted for in Table 2.

Among the largest groups of absentees were workers, domestic servants, and proprietors. Workers will be examined in more detail below. Domestic servants were a rural class, cut off from city life and from one another; most worked as single maids of all work in middle-class households. (These and cooks disappeared most completely between 1918 and 1920.) Nor did domestic servants produce dependents for future urban generations.[45] Their disappearance would have little negative effect on urban political life; furthermore, if they were reabsorbed into the urban work force in other occupations, their exposure to political culture might actually increase.

The departure of individual proprietors for Paris, Berlin, Odessa, Vladivostok, or wherever else they escaped to, like the departure of their servants, probably did not directly affect socialist political relationships in Moscow.

TABLE 2

**Net Change in Moscow Working Population by Occupational Group
from 1918 to 1920**

Group	Male	Female	Total
Workers	−90,760	−9,680	−100,440
Servants	−25,390	−56,270	−81,660
Employees	−59,460	+24,400	−35,060
Free professions	−720	+1,340	+620
Proprietors	−46,960	−14,530	−61,490
Other	+65,690	+14,320	+80,010

Source: *Statisticheskii ezhegodnik goroda Moskvy i moskovskoi gubernii*, vyp. 2 (Moscow, 1927), pp. 46–51.

Note also that 60,000 male employees left; their leaving was partially balanced by an influx of 24,000 women employees, primarily typists and other clerical personnel (messengers and couriers were classified as servants). Many of these office workers presumably worked for Soviet institutions, the biggest growth sector in Moscow, but others replaced departed or drafted men in business, factory, or cooperative society offices. Finally, an additional 80,000 residents in other categories came to the city, including 14,000 wards of the state (orphans, invalids, prisoners) and 50,000 people classified simply as "other occupations." Since these were almost all males, this large group of newcomers certainly represents the Moscow Red Army garrison. Many of these may not have been newcomers at all, but workers reassigned from Moscow factories to Moscow barracks.

Returning to the change among workers between 1918 and 1920, note that 90 percent of the decline is accounted for by men. Working women did not leave the city, unlike their economically dependent counterparts; from 90,000 in 1918, their numbers dropped only to 80,000 in 1920, whereas the number of male workers fell from 215,000 in 1918 to 124,000. In Petrograd, too, women dominated the labor force after 1918, especially in the age group fifteen to twenty-five.[46] During the Civil War, Moscow women continued to work in the same occupations they had held during the war and in 1917: textiles, clothing manufacture (especially army uniforms), and food and tobacco production.

Among men, skilled workers suffered the greatest numerical losses (although in percentages, their proportionate loss was less than among semiskilled or unskilled workers). It is this group that included the most committed of the revolutionary activists of 1917. Indeed, a different set of figures that permits comparison of 1920 and 1917 shows that the number of metalworkers, the quintessential urban proletarian activists, declined in Moscow by almost 40,000, or 66 percent: 25,000 of these left between 1917 and August 1918, a loss therefore only marginally represented in the comparison of 1918 and 1920.[47] By virtue of their scarce and flexible skills, these metalworkers were among the most employable men in Russia, and many of them traveled the countryside during these years, finding work at the big state munitions plants in centers such as Sormovo, Tula, and Izhevsk; here they received the same food ration as Red Army men and were closer to sources of food supply.[48]

Like Moscow's, Petrograd's losses included large numbers of skilled and valuable longtime workers. In fact, none left in such great numbers, both absolute and relative, as the skilled metalworkers, so that by October 1918, when the Red Army's need for armaments caused metal production to revive, metal union officials pleaded for a return of workers to the city:

> We still have raw materials, coal, and iron. We still have machines. We can and know how to work. But few of our metalworkers have stayed in Petrograd. Some died in the fight for freedom, others have gone to the front, still others have left the red capital during the evacuation, and still others have dispersed

all over the country in search of bread for themselves and their families. Many, after the closing of their factories, moved to other branches of industry, joined the militia, or engage now in petty trade.[49]

But despite the allegations of declassing, of workers returning to their native villages, statistical evidence suggests that the overwhelming majority of Moscow's skilled workers were lost to the Red Army itself. And the loss of such activists surely diminished the reserves of Bolshevik agitators and Bolshevik supporters. On the other hand, of more than 300,000 Muscovites mustered into the army,[50] not all were hereditary proletarian cadres—workers of the family types A, B, and C. Scattered evidence compiled from biographies and from figures on aid to army dependents suggests that many recruits came directly from tsarist army units on active or reserve status in Moscow, and from families of white-collar employees as well as of workers.[51] Recruits, however, were overwhelmingly young, unmarried, and childless; workers of this type had enthusiastically supported Soviet power in 1917, and their physical absence from the city would clearly affect the political climate.

Not all eligible workers joined the Red Army, however. Reports about the initial May 1918 mobilization suggest that from 15 to 25 percent of those called were too ill to report; others were rejected on initial examination, so it is likely that only half of those called up left the city. Many other workers also remained in Moscow in reserve units, working their jobs during the day and training evenings and on weekends.[52] Still others, especially skilled workers, received permanent assignments as army instructors in Moscow. A young printer who volunteered for duty in May 1920 was trained as an instructor and spent the remainder of the Civil War training reserve units of printers in his original Moscow neighborhood.[53] Finally, just as had happened in 1914 and 1915, skilled workers were deemed too valuable for production to be used as soldiers, and beginning in late 1918, they began to return to their original industrial occupations.[54]

It is important now to evaluate the nature of the change in the social composition of Moscow during the Civil War years, and especially to suggest something about the fate of the politically active urban workers who helped make the revolution in 1917. First of all, they did not rusticate themselves in large numbers. Those that returned to the countryside were those with the closest ties there—unskilled recent migrants, servants, and nonworking dependents. Second, although many of the urbanized workers served in the Red Army, many also remained in the city. Moscow experienced what a Soviet analysis of the 1918 census called a "middling-out" of the working class.[55] Many of the most politically committed workers left the work force for military service or for posts in the Soviet government. The least politically active workers (for example, the nonvoters in 1917) returned to their villages, leaving the middle strata, including women, in the labor force. But the skilled workers whose class consciousness and revolutionary zeal had helped win the October Revolution did not entirely disappear, and the women who remained were likely to be family members of these veterans of 1917.

Unquestionably, the population was older; the median age of Moscow residents rose by a year between 1917 and 1920, and other evidence confirms the commonsense assumption that the skilled workers who stayed in the city and continued to work were older family men. They were less likely to have been Bolshevik supporters than their younger brothers or sons. Eduard Dune's father, a skilled worker and a family man, sympathized with his son's determination to fight for Soviet power in October 1917, but he himself chose to stand aside. Thus it was the loss of young activists rather than of all skilled and class-conscious urban workers that caused the level of Bolshevik support to decline during the Civil War. Older workers had tended to support the Menshevik Party in 1917;[56] the Menshevik resurgence in 1918 was made possible in part by the Red Army's mobilization and removal from the urban political scene of the activist young workers. Such an analysis suggests that revolutionary consciousness may have been based as much on generational as on class distinctions, a fact that was not part of the Bolshevik canon of revolutionary theory.

The changed social composition of the Moscow work force can be summarized by returning to the five types of urban workers described above. Urban Type A workers had no place to go except the Red Army. Young men from this group may have disappeared during the Civil War; their parents and sisters remained. Type D workers, husbands and fathers alone in the city without families, were the first to leave in search of land even before the serious crises began. Many workers of Types B and C, whose attachment to the countryside depended upon the length of the family's stay in the city as well as the economic viability of their village property, may have chosen to stay in the city; young sons in these groups would also provide Red Army recruits. Finally, some young workers of Type E, the first-generation migrants, may have also chosen to stay on, especially those who had begun to take advantage of city life. A number of Red Army veterans came from this stratum, and some recalled having attended evening schools while in the city.[57] Workers of this type who were least assimilated would have returned home with the first wave of refugees in 1917, but social origin is an especially poor predictor of the outlook of such young unattached workers. Further research on the formation of the Soviet working class after 1921 would do well to observe the career paths of similar young workers who migrated from the countryside without the baggage of strong rural ties. It is likely that some of these Type E workers would interact with and be assimilated into the urban core of the working class that had remained in the city.

Deurbanization in Moscow: Cultural Changes

The prevailing analysis of the "declassed" proletariat in 1920–21 by Mensheviks and Bolsheviks was based on two assumptions: one was the physical disappearance of former proletarians and the other was the changing consciousness of the proletarians who remained. The demographic data for Moscow reveal that a sizeable core of veteran urban proletarians remained in the city; they did not all disappear. Lenin assumed that a worker who manufactured cigarette lighters in his darkened former factory was less class conscious than his neighbor who used his skills to manufacture machine guns or locomotive parts. And while one may argue with Lenin's rather narrow definition of consciousness, there is no question that the dislocations of the Civil War produced changing attitudes and caused workers to rearrange the priorities of their value systems. The question is, Were urban workers' values, their political consciousness, declassed or deurbanized? Did workers forget the class origins and class pride that had been so important in 1917? How did the dislocation of the Civil War alter the specific elements that had contributed to the prevailing political consciousness as of October 1917?

Urban workers were especially prone to participate in political activity because of four factors: the educational and cultural opportunities afforded as part of an urban upbringing; the awareness of class interests fostered by ideology, employment patterns, and the settlement of workers in specific neighborhoods; the ease of organization for workers whose education and skills gave them resources with which to act; and the fact that the cities themselves were centers of political life.

The Civil War exodus from Moscow affected some of these factors and not others. Education and culture continued, although at reduced levels. All children, regardless of social class, were given free noon meals, provided they attend city schools for an hour each day. The city could not afford to heat the school buildings, but the idea, explained Moscow Soviet chairman M. N. Pokrovskii, was to feed them and at the same time to teach the habit of attending school. The city's cultural life, especially its theaters, seemed to visitors more vibrant than ever before. The number of libraries in Moscow nearly tripled and in Petrograd doubled between 1917 and 1919; educational institutions, especially for workers, expanded at the same rate.[58] The theater, always one of the most popular Russian art forms, was especially lively. An American visitor in 1918 wrote, "In the days before the war, the cheaper seats at the Moscow Art Theatre and at the opera and ballet were fought for by long queues of students and workmen in blouse and belt. The only difference today, with the ascendency of the proletariat, is that the workman's greater comparative wealth has enabled him to move down into the parterre."[59] A year later, Arthur Ransome attended a performance of *Uncle Vanya* at the Art Theatre, and was "struck by the new smartness of the boy officers of the Red Army, of whom a fair number were present."[60] Factory theaters were also springing up, twenty of them by late 1920.[61]

Working-class neighborhoods continued to exist through the Civil War and became ever more autonomous units of public and daily life. Workers in these neighborhoods often became responsible for maintaining their factories, domestic safety, and housing: as landlords fled, more and more apartment buildings, for example, became "wild"—that is, were managed on an ad hoc basis by residents themselves.[62] Unemployment and even cooptation of workers into official Soviet positions would not necessarily have taken workers away from these neighborhoods, and thus their proletarian character was not likely to change despite the social changes going on in the city at large. There were substantial population shifts within the city, as workers resettled in formerly middle-class residential areas. On the other hand, because of the breakdown of local transport and the strong sense of neighborhood and district loyalty that appears again and again in workers' memoirs, it is unlikely that workers moved far from their original places of residence.

The neighborhood may well have replaced the factory as the focus of working-class identity during these years. And the consolidation of these neighborhoods may have been aided by a curious new phenomenon appearing in the statistical record: the absolute number of marriages began to climb in 1918, doubled in 1919, and remained at a high level well into the 1920s (see Table 3).[63]

A number of explanations were proposed and dismissed at the time by Soviet officials. First, only a small part of the increase represented marriages deferred from the war years; these had been "made up," based on prewar rates, by mid-1919. More influential was the award of cloth and later cash to wedding couples, and some marriages may have been fictitious, made to qualify women for the special Red Army ration.[64] But even when these nuptial incentives were repealed in mid-1920, the rate remained high.[65] It is more pertinent that early in 1918, civil marriage replaced church ceremonies; one might guess that urban workers most likely preferred to marry outside the church and that such urban couples accounted for much of the marital increase.[66] A British Labour Party delegate to Russia was told (probably by Inessa Armand) in 1920 that such people before the revolution preferred to live together without benefit of clergy rather than submit to the institution of the church; now, "as a rule, they prefer to be legally married."[67] Urbanized workers rather than peasants more strongly preferred a secular culture; the rise in the civil marriage rate was thus surely

TABLE 3

Marriages and Marriage Rates in Moscow from 1912 to 1923

Year	Marriages	Marriages per 10,000 Population
1912	9,564	58
1913	10,093	60
1914	9,679	55
1915	7,478	41
1916	7,623	39
1917	9,918	54
1918	12,650	75
1919	24,693	174
1920	21,363	191
1921	19,863	169
1922	21,072	153
1923	25,342	156

Source: *Statisticheskii ezhegodnik goroda Moskvy i moskovskoi gubernii*, vyp. 2 (Moscow, 1927), p. 88.

facilitated by the fact that the women remaining in the city were relatively more urban than peasant, as were the men. They were the children of Type A and B families, and in marrying they were not only expressing hope in the future, but helping perpetuate the elements of urban culture that had been evolving since well before the revolution. The families they would produce (slowly, because the number of births continued to fall during these years) would be purely urban, too. Consequently, this surge of marriages (equaled elsewhere in Russia only in Petrograd) represented a consolidation of urban working-class society in the midst of what otherwise has been portrayed as urban collapse. One might also expect that the frequency of marriages added a new element of kinship ties to reinforce or to rival the existing bonds of class and neighborhood.

The advantage of urbanism most negatively affected by the crisis of 1917–20 was the urbanized worker's special reservoir of resources and organizational facility. Economically, the period was a nightmare. Real wages plummeted, and nominal wages became meaningless as more and more compensation came in the form of uniform food rations. On the other hand, Moscow workers all had a great deal of time off work, which they might have used for culture, political activity, and organization. In 1919, the darkest year of the Civil War, the average worker spent 18 days a month at work and 12 days off. Of those 12, 6 were missed for personal reasons; the figure was even higher (9.5 days) for the stalwart metalworkers: for every 2 days on the job, they took 1 off.[68] Most of these days were not spent in political activity, however, or in idle carousing, but in the search for food, on personal trips to forage in the country-side. Thus the city's advantage as a cultural center was offset in this period by the total absorption of its residents in the struggle for daily existence.

Still the workers who remained in the city were among the most urbanized elements, and although the urban propensity toward working-class activism may have been slowed, it was not reversed. But activism, even working-class activism, was not necessarily identical to Bolshevism, and other short-term changes occurred during the Civil War years that may have helped alter the class consciousness and Bolshevik support of 1917. They were probably not the changes blamed by Lenin for the deterioration of workers' consciousness, such as trading homemade cigarette lighters on the Moscow black market.

What then were these changes? First of all, Bolshevik consciousness in 1917 had been reinforced by a sense of class separateness and class identity. Separate neighborhoods remained after 1917, but there was a tendency toward more interclass mingling, not less. For example, British labor delegates visited a nine-room apartment occupied in 1920 by its former sole resident, a rich widow, as well as a factory worker, a tram conductor, a military student from rural Smolensk, and a former lawyer now employed in a Soviet bureau, all with wives and children.[69] Moreover, once the government had chased out its class enemies, the need for a class-pure government might not remain as essential as it had in 1917. With the departure of so many manufacturers, bankers, and traders, maybe the Bolsheviks' extremist vision of class struggle no longer seemed so important. This may be why party membership dropped in 1918.[70]

On the other hand, William Chase argues with some evidence that the place of the big bourgeoisie was taken by petty traders selling foodstuffs and manufactured goods on the Sukharev market.[71] Moreover, the class enemy was alive and well and fighting in the White Armies, as newspapers stressed throughout the period, although, despite the appeals for Sunday work to produce more arms and all-out drives such as "Front Week," this confrontation was removed from the direct daily experience of most workers.

A second short-term factor in the Bolsheviks' success in 1917 had been their identification as a peace party. Once Russia had withdrawn from the international war, this appeal must have been diminished, too. Careful research in the varied periodical press of the period may help determine how the populace felt about the civil war that their boys were mobilized to fight, but memoir sources give the strong impression that the Civil War was perceived as a just and necessary conflict: Mensheviks, Bolsheviks, and nonparty citizens all volunteered to defend the social revolution.

The economic situation had unquestionably been a major, critical factor in the formation of the particular class consciousness of 1917. Factories closed, workers were laid off, and the devastating supply crisis haunted the cities throughout 1917. If the economic crisis owed to sabotage, as workers believed, then the socialists in the Provisional Government had been powerless to stop it. The Bolsheviks received a great deal of support precisely because they had not been implicated in the economic debacle of 1917.

But the economy continued to collapse in 1918, 1919, and 1920. Did the urban cadres of 1917 face the continuing crisis with the same sense of class consciousness that they had shared in October? Ralf Dahrendorf has argued that under varying conditions, class identity can lose its power as a focus of unity, and that other factors—workplace, neighborhood, skill, kin—may become more important.[72] The struggle for existence that workers in 1917 tried to solve as a class, through the soviets, was not solved, and to survive, workers turned to other sources: individual trading and foraging for food, local institutions, workplace control. The result was that the Bolshevik Party had to scramble politically to keep the backing of its former supporters. That no other organization arose to challenge them successfully may be ascribed in some measure to the utter lack of resources that workers had for any new mobilization of their energy and support, but also to Bolshevik control of the means of repression, including control over food distribution, housing, and, of course, the Cheka—the new government's secret police.

Concluding Remarks

This examination of the Civil War years, particularly in Moscow, suggests that the deurbanization of those years represented a change in quantity but not entirely in quality in the cities. The proletariat declined in the city, but it did not wither away. Thus its basic urban character remained, reinforced in marriage and in the location if not the quality of its experience. Despite substantial turnover and the presumed influx of new generations of nonurbanized peasants after 1921, a core of the city's working class remained to impart its own brand of urban culture.

If the relationship between the urban working class and its representative Bolshevik Party changed during these years, it changed not entirely because the cadres of 1917 left the factories for the front, the villages, the black market, or the commissariats. Rather, it changed because the political and economic conjuncture of these years called for different responses and fostered a different set of priorities from those of the preceding revolutionary years. If Lenin's perceptions of the situation were at all representative, it appears that the Bolshevik Party made deurbanization and declassing the scapegoats for its political difficulties when the party's own policies and its unwillingness to accept changing proletarian attitudes were also to blame.

A number of writers have suggested that the Civil War years be viewed as a generational experience, in Karl Mannheim's sense, during which new values are acquired that are retained by members of a generation throughout their active lives.[73] What characteristics were acquired during these years that might have become part of a new Russian urban culture? One must look to the many negative elements of the period: the atmosphere of political emergency and terror against opposition; the prevalence of crime and utter lawlessness in working-class districts; the collapse of any semblance of a market economy; the erosion of industrial discipline and of productivity; the decline of the workplace as the center of one's life; the experience of unemployment, of living on the dole, and, later in the period, of labor mobilization; and the wholesale militarization of society. But we should not ignore, in assessing the formative elements of the period, the continuing positive aspects of urban life: theater, libraries, schools, recreation, family formation, associations, newspapers, political participation, and the sense that a new society was being created even in these dark years.

The demographic and social evidence presented here thus modifies the hypothesis that Russia "deurbanized," that its workers were "declassed" during the years from 1917 to 1921. Just as urban growth and urbanization are not synonymous, so too we should distinguish between the numerical decline of the urban population, or "urban contraction," and "deurbanization," which suggests a reversal of all of the elements of the urbanization process. Despite the years of hunger, cold, and disease in the cities, despite the antiurban utopian dreams that these years encouraged,[74] urban life and urban culture were not extinguished during the Russian Civil War, only transformed. The full nature of this transformation remains to be explored.

NOTES

1. This essay originally appeared in the *Journal of Modern History*, September 1985, vol. 57, pp. 424–50.

2. *Statisticheskii ezhegodnik goroda Moskvy i Moskovskoi gubernii* (hereafter *Stat. ezhegodnik g. Moskvy*), vyp. 2 (Moscow, 1927), p. 15; Tsentral'noe statisticheskoe upravlenie (TsSU), *Trudy*, vol. 8, vyp. 1, part 32, p. 342.

3. For 1910 population, B. R. Mitchell, *European Historical Statistics, 1750–1970*, abridged ed. (New York, 1975), pp. 12–15; Baedeker, *Russia*, facsimile of the 1914 ed. (New York, 1970), passim. For 1920, TsSU, *Trudy*, vol. 8, vyp. 1, part 1, table 3.

4. See E. H. Carr, *The Bolshevik Revolution* (Harmondsworth, Eng., 1966), 2:196; Leopold H. Haimson, ed., *The Mensheviks: From the October Revolution to World War II* (Chicago, 1974), pt. 2.

5. Quoted in Carr, 2:196.

6. Lenin, *Polnoe sobranie sochinenii*, 5th ed. (Moscow, 1963), 43:42 (my translation).

7. John L. H. Keep, *The Russian Revolution: A Study in Mass Mobilization* (New York, 1976), pp. 261–62. See also Sheila Fitzpatrick, *The Russian Revolution* (Oxford, 1982), pp. 85–86.

8. S. A. Smith, *Red Petrogad* (Cambridge, 1983); David Mandel, *The Petrograd Workers and the Fall of the Old Regime* (London, 1983) and *The Petrograd Workers and the Soviet Seizure of Power* (London, 1984); Diane Koenker, *Moscow Workers and the 1917 Revolution* (Princeton, 1981); Israel Getzler, *Kronstadt, 1917–1921* (Cambridge, 1983); Rex A. Wade, *Red Guards and Workers' Militias in the Russian Revolution* (Stanford, 1984); Ronald G. Suny, *The Baku Commune* (Princeton, 1972); William G. Rosenberg, "The Democratization of Russia's Railroads in 1917," *American Historical Review*, December 1981, 88, no. 5, pp. 983–1008.

9. Mandel, *Petrograd Workers and Soviet Seizure*, pp. 390–413; see Vladimir Brovkin, "The Mensheviks' Political Comeback: The Elections to the Provincial City Soviets in Spring 1918," *Russian Review*, 1983, 42, pp. 1–50.

10. *Istoriia rabochikh Moskvy 1917–1945 gg.* (Moscow, 1983), p. 93.

11. Lenin, 43:42.

12. Mitchell, pp. 12–15.

13. Gaston Rimlinger, "The Expansion of the Labor Market in Capitalist Russia, 1861–1917," *Journal of Economic History*, 1961, 21, pp. 208–15, esp. 211; E. G. Gimpel'son, *Sovetskii rabochii klass, 1918–1920* (Moscow, 1974), p. 51.

14. (There will be occasion to refer to Riazan again later in this essay.) *Statisticheskii ezhegodnik Rossii* (Petrograd, 1915). The 1915 definition of "urban" is not clear. One study of Russian urbanization restricts the term to settlements of at least 15,000 people, or 20,000 in some cases (Robert A. Lewis and Richard H. Rowland, "Urbanization in Russia and the USSR, 1897–1970," in Michael Hamm, ed., *The City in Russian History* [Lexington, Ky., 1976], p. 206). Using these criteria, Lewis and Rowland claim that 9.4 percent of the population was urban in 1897, a figure that is considerably lower than those used here. Therefore, the definition of "urban" used by Russian census officials must include cities smaller than 15,000. See also Chauncey D. Harris, *Cities of the Soviet Union* (Washington, D.C., 1972), chap. 7.

15. R. E. Johnson, *Peasant and Proletarian* (New Brunswick, N.J., 1978); *Pervaia vseobshchaia perepis' naseleniia 1897 goda* (St. Petersburg, 1903).

16. A classic memoir of the genre is S. I. Kanatchikov, *Iz istorii moego bytiia* (Moscow, 1929); see an abridged translation of this and other memoirs in Victoria E. Bonnell, ed., *The Russian Worker* (Berkeley, 1983). See also Reginald E. Zelnik, "Russian Bebels: An Introduction to the Memoirs of Semen Kanatchikov and Matvei Fisher," *Russian Review*, 1976, 35, pp. 249–89, 417–47; and L. M. Ivanov, "Preemstvennost' fabrichno-zavodskogo truda i formirovanie proletariata v Rossii," in Ivanov, ed., *Rabochii klass i rabochee dvizhenie v Rossii* (Moscow, 1966), p. 105.

17. I. M. Koz'minykh-Lanin, *Ukhod na polevye raboty fabrichno-zavodskikh rabochikh Moskovskoi gubernii* (Moscow, 1912).

18. *Istoriia Leningradskogo soiuza rabochikh poligraficheskogo proizvodstva*, vol.

1 (Leningrad, 1925); V. V. Sher, *Istoriia professional'nogo dvizheniia rabochikh pechatnogo dela v Moskve* (Moscow, 1911); Koenker, *Moscow Workers*, chap. 2; Mandel, *Petrogad Workers and the Fall*, chap. 2.

19. Koenker, *Moscow Workers*, pp. 45–46.

20. Diane Koenker, "Urban Families, Working-Class Youth Groups, and the 1917 Revolution in Moscow," in David L. Ransel, ed., *The Family in Imperial Russia* (Urbana, Ill., 1978), pp. 280–304.

21. V. Iu. Krupianskaia, "Evoliutsiia semeino-bytovogo uklada rabochikh," in L. M. Ivanov, ed., *Rossiiskii proletariat: oblik, bor'ba, gegemoniia* (Moscow, 1970), p. 283; Anna Litveiko, "V semnadtsatom," *Iunost'*, 1957, no. 3, pp. 3–18; I. V. Babushkin, *Vospominaniia, 1893–1900* (Moscow, 1951), p. 39. On the role of theater, see Gary Thurston, "The Impact of Russian Popular Theatre, 1886–1915," *Journal of Modern History*, 1983, 55, pp. 237–67.

22. See the memoir by Eduard Dune, "Zapiski krasnogvardeitsa," MSS in the Nicolaevsky archive, Hoover Institution, Stanford, California.

23. On neighborhoods, see Laura Engelstein, *Moscow, 1905* (Stanford, 1982); and Mandel, *Petrograd Workers and the Fall of the Old Regime*.

24. Reading habits before and after the 1917 revolution were surveyed by E. O. Kabo in 1923 and reported in *Ocherki rabochego byta* (Moscow, 1928).

25. Heather J. Hogan, "Labor and Management in Conflict: The St. Petersburg Metal-Working Industry, 1900–1914," Ph.D. dissertation, University of Michigan, 1981; Victoria E. Bonnell, *Roots of Rebellion: Workers' Politics and Organizations in St. Petersburg and Moscow, 1900–1914* (Berkeley, 1983); Smith, *Red Petrograd*.

26. Bonnell, *Roots of Rebellion*, p. 263; Koenker, *Moscow Workers*, chap. 2.

27. In 1912, 11 percent of women in factories and 23 percent in nonfactory manufacturing were urban born, compared to figures of 9 percent and 7 percent for urban-born men. Since many replacements for drafted workers after 1914 were wives of factory workers, the percentage of urban-born women in the work force was probably even higher in 1917.

28. Litveiko; *Krasnaia Presnia 1905–1917 gg.* (Moscow, 1930), pp. 455–57; *Prechistenskie rabochie kursy* (Moscow, 1948).

29. Koenker, "Urban Families," p. 301.

30. *Moskovskie bol'sheviki v ogne revoliutsionnykh boev* (Moscow, 1976), pp. 275–76 (my translation).

31. Wade, *Red Guards*; V. I. Startsev, *Ocherki po istorii Petrogradskoi krasnoi gvardii i rabochei militsii* (Moscow-Leningrad, 1965).

32. *The Bolsheviks Come to Power* (New York, 1976).

33. L. M. Spirin, *Klassy i partii v grazhdanskoi voine v Rossii* (Moscow, 1968), pp. 59–60.

34. Lenin, 43:311.

35. *Stat. ezhegodnik g. Moskvy*, pp. 15, 88.

36. William Chase, "Moscow and Its Working Class, 1918–1928: A Social Analysis," Ph.D. dissertation, Boston University, 1979, p. 89. See also the discussion in his *Workers, Society, and the Soviet State: Labor and Life in Moscow 1918–1929* (Urbana, Ill., 1987), chap. 2.

37. The published February census groups fifteen to fifty-nine-year-olds, without further division.

38. G. S. Ignat'ev, *Moskva v pervyi god proletarskoi diktatury* (Moscow, 1975), p. 281.

39. The census by geographic districts—precincts and later commissariats—was reported in *Biulleten' Tsentral'nogo statisticheskogo upravleniia*, 1920, no. 33.

40. *Professional'nyi vestnik*, April 20, 1918, p. 18.

41. TsSU, *Trudy*, vol. 6, a study of the economic stratification of the peasantry in 1917 and 1919.

42. *Ekonomicheskaia zhizn'*, December 1, 1920, p. 3.

43. The natural decrease in this period was 56,000, but since mortality statistics were not provided by sex, net out-migration must be calculated without regard to sex. In order to preserve the value of sex-ratio information, it is preferable here to refer to net loss of population rather than net out-migration.

44. See the worker families reported on in Kabo.

45. *Stat. ezhegodnik g. Moskvy*, p. 73. In 1912, 4 percent of domestic servants were urban born (the city average was 29 percent). For servants, there were sixteen self-supporting individuals for every one dependent, while the overall ratio was about two dependents to one independent (ibid., p. 74).

46. TsSU, *Trudy*, vol. 26, vyp. 2, tables 3 and 4.

47. *Fabrichno-zavodskaia promyshlennost' g. Moskvy i moskovskoi gubernii 1917–1927 gg.* (Moscow, 1928), p. 1. These industrial figures presumably derive from the August 1918 industrial census, taken four months after the urban population count that provides most of the occupational information used here.

48. D. A. Baevskii, *Rabochii klass v pervye gody sovetskoi vlasti (1917–1921 gg.)* (Moscow, 1974), p. 250.

49. V. Z. Drobizhev, A. K. Sokolov, and V. A. Ustinov, *Rabochii klass sovetskoi Rossii v pervyi god proletarskoi diktatury* (Moscow, 1975), p. 91 (my translation).

50. *Krasnaia Moskva 1917–1920 gg.* (Moscow, 1920), p. 618.

51. *Krasnaia Moskva*, pp. 435–38.

52. *Uprochenie sovetskoi vlasti v Moskve i moskovskoi gubernii* (Moscow, 1958), pp. 443–52.

53. *Leninskii zakaz: sto let tipografii 'Krasnyi proletarii'* (Moscow, 1969), p. 97.

54. Baevskii, pp. 246–48.

55. Drobizhev, et. al., p. 151.

56. Koenker, *Moscow Workers,* chap. 5.

57. *Geroi grazhdanskoi voiny* (Moscow, 1974).

58. Arthur Ransome, *Russia in 1919* (New York, 1919), pp. 183–84, 187–88.

59. Oliver M. Sayler, *Russia, White or Red* (Boston, 1919), p. 87.

60. Ransome, p. 139.

61. *Rabochii klass sovetskoi Rossii v pervyi god diktatury proletariata. Sbornik dokumentov i materialov*, ed. D. A. Chugaev (Moscow, 1964), p. 322. Indeed, the broad popularity of drama among the Russian working populace raises the heretical notion of the revolution as theater. Angelica Balabanoff suggests as much in her recollections of 1919, although she did not seem to appreciate the importance of drama in Russian popular culture: "I had already been shocked by the display and theatricality of public life in revolutionary Russia (the Bolsheviks seemed to be masters of stage direction), which seemed to me unsuited to the Revolution's proletarian character." (Angelica Balabanoff, *My Life as a Rebel* [Bloomington, Ind., 1973], p. 219.)

62. Kabo, p. 78.

63. *Stat. ezhegodnik g. Moskvy*, p. 88.

64. *Krasnaia Moskva*, p. 65.

65. Nor were easy divorces a significant factor, since the divorce rate was low during this period (*Otchet Moskovskogo gubernskogo ekonomicheskogo soveshchaniia na 1-e oktiabria 1921 g.* [Moscow, 1921], p. 8).

66. G. V. Zhirnova, "Russkii gorodskoi svadebnyi obriad kontsa XIX-nachala XX vekakh," *Sovetskaia etnografiia*, 1969, no. 1.

67. *Report of the British Labour Delegation to Russia* (London, 1920), p. 21.

68. *Krasnaia Moskva*, p. 65.

69. *Report of the British Labour Delegation*, p. 138.

70. Ignat'ev, *Moskva v pervyi god*, p. 91.

71. William Chase, "Moscow and Its Working Class, 1918–1928: A Social

Analysis," Ph.D. dissertation, Boston College, 1979, pp. 36–39; Marguerite Harrison, *Marooned in Moscow* (New York, 1921), pp. 151–57.

72. Ralf Dahrendorf, *Class and Class Consciousness in Industrial Society* (Stanford, 1959), and *Conflict after Class* (London, 1967).

73. Fitzpatrick, *Russian Revolution,* pp. 64–65; Robert C. Tucker, "Stalinism as Revolution from Above," in Robert C. Tucker, ed., *Stalinism* (New York, 1977), pp. 91–92; Stephen F. Cohen, "Bolshevism and Stalinism," ibid., pp. 3–29; see also Alan B. Spitzer, "The Historical Problem of Generations," *American Historical Review,* December 1973, 78, no. 5, pp. 1353–85.

74. See, for example, the pseudonymous work of the agricultural economist A. V. Chaianov: Ivan Kremnev, "The Journey of My Brother Alexei to the Land of Peasant Utopia" (Moscow, 1920), reprinted in the *Journal of Peasant Studies* October 1976, 4, no. 1, pp. 63–117.

THE EFFECTS OF THE CIVIL WAR ON WOMEN AND FAMILY RELATIONS

Barbara Evans Clements

People caught up in great revolutions often feel that the massive social turmoil is changing everything. So it was during Russia's Civil War. By 1918, the pillars of tsarist society—the monarchy, the nobility, the church—had been brought down, and even the patriarchal family was being shaken by the chaos of the times. Speakers from the new revolutionary government declared their intention to abolish the "bourgeois" family and replace it with a new Soviet family based on romantic love between the spouses and on the full equality of women within marriage and in the larger society.

It seemed possible during the Civil War that the Bolsheviks actually could undertake so enormous a task as rebuilding the family. Millions of marriages had been shattered, millions of children were homeless wanderers, and, in the midst of all this destruction, there were signs that the liberation prophesied by the Marxist fathers was beginning spontaneously. Women joined the Red Army and rode into battle in men's overcoats. Young people embraced the Marxist doctrines of sexual liberation with delight, not only in the capital cities where they could hear Bolshevik feminists such as Inessa Armand or Aleksandra Kollontai, but in the hinterland as well. In Vladimir in 1918 some of these enthusiasts established a "Bureau of Free Love" within the Commissariat of Welfare and issued a proclamation requiring all the unmarried women in the city between the ages of 18 and 50 to register with the Bureau. "Registration in the Bureau of Free Love," the proclamation declared, "grants [young women] the right to choose for themselves men 19 to 50 years old for cohabiter-spouses [sozhiteli-suprugi]." The anonymous authors of this decree do not seem to have fully grasped party principles on women's emancipation, for they also declared all "girls" (devitsy) over 18 to be "state property" and gave men "the right to choose a girl registered in the Bureau [to marry] even without the consent of the latter, in the interests of the state."[1] That such manifestoes, however muddled their thinking, could come from a provincial city testified to how quickly traditional values were being overthrown, or at least so it seemed to Bolsheviks and non-Bolsheviks alike.

Fifteen years later, the Soviet government had denounced the "free-love" visions of its utopian members and was endorsing a family form for the USSR that bore all the characteristics of the nuclear family that had already developed in Western Europe and had begun developing in Russia before the revolution. This family consists of couples living together with their minor children and supporting themselves by working for wages. The values of the nuclear family are based on doctrines of individualism that condemn parental control over adult children. Instead the appropriate sources of family solidarity are seen to be the love between husbands and wives and parents and dependent children. Women are charged with being the chief nurturers of these comforting emotions. They are also expected to do most of the housekeeping. Despite an ideology that had once condemned such values as bourgeois, despite the war that had wrenched millions of families apart, by 1935 the Soviet people had arrived at the point in family evolution toward which they were already moving under the tsar.[2]

What was the impact of the Bolsheviks on this evolution? Did the Civil War affect it, and if so, how? Is this change from extended to nuclear family so inexorable a process, so direct a consequence of the modernizing values now universally associated with urbanization that short-term upheavals such as revolutions and radical regimes such as that of the early Bolshevik can do little either to stop it or to mold it to more nearly conform to their ideological preferences?

I cannot hope to answer such large questions in a short essay. But I can advance an interpretation of the impact of the Civil War on the family, of the Russians' perception of that impact, and of the consequences of both war and perceptions for policymaking in the 1920s. I shall look too at the effects of the war years on women, concentrating on them rather than on men or children because women were so often seen as the key to change in the family. Women's liberation in its entirety is not our subject here, however, and therefore changes in their participation in the public arena—civic and legal equality and educational and employment opportunities—will be examined primarily for their impact on women's relationship to the family.

Several additional distinctions must be made at the outset. First, it is important to distinguish between short-term and long-term effects of the Civil War. Second, one must of course differentiate between the peasantry and the proletariat. And, third, I am leaving the non-European nationalities out of consideration altogether and concentrating primarily on the Great Russians. This essay will contend that the short-term effects of the Civil War on women and families was devastating, so devastating that they seemed to contemporaries to produce far more change in the situation of women and in the institution of the family than had in fact occurred. Actually, the Civil War only accelerated changes already underway. But because it seemed to have shaken the very foundations of Russian society, the war produced a reaction that played a part in conserving, perhaps even strengthening, altered but still pow‿ ful institutions of marriage and family.

First we must consider the short-term effects of the Civil War on the peasantry. There the immediate effects were disastrous. Millions of families had already lost sons to World War I; millions of women were farming their allotments alone or with the aid of their children. The Civil War took more men away, destroyed farmland, separated families, and left in its wake drought, famine, and disease. "We are dying off," crooned women begging in the streets of Ivanovo-Voznesensk in 1921. "The people are dying off."[3]

Amidst all the misery the patterns of village life were changing. World War I had drawn millions of young men away, leaving some wives to farm their allotments alone or with the aid only of children. There are no precise statistics on the numbers of such women during the Civil War, but we do have figures from the 1920s. As late as 1929, 3 million peasant households (15 percent of the total) were still headed by women.[4] Their lot was a difficult one, not only because of the grueling nature of their work, but also because they had to contend with pressure from the village. Women farming alone had not fared well since emancipation; the peasants did not believe that single women could use the land as productively as men and therefore pushed them to give up their shares for redistribution by harassing them and refusing them much-needed help. Male peasants continued to do this throughout the Civil War period. Those single women who were determined to hold out fought back by complaining loudly at commune meetings, by threatening vengeance when their husbands returned, and by going to the Bolsheviks for help. But of course this last tactic laid them open to charges of disloyalty to the village, and, given the paucity of Bolshevik personnel and funds available, as well as the weakness of the party politically among the peasants, the appeals probably did the women little good.[5]

Ironically, the lot of women left without men was made more difficult by the men who returned. Most of the soldiers came home, at least temporarily, in waves that began to sweep through the countryside in 1917 and continued into the twenties with the demobilization of the Red Army. There is evidence that these men, often bearing with them the new notions of liberty that they had heard on city streetcorners, were unwilling to sink peacefully into the established routines of country life. Rather, they were eager to claim a portion of village land, newly enlarged by the confiscation of the landlords' property. In the repartitions that resulted, widows and women whose husbands had not yet come home often found their holdings reduced or exchanged for inferior plots.

It is also here, in the calls of young men for land, that perhaps the most significant change in family life of the Civil War years began. Again we are dealing with fragmentary evidence, but there is some indication that the young were seeking allotments independent of their parents, that is, that they were calling for a breakup of the extended family so that they could set up their own households. This development had begun before the revolution, in the

entury.[6] During the Civil War the push of sons for separate
...w more widespread and met with greater success than previ-
...Shanin has found testimony that the wives of these young men,
...ut from under the control of their mothers-in-law, cheered their
...i. Some anecdotes even credit wives with pushing their reluctant
...confrontation with parents.[7] Thus, at the same time that the war
was ...ng enormous deprivation, it was also heightening conflict within the
village by pitting single women against the group, sons against fathers, and
perhaps even younger against older women.

Although peasant women were willing to rebel against their in-laws, they
do not seem to have possessed an equally strong desire to alter their relationships with their husbands, that is, to rebel against the patriarchal power of
the husband as well as the father. Again, as yet little is known about this
subject, but such evidence as we do have about the attitudes of women toward
marriage during the Civil War indicates that they were defending it from
change. Most women were probably frightened by the war and by the unrest
all around them. Social upheaval, especially if it destroys families, imperils the
weak in a society, and women had always been far weaker than men in Russia.
If a woman lost her husband she might be cast adrift, usually with children,
into a war-torn world that no longer offered even the uncertain refuge of
employment in the city. Far from weakening the loyalty of the great majority
of peasant women to a traditional marriage, which granted the husband great
power over the wife, the Civil War may even have strengthened their beliefs
by demonstrating forcefully how crucial marriage was to their survival. It was
a family in transition to which they clung, but they defended it as unchanged
and unchanging.

The best evidence we have of these attitudes is the reaction of peasant women
to the occasional itinerant Bolshevik organizer who came among them preaching women's liberation. The women's responses ranged from avoidance to
sullen silence to outright attacks. Workers for the Women's Department (the
Zhenotdel) were waylaid on the road and beaten, meetings were broken up
by cursing men, groups of older women set on younger ones accused of having
attended Bolshevik-sponsored gatherings, women who criticized the commune
were ostracized by other women—all in a defensive reaction against not just
the few Bolsheviks who penetrated the countryside, but also against the chaos
out of which they came, chaos that seemed to be endangering custom and the
village.[8]

Of course the women were not acting alone. Peasant men enforced con-
formity too, using all the time-honored, often violent means at their disposal.
Yet women were motivated not just by fear of their men but by the deep and
genuine loyalty they felt for traditional institutions. The Russian peasant family
was deeply rooted in the lives of women as well as men, as family structures
always are. All the sanctions of a traditional society legitimated it: it was
ordained by God, it was the way things had always been, it was an organic

part of the world of the village. The traditionalism of most peasant women was neither fully rational and calculating, as much of the foregoing argument may seem to imply, nor fully irrational and unconscious, as the Bolsheviks often charged. Rather, it was both. Peasant women saw in the Civil War compelling reasons to preserve family mores, mores they had been taught to accept unquestioningly as part of the natural order.[9]

To sum up, available evidence supports the generalization that peasant women as well as men wanted to change the traditional extended family by weakening the power of the patriarchs and that younger women were willing also to weaken the matriarchs. Civil war conditions permitted, perhaps even encouraged them to do so. This in itself was probably immensely unsettling. Most female and male peasants did not want to go beyond challenging their parents. Women in particular weathered the desperate privations of the times by clinging to the village and to marriage and defending both against outsiders.

In the cities the extended family was already giving way to a more nuclear household before World War I. The pattern was much like that in Western Europe in the early nineteenth century—a pattern created by large numbers of single men and women who had left families behind in the country, often with the intention of later returning to them, joining a growing proletariat that had settled permanently in the city. Those members of the urban working class who did not move back to the country married later than the peasants, had fewer children, and tended to live together without parents or collateral relatives sharing their quarters. One recent Soviet demographic study estimates that the urban family consisted on average of 4.4 people as early as 1897.[10] For these people the patriarchal ways of the rural *dvor* had been sinking rapidly into the past even before war and revolution swept over them.

City dwellers did share with the peasants the experience of having men drawn off to war, leaving women alone to support themselves and their children. Initially this task was made somewhat easier by the opening up to women of better paying jobs in industry; the female percentage of the total industrial labor force grew from 25 percent in 1913 to 40 percent in 1917. This process continued during the Civil War; by 1920 women made up 46 percent of the workers in heavy manufacturing. In Petrograd, where so many men were drafted into political or military work, women held 65 percent of all civilian jobs by 1920.[11]

But the collapse of the economy after 1917 meant that surviving in the city became a struggle for all women, the employed as well as the unemployed, the married as well as the single. Urban conditions were even more desperate than those in the countryside, and millions of people eventually fled the crumbling cities for their native villages where food could still be found. One set of figures speaks eloquently of this exodus: the aforementioned 40 percent of the industrial labor force in 1917 consisted of 881,000 women. By 1920, women had come to compose 46 percent of the labor force, but this percentage represents only 434,000 women.[12] In other words, half of the women employed in the cities in 1917 had left their jobs by 1920; some doubtless went to work for the Bolsheviks elsewhere, but the vast majority streamed back to the countryside.

Those who stayed in the cities adopted various strategies for getting themselves through the calamity. The wives of soldiers and some female factory workers began to organize women's unions in 1917. The *soldatki* unions bargained with the government for increased allotments and shared clothing, food, medical knowledge, and consolation. The women workers' unions lobbied with male-dominated unions for improved wages and working conditions and also set up co-ops, as well as day care for children. Both types of women's unions seem to have been widespread; there is evidence of their existence in Petrograd, Ivanovo-Voznesensk, Kiev, Kazan, Kharkov, and Kaluga. How long the unions lasted is unclear, but some seem to have endured, although weakened by falling membership and government pressure, into the early twenties.[13]

Organizing, however, was not the most common way working-class women chose to deal with the Civil War crisis. Most women resorted to more traditional defenses. As we have already seen, many left the cities. Many others married. In 1915 the marriage rate in Petrograd was 5 marriages per 1,000 people. In 1919 it ballooned to 23 per 1,000. In Moscow too the marriage rate soared to the highest recorded in Europe that year.[14] A student of Soviet marriage, Wesley Fisher, has documented a long-term trend in Russian history for couples to postpone marriage during emergencies such as wars, thus building up a backlog of demand that results in high marriage rates after the crisis is over.[15] The crisis was not over in 1919, but, at least in Moscow and Petrograd, men on their way from one conflict to the next and the women left on their own in the meantime seem to have decided to regularize their relationships. Far from letting loose an orgy of free love, the revolution was ushering in a period of marriages in unprecedented numbers.

The reasons for the astonishing rise in the marriage rate deserve further study. Doubtless there were several fairly ephemeral causes, such as the possibility that one could obtain benefits (a soldier's allotment, a worker's ration card, or a residency permit) more easily if one were legally married. Perhaps the new Soviet civil marriage procedures were just becoming widely enough known by 1919 for large numbers of people to take advantage of them. The legalization of divorce in 1918 may also have boosted the marriage rate by permitting remarriage. And finally, it may be that by 1919 the government apparatus charged with registering marriages (ZAGS) was able for the first time to process substantial numbers of applications, so that some of the increase recorded resulted simply from clearing an administrative logjam.

The marriage rate may also indicate that women and men were responding to the Civil War by seeking the security of a legally binding tie, that marriage was seen as a pooling of resources in a time of fear, anxiety, and deprivation. Analyzing motives for marriage is difficult, never more so than in a period such as the Civil War, about which information is so scattered and impressionistic. Evidence about the attitudes of women is presently available, however, that will support, albeit somewhat indirectly, the proposition that the soaring marriage rate of 1919 resulted from more than just efforts to manipulate the rationing system.

I shall deal first with working-class women, about whom we know rather a lot, then briefly mention middle-class and aristocratic women, about whom we know practically nothing. The issue of whether women sought refuge in marriage is part of a larger question: do crises such as wars and revolutions loosen the hold of traditional institutions on women, thereby enabling them to move more freely through society? For the great majority of Russian women, the answer seems to be no. Undeniably, the war left many women fending for themselves. Some chose to do so in new ways, by organizing unions, for example. A few, whom we shall study in more detail later, joined the Communist Party and embraced its vision of emancipated womanhood. But most simply endured, struggling along with their jobs in the cities, scrounging for food and fuel and clothing. They did not view the Civil War as an emancipating experience, judging by what they told the Bolsheviks who came to preach to them. Working-class women seem to have shared their men's joy in the destruction of the ruling class, but they did not like the hardship that followed, often blamed the Bolsheviks for it, and were openly skeptical of, if not downright hostile to, party proposals for marriage reform, day care, and communal living. They also did not like what they had heard about the party's attitude toward religion.[16]

Living amidst the liberalizing influences of the city, working-class women were more cosmopolitan than the peasants: they experimented with city-bought clothes, allowed their daughters some courting with young men, and even read newspapers, magazines, and the Russian equivalent of dime novels.[17] During the mass protests against the tsarist government in 1905 and again in 1917 women took part in demonstrations and attended meetings, although they remained more reluctant than men to become politically active. Not only were they tied down by their domestic responsibilities, but they also shared with their men a belief that politics was a male domain. Like the peasants, to whom they were so closely linked by kinship and experience, most working-class women remained loyal to a traditional division of labor and spheres between women and men, and to a traditional division of power within marriage.

The hostility of working-class women toward the Bolsheviks was caused in part by their fears that the party was trying to change the family and the church, institutions they cherished. In fact, the party's leaders of work among women realized how sensitive their audiences were to these issues and deliberately avoided discussing the more radical proposals for family reform with them. Instead, when addressing the female proletariat, the party appealed to women's common interests with men, urging them to support the revolution because it had destroyed the oppressors and was ushering in a just new world. This careful sanitizing of appeals to women was not enough to quell rumors, however.[18] Stories circulated among women that the Bolsheviks were plotting to take children away from their mothers, encourage promiscuity among the young, even destroy the icons hanging everywhere. To a degree, of course, these rumors were an accurate reading of the party's intentions, but to an even greater extent they reflect the fears of working-class women, caught, like the peasants, in a terrifying crisis. They could support the revolutionaries when they were smashing the ruling class, but not when they criticized the institutions on which the lives of the working class were built.

Of course some women did come to meetings and even joined the party. According to its own reports, in 1921, after two years of work, the Woman's Department was able to persuade 6,000 women from Petrograd and its environs to serve as *delegatki*, that is, to attend a series of meetings as representatives of their factories. Forty-five hundred women participated in Moscow that year, up from 900 in 1920.[19] These precious few were a small minority of the female labor force, though. Furthermore, according to one source, the percentage of working-class women among women joining the party actually fell substantially during the Civil War years, from 46 percent of all female recruits in 1917 to 34 percent in 1920.[20] These figures might have been higher, the resistance of working-class women might have been allayed by the reassurance of carefully coached Zhenotdel workers had the Bolsheviks been able at the same time to do more to relieve women's suffering. But the programs the women might have been persuaded to accept, such as the establishment of day-care centers, could not be funded. Attempts to rouse women to set up their own dining rooms or nurseries also foundered on shortages of equipment and personnel. The crisis of the Civil War was so grave and all-consuming that it did not create substantial opportunities for women; it simply increased their burdens while opening few doors for them. In such a situation they naturally relied on the institutions that had brought them through before— marriage and the family—and responded defensively to threats to those institutions.

The commitment of some working-class women to religion and to marriage may even have been strengthened by the crisis. This may account, in part at least, for the record marriage rates of the Civil War period. Rather than postpone marriage, as they had done throughout the years of World War I, women were now rushing to it, as an economic and perhaps also as a psychological defense. H. Kent Geiger has suggested that subsequent crises in Soviet history, particularly the purges, may have had the effect of drawing people into closer family alliances.[21] Could the same not have been the case in the Civil War, particularly for women, who were more vulnerable economically than men and more likely to be bearing the responsibility for children?

The immediate effects of the Civil War were equally devastating for aristocratic and middle-class women. There is little solid information available on such women, since they were officially designated class enemies and persecuted by the Bolsheviks. What follows is a sketch of their fate based on impressions culled from memoirs.[22] Aristocratic and middle-class women coped with the crisis by fleeing Russia or by finding work under the new regime. Women of the *sluzhashchie*, or white-collar group that made up much of Russia's small middle class, and of the intelligentsia had skills desperately needed by the burgeoning Bolshevik bureaucracy. They served as clerical workers, as teachers, and as medical personnel. It was from this group as well that the majority of female Bolsheviks was recruited, but as there were only 30,000 to 40,000 such women in the party during the Civil War years, this choice seems to have appealed only to a tiny percentage of middle-class women.[23] There are hints as well that bourgeois women sometimes prospered by marrying into Soviet officialdom. Kollontai denounced such brides more than once, calling these "doll-parasites" a sign of the corruption of the party during the NEP. How many middle-class women actually used marriage as a route into the emerging elite we do not know.[24]

In sum, the immediate impact of the Civil War on women and family relations was complex. It broke up families, cast women and children adrift, beckoned some women into new sorts of alliances, and probably convinced others of the wisdom of tradition. We cannot measure such a diversity of attitudes with any precision; we can only conjecture, based on the sketchy evidence we have, that most Russian women, urban and rural, survived the Civil War by relying as heavily as they could on the support of marriage and family.

In the long-term the Civil War seems to have speeded up the evolution toward a nuclear family. I have earlier alluded to the emergence of a more nuclear family in the cities before the revolution and to the small but perceptible changes going on in the rural areas. We have seen that this latter development— the splitting up of the peasant family—became commonplace during the Civil War; Teodor Shanin estimates that 50 percent of the richest households were divided by voluntary repartitioning during those years. Shanin also documents a shrinkage in allotments among the middle peasantry that he attributes in part to the push of sons for independence.[25] The new households thus formed endured into the twenties, becoming a lasting consequence of the Civil War. Although the patriarchs remained powerful, continuing to influence their adult children and to work together with them in the fields, they did not require in the 1920s that their children move back in with them.

Of course simply allowing sons to set up their own households did not necessarily strip the senior men of the village of control over decisionmaking in the commune; Shanin believes that they kept this power until collectivization. Greater attention should be paid, however, to the issue of generational conflict within the peasant family and within the village as well. In particular further studies could consider the extent to which rebellion against paternal control figured in support for the Bolsheviks and in political activism more generally and whether this rebellion cut across the socioeconomic layers of the peasantry and thus characterized *bedniaki* as well as *kulaki*. We also need to explore differences among the European nationalities, particularly between the Russians, on whom Shanin concentrates, and the Ukrainians.[26]

The potential significance of the movement of adult sons away from their parents' households becomes apparent when we consider that such movement served all over Europe as the first stage of the transition from an extended, clan-based family form to the nuclear. Historically the breakup of the patriarchal family did not mean, however, a lessening in the power society granted husbands over wives. Indeed, some scholars have argued to the contrary, that as the authority of the father over his adult children diminished, the authority of husband over wife grew, in a compensating attempt to validate the solidarity of the conjugal couple.[27]

Did the Russian peasant son reach for increased power over his wife as a consequence of his new status, as had the Protestants of the Reformation? We have no evidence that he did so. Nor could he do so as easily as could men of earlier times, for the more egalitarian notions of modern courtship and marriage were continuing to penetrate the village. To some degree at least these modern notions discouraged the more brutish husbandly behavior once deemed appropriate. The belief that marriage should be based on romantic attraction also continued to undermine the considerations that had earlier governed the choice of mates. And the ideology of the emerging Bolshevik elite did not sanction strengthening the role of the newly independent husband, as did sixteenth-century Protestantism or the Victorian "Cult of True Womanhood." Finally, one might argue that existing peasant values already gave the peasant male so much authority over his wife that he had no need to seek more.

Thus, we have no reason to believe, and no evidence to suggest, that the peasant wife living in her own *izba* had suffered from her move. She probably benefited from the distance she had put between herself and her in-laws. One can detect among peasant women in the 1920s a slight weakening of their earlier resistance to the Bolsheviks that may be both a sign of women's improving position and a consequence of it. By the mid-twenties the number of peasant women willing to participate in projects organized by the Zhenotdel had climbed into the hundreds of thousands.[28] In these far less desperate times, peasant women were more willing to listen and to take advantage of the few benefits the party was now able to offer, but they still rejected most of the party's proposals for reform in the family. Even their innocuous stirrings toward change were enough to provoke peasant men, and Zhenotdel workers reported numerous incidents of men harassing and even assaulting them. The defenses of the village, although weakened, were still up.[29]

What about city folk? What enduring effects did the Civil War have on the decimated proletariat? As in the countryside, the war seems to have speeded the pace of changes already underway. The evidence available from the twenties suggests that the urban patterns of marriage, childbearing, and childrearing established before the revolution had been intensified by the years of war. The demographic data are revealing. In the mid-twenties marriage rates leveled off at a rate considerably lower than the peak years of 1919 and 1920, but still higher than before World War I.[30] Fewer men were available for women to marry because of the wars, however, and the twenties saw the beginning of the development of a sex ratio unfavorable to women that would persist through the thirties and reach dramatic proportions after World War II.[31] The phenomenon that had characterized Western Europe for hundreds of years— substantial numbers of single adults in the population—came to Russia through the agency of war, and therefore those who remained single were primarily women.

Other characteristics of the marriage patterns of the twenties can be described as "modern" and "urban." The age at first marriage rose two years over its late nineteenth-century level.[32] There is as yet no thorough analysis of this change, but there are several possible reasons. Most obvious, and almost universal, is the tendency of urban youths to postpone marriage until after they worked for several years. This motive had operated throughout the first decades of the twentieth century, augmented powerfully by the years of war. With the return of peace in the twenties, the new opportunities for education and employment, combined with shortages, particularly of housing, provided additional reasons for delaying marriage.

The divorce rate in the cities was high; perhaps as many as half of the marriages among the urban population of European Russia were ending in divorce in the 1920s. This figure seems all the more remarkable when it is compared to divorce rates elsewhere. The U.S. had led industrialized nations in divorce since 1914; during the twenties the U.S. rate stood at approximately 10 percent of marriages.[33] By comparison the Soviet rate seems phenomenally high, but understanding its significance, particularly its relation to changed values and social instability, is a formidable task.

First, it must be noted that divorce was almost exclusively an urban phenomenon. In the rural areas of Leningrad raion, for example, the rate in 1927 was 1.5 divorces per 1,000 people, in the city of Leningrad it was 9.8 per 1,000. Leningrad was an extreme case in that year, having the highest divorce rate in the USSR. Moscow was also high at 9.3 per 1,000, but its rural hinterland recorded a rate of only 2.1. The people of the capitals also divorced more than those in other urban areas; for example, the rate in the cities of the Urals was 6.5 per 1,000 and that in the cities of the Right Bank Ukraine 2.1.[34]

Second, to assess the significance of these figures one must have some sense of the divorce patterns that prevailed in the cities before the revolution. Legal divorce was virtually unobtainable until 1918, but as early as the 1890s working-class neighborhoods were rumored to be full of unmarried couples living together and of permanently separated spouses. The intelligentsia was also cultivating a liberal attitude toward common-law marriage and remarriage as the revolution drew on. The resourceful scholar who manages to sort through all the impressionistic and statistical material available and arrive at a sense of the rate of marital dissolution in the prerevolutionary city will shed much light on the extent to which the new divorce laws of the revolutionary era, and the disruptions of the times, led to an increase in divorce. Until such work is done, we will not know the effect of the Civil War on marriage; we will only know that contemporaries perceived it to have caused great marital instability.

The birth rate in the twenties climbed but remained below its prewar level; infant mortality resumed a decline that had been halted by the war. The urban family continued to shrink, with average size of families living together falling to 3.5 persons from its 1897 level of 4.4, according to one recent Soviet study.[35] These last figures must be crosschecked against other data. If they hold up under such scrutiny, they, like the rise in age at first marriage, indicate substantial change in progress. Indeed, the shrinkage in the size of the urban family and the rise in the age at first marriage are probably linked. Both occurred initially in response to the conditions of urban life, and both were probably accelerated significantly by the Civil War crisis. The shrinking family may be one of the best indications available of the fragmentation caused by the disintegration of the cities.

The signs of change in the urban family in the 1920s, then, were these: families were growing smaller, brides and grooms older, and divorce more common. But there were also signs of continuity with the past. The urban population continued to marry in record numbers. Within marriage the division of labor and power between women and men remained virtually unchanged. Time-budget studies from the period bear eloquent testimony to the continuation of woman's domestic labor.[36] The evidence, considered in its entirety, leads to the conclusion that the institution of the urban family had survived the war intact, its demographic development hastened, its values little changed. If this was the case, it lends support to the proposition that the Russian working-class family took its form primarily from the physical and economic demands of urban life and the ideals of the nuclear family circulating in the city. The temporary crisis of war had not been strong enough to reverse the far more powerful processes already at work; rather, it had intensified them.

The situation seemed different to many in the Soviet Union in the twenties; they feared that the urban family was about to collapse. There had been such tremendous disruption of individual families. Orphaned children were roaming the streets in gangs. The divorce rates were soaring all over the RSFSR but nowhere more so than in Moscow and Leningrad, long considered the bellwethers of change in the country. The legalization of abortion, condemned even by Bolshevik spokesmen as a necessary but temporary evil, appeared yet another threat to the survival of marriage.[37] And the threats were made to seem all the greater by reports of the hedonism of the young, who were alleged to be preaching a variety of theories of sexual liberation in order to defend the practice of old-fashioned promiscuity.

Among the students, as among other groups in the population, however, the appearance of radical change masked a more moderate reality. A survey of students at Moscow University in 1922 revealed that only 8 percent of the women were opposed on principle to marriage.[38] The vast majority of the female students surveyed aspired to marriage based on romantic love, as did most of their male counterparts. Probably these young people, particularly the women, were more sexually active outside marriage than had been the case with youths before the war. But in their conceptions of marriage and eventually in their married lives, most adhered to liberal but still predominantly "bour-geois" values—monogamy, the nuclear family, and a division of labor and power between the sexes that granted men authority over women and assigned to women most of the domestic chores and a central, nurturing role in the family's emotional life. The free love advocates, a tiny minority of the students, attracted far more attention than they deserved, in large part because they raised fears among populace and party alike.[39]

So too did the *bolshevichki*, the female members of the party who were hailed as the vanguard in the liberation of women that was believed to be underway. For the tens of thousands of women who had joined the party by 1921, and the thousands of others who worked for the revolution without actually joining, the experience was undoubtedly emancipating.[40] Riding with soldiers into combat or trudging along muddy roads bundled up in men's greatcoats, these women seemed the very embodiment of the new freedoms. They were ardent socialists who accepted the Marxist doctrines of female emancipation: they believed that it was the responsibility of woman to dedicate herself to social reform, they argued for egalitarian relationships with men, and they rejected parental authority, as well as religion.

Like the students, however, most Bolshevik women, both those of the Civil War generation and those who had joined the party before 1917, were in fact less radical than the proclamations that applauded their coming. A gender-based division of labor and power within the party influenced strongly the types of jobs available to these women and the progress of their careers, even during the most desperate and therefore liberating days of the Civil War. The majority of them served in the army as nurses or clerks. Those working else-where in the government or party were also for the most part clerical workers; women achieved leadership only in the Zhenotdel or the Commissariat of Enlightenment. In the twenties they moved into teaching, writing, editing, and other equally "soft" jobs; only a few joined the ranks of the leather-jacketed "hard" commissars during the Civil War, and even these left politics during the twenties.

As far as the private lives of Bolshevik women were concerned, most of the evidence supports the conclusion that they sought monogamous marriages based on romantic love and that they wanted to have children. Kollontai's dreams of a variety of sexual relationships governed only by personal taste or need, and of a total relegation of childrearing to public institutions, found little support among these women. Their conceptions of marriage and motherhood were modern by contrast with those of their peasant sisters, but not radical. This is not to denigrate the feminism of many Bolshevik women; they were genuinely committed to reforms for women. Nor is it intended to belittle the accomplishments of both the Zhenotdel and the party in bringing improve-ments in the lives of Soviet women. The subject here is the effect of the Civil War on the Russian family and, more specifically, the fears of many Soviet people, within government and without during the twenties, that the family was in serious jeopardy. The liberated Bolshevik woman seemed a sign of the radical change that had swept over Russia, and thus the true extent of her rebellion against family norms is relevant to a consideration of how much change had in fact occurred, and how much the cries of alarm that the family was disintegrating were exaggerated. If one looks at her beliefs and behavior with this question in mind, one finds her a liberal on matters of family life and woman's roles, but not a radical utopian. Although more emancipated than the peasant, she was not ready to leave her husband and children and rush off to live in a commune. Rather, she was at the forefront of the evolution toward the modern, nuclear family.[41]

This evidence seems to support the conclusion that the revolution and war had left much in the structure of the urban family and the values governing it intact. It seemed quite otherwise to many in Soviet Russia in the twenties. Contemporaries, among them Bolsheviks, saw the divorces, the abortions, the orphans, and the liberated youth at the universities as indicators of a society come apart. After years of conflict, Russians of all classes profoundly desired stability; reacting to war they wanted peace. Any signs of fundamental change in that most stabilizing of all institutions, the family, were frightening, and thus the changes were seen as a threat, and a movement was launched to restore order.

I am referring specifically to the debates over marriage law reform and over the sexual behavior of the young that began in the mid-twenties and led ultimately to Stalinist puritanism and blessings on domesticity. Lower-ranking Bolsheviks during the marriage law debates repeatedly asserted that family and social stability were linked, that both were desirable, and that instability in the family originated in the licentious cities. Rank-and-file party members and learned commentators on contemporary morality worried that men unrestrained by the legal ties of marriage had become irresponsible, lustful creatures who were victimizing women. Sophisticated Marxists such as Emelian Iaroslavskii condemned the sexual permissiveness of youth for weakening the construction of socialism, the success of which was, of course, crucial to the survival of the revolution. The fears of youthful dissoluteness also reveal a reaction to the freeing of the young that had occurred during the revolution and suggest that generational conflict was occurring in the cities as well as in the countryside. By the mid-twenties there was a widespread desire among the leadership, probably shared by many lower down in the hierarchy, to get homeless children, rebellious youths, vulnerable women, and promiscuous men back into institutional arrangements that guaranteed stability.[42]

The family form that ultimately received the state's blessing was not that of the traditional peasant, of course, but the modernized, nuclear family described earlier. By the late twenties the party was more radical than the urban public only in the extent to which it continued to endorse egalitarian relations between husbands and wives. This is not to deny the role of Stalin's revolution in completing all the processes discussed here—destroying what remained of the extended peasant family, accelerating the move to the cities, granting government approval to motherhood, romantic love, and housekeeping, as well as drawing women into paid labor in unprecedented numbers. It is to suggest, however, that Stalin's government was less responsible for the embourgeoisement of Bolshevik visions of the family than has earlier been thought.[43] The decade of the twenties, often portrayed as a time of radical experimentation and free thought about the family, was also a time of consolidation in the aftermath of war, a consolidation desired by party elite and masses alike. The marriage law reforms and the sexuality debates did not halt the evolutionary processes already underway within the family. Rather, they signified an emerging societal consensus: the government should disavow experimentation with the family. It should support the existing order developing in the cities. There had been enough disorder.

This reaction might have come had the Bolsheviks gained power without civil war. Perhaps any revolutionary party must moderate its stand on family reform in the face of deep opposition from those it governs. Perhaps it is true also that socialist visions of communes and of free love are simply too utopian to be realized anywhere. In Russia, some accommodation with popular attitudes, which still attached enormous importance to the family and woman's roles within it, was inevitable. Furthermore, the party's voice was never certain and unanimous in its support for plans to restructure the family radically. The utopians on this issue were always a minority, particularly after the mass recruitments of the Civil War and early twenties. What the Civil War seems to have done is to provide such a graphic example of social dissolution that it generated a strong reaction in the party (at least as evidenced in the fears of promiscuity and divorce) and helped persuade the Bolsheviks to disavow their proclamations of hostility to the family. Whether they would have done so under any circumstances we shall never know; they did so in response to fears produced by the Civil War. The war accelerated changes already underway while at the same time serving as a warning against too rapid change.

NOTES

1. A. G. Kharchev, *Brak i sem'ia v SSSR*, 2nd ed. (Moscow, 1979), p. 133. Professor Kharchev tells about this incident with great distaste, as an example of the way things got out of hand among the young during the Civil War. As we shall see below, this was precisely the response of many in the party at the time.

2. For a discussion of Stalinist doctrines on the family see H. Kent Geiger, *The Family in Soviet Russia* (Cambridge, Mass.: 1968), pp. 76–106. The best treatment of post-Stalinist developments in approved notions of the family is Vladimir Shlapentokh's *Love, Marriage and Friendship in the Soviet Union* (New York, 1984), especially pp. 19–38. For a contemporary and scholarly Soviet study of family structures and values that endorses a nuclear family precisely like that described here see Kharchev, *Brak i sem'ia v SSSR*.

3. *Kommunistka*, 1922, no. 1, p. 13.

4. Moirova, "Rabota sredi krest'ianok," *Kommunistka*, 1924, no. 3, p. 23; P. M.

Chirkov, *Reshenie zhenskogo voprosa v SSSR (1917–1937 gg.)* (Moscow, 1978), p. 137.

5. For the plight of single women during the Civil War see E. N. Tsellarius, "Put' v kolkhoz," *Oktiabrem rozhdennye* (Moscow, 1967), pp. 262–69; O. Sokolova, "Opyt vovlecheniia krest'ianok Penzenskoi gubernii v sovetskoe stroitel'stvo," *Kommunistka*, 1921, nos. 12–13, pp. 66–68; V. Romanov, "Krest'ianka i derevenskii mir," *Kommunistka*, 1922, nos. 8–9, pp. 35–36.

6. Teodor Shanin in *The Awkward Class: Political Sociology of Peasantry in a Developing Society: Russia 1910–1925* (Oxford, 1972), pp. 29–30, alludes to an increase before 1914 in partitioning of households to allow sons to establish their families separately. But he also argues, as do most observers, that the traditional family remained the dominant family form among the peasants until collectivization. For a description of the sons' pressure for their own property in the prerevolutionary period see Sula Benet, ed., *The Village of Viriatino* (Garden City, N.J, 1970), pp. 55, 93–94.

7. Shanin, *Awkward Class*, pp. 157–59, 175–77.

8. For a fuller discussion of this topic see Barbara Evans Clements, "Working-Class and Peasant Women in the Russian Revolution, 1917–1923," *Signs* 1982, 8, no. 2, pp. 215–35.

9. This paragraph has benefited from J. Jackson Lears's stimulating discussion of the problem of analyzing the consciousness of subordinated groups in "The Concept of Cultural Hegemony: Problems and Possibilities," *American Historical Review*, June 1985, 90, no. 3, pp. 567–93.

10. E. O. Kabo, *Ocherki rabochego byta—Informatsionnyi biulleten' No. 13. Byt, vremia, demografiia* (Moscow, 1968); as cited in Kharchev, *Brak i sem'ia v SSSR*, p. 233. See also Diane Koenker, "Urban Families, Working-Class Youth Groups, and the 1917 Revolution in Moscow," in *The Family in Imperial Russia*, David Ransel, ed. (Urbana, Ill., 1978), pp. 282–87.

11. Chirkov, *Reshenie zhenskogo voprosa v SSSR*, pp. 117, 158.

12. Ibid., p. 117.

13. Ibid., p. 39; P. M. Dvoretskaia, "Soiuz soldatok," *Zhenshchiny goroda Lenina* (Leningrad, 1963), pp. 77–86; M. Levkovich, "Otvazhnye docheri ukrainskogo naroda," *Zhenshchiny v revoliutsii* (Moscow, 1959), pp. 258–59; Nina N. Selivanova, *Russia's Women* (New York, 1923), p. 198; P. Voronova, "Stranitsy geroicheskoi istorii," *Zhenshchiny v revoliutsii*, p. 166; E. Zelenskaia, "Soiuz soldatok," ibid., pp. 172–77. For the existence of the women's unions see *Kaluzhskie bol'shevichki; sbornik vospominanii* (Kaluga, 1960), p. 45; A. Pomelova, *Slovo o zhenshchinakh severa* (n.p.: Severo-zapadnoe knizhnoe izdatel'stvo, 1968), pp. 33–43, 107, 109; *Pravda*, June 3, 1919, p. 2; October 24, 1919, p. 5; June 5, 1921, p. 2. For a modern Soviet scholar's discussion of the unions see Chirkov, *Reshenie zhenskogo voprosa*, pp. 38–40.

14. Bystrianskii, *Kommunizm, brak i sem'ia* (Moscow, 1921), pp. 64–65; Wesley Andrew Fisher, *The Soviet Marriage Market: Mate Selection in Russia and the USSR* (New York, 1980), pp. 90–91.

15. Ibid.

16. The evidence of women's hostility is so extensive that only selected sources can be cited here. See for example Maxim Gorky, *Untimely Thoughts: Essays on Revolution, Culture and the Bolsheviks*, Herman Ermolaev, trans. (New York, 1968), pp. 207–13; *Kommunistka*, 1920, nos. 1–2, p. 35; 1920, nos. 3–4, p. 31; 1922, nos. 16–17, p. 3; *Pravda*, May 8, 1919, p. 4; July 3, 1919, p. 4; July 17, 1919, p. 3; October 16, 1919, p. 4; M. N. Sveshnikova-Vydrina, "V organizatsii—sila!" *Zhenshchiny goroda Lenina*, pp. 96–97.

17. The essay by Jeffrey Brooks, "The Breakdown in Production and Distribution of Printed Material, 1917–1927" (*Bolshevik Culture, Experiment and Order in the Russian Revolution*, Abbott Gleason, Peter Kenez, and Richard Stites, eds. [Bloomington, Ind., 1985], pp. 151–74), contains some illuminating statistics about the reading

habits of the working class and peasantry before 1917. His data reveal a large, if unsophisticated audience among the lower classes. See also Jeffrey Brooks, *How Russia Learned to Read* (Princeton, 1986).

18. For a discussion of the content of party agitation aimed at working-class women see Barbara Evans Clements, "The Birth of the New Soviet Woman," in *Bolshevik Culture*, Gleason, Kenez, and Stites, eds., pp. 223–26.

19. "Otchet otdela Ts.K.R.K.P. po rabote sredi zhenshchin," *Izvestiia Ts.K.R.K.P. (b)*, March 1922, p. 49.

20. See Appendix 2 (part 2) in Barbara Evans Clements, "Baba and Bolshevik: Russian Women and Revolutionary Change," *Soviet Union*, 1985, 12, pt. 2 p. 176.

21. Geiger, *Family in Soviet Russia*, pp. 126–27.

22. Among the most touching and revealing of these memoirs are the following: Princess Anatole Marie Bariatinsky, *My Russian Life* (London, 1923); Countess Kleinmichel, *Memories of a Shipwrecked World* (New York, 1923); Marie, Grand Duchess of Russia, *Education of a Princess* (New York, 1931); Irina Skariatina, *A World Can End* (New York, 1931); Alexandra Tolstoy, *I Worked for the Soviet* (New Haven, 1934); *Woman under Fire: Six Months in the Red Army* (London, n.d.).

23. F. M. Knuniants-Rizel', "Docherii partii," *Uchastnitsy velikogo sozidaniia* (Moscow, Politizdat, 1962), pp. 14–17; E. Smitten, "Zhenshchiny v R.K.P.," *Kommunistka*, 1923, nos. 1–2, p. 30.

24. Kollontai's attack on bourgeois women who were marrying Bolsheviks appears first in her article "Novaia ugroza," *Kommunistka*, August-September 1922, nos. 8–9, pp. 5–9. This is the source of the appellation "doll-parasites." The theme later appears in her fiction, most notably in the short story "Vasilisa Malygina," which was first published in a 1923 collection of short stories entitled *Liubov pchel trudovikh* (Petrograd, 1923). A recent translation by Cathy Porter is available in *Love of Worker Bees* (Chicago, 1978), pp. 21–181.

25. Shanin, *Awkward Class*, p. 158. The ethnographic study of the village of Viriatino in Tambov guberniia also offers evidence for this proposition. Between 1918 and 1930 the number of independent households grew by 30 percent; the splitting up of the larger families was particularly common during the Civil War and was provoked in large measure by returning sons. See Benet, *Village of Viriatino*, p. 243.

26. Statistics indicate substantial differences between the two regions. Fertility rates in the Ukraine had dropped below those of central Russia before the revolution. See Ansley J. Coale, Barbara Anderson, and Erma Harm, *Human Fertility in Russia since the Nineteenth Century* (Princeton, 1979), pp. 113, 116. In the 1920s, the urban marriage and divorce rates in the Ukraine were virtually the same as the rural rates, whereas in Russia urban rates were much higher than rural. For statistics from 1927 see Tsentral'noe Statisticheskoe Upravlenie, *Statisticheskii spravochnik SSSR za 1928* (Moscow, 1929), pp. 76–79.

27. One of the most elegant statements of this argument is Lawrence Stone's *Family, Sex, and Marriage in England, 1500–1800*, abridged ed. (New York, 1979).

28. One source reports that 386,000 peasant women attended delegate meetings in 1926—this in a population of adult peasant women of the European nationalities that numbered at least 20 million *Opyt KPSS v reshenii zhenskogo voprosa* [Moscow, 1981], p. 56; *Zhenshchiny v SSSR* [Moscow, 1975], p. 9).

29. Another indicator of women's continuing resistance to Bolshevik overtures is participation in the work of the soviets. Zhenotdel reports from 1924 claim that peasant women made up 10 percent of those voting in elections for rural soviets and 1 percent of the delegates. These percentages had not changed since 1919. They compare to a participation rate for urban women of 14 percent, up from 7 percent in 1919 (P. Zaitsev, "Krest'ianka v sovete," *Kommunistka*, 1924, no. 4, p. 14). For additional figures on peasant women's participation in various sorts of government-sponsored activities, see B. Kanatchikova, "Svodka raboty zhenotdelov po 15 guberniiam," *Kommunistka*,

1921, nos. 11–12, pp. 39–41; O. Sokolova, "Odna i ocherednykh rabot," ibid., 1923, no. 8, p. 6–7; "Uchastie zhenshchin v organakh upravleniia Sovetskoi Respubliki," ibid., 1923, nos. 1–2, pp. 32–33. For peasant women's attitudes toward changes in the 1920s see Levkovich, *Zhenshchiny v revoliutsii*, p. 273. For male violence against female Bolsheviks and women consorting with them see *Kommunistka*, 1922, nos. 8–9, p. 35; *Kaluzhskie bol'shevichki*, pp. 114–15; Pomelova, *Slovo o zhenshchinakh severa*, pp. 70, 78–82.

30. The rate in Leningrad in 1927 was 15: 1,000, down from 23: 1,000. The marriage rate for European Russia in 1911–13 was 8: 1,000; in 1924 the RSFSR recorded a rate of 11: 1,000. See *Statisticheskii spravochnik*, pp. 74, 76–77.

31. Fisher, *Soviet Marriage Market*, pp. 77–119.

32. In 1897 the age at first marriage for men was 25.3, for women 21.9; in 1925 those figures were 27.8 and 24.2. (Ibid., pp. 150–51.)

33. *Statisticheskii spravochnik*, pp. 76–79; *Historical Statistics of the United States: Colonial Times to 1970*, part 1 (Washington, D.C., 1976), B.214–220; Nelson Blake, *A History of American Life and Thought* (New York, 1972), p. 408.

34. *Statisticheskii spravochnik*, pp. 76–79.

35. Fisher, *Soviet Marriage Market*, p. 96; Chirkov, *Reshenie zhenskogo voprosa*, pp. 227, 228. The figures on family size are from Kabo, *Ocherki rabochego byta*, as cited in Kharchev, *Brak i sem'ia v SSSR*, p. 233.

36. P. Kozhanyi, *Rabotnitsa i byt* (Moscow, 1926), pp. 13–19; S. Strumilin, "Biudzhet vremeni russkogo rabochego," *Kommunistka*, 1923, no. 6 pp. 17–21; 1923, no. 8, pp. 21–23.

37. For two early, but characteristic Bolshevik treatments of the abortion question see N. Krupskaia, "Voina i detorozhdenie," *Kommunistka*, 1920, nos. 1–2, pp. 18–20; and N. Semashko, "Eshche o bol'nom voprose," ibid., nos. 3–4 (1920): 19–21.

38. I. Gel'man, *Polovaia zhizn' sovremennoi molodezhi* (Moscow, 1923), p. 84.

39. This paragraph is a synopsis of all of Gel'man's findings. For discussions of studies with similar results see Chirkov, *Reshenie zhenskogo voprosa*, p. 203; and Sheila Fitzpatrick, "Sex and Revolution: An Examination of Literary and Statistical Data on the Mores of Soviet Students in the 1920s," *Journal of Modern History*, June 1978, 50, pp. 252–78.

40. For figures on female party membership, see E. Smitten, "Zhenshchiny v RKP," *Kommunistka*, 1923, nos. 1–2, pp. 30–32; 1924, no. 4, pp. 8–10; F. M. Knuniants-Rizel', "Docheri partii," *Uchastnitsy velikogo sozidaniia*, pp. 14–18.

41. These generalizations are based on a study of a sample of 314 Bolshevik women who joined the party before 1922. For a more detailed treatment, see my essay "Baba and Bolshevik: Russian Women and Revolutionary Change," *Soviet Union*, 1985, 12, pt. 2 pp. 161–84.

42. For an extended discussion of the marriage law debates, see Wendy Goldman, "Freedom and Its Consequences: The Debate on the Soviet Family Code of 1926," *Russian History*, Winter 1984, 11, no. 4, 362–88. Rudolph Schlesinger, ed., *The Family in the U.S.S.R.* (London, 1949), pp. 81–168, contains lengthy excerpts from the debates. Complementing Schlesinger is a recent Soviet account of regional opinion in Pomelova, *Slovo o zhenshchinakh severa*, pp. 46, 61. See also E. Iaroslavskii, "Moral i byt proletariata v perekhodnyi period," *Molodaia gvardiia*, May 1926, no. 3, pp. 138–53.

43. This is Geiger's implication throughout *Family in Soviet Russia*. For an explicit discussion see pp. 88–116.

COMMENTARY
THE ELEMENTS OF SOCIAL AND DEMOGRAPHIC CHANGE IN CIVIL WAR RUSSIA

William G. Rosenberg

Understanding social and demographic change in Civil War Russia is a weighty problem in both substantive and analytic terms, and one fraught with implications for subsequent Soviet history. The principal issues turn not only on how objective indices of Russian social order changed between 1918 and 1921, but also on how these objective changes affected attitudes, social identities, and political commitments and the degree to which the aftermath represented a social order different both qualitatively and quantitatively from the one the Bolsheviks came to govern in October 1917. Involved here, consequently, are not only estimates of population changes and measurements of changing social strata, but also conceptions of class and of the processes of class formation; transport statistics and interpretations of the ways in which economic activities related to political attitudes; estimates of real and relative standards of living; and an analysis of how marriage, family structures, and other similar social formations relate institutionally to revolutionary social values. It is hardly surprising that many of the arguments presented in these papers produced spirited discussion. As Carol Hayden observed in her role as one of the seminar's formal commentators, the Civil War had an overwhelmingly traumatic effect on Russian society, created a deep "longing for stability," and hence "contributed to the rise of Stalinism." If some disagreed with her conclusion, few doubted its premise or the importance of the trauma itself to other aspects of Civil War history.

The relationship between objective indices and broader patterns of social change is the central problematic of all three papers here, but each author has different views of how these two types of social phenomena were related. Daniel R. Brower and Diane Koenker both describe in detail the depopulation of Russia's major cities and towns in 1918–21, yet Brower's aggregate estimates

123

do not attempt to differentiate with any precision between the types of inhabitants who left. This is partly (and properly) because his focus is on the city as a whole, on the changing characteristics of urban life during the Civil War that were essentially shared by everyone. The "grim story of destruction" he presents structured the tasks of postrevolutionary reconstruction, but even more important, in his view, "gave new meaning to urban life among the remaining inhabitants," whatever their occupation or social identity. In important ways, he suggests, the "survivors" had a great deal in common simply as a result of the nature of their struggle, and especially as a result of the ways in which they uniformly fought to survive.

Thus as transport began to break down and as the established market mechanisms soon proved unable to supply cities with essential goods and resources, all sorts of urban dwellers became petty traders, seeking to barter goods or to make their living by trading for others. By necessity, workers and former members of the *patronat* both assumed the guise and functions of *meshchanstvo*, as the "struggle to survive" turned cities "into the kingdom of petty traders, the *meshochniki*." Class distinctions soon became meaningless in characterizing the social groups involved in this trade, who came, Brower indicates, from all walks of life. Thus Briansk metal workers made axes to trade for grain, soap workers bartered their wages in kind, and whole enterprises began to shift their production, however meager, toward products that could be readily exchanged. "Such a process" in Brower's view, represented not so much a transformation or disintegration of the working class, as it has often been depicted, as "its assimilation into the mass of trading townspeople."

Brower is surely correct in suggesting the emergence of a "second economy" of black and grey markets between 1918 and 1921. His vivid and careful depiction of the cityscape and his portrait of the urban dwellers' struggle to survive through the use of these markets is an important corrective to simplisitic perspectives on the realities of War Communism. But whether the entry into market practices "destroy[ed] the very class distinctions on which [Soviet leaders] relied for working class support," as Brower also argues, depends on one's understanding of the nature of class, and particularly on how strongly one identifies socioeconomic behavior with class perspectives or consciousness. Do workers with many years of factory experience, who had recently participated in a massive proletarian revolution, shed their identities and outlooks as their factories reduce or stop production? Do they change their politics? Their attitudes toward the "bourgeoisie?" Are class distinctions destroyed, in other words, as socioeconomic functions become themselves less distinct?

Such questions are contentious ones, partly because overt worker protests are readily construed as evidence of anti-Bolshevik politics during the Civil War, especially in late 1920 and 1921 on the eve of the Kronstadt debacle. One can only begin to resolve them by offering sharper definitions of the objective parameters of class, and by reassessing social and demographic changes during the Civil War in terms of how, more precisely, they affected particular social groups. This is one of the great merits of Diane Koenker's contribution. One need not agree with every aspect of her typology of "urbanized" workers to appreciate the soundness of her approach and the important analytical implications of her argument.

In her view, politically active urban workers who helped make the revolution of 1917 did not rusticate themselves in large numbers during the Civil War, despite a mass exodus from the cities. Those who returned to the villages were among the least active politically, and even though large numbers of politically committed workers entered the Red Army, the party administration, and state service, many who did so remained in cities and towns and in close proximity to their former factory comrades. The numbers (and political role) of skilled workers remaining in urban industry clearly declined; so, too, in all likelihood, did the practical meaning of occupational differences (and skill levels) in the factories themselves. But none of this suggests to Koenker a radical transformation of class consciousness or even political commitment. Because a great deal of Bolshevik strength had earlier rested on relatively young worker activists, and because the size of this cohort contracted for a whole range of reasons during the Civil War, an older (and increasingly female) urban proletariat was more likely to be critical of Bolshevik policies and practices as it suffered increasingly the depredations involved in struggling to survive. But precisely because the political commitments of this relatively stable cohort were deep and of long duration, it is unlikely that overt criticism and even active protests signified an abandonment of support for Soviet power, and even less an identification with the attitudes and values of the *meshchanstvo*, however much workers were involved in trade. Class formation in Russia and elsewhere, in other words, while obviously related in important ways to one's position in the socioeconomic order, also necessarily involved elements of culture and consciousness that, while more gradual in their development than the process of occupational change, are also by nature deeper and more permanent.

What, then, changed regarding class in Civil War Russia, and especially about workers? Koenker points to important modifications of urban culture in this period and suggests the ways in which they affected workers' particularly. Neighborhoods tended to become more important than factories in structuring day-to-day life; the struggle for existence meant a radical change in the use of one's time, especially in the workplace; and traditional cultural prerogatives of the "bourgeoisie" like the theater became much more a part of proletarian culture. Social distinctions in the neighborhood also diminished, as members of formerly distinct (and even antagonistic) social strata intermingled to a far greater extent than they ever had before October 1917. As Koenker suggests, the class enemy "was alive and well," but fighting in the White armies rather than in factories and plants.

What this suggests, however, is not simply an *extension* of proletarian outlooks rather than their absorption by the mentalities of the *meshchanstvo*, but also a significant change in the very nature of the processes of class formation in Russia. For many years, and especially in 1917, one's identity as a worker was defined not only by an understanding of who and what one was, but also by clarity about who one was *not*. The very nature of struggle in the workplace acted to consolidate different groups of workers who often had different crafts, values, and outlooks, largely because they were all "workers" in the eyes of employers, were treated as such, and shared the limitations of power and welfare that redounded to all who earned wages. In important ways, the processes of expropriation in 1917 and 1918 deprived workers of a critical means of taking their own measure, and not the least of the Bolsheviks' tasks after 1918 was again to give political meaning and tangible value to proletarian identity.

Some would argue that Lenin's party ultimately failed to do so because of obvious linkages between class consciousness and collective action. Bolsheviks in power, whether workers or not, idealized class identities while constraining their natural and logical political inclinations. In these circumstances, other attributes, like gender, took on added meaning. To be a woman came to matter as much or more than one's social origins or the type of work one did, at least for some.

The relationship between gender and class as structural determinants in early Soviet society is a matter of continuing debate, but Barbara Evans Clements's study of women and the family leaves no doubt about the importance of gender in social relations during this period. The data she presents about the devastating effects of the Civil War display the staying power of cultural prejudices and remind us of the limitations of revolutionary transformation on women. At the same time, her argument that these short-term dislocations were actually less significant in the long run than one might think, especially in terms of their effect on family or marriage patterns, suggests the power of social relationships complementing (and perhaps even superseding) those of class. Insofar as marriage and the family, especially the nuclear family, were long-term sources of stability and support, it is possible, she suggests, that the commitment of some working-class women to marriage was even strengthened by the crisis, despite popular perceptions and the dominant rhetoric.

In her formal commentary at the seminar, Carol Hayden accepted Clements's suggestions about the possible conservative effects of the Civil War on marriage and family relations, but "not for the reasons or through the processes she describes." In Hayden's view, the impact of the Civil War itself depended greatly on class, and any implication that women in general, "both from the peasantry and the working class, responded to Bolshevik assaults on traditional family relations and to the insecurity and hardship of the Civil War by becoming more conservative" was an exaggeration at best.

Hayden argued that while the Bolshevik Party accepted in principle Marx's and Engels's critique of the bourgeois family, it never took a position against the family per se, despite the sometime projections of Bolshevik figures like Alexandra Kollontai. Instead, it was the oppressive and exploitative nature of relations within the family that Bolsheviks as a party sought to abolish, and they did so through explicit political activity carried out during the revolution and Civil War almost entirely among workers. Here, moreover, they had "considerable success . . . especially in Petrograd, where thousands of working women embraced Bolshevik-organized child care centers, and hundreds of like institutions were set up in factories even at the height of the Civil War." Opposition to efforts on behalf of women, particularly through the Zhenotdel, "came overwhelmingly from men," and sympathetic women "frequently feared the brutal attacks of their husbands, brothers, and fathers should they respond to Zhenotdel appeals."

In several important ways, however, Hayden's criticism strengthens rather than weakens Clements's suggestions about the power of longer-term social and cultural processes. The disinterest and hostility of many men to women's issues or welfare, itself a deeply rooted pattern in prerevolutionary Russia, was neither imcompatible with a strengthening commitment on the part of women to nuclear as opposed to extended families, nor to the role of marriage per se as a stabilizing institution. The question was largely one of content rather than of form, and once restrictive laws on marriage rights were lifted, concerned the end of exploitation of women everywhere. If party figures soon raised exaggerated cries of alarm about the disintegration of the family, popular (and official) denigration of radical feminism was itself as much a reflection of challenged cultural values and norms as an indication of desire for social stabilization.

As noted above, Hayden also suggested the "inescapable conclusion that the Civil War had an overwhelmingly traumatic effect on Russian society," leading in her view to a generalized longing for "stability and normality in social and economic relations." What these three essays suggest, however, and what further research is needed to demonstrate, is just what "stability" and "normality" came to mean in the aftermath of such traumatic and universal social dislocation.

III

Administration and State Building

INTRODUCTION
BOLSHEVIK EFFORTS AT STATE BUILDING

Victoria E. Bonnell

The phenomenon of "statism" during the Civil War—that is, the creation of a centralized administrative apparatus and the application of the principle of state intervention in the name of socialism—has been noted by many scholars. Moshe Lewin has argued, for example, that by the end of the Civil War "it was not a social class any more—the proletariat—that served as the epitome and bearer of socialism through the state, but . . . the state itself was now replacing the class and becoming the epitome and carrier of the higher principle with, or without, the help of the proletariat."[1] Three of the four chapters in this section—by Daniel T. Orlovsky, Alexander Rabinowitch, and Thomas F. Remington—help us see some of the ways in which the Bolsheviks went about the task of state building during these years and the implications this had for social, political, and institutional structures of the new regime. The fourth chapter—by Mary McAuley—deals with a related but different topic: the impact of Bolshevik policies and administration on daily life—with particular attention to the food situation—in Petrograd during the Civil War years.

In their efforts at state building that immediately followed the October Revolution, the Bolsheviks proceeded along three different paths. In the first instance, the Bolsheviks took over a preexisting governmental institution, such as the state *kontrol'* bureaucracy discussed by Remington, in an effort to make it serve the purposes of the new Soviet state. There were many such organs of government at the central, regional, and local levels that the Bolsheviks inherited from the old regime, and with them came many thousands of former tsarist officials and a large bureaucratic stratum recruited from the ranks of what Orlovsky calls the "lower-middle stratum."

The second path involved the subordination and transformation of former nongovernmental organizations, which, under conditions of Soviet rule, were incorporated into the state apparatus. The workers' control movement, the soviets, and the cooperatives illustrate this development. Each chapter takes up this problem in a different context. Finally, a third approach to state building involved the creation of an entirely new bureaucratic structure, one that combined functions hitherto dispersed in governmental and nongovernmental institutions. The establishment of Rabkrin in 1920, examined by Remington, exemplifies this approach.

In their efforts to explore various aspects of the Bolsheviks' state building efforts in the Civil War era, the authors present a number of important themes. The social composition and social bases of state institutions and organizations in the post-October period is one such theme. Orlovsky focuses on the role of the "lower-middle strata" in governmental institutions. Remington investigates the interrelationship between the state *kontrol'* bureaucracy and the working population, and Rabinowitch looks at linkages between the Bolshevik-dominated First City District soviet in Petrograd and the workers who had previously given it support.

Another recurrent theme is the problem of bureaucratic outcomes. In one way or another, each of the three authors presents material that seeks to account for why, in a period characterized by a great variety of bureaucratic proposals and experiments, certain bureaucratic solutions prevailed and others did not. Orlovsky, for example, poses the question of "why Lenin and his immediate circle opted for the old ministerial form of government in the new revolutionary workers' and peasants' state"? Rabinowitch examines this problem in relation to the development of the local soviets. Similarly, Remington's study of workers' control explores the circumstances that transformed the once highly popular and mass-based workers' control movement; drained of its radical content, it was turned into an instrument of state domination and labor discipline, all in the name of socialism. Readers will note that the variety of analytic approaches—ideological, organizational, social structural, functional, cultural—to the problem of bureaucratic outcomes evident in these papers provides further incentive for research and reflection on the Civil War period.

Looking at the emerging bureaucratic system in Russia from another perspective, McAuley examines the issue of governmental institutions from the bottom up, focusing on popular perceptions of the new state administration as it struggled to deal with the problem of food provisioning. Her contribution complements the others by emphasizing the impact of the emerging state system on the lives of ordinary citizens. Taken together, the four chapters offer valuable new perspectives on the process of state building during the Civil War period.

NOTE

1. Robert C. Tucker, ed., *Stalinism: Essays in Historical Interpretation* (New York, 1977), p. 114.

THE PETROGRAD FIRST CITY
DISTRICT SOVIET DURING
THE CIVIL WAR

Alexander Rabinowitch

Between 1917 and the end of the Russian Civil War, city and district soviets in revolutionary Russia went through a three-stage process of change. During the initial stage of development in the Provisional Government period, these institutions were lively, relatively democratic forums for the articulation of popular concerns and interests, but not much more. In the next stage, during the first eight months after the October Revolution, as the workers, soldiers, and sailors who had supported the overthrow of the Provisional Government rushed to realize their aspirations—most fundamentally power to ordinary citizens exercised through revolutionary soviets—they became the new regime's primary institutions of urban local government. In their final stage of development during the Russian Civil War (roughly speaking between June 1918 and January 1920), the power and independent authority of these institutions were gradually decisively undermined, with the result that by war's end, generally speaking, they were effectively eliminated as significant autonomous political entities. In this essay, I will focus on the evolution of these institutions in this final stage as it is reflected in the history of just one Petrograd district soviet—that of the First City District of Petrograd. My primary purpose is to see what an understanding of the dynamics of change in this stage brings to bear on one of the central historiographical issues in Soviet history, namely, the relative importance of historical events and responses to them as opposed to a preconceived Bolshevik revolutionary ideology or a firmly established pattern of dictatorial behavior, in shaping Soviet Russia's highly centralized, authoritarian political system. So that the significance of developments in this culminating period may be fully understood it is necessary first, however, to summarize, if only in brief, the socioeconomic character of the First City District in the revolutionary period and the evolution of the First City District soviet to June 1918.[1]

The First City District and the First City District Soviet in 1917

As definitively established at the end of April 1917, the First City District, centrally situated, was Petrograd's largest administrative unit both in territory (it comprised 25 percent of the land area of Petrograd) and in population (approximately 546,000 people lived in the district, out of a citywide population of 2.5 million). Located in the district were the former Liteinyi, Moskovskii, and Aleksandr Nevskii police sections, which became in effect administrative subdistricts. Within this sprawling area there were sharp socioeconomic differences. Thus, while southern portions of the district, including most of the comparatively thinly populated Alexander Nevskii subdistrict, were inhabited mostly by workers, the Liteinyi subdistrict was one of the more well-to-do, politically conservative parts of Petrograd. There were a few large factories and railway yards in the district; more typical were smaller industrial and commercial enterprises—electrical generating plants, textile and paper mills, construction firms, cigarette factories, printing and other small craft workshops, laundries, bakeries, shops, hotels, restaurants, cafes, casinos, houses of prostitution, and theaters and clubs of all kinds. Quartered in the district as well were several large and strategically important military units. Nonetheless, the approximately 30,000 workers and roughly similar number of soldiers in the district in April 1917 constituted less than 15 percent of the total population. The large majority of inhabitants belonged to the lower and middle bourgeoisie.[2]

In view of the socioeconomic structure of the First City District in 1917, a soviet of workers' and soldiers' deputies was something of an anomaly there. Much more appropriate to the locale, it would seem, were district dumas, formed as an extension of the Provisional Government in the first weeks and months after the February Revolution and in which all classes of the population were represented. Thus, in March 1917 district dumas, with a panoply of associated militia commissariats and food-supply and other administrative boards, were established in each of the First City District's three subdistricts. As elsewhere in the city, however, at roughly the same time a First City District soviet, headed by an elective executive committee, came into being, in principle as the district-level arm of the Petrograd Soviet.[3]

From the time of its inception until May 1917, the First City District soviet was composed overwhelmingly of moderate socialists; only a very few Bolsheviks disrupted a solid phalanx of middle-of-the-road Mensheviks and SRs. Under the latter's tutelage, the district soviet set for itself the relatively modest aims of carrying out directives of the Petrograd Soviet, helping ensure democratization of other local political and administrative institutions then being formed, defending the professional interests of workers and soldiers, and carrying out a broad program of educational activities.[4]

In May, however, the Bolsheviks took advantage of rapidly rising popular dissatisfaction with the cautious internal and traditional foreign policies of the first Provisional Government to win a majority in the First City District soviet,[5] and from that time on a bloc of left deputies headed by the Bolsheviks and including left Mensheviks and Left SRs, as well as Interdistrict Committee representatives, directed the First City District soviet's work. Of course, if a soviet of workers' and soldiers' deputies was out of place in the First City District in 1917, this was all the more true of one directed by the extreme left. The results of district duma elections also held in May, in which the Bolshevik/Menshevik-Internationalist slate was completely overwhelmed by the moderate socialist slate and even the Kadets, were a more accurate barometer of the political outlook in the First City District at this time.[6]

The few Soviet memoirists and historians who have written about the work of the First City District soviet after the reorganization of its leadership at the end of May have tended to emphasize the fierce arguments about vital national issues that erupted from time to time between the Bolsheviks, on the one hand, and the moderate socialists, on the other.[7] This emphasis is not entirely misplaced. Yet, when one studies the primary documents of the time from the perspective of nearly seventy years, what seems remarkable is less the existence of such conflict over national political issues than the broad general agreement that seems to have prevailed among most deputies on local problems, which, it should be underscored, were the soviet's main concern. Also worthy of note is the degree to which, even after the Bolshevik surge in May, the soviet continued to operate as a relatively democratic forum, by and large still unified behind the relatively modest objectives set in April.[8]

The First City District Soviet, October 1917–June 1918

During the first nine months after the October Revolution, the role of the First City District soviet in local governmental and administrative affairs expanded quickly, despite the fact that still only a small percentage of the local population was represented in it. By early summer 1918, the district soviet had all but entirely displaced subdistrict dumas and municipal boards and was the primary institution of government at the local level.

Several aspects of this development seem particularly germane. One factor is what might be called the democratic legacy of 1917 in the First City District soviet—that is, a tradition of populist inclinations and democratic collaboration among representatives of political parties and worker-soldier delegates generally, especially on matters of local concern. This tradition broke down in the wake of October, the suppression of the Constituent Assembly, and the eruption of worker frustration with Soviet power in the early spring of 1918. But it was subsequently revived for a fleeting time. A second significant characteristic is the degree to which early changes in the role and position of the First City District soviet appear to have been gradual, unplanned, and unsystematic, with surprisingly little direction or attempts at control by higher governmental or party authorities. Probably at work here were in part the horrendous political, social, cultural, and economic problems that Bolshevik authorities faced on the morrow of October; conditions in the sprawling First City District mirrored the plight of the Bolsheviks nationally in these first months. City and district authorities, attempting to cope with expanding chaos and to keep Petrograd running, at first sought to utilize, insofar as possible, existing municipal legislative, administrative, and even police and judicial institutions, and whatever specialized personnel in these agencies were willing to remain on the job. This was especially true in such areas of fundamental leftist weakness as the First City District.

In developing initial policies toward holdover political and economic institutions, the First City District soviet appears to have been largely on its own.[9] To be sure, during this initial period some of the First City District soviet's new functions were added at the direction of higher bodies; most, however, were self-generated. That is to say, the district soviet itself, as much as any outside body, defined its new and vastly enhanced role in response to emerging local needs and concerns. At the same time, despite this expansion and diversification of functions, the soviet's structure remained essentially unchanged. More often than not, existing sections of the soviet simply took on new and different responsibilities. Two important new permanent institutions established early by the First City District were a network of people's courts and an investigating commission. These were, however, exceptions. By and large, it was not until well into the spring of 1918 that more or less permanent sections of the district soviet, and other permanent soviet institutions with clearly defined responsibilities, began to be formed.

By the end of May the separate sections and commissions belonging to the First City District soviet numbered over twenty. There now existed, among others, a legal section that provided legal advice and notary services to the soviet and to private individuals, registered and examined regulations from the prerevolutionary period, offered instruction on the direction and responsibilities of people's courts, and codified official decrees and directives of district authorities; a housing section, the primary purpose of which was to locate space for labor organizations and new administrative institutions and to resettle workers, their families, and Red Army personnel and their dependents in apartments and rooms requisitioned from the bourgeoisie; a social welfare section concerned with such matters as pension and rationing problems, orphan care, poor relief, and the establishment of food kitchens for the unemployed; and a culture and education section, with separate subsections for preschool training and childcare, schools, adult continuing education, and theater and cinema. Additionally, attached to the soviet was a press section, which in April began to put out a substantial district newspaper, *Vestnik pervogo gorodskogo raiona* (News of the First City District).[10]

A brief accounting of the formation and responsibilities of these various sections and commissions may convey a sense of order and rationality in the First City District soviet's development that, the record shows, was often absent.[11] Probably the most serious difficulties encountered by the district soviet related to the all-important food-supply problem, which had contributed mightily to the downfall of both the tsarist government in February 1917 and the Provisional Government in October. Trying to avoid a similar fate the Sovnarkom under Lenin had resorted to a variety of strong regulative measures, culminating in the spring and summer of 1918 with the dispatch to the countryside of massive numbers of workers, the so-called food-procurement detachments, to obtain agricultural products from peasants by force if necessary.

At the district level, beginning in the spring, the First City District soviet had gradually managed to purge and impose effective control over subdistrict food-supply boards. However, this lower-level streamlining went largely for naught because of an increasingly strained relationship between the subdistrict boards and the city food-supply bureaucracy, in which opponents of Soviet power remained firmly and prominently entrenched.

Such problems notwithstanding, by June 1918 virtually all of the functions of the former subdistrict duma boards and agencies had already been transferred or were in the process of being shifted entirely to the district soviet. By an order of July 24, 1918, remaining nonsoviet public agencies were officially dissolved,[12] leaving the district soviet, for all intents and purposes, master in the district, responsible for all aspects of local government, administration, and police protection. The vastly expanded role and status of the First City District soviet, and that of other Petrograd district soviets, were succinctly defined in a carefully formulated declaration, "District Soviets, Their Functions and Organization," featured in the June 1 *Vestnik*.[13]

Laying claim to supreme authority was one thing; finding loyal, qualified personnel to meet constantly expanding obligations was quite another. In 1917 a handful of unpaid volunteers easily recruited from among elected deputies was all the staff that operation of the soviet required. Beginning immediately after the October Revolution, however, the district soviet's need for personnel and demands on it for detachments of individuals to serve here, there, and everywhere were endless. In November and December 1917 the plea was for experienced organizers and agitators to help consolidate the revolution in the provinces and for personnel to fill positions in the national government and city bureaucracies. Beginning in January and February 1918 came insistent demands for Red Army recruits, while a bit later the call was for personnel to staff food procurement detachments. And so it went. And in every case the call was for "the very best people." Because of the First City District's relatively large size and the hostility of much of the citizenry to the Bolsheviks, the local immediate need for cadres far outstripped the pool of qualified individuals upon which the soviet could draw. With the curtailment of production in the few larger factories in the district, and the mass exodus of workers from Petrograd that began in January 1918, this already restricted pool was further reduced.[14]

Earlier, the First City and Liteinyi Bolshevik Party committees could be counted on to provide personnel in an emergency. By spring 1918 this was no longer the case. By then many of the best known and most effective Bolshevik and Left SR First City District soviet leaders of 1917 were no longer in Petrograd. Able, experienced, dedicated individuals who remained filled two and sometimes three full-time administrative positions, for which they were in any case completely unprepared. In these circumstances, to an ever-increasing degree, a good part of the district soviet's work was perforce in the hands of hastily recruited paid administrators, clerks, militiamen, agitators, foremen, and technical personnel. With experienced and committed deputies trying to do so much, and with many vacancies at any one time because of transfers, plenary meetings of the soviet were convened less and less frequently and, even so, were poorly attended. Links with factory workers, so important for leftist success in 1917, were broken (who had time for reports or agitation among constituents when the Germans were at the gates?). More often than not, even important decisions rested with whatever few members of the district soviet happened to be on hand; it is difficult to see how it could have been otherwise. Bolshevik party members, in alliance with Left SRs, continued to direct the First City District soviet in the spring of 1918. By now, however, effective collaboration with moderate socialist deputies had broken down almost completely. Nonetheless, if in practice the policies of the soviet were at this point determined and supported almost exclusively by the Bolsheviks and Left SRs, there is little indication that the Bolshevik citywide Petersburg committee, or lower-level party committees, controlled or even attempted systematically to guide the district soviet's work.

This relatively weak leadership appears to have been the result of three factors, all of them connected with the Bolshevik party organization itself during this period. Far and away the most important factor was the lack of any special concern on the part of most veteran Bolsheviks with the institutionalization of an authoritative and exclusive directing role for party organs in the building of socialism. Among contemporary Soviet historians and many Western specialists in Russian history there is a strongly ingrained assumption that the development of a highly centralized, party-directed authoritarian political system was one of the keys to the ability of the Bolsheviks to survive their early crises and that this organizational model was clearly envisioned and energetically pursued from the start. Leaving aside the development of Lenin's views on this subject, the relevant available sources leave no doubt that the need for a highly structured, all-powerful party dictatorship was by no means apparent to most Petrograd Bolsheviks during the first several months of Soviet rule. In 1917 the Bolsheviks' rallying cry had been "all power to democratic soviets." Then the party had tolerated, indeed even encouraged, a significant measure of decentralization, local initiative, and organizational flexibility, which, as I have argued elsewhere, was of great importance to its ultimate success.[15] In the aftermath of the October Revolution there did not appear to be any need to abandon this tradition—in the short run the egalitarian impulses unleashed by the revolution, coupled with the vacuum caused by the breakdown of old authorities, only served to reinforce it.[16]

A second factor contributing to the Petrograd Bolshevik organization's ineffectiveness at this time was the same colossal attrition of loyal, qualified personnel, and the resulting staffing pressures, that contributed greatly to the fundamental transformation of the First City District soviet. A final factor that helps explain the weak leadership of the Petrograd Bolshevik organization in these early months was the fact that between January and April 1918 it was a participant in, and on occasion it was virtually paralyzed by, the bitter intraparty struggle over ratification of the Treaty of Brest-Litovsk. This relative absence of centralized party controls, then, along with the great independent power at the local level that the district soviet managed to amass in the first months after October, are also noteworthy aspects of the First City District soviet's development at this stage.

The Workers' Conference, the June Soviet Elections, and the Breakdown of the Bolshevik–Left SR Alliance in the First City District

While staunchly proud of their accomplishments and protective of their independent power and importance in the spring of 1918, leaders of the First City District soviet were by no means unconcerned about their increasing isolation and arbitrary methods. In late May 1918, amid ever-increasing signs of imminent famine and of skyrocketing worker discontent, which overnight seemed to revitalize opposition to Soviet rule in the factories, the leadership of the district soviet convened an elected, democratically organized, representative workers' conference. This conference, which lasted some ten days, appears to have been viewed by at least some local leaders not simply as a one-time means of helping undercut opposition movements and attract new cadres to the soviet (in short as an extraordinary means of dealing with an extraordinary emergency), but as just the first of periodic public grass-roots assemblies at which they would have to account formally for their policies before their working-class constituents and seek their advice in regard to future programs—in a sense to renew their popular mandate. It is important to note, as well, that the First City District Workers' Conference was not at all an exclusively Bolshevik–Left SR enterprise. All political groups in the First City District soviet, including Mensheviks and SRs, helped plan and took an important part in its work.

At virtually every session of the conference, the soviet leaders were subject to unrestrained criticism by both factory worker representatives and opposition group spokesmen; in part as a result, the published proceedings of the conference provide a fascinating glimpse into local problems and attitudes.[17] The soviet leadership was constantly and bitterly attacked for, among other things, its handling of virtually all political, economic, social, and military problems (which were pushing Russia into an abyss!), for ignoring the desperate needs and aspirations of the very workers who had put them into power, and for facilitating the transformation of the soviet from an institution for furthering lower-class interests into an arbitrary, isolated, cumbersome paid bureaucracy.

Indeed, almost all of the speeches by representatives of non-Bolshevik political groups at the First City District Workers' Conference reflected confidence that the Bolsheviks were near the end of their rope and that the revolution would soon be put back on track toward a Constituent Assembly and the establishment of a more democratic and broadly based political and social system. Whether the conference discussion concerned administrative mismanagement of the shift from wartime to peacetime industrial production, or food procurement and distribution policies as symbolized in the dispatch to the countryside of armed detachments of workers in search of grain, or the attempt to build a modern army composed virtually exclusively of raw recruits united by no more than a readiness to pledge unswerving obedience to the existing regime, or, finally, the impossibly harsh terms of the Treaty of Brest-Litovsk, it clearly seemed to Menshevik and SR spokesmen that Bolshevik policies, and the Bolsheviks themselves, were bankrupt. The anguished reports of many factory representatives strengthened the opposition's conviction that time was on their side. This underlying assumption was reflected in remarks by opposition spokesmen, such as the Menshevik Segal's declaration to the Bolsheviks during debate on "the current moment": "You want history to surround your name with fine pages, such as surrounded the names of the Paris Communards, but the horror and tragedy of your historical fate lies in the fact that the working class is abandoning you and uniting ever more strongly around the slogan 'Long Live the Constituent Assembly.' "[18]

Was there any justification for such confidence, clearly widespread among Menshevik and SR leaders in the spring of 1918? Had the situation of the Bolsheviks among Petrograd factory workers been decisively undermined, as many reports of factory representatives and the apparent success of opposition agitation among workers seemed to suggest, or were workers, however hungry and disappointed, at bottom still loyal to the soviets, as the Bolsheviks naturally hoped? Did workers criticize the soviets "like a loving mother scolds her children fearful that they might become spoiled," as a Bolshevik factory representative insisted, also during debate on "the current moment,"[19] or did their disaffection go significantly deeper than that? An early, if somewhat ambiguous answer to such questions was provided by partial elections to the First City District soviet in mid-June and comprehensive elections to the Petrograd Soviet in the second half of the month.

A short time after leaders of the First City District soviet responded to signs of deepening worker unrest by convening a representative worker conference, that is, during the second week in June, the leadership of the Petrograd Soviet agreed that new elections, the first comprehensive reelection of Petrograd Soviet deputies since March 1917, would be held during a seven-day period ending June 25.[20] The First City District soviet, for its part, resisted demands for comprehensive elections,[21] obligating itself only to the organization of elections to fill existing vacancies and to replace elected deputies who for one reason or another were unsatisfactory to their electors.[22]

At this time moderate socialist opposition leaders in Petrograd looked to gains in district soviet elections to provide momentum for the vastly more important campaign for control of the Petrograd Soviet. But in the case of the First City District soviet, at least, these hopes were not realized. While the partial elections for district soviet deputies in June 1918 resulted in the Bolsheviks temporarily losing the absolute majority in the soviet that they had previously enjoyed, they nonetheless remained far and away the largest single party. Most important, with the support of their own sympathizers, and that of the Left SRs and their followers, the Bolsheviks were able to retain firm control of the district soviet leadership.[23] This became apparent at a soviet meeting on June 30, when the principle of proportional representation, which had up to now governed composition of such key organs as the executive committee, was discarded. A majority of deputies voted to accept a joint Bolshevik/Left SR slate of committee candidates composed of six Bolsheviks and three Left SRs.[24] In short then, the significant expansion of opposition sentiment at the First City District Workers' Conference was not translated into enhanced Menshevik–SR influence in the district soviet; to the contrary, at this point, for the first time, the opposition was excluded from the district soviet leadership altogether.

Meanwhile, the campaign for control of the Petrograd Soviet had begun as soon as the election dates became known. As specified in the rules governing this election, perhaps the most significant innovation in the make-up of the new city soviet was that now numerically significant representation was given to trade unions, district soviets, factory-shop committees, and district worker conferences, in which the Bolsheviks had overwhelming strength. Significant representation was also given to Bolshevik–Left SR–dominated Red Army and naval units; in fact, only about 260 of 700 plus deputies in the new soviet were to be elected directly in the factories.[25] It was this arbitrary "stacking" of the new soviet, much more than election of "dead souls" from shut-down factories, unfair campaign practices, falsification of the vote, or direct repression, that gave the Bolsheviks an unfair advantage in the contest (press controls, for one, were significantly eased during the campaign). The revised system's advantage for the Bolsheviks was well illustrated by the representation of the First City District Workers' Conference in the new soviet. The workers' conference was reconvened for just one session on June 22, and by majority vote "slate" electoral procedures were also adopted there. As a result, all 28 individuals elected to the Petrograd Soviet by the conference were either Bolsheviks or Left SRs; the sizable Menshevik/SR minority in the conference (27 percent) received no representation at all.[26]

The city soviet election campaign itself, predictably heated and bitter, was a primary focus of popular attention in Petrograd throughout the second half of June; this was the case even in the First City District, where the vast majority of residents were disenfranchised. The Bolsheviks, it is apparent, attached considerable importance to a good showing. While an overall majority in the new soviet was all but assured from the start by the "stacking" described above, and while one should take with a grain of salt a comment attributed to Zinoviev that the Bolsheviks would give up the government in the event of defeat,[27] a failure by the party to retain a solid following among workers in "Red Petrograd" was realistically viewed by local party leaders from Zinoviev on down as a potentially stunning blow. Virtually all the chief figures in the Bolshevik and Left SR Petrograd party hierarchy were mobilized for in the campaign. By means of an intensive "blitz," Soviet spokesmen now attempted to gain back in a few days the popular support that had clearly eroded in the preceding weeks and months of continual crises, when agitation and "party work" had been neglected. The Bolshevik campaign was directed by V. Volodarskii until his assassination by an SR terrorist on June 20. The central theme of the campaign planned by him, trumpeted daily in the Bolshevik press and in round-the-clock factory assemblies and political rallies was that, among the contending parties, only the Bolsheviks and Left SRs stood for the realization of revolutionary goals. The Mensheviks and the SRs, on the other hand, stood for a return to power of the capitalists and for early restoration of all the hated ways of the old regime. A vote for them, so the Bolsheviks contended, was a vote for counterrevolution—there was no middle ground.[28]

Not only the Bolsheviks and Left SRs took the elections seriously; after some initial hesitation, so did the Mensheviks and SRs. In a sense, the emphasis of their campaign was the reverse of that of the Bolsheviks. While the Bolsheviks sought to shift popular attention away from immediate economic troubles to long-term revolutionary goals and emphasized that opposition demands for reconvocation of the Constituent Assembly were no more than a vehicle for the restoration of traditional injustices, the Mensheviks and SRs tried to play on popular anxieties over the threat of famine and the spread of disease, the negative effects of the Brest Treaty, and the horror of expanding civil war to underscore the bankruptcy of the Soviet experiment and the importance of the Constituent Assembly as perhaps the only means of averting total catastrophe.[29]

The election campaign and balloting dragged on for nearly three weeks; as soon as the first scattered returns became available, however, each side tried to interpret them to advantage.[30] Close to final, detailed vote breakdowns appearing in *Severnaia Kommuna* during the first week in July revealed that the Bolsheviks had done surprisingly well.[31] As expected, their greatest successes were among Red Army soldiers and, to only a slightly lesser degree, in the trade unions, district soviets, and worker conferences. But at the same time, approximately 50 percent of the deputies elected directly in the factories were Bolshevik (127 of 260 deputies). While the opposition registered some gains in the Putilov factory and a few other large plants, the Bolshevik party clearly remained the political group with the strongest support among Petrograd workers generally. Comparison of election results in the First City District with the reports of factory representatives at the First City District Workers' Conference suggests the effectiveness of the Bolshevik electoral campaign. The party held its own in factories where it had been strongest in late May and early June and managed to regain a measure of respectability in at least some plants where the anti-Bolshevik mood had seemed most intense earlier. In the aftermath of the election, even some opposition representatives appeared to concede the legitimacy of the results. As a commentator, no friend of the Bolsheviks, lamented in the July 2 *Novaia Zhizn'*, "one cannot escape the fact that many workers still have not outgrown Bolshevik 'communism' and continue to consider soviet power, for better of for worse, the representative of their interests. They associate it with their fate and the fate of the workers' movement."[32]

These results of the June 1918 soviet elections inevitably strengthened the Bolsheviks' hand in Petrograd local politics. The abortive Left SR rising that erupted in Moscow on July 6, and spread to Petrograd the next day, had a similar effect, at least in the short-run. Details of this unmitigated fiasco fall outside the scope of this essay.[33] Suffice it to record here that at this juncture the Left SRs, fundamentally opposed to the Brest Treaty and to Bolshevik grain procurement policies and also frustrated in their attempts to win majority support for their positions on these issues in the soviets, masterminded the assassination of the German ambassador to Moscow, Count Mirbach. His sensational killing was intended to precipitate military reprisals by the Germans and make "revolutionary war" unavoidable. In the event, however, the Soviet government was able to mollify the Germans with respect to Mirbach's death and to quickly suppress the Left SR risings in Moscow and Petrograd. Following this debacle, Left SR officials in the Petrograd Soviet who did not publicly disassociate themselves from their central committee and pledge their support of the resolutions of the just completed Fifth All-Russian Congress of Soviets were banned from the soviet leadership. Most rejected the pledge, and fifteen seats allotted to them in the new Executive Committee were left vacant.[34]

The fate of Left SR leaders in the First City District soviet was more complex. As we have just seen, a new district soviet executive committee with three Left SRs had only recently been installed. Two of these Left SRs had immediately disassociated themselves from the insurrection and put themselves at the soviet's disposal (the third went into hiding). It was clear to Bolshevik district soviet leaders that the two had had no inkling of the plans being hatched by their central committee in Moscow and indeed were not even party to subsequent related actions in Petrograd. After the entire Left SR district soviet fraction agreed to condemn the actions of the Left SR central committee as "wrong" and "shameful," the Left SRs were permitted to retain their positions.[35] Several district soviet deputies registered as Left SR sympathizers, however, now joined the Bolshevik camp. As time went on, the relationship between Left SRs and Bolsheviks in the First City District soviet became increasingly strained. In retrospect, it is clear that the significant influence the Left SRs had hitherto enjoyed in the district soviet was never restored.

Coming on the heels of the June soviet elections, the breakdown of the Bolshevik–Left SR alliance left the Bolsheviks with a virtual monopoly of power in the First City District soviet. For local workers and soldiers, all this effectively eliminated practical alternatives to the political course being pursued by the Bolsheviks. As far as Bolshevik leaders were concerned, this was the positive side of the events of June and July. The negative side was that with the breakup of the Bolshevik–Left SR alliance, the district soviet's already limited base of support was further narrowed. Responsible party leaders were uneasy about this, and it is no coincidence that at the same soviet meeting at which a policy toward the Left SRs was decided on, it was also unanimously agreed to immediately convene another broadly representative workers' conference.[36] This conference, however, does not appear to have been held.

The Petrograd Soviet versus the First City District Soviet, June 1918–May 1919

The immense independent power and governmental authority that the First City District soviet acquired during the first nine months after the October Revolution was not destined to last long. In the spring of 1918, the relatively passive orientation of the local Bolshevik party organization toward governmental and administrative affairs had begun to change. During the second half of the year, the district party committee started to play a systematic and direct role in the soviet's direction. This was still a far cry from party dominated "democratic centralism," but it was a start. Roughly concomitantly, a variety of governmental institutions at the regional and city levels gradually began to overcome local resistance and assert effective authority over the district soviet's myriad activities. If anything these trends greatly accelerated in the course of the economic and military emergencies of 1919, with the result that by 1920, the First City District soviet was all but bankrupt as an independent democratic political authority, its numerous sections and agencies having become no more than territorial extensions of corresponding city administrative departments.

Framed against specific crises of the Civil War period, the dynamics of these changes emerge fairly clearly. For example, as early as April 1918, the Bolshevik Petersburg Committee, increasingly alarmed by the separateness and independence of district soviets, had formally agreed that "the weakness and incompleteness of party control over soviet work in the districts in the post-October period has led to a number of harmful consequences and first of all, has had a disastrous effect on the activity of district soviets themselves."[37] Nonetheless, not until the early summer, it seems, was a Bolshevik district soviet fraction formally responsible to the district party committee actually established (from then on fraction meetings normally preceded all general meetings of the soviet). This systematization of the relationship between party and soviet appears to have been directly connected to organizational streamlining undertaken in response to, among other things, deepening economic chaos and the significant expansion of the Civil War.

It is noteworthy that while relations between the Bolshevik Party organization at the city level, on the one hand, and the leadership of the Petrograd Soviet and of the Union of Communes of the Northern Region,[38] on the other, were confused and contentious throughout the Civil War period,[39] this does not appear to have been the case in the districts. In the First City District, at any rate, a stable, mutually supportive relationship between party and soviet seems to have developed naturally early on. Despite continuing emphasis on party recruitment, the fundamental critical shortage of reliable, qualified leadership personnel, aggravated by the breakdown of the Bolshevik–Left SR alliance, inevitably led to a situation in which the chief figures in the Bolshevik district party committee and the district soviet were practically the same. (Thus, while serving as chairman of the district soviet, Anton Korsak, for one, also presided at party meetings.) At this time, nominations of individuals for soviet leadership posts began to be initiated by the local party committee. First City District soviet officials made frequent reports on their work at party meetings; moreover, with the district soviet's blessing, the district party committee attempted as best it could to establish reliable party collectives in all of the main district soviet sections and organs.[40]

At moments of particularly grave crisis beginning early in 1919, when both the soviet and the party organization were virtually emasculated by personnel transfers, the First City District Bolshevik committee and the executive committee of the First City District soviet developed the practice of meeting jointly.[41] Indeed, later in 1919, when Petrograd was directly threatened by White military forces, distinctions between party and soviet often appeared to break down altogether.[42] Already in mid-November 1918, lengthy "Party Life" sections and summaries of district party meetings and activities had begun to appear in the *Vestnik*.[43] They were soon regular *Vestnik* features, and by spring 1919, the *Vestnik* sometimes contained almost as much news of party activity as of soviet affairs. Earlier, in February 1919, at the height of the controversy between city party and soviet organs over their respective authority and roles, the relationship of the party to soviets was the main agenda item of a First City District Bolshevik party committee meeting.[44] But this discussion does not appear to have reflected any fundamental problem at that level; all the while, as nearly as I can tell, relations between party and soviet in the First City District were harmonious.

Efforts by higher governmental organs in Petrograd to assert authority over district soviets fall into two main categories: (1) those involving promulgation of comprehensive legislation to significantly restrict the authority of district soviets and to integrate district soviet sections generally into the city bureaucracy and (2) a more gradual, piecemeal, and natural centralizing process whereby individual city administrative departments sought to systematize the organization and control the activity of district soviet sections in their own spheres of competence. One of the first proposals falling into the first category was embodied in a draft organizational plan apparently drawn up in April 1918 in connection with the establishment of the Petrograd Labor Commune following the transfer to Moscow of the Soviet national government.[45] According to this plan, the Petrograd Soviet was to be the highest organ of local government in Petrograd. City administrative departments (commissariats of the Petrograd Labor Commune) were to be responsible to the Petrograd Soviet. They were to be in charge of all institutions and activities in their respective fields; in this connection, district soviet sections were to be removed from the control of district soviets and turned into local agencies of city departments.

These provisions were not implemented at the time, in all likelihood primarily because of the fierce opposition of district soviets acting individually or in concert through the Interdistrict Conference. The response at the local level to centralizing proposals such as this was reflected in, among other things, the *Vestnik* declaration of June 1, 1919, "District Soviets, Their Functions and Organization," described above, and an editorial, "Centralization and District Soviets," which was prominently featured in the July 6 *Vestnik*. The explicit purpose of the editorial was to discuss whether district soviets were needed at all and what their proper role ought to be if they were retained. "These questions have been discussed at the center and at various conferences," the editorial explained, "and the conclusion has always been that keeping district soviets is a matter of life and death." According to the editorial, not only were district soviets absolutely essential, the unifying role played by the Interdistrict Conference was equally crucial as well.[46] Hence, the primary conclusion of the editorial was that a critical immediate need in the prevailing situation was the regularization and formalization of the relationship and status of district soviets and the Interdistrict Conference, on the one hand, and central organs of the Petrograd Labor Commune, on the other.[47]

The editorial went on to convey the substance of two related organizational proposals then pending in the Interdistrict Conference. One was a draft constitution for the Petrograd Labor Commune as a whole introduced by the Novoderevenskii district soviet, presumably as an alternative to the comprehensive organizational plan proposed by higher authorities, and the other was an organizational scheme for district soviets put forward by the Petrograd district soviet. Far from encouraging centralization under the aegis of higher authorities, the organizational proposals pending in the Interdistrict Conference were most of all a clear and unequivocal assertion of district soviet individual and collective authority. For example, paragraph one of the proposed constitution for the Petrograd Labor Commune as a whole specified that individual districts were to be self-governing insofar as possible; only such "indivisible" functions as street car transport, water supply, telephone service, communication with other cities, and so on were to be responsibility of centralized institutions. According to paragraph two of the proposed constitution, distinctions between state, municipal, and district governmental functions were to be abolished and district soviets were to be simultaneously state, city, and district organs. Parallel institutions not under the district soviet's control, except those concerned with indivisible functions provided for in paragraph one, would no longer be permitted.

The task of coordinating and, if necessary, regulating the work of district soviets, as stated in paragraph three of this proposed constitution, was to be delegated not to the Petrograd Soviet but to interdistrict conferences of district soviet section heads, or, in exceptional circumstances, of general interdistrict meetings of section members. Indeed, even the "individual" communewide functions alluded to in paragraph one were to be the responsibility of special central administrative boards. The Petrograd Soviet was only to act on important policy matters relating to life in the Petrograd Labor Commune generally, whatever that meant. This not enough, the Petrograd Soviet was henceforth to be made up of all district soviet deputies and board members; it was no longer to be elected independently. One of the few fundamental questions relating to city government not touched on in the draft constitution, that of taxing power, was settled in favor of district soviets in the proposed district soviet organizational plan. Thus paragraph three of the plan specified that the district soviet was the collection agency for national and city taxes and also had the right to levy an independent tax for its own upkeep.[48]

No doubt in part because of conflict over such diametrically opposed organizational plans, during the second half of 1918, higher governmental authorities' policies toward Petrograd district soviets were ambiguous. For the time being, district soviets were the only viable administrative institutions in the districts, and city officials had no alternative to relying on them as need arose; consequently, at the same time that efforts were continued to impose comprehensive controls over district soviets, they were delegated important new responsibilities. A good illustration of this is a government decree of fall 1918, relating to the creation of "house committees of the poor."[49]

Initially formed by residents of larger apartment houses in the immediate aftermath of the February Revolution, apparently primarily for protection, elective house committees soon became responsible for overseeing general housekeeping tasks, for a variety of civic duties, and for representing tenant concerns. After October, a high percentage of these committees, especially those in more prosperous areas of Petrograd such as the First City District, were naturally hostile to the Bolsheviks and actively opposed Soviet power. Hence it is not surprising that by a decree issued by the Department of Justice of the Petrograd Labor Commune in September 1918 existing house committees were dissolved; district soviets were now given the responsibility of supervising the election and operation of new, hopefully supportive "house committees of the poor."

For the First City District soviet, establishing these new house committees of the poor was a gigantic undertaking, clearly one of its main preoccupations during the fall and winter months of 1918–19. The difficulties it encountered in carrying out this task, which among other things involved an attempt to move substantial numbers of factory workers into apartment buildings with insufficient numbers of tenants classified as workers and to organize and certify elections in something on the order of three thousand buildings, were reported in great detail in the *Vestnik*. In the context of our present concern, however, the main point is that for a time in 1918 and 1919, work connected with establishment of house committees of the poor significantly enhanced the importance of Petrograd district soviets, the First City District soviet among them, and in this way temporarily undermined efforts by higher authorities to bring district soviets to heel.

While attempts to impose comprehensive controls over district soviets and their sections remained at a standstill, and district soviets were even delegated new tasks, in retrospect it is clear that pressures on them were not eased and that they were in fact dealt two major blows at this time. The first of these was apparently suffered around the middle of 1918, when district soviets appear to have lost much of the budgetary autonomy that they had previously enjoyed. To ascertain precisely how and when this change occurred is difficult, but, in any case, by the end of 1918 the independent taxing powers of district soviets were greatly restricted and many, if not all, major budget allocations were subject to prior approval by the Petrograd Soviet. To complicate matters further, even officials in Moscow were involved in district soviet financing.[50] This power over district soviet funding was subsequently used by higher authorities as a means of applying pressure on district soviets and led to continual friction between district finance sections and the Petrograd Soviet's budget office.

The second of these blows to the independence of district soviets came in December 1918, when by action of the Petrograd Soviet, separate district soviet elections were discontinued.[51] From then on, for the duration of the Civil War, the First City District soviet was made up exclusively of Petrograd Soviet deputies from the First City District (this was obviously the reverse of the district soviet proposal that the Petrograd Soviet be composed of district soviet deputies). Probably motivated largely by the aim of stretching scarce human resources, and likely accepted on this basis in the districts, this practice had negative effects on the operation of district soviets that were felt almost immediately. In the First City District soviet, attendance at general meetings in January and February 1919 dropped to new lows; continual appeals to absent deputies, alternating with threats of expulsion, failed to measurably improve the situation.[52]

Meanwhile, during the second half of 1918 and the beginning of 1919, gradual centralization began to prevail in specific administrative areas. The pages of the *Vestnik* provide valuable examples of this process in the areas of education, sanitation and health, crime control and the courts, and perhaps most importantly economic administration. As early as July 1918, for instance, the Soviet of the Economy of the Union of Communes of the Northern Region (SNKhSR) had issued organizational guidelines for district economic sections that set forth their goals and tasks, attempted to systematize their organization, and established their relation to the SNKhSR and to parent district soviets.[53] In this regard, these guidelines were sufficiently ambiguous and sensitive to the aspirations of district soviets to be mutually acceptable. Thus, while district economic sections were said to be responsible for controlling and organizing the local economy under the direction of the SNKhSR, the sections were expressly identified as organs of the district soviet, not the SNKhSR. Permanent contact between the SNKhSR and district soviets was to be maintained through the mutual exchange of delegates (this was deemed especially important during the period of socialist construction; after that, presumably, the district soviet might be more, not less, independent). Representatives of economic sections, one per district, were given the right to participate in plenary meetings of the SNKhSR, albeit without voting rights. Moreover, a specific role was established for interdistrict conferences of economic section representatives; these were to be convened no less than twice a month to discuss current issues and to coordinate activities.

These guidelines appear to have enabled the SNKhSR and the district soviet sections to develop a fairly stable relationship in the short run. Economic administration, however, remained extraordinarily inefficient, the city and districts each possessing substantial bureaucracies with overlapping functions and responsibilities; each side remained jealously protective of its prerogative and highly critical of the other. Spurred on by a sudden worsening of the economic situation at the end of 1918, the SNKhSR developed a plan to further centralize economic administration under a new organ, the Petrograd Communal Economy Council. Under this plan, first announced in December 1918, all soviet sections concerned with any aspect of economic administration were to be consolidated into district communal economy councils and to be strictly subordinated to the Petrograd Communal Economy Council. At this critical juncture even most First City District soviet officials acknowledged the need for consolidation and streamlining of local government economic institutions. But in contrast to higher authorities, who insisted on immediate centralization from above to bring order out of the existing chaos, district soviet spokesmen, acting jointly through the Interdistrict Conference and interdistrict conferences of district soviet section heads, remained thoroughly suspicious and critical of central institutions. Believing that the latter were still dominated by carry-over officials hostile to the revolution, they steadfastly demanded stronger autonomous district level administrative and coordinating institutions, and "controls from below," to remedy existing problems.[54] Furious debate over the new SNKhSR plan dragged on for months and was in fact still going on well after February 1919, when the SNKhSR itself was dissolved.[55] Meanwhile, both at the city and district levels, reform of economic institutions was stalled. In March, after being threatened with severe budget penalties, the First City District soviet shifted some economic management functions to the city.[56] Moreover, in early April the First City District soviet amalgamated its economic, labor, housing, food supply, and fuel sections, among others, into a single consolidated communal economy section.[57] Not until May 1919, however, when a seemingly dire military emergency suddenly intensified pressures for immediate, more drastic economic reform, did the First City District soviet tacitly approve a revised organizational plan for communal economy councils put forward by the Petrograd Soviet. This plan incorporated some modest new concessions to district soviets but, overall, greatly enhanced the controlling authority of the center. While the revised plan provided for the convocation of periodic interdistrict conferences of district soviet representatives to help coordinate the work of new, consolidated district communal economy sections, the latter were formally designated "executive organs of the Petrograd Communal Economy Council"; in time, they were effectively incorporated into the city economic bureaucracy.[58]

The Impact of the 1919 Military Emergencies in the First City District Soviet

It was during the two great military emergencies of 1919 in Petrograd—the danger presented by the victories of White forces in Finland in May and June 1919 and the threat posed by the apparently irresistible advance of Yudenich's troops the following fall—that the autonomy of the First City District soviet and other Petrograd district soviets was completely and irreversibly undermined. Here again, a major contributing factor was horrendous personnel losses, which had already begun to sap the soviets' vitality soon after October. During the second half of 1918 and the first months of 1919, the First City District Bolshevik Committee had been continually both purging its ranks of undesirables and adding new recruits,[59] at least a portion of whom were assigned to the First City District soviet. However, at the height of the May emergency, the district party organization was suddenly ordered to ready 20 percent of its membership for service at the front. The response to this mobilization was apparently so effective that most of the party collectives that had been built up with great effort in the preceding months were either stripped to the bone or rendered totally inoperative. Included in the mobilization were virtually all experienced lower level leaders who were at all familiar with the use of weapons. In the First City District soviet, the last remaining Bolshevik veterans of 1917, as well as a high percentage of party leaders who rose to prominence after October, were now transferred, most to service on the Northwestern Front or on the Don.[60]

During these critical months, largely as a result of the severe personnel shortage, structural distinctions between party and soviet all but disappeared.[61] Indeed, in the early summer of 1919, the district soviet as such, and even its executive committee, virtually ceased to function. Mobilization of recruits and other defense preparations were directed by an authoritative party-designated revolutionary troika "behind closed doors."[62] Municipal services were supplied by appropriate district soviet sections, all of them hopelessly understaffed. In the prevailing circumstances, the district sections had only the city to turn to for leadership and help; consequently, while ties between district soviet sections and the district soviet leadership were significantly weakened in the spring and early summer of 1919, the reverse was true of linkages between the district sections and city departments.

A new First City District soviet was formed following elections to the Petrograd Soviet in mid-July 1919, and at this point some local level leaders still hoped the district soviet might be rejuvenated. Commenting on the first general meeting of the soviet in over two months, a *Vestnik* observer confidently wrote that the session showed that "the activity of the district soviet was once again on a normal course."[63]

But this was not to be. In retrospect, it is clear that the press of events had by now rendered the First City District soviet all but helpless. At the end of August 1919, a clash between an interdistrict conference of heads of district soviet financial sections and the Petrograd Soviet over taxing authority ended with the suppression of the former[64]—a sign of the times. More fundamentally, on September 3, 1919, the Executive Committee of the Petrograd Soviet issued special new statutes that harnessed all district soviet sections to city departments and effectively emasculated district soviets along the lines first proposed and then dropped a year and a half earlier.[65] According to these statutes, district soviet sections were placed under the exclusive control of corresponding departments of the Petrograd Soviet; district soviet executive committees were restricted to "general control" over the activities of their own sections—under no circumstances were they to "meddle" in section affairs; and transfer of personnel in district soviet sections was permitted only on the approval of the Presidium of the Petrograd Soviet.[66]

These statutes were realistically perceived in the districts as stripping district soviets of all real power and authority; predictably, they stirred another howl. At the end of November 1919, the tip of this controversy was revealed in an unusual exchange of letters published on *Petrogradskaia pravda*'s front page. In the course of this exchange, an individual identified only as A. Mushtakov defended centralization and the harnessing of district soviets, contending that while autonomous soviets had been forced to devise new organizational forms on their own as they engaged in the task of destroying the old bourgeois order, by about April 1918 the smashing of the old order had basically been completed. From then on centralized planning and organization had rightfully become the order of the day and, indeed, had already been significantly advanced. Letters from D. Trilisser and Nik-Bergen, not otherwise identified, however, passionately defended district soviets, arguing, among other things, that the possible economies that would result from centralization were more than outweighed by the absolutely crucial organizational roles that district soviets possessing considerable freedom of initiative could continue to play, and that the masses had become accustomed to their district soviets and related to them in ways that they could never relate to centralized city departments. Moreover, they reiterated the familiar claim that it would be downright dangerous to tie district soviets too closely to city departments inasmuch as the latter were still dominated by bureaucrats from prerevolutionary times. As Nik-Bergen's letter put the matter,

> to deprive district soviets of the possibility of spontaneous activity and to transform them into nothing more than technical organs of central municipal institutions means that they will be irreversibly reduced to hopeless bureaucracies, mired in red tape. The city departments have not undergone much of an internal

purge and if one is to consider administrative centralization, surely this should not come before all of them have been sanitized and vitalized through the influence on them of district soviets.

"We are heading toward centralization," concluded Trilisser, "but now is too early for it."[67]

In the prevailing circumstances, the arguments of the proponents of "district power" fell on deaf ears. In a recent history of the Petrograd Soviet during the Civil War, the Leningrad historian A. V. Gogolevskii implies that the provisions of the fall 1919 district soviet statutes were effectively implemented.[68] Although I have not yet studied this phase of the First City District soviet's evolution in detail, it seems likely that this was the case. Even earlier, in July 1919, the complete demoralization of the First City District soviet was mirrored in the fate of the *Vestnik*, which during its fourteen-month existence had been the voice of the First City District soviet, if not of Petrograd district soviets generally. On more than one occasion in 1918 and 1919, higher authorities in Petrograd had attempted to shut the paper down, ostensibly because of a critical shortage of newsprint.[69] On each of these occasions, the leadership of the First City District soviet had mounted a strong public protest and higher authorities had backed off.[70] The city administration issued the last of their shut-down orders on July 24, 1919; the very next day, the district soviet's leadership responded by appointing a special *Vestnik* "liquidation" commission.[71] The final issue of the paper, which announced the *Vestnik*'s demise on the back page, was published on July 30.

Conclusion

What then does the experience of the First City District soviet contribute to discussion of the role of various causal factors, in particular the Civil War, in shaping the early Soviet system? Clearly, the evidence as presented here tends to support the side of those who stress the importance of events and responses to them in shaping the outcome of the revolution. To be sure, revolutionary ideology and organizational habits rooted in the prerevolutionary period helped shape the behavior of Bolshevik party veterans in times of crisis after October; this factor deserves significantly greater attention than the scope of this paper has permitted. Nonetheless, it seems clear that during the period focused on in this essay, the main justification for centralization on the part of higher authorities was invariably that of eliminating organizational chaos and making optimum use of critically scarce resources in a time of dire national emergency. Although many First City District soviet officials clearly operated on the assumption that decentralization and proletarian self-government were good in and of themselves, their primary argument in resisting limitations on their authority was that district soviets, standing closest to the masses, were best able to define revolutionary goals and to mobilize and organize the masses for their realization.

At the same time, the dynamics and chronology of political developments in early Soviet Russia, at least as they are reflected in the early evolution of the First City District soviet, appear somewhat more complex than even those who stress the importance of events over ideology usually suggest. On the one hand, within the district soviet itself the breakdown of democratic practices and the bureaucratization of political affairs began almost at once after October, and certainly well before the full explosion of what is usually considered the Civil War crisis in May and June 1918. (The first workers' conference in the First City District, which can fairly be viewed as an honest attempt to restore meaningful reciprocal linkages with the masses and, more fundamentally, to return to the populist and more democratic ideals and practices of 1917 was, as nearly as I can determine, the last effort of its kind.) On the other hand, not until the emergencies of early summer 1918 did the Bolshevik party committee in the First City District begin to play a systematic, direct role in the direction of the district soviet. Higher governmental authorities initially sought to impose comprehensive controls over the district soviet in April 1918; however, in the face of strong individual and collective district soviet opposition to this threat, city-level officials were for the time being forced to make do with gradual, piecemeal centralization. Not until after the strength and integrity of the district soviet had been decisively undermined by the economic and military crises of 1919 was local resistance finally overcome and the district soviet effectively eliminated, once and for all, as a significant autonomous political entity.

In conclusion, it is worth noting that the local government established by the First City District soviet following the October revolution does seem to have been a revolutionary dictatorship of the proletariat in that many of the most influential leaders in the soviet, not to speak of rank-and-file section staff, appear to have been of working-class origin, wholly new to government, and earnestly committed to effecting meaningful revolutionary change in a largely hostile environment. An important related issue that also merits further study is the degree to which the accusations of district soviet spokesmen like Nik-Bergin regarding the continued strong influence in the city bureaucracy of representatives of the old regime were grounded in fact. If these claims were well founded, then, ironically, a genuine workers' government in the First City District was in a sense suppressed during the Civil War period by the very elements against whom the Civil War was being waged.

NOTES

1. The first two sections of this essay are abridged adaptions of a companion paper, published as "The Evolution of Local Soviets in Petrograd, November 1917-June 1918: The Case of the First City District Soviet," *Slavic Review*, Spring 1987, pp. 20–37. Both papers are part of a broader study, "Petrograd Politics and Society, 1917–1920," currently in progress.

2. For a useful description of the First City District in 1917–18 see E. R. Levitas, "O partiinoi i sovetskoi rabote v 1-m gorodskom raione," in *V ogne revoliutsionnykh boev: Raiony Petrograda v dvukh revoliutsiiakh 1917 g.* (Moscow, 1967), pp. 411–14. See Z. V. Stepanov, *Rabochie Petrograda v period podgotovki i provedeniia Oktiabr'skogo vooruzhennogo vosstaniia* (Moscow-Leningrad, 1965), p. 30, for data on workers in the First City District.

3. The formation of district soviets in Petrograd and their role in 1917 are discussed in Akademiia nauk SSSR, Leningradskoe otdelenie instituta istorii, *Raionnye sovety Petrograda v 1917 godu: Protokoly, rezoliutsii, postanovleniia obshchikh sobranii i zasedanii ispolnitel'nykh komitetov*, 3 vols. (Moscow-Leningrad, 1964–16), 3–8. A fuller discussion is contained in B. D. Gal'perina, "Raionnye sovety Petrograda v 1917 g.," Kandidat dissertation, Leningrad Branch, Institute of History, USSR Academy of Sciences, Leningrad, 1968. See also Rex A. Wade, "The Raionnye Sovety of Petrograd: The Role of Local Political Bodies in the Russian Revolution," *Jahrbücher fur Geschichte Osteuropas*, 1972, vol. 20, pp. 226–40.

4. *Raionnye sovety Petrograda v 1917 godu*, 1:183.

5. Gal'perina, "Raionnye sovety Petrograda v 1917 g.," p. 161.; *Pravda*, June 8, 1917, p. 4; *Vestnik soveta 1-go gorodskogo raiona*, August 28, 1918, no. 28, pp. 4–5.

6. *Novoe vremia*, June 2, 1917, p. 2.

7. Lending special piquancy to these clashes between opposing sides in the First City District soviet during this period was the fact that, while the chief spokesman for the Bolshevik side was the veteran revolutionary Semen Nakhimson, the leader of the Menshevik-SR bloc was the Menshevik Fedor Nakhimson, a lawyer by profession, a persuasive orator, and Semen's brother. In the First City District soviet the warring brothers were commonly referred to as Nakhimson I (Semen) and Nakhimson II (Fedor) and were usually at each other's throats. Levitas, "O partiinoi i sovetskoi rabote," pp. 422–23.

8. Thus, in early June, when the district soviet was invited to send representatives to reorganized district and subdistrict food-supply and distribution committees, the deputies, including the Bolsheviks, turned down the invitation. That Bolsheviks should have abjured participation in "coalition" organs was fully consistent with their opposition to socialist collaboration with liberals nationally. What is unexpected is that the Bolshevik deputies justified leaving management of food supplies exclusively in the hands of district dumas, then under the control of Kadets and moderate socialists, because, in the words of the Bolshevik-sponsored resolution on the issue, they had been elected on a "broad democratic basis" (*Raionnye sovety Petrograda v 1917 godu*, 1:199).

9. For example, not until the end of 1917 did it receive direction regarding the handling of counterrevolutionary subdistrict dumas; at that time, the central authorities encouraged all district soviets to dissolve local dumas if this seemed warranted. Shortly thereafter, dumas in the Liteinyi, Moskovskii, and Aleksandr Nevskii subdistricts were deposed and new elections promised. In practice, neither in the three dumas in the First City District nor in any other lower-level duma in Petrograd were these elections ever held. For the time being, however, the First City District soviet continued to try to work through the old subdistrict duma boards and militia commissariats as best it could. Only gradually did many of these agencies come to be headed by district soviet appointees and become formally responsible to the soviet; this process was not completed until the late spring.

10. *Pervaia konferentsiia rabochikh i krasnoarmeiskikh deputatov l-go gorodskogo raiona (stenograficheskie otchety 24 maia-5 iiunia)* (Petrograd, 1918), pp. 320–23. The paper's primary purpose was to keep residents informed about district soviet activities and about developments relating to food supply, health and sanitation problems, the organization of local militia and Red Army forces, and other matters of particular importance to them. Usually published on Wednesday and Saturdays in eight- to ten-

page editions, from May 1 (April 18), 1918, until July 30, 19:9, when the paper was ordered shut down, it is a mine of detailed information about varied phases of daily life in the district.

11. For example, for nearly three months the soviet continued to try, largely unsuccessfully, to assert control over and to reshape the existing militia. *Vestnik*, May 15 (2), 1918, no. 3, pp. 2–3; May 18 (6), 1918, no. 4, p. 3; May 29 (16), 1918, no. 7, p. 5.

12. B. D. Gal'perina and V. I. Startsev, "Sovety rabochikh i soldatskikh deputatov Petrograda v bor'be za ovladenie aparatom gorodskogo obshchestvennogo upravlevniia (noiabr' 1917-noiabr' 1918 g.)," in *Rabochie Leningrada v bor'be za pobedy sotsializma* (Moscow and Leningrad, 1963), p. 101.

13. According to this declaration, within the boundaries of the district the power of the district soviet was absolute. Local Red Army commissariats, while retaining autonomy in non–district-specific matters, as well as separate chains of command, constituted special organs of the district soviet for the settlement of local problems. Among other bodies responsible to the district soviets, apart from the sections and commissions of the soviet itself, were district food-supply and municipal boards, which concomitantly retained their national and regional authority and their links to corresponding central authorities. On the same basis, people's courts were district soviet organs. Moreover, lest anything had been left out, the declaration specified that all commissars and heads of sections and boards within district boundaries were at the disposal of district soviet executive committees and subject to their directives, albeit with the qualification that these accord with the directives and decrees of central authorities. See *Vestnik*, June 1 (May 19), 1918, pp. 1–2.

14. By June 1918 the population of the First City District, along with that of the rest of Petrograd, had declined drastically, from 546,000 to 333,539 residents (*Vestnik*, July 20, 1918, no. 19, p. 8). Nonetheless, the district remained the city's most populous.

15. A full elaboration of this interpretation is contained in Alexander Rabinowitch, *The Bolsheviks Come to Power: The Revolution of 1917 in Petrograd* (New York, 1976).

16. Our knowledge of Petersburg Committee politics in 1918 is significantly limited by the fact that the committee's protocols for that year, prepared and announced for publication in 1928, never appeared. A substantial five-part memoir by the former prominent Petersburg committee leader K. I. Shelavin published at the end of the 1920s, however, describes in considerable detail differing views within the Bolshevik leadership regarding the party's role. Judging by his account, during the first six months of Soviet rule virtually no one in the local party organization stressed that party committees at the city or district levels should attempt systematically to control nonparty political and administrative institutions and important decisionmaking generally (K. I. Shelavin, "Iz istorii Peterburgskogo komiteta," *Krasnaia letopis'*, 1928, no. 2 [26], pp. 106–24; 1928, no. 3 [27], pp. 146–72; 1929, no. 1 [28], pp. 68–88; 1929, no. 2 [29], pp. 24–25; 1929, no. 3 [30], pp. 120–53).

17. See *Pervaia konferentsiia rabochikh i krasnoarmeiskikh deputatov l-go gorodskogo raiona*. Detailed reports on the conference also appeared in the *Vestnik*.

18. *Pervaia konferentsiia rabochikh i krasnoarmeiskh deputatov l-go gorodskogo raiona*, p. 283.

19. Ibid.

20. *Novaia zhizn'* (Petrograd edition), June 11, 1918, p. 2.

21. These demands became especially insistent at the First City District Workers' Conference.

22. According to procedures announced in the soviet on June 6, these elections were to be completed in two weeks, after which the district soviet leadership was to be reorganized. At the June 6 district soviet meeting during which all this was decided, the chairman, Anton Korsak, insisted that early election of a new executive committee

was absolutely essential "inasmuch as the existing committee considered its mandate to have expired on the conclusion of the worker's conference (that is, on June 5). See *Vestnik*, June 12 (May 20), 1918, no. 11, pp. 7–8.

23. *Vestnik*, July 4, 1918, nos. 16–17, p. 8. The party affiliations of the 132 deputies elected and still available to serve in the district soviet at the beginning of July broke down as follows: Bolsheviks, 52; Bolshevik sympathizers, 17; Left SRs, 14; Left SRs sympathizers, 13; Socialist Universalists, 1; Centrist SRs, 2; Mensheviks, 7; Menshevik sympathizers, 1; Nonparty, 25.

24. *Vestnik*, July 4, 1918, nos. 16–17, p. 8.

25. *Severnaia kommuna*, July 5, 1918, p. 3.

26. *Vestnik*, July 4, 1918, nos. 16–17, pp. 8–9.

27. *Gazeta-kopeika*, June 19 (6), 1918, p. 3.

28. These were the main campaign themes of headlines and daily editorials in the major Bolshevik daily papers, *Petrogradskaia pravda* and *Krasnaia gazeta* (which appeared in both morning and evening editions), and in the Petrograd Soviet's press organ, *Severnaia kommuna*.

29. *Novaia zhizn'* (Petrograd edition), June 18, 1918, p. 2.

30. See, for example, interpretations of fragmentary election results on July 20 in *Severnaia kommuna* and *Krasnaia gazeta*, on the one hand, and *Gazeta-kopeika*, on the other. See also *Delo naroda*, June 22, 1918, p. 4.

31. *Severnaia kommuna*, July 5, 1918, p. 3; July 6, 1918, p. 3.

32. *Novaia zhizn'*, July 6, p. 1.

33. A useful account of the Left SR rising is contained in V. Vladimirova, *God sluzhby "sotsialistov" kapitalistam: Ocherki po istorii kontr-revoliutsii v 1918 g.* (Moscow-Leningrad, 1927), pp. 265–89. Valuable related documents are in *Krasnaia kniga V. Ch. K.* (Moscow, 1920), vol. 1.

34. *Novaia Petrogradskaia gazeta*, July 17, 1918, p. 3.

35. *Vestnik*, July 20, 1918, no. 19, p. 4; July 24, 1918, nos. 20–21, pp. 3–4.

36. *Vestnik*, July 24, 1918, nos. 20–21, pp. 3–4.

37. K. I. Shelavin, "Iz istorii Peterburgskogo komiteta," *Krasnaia letopis'*, no. 2 (29), p. 36.

38. The Union of Communes of the Northern Region was formed at the end of April 1918 and included eight neighboring provinces. Under Zinoviev's direction, the Sovnarkom of the Union of Communes of the Northern Region, with headquarters in Smolny, often behaved much like a national government, at one point even going so far as to appoint a foreign minister. During its ten-month existence, it operated alongside the Petrograd Soviet and its Executive Committee and Presidium. Its economic arm was the Soviet of the Economy of the Northern Region.

39. For example, see discussions of this issue in *Petrogradskaia pravda*, Feb. 4–6, 1919. The question of the relationship between party and soviet stimulated lively discussion at the Petrograd Bolshevik Ninth City Party Conference, the Third Bolshevik Petrograd Provincial Party Conference, and the Bolshevik Eighth Party Conference, all held in March 1919 (A. V. Gogolevskii, *Petrogradskii sovet v gody grazhdanskoi voiny* [Leningrad, 1982], p. 83).

40. *Vestnik*, November 30, 1918, no. 49, p. 5.

41. A summary of such a joint meeting can be found in *Vestnik*, June 7, 1919, no. 34–35 (92–93), p. 1.

42. See below.

43. For example, see *Vestnik*, November 13, 1918, no. 45, pp. 2–3.

44. *Vestnik*, February 14, 1919, no. 11–12 (69–70), p. 3.

45. *Sbornik dekretov i postanovlenii Soiuza kommun Severnoi oblasti*, 2 vols. (Petrograd, 1919), 1: 22; A. V. Gogolevskii, *Petrogradskii sovet v gody grazhdanskoi voiny* (Leningrad, 1982), pp. 78–79. On the history of the Petrograd Labor Commune generally, see M. N. Potekhin, *Petrogradskaia trudovaia kommuna* (Leningrad, 1980).

46. Initially formed in May 1917 and composed of representatives of all Petrograd district soviets, the Interdistrict Conference helped coordinate the activity of district soviets and played an important independent, as yet little-studied role in city political affairs until the middle of 1919.

47. *Vestnik*, July 6, 1918, nos. 16–17, pp. 2–3.

48. Ibid.

49. *Vestnik*, September 19, 1918, nos. 32–33, p. 1. See *Severnaia kommuna*, January 30, 1919, for regulations on house committees of the poor that define their duties.

50. *Vestnik*, March 29, 1919, no. 23 (81), p. 3.

51. A. V. Gogolevskii, *Petrogradskii sovet*, p. 16; A. V. Gogolevskii, "Struktura Petrogradskogo soveta rabochikh i krasnoarmeiskikh deputatov v 1918–1920 g.g.," in *Gosudarstvennye uchrezhdeniia i klassovye otnosheniia v otechestvennoi istorii: sbornik statei* (Moscow-Leningrad, 1980), pp. 26–27.

52. See especially *Vestnik*, February 19, 1919, no. 13 (70), p. 1; and April 26, 1919, no. 26 (84), p. 2.

53. *Vestnik soveta l-go gorodskogo raiona*, July 24, 1918, no. 20–21, p. 6.

54. See, for example, A. Tverskoi's editorial in *Vestnik*, March 8, 1919, no. 18 (76), p. 5.

55. *Vestnik*, March 8, 1919, no. 18 (76), p. 2. In late February 1919, the Union of Communes of the Northern Region and its associated organs were dissolved at the insistence of the national Sovnarkom in Moscow.

56. *Vestnik*, March 8, 1919, no. 18 (76), p. 7.

57. *Vestnik*, April 17, 1919, no. 25 (83), p. 2.

58. *Vestnik*, May 21, 1919, no. 30 (88), pp. 1–2.

59. The party's emphasis on recruitment is mirrored in *Vestnik* reports in this period. A portion of virtually every meeting was devoted to discussion and confirmation of numerous new members, as well as consideration of candidates for expulsion.

60. *Vestnik*, May 17, 1919, nos. 27, 28, 29 (85, 86, 87), pp. 3 and 6. See also *Vestnik*, June 7, 1919, nos. 34–35, (92–93), p. 3. For an interesting evaluation of the impact of the May mobilization generally see A. V. Gogolevskii, *Petrogradskii sovet*, p. 139.

61. See above, p. xxx.

62. *Vestnik*, May 17, 1919, nos. 27, 28, 29 (85, 86, 87), pp. 3 and 6; June 14, 1919, nos. 36–37 (94–95), pp. 2 and 4.

63. *Vestnik*, July 19, 1919, no. 44 (102), p. 1.

64. *Vestnik*, March 29, 1919, no. 23 (81), p. 3; A. V. Gogolevskii, *Petrogradskii sovet*, p. 99.

65. See above, p. xxx.

66. A. V. Gogolevskii, *Petrogradskii sovet*, p. 99; A. V. Gogolevskii, "Struktura Petrogradskogo soveta," p. 27.

67. *Petrogradskaia pravda*, November 28, 1919, p. 1; November 30, 1919, p. 1; December 2, 1919, p. 1.

68. A. V. Gogolevskii, *Petrogradskii sovet*, p. 99.

69. This occurred, for example, at the end of December 1918; in March 1919, when the budget office of the Petrograd Soviet's finance department refused to approve expenditures for the *Vestnik*'s biannual budget; and at the beginning of April, when the *Vestnik* was shut down for two weeks.

70. See, for example, *Vestnik*, December 31, 1918, nos. 57–58, p. 4; January 16, 1919, nos. 3–4 (61–61), pp. 7–8; March 8, 1919, no. 18 (76), p. 1; and April 1, 1919, no. 24 (82), p. 2.

71. *Vestnik*, July 30, 1919, no. 45 (103), p. 4.

BREAD WITHOUT THE BOURGEOISIE

Mary McAuley

The food situation in Petrograd worsened steadily after August 1917. By October stocks were dangerously low, rations down, and prices rising fast. The following year saw a catastrophic decline in living standards. The population shrank by almost a million, but even that could not prevent the city from nearly starving to death. December 1918 to March 1919 were perhaps the worst months in the city's history until World War II made the Civil War seem a time of plenty in comparison. In "breadless December" oats were for a time the only staple available for distribution. The Food Commissariat, paralyzed by charges of corruption and inefficiency, simply failed to cope. Sickness and starvation stalked the city. Death rates rose above 80 per 1,000 in the first few months of 1919. By March, with calorie consumption down to little more than 1,500 per day, there were political disturbances and a rash of strikes in the factories. It was a desperate time. The Whites were massing to the north and east. The Bolsheviks had to muster all their resources to calm the angry workers, some of whom were spreading the slogan:

> Down with Lenin and horsemeat
> Give us the Tsar and pork.

Lenin came from Moscow to address the problems of food shortages directly before a huge meeting at the *Narodnyi dom*, and a new rationing system was worked out. Conditions were never quite as bad again but the three-quarters of a million inhabitants who survived the Civil War were emaciated and sick by the end of 1920. Years of near subsistence diet had taken their toll physically and psychologically. The announcement of factory closures (because of the fuel crisis) and of a temporary cut in the bread ration in February 1921 was enough to produce the most serious disturbances the Bolsheviks had faced since the bad spring of 1919.[1]

At the Petrograd Soviet, called to discuss the crisis, one of the delegates reported facing a woman, aged about fifty, who, standing there with her torn

158

coat flapping in the icy wind, upbraided him with, "Who are you aiming your rifle at, sailor? You should be helping us to go to Smolny and ask for bread." The crowd on *Vasilevskii ostrov* "consisting mainly of women and youths behaved very badly toward the soldiers—threw snow at them, swore, and there were incidents when they tried to disarm them." But, apart from the demand for more bread—which takes us back to February 1917—what did the angry crowds want? According to Lashevich, the Bolshevik commissar who gave the official report, "the basic demands are everywhere the same: free trade, free labor, freedom of movement and so on." A delegate from Skorokhod who went with a group of fellow workers to find out what was happening on *Vasilevskii ostrov* met with the response "more bread, clean out the top jobs where lots of the bourgeoisie have tucked themselves in, and reelections to the Petrograd Soviet—those are our slogans."[2] Perhaps the two key demands, which already came to the fore in 1920 and dominated the debates of early 1921, were for free trade and an end to privilege. The first of these, the demand for "free trade," does suggest a shift in attitudes from 1917, whereas the attack on privilege echoes the sentiments of that year. Yet we need to look at them both more closely to understand what they meant. How are we to reconcile the demand for free trade with continued hostility toward traders and the bourgeoisie whose existence had always been associated with the market? Which privileges were considered unacceptable and by whom? Factory representatives might follow a demand for equality with a plea for special treatment for their factory. And, to take an example from the other end of the social spectrum, Princess Skariatina, calling at an "Important Man" 's house in December 1920 in a fruitless attempt to get her elderly mother released from her fourth detention in prison, was shocked to find a chef in starched uniform preparing a prerevolutionary dinner of "thick rich soup, a great big roast, vegetables, dessert, coffee and wine, not to mention such trifles as hors-d'oeuvres, white rolls and candy . . . 'Well, if *this* isn't counterrevolution', I caught myself thinking as I stared at the chef in amazement, and then wondered if I wasn't becoming a Bolshevik too!"[3]

Skariatina's entry in her diary suggests that Civil War experience could and did influence previously held beliefs, although not in a predictable or straight-forward fashion. The incoherent and sometimes contradictory set of popular attitudes that prevailed in 1920/21 can only be understood in terms of the ideas and convictions of 1917 trying unsuccessfully to make sense of a new world. In Petrograd the Civil War meant living in Petrokommuna, the first city commune of its kind, where radical Bolshevik policies on trade and food distribution went into action and where the struggle to survive affected all. But it was not simply that the pattern of life changed. Some of the demands of 1917 had become the ruling ideas, but still the food supply failed and new and unexpected consequences of that failure appeared. Who or what was responsible? A whole range of responses was theoretically possible. But, not surprisingly, those which came had their origins in the beliefs and attitudes of 1917. These, however, had stemmed from and made sense of a different prerevolutionary environment. Some of them were responsible for the creation of Petrokommuna. But by this very act it is as though they signed their own death warrant. The understanding, let alone resolution, of the new social and political relationships that came into being required a new set of ideas. But it takes time for new ideas to arise, coalesce, and to convince (and maybe some social orders cannot produce a meaningful set of ideas). In any event, the Civil War experience was too short and owed too much to a powerful set of revolutionary ideas to be able to produce its "own" coherent set. Neither rulers nor ruled could do it; both were still in thrall to ideas that became more and more distorted and confused as they were applied to a new and intractable reality.

This we try to show by describing, briefly, Bolshevik policy toward "the food question," the impact it had on city life, and the responses it engendered both among the Bolsheviks and from other sections of the community.

Petrokommuna

When the Bolsheviks came to power in October, responsibility for the city's food supply lay with the Food Administration, whose task was purchasing of grain, fixing and administering of the ration system, and, where possible, controlling the prices of basic food items. It had departments in each district and municipal outlets. Much of the food, though, was distributed through the cooperatives that had flourished since February. There were two main rival cooperative organizations and countless small ones, often based in a house to facilitate the purchasing of rations by some on behalf of all. And then there was the private sector, which ranged from the smart shops on Nevskii to the bakeries (large and small), the little stalls, and last, but far from least, the city markets and the street peddlers.[4]

The Bolsheviks had little if any support from those occupied in any of these sectors. They had no ready-made policy, but they believed, without question, that free trade was bad—bad because, with a free market, those with money ate better than the poor, because the traders benefited and exploited the workers, and because, at a time of scarcity, free trade pushed prices so high that almost everyone ended up worse off. At the Seventh City Party Conference in September 1918, one delegate did question these beliefs but he was in a minority of one, and *Petrogradskaia pravda* asked in surprise "how can he be a Marxist and believe in free trade?"[5] Some of the more sophisticated referred to the theoretical distinction between production and distribution, but evident in the attitudes of different types of Bolsheviks is the firm conviction that in the markets, in the kids trading lumps of sugar or typhus lice on street corners, was a class enemy, a parasite to be destroyed. Free trade could and would eat away at a healthy society. In Civil War Petrograd the evil social consequences of free trade were plainly visible—children skipping school, juvenile crime (by 1920 juveniles both accounted for the largest group of criminals and their victims), gangs who hung around the cigarette factories, dealing with the women workers in cigarettes, gold rings, and cocaine. Free trade distracted workers from their jobs and it lured Red Army soldiers into the markets (in the August 1920 swoop on the markets, 1,000 of the 4,000 detained turned out to be garrison soldiers).[6] Socialists from abroad were taken aback by this extreme attitude: the perception that a flighty seventeen-year-old girl trying to sell a pair of shoes to get a bit more food or a peasant woman selling a few potatoes was a class enemy. And it *was* extreme. It was nonetheless real. There is no mistaking the conviction with which the city leadership and its supporters moved time and time again against the traders, the reluctance with which they authorized the bringing in of personal supplies, and the feeling of defeat that is present in the Ispolkom authorization of the free buying and selling of farm products on April 16, 1921, following the Sovnarkom decree of March 28.[7]

This bedrock belief lay behind Bolshevik attempts to control and organize food distribution in such a way that free trade would be a thing of the past. At the start there was confusion as the Food Administration set up by the Military Revolutionary Committee, the Petrograd Soviet, and old and new duma departments jockeyed for control of city services, but, by the outbreak of the Civil War, the main institution responsible for procuring and distributing food was one of the new commissariats, Petrokomprod. In theory it was subordinate to Narkomprod in Moscow, but, even in theory, the relationship was not entirely clear. Much of its activity was concentrated on procuring of grain and other food stuffs for the city. Even before the Civil War started, supplies getting through were less than half those of a year earlier, and henceforth the city lurched from one crisis to another. At times all passenger traffic was stopped to try to get the trains through, Lenin made special appeals for "bread for Piter," and detachments of workers were sent out far and wide to scour the countryside. The inability to get enough food to the city through organized channels remained the basic problem: it meant both that the state could never provide adequate provisions and that the authorities thereby were forced to allow initiatives of which they disapproved. Whether an alternative policy could have fed the city better is an important and valid question but one we cannot address here; nor can we deal with Petrokomprod activities outside the city. Our concern is with what was happening within.

Petrokomprod was the institution responsible for administering the rationing system and, increasingly, for controlling all the trade outlets in the city. In the summer of 1918 the cooperatives and private traders still supplied the population with the bulk of the foodstuffs, and indeed in the first half of 1918 the number of little cooperatives shot up. But in the autumn the city government began to move in earnest toward the municipalization of all trading outlets and, as part of this, sought either to squeeze out the cooperatives or to fashion a new role for them. The situation was complicated by rivalry between the big cooperatives, by the presence of strong Menshevik elements within the cooperative movement and hence the emergence of a rival Bolshevik-led workers cooperative and by a countergroup of Bolsheviks within SNKh that wanted to abolish all cooperatives. One wing within the city party and administration was now strongly centralist, that is, in favor of nationalizing all outlets, putting all under a strong central authority. This group, of whom Molotov was one of the key spokesmen, disliked the cooperatives on principle and also disliked "district autonomy" in whatever form—soviet, district food administration, and so on. With such a shortage of food, they argued, the most efficient method of distribution was centralization, reduction in the number of institutions, standardization. And indeed the mass of tiny cooperatives, dependent on the state authorities for supplies and lacking either financial resources or other means of obtaining products for their members, were unable to offer a better service than the multiple outlets. In October the anticooperative wing won, but a month later Lenin's stance on the need for cooperatives reopened the issue. Zinoviev tried to find a compromise position, but anticooperative feeling within the Petrograd party was too strong to permit anything more than a stalemate. In April 1919 the Petrograd Soviet returned to the matter and set up a commission; conferences were called but then deferred until, finally, in September 1919 it was decided that all production and distribution should be concentrated in a new organization, Petrokommuna, the consumers' commune. This took over from Petrokomprod and absorbed the cooperatives.[8] Petrokommuna had a board and elected representatives from the districts but, effectively, it was Petrokomprod in another guise, the centralized authority Molotov had demanded. Headed by Badaev, it brought the grain into the city, ran the 2 mills, the 8 bread factories and 11 bakeries (which had replaced the 2,000 pre-October bakeries); it was responsible for distributing the bread and other foodstuffs to the warehouses, depots, then to the hospitals, cafeteria, to the distribution points in the districts from whence it went to the now municipalized stalls and shops.

All this meant that Petrokommuna became a gigantic organization: in the spring of 1921 it employed 36,000 white-collar workers alone or nearly 10 percent of the adult population of the city. Roughly 5,000 of these were salespeople in the 3,948 stalls, 398 shops and 808 depots. Others were employed in the communal eating sector and in the rationing administration. Providing basic foodstuffs and items of mass consumption (shoes, clothes, material, kerosene, soap) and running the canteens were its basic task.

The first famous canteen for the unemployed and the poor was opened in the *Narodnyi dom* on November 1, 1917.[9] In the early months, the Petrograd Soviet assigned huge sums for this purpose (while squeezing and requisitioning private restaurants), and both central and district canteens sprang up. By the autumn of 1918 there were 10 central canteens run by Petrokomprod but (at one count) 189 small district canteens that jealously guarded their independence. Again the central versus district issue was fought out with each side arguing that it could husband the scarce resources most efficiently, and again the districts lost.

Private restaurants were officially closed in October 1918, and communal eating facilities came to dominate the life of the city. By the late summer of 1919 there were approximately 250 large central canteens out of a city total of perhaps 700. By June 1919 all children under the age of 14 were entitled to free meals. By 1920 the canteens were catering for the whole population, but the family surveys suggest that only 60 to 70 percent of the adult population made use of them. The hope was that by distributing part of the ration through the "communal cooking-pot," fuel, time and labor would be saved. In theory this sounds right; whether in practice it was we cannot tell. In any case, the canteens were never popular. The tasteless food caused strikes in the summer of 1919. Badaev rushed from one angry meeting to another (Skorokhod, Putilov, Obukhov), tasting the soup, trying to calm down enraged workers who threatened "Into the cooking-pot with him, into the pot!" New arrangements were made for volunteer squads to act as inspectors in the kitchen and to try to prevent the thieving, but inevitably fights broke out as tired, hungry people lost their patience over delays, food running out, and suspected injustices.[10]

The Ration System

If the Petrograd Bolsheviks held a common conviction that socialism meant replacement of free trade by state control, they had no particular view on what constituted a socialist rationing system. They inherited a system from the Provisional Government in which elements of differentiation based on need (for those involved in heavy physical labor and for children) had already been introduced, and initially they made no changes. The new Red Army and the fleet received privileged rations, but this was nothing new. In the spring of 1918, however, a commission was set up by the Petrograd Soviet to consider the rationing system, and in May, a time of disturbances in the factories with the Putilov workers demanding rations equal to those of the Red Army, it put a draft before the soviet and the trade unions for discussion.[11] The proposal was for a new class-based ration, and it was this that went into effect from July 1. The adult population was classified by occupation: those engaged in heavy physical labor in category 1, those in less heavy manual labor and white-collar employees in category 2, members of the intelligentsia and free professions in category 3, and rentiers, house-owners, stall-owners, and so on in category 4, the "bourgeois" category. It was they who, in Zinoviev's words, were to receive just enough bread so as to not forget the smell of it. The unemployed were to be put in their appropriate category; nursing women, women with several dependents, and children received special treatment.[12]

The city government spelled out the justification for such a system as follows:[13]

> We have little bread. In the first place we must give it to the workers and their families. Justice and expediency demand that. Workers do not have money, they cannot buy bread at high prices. Workers need to eat better so that they can work more and thus improve transport and output. Both bread and unrationed food—to the workers first of all.

Both the principle of physiological need and a new argument that since poorer members of the community could not afford free market prices they must be given a larger ration if they were not to be worse off than the wealthy form part of the justification. As we shall see, neither at this time nor subsequently could any but a few live off the rations; hence, with free market prices rocketing, only unequal rations could make consumption more equal. But it proved impossible to make the classification system work and the "savings" made by cutting the ration for categories 3 and 4 were far too small to benefit those in category 1. Even when the system was introduced only 1 percent of the population appeared in the "bourgeois" category, and by October 1918-their numbers were down to 2,000. The four-category system was replaced by one with three categories, but the following table shows the story.[14]

Percentage of Population in Ration Categories

Category	Oct. 1918	Jan. 1919	Jan. 1920	Apr. 1920
1	52.3	81.1*	63.0	63.0
2	38.6	16.5	7.0	6.5
3	8.9	2.2	.2	.1
4	.2		30.0	30.0

*Of the 81.0 percent, 20.0 percent were children.

It was not just that aristocrats took jobs as clerks, traders went to work in the Izhorskii factory and that cheating occurred. City authorities also came under continual pressure to reclassify professions, and frequently did so. Doctors and other medical personel, and those in water transport, got category 1 in the cholera epidemic of 1918, and academics and professors of forty-five years and over were transferred to category 1 in the autumn. By the autumn of 1919 the system was meaningless: in the Porokhovskii district, for example, of the 8,000 adults, 2 received category 2 rating and a single individual had a category 3 ration card.[15] Only if category 1 had been tightly restricted could the workers have benefited substantially from such a system. Narkomprod economists recognized by the end of 1918 that, although the class ration was politically important, its economic effect was negligible.[16] And, ironically, as category 1 expanded, manual workers lost the edge they had had under the old system. In the spring of 1919, after the terrible winter, the city authorities resolved to try to get extra rations for 200,000 workers and set the date for March 5. When the rations failed to materialize, strikes broke out at Putilov and spread to a number of other factories. Lenin's appearance and Zinoviev's promises of bread in a few days failed to end the stoppages. As a party spokesman reporting on a meeting in Smolny with a nonparty delegation from a large factory argued: "the stomach has become all important."

When the discussion was of questions of principle—on the essence of Soviet power, on its struggle with Imperialism, on communes—not a single delegate disagreed. On the contrary all our positions were accepted more or less sympathetically. But as soon as the talk turned to other issues, it was another matter altogether. "It's impossible to live," said one delegate, "when *za podoshvu* you are paid only a few hundred rubles." "We are all dying," said another despairingly and angrily. And when discussion touched on the unsatisfactory state of distribution and the amount of theft the delegates' eyes glowed. "They are stealing," shouted one them, "they are stealing up to nine railway wagons a day, there you are!" Why not 10, 15 up to 20? The delegate said nine but the masses say 99 . . . it would be stupid to argue that the recent troubles were all the work of the SRs.[17]

The city authorities hurriedly introduced a new "labor ration" for certain factories and officially authorized this new system from April 11. The crucial difference between the labor ration and the old class ration (which remained in force) was that the labor ration of an extra half pound (*funt*) of bread a day was only awarded to certain occupations and only for a full day's work. It was administered by the factory committee; only with the *fabkom*'s stamp for the day's work, could the worker collect it. The intention was clearly stated: to increase the food supply for workers in key sectors, to raise productivity, and to improve labor discipline.[18]

But again practice confounded principles or intention. To summarize the consequences briefly: The labor ration did, for the first time, push the workers' families' calorie consumption above that of white-collar employees and helped maintain it there. But, as the months passed, the list of those occupations entitled to the labor ration grew longer (by October 1919 the second largest profession listed was "workers of different institutions") until in December the authorities decided the only solution was to differentiate it. A new "A" labor ration of three-quarters of a pound for workers in heavy manual labor was brought in, and a "B" category (one-half pound) for other workers and seven-month's pregnant and nursing mothers (a *labor* ration?). This opened the floodgates. In January 1920 soviet employees got a "C" ration of one-quarter pound and a meal; 1,800 scholars got Red Army rations, the militia a 1.5-pound labor ration. All these in addition to the still existing class rations. In April teachers got the "B" category, in May invalids qualified (for a day's productive work?), and sculptors were granted "A." Who was left? From June 1 housewives got "C" (soviet employees had since been upgraded to "B"), now a category for anyone not employed in a state institution. A final blow to the principle of the labor ration being tied to work came in July when the Ispolkom resolved that it should be paid for Saturdays, Sundays, and holidays too. This decision was subsequently and grudgingly revoked on Narkomprod's orders, but, in effect, the labor ration had long ceased to serve its original purpose.[19]

By October 1920, approximately 300,000 out of an adult population of 500,000 were receiving a labor ration, clearly not everyone. But then there were also factories that had been put on Red Army or Red Fleet rations, there were the Red Star rations for Red Army wives, and the "extra" ration for "responsible workers" (that is, political officials and administrators), Cheka officials, professors, and certain members of the artistic community.[20] Whether we are talking of the autumn of 1920 or January 1921, when a new, simpler, yet differentiated variant was introduced, the system had become too complex to be effective. The authorities had steadily added to its objectives: it was to cater to different physiological needs, iron out social inequalities, raise productivity, reward key groups within the industrial labor force and the intelligentsia, ensure the survival of political activists, stave off unrest in particular groups, and, in the end, simply keep people alive.

Even if all of the figures were available it would be difficult to compare the differentials in 1918 and 1921 because of the changing content of the ration and the groups involved. And, given that rations only accounted for part of consumption, knowledge of the ration does not necessarily tell us how a particular group lived. For example, Red Army soldiers were a privileged ration group throughout (in August 1918, it was reckoned that they received 13.5 pounds of bread to the average worker's 3.5 pounds), but in 1920 (when trade union handouts and the bringing in of provisions were available to workers but not to soldiers) they may well have been worse off than the average worker.[21] In terms of official policy, the basic differential for the civilian population narrowed from 8:1 under the class ration of May 1918 to perhaps 4:1 in January 1921. But in 1921 workers in selected defense industry factories were getting the naval ration, which was approximately double that of the top civilian worker's ration (the Red Army ration earned by some other workers came somewhere in between)—which would again give us a ratio of 8:1. But by this time, even the bottom category was entitled to at least one-quarter pound of bread and a bowl of meat soup or a plate of kasha a day, whereas in the summer of 1918, category 4 sometimes received only one-eighth pound of bread or no bread at all and three salt herrings—and no bread at all makes a qualitative difference.[22] Yet again entitlement to chocolate or soap means one thing in a situation where they are available, if at a price, and something quite different when the ration is the only source of scarce goods.

The most we can say is the following. In 1918, four groups—Red Army soldiers, a small group of responsible administrators, nursing and pregnant women with large families, and children—were the beneficiaries of the rationing system. In 1919 the workers as a whole improved their position relative to other groups; by 1921 a segment within the industrial labor force had improved its position even more, and a small group within the intelligentsia had made a huge leap upward. But only those who received the sought-after and privileged "extra" (consisting of 16 pounds of bread, 8 pounds of sturgeon or caviar, 4 pounds of butter, 4 pounds of cheese, 4 pounds of sugar and 4 pounds of chocolate in January 1921) could live off the rations.[23] Bread, thin soup, cabbage, and salt-fish were not simply the staples but indeed all that the state could provide for most of the population most of the time. As Strumilin noted in mid-1919, "Sugar, cereals, fats, eggs have long since disappeared from the markets and have not been given out as part of rations for months on end."[24] Even where the calorie content was maintained, the protein and fat element was derisory. Potatoes were a luxury. Buckwheat kasha and raisins only appeared in rations for the privileged. For most it was bread and *vobla*, an awful salt-fish, nicknamed "Soviet ham," whose bones would splinter and damage the intestines. Even those who did not share Princess Wolkonsky's background ("How can I convey the real meaning of the word 'vobla' to the mind of the European reader, for whom 'fish' is naturally associated with the appetizing picture of *sole frite* or *turbot au vin blanc?*")[25] found the fish nauseating. When the government could, especially at holiday times, it issued more. Easter 1919 brought white flour (though not to category 3), sugar, vinegar, and salt, and at Passover the Jewish population received a special allowance of wheat flour. But in the spring of 1921, after an improvement, the rations were cut down to one pound of bread, and a monthly issue of three pounds of cereal and meat, one-half pound of sugar and 250 cigarettes for the top-category worker, while the average employee was back to a half pound of bread, one pound of cereal, and two pounds of *vobla*.[26]

Keeping Alive

A daily calorie intake of 2,300 was the recommended minimum, but even in the better months the average ration and canteen meal consisted of less than half of that. How then did the average family survive? The first budget survey (of May 1918) showed that workers and white-collar employees spent 71 percent and 63 percent of their incomes, respectively, on food, 80 percent of that on the free market, but still spent more than they earned. The workers were drawing on savings; the employees had exhausted their savings and were borrowing; the poorest were selling possessions or begging.[27] By mid-1919 Strumilin was suggesting that workers were surviving by earning on the side, canteen eating, and trade-union hand-outs.[28] What he did not mention but what was of great importance throughout was the bringing-in of produce from the countryside and the buying, selling, and bartering of goods. Again the family budget surveys tell the story:[29] in 1919 and 1920 roughly 40 percent of a family's bread consumption alone came from the free market or from bringing-in from outside. Workers bought less than employees on the open market; they fared better on factory hand-outs and had more opportunities to bring food in. As this shows (and thinking back to the example of the Red Army soldier), a group's consumption depended on the size of the ration, trade union hand-outs, income and possessions (the ability to buy and barter on the free market), and the opportunity to bring food in from the countryside. The combination of these determined consumption.

Until the spring of 1919 the average employee's family was eating slightly better than the worker's; by the summer, employees had slipped below the workers, and although 1920 was a better year for both with daily calorie consumption ranging from 2,500 to over 3,000, henceforth employees lagged behind. The family budget surveys do refer to an "other" group, which was consuming perhaps 30 percent more than the workers and twice as much as the employees. Whether this refers simply to the responsible administrators, the Cheka, specialists, professors, and leading artists—that small group that received the valuable extra rations—or whether it includes soldiers and sailors, we cannot tell. Yet even including this group, the two most striking features of the period were, first, the drastic fall in the standard of living for the great majority of the population. In 1920 the worker was eating only half as much as in the period 1912–14; the population as a whole consumed even less. To make these figures more concrete: in 1919 the average Petrograd worker or employee family was eating less than half as much bread, only a third as much meat, and roughly the same quantity of potatoes as a Petersburg textile work-er's family in 1908.[30] No professional family in 1908 surely ever dreamed that in ten years' time they would be eating only half as well as the often poverty-stricken spinners and weavers from the Nevskii mills of their day. And this draws attention to the second feature: the great leveling process that occurred.

This leveling was surely the most important social change of the period, but not all ate equally badly and this—at a time of dire hardships—could be of great significance. "Where do the eggs go?" asked a passenger on a tram in April 1919. Someone suggested to the hospitals, but few thought that was true; most reckoned that the Bolsheviks and the employees of Petrokomprod ate them all.[31] And two years later the same question was posed, this time by a worker from the Lessner factory, at the Petrograd Soviet: why do the factories get consignments of chicken claws? "Aren't there comrades here who have eaten the chickens and sent the claws to the factories? There's agitation for you' [Applause]."[32]

Only a few had the skills that brought them face to face with a commissar's second wife who wanted English and French lessons:

> "To come to my terms. I shall want you four hours a week. I can give you a pound of black bread per lesson. I have heard that this is extremely generous." On the table before her stood the remains of a meal, bones of a chicken leg, a broken white roll, butter in a dish, caviar in a china pot.[33]

But first-hand evidence is not of primary importance in encouraging or sus-taining beliefs. Official privilege was popularly considered to give its holders an unwarranted and luxurious lifestyle, but there were others, too, who, it was reckoned, lived well at the expense of the poor. To a British observer in the spring of 1919, the ability to trade and speculate could be as important as government privilege.[34]

> in spite of ghastly facts one is witness to every day, it cannot be said that Petrograd is suffering famine in the fullest sense of the term as applying to the whole population, for the Government strains its utmost to supply the wants

of the masses it fears, and though the food is bad, all the higher Soviet employees, the Jews, and the workmen who by insurrection have won for themselves Red Army rations, as also the host of food speculators and those of the bourgeois class who still have some savings, are either fed at the expense of the rest of the population by order of the Soviet government or feed through the medium of "bag-men".

It is to these other sources of consumption—trade, barter, and the bringing-in of food—that we now turn our attention.

The bringing-in of extra food became an issue in the late spring of 1918 and a bone of contention thereafter. In its history, we see all the problems associated with either allowing free trade or trying to abolish it. Before October, the inhabitants of the city could come and go as they wished, bringing in goods for their own consumption or to sell in the markets. After October, with the campaign against speculation and in a vain attempt to curb rising prices, Red Guards, courts, and enraged groups of citizens took action, sometimes violent, against those who brought food in and sold it at high prices. By the new year, with the transport system unable to cope with either the bringing-in of grain or the flood of evacuees, restrictions were placed on movement in and out of the city and, it seems, on what could be brought in. In May, however, with state supplies failing, the city government authorized the bringing-in and selling of potatoes by organizations and individuals, and an allowance of one-and-a-half *puds* of produce, including grain, per passenger.[35] Whether this was subsequently rescinded is not known, but, following a Sovnarkom authorization of one-and-a-half *puds* to run from August 24 to October 1, the Petrograd commissars reaffirmed the one-and-a-half *pud* allowance on September 5 and stated that any guilty of requisitioning such "personal baggage" would be dealt with severely.[36] But how could one distinguish an honest citizen from a bagman? A week later, Strievskii, the food commissar, was complaining that 25,000 bagmen had traveled to one station alone on the previous Sunday to sell their potatoes.[37] And this remained the official argument throughout: bringing-in encouraged bagmen and prices on the free market went up. Hence, official policy favored the authorizing of organizations—trade unions, factories, institutions—to send out detachments and bring back food for their members. Sometimes they were obliged to hand over half of what they obtained to Petrokommuna, sometimes they were charged a 10 percent levy, sometimes the individual members were allowed to bring in their own one-and-a-half *puds* as well.

In December 1918, belatedly and after heated disagreement within the Petrograd party, workers' organizations and trade unions were allowed to bring in potatoes, vegetables, milk, curds, and mushrooms, and at the end of the month the right was extended to individuals.[38] In July 1919, with discontent in the factories over canceled holidays and short rations, the city government gave in again: holidays would be granted, on a rota system, and those returning could bring one-and-a-half *puds* with them. At the Petrograd Soviet, an official spokesman stated that women workers would be the first to go, that wives would have the right to go, and, it was to be hoped, party members, soviet members, and Red Army soldiers would not apply. But the question could not be resolved so easily. As Ivanov reported to a later session:

> Everyone wanted to go, to have a holiday and above all to bring something back . . . first we sent the textile and tobacco workers, then the metal-workers with their families. We tried to keep it to 3,000 a day but many more went . . . factory workers have been streaming into the Labor and Food Commissariats asking for a holiday; they simply say, if you don't grant it, we'll just go anyway. And now we are being blamed for not having foreseen it would bring the railways to a halt and undermine the whole food policy.[39]

Not all managed to bring back supplies, but some brought back five *puds* rather than two. Each Ispolkom session had to deal with complaints from those who had not gone. Criticisms were made of Red Army wives going twice and of some Vyborg workers coming back with twelve *puds*. One suggestion was to promise one-and-a-half *puds* of flour to those who had not been, another to raise the ration. The debate dragged on, with recriminations from all sides. Thereafter, it seems, individuals were allowed to bring in small personal amounts and particular groups (for example, returning Red Army soldiers or students) given a maximum allowance. But the checkpoint patrols remained. Acting in an arbitary and at times unlawful manner, they became one of the main targets of popular hostility.

Despite all of the Bolsheviks' efforts, the private sector never disappeared entirely. It did not spring up like mushrooms after rain as was to happen in 1921, but, in Bolshevik eyes at least, it appeared like weeds through the cracks in the cobblestones whenever the commissar disappeared around the street corner. It changed its character as the population shrank, grew poorer, and yet had to trade to keep alive. As early as the spring of 1918 the traditional stall-holders and the well-known Tatars in the Aleksandrovskii market found themselves joined by a motley band of amateurs, women and children:

> In their rows stand women with tired, downcast faces. One holds some linen, another a coffee-pot, a third some second-hand dress or other. Then there's a woman with a samovar, after her comes one with a couple of pillows and so on. . . . You look at these women's faces and it seems as though in the expression of their tired eyes, in their weary stance, you can read the whole history of today. Stories of hungry children, of sons who have been made redundant by "socialized" or "taken under control" and now dying factories . . . Court dress coats, pictures, lamps, clocks, dresses, shoes. . . . There are all kinds of strange items. For example, a single boot. "Who on earth would want one boot?" you ask in amazement. "What do you mean—who?" answers the trader philosophically. "Are there so few one-legged people around? Look how many have come back from the war." . . . There's a soldier selling his cap, another his boots . . . foul slices of bread, tobacco, lumps of sugar.[40]

In the better-off districts, in the early months, the private sector could be quite tasteful. Along the aristocratic streets such as Sergievskaia, Furshtadt-skaia, or Kirochnaia, curio shops opened up, even taking over from bakeries. Clavichords, mirrors, exotic carpets, antique furniture appeared; there was a roaring trade in medals and badges; Prussian eagles and tsarist insignia were especially popular. In a "This and That" shop on Sergievskaia run by four aristocrats, one of the ladies might break off her conversation (in French, of course) with the owner of a marble table, sold yesterday, to sell a statuette to a sailor for 550 rubles.[41]

Speculation was already illegal but it was not until August 1919 that the Ispolkom officially prohibited all street trading and any juvenile traders, and restricted buying and selling to goods of prime necessity in a limited number of markets.[42] But all types of trading survived. As Ravich reported to the Petrograd Soviet a year later, private trade had again reached significant proportions: both basic foodstuffs and luxury items slipped out of the state network to appear in the markets where they could be sold for ten times the official price; perhaps 8,000 children were involved in street-trading. The decision to try and wipe it out altogether was taken by the Ispolkom in March 1920 but its execution was delayed until July 23, when a task force of 10,000 party members and 3,900 Red Army soldiers swooped on the shops and markets—requisitioning, sealing up shops and stalls, and detaining those involved. In all 2,566 stall and shops were closed as well as 2,000 tiny booths, most in the central-city district. The following day the eleven remaining markets were closed; 4,100 able-bodied citizens were detained.[43] This represented the most determined effort by the city government to wipe out trade but again it failed. It was not just that traders began, cautiously, to appear in the markets again but that (as even official spokesmen agreed) when trading was forced off the streets, it took place in courtyards, on the staircases, and inside apartments. Those with real wealth and daring engaged in the buying and selling of antiques, pictures, and valuable jewelry:[44]

> I always preferred pictures to jewels, for such an investment spared a great deal of anxiety during the possible perquisitions. Something small, old, and dark hanging on the wall in the dark passage does not draw the attention, though it be a Leonardo da Vinci. Having held a family council, my friends decided to invest their money in the Estonian's brooch.

But their numbers dwindled and their activities were largely hidden. It was the ordinary citizen who, at a time of such desperate shortage, had to buy and sell, and barter for pitiful amounts of food. People still gravitated to the former markets; outside the railway stations and factory gates, inside the factory apartments, people hawked their wares and the street urchins with their battered noses (tell-tale evidence of encounters with the patrols) sold everything imaginable including themselves.

This is the context that produced the insistent demands for the free bringing-in of products and free trade by the spring of 1921. Did this mean that the hostility toward the trader who in 1917, together with the civil servants and the bourgeoisie, was blamed for the high prices and for cheating the poor had disappeared? In 1918 and 1919 evidence of such hostility is present both in actions and in readers' complaints to the press. One of the first cases to be tried by the new Vyborg people's court involved two men charged with bringing meat into the city and selling it at exorbitant prices. A man selling bread for five rubles a pound, who refused to drop his price, was thrown into the Fontanka by a crowd of angry women and drowned.[45] And one of the demands in the discussion of the draft of the class ration was that all traders should be put in category 4. These cases of rough justice toward traders seem to grow more infrequent as the Civil War gets underway, yet the antipathy remained. The worker from the Nevskii spinning mill who returned home to a hungry family in the factory barracks with a daily pay of 27 rubles and found a trader lurking in the corridor asking 9 rubles for a pound of partly frozen potatoes, 20 rubles for a loaf of bread, and 45 rubles for a pound of meat wrapped in a dirty cloth inside his even dirtier shirt felt little sympathy for the traders when the authorities shut the markets.[46] And there is no suggestion that the authorities found it difficult to muster an enthusiastic task force for these operations. It is true that at the Petrograd Soviet discussion of the closures in August 1920, one of the Menshevik delegates argued that although the markets bred theft and speculation, shutting them and the shops could not solve the problem.

> And how has shutting the stalls helped? You say the workers demanded it. I must say I have heard the opposite from workers. Closing the markets drives speculation indoors where the Soviet bourgeoisie can indulge in it. We ask for higher wages—not so as to wallpaper our rooms with notes but so as to survive. You can't spend more than 150 rubles in a state stall but we are given 5,000 rubles—therefore we're meant to go and buy things with it.[47]

But the part of his speech that brought him applause was the demand for the free bringing into the city of grain and flour by horse and cart. And at a stormy meeting of the soviet a month later, a nonparty delegate from the Obukhovskii factory, who delivered a swinging attack on several aspects of Bolshevik policy, criticized the government for *lack* of toughness toward the trader.

> It is true that we from the Obukhovskii factory asked for trading to be stopped but I still see it everywhere. What are the militia doing? The traders should be sent to work. Whoever wants to have his boots cleaned (I don't have my bark slippers cleaned and I don't have any boots) can do them at home himself, and we should set such citizens to work.[48]

A number of factors influenced popular attitudes. More and more of the population had to engage in bartering, buying, and selling in order to keep alive; ironically, the attempt to introduce centralized state administration in place of the market produced a population of traders, but unwilling traders. It was a degrading, wretched business. And worst of all was being treated as a trader by a checkpoint patrol who seized the sack of provisions you had bought out in Kolpino from the German farmers so as to survive for the next two months. If only you could bring in freely what you needed, you would not have to turn to the trader. The official defense of the checkpoint patrols fell on deaf ears, and not simply because of the squads' arbitrary actions. If the state could not provide enough food, then surely individuals had the right to go and get it, as cheaply as possible; prohibiting this threw the individual back into the speculator's hands. Official policy seemed plainly perverse. Was it not obvious that with free bringing-in, people would be able to feed themselves, and with more food available the traders' prices would come down? Although at a time of shortage such reasoning was probably faulty, the manifest failure of Bolshevik counterplans to feed the population naturally gave it a plausibility. The image it presents is of some state provision and a free market of nonprofitmaking buyers and sellers trading to meet their needs. If we think back to the pre-October image of poverty, speculation, and high prices being caused by the existence of a bourgeoisie, aided and abetted by an alien and privileged civil service, we can see how—with the destruction of the bourgeoisie, and the creation of a new workers' administration—such a harmonious and just world could seem not only possible, but also probable. If it did not exist, it must be because of fairly simple, removable factors. And when we look at the attempts to make sense of the situation and the remedies proposed or demanded, we see this framework underlying them.

The Impact on Ideas

Until the autumn of 1918, high prices could still be blamed on the existence of a wealthy community; readers' letters complaining, for example, of fancy restaurants where "beefsteaks" were still available for a price would link them with the rich. But as the old bourgeoisie and the aristocracy shrank, and their remaining members were compelled to live discreetly, they could no longer be held responsible. From time to time charges were made that "old society" still existed:

> The House of High Art with its surfeit of rations
>> Dinner-jackets with asters in their button-
>> holes, fantastic trousers,
> Glossy hair, French conversation, and silk
>> stockings[49]

But it was the members' access to rations that was noted, not their inherited wealth, and all could see that the majority of the intelligentsia was living in poverty. Those who lived well because of privileged rations could not be held responsible for the high prices—at most they could be accused of having an unfair share of scarce goods.

What, though, was thought to be a fair or just distribution? As money became less important, the debates over what constituted a just wages system shifted their focus to rations. In May 1918 the Putilov workers demanded that their rations be made equal to those of the Red Army and the railway workers, and, henceforth, there were repeated claims from different factories and occupations that their work warranted a higher ration category. In April 1919 the Commissariat of Labor was flooded with claims for entitlement to the labor ration.[50] In both 1919 and 1920 demands might be accompanied by requests for specific goods. The Pal factory in March 1919 wanted higher rations—20 *arshins* of material and 1.5 *puds* of flour per worker and an increase in wage rates. In the summer of 1920 the Izhorskie demanded better rations, material, shoes, and steel knives; the Skorokhodtsy wanted shoes and boots, material, 10 pounds of salt, Red army rations, and priority for holidays.[51]

Inevitably the complexity of the criteria governing the rationing system and the government's willingness to make readjustments for different occupations meant that almost any occupation could claim an improved ration category and feel aggrieved if their claim was unsuccessful. The absence of clear criteria by which the fairness of the ration could be measured encouraged interfactory and interoccupation rivalry. A delegate from five textile factories argued at the Petrograd Soviet in February 1921 that for the past month shock workers had been given 7 pounds of meat whereas they had only received 2 pounds and had no canteen: "I don't say that the complaints are right but that's what hungry workers are saying, not counterrevolutionaries."[52] This was mild enough, but a week later there were bitter exchanges when a delegate from the Baranovskii plant claimed that they had received nothing extra for the past two-and-a-half years until finally the union had got them some boots and clothes; their neighbors, however, were still getting food privileges. A peasant delegate replied that it was the peasants who got nothing, they worked eighteen hours a day for nothing while the Baranovskii workers at least got something. He had worked at the Baltiiskii plant (where naval rations operated) and it was a piece of cake. An army delegate suggested that the Baltiiskii workers should be shot, another claimed that the soldiers were much worse off than the workers but they were not causing trouble.[53]

But if the nature of the ration system and the desperate struggle to survive combined to reduce the notion of justice to one of maintaining or improving one's own position (a poor, narrow view), it also perpetrated an idea of equality—albeit in a simple form. Perhaps, inevitably, at times when survival is at stake, "justice" and "equality" can only retain a bare, essentialist vision. In May 1918 the Mensheviks had argued that the workers would reject the class ration because of the principles on which it was based. There is no evidence of objections from any groups within the working class, but, in March 1919, the Rechkin coach-building plant demanded equal rations for all *workers*. A later commentator suggested that the two most characteristic demands of the striking workers at that time were for the free bringing-in of food and for an increase in the bread ration for the workers without a reduction for anyone else. And even *Petrogradskaia pravda* ran an article in which the author argued for equal rations.[54] But those in favor of differentiation, *albeit to achieve a greater measure of equality*, won easily. And this was part of the problem: a great measure of equalization had taken place; new types of inequality were emerging. Everything needed rethinking but there was no energy to spare. All that remained was anger at blatant privilege associated with office. This surfaced in a reader's letter to *Krasnaia gazeta* complaining of the preferential treatment given Ispolkom members in the cafeteria of the First City District soviet or at a garrison conference in August 1919, where arguments that officers and commissars should not receive any food privileges won the day.[55] By 1920 it was the special rations and access to clothing that had become a focus for discontent. A nonparty delegate at the Petrograd Soviet in September found himself addressing a receptive audience:

> Comrades, under the bourgeoisie I wore a dirty blouse and the parasites who killed our working brothers and drank their blood wore ties and starched collars, and now our comrade members of the (union) organization have inherited those ties . . . and begun to look cleaner than the bourgeoisie (applause). . . . I suffered under the bloody Nicholas II, and I have been arrested five times under Soviet power for speaking the truth to a commissar. I suggest all the bosses should be more polite in their dealings with the working classes (applause) . . . provisions must be made equal . . . commissars eat well . . . and your ordinary worker who gets a pound of flour is not prepared to work for that. I propose that all the leather jackets should be handed in and sent where they are needed (applause).

Evdokimov, in an unusually conciliatory reply, suggested:

> had comrade Golgin spoken not here in the Petrograd Soviet but at a factory where, for one reason or another, misunderstanding was rife and a work-stoppage threatened, it would be difficult for even a very experienced comrade, going to that meeting, to answer him and clear up the misunderstanding because when they become part of daily existence then it's very difficult to explain basic and important questions to exhausted hungry workers when simultaneously people are playing on minor grievances, albeit very irritating and painful ones. And even here, in the Petrograd Soviet, comrade Golgin's speech did not get the reception it should have. What was most important in his speech? First he pointed to a number of failings. He pointed out that people holding positions of power are sometimes not worthy of it. Why? Because they put their personal comfort before that of the working class, sometimes so much so that it hits you between the eyes. Even over clothes they are so tactless, simply lacking in any tact, they forget that in front of them is a hungry, bare-footed, suffering worker and this cuts them off, sharply, from the workers.[56]

But even though commissar privilege was attacked, it was not usually considered the reason for the shortages the workers suffered. The most popular culprit was Petrokomprod and its successor Petrokommuna. This was, after all, the institution responsible for the procurement and distribution of food, whose employees thereby had access to scarce goods. The sideways shift of goods by storekeepers, accountants, clerks, and salespeople was endemic and lucrative—and the ramifications extensive.[57]

> In those days (the end of 1919) delicacies like wheat flour, eggs, butter, sardines, jam, even cocoa and chocolate, were still to be had in the city but people had to get doctors' prescriptions to receive them from a special depot. If a doctor certified that you were suffering from say, acute appendicitis, some "liver disorder, or even gout," you might be solaced with a tin of Norwegian sardines or else a slab of German chocolate. The prescription, issued by specially appointed doctors, had to be countersigned by officials detailed to deal with such matters. Each district had its own "prescription" store, guarded day and night by armed sentries.

To be manager of such a store was a plum of a job. One such had fallen to a grocer from a tiny town near Pskov because his wife's cousin held an important position in the Kremlin.[58]

> Of course he stole from the store. They all did. Some doctors plied a successful trade in issuing prescriptions; no price could have been considered too high for soap or chocolate, and there was no other way of obtaining them—unless people belonged to the privileged Party circle.

But while doctors (or Cheka officials with the power their job afforded) could misuse the system, the employees of the Food Administration remained the main target of popular criticism. When the rations ran out before all had been served, the stall-holder would be accused of selling the bread on the side to make a profit. And, during the food crisis of December 1918, charges of corruption and maladministration culminated in the setting up of a commission to investigate the activites of leading officials, including Strievskii, the commissar, and a call went out to the districts to provide 200 communists to join the commissariat.[59] Similar charges, both at central and district level, occurred throughout the period. But, despite the corruption and inefficiency (which was real enough), the idea of state control per se was never questioned. Those who thought state control alone could solve the food problem may have become disillusioned, but—perhaps surprisingly—no groundswell in favor of bringing back the cooperatives developed. In May 1918 a larger role for them was one of the Putilov demands, and in March 1919 Left SR leaflets called for making cooperatives and trade unions responsible for food administration but no such demands surfaced in 1920 or 1921.[60] Perhaps this was because the cooperatives had been no more successful than the state network. More important, though, there was a ready explanation for the malfunctioning of the state apparatus:

it was because the bourgeoisie had crept into the state administration that such things could happen. Such an explanation followed naturally from a belief that lack of food, high prices, and injustices stemmed from the existence of a bourgeoisie and an alien civil service. If such evils still existed under a workers' government it must be because the bourgeoisie was still at work. That was why the Food Commissarist worked so badly.

The belief that a workers' government would ensure an ideal world could remain unchallenged, and present evils could be seen as easily curable—remove those members of the "soviet bourgeoisie," allow free trade, and all would be well. Bolsheviks felt in their bones that the free-trade arguments were wrong, but they shared the other beliefs—and hence could make even less sense (to themselves) of what was going wrong. Viewing social reality through the prism of old categories produced a curiously blurred picture. To use "the bourgeoisie" as an example, if it was responsible for social ills then, when faced with a perpetrator of privilege or injustice, the worker or Bolshevik "recognized" a member of the bourgeoisie. The result was that a heterogeneous collection of individuals—the dispossessed and often penniless members of once privileged society, higher Soviet officialdom, speculators, and, subsequently, NEP men— whose relationships to each other and whose social power or significance was wholly unclear—acquired the persona of a social group, a fictitious social group. Whether it would survive and play a part in the construction of the new soviet structure of the NEP city, remained to be seen.

NOTES

1. This essay is based on a chapter in the first volume of a study of Leningrad in the interwar period (Oxford, forthcoming).

2. *Stenograficheskii otchet Petrogradskogo soveta*, February 26, 1921, pp. 4, 33, 41.

3. I. Skariatina, *A World Can End* (n.p., 1931) p. 294.

4. Of the numerous sources on the state and private sector and the setting up and subsequent working of Petrokoprod and Petrokommuna, the following are among the most important: A. E. Badaev, *Desiat' let borby i stroitel'stva* (Leningrad, 1927) and the same author's contribution to *Leningradskaia kooperatsiia za 10 let* (Leningrad, 1927); *Izvestiia petrokommuny*; A. I. Puchkov, ed., *Petrokommuna* (Petrograd, 1920).

5. September 20, 1918, p. 2.

6. *Krasnaia gazeta*, April 7, 1920, p. 4; August 12, 1920, p. 3; *Stenograficheckii otchet Petrogradskogo soveta*, August 20, 1920, p. 157.

7. *Novaia prod-politika* (Petrograd, 1921), pp. 148–49; and see *Petrogradskaia pravda*, May 5, 1921, p. 3, for the hope that street-trading would soon again be curbed.

8. The cooperatives are discussed by Badaev and Puchkov; the debate within the party is reported in *Petrogradskaia pravda* from October till the end of December 1918; a recent article that discusses the question of the cooperatives more generally is that by V. V. Kabanov, in *Istoricheskie zapiski*, 1988, vol. 82 pp. 3–39.

9. Contemporary Soviet historians, often drawing on Badaev, Puchkov, and others, have described the early canteen movement. Figures differ quite considerably.

10. Badaev describes the incidents of 1919. For a different example, see Irina Odoev-tseva in *Na beregakh nevy* (Washington, D.C., 1967), who recounts her tearful dismay when Mandelshtam unthinkingly ate her portion of kasha in the House of Writers.

11. *Izvestiia petrokommuny*, 1919, p. 3.

12. For the decree, *Sbornik dekretov i postanovlenii po SKSO* (Petrograd, 1919), vyp.1, pp. 321–24.

13. Ibid., p. 325.

14. Compiled from *Izvestiia petrokommuny*, 1920, p. 12; and Badaev, in *Leningradskaia kooperatsiia*, p. 283.

15. All examples taken from the press except the Porokhovskii data, which are given in a district study, reported in *Izvestiia petrokommuny*, 1919, p. 10. Census returns too show a clear discrepancy between professional groups and ration categories.

16. *Izvestiia narod. kom. po prodovol'stviiu*, 1918, nos. 18–19, p. 41.

17. *Petrogradskaia pravda*, March 23, 1919, p. 1.

18. *Izvestiia petrokommuny*, 1919, p. 16.

19. Ibid.; the press of the early spring of 1920; for the holiday issue, see Badaev, and *Krasnaia gazeta*, August 4, 1920, p. 2; August 5, p. 3.

20. *Krasnaia gazeta*, October 6, 1920, p. 3; *Krasnaia gazeta*, February 5, 1920, p. 3, refers to the injustice of the Putilovtsy only getting "A" rations while the Baltiiskie were getting naval rations. Red Star rations feature in *Izvestiia petrokommuny*; the "extra" rations pose more of a problem, at least for political officials, for whom data are scanty.

21. *Petrogradskaia pravda*, September 20, 1918, p. 2 for the August figures. In December 1920 the Petrograd soviet set up a commission to look into the appalling conditions in the garrison and the destitution of some of the soldiers.

22. *Petrogradskaia pravda*, August 17, 1918, p. 5; Bakhmeteff Archive (Columbia), Russian National Committee: Finland—Related Material.

23. For the extra ration, see Bakhmeteff Archive, RNC: Finland-Related Material. How well leading officials lived is difficult to tell. There are reports of individuals being hungry after scanty meals, but these may have been the most committed communists. The general conclusions are based on some careful statistical work done by economists of the time and my own calculations.

24. *Novyi put'*, 1919, nos. 4–5, p. 20.

25. P. Wolkonsky, *The Way of Bitterness* (London, 1931), p. 157.

26. P. Dukes, *The Story of "ST25"* (n.p., 1938), appendix, p. 369; *Petrogradskaia pravda* and *Krasnaia gazeta*, April 13, 1919, for repercussions from the distribution to Jews; Bakhmeteff Archive, RNC: Finland-Related Material for 1921.

27. I. Dubinskaia, in *Materialy po statistike truda severnoi oblasti*, 1918, vyp.I, pp. 20–32.

28. In *Novyi put'*, 1919, nos. 4–5, p. 20.

29. Dubinskaia's survey was the first of a whole series, reported in a number of different publications. Unless stated otherwise, data quoted here are from *Trudy TsSU*, vol. 8, pt. 7; vol. 30; *Statisticheskii sbornik po Petrogradu i Petrogradskoi gubernii* (Petrograd, 1922); *Biulleten' otdela statistiki truda pri Petrogradskom otdele truda i sovete profsoiuzov*, 1921, no. 32. My attention was first drawn to some of these by an unpublished paper by Horst Temmen (Bremen), given to me by the author, "Materielle Lage der städtischen Bevölkerung von 1917–1921." A number of studies estimating the cost of the standard of living or the fall in real wages also exist, but these are less relevant for our purposes than the consumption data.

30. E. Kabo, *Pitanie russkogo rabochego do i posle voiny* (Moscow, 1926), p. 35, gives the 1908 data; A. Lozitskii, in *Trudy Tsentral'nogo Statisticheskogo upravleniia*, vol. 30, p. 14, the 1919 data.

31. *Krasnaia gazeta*, April 24, 1919, p. 3.

32. *Stenograficheskii otchet*, March 4, 1921, pp. 33–34.

33. E. M. Almedingen, *Tomorrow Will Come* (Woodbridge, 1983), p. 173.

34. Dukes, *Story of "ST25,"* p. 367.

35. *Sbornik dekretov*, p. 312.

36. Ibid., pp. 336–37.

37. Ibid.

38. *Petrogradskaia pravda*, December 13 and 14, 1918, p. 1; *Krasnaia gazeta*, December 31, 1918, p. 2.

39. *Stenograficheskii otchet*, August 29, 1919, pp. 15, 27.

40. *Nash vek*, January 25, 1918, p. 1.

41. *Novyi vechernyi chas*, May 27, 1918, p. 4.

42. *Petrogradskaia pravda*, August 30, 1919, p. 3.

43. *Stenograficheskii otchet*, August 20, 1919, pp. 155–57, and press reports of the time.

44. I. Doubassoff, *Ten Months in Bolshevik Prisons* (London, 1926), p. 14. In fact this transaction landed Doubassoff in prison.

45. *Petrogradskii golos*, January, 17, 1918; Iu. S. Tokarev, V. A. Zubkov, "Pervye narodnye revoliutsionnye sudy v Petrograde," *Istoricheskii arkiv*, 1957, no. 1.

46. *Petrogradskaia pravda*, March 6, 1919, p. 3; May 7, 1919, p. 4.

47. *Stenograficheskii otchet*, August 20. 1920, pp. 162–63.

48. *Ibid.*, September 17, 1920, p. 162.

49. This poem appeared in *Krasnaia gazeta* in February 1921, above the signature of Brauning no. 215, following the anonymous author's attendance at a closed evening in *Dom iskusstv*. It drew an angry but defensive reply from the secretary in *Zhizn' iskusstva*, March 2–4, p. 3. (Gumilev had caused a stir by attending the Pushkin anniversary celebration in evening dress, and this may have prompted the attack.)

50. *Nash vek*, May 9, 1918, p. 3; *Krasnaia gazeta*, April 10, p. 2.

51. *Petrogradskaia pravda*, March 21, 1919, p. 1; March 23, p. 1; *Krasnaia gazeta*, June 11 and 22, 1920.

52. *Stenograficheskii otchet*, February 26, 1921, pp. 40–41.

53. *Ibid.*, March 4, 1921, passim.

54. *Petrogradskaia pravda*, March 28, 1919, p. 4; April 13, 1919, p. 4. The later commentator was A. N. Anishev, in his *Ocherki istorii grazhdanskoi voiny 1917–1920* (Leningrad, 1925) p. 125.

55. *Krasnaia gazeta*, March 30, 1919, p. 4; *Stenograficheskii otchet*, August 6, 1919.

56. *Stenograficheskii otchet*, September 17, 1920, passim.

57. Almedingen, *Tomorrow Will Come*, p. 148.

58. Ibid.

59. *Petrogradskaia pravda*, December 20, 1918, p. 1; December 25, 1919, p. 2.

60. *Nash vek*, May 9, 1918, p. 3; Left SR leaflet: *Otvet fraktsii levykh s-r* (Petrograd, n.d.). this is probably the same as the one referred to by Dukes, *Story of ST25*, p. 256.

STATE BUILDING IN THE CIVIL WAR ERA

THE ROLE OF THE LOWER-MIDDLE STRATA

Daniel T. Orlovsky

Lost among the debates over the bureaucratization of the party and the soviets at the eighth Party Congress of the Bolshevik Party in March 1919 was the following comment by the Bolshevik Antonov pertaining to the reemergence of the "petty bourgeoisie" [*melkaia burzhuaziia*] in Russia's state and party institutions:

> although the petty bourgeoisie is dispersed and at the present time does not have a specific political organization, it continues to exist as a defined social stratum and out of a desire to save itself is attracted to a well-known type of social mimicry. It began to adapt to the new conditions and to penetrate everywhere. After the October Revolution when the colossal advance began, the petty bourgeoisie strove to save itself and gradually began to penetrate the institutions created by the working class. In the end they filled our soviet institutions and even supplanted a significant part of those functionaries who had earlier worked in those institutions—and as a well-defined stratum with a specific psychology infected our own workers [*rabotniki*] with that psychology.[1]

Antonov went on to define the petty bourgeoisie as those who had worked in the old state and public organizations and to claim that this group was the social bearer of bureaucratism. The party, he argued, had taken the line of least resistance and, instead of building new forms, "the party had not built what was necessary, but had absorbed what was suggested by alien elements that had corrupted our soviet institutions."[2] In testing Antonov's assertion about the "petty bourgeoisie" in early soviet government institutions, we shall consider some theoretical and comparative dimensions of the "petty bourgeoisie" as historical problem as well as what I term the social revolution of the lower-middle strata, which took place in Russia between 1905 and 1917.

180

This background will put into sharp focus the dynamic role of the lower-middle strata in politics and state administration during 1917 and Soviet state building. In fact the lower-middle strata's contribution should be viewed as a key, if neglected, cause of the Bolshevik victory in the Civil War.[3]

It has been the party's goal from the beginning of Soviet power to play down the role of non–blue collar workers in the revolution and especially in the construction of the Soviet state and the Bolshevik Party during the early years of soviet power. That the party, then and now, has been interested in pointing up the leading role of the working class in what it proclaimed to be a worker's revolution comes as no surprise. It is also not surprising that peasants and soldiers (and sailors) have received a place in the pantheon of revolutionary classes or social groups both before and after October. The party and official historians have made a great effort to show that the working class played the leading role in state building and that workers and peasants (but especially workers) participated in growing numbers in the early institutions of the Soviet state. The leading Soviet historian of the soviets and of War Communism, E. Gimpelson, in a monograph titled *The Working Class in the Administration of the Soviet State: November 1917–1920,*[4] has used copious statistics to show that in all important areas of state administration, from the economy to culture, workers participated in ever increasing numbers and therefore that the Soviet state had completely fulfilled its promise as a proletarian state. He makes this claim despite the obvious existence of large numbers of the lower-middle strata in virtually all of the institutions under discussion.

The point is that there exists a systematic effort to eliminate from the historical record the presence of the lower-middle strata in the process of state and party formation, and more important, to eliminate consideration of how this group interacted with and influenced the working class, the party, and the workers' and peasants' state. This is not to deny the commitment of the party to its proletarian ideology or to deny the substantial participation of blue-collar workers in Soviet administration. The October Revolution, as Sheila Fitzpatrick has argued, most certainly opened numerous channels of social mobility for blue-collar workers and agrarian laborers.[5] Furthermore, the revolutionary energy of the blue-collar workers and peasants must be recognized as decisive in the establishment of Soviet power and in solving numerous tasks put before the government during the period from October through the Civil War. White-collar workers, statisticians, and feldshers are far less likely to go to the barricades, and factory workers and peasants are less likely to follow them. The major revolutions of the twentieth century have not been made in the name of clerks, sales personnel (*prikazchiki*), village school teachers, and middle and lower-level technical personnel. Yet this does not mean that such people were unwilling participants in the revolution or that their presence as neutrals, or even as opponents of a dominant party or ideology, is a factor to be ignored in a *social* history of the revolution.

For the Bolsheviks before and after October, the "petty bourgeoisie" was a declared class enemy and opponent of Leninist revolution. This "petty bourgeoisie" provided the social support of the left parties that participated in the Provisional Government and stood for a *democratic* revolution that embraced the aspirations of a variety of social groups including the lower-middle strata. In this view, the Bolsheviks followed the prescriptions of classical Marxist theory. Yet in 1917, despite their rhetoric, the Bolsheviks recognized how crucial this group was to a proletarian revolution.[6] The party was skilled at appealing to the growing radicalism and hostility to capitalism of the urban lower-middle strata during 1917. From the Bolshevik perspective, this "petty bourgeoisie" was not revolutionary material when acting in its own name, but if it could bring its radicalism and talents to the side of the blue-collar proletariat, if it could recognize that objectively its class interests were identical, then it could be welcomed into a Bolshevik workers movement. During 1917, Lenin often chided the non-Bolshevik left for viewing the revolution in purely theoretical terms of proletariat and bourgeoisie and "not soberly evaluating the more numerous petty bourgeoisie from either the economic, political, or military point of view."[7] For Lenin, support of the "petty bourgeoisie" was essential to the *making* of a revolution. "The necessary 'majority' of the petty bourgeoisie at the last and decisive moment and at the decisive place joins the revolutionary proletariat."[8] And indeed this occurred in numerous instances in 1917 as white-collar strikers joined their blue-collar counterparts to extract concessions from both factory owners and the Provisional Government.[9]

The lower-middle strata were far from putty in the hands of history. Many social groups in this category had already been radicalized by the 1905 revolution and the experience of World War I. They had exhibited excellent organizational skills in forming trade unions and other organizations and had played a far larger role in a variety of institutions, including the soviets and factory committees both before and after October, than we have recognized. Materials from 1917 and after show that we must begin to see the lower-middle strata alongside the working class and peasantry as a prime mover of the revolutionary process that included the creation of the Soviet state. If we want to understand how the Bolsheviks maintained power in the Civil War era, how they managed to build a remarkably efficient apparatus that could arm and supply the Red Army and administer the Soviet state; if we want to understand the significance of nationalization and economic administration during this period, that is, how they really worked, then we must look to the lower-middle strata.

The lower-middle strata were distinct from earlier groups of shopkeepers and artisans and peasant accumulators—the classic petty bourgeoisie of nineteenth-century Europe and groups often scrutinized in relation to the revolutions of 1848 and in early explanations of the social roots of twentieth-century fascism.[10] Even recent Marxist analyses of the petty bourgeoisie that see the group as the inevitable offspring of capitalist development differ markedly on such issues as the relationship of "old," and "new" petty bourgeoisie, whether or not the entire group constitutes a class, and the historical and contemporary possibilities of solidarity with the proletariat as opposed to the bourgeoisie. Nicos Poulantzas, for example, does see the combined group as a class that, despite its often anticapitalist ideology, aspires to upward mobility and individualism and maintains values of order, discipline, and legitimate hierarchy.[11] Poulantzas argues that a worker-petty bourgeois alliance can only be accomplished by prior recognition of the class differences between the two troupes and working-class hegemony and leadership through all stages of the political process. For Poulantzas, this alliance is not a matter of formal concessions to petty bourgeois interests, but of transforming those interests through the class struggle itself.[12] Erik Olin Wright, in opposition to Poulantzas, argues that the ambiguities in class relations should be studied in their own right and not forced into rigid class categories. In a theoretical approach similar to that used here, Wright adopts the term "contradictory class locations" to describe social groups or layers located between accepted class divisions.[13] From these contradictory class locations, Wright sees the full possibility of the unity of various layers in enlarged classes such as the proletariat.[14] The case of revolutionary Russia offers fertile ground for fulfilling Wright's and Arno J. Mayer's calls for analysis of the lower-middle strata in their own right and their relation to "classes" and the revolutionary process.[15]

In a recent work on late nineteenth-century Paris shopkeepers, Philip G. Nord has captured the shifting political allegiances of the Parisian petty bourgeoisie and in so doing has rejected older sociological conceptions of the problem that posit an almost inevitable shift from lower-middle-class liberalism to the radical right and then to twentieth-century fascism.[16] According to Nord, the Parisian shopkeepers did shift from left to right during the late nineteenth century under the influence of "Haussmannization" of the urban landscape and a variety of economic pressures including depression, transformations in the shape and structure of the urban retail market, the development of the department store, imports of consumer goods, and the selective decline of certain luxury good and artisanal enterprises. Yet, for Nord, this shift was neither inevitable nor solely dictated by economic decline. Such decline was always selective, and in fact many shopkeepers flourished under the new regime of commercial capital. In fact the organized shopkeeper movement emerged not out of a "liberal" tradition (this argument is a fantasy of Western liberal historiography and social science), but out of a radical republican or populist tradition that was at once anticapitalist and nationalist, that believed in public virtue and "democracy," in the threat of a parasitic new aristocracy of wealth and political power. In a telling comparison to American populism, Nord writes:

> American populists combined moral conservatism and faith in small ownership with a genuine radicalism that focused on citizen participation and issues of social welfare. The same can be said of the *Ligue syndicale*, and it is possible to recognize in the *Ligue* the embryo of a French populism.
>
> However the *Ligue*'s politics are to be characterized—radical republican, populist, Radical-Socialist or Boulangist—they were left wing, but not liberal,

or even pseudo-liberal. On this point the French case deviates from the "liberal to fascist" schema. Just the same, the shopkeeper movement still ended up on the right, as predicted by the sociological school.[17]

Not only did this petty bourgeoisie begin on the left, but it easily switched over to the right. The question is why, and here Nord goes beyond the depression experience to the realm of politics and ideology. The organized shopkeeper's relations to the left deteriorated during the 1890s when it appeared that collectivist ideologies no longer took stock of shopkeeper interests. At the same time the shopkeepers attacked organized labor with a campaign against consumer cooperatives. The bourgeoisie, for its part, helped block reform and leave the shopkeepers politically isolated. From their perspective, neither the left nor the center appeared willing to take up their cause. Calculation demanded then a search for new political allies, and these they found on the radical right with its language of "small owner utopianism and cultural reaction."[18] According to Nord, "The *petit commercant* recognized in the man of letters a common defender of a commercial and cultural milieu threatened with extinction. It was not just demogoguery and manipulation that drew the shopkeeper movement to Nationalism, but a shared perspective based . . . on a shared experience of disruption."

The great secret of the new radical right was its ability to coopt and assimilate both the doctrines and values of the small proprietors. These included the ideology of smallness, integrity of neighborhood, workshop, and family; independence, thrift, hard work, and paternal authority. Of prime importance was patriotism and belief in the state as protector of social equilibrium and regulator of the hegemonic apsirations of labor and capital. Thus, lower-middle-class political allegiance is always an open question whose answer is determined by a mixture of economic, political, and ideological factors. The Russian lower-middle strata provide an illuminating counterpoint to the French example. In Russia, these groups also began on the left, largely as populist believers in democracy and the moral worth of the "people" as compared to the interests of capital or the older landed or service nobility. They too made political choices during the revolutionary upheavals, choices that conformed to their interests. At first these choices amounted to full support of various grass-roots political and social organizations that received the sanction of the Provisional Governments. When this version of the "democratic" left failed to fulfill its promises, its guarantees of social mobility and political stability with large-scale lower-middle strata participation, these social groups joined and were absorbed into the new Bolshevik state. This new state, of course, espoused a radical, transformative doctrine based on the proletariat and peasants. Yet its social content was far more diverse, and indeed one might argue that Bolshevism too would shortly become a radical movement of the right, despite its worker and peasant supporters.

The revolutionary year, 1917, witnessed the completion of a quiet but deeply rooted social movement of the lower-middle strata. The lower-middle strata helped provide the dynamism for the revolution. Not only did this group supply many leaders of the parties of the non-Bolshevik left and center, but the social movement of the lower-middle strata also took several forms.

The Provisional Government made a large commitment to the lower-middle strata in the cities as well as in the provinces. This commitment or wager on the non–blue-collar, nonpropertied elements of Russian society was expressed in the almost ritualistic proclamations and policies in favor of "self-government" and "democratization" within the organs of self-government.

In 1917, the zemstvos also experienced a social transformation. Even before the first elections of new zemstvo assemblies and executive boards, the movement for democratization brought to the fore smoldering social and political conflicts between the Third Element experts and white-collar workers and the older zemstvo leadership in the assemblies and among the permanent executive board staff.[19] The zemstvos with their many departments and industrial and commercial enterprises were among the larger employers in many nonindustrial provinces.[20] The February Revolution unleashed the pent-up desires of middle- and lower-ranking members of the provincial lower-middle strata working in these departments and enterprises, and indeed from all available evidence, they succeeded in wresting control of the assemblies and executive boards from the property owners and their collaborators during the first months of the revolution. This democratization from below took place prior to the elections meant to produce that result. It was important that members of the lower-middle strata had taken political power in their local spheres, but equally important is the fact that during 1917 they took over *management of state functions*.

The Provisional government created two types of local bodies that were immediately dominated by the lower-middle strata—the land and food supply committees. A striking aspect of the historiography of the Provisional Government is the curious inattention of both Soviet and Western scholars to the social composition of these bodies and their place in either the *social* revolution of 1917 or Soviet state building.[21]

Here clarification is necessary about the category "peasant" as applied to statistics. In 1917, Lenin claimed that the provincial-level land committees, for example, were the least democratic (implying that the bourgeoisie dominated them), that the district committees were more democratic, and that the volost committees were most democratic.[22] The implication is that these volost committees were staffed by peasants who had proper revolutionary class interests. We are to believe that these peasants were all agricultural laborers and not village intelligentsia—agronomists, teachers, statisticians, doctors, feldshers, or cooperative workers who were born into the peasantry and would have declared themselves "peasants" whenever required to do so on official documents or election lists before or after October 1917. The village intelligentsia and other members of the lower-middle strata played a leading role on these committees at all levels. The committees and their experts, primarily agronomists, statisticians, and cooperative workers, helped build the Soviet state during the Civil War period.[23]

Two important types of peasant institutions that advertised themselves as "class" institutions of the toiling narod were, in fact, dominated by village *intelligenty*, specialists, and other individuals often born into the peasant estate (*soslovie.*) These were the local branches of the All-Russian Peasant Union, and the peasant soviets themselves as well as the expanding cooperatives that came to dominate commerce and supply well beyond their original Provisional Government mandate in the area of foodstuffs.

As shown above many of the peasant volost committees that were formed during the first days of the February Revolution included village *intelligenty*, teachers, feldshers, and cooperative workers. In fact these often were the leaders to whom the peasants turned during the heady March days to establish the new committees to replace the largely discredited and ineffective volost administration of the old regime. It may be that village *intelligenty* were respected because of their knowledge or because they were perceived to be "of the people" or peasants themselves. What has been overlooked in treatments of the revolution, however, is not the existence of these committees, but their social content and historical roots going back to the 1905 revolution. What becomes abundantly clear about the committees, the Peasant Union and soviets, and the cooperatives is how closely their organizational forms and participants resembled those of the 1905 revolution and, in the case of the cooperatives at least, the period of growth brought on by World War I as well.

In addition to the formation after February 1917 of volost and village committees and local peasant unions, the lower-middle strata in the unions and cooperatives moved immediately to call the first district and provincial peasant congresses.[24] The first provincial congresses were organized three to four weeks after the revolution in Nizhnii Novgorod and Iaroslavl' provinces as the Peasant Union and cooperatives responded to the Provisional Government's March 19 edict calling on local committees to supply materials to the government on the land question.[25] The over six hundred delegates who attended the Nizhnii congress and Smirnov's silence about the social composition of these and other congress delegates speaks eloquently for the presence of significant numbers of lower-middle strata employees and *intelligenty*. As a testament to the significance of the lower-middle strata acting through the Peasant Union and its successor, the All-Russian Congress of Soviets of Peasants' Deputies, in 1917 we may refer to the Shestakov's document collection on the peasant soviets. A significant portion of this volume is devoted to the Peasant Union and acknowledges its role in the creation and development of peasant soviets.

Running like a thread through the Peasant Union and their successor soviets in the provinces were the employees and organizations of Russia's cooperative movement. In many ways the cooperatives are a paradigm of the entire state-building process since they illustrate clearly the connections between the lower-middle strata and both blue-collar workers and peasants, and they were functioning economic organizations that became a growing infrastructure absolutely indispensable to the Provisional Government and its Bolshevik successor alike. Although Soviet scholars have tended to view the pre-October cooperatives and post-October cooperative leadership as petty bourgeois representatives of a capitalist economy, the key to understanding the dynamics of the movement and the social forces represented is the fact that cooperative employees as well as their theoreticians espoused a deeply anticapitalist ideology. One might well argue that the cooperatives prior to October did function within the framework of a "capitalist" economy. But the entire program was directed against capitalist control of the marketplace and particularly of distribution. As with the zemstvo employees, rural teachers, agronomists, and others, cooperative workers were populist in orientation; their mission was serving the *narod* and saving them from capitalist exploitation. In the words of two of the movement's leaders:

> The cooperative movement, representing a compact organization of thousands of self-governing economic units interlaced in district and regional unions, and served by practical experts, statisticians, engineers, and economists, seemed the only assembly and distributing agency of a public character remaining in the open—at a time of universal disintegration and imminent economic catastrophe. The leaders of the movement became conscious of their power; they felt that should the government permit them in the future to work without hindrance, they would free producers and consumers, in the country and city, from their subjection to speculative middlemen, and bring Russian agriculture in particular into a closer economic contact with the national and international markets. . . . The members were essentially their own shopkeepers acting through their elected representatives. The cooperative store was thus more than a retailing business; it was a school of social and economic responsibilities for the inculcation of self-help, thrift and loyalty to mutual interests.[26]

The cooperative movement, and consumer cooperatives in particular, made great advances after the outbreak of World War I in 1914—advances that continued almost unabated after both the February and October Revolutions of 1917.[27] Although the major cause of this growth was the economic crisis exacerbated by the war, and more particularly the supply crisis, we must not lose sight of the more general cultural and political motivations of many cooperators. Consonant with the theme of this book, a major goal of the movement was to build democracy in Russia. The cooperative experience was meant to instill the spirit of democracy among the people. In describing these motivations, the Menshevik cooperative activist M. D. Shishkin put it clearly: "Some believed that through cooperation the people would come to democracy. Others nourished the even greater faith that through cooperation the people would come to socialism. All agreed that through cooperation the people would gain the habits, experience and knowledge necessary for the building of a better future."[28] This sense of cultural mission, of course, had its political as well as moral overtones. The cooperatives represented an already existing and growing infrastructure that provided, perhaps even more than teachers, a direct link to the peasant masses on the eve of the revolution. As one cooperator put it in 1915: "At the present time there is no other road to the peasant masses than that through cooperatives."[29]

Before discussing the cooperatives' role in the 1905–7 revolution, World War I, and 1917, a few words about the social composition of the movement are in order. Salzman provides data on the representatives to the twenty-fifth, twenty-sixth, twenty-seventh meetings of the Moscow Society for Consumer Cooperatives held in 1912 and 1913.[30] She notes that after 1905–7, "cooperators came more and more frequently to have third element backgrounds."[31] And indeed, the representatives included numerous public and private sector "employees"—teachers, agronomists, bookkeepers, professionals, and the like. Over 80 percent of the delegates to the twenty-sixth meeting were under forty years of age: 53 of the 187 were between the ages of twenty-six and thirty. These figures seem to say nothing about social origin or status, but the fact is that the vast majority of these "employee" and professional cooperators had been born into the peasantry. Before and during World War I, the cooperatives provided horizontal links to the trade unions, zemstvos and town dumas, War Industries Committees, and other provincial and municipal organizations. During the war, the cooperatives played a key role in supplying the army and the general population. At a 1915 congress, the Central War Industries Committee resolved to give representation on War Industries Committees to unions of cooperative societies. The cooperatives joined with the zemstvo and municipal employees to form a solid bloc of lower-middle strata power over and against representatives from the propertied social groups.

The cooperative movement was of enormous importance to the Provisional Government as it would be to the Bolsheviks after October. The Provisional Government denied the commercial bourgeoisie its traditional role in supplying food and instead threw its support entirely to the cooperatives. These were to work together with the food supply committees dominated by the lower-middle strata and to some extent with zemstvos and even soviets as well.[32] Many leaders of the cooperative movement were coopted into the Provisional Government as high officials (for example, Prokopovich, Zel'geim) and the entire movement with its anticapitalist, populist ideology organized during 1917 to meet Provisional Government overtures and to deal the capitalist commercial infrastructure a mortal blow.

Provincial economic administration provides parallel examples of the lower-middle strata social movement. This movement helps explain just how the Bolsheviks managed to raise and supply the Red Army and win the Civil War with an industrial base that was shattered in comparison to prewar statistical levels. Lower-middle strata organizations of World War I and 1917 in particular provided the foundation for the local economic councils (sovnarkhozy and glavki)—the provincial and district organs of the post-October Supreme Council of the National Economy (Vesenkha).[33] The roots of this participation in economic management during the Civil War and the prominent role of industrial white-collar workers in the young Soviet state can be seen clearly in 1917 and indeed as far back as the Revolution of 1905.

White-collar trade unions and mixed blue- and white-collar unions provide a final base for the social and organizational revolution of the lower-middle strata during 1917. As in the case of the soviets and cooperatives these unions drew white-collar employees closer to the blue-collar working class and set them in opposition to both factory owners and the Provisional Government.[34] Of 111 unions that existed at least one month in Petrograd in 1917, no fewer than 72 were white collar or mixed white and blue collar in composition. These included 222,300 individuals or 37 percent of the membership of unions that reported statistics. In Moscow, there were, in 1917, 40 unions of white-collar workers and semiproletarian elements.

In Siberia, July 1917 statistics reveal that of 418 unions, 158 were white collar and 40 were mixed, white and blue collar in membership. In the Urals, 84 white-collar unions existed out of 204 total. In many instances white-collar workers in individual factories led or participated in strikes, organized regional and national congresses, and searched for ways to protect and assert their interests. Unions were created in the various ministries of the Provisional Government (as well as among provincial *chinovniki* and other state employees) as were soviets of deputies of the "laboring intelligentsia." The latter were created in May 1917 in Moscow to emulate the Union of Unions of the 1905 revolution.[35] They aimed to become a center for "the attraction of all creative forces for constructive work in all areas of the economy and culture." These lower-middle strata soviets were neither class nor party organs, and by July they had over 100,000 members in 100 organizations. It was this kind of movement in the provinces that produced slates of white-collar candidates for elections to the dumas, zemstvos, and eventually, under party labels, for the Constituent Assembly.

By October 1917, there were approximately one million members in unions of mixed white- and blue-collar membership representing about one-third of all union members.[36] The creation of many joint unions with blue-collar workers, the organization of national union institutions and congresses, specialization according to branch of industry, and assimilation of the white-collar groups into the larger All-Russian Trade Union movement and its organizations eased the lower-middle strata's transition into the institutions of the workers' state after October. National (and local) trade union organizations and the Bolshevik Party were responsible for selecting cadres and managers and thus for promoting blue-collar workers into white-collar positions during the Civil War period.[37]

Union bureaucracies had a significant lower-middle strata membership. The composition of the Third and Fourth Trade Union Congresses during the Civil War and transition to NEP reveals this pattern as well as the cooptation of the unions into the state structure.[38] Among delegates to the Fourth Trade Union Congress (May 17–25, 1921), for example, 41 percent of the voting delegates (988 of 2,357) and 47.3 percent of the delegates with advisory votes (355 of 748) were engaged in nonmanual or "mental" labor as opposed to 59 percent and 52.7 percent, respectively, who were engaged in manual labor.[39] By union *stazh*, the overwhelming majority of delegates entered the unions during 1917 and after (1,942 of the voting and 623 of the advisory delegates) and were elected (95.2 percent of the decisive and 88.8 percent of the advisory votes) to the congress by provincial and district-level trade union departments and conferences. This suggests that the vital 1917 trade union movement had already included an important white-collar component and that, after October, it increasingly drew into its ranks provincial white-collar types who imparted attitudes and patterns of organization to blue-collar workers. The lower-middle strata were a vital catalyst in the absorption of blue-collar unions into a statist framework.

Party and union leaders could speak at this congress of the break-up of the working class during the Civil War or, as Bukharin did, of the nonexistence in Russia of a working class, but the same could not be said for lower-middle strata functionaries. They were survivors who more than survived. Wherever we look, whether to the soviets, the economic councils, the trade unions, or to the party itself, we see evidence of their staying power and their rise to prominence through the expanding organs of the new party-state. The Bolsheviks counted on the proletarianization of the lower-middle strata and their attraction to the working class both to make the revolution and build a Soviet state. Yet the question remains open as to whether the lower-middle strata became proletarianized or the opposite occurred, that blue-collar workers (and peasants) fell under the influence of the lower-middle strata.

The Lower-Middle Strata and State Building after October

Recent studies have increased our knowledge of the early Soviet state and the state building process, 1917–21.[40] Yet, the topic is vast and as is the case in virtually all areas of Soviet history, the waters remain relatively uncharted. The diligent reader can now find, however, basic materials on the institutions of the early Soviet state—ranging from the Council of People's Commissars at the center to the provincial soviets. The same can be found for the political and administrative work of state and party institutions. Yet important social and cultural dimensions of the state-building process have been ignored. Continuities in administrative forms, practices, and ethos are treated only tangentially, and most scholars, to the extent that they consider ideology, focus strictly on Bolshevik factions and individuals during the post-October period. Thus, political culture is equated with Bolshevik ideology, and we are absolved from considering how uncodified cultural norms and traditions of power may have shaped Bolshevik ideologies. What remains unanswered is why Lenin and his immediate circle opted for the old ministerial form of government in the new revolutionary workers' and peasants' state and the implications of this choice for the development of that state.[41]

The state building process cannot be reduced to formal administration or the dysfunctions, abuses, and record of conflicts among rival Soviet institutions during the Civil War. The sources are quick to reveal this formal story of administrative conflict and ostensible incompetence that supports a jaundiced view of post-1921 Soviet history and institutions. What is missing is the social dimension and the dynamic interaction between state and society that marked the entire revolutionary era in Russia, including the two decades prior to 1917. Revolutionary state building was more than the proliferation of formal institutions and government decrees, though these do outline the course of government domestic policy.[42] One shortcoming in our approach to state building has been to treat both the party and the state as reified historical actors, set apart from society, that after internal debates enunciated and implemented policies despite institutional and ideological divisions. Another is to concentrate excessively on those formal divisions and institutional conflicts. In the area of economic administration, for example, the People's Commissariat of Finance (*Narkomfin*), *Vesenkha*, the Council of Labor and Defense, military supply organs, the *glavki*, and *sovnarkhozy* all fought for autonomy, resources, and control.[43] Similarly, the soviets and the Central Executive Committee struggled against the party and Sovnarkom; Soviet departments relived the old tsarist debates about dual responsibility, that is, the allegiance of Soviet departments to Soviet executive committees on the one hand and central commissariats on the other; and the new food supply dictatorship under Narkomprod with its helpmate committees of the poor peasants also fought for power against established Soviet organs in the face of the ongoing food supply crisis.

The one question never asked as historians describe the numerous Bolshevik state and party institutions and policy struggles is how was it possible in such a short time for the young Soviet state to have produced hundreds of institutions with tens of thousands of functionaries? What was the social source of the remarkably elaborate infrastructure that embodied the economy and the larger realm of administration by mid-1918? The fact is that revolutionary state building was a dynamic social and cultural process with roots in the institutions of tsarist Russia and especially in the social revolution of the lower-middle strata that had reached its crescendo in 1917. When speaking of the state or the party, it is necessary to recognize that this social movement, which had provided mobility and status for several decades, now offered these in even greater measure, and *power* as well. The social movement provided much of the infrastructure for the new state in the form of the numerous institutions, offices, and life possibilities that became that party/state. Thus, the lower and middle levels of the various hierarchies that were in the process of becoming the state may be viewed as membranes through which society nourished that state. Functioning as a surrogate marketplace that in turn could shape social development, this new state grew rapidly as it absorbed the lower-middle strata and upwardly mobile workers and peasants.

In this sense the state as historical actor, particularly at middle and lower levels, must be viewed as a dynamic and developing social entity. This does not mean that we should abandon entirely the idea of separation between state and society. Indeed, such a model remains valid when describing the power position of the highest central and provincial authorities or the application of state power to individuals or groups who have formal, but not substantial, legal protection against officeholders or institutions claiming legitimate authority as part of that state. The same holds true for economic dependence. To the extent that individuals and groups are dependent on the state rather than the marketplace for shares of national resources, the concept of subordination of individuals or social groups to the state takes on meaning.[44] There remains no elegant English translation for *ogosudarstvlenie* (statization), yet this term appeared frequently in Civil War era debates to describe the state-building process, and particularly what appeared to be the absorption of an independent infrastructure into the state. Revolutionary state building exemplified both the creation of the state from below and the reestablishment of "statehood" (*gosudarstvennost'*) with authority patterns that often pitted social groups against one another or left them defenseless against state power.

The central administrative commissariats (heirs to the ministerial bureaucracy), soviets, cooperatives, and professional congresses are just several of many examples of the state-building process at work during the Civil War period. They illustrate continuities with the pre-October social movement of the lower-middle strata and the importance of existing infrastructures and patterns of administration and authority to the new state.[45]

Lenin and his government opted immediately to make use of the ministerial bureaucracy of the old regime and Provisional Government. Of course, these were renamed as people's commissariats, but essentially the structures and even personnel of the old regime and Provisional Government remained in place. Only in such highly politicized ministries as the Commissariat of Internal Affairs did substantial purging of Provisional Government officials take place."[46] Not only was carryover high (50 to 80 percent) in the upper and middle reaches of the central government commissariats, but the social origin and occupation of these men and women clearly places them within the lower-middle strata. According to Iroshnikov, "employees" comprised more than 50 percent of leading central government officials in eleven of the fifteen central state institutions examined."[47] Among the so-called top management (*rukovoditeli*) the percentages were even higher. Iroshnikov is one of the few Soviet scholars to recognize the dominant role of "employees" drawn from the old regime, public and private sectors (and not workers or peasants) in the Civil War–era administration. The new government coopted holdover and non-government specialists into the state-building project.[48]

From the beginning of Soviet power, Lenin wrote frequently of the cooperatives as essential building blocks of socialism. In notes to the "Project on Consumer Communes," he wrote as follows about the organization of supply and distribution:

Cooperative units should be both consumer and production (this is better than wholesaling and trading etc.) volost unions that also play the role of supply committees and organs of requisition. Volost borders may be changed if necessary. In cities, perhaps similar committees could be organized by neighborhood or parts of streets. These would provide a network capable of organizing distribution of necessities to the entire population as well as production on a general state scale.[49]

Lenin and other Bolsheviks foresaw the nationalization of the consumer and credit cooperatives, but as in the case of industry this was a tricky business, especially since the cooperatives were far more experienced and able than any possible soviet rival in the countryside. Moreover, the cooperatives in many provinces were *already* functioning as the legitimate ("state") supply organs. In March 1918, Sovnarkom and Narkomprod issued decrees ordering soviets to halt interference in "general state procurements policy" and in the activities of the cooperatives, some of which had been forcibly nationalized or shut down by overzealous local "functionaries."[50] The result was the so-called compromise decree "On Consumer Cooperative Organizations" of April 11, 1918, in which the cooperative leadership agreed to limit government control in exchange for permission to continue operations under pre-October leadership and functionaries. The cooperatives maintained enrollment fees and managed to stave off the desires of more ideologically minded Bolsheviks to "proletarianize" the movement and its institutions.[51]

By early summer 1918, in the wake of the spring food procurement crisis and on the eve of the Civil War itself, the cooperatives were extremely active in supply and credit operations—and they would become even more so during the Civil War. The reports from the provinces at the Conference of Representatives of Tsentrosoiuz, the largest national cooperative organization, held in Moscow, April 24–2 May, 1918, illustrate not only a business-as-usual attitude, which might be surprising enough, but also a clear recognition of cooperative expertise and power that pointed toward future domination of supply function.[52] Representatives of Simbirsk, Voronezh, Viatka, and Urals, to name just a few, claimed that the cooperatives were growing rapidly, that they were the only competent economic organs in the localities, and that they had help from the local soviet authorities. As one put it: "In terms of businesslike work, the local commissariat of supply wants to enlist cooperative forces to supply the population with goods.[53] This same Ural representative spoke also of nationalizations and claimed that the cooperatives' only weapon was to insist that all economic activity would stop as a result. Faced with this threat, local authorities reversed the nationalizations.

As with most policy during the Civil War, there was no single Bolshevik attitude toward the cooperatives. Lenin steered clear of emphasizing the "bourgeois" nature of these institutions, preferring instead to coopt the mid- and lower-level functionaries and the entire apparatus while supporting the further development of class-dominated proletarian cooperatives."[54] Lenin and other central government figures repeatedly had to defend the cooperatives by emphasizing that they were indispensible to the war effort and the construction of socialism and that since they no longer existed in a capitalist environment, their essence had in fact changed.[55] One point of agreement for all Bolshevik leaders, however, was the need to absorb them into the state, to control and indeed eventually destroy the independence with which they operated. The result was the Sovnarkom decree of March 20, 1919, on consumer communes, which recognized their primary role in the economy but only as state institutions.[56] The decree mandated transformation of the cooperatives "so that the main apparatus of correct mass distribution, namely the cooperatives, created and proven by many years of development and practical experience under capitalism, will not be destroyed or cast aside, but placed upon a new, secure, developed and mature foundation."[57]

The situation was similar in the area of cooperative credit institutions. Provincial credit cooperatives flourished after the October Revolution. On a larger scale, during 1917–19, the Moscow People's Bank became a powerful financial center, active in foreign markets as well as in the Soviet state. It financed cooperatives, received deposits, and was a large supplier of farm implements and other goods to the countryside. For most of 1918, it was the only private bank not nationalized by the Bolshevik government. On December 2, 1918, the government finally nationalized the Moscow People's Bank and the provincial credit institutions, but unlike the earlier nationalizations of private banks, the Moscow Bank was left as a largely autonomous "cooperative department" of the People's Bank of the RSFSR.[58] The technical and managerial personnel continued their work in this new framework.

In the autumn of 1918, Tsentrosoiuz leader A. N. Lavrukhin noted that "a whole range of food supply organizations have found it necessary, despite prejudice against the cooperatives, to transfer to them all technical functions of goods distributions."[59] Throughout 1918, Tsentrosoiuz and its organs had distributed goods in twenty-seven provinces. In fifteen of these, cooperatives controlled all distribution. In the remaining twelve provinces, cooperatives distributed more than one-half of all products.[60] The cooperatives served approximately 70 percent of the entire population (close to 100 million people) through 53,000 consumer and 17,500 credit institutions. By 1919 there were 18 million members of the consumer cooperatives, up from 11 million at the end of 1917.[61] Cooperative production enterprises also grew. Cooperative workshops and factories produced leather and metal goods, paper and other wood products, foodstuffs, printed material, and chemicals and minerals. At a time when many factories were closed, cooperative enterprises flourished. The leading Soviet scholar of the cooperatives, V. V. Kabanov, agrees with the claims of the cooperative leadership during the Civil War: "Cooperation was about the only organization that retained virtually all its power during the years of war and revolution: its apparatus, cadres, capital and well developed business relations in Russia and abroad."[62]

Officially, the soviets, as institutions of proletarian democracy, were the building blocks of the post-October revolutionary state.[63] The outlines of "soviet construction" are now well known, but again mainly from a formal perspective. We know that the soviets existed, helped seize power, multiplied, became bureaucratized, and had conflicts with the provincial apparats of the various commissariats (ministries) and eventually with the Bolshevik Party itself. In fact, bureaucratization of the party and its centralizing, authoritarian approach to government (creation of the party/state) in 1918–21 have been explained as a response to the manifold crisis of the Civil War, which included the excessive independence and political unreliability of the soviets.[64] In relation to the social dimension of state building, the following points are important. First, even before October the soviets had become bureaucratic administrative organs with significant lower-middle strata participation. They actively participated in the October Revolution (which extended on into 1918) to the extent that they had come under the control of reliable Bolshevik cadres or to the extent that Soviet functionaries believed that the revolution signified a devolution of power to the localities under their hegemony. In many cases the transfer of power to the Bolsheviks was effected through the use of military revolutionary committees and plenipotentiaries—representatives of personal and noninstitutionalized power, which were the heirs of prerevolutionary political culture and the forerunners of provincial party institutions and secretaries.[65] The central Bolshevik leadership's authority and articulated ideology of "democratic centralism" were crucial, as the leadership moved in 1918 to purge the still popular SRs and Mensheviks from elected and appointed positions, to set up the system of dual subordination of soviet departments to provincial and district soviet executive committees as well as central commissariats, and to use the soviets (among many other institutions as we have seen) to integrate and mobilize the provinces for the Civil War effort.[66]

Local politics had much to do with the construction of soviets before and after October, but so did the existing institutions of the lower-middle strata. The evidence is clear. Zemstvos and town dumas, for example, did not disappear when abolished by decree: rather, they became soviet departments staffed by Third Element functionaries.[67]

A Bolshevik plenipotentiary filed a revealing inspection report on the 1918 work of a district Soviet executive committee in Viatka Province.[68] After the ritual complaints that the district had existed in "full chaos and with the absence of power (*bezvlastie*)," he chided the old zemstvo and peasant executive committee for weakness, lack of energy, and, perhaps more important, lack of funds to conduct business. The peasant committee was also politically unreliable as it consisted of many former Right SRs or nonparty types. Typically, both ignored the edicts of the central government. In January 1918, Bolsheviks, with the help of soldiers returned from the front, engineered a counter–peasant conference, which declared itself to be in power. The problem, according to the plenipotentiary, was that this new group lacked the knowledge and experience of soviets and administration. As a result, the new soviet took over all existing organs of self-government and state administration. These were ordered to continue work under "soviet control." Commissars would be the controllers and elected representatives were eliminated. Officials (*rabotniki*) took over all responsible posts (which for some meant remaining in place). Provisional Government food supply and land committees were renamed as Soviet sections and all employees and officials were mandated to remain on the job. Soviet commissars and the trade unions took over all appointments and dismissals with appeals in this area referred to the Soviet executive committee. The district economic council (*sovnarkhoz*) was to be organized within the agricultural department of the zemstvo executive board, and all judicial personnel were to remain in place.

Administration went more smoothly, despite the inability of this "new" infrastructure to collect taxes, and the central government representative listed the well-known revolutionary edicts (on land, marriage, workers control, and the like) implemented by the soviet. Despite persistent political problems—usually resulting in battles as district soviet congresses and always won by the Bolsheviks with the help of the Red Army—this administrative mechanism (which now included more sophisticated economic, statistical, and technical departments) with its former Third Element, cooperative, and other economic functionaries continued to develop through further annexations of lower-middle strata infrastructure. This kind of development prepared the Bolshevik regime for the Civil War as much as did creation of the Red Army and re-establishment of the central ministerial bureaucracy.[69]

The debates over centralization during the Civil War–era party and soviet congresses are well known, as is the fate of the "democratic centralists." What must be emphasized, however, is that both parties to this conflict promoted the primacy of administration and lower-middle strata functionaries and specialists. Despite this, the official line maintained that it was a worker and peasant state. At the First Congress of Representatives of Provincial Soviets and Directors of Provincial Departments of Administration, speakers proclaimed the need for further centralization in line with NKVD policy and described the successes of 1918 as clear evidence "that workers and poor peasants could run the country, on new principles, without *chinovnichestvo*, or appointments from the center."[70] This was certainly the official view repeated at the conference by the commissar of internal affairs, G. Petrovskii, who raved against localism, administrative parallelism and conflicts. The NKVD had created the departments of administration to centralize administration within the soviets themselves—to keep the various soviet departments from working at cross purposes. It appears from such documents that the frequency of terms such as worker and peasant state and centralization masked the realities of local power and the hybrid social composition of Soviet institutions.[71]

Professional congresses and organizations, often deeply rooted in the lower-middle strata, offered the new regime yet another source of strength for the state-building project. The Civil War era continued the proliferation of such organizations and congresses begun during 1917 or earlier.

Functionaries and specialists from such diverse branches as the judiciary, education, health sciences, agriculture, statistics, local treasury offices, transportation, State Bank employees, Labor Ministry, Post and Telegraph, engineering, and the like held regular meetings and developed provincial and national organizations that served to leaven the revolutionary loaf.[72] White-collar workers, specialists, professionals, and technical personnel of all sorts organized to protect material interests and status, and the records of these congresses reflect the desire of professional groups to find ways to continue their work, despite disagreements with local officials or party leadership. In the words of the director of the Department of Customs Duties to union member employees: "the present moment of political unrest does not permit us to speak seriously to reforms in our institution. Our task today is to secure our Department in its entirely and unity until better times."[73] The message was that professional service was a social obligation. Some unions such as that of post and telegraph workers, were pro-Bolshevik from the beginning, whereas others, such as the engineers, worked to stave off the claims of workers' control. Congresses of judicial and labor commissars also reflected the official party line as pro-Bolshevik functionaries moved to establish control over the administration of justice and labor relations. Yet the web of relations between this new officialdom and society helped forge the links of future state power. Despite the chaos and brutality of the Civil War, the state-building process was remarkably elaborate and possessed deep social roots. The record of persistent organized activity on the part of administrative units of all sorts and the widespread participation of the lower-middle strata in numerous professional, technical, and service positions stand as monuments to the power of society and culture to shape revolution.

In 1924 one of the principal architects of early Bolshevik economic policy, Iu. Larin (Lur'e), clearly enunciated the role of the lower-middle strata in revolutionary state building.[74] Larin began a review of the intelligentsia's relationship to soviet power since the October Revolution by dividing it into three layers. The highest, or elite level, included leading scholars, engineers and high-status professionals. These most often openly opposed soviet power, and many chose to leave Soviet Russia. Nonetheless, Lenin and the party appealed to them to join in constructive work under the protective umbrella of high wages promised to bourgeois specialists. Many did join in the work of the new regime. Next Larin pointed to a larger group of middle intelligentsia embracing the broad categories in the free professions and middle-management levels in the state and private sector. This group was more politically neutral during the October Revolution and establishment of soviet power during the Civil War. But, he argues, they were most definitely bourgeois in psychological orientation. Larin claimed that without constraint this middle layer would naturally gravitate toward the culture and institutions of bourgeois society. They might be used to build socialism, but only under strict control. They were an unlikely target group for conversion to proletarian consciousness or point of view. Finally, Larin claimed that there existed a third layer of intelligentsia *that had been instrumental in the establishment and securing of soviet power*—a mass group of semiproletarian intelligentsia who shared many elements of proletarian class consciousness and who had fought alongside workers to establish the Soviet state. Larin's admission of the lower-middle strata's historic role carries extra weight since he and most other top party leaders depended so much on this social movement to manage the economy and administer the state during the Civil War.

Statistics support this thesis and suggest numerous lines of future inquiry in early Soviet history, in the theory of revolution, and in the comparative history of Soviet society and that of the more highly industrialized societies of the West. Communist Party membership statistics for 1922 set the parameters of the discussion.[75] (See Table 1.)

TABLE 1

Social Composition of Party Members, 1917–20
(thousands/percentage at beginning of year)[76]

Year	Party Members	Social Origin Workers	Peasants	Employees	Others
1917	23.6	14.2/60.2	1.8/7.6	6.1/25.8	1.5/6.4
1918	115.0	65.4/56.9	16.7/14.5	25.8/22.4	7.1/6.2
1919	251.5	120.1/47.8	54.9/21.8	60.1/23.9	16.4/6.5
1920	431.4	188.8/43.8	108.4/25.1	104.7/24.3	29.5/6.8

These facts are well known to historians but are never linked to the rising tide of the lower-middle strata in revolutionary Russia. No fewer than 104,700 party members in 1920 (of a total 431,400), or 24.3 percent, declared their social origin as white-collar worker *sluzhashchie* in the *proletarian* state. Another 29,500 (6.8 percent are found in the category "other" (*prochie*), that is, neither blue- nor white-collar workers or peasants. If they were not engaged in blue-collar or agrarian labor, then it seems likely that they too belonged to the lower-middle strata. Furthermore, as argued above, Soviet statistical categories do not indicate whether they refer to social origin or present function.[77] If they reflect social origin, then the peasant category is certainly misleading, since many who claimed peasant birth functioned as within the lower-middle strata. This is certainly less of a problem with regard to blue-collar workers since the party was far more scrupulous in reserving this title for its rightful holders and elevating blue-collar proletarians to staff positions in the state and the party. The problem with using party composition statistics to imply proletarianization of the soviets is evident in the following tables on the party affiliation and social composition of delegates to soviet congresses and officials *rabotniki* of soviet executive committees. (See Tables 2 and 3.) As can be seen, there were many Bolsheviks represented at the congresses and on soviet executive committees and few members of the "petty bourgeois" parties. We learn nothing of the social composition of these communists, and the statisticians try to create the impression that the soviets were firmly Communist in

TABLE 2

Party Affiliation of Delegates to Soviet Congresses and
Soviet Executive Committee Employees, 1918–20 (percentage)[78]

Party Affiliation	1918	Congress/Ex Comm 1919	1920
Communists and "Sympathizers"			
Provinces	71.4/83.9	79.9/88.9	78.6/91.3
Districts	60.6/83.5	55.4/85.9	43.0/79.9
"Petty Bourgeois" Parties			
Provinces	14.2/16.1	4.7/0.7	0.2/0.8
Districts	14.2/16.5	4.9/1.0	0.7/4.7
Nonparty			
Provinces	14.4/——	15.4/10.4	21.2/7.9
Districts	25.2/——	39.7/13.1	56.3/15.4

TABLE 3

Social Composition of Soviet Executive Committees, 1919–20 (percentage)[79]

| | Provincial Executive Committees | | |
	Workers	*Peasants*	*Employees*
1919	29.7	13.0	57.3
1920	34.1	8.8	57.1

| | District Executive Committees | | |
	Workers	*Peasants*	*Employees*
1919	37.9	22.6	39.5
1920	32.8	20.8	46.4

composition. Yet chosen delegates were likely to be the most politically active in their localities or those most willing to join the party for either reasons of ideology or career. Party composition of the delegates tells us almost nothing about the social composition or ideological inclination of the soviets as working administrative bodies. It also is mute on the political struggles within local communities and the soviets, which were reflected in significant electoral gains and soviet participation by SRs and Mensheviks as late as 1919.[80]

At the provincial level, white-collar workers and specialists accounted for 57.3 percent and 57.1 percent of soviet executive committee officials in 1919 and 1920 respectively. Blue-collar workers accounted for approximately one-third of these officials, and peasants 13 percent and 8.8 percent in 1919 and 1920. District-level executive committees contained more peasants and blue-collar workers and fewer white-collar workers. The statistics obscure social dynamics by not informing us whether these peasants were agrarian laborers, village intelligentsia, or those in transition to white-collar status. Archival evidence supports the idea that many were teachers, feldshers, statisticians, and cooperative workers who were born into the peasant estate *soslovie* and rose rapidly to high positions in soviet and party organs in the districts and volosts.[81]

Official census statistics shed further light on the nature of party membership in the provinces.[82] White-collar workers comprised 17.5 percent of party members in four major industrial provinces excluding Moscow and Petrograd provinces (over 25 percent in the cities of those provinces) and 23.2 percent of the party members in nineteen agrarian and cottage industry provinces. The figures for Siberia and the Ukraine as well as for the other non-Russian borderlands follow this pattern. In addition, the statistics for length of party membership (*stazh*) reveal that the vast majority of party members joined during 1918 and 1919 (not 1920 or 1921) and that the rate of increase of white-collar workers who admitted their status on the questionnaires (*ankety*) was higher during 1918 and 1919 than the rate of increase of blue-collar workers and peasants.

The same trends hold for the soviets.[83] The aggregate figures for urban (capital) and rural provincial and district executive committees (corresponding to the old split between zemstvo and municipal duma administration) shows 22.4 percent office and commercial white-collar workers, another 4.7 percent classified as technical personnel with secondary education, 0.8 percent technical personnel with higher education, 0.8 percent medical doctors (*vrachi*), 0.8 percent lawyers, 6.8 percent teachers, 1.9 percent students of higher educational institutions, 3.2 percent other professions. Blue-collar workers comprised 37.7 percent and agrarian laborers 19.9 percent of these officials. In provincial executive committees alone, blue-collar workers drop to 29.7 percent, agrarian laborers to 13 percent, whereas white-collar workers and professionals, specialists, and the like increase significantly: office and commercial white-collar workers 23.6 percent, technical personnel with secondary education 8.5 percent, technical personnel with higher education 1.6 percent, doctors 1.6 percent, lawyers 2.9 percent, teachers 10.1 percent, students 5 percent, and other professions 3.9 percent. Rarely in Soviet writings of the time and never in recent Soviet scholarship are such basic facts or their implications set out clearly. For example, in the articles and monographs by V. Z. Drobizhev and his associates, who are among the few Soviet scholars to have access to raw census materials (*ankety* and supporting documents in Soviet archives) there is not a word about the significance of the large numbers of white-collar employees (lower-middle strata) in the institutions or groups of officials under investigation."[84] This is obvious in Drobizhev's analysis of the extremely valuable *All-Russian Industrial and Professional Census of 1918*, a vast compilation of factory statistics published by the Central Statistics Administration only in 1926."[85] This census covered 6,973 factories with 1,142,268 blue-collar and 103,975 white-collar workers. A tantalizing point for the social historian of the revolution is found buried in the hundreds of pages of statistics when we learn that fully 91,749 white-collar workers served in administration (presumably of the factories) or in "other social organizations in the province."[86] Drobizhev is unable or unwilling to take up such leads, and we are left with the crudest statistical aggregates shorn of their historical and social context.

During the Civil War, lower-middle strata participation in economic administration may be charted in the statistics published in 1920 by *Vesenkha*.[87] These cover the social composition and work experience of staff members of the central *Vesenkha* apparat, the main committees (*glavki*), and the provincial (*sovnarkhozy*) and economic sections of provincial soviets. The statistics for the central organs pertain to August 1, 1919; those for the provinces were gathered in May and June 1919. Let us examine first the professions of 287 members of *glavki*, centers, and production departments of *Vesenkha* itself as well as from trade unions and workers' groups, factory committees, congresses and conferences, and other unidentified sources. The total breaks down as follows: Blue-collar factory workers and artisans, 58 (20.2 percent); salaried or elected employees of trade unions, 9 (3.1 percent); directors and members of enterprise management, 42 (14.6 percent); employees with high technical qualifications, 43 (15 percent); office, mid-level management and bookkeeping personnel, 34 (11.8 percent); mid-level technical personnel, 31 (10.85 percent); government officials (including those of the old regime, Provisional Government, and Soviet institutions, 30 (10.5 percent); employees of public organizations, 10 (3.5 percent); professors and instructors in institutions of higher learning, 14 (4.9 percent); free professions, cooperative employees, railroad and water transport employees, 16 (5.6 percent).[88] As these figures show, blue-collar factory workers comprised fewer than 20.2 percent of the group since that figure also included artisans. The remainder, 79.8 percent, was drawn from the various lower-middle strata, with the possible exceptions of some of the highest qualified technical and managerial personnel and some trade union delegates and employees. Even more striking are the data for trade union, factory committee, and congress representatives. Only 38.6 percent of the trade union representatives, 39.2 percent of the factory committee representatives and 26.5 percent of the congress representatives were blue-collar factory workers and artisans. All the remaining functionaries drawn from these "workers'" institutions came, as in the above examples, from managerial, technical, and other white-collar cadres.

The same holds for provincial organs. Presidiums of provincial and regional economic councils had 26.3 percent blue-collar factory workers and artisans.[89] Remaining members included: state officials, 22.1 percent; free professions, teachers, and cooperative workers, 5.3 percent; middle-level management and technical personnel (including both higher and middle-level technical qualifications) 17.9 percent; sales clerks and shop emplyees, 4.2 percent; trade union employees and representatives, 5.3 percent; agrarian laborers, 3.1 percent; representatives of various provincial, district, and volost soviet and *sovnarkhoz* organs, 13.7 percent. Presidium personnel were drawn mainly from provincial soviet executive committees (52 percent), trade unions (15.3 percent), and the provincial economic councils themselves (7.1 percent). Since the presidiums were usually control organs, we can assume an even greater percentage of lower-middle strata employees in working departments of the *sovnarkhozy*. In the district-level economic councils and soviet economic departments the figures for blue-collar factory workers and artisans (again in the presidiums) are 29.5 percent and 23.7 percent respectively. The figures for state employees drops by about 10 percent while agrarian laborers increase correspondingly. Only 1.1 percent admitted previous employment in the zemstvos or city dumas. This is most likely because of suspicions of political unreliability, which kept such Third Element types from rising easily into *sovnarkhoz* presidiums and soviet executive committees. The provincial economic conference reports claim significant numbers of Third Element, Zemstvo, duma, cooperative, and War Industries Committee's personnel at work in provincial and strict *sovnarkhoz* departments.

What do such figures tell us about social processes during the Russian Revolution? Returning to the history of the Provisional Government and the social movement of the lower-middle strata during 1917, we remember the defeat of such ideals as "democracy" and the various socialist (and in some cases nonsocialist) visions of ameliorated class conflict and a broad social movement embracing not just workers and peasants, but also the lower-middle strata and progressive elements of the bourgeoisie. Broad segments of the working class and peasants in the military and in the countryside rejected alternatives to the Bolshevik notion of class conflict, workers' control, and soviet power. The October Revolution, however, failed to block the social movement of the lower-middle strata despite the apparent political defeat of their would-be spokesmen. These groups grafted themselves onto the workers' and peasants' revolution and indeed managed to infiltrate a wide range of revolutionary class institutions. The presence of large numbers of intelligentsia, specialists, protoprofessionals, and the like imparted stability, skills, and the promise and reality of an effective apparatus for the new soviet state.

This exploratory essay does not treat the lower-middle strata's role in the building and supply of the Red Army, the management of food supply, industry and commerce, education, forestry, and agrarian policy—in short the entire range of functions performed by the soviets, economic councils, and the multitude of specialized departments that had come of age in the years leading up to 1917. The impact of these *obyvately* on the course of the revolution and on the working class that in so many cases they helped sponsor and integrate into the new institutions of the Soviet state remains to be explored more fully. Far from being simply "survivors," the lower-middle strata quickly became part of the new elite including the Bolshevik Party. Although many would have preferred an SR or perhaps even Menshevik outcome in the revolution, those in the lower-middle strata could or would offer little resistance to the revolutionary energy of the worker and peasant masses. Their commitments to ideological alternatives to Bolshevism appear not to have been deep. Instead of following through on the radicalism that grew out of their worsening economic situation during World War I, they preferred to opt for the security and order that a Bolshevik state might provide, especially to those who became part of that state as it was being created.

As has been observed among other social groups in late imperial and revolutionary Russia, radical impulses and the search for stability go well together. In the case of the lower-middle strata, their radicalism helped make the October Revolution possible, and their conservatism and knowledge and skills helped secure the Bolshevik state during the Civil War. The result was a state and a party heavily indebted to and influenced by this forgotten group. The legacy was a contradiction between the idea of a workers' revolution and a workers' state and the complex social and cultural realities of the Soviet state that has yet to be resolved.

NOTES

1. *Vos'moi s"ezd RKP(b) mart 1919 goda: Protokoly* (Moscow, 1959), p. 199.
2. Ibid., pp. 199–201. The debate also brought out the hostility of the so-called Democratic Centralists to the bureaucratization of party and soviets in late 1918 and early 1919. The Democratic Centralists were not against administration per se, but they wanted a Soviet administration with considerable devolution of power to provincial functionaries based in the soviets. They particularly resented party bossism and the beginnings of the *nomenklatura* system that made all key local offices subject to local or central party appointments.
3. Recent work in European and American history on white-collar workers and the lower-middle "class" and their relationship to fascism and parliamentary democracy has shown the way to a new understanding of the vitality and political power of groups of people formerly thought to have been on the fringes of society or in an ever-weakening position in the face of the social and economic changes wrought by capitalism. As I began to examine War Communism and state building in the Civil War era, I became increasingly aware of the obfuscations and tendentiousness of most Soviet accounts (not to mention those of many political activists during the revolution) of the role of the lower-middle strata or large groups of people who were neither blue-collar workers nor agrarian laborers. I began to look at well-known statistics in a new light— for example, those pertaining to party membership at the end of the Civil War and those relating to mentorship in the provincial economic councils *(sovnarkhozy)* or in the central organs of the Supreme Council of the National Economy *(vesenkha)*—and began to see that these and other data told a story very different from official interpretations. The obvious prominence of the lower-middle strata necessitates rethinking many problems of the revolution. It has been like a missing puzzle piece whose placement permits many new connections.
4. E. G. Gimpel'son, *Rabochii klass v upravlenii Sovetskom gosudarstvom noiabr' 1917–1920 gg.* (Moscow, 1982). See my review essay, "Gimpel'son on the Hegemony of the Working Class," *Slavic Review*, vol. 48, no. 1 (spring, 1989).
5. Sheila Fitzpatrick, *The Russian Revolution 1917–1932*, (Oxford, 1984); and ibid., *Education and Social Mobility in the Soviet Union, 1921–1934* (Cambridge, 1979).
6. S. S. Fediukin, "Oktiabr' i intelligentsiia (nekotorye metodologicheskie aspekty problemy," in K. V. Gusev, ed., *Intelligentsiia i revoliutsiia: XX vek* (Moscow, 1985), pp. 20–33; and K. V. Gusev, "Intelligentsiia Rossii i bor'ba partii," in ibid., pp. 34–

43. The point is made most forcefully in the important collective volume of V. P. Buldakov, A. E. Ivanov, N. A. Ivanova, and V. V. Shelokhaev, *Bor'ba za massy v trekh revoliutsiiakh v Rossii: Proletariat i srednie gorodskie sloi* (Moscow, 1981), pp. 164–256.

7. V. I. Lenin, *Polnoe sobranie sochinenii*, 5th ed. (Moscow, 1958–65), vols. 34, 38–41. Lenin was correct only in terms of tactics since the lower-middle strata were crucial to the moderate left's vision of a "democratic" revolution and conception of "the Democracy." The fact that the non-Bolshevik left could not effectively mobilize its own potential support among the lower-middle strata may well have been the result of excessively rigid ideological categories and modes of discourse.

8. Ibid., p. 41.

9. V. P. Buldakov, et al., eds., *Bor'ba za massy*, pp. 196–208.

10. Here we cannot consider the relationship of the lower-middle strata to fascism or to parliamentary democracy in Western societies, but it is important to note, as Jurgen Kocka has shown, that lower-middle strata white-collar workers were capable of generating or following conservative nationalist appeals cloaked in populism or joining forces with broader labor movements on the left. Much depended on the "social constellation and social psychological configuration of each society." See Kocka, *White-Collar Workers in America, 1890–1940: A Social-Political History in International Perspective* (London, 1980), p. 281; and ibid., "Class Formation, Interest Articulation and Public Policy: The Origins of the German White-Collar Class in the Late Nineteenth and Early Twentieth Centuries," Suzanne Berger, ed., *Organizing Interests in Western Europe: Pluralism, Corporatism, and the Transformation of Politics* (Cambridge, 1981), pp. 63–101. For an excellent critique of Kocka's comparative approach and theoretical framework that at the same time substantiates the role of the lower-middle strata in the rise of fascism, see Geoff Eley, "What Produces Fascism: Pre-Industrial Traditions or a Crisis of the Capitalist State" *Politics and Society*, 1983, vol. 12, no. 1, pp. 53–82; and David Blackbourn and Geoff Eley, *The Peculiarities of German History: Bourgeois Society and Politics in Nineteenth-Century Germany* (Oxford, 1984). See also, David Blackbourn, "The *Mittelstand* in German Society and Politics, 1871–1914," *Social History*, January 1977, no. 4, pp. 409–33; and Geoffrey Crossick, ed., *The Lower Middle Class in Britain 1870–1914* (New York, 1977).

11. In short, the "class" is profoundly antirevolutionary. Nicos Poulantzas, *Classes in Contemporary Capitalism* (London, 1975), pp. 191–336.

12. Ibid., pp. 334–36.

13. Erik Olin Wright, *Class, Crisis and the State* (London, 1978), pp. 61–63. Examples include managers and supervisors who occupy a contradictory location between bourgeoisie and proletariat; semiautonomous employees who occupy a contradictory location between the working class and petty bourgeoisie; and small employers who are located between the bourgeoisie and petty bourgeoisie. Wright has since modified his position to place more emphasis on exploitation within class relations as opposed to pure domination related directly to the means of production. See Erik Olin Wright, "What Is Middle About the Middle Class?" in J. Roemer, ed., *Analytical Marxism* (Cambridge, Eng., 1986).

14. Ibid., p. 63.

15. In a telling passage, Mayer explains intellectuals' aversion to the topic thus: "It is far more likely that non- and anti-Marxist scholars and intellectuals have in large measure avoided dealing with the *Kleinburgertum* precisely because they, too, approvingly prophesied its extinction. Furthermore, this intermediate class seems to enjoy little sympathy and still less empathy in academic circles. Could it be that social scientists are hesitant to expose the aspirations, lifestyle, and world view of the social class in which so many of them originate and from which they seek to escape? Whatever the answer to this question, the petite bourgeoisie has had a harder time commanding scholarly attention than either the power elite or the proletariat; it has no patronage

to dispense, it is not seen as a revolutionary threat, and it lacks the romance of utter wretchedness, once removed, that commands empathetic scrutiny" (Arno J. Mayer, "The Lower Middle Class as Historical Problem," *Journal of Modern History*, (September 1975, vol. 47, p. 409).

16. Philip G. Nord, *Paris Shopkeepers and the Politics of Resentment* (Princeton, 1986).

17. Ibid.

18. Ibid., pp. 488–90.

19. This assertion is based on close reading of such provincial newspapers as *Tambovskii zemskii vestnik*.

20. See Thomas Fallows, "Forging the Zemstvo Monument: Liberalism and Radicalism on the Volga, 1890–1905" (Ph.D. diss., Harvard University, 1981).

21. The most recent studies are Graeme J. Gill, *Peasants and Government in the Russian Revolution* (London, 1979); and V. I. Kostrikin, *Zemel'nye komitety v 1917 godu* (Moscow, 1975). Both have almost nothing to report on the composition of these bodies as they review the legislation governing their activities and their role in policy debates over agrarian reform and food supply. Despite archival access, Kostrikin downplays the social dimension as part of the Soviet denigration of the lower-middle strata. Provincial archives contain the evidence on social composition, and Soviet dissertations show that these committees were similar to the volost peasant committees, cooperatives, and zemstvos in their inclusion of many specialists and village *intelligenty*. See Baranov, "Mestnye organy," and E. D. Popova, "Zemel'nye komitety severnogo priural'ia v 1917 godu (po materialam Viatskoi i Permskoi gubernii)" (Candidate Dissertation, Moscow State University, 1965).

22. Kostrikin makes the same argument.

23. See Bertram Patenaune, "Bolshevism in Retreat: The Transition to the New Economic Policy, 1920–1922" (Ph.D. dissertation, Stanford University, 1987). For a Soviet approach see M. A. Molodtsygin, *Raboche-Krest'ianskii Soiuz 1918–1920* (Moscow, 1987).

24. A. S. Smirnov, *Kresti'ianskie s"ezdy v 1917 godu* (Moscow, 1979), pp. 40–41.

25. Ibid., p. 41.

26. Eugene M. Kayden and Alexis N. Antsiferov, *The Cooperative Movement in Russia during the War* (New Haven, 1929), pp. 22, 46.

27. Two excellent works that place the history of the cooperatives against the backdrop of the revolutionary process and lay bare the cooperatives' role in grass-roots social and political life as well as in revolutionary state building are: Catherine L. Salzman, "Consumer Societies and the Consumer Cooperative Movement in Russia, 1897–1917," (Ph.D. diss., University of Michigan, 1977), p. 123; and V. V. Kabanov, *Oktiabr'skaia revoliutsiia i kooperatsiia (1917 g.-mart 1919 g.)* (Moscow, 1973).

28. Quoted in Salzman, "Consumer Societies," p. 173.

29. Ibid., p. 188. Salzman provides important statistics on the cooperatives' role in the dissemination of various forms of printed material in the countryside.

30. Ibid., pp. 251–52.

31. Ibid., p. 249.

32. V. V. Kabanov, *Oktiabr'skaia revoliutsiia*, especially pp. 109–121; and Salzman, "Consumer Societies," pp. 413–78. See also L. F. Morozov, *Ot kooperatsii burzhuaznoi k kooperatsii sotsialisticheskoi* (Moscow, 1969).

33. V. Z. Drobizhev, *Glavnyi shtab sotsialisticheskoi promyshlennosti: Ocherki istorii VSNKh, 1917–1932 gg.* (Moscow, 1965); V. Z. Drobizhev and A. G. Medvedev, *Iz istorii sovnarkhozy (1917–1918 gg.)* (Moscow, 1964). Here, too, the literature distorts or plays down continuity and social composition. No Moscow library would yield out of closed collections (*spets khran*) the published protocols of the congresses of *sovnarkhozy* for 1918–21. Further evidence on these matters can be found in the *Vesenkha* archive (TsGANKh F. 34—) and in a series of publications of the provincial

economic conferences (*ekonomicheskie soveshchaniia*), successor organs to the *sovnarkhozy* in 1922, which reported directly to the Council on Labor and Defense (STO). The Kaluga conference, a province for which I was able to obtain archival materials as well, states openly that in 1922 the provincial economy was entirely managed by the lower-middle strata who had participated in the social revolution of 1917–18 (*Otchet Kaluzhskogo gubernskogo ekonomicheskogo soveshchaniia za vremia ot 1-go ianvaria do 1-go oktiabria 1921 goda,* vyp. 1-i [Kaluga, 1921], pp. 15–16.

34. Buldakov, et al., *Bor'ba za massy,* pp. 164–267.

35. Ibid., pp. 174–176.

36. For example there were 153,500 white- and blue-collar employees in six unions representing state and municipal enterprises.

37. Gimpel'son, *Rabochii klass,* pp. 99–118.

38. This was similar to the cooptation of the cooperatives and other autonomous or semiautonomous bodies (*Chetvertyi Vserossiiskii s"ezd professional'nikh soiuzov [17–25 maia 1921 g]): Stenograficheskii otchet,* [Moscow, 1921]).

39. Ibid., pp. 109–110.

40. There are several landmark studies already in print and excellent dissertations that soon should follow. See, for example, T. H. Rigby, *Lenin's Government: Sovnarkom, 1917–1922* (Cambridge, 1979); Thomas F. Remington, *Building Socialism in Bolshevik Russia: Ideology and Industrial Organization 1917–1921* (Pittsburgh, 1984); Robert Service, *The Bolshevik Party in Revolution: A Study in Organizational Change, 1917–1923,* (New York, 1979); A. A. Nelidov, *Istoriia gosudarstvennykh uchrezhdenii SSSR, 1917–1936 gg.* (Moscow, 1962); M. P. Iroshnikov, *Sozdanie sovetskogo tsentral'nogo gosudarstvennogo apparata: Sovet narodnykh komissarov i narodnye komissariatii: oktiabr' 1917 g.-ianvar' 1918 g.* (Moscow-Leningrad, 1986); V. Z. Drobizhev and A. B. Medvedev, *Iz istorii Sovnarkhozov (1917–1918 gg.)* (Moscow, 1964); Iu. K. Avdakov, *Organizatsionno-khoziaistvennaia deiatel'nosti VSNKh v pervye gody sovetskoi vlasti (1917–1921 gg.)* (Moscow, 1971).

41. Two recent works tackle some of these issues. See Remington, *Building Socialism in Bolshevik Russia;* and George L. Yaney, *The Urge to Mobilize: Agrarian Reform in Russia, 1880–1930* (Urbana, Ill., 1982). Remington places "mobilization" at the core of Soviet state building (see also his chapter in the present volume) but posits a fundamental contradiction between the two processes. "For the Bolsheviks, the mobilization of society was more than a temporary expedient required by the civil war. The regime saw in mobilization the means to draw the independent initiative and organizational authority of working class and industrial bodies into the new state and to place them under its formal authority. Doing so deprived the regime of the support that social institutions outside the state such as independent factory committees, industrial managers, trade unions, educational institutions, professional associations, newspapers, and the like might have given it. In early 1921 the Bolsheviks were forced to abandon the mobilization model when the system they were seeking to establish collapsed, and they demobilized society by restoring market relations. The socialist sector remained weak and entirely dependent on the state. . . . The consequence, therefore, of building a socialist state through societal mobilization was that only through a renewal of mobilization could the state resume the construction of socialism. This method of state-building prevented the Bolsheviks from creating the socialist society to which their doctrine pointed and on which their legitimacy depended. . . . In short, where revolutionaries seek to mobilize society as a means of building a new state, the result is likely to be self-defeating: either the creation of an autonomous state makes the state the sole source of power and purpose, or the state concedes power to the social institutions which join the cause" (*Building Socialism,* pp. 12–13). Notice here Remington's emphasis on the "regime" and the "state" as actors quite apart from the social dynamic described above. Yaney, too, develops a mobilization concept that he ascribes to various administrative ideologies and to Bolshevism. He is particularly good at showing how

agrarian realities shaped these ideologies and how lower ranking agrarian specialists influenced policy.

42. See Sylvana Malle's study of economic and social policies, *The Economic Organization of War Communism, 1918–1921* (Cambridge, 1985). Malle's book is based on extensive published sources. The author provides a first-rate guide to the ideological positions of the various framers of Bolshevik policy and a reliable summary of the policies themselves. To her credit, she recognizes explicitly the enormous Bolshevik debt to the economic institutions of the Provisional and late tsarist governments. Yet she cannot escape an excessively formal approach involving long passages recording administrative disputes over turf, the agendas of centralizers versus those in favor of this or that vision of decentralization, and the like. The book lacks entirely a social dimension or a sense of the social forces that propeled the party/state forward.

43. See Malle, *Economic Organization of War Communism*, pp. 202–292; and E. G. Gimpel'son, *Velikii Oktiabr' i stanovlenie sovetskoi sistemy upravleniia narodnym khoziaistvom (noiabr' 1917–1920 gg.)* (Moscow, 1977).

44. I treat this topic more fully in "State and Society in Russia: Rethinking the Paradigm" (Paper delivered at the American Historical Association, annual meeting, Chicago, 1984).

45. We could have chosen the economic councils, trade unions, Rabkrin, the various commissariats, Sovnarkom, and the like. The soviets best illustrate the absorption of the old organs of self-government and tsarist administration, whereas the cooperatives and professional congresses were crucial to the establishment of Soviet power yet are overlooked in the historiography of the early Soviet state.

46. M. P. Iroshnikov sets out the full story well in his *Predsedatel' soveta narodnykh komissarov V. I. Ul'ianov (Lenin): ocherki gosudarstvennoi deiatel'nosti v 1917–1918 gg.* (Leningrad, 1974).

47. Ibid., p. 421.

48. Gimpel'son in *Rabochii klass* provides similar data on the presence of significant numbers—most often clear majorities—of "employees" in the new Soviet state, but he uses the material to argue the case for "worker" participation and mobility (*vydvizhenie*). For him the presence of any percentage of workers is all that matters to prove his case. He makes no attempt to analyze the symbiotic relationship between blue- and white-collar types, the patterns of mutual influence, or the impact of both on state building.

49. Lenin, *Sobranie sochineniia*, vol. 35, p. 206.

50. Kabanov, *Oktiabr'skaia revoliutsiia i kooperatsiia*, pp. 146–47.

51. Ibid., pp. 154–155.

52. *Soveshchaniia predstavitelei tsentrosoiuza, soiuznykh ob"edinenii i otdel'nykh obshchestv, vkhodiashchikh v sostav tsentrosoiuza 24–27 maia 1918 goda v Moskve* (Moscow, 1918). The reports also reflect early conflicts with soviets, which often seized cooperative property or attempted to "socialize" or "nationalize" them.

53. Ibid., p. 22.

54. P. A. Garvi, *Zapiski sotsial demokrata (1906–1921)* (Newtonville, Mass., 1982).

55. See Lenin's February 2, 1919, letter to Narkomprod, Narkomfin, and Vesenkha, in which he writes of the need for practical measures leading to a transition from bourgeois to proletarian cooperation and "communist supply and distribution" (Lenin, *Sobranie sochinenii*, vol. 37, pp. 471–72.

56. Kabanov, *Oktiabr'skaia revoliutsiia i kooperatsiia*, p. 194.

57. Ibid., p. 194.

58. Ibid., p. 206.

59. *XXXIII sobranie upolnomochennykh Tsentrosoiuza. 26 sentiabria-1 oktiabria 1918 g.* (Moscow, 1918), p. 15.

60. Kabanov, *Oktiabr'skaia revoliutsiia i kooperatsiia*, p. 230.

61. Ibid., pp. 210–11.

208 Administration and State Building

62. Ibid., p. 224.

63. The standard works include E. G. Gimpel'son, *Sovety v gody interventsii i grazhndanskoi voiny*, 2 vols. (Moscow, 1968); Malvin M. Helgesen, "The Origins of the Party State Monolith in Soviet Russia: Relations between the Soviets and Party Committees in the Central Provinces, October 1917-March 1921" (Ph.D. diss., State University of New York at Stony Brook, 1980); Robert Abrams, "The Local Soviets of the RSFSR, 1918–1921" (Ph.D. diss., Columbia University, 1975); A. I. Lepeshkin, *Mestnye organy sovetskogo gosudarstva (1917–1920 gg.)* (Moscow, 1957). See also Vladimir Brovkin, *The Mensheviks after October* (Ithaca, 1987).

64. Helgesen, "Origins of the Party State Monolith," pp. iii-iv. Helgesen's point is valid, especially insofar as he deemphasizes ideology in state building. Nonetheless he too ignores the social and cultural context of Soviet construction.

65. R. G. Tsypkina, *Voenno-revoliutsionnye komitety v oktiabr'skoi revoliutsii (po materialam gubernii tsentral'nogo promyshlennogo raiona, urala i povolzh'ia)* (Moscow, 1980).

66. See the official NKVD journals, *Vestnik NKVD* and its successor *Vlasti sovetov*, especially for late summer and autumn 1918 and the beginning of 1919.

67. See, for example, I. Galperina and V. Startsev, "Sovety rabochikh i soldatskikh deputatov Petrograda v bor'be za ovladenie apparatom gorodskogo obshchestvennogo upravleniia (noiabr' 1917- noiabr' 1918 g.)," and V. I. Aver'ev, "Likvidatsiia, burzhuaznikh organov mestnogo samoupravleniia posle Oktiabr'skoi Revoliutsii," in *Sovetskoe gosudarstvo*, August 1936, no. 4, pp. 100–115; and "Perestroika mestnikh organov vlasti v sviazi s priniatiem konstitutsii 1918 g." in *Sovetskoe gosudarstvo*, 1937), nos. 3–4, pp. 97–113. As in all Soviet accounts, Aver'ev emphasizes zemstvo hostility to the new order, but he does recognize that by late 1918 zemstvo executive boards could still be found in most volosts and many districts—though they functioned under the Soviet umbrella. I found examples in TsGAOR F. 393 in reports of volost Soviets for 1918, of pre-October peasant committees, and zemstvo executives simply renaming their operations as soviets.

68. "Otchet o deiatel'nosti malmyzhskogo uezdnogo ispolkoma (Viatskaia guberniia)," in *Sovety v Oktiabre* (Moscow, 1930). The best sources on provincial state building remain the local newspapers. Some material, as in the present example, can be gleaned from the collections of documents published by provincial party organizations on the various anniversaries of the revolution. See, for example, *Oktiabr' v Tule* (Tula, 1957); and *Ustanovlenie sovetskoi vlasti v Pskovskoi gubernii*, (Pskov, 1957).

69. The technical apparatus was responsible for drafting recruits into the Red Army and, of course, played a large role in production, supply, and transport.

70. *Protokoly 1-ogo s"ezda predsedatelei gubernskih sovetov i zaveduiushchikh gubernskimi otdelami upravleniia* (Ekaterinoslav, 1919), pp. 3–5. The report was published on the printing press of the provincial zemstvo executive board.

71. Again, this state-building process did provide mobility for workers and peasants as they were removed from factory and land and placed in the lower-middle strata infrastructure. See Gimpel'son, *Rabochii klass*.

72. See, for example, *Protokoly II vserossiiskogo s"ezda komissarov truda, predstavitelei birzhi truda i strakhovikh kass 18–25 maia n/s 1918 goda* (Moscow, 1918); *Trudy malogo s"ezda vserossiiskogo soiuza sluzhashchikh kasnacheistv (15–24 maia 1918 g.); Protokoly tsentral'nogo ispolnitel'nogo komiteta vserossiiskogo proletarskogo pochtovotelegrafnogo soiuza za 1918 god* (Moscow, 1918); *Vtoroi vserossiiskii s"ezd tamozhennikh sluzhashchikh 19 iiunia-5 iiulia 1918, Protokoly* (Moscow, 1918); *Materialy narodnogo komissariata iustitsii. Vyp. I: Pervyi vserossiiskii s"ezd oblastnikh i gubernskikh komissarov iustitsii. Protokol vserossiskogo s"ezda* (Moscow, 1918); *Biulleten' Moskovskogo oblastnogo biuro i Moskovskogo otdeleniia vserossiskogo soiuza inzhenerov (no.1): zaniatiia 1-go Moskovskogo oblastnogo delegatskogo s"ezda 4–6 ianvaria 1918 g.* (Moscow, 1918); *Vserossiiskii soiuz inzhenerov: Otchet c zaniatiakh*

2-i moskovskoi oblastnoi konferentsii 18–21 oktiabria 1918 goda (Moscow, 1918). Also, K. Bazilevich, *Professional'noe dvizhenie rabotnikov sviazi (1917–18)* (Moscow, 1927).

73. *Vtoroi vserossiskii s"ezd tamozhennikh sluzhashchikh*, p. 3.

74. M. A. Lur'e, *Intelligentsiia i sovety: khoziaistvo, burzhuaziia, revoliutsiia, gosapparat* (Moscow, 1924).

75. Many statistical tables used by Soviet historians to discuss the social history of the early Soviet state are cast in terms of party composition of institutions.

76. *Izmenenie sotsial'noi struktury*, p. 156.

77. These same four categories are used in all censuses of party and state institutions for the early Soviet period.

78. *Izmenenie sotsial'noi struktury*, p. 154.

79. Ibid., p. 149.

80. Brovkin, *The Mensheviks after October.*

81. TsGAOR SSSR F. 393 op. 3 d. 160.

82. *Vserossiiskaia perepis' chlenov v R. K. P. 1922 goda: itogi predvaritel'noi razrabotki po 45 guberniiam i oblastiam*, vyp. 2 (Moscow, 1922), pp. 5–47.

83. M. Vladimirskii, *Sovety, ispolkomy i s"ezdy sovetov*, vyp. 1, *Ispolkomy* (Moscow, 1920), pp. 3–14. This offers one of the few breakdowns of early Soviet officialdom by profession.

84. See, for example, V. Z. Drobizhev and E. I. Pivovar, "Statisticheskie obsledovaniia intelligentsii i sluzhashchikh SSSR (obzor istochnikov)," *Istoriia SSSR*, 1978, 3, pp. 70–88; A. K. Sokolov, "Metodika vybornoi obrabotki pervichnikh materialov professional'noi perepisi 1918 g.," *Istoriia SSSR*, 1971, 4, pp. 76–96; O. V. Naumov, L. S. Petrosian, and A. K. Sokolov, "Kadri rukovoditelei, spetsialistov i obsluzhivaiushchego personala promyshlennikh predpriiatii po dannym professional'noi perepisi 1918 goda," *Istoriia SSSR*, 1981, 6, pp. 92–108.

85. *Professional'naia perepis' 1918 goda* in *Trudy TsSU*, vol. XXVI, vyp. 1 and 2 (Moscow, 1926).

86. Ibid., pp. 170–71.

87. Contained in the *Vesenkha* journal *Narodnoe khoziaistvo*, 1920, nos. 3–4 and 7–8. The data offer clues to the post-October merging of the public and private sectors.

88. *Narodnoe khoziaistvo*, 1920, nos. 3–4, pp. 62–66.

89. Ibid.

THE RATIONALIZATION
OF STATE *KONTROL'*

Thomas F. Remington

A statewide system of supervisory agencies for monitoring the bureaucracy has been present in some form since the inception of the Soviet regime. Generally it has combined mass participatory and centralized, bureaucratic elements, and in practice the emphasis has oscillated between them. In the Civil War period, the establishment of an integrated system of inspectorates, Rabkrin (the worker-peasant inspectorate, or RKI), grew out of three distinct processes of organizational evolution.

In the first, between the October seizure of power and mid-1918, the widespread intervention by factory workers into the sphere of managerial power in state and private enterprises acquired systematic institutional form under trade union and state organizations. In the course of this process, the concept of "workers' control" ceased to refer to the aim of shop-floor managerial power, which many in the factory committee movement had sought, and came to refer instead to the exercise of auditing and discipline-enforcing powers. The second process, which also began shortly after the assumption of Soviet power and continued throughout the period, consisted of a series of attempts to reform the inherited state *kontrol'* bureaucracy so as to force it to serve the needs of the Soviet state. These measures changed both organizational form and assigned functions of the state *kontrol'* commissariat and, broadly speaking, aimed at providing the central government with an efficient, fully centralized organ of state supervision that at the same time enlisted wide strata of the working population.

Finally, the third process comprised efforts to integrate state *kontrol'* with the many accounting and inspection bodies under trade union auspices, including control commissions in the enterprises (heirs to the factory committees) as well as the "workers' inspectorates," formed by trade union councils to uncover and prevent abuses and breakdown in certain critical economic sectors, particularly the railroad network and the food supply system. Although state *kontrol'* formally merged with the workers' inspectorates and factory control bodies under a decree of February 1920, which created the People's Commissariat of Worker-Peasant Inspectorates, it would be more accurate to say that the 1920 merger achieved a kind of nonaggression agreement rather than full merger. Through 1920, cooperation between the state controllers and the trade unions remained limited. Only after a decision of the Tenth Party Congress to the effect that Rabkrin was obliged to work through the trade union organs, followed by a corresponding decision of the Fourth Trade Union Congress in late May 1921, did control "from above" finally unite with control "from below."

State *kontrol'* affords an instructive example of the different directions in which national policy was tugged during the Civil War era by powerful social forces. Particularly visible in this case are the hardy tenacity of an inherited bureaucracy, the state control agency; the rear-guard struggle for independence on the part of various elements of the trade union movement; and the regime's desperate struggle against chaos and the ravages of war. Against these nearly insurmountable obstacles, the Bolshevik leadership's persistent demands for a control commissariat able to serve as ombudsman, management consultant, policeman, and business school were too ambitious to be realized but did prompt the state *kontrol'* commissariat to become an active, if often intrusive and self-aggrandizing, element in the young Soviet state.

At the heart of the government's efforts to rationalize and systematize the work of *kontrol'* are two related dilemmas. The first of these is the problem of defining *kontrol'*. The concept of *kontrol'* had lost focus in the course of 1917, as factory workers interpreted the recognized powers of *kontrol'* broadly or asserted a variety of executive rights and christened them *kontrol'*. Even after the Bolshevik government made it clear that *kontrol'* was not a surrogate of management, a bifurcation in the sense of the term remained. One set of functions derived from the traditional review of budget estimates and after-the-fact auditing of financial records that had been conducted by tsarist controllers in government agencies and enterprises. The other consisted of the active, open-ended custodial responsibilities entailed in monitoring, guarding, preventing, assisting, correcting, exposing, and even punishing the actions of executive authorities inside and outside the workplace—a sphere of authority into which *kontrol'* not infrequently crossed. This dichotomy was sometime identified as ex ante versus ex post facto *kontrol'*, or as "paper," "financial," or "documentary" *kontrol'* versus factual," "genuine," and "socialist" *kontrol'*, none of which were satisfactory functional distinctions, since, among other things, traditional *kontrol'* embraced the triad of prior, factual, and post-facto review.

The second dilemma is the jurisdictional disjunction among the many organizations carrying out *kontrol'*. These included the internal inspectorates in numerous commissariats, VSNKh, and the War Department, but, as *kontrol'* activity was gradually concentrated in the state control commissariat, the jurisdictional gap was most severe between state control and workers' control.

Politically this was manifested in the state control commissariat's efforts to draw the trade unions' *kontrol'* organs under its wing and in the trade unions' resistance to this pressure.

To a large degree, of course, these two dilemmas overlap. The Sovnarkom's frustration in dealing with the State Control Commissariat, its inability to push the agency beyond the preoccupation with reviewing budget and financial transactions, and the difficulty in combining the state *kontrol'* agency's efforts with those of the trade unions and factory committees may be explained by the different nature of the tasks to which each side was fitted. Workers' control, as it developed in 1917, was the factory-floor response to immediate crisis. In some instances the crisis was the hostility or breakdown of management, in others the collapse of the normal flow of orders, revenues, raw materials, fuel, and other requisites of production. Under these circumstances, as the research of all who have studied this compelling movement has shown, the very content of "workers' control" changed from the more narrowly defined traditional understanding of *kontrol'* as supervision external to administration that is concerned with ensuring the legality, propriety, and expediency of transactions to executive responsibility for a variety of politically and economically motivated duties.

Consequently, through the end of 1917 the direction of evolution was towards the broadening of powers of workers' control into management itself, however this function would be adapted to local structures of administrative authority. While examination of records formed part of the work of the committees involved in workers' control, it was a comparatively minor aspect of it—partly because of the workers' inexperience with the task—and one that tended to be superseded by more direct executive responsibility. Only when new management took over and the central government finally made it clear that factory committees were to be control commissions of their branch trade unions did the *kontrol'* function become focused on oversight and review of production and exchange. For its part, state control, as we shall see, gradually dropped after-the-fact audits from its sphere of activity and reduced its attention to prior review of budget estimates (both became ludicrously irrelevant under the circumstances of the time), instead devoting a greater share of its resources to "factual" reviews—inspections and examinations of various Soviet institutions, often in response to citizens' complaints. Thus, through the Civil War period, the duties of "*kontrol'* from above" and "*kontrol'* from below" gradually converged.

1. Workers' Control and the Factory Committee Movement

With the establishment of Soviet power the relationship between the factory committees, soviets, and similar bodies that had assumed active powers in economic administration and management in state and private enterprises needed to be clarified. While the party's support for "workers' control" as a rallying cry of revolutionary democracy in the workplace as well as an endorsement of workers' efforts to maintain order in production and distribution gained legal force with the regime's decree on workers' control of November 14, 1917, the question of the relationship between *kontrol'* and executive power, and that of the powers of the local enterprise vis-à-vis central authority, remained to be worked out. On these issues pre-October party resolutions offered little concrete guidance, and the comments by Lenin and other party leaders were studiously ambiguous.

Three times between October 1917 and January 1918 the factory committee leadership outlined a conception of control institutions that ultimately pointed toward a self-managing model of proletarian socialism. On each occasion the party leadership opposed them.[1]

The first occurred on the day after the seizure of power when three Petrograd factory committee leaders called on Lenin and offered a scheme for a "Supreme Economic Council" that would exercise administrative authority via the factory committees, overseeing workers' control, output norm-setting and organization of production, regulation of retail distribution and consumer cooperatives, and general policy.[2] Lenin expressed interest in the proposal but demurred at the suggestion that it be published as an official degree, promising instead to send a party leader to help redraft it into the form of a proper legislative act.[3] In the event, however, Lenin immediately separated the issue of control both as function and as hierarchical structure from that of management and general economic administration. Design of an institution to perform the latter functions he vested in three party leaders not affiliated with the factory committees, Osinskii, Smirnov, and Savel'ev, who opposed making workers' control the centerpiece of their proposed new Supreme Economic Council.

Meantime the factory committee movement sought to inject its views into a general decree on workers' control. Their draft proposal still circulated, as did drafts initiated by Lenin, Larin, and Shliapnikov, and A. Gol'tsman on behalf of the metal workers' union. At a general meeting on November 5 held to discuss the various proposals, the outcome was the defeat of the proposals by Larin—which restricted control to technical functions—and by the metal workers' union, which emphasized a territorial hierarchy.[4] Lenin's proposal empowered workers in all but the smallest enterprises to assume control powers but did not specify central bodies of control or of administration and failed to define the powers of control vis-à-vis management. Once the Gol'tsman and Larin versions were dropped, the factory committee group withdrew its proposal in favor of Lenin's.

At the suggestion of A. L. Lozovskii, Secretary of the All-Russian Council of Trade Unions and an opponent of the factory committee movement, Lenin's draft was amended by adding a hierarchical chain of control councils culminating at the center in an All-Russian Council on Workers' Control. This body, evidently superseding the pyramid of factory committee organizations directed by the Central Council of Petrograd Factory Committees, remained spectral. After but two meetings and almost no activity it was absorbed into VSNKh, the Supreme Economic Council[5] It should be added that this council served essentially as a sounding board for Larin, the energetic opponent of factory committee autonomy and of administrative decentralization. Lenin's draft as amended was adopted and published by the Central Executive Committee on November 14 and 16, respectively, and immediately afterward was discussed and approved at the Fifth Conference of Petrograd Factory Committees, at which the decree was welcomed for creating the basis for further industrial regulation leading eventually to socialism.[6]

At the time of the October Revolution, the factory committee movement had developed an extensive system of specialized bodies and participated in a number of major economic coordinating and regulatory bodies that bridged state and society in the interests of maintaining production and distribution. Since summer the "supply conferences" and "factory conferences" had recruited workers from the soviets, trade unions, and factory committees on a parity basis with owners and managers. This half and half system of representation underlay the Menshevik conception of state control, which the Bolsheviks considered a deliberate evasion of the central problem of overturning state power, but the Bolsheviks never committed themselves to the principle of proportional representation of workers or institutional participation by factory committees in laying out the system for postrevolutionary economic administration. By the beginning of October, the Central Council of Petrograd Factory Committees had formed a system of twelve district councils and specialized commissions for resolving disputes, overseeing control, and planning the demobilization of industry.[7] It had ties to the Ministry of Labor, the Petrograd Soviet, and the supply conferences. It maintained liaison with similar councils in other cities. Although the Central Council was frequently faced with demands for assistance that were beyond its powers, it is worth observing that Lozovskii wrote in 1922 that at the time of the October Revolution, the Central Council had actually been running the industry of Petrograd.[8]

It was reasonable, therefore, for factory committee leaders to envision the transition from the power their committees exercised under the broad rubric of "workers' control" to a formalized system for general economic administration. Such an act would legally recapitulate the evolution of powers and functions that the factory committees had assumed under the pressure of circumstances and with the general though vague approval of the party's leadership. The refusal therefore of the Leninist center of the party to endorse their scheme explicitly cannot be explained by an oversight. Transferring nominal rights of control to a shadowy network of "control councils" while transferring statewide economic responsibility to a new supreme economic council left the factory committee movement with no rationale for a separate existence. Accordingly (and perhaps following party instruction), the Sixth (and final) Conference of Factory Committees, meeting on January 22, 1918, voted to dissolve itself into the trade unions, making each factory committee a cell of the union for the particular firm. Somewhat later the Central Council itself entered the state Economic Council for the Northern Region.[9]

Shortly before this took place, the third attempt by the factory committee leadership to specify a broad definition of the meaning of workers' control occurred, and met with little success. In response to a set of instructions elaborating the powers granted factory workers under the workers' control decree that had been issued in the name of the "All-Russian Workers' Council" in December 1917 by a commission headed by Larin and including Miliutin, Lozovskii, Antipov, and Smidovich, all opponents of a "broad" definition of control, the Petrograd Factory Committee movement leadership issued its own set of instructions in mid-January. These claimed the right for factory committees to intervene in management of enterprises when necessary. Indeed, the Central Council envisioned that a public control *(obshchestvennyi kontrol')* would replace capitalist ownership and management and would lead toward the placement of the entire economy "on social principles" *(na sotsial'nykh nachalakh).*[10]

Yet when Kaktyn', Amosov, and Ivanov-Mikhailov, on behalf of the Central Council of Petrograd Factory Committees, went to see Lenin in January to gain his explicit endorsement of their Instructions in preference to those issued by Larin, Lenin equivocated and advised them to base themselves on "life" rather than on "law."[11] Shortly thereafter life took the course of dissolving the Central Council of Factory Councils of Petrograd into the trade unions and the *sovnarkhozy,* and the theoretical problem of relating control to management and local to central power was resolved. Lenin refrained from granting approval to a conception that risked political decentralization; shortly afterward, the self-dissolution of the factory committee movement confirmed that the party leadership tacitly but deliberately sought to prevent workers' control from hindering the process of administrative centralization. The three occasions when factory committee leaders sought explicit approval for an expansion of workers' control and an endorsement of their de facto power demonstrate the skill with which Lenin disarmed a potentially provocative challenge to the party's authority. Having made it evident by degrees that both control and management were forms of authority that were hierarchical rather than democratic, state rather than public, the party leadership now needed to establish working institutions of control and management.

2. Reforming State *Kontrol'*

Reforming the inherited state *kontrol'* agency to make it an effective arm of bureaucratic oversight and control occupied Sovnarkom and the Central Executive Committee intermittently over the entire Civil War period and into the 1920s. Initially the task was to gather together the diverse agencies of internal inspection and control that formed in the early weeks after the October seizure of power when the state *kontrol'* was effectively defunct owing to the clerks' strike.[12] Among these were two agencies under the War Commissariat, as well as organs in the Food Commissariat, the Commissariat for Internal

Affairs, VSNKh, individual *glavki* under VSNKh, and individual trade unions. Later certain trade unions and enterprises formed "workers' inspectorates"; as will be discussed below, these were ultimately merged with state *kontrol'* to form the Worker-Peasant Inspectorate.

Despite a hiatus caused by the clerks' strike and the resulting need to improvise transitional forms, institutional continuity—with only the lightest anointing with Soviet oil—is the most striking feature of state *kontrol'* as it took form after October. The Sovnarkom discussed what to do with the agency on November 15 and deferred action; on November 19 it named the old Bolshevik E. E. Essen to be "deputy commissar of state *kontrol'* " (the title "deputy commissar" was apparently used in several early acts of appointment, in order to convey the provisional nature of the appointment).[13] Essen formed the senior controllers still at work into a collegium, which Sovnarkom charged with direction of *kontrol'*.[14] Immediately resuming the job of reviewing the financial transactions of other state bodies, the collegium soon found itself at odds with the commissar of finance.[15] The unique status of state *kontrol'*, that is, its lack of executive power, together perhaps with a mistrust of the collegium's political loyalty, lay behind Sovnarkom's decision on December 5, 1917, to give the commissar of state *kontrol'* a full vote on political issues but only an advisory vote on financial and economic matters.[16]

On January 18, 1918, Sovnarkom approved a statute on the functions and organization of state *kontrol'* that the collegium proposed. Under it, the "Central Control Collegium" was to oversee a network of local commissions attached to local soviets; these would review the economic and financial activity of local government. Although Sovnarkom intended the decree to ensure more "vital and rational" forms of local *kontrol'*, the decree's effect was to reestablish the old "chambers of *kontrol'* " of tsarist times. On May 9, Sovnarkom named K. I. Lander, a party member since 1905, commissar (he remained in the post until replaced by Stalin on March 30, 1919). In early June, Sovnarkom abolished the earlier collegium and at the same time specified that *kontrol'* must move past financial audits and must check the correctness and expediency of all material transaction of state bodies.[17] At both central and local levels, the staff of state *kontrol'*, not surprisingly, showed a remarkably high degree of continuity between the pre- and post-October periods: over 90 percent of the controllers were former controllers.[18] In fact, the census of autumn 1918 determined that, of all state branch agencies surveyed, the commissariat of state *kontrol'* had the lowest proportion of Bolshevik and pro-Bolshevik employees. Of 937 employees, only 12 were party members and another 10 sympathizers. At 2.3 percent of the staff, this was lower than the average for all 22,432 employees, 13.3 percent. If it is fair to conclude, as do Gaponenko et al. in their recent synoptic history of the Soviet working class, that the revolution merely removed the very top administrative stratum from the state bureaucracy, in no branch does this apply more aptly than in state *kontrol'*.[19] Still later, Stalin, shortly after being named commissar of state *kontrol'*, pointed out that the commissariat was the only Soviet agency not yet subjected to a thorough *chistka i lomka* (purging and smashing).

From the publications of the commissariat (the *Izvestiia gosudarstvennogo kontrolia* and the *Biulleten' izvestii gosudarstvennogo kontrolia*, the latter of which ceased publication at the end of 1918 and was combined with the *Izvestiia*) as well as from the fulminations of *kontrol'*'s numerous critics in VSNKh and the trade unions, it is clear that the commissariat's leaders shared an institutional outlook that saw *kontrol'* as a force for order and reason in state administration. Far from evincing hostility or suspicion toward the Soviet regime, this group, largely non-Bolshevik, supported the new order, sharing the adherence to the values of statism and centralism that led many members of the old intelligentsia to cooperate with it.[20] Moreover, the controllers actively sought to draw in fresh proletarian forces, grasping that the poor reputation of the commissariat, its lack of authority and frequent collisions with other agencies, might be overcome if workers and Communists shared responsibility for its activity. This point was a constant refrain in the articles appearing in the *Izvestiia*. A typical example is an article by a former general in the tsarist auditing department, Sergei Gadziatskii, who vigorously supported the new order and the place of *kontrol'* in it, about the poor image state *kontrol'* enjoyed. Other agencies, he wrote, need to see state *kontrol'* as a Soviet, people's organ, not as something bureaucratic and alien; it needs reform to become strong and authoritative; and so as to merge state and workers' *kontrol'*, trade union and other workers' bodies performing *kontrol'* functions should be integrated into the state *kontrol'* commissariat.[21] Defending the commissariat against its critics, Commissar Lander pointed out in March 1919 that not one case of sabotage by the old staff had been uncovered. Lander noted proudly that in its "factual" control work—that is, inspections of transport, fuel, food, and similar sectors—300 Communists took part.[22]

State *kontrol'* sparred with Vesenkha and the unions incessantly. Critics, among whom Mikhail Larin was particularly vocal, accused state *kontrol'* of being dominated by tsarist *chinovniki*, which was true of many Soviet agencies; of bureaucratism and pettifoggery; and even of providing grist for the mills of the regime's enemies through its reports of deficiencies in the state apparatus.[23] When in early 1919 the VTsIK discussed how *kontrol'* should be reformed, Vesenkha urged that it be abolished.[24] In the case of inspections on the railroads, workers' bodies flatly refused to cooperate with state *kontrol'*.[25] In this case the strongly independent railway workers would not recognize controllers from the commissariat, despite a direct order from the commissar of communications on April 6, 1918, and another from Lenin on April 16, 1918.

The principal reason state *kontrol'* provoked such antagonism from other agencies was its insistence on continuing the forms and methods of work inherited from the prerevolutionary period, which inevitably brought it into conflict with agencies whose budget requests it passed on and whose books it examined. Moreover, in the absence of a governing statute detailing how audits and reviews were to be conducted, the controllers themselves determined their procedures and selected the units to be audited. Claiming that since the state's books for the war years had not been audited, the new government lacked accurate information about what resources it had, the commissariat worked throughout 1918 to close out the books on 1915, 1916, and 1917. In mid-December 1918, the commissariat published a notice that its audit of the year 1915 was complete.[26] Irritating to other commissariats and local governments was the commissariat's insistence that it pass on budget estimates before funds were appropriated from the state treasury. The commissariat condemned the common practice among government agencies of keeping large sums of cash on hand for expenses rather than clearing expenditures through the treasury. Many budget documents were sketchy and incomplete; the commissariat's refusal to accept them caused resentment. The commissariat's inspections almost invariably uncovered serious lapses from proper fiscal practices as well as losses of huge sums. It is understandable that when the union of employees and workers of the central offices of state *kontrol'* held a conference in late 1918, the major topic of discussion concerned how the physical security of inspectors could be protected from the "dark elements" that were squandering the nation's inheritance.[27]

Despite the commissariat's persistence in the old routines, its representatives articulated a grand vision of the role *kontrol'* could play in systematizing and rationalizing state administration. The commissariat proposed, unsuccessfully, a statute on the organization of *kontrol'* that would have made the local *kontrol'* offices independent of local soviets and, at the center, would have placed the commissariat under the Central Executive Committee rather than Sovnarkom. This of course would have made it effectively autonomous.[28] The commissariat defended its proposal on the grounds that as an agency without executive responsibility, it should be "independent and subordinate directly to the legislative authority."[29] On the same grounds, the commissariat sought to escape the burden of collective responsibility for government decisions implied by its full vote on political questions in Sovnarkom.[30] Carried away with his vision of a centralized, universal agency of supervision, the anonymous editorialist in the *Bulletin* of the commissariat demanded that state *kontrol'* become "the all-seeing eye of the republic" and proclaimed: "From a dead, post hoc, paper thing, *kontrol'* must become living, real *kontrol'* over all organs of economic construction, with the power to intervene everywhere and direct everything, and as the regulator of economic policy, to verify the implementation of all laws and orders."[31]

The almost ludicrous discrepancy between the commissariat's aspirations and its capabilities was a product both of the adherence to standing procedures for monitoring the flows of goods and money, which required a standard of recordkeeping that no Soviet office could meet, and of the institutional attitude this engendered—that only the *kontrol'* agency could straighten out the abuses, carelessness, and confusion in economic transactions pervading the state bureaucracy. Few in the Soviet government shared the commissariat's confidence:

apart from a portion of a provisional statute on auditing (*ustav revizii*), none of the decrees proposed by the commissariat was approved by Sovnarkom until the April 1919 reorganization.[32] The best explanation for the commissariat's endurance in the face of all efforts at reform, reorganization, and merger was the powerful belief in centralism professed by all who dealt with the subject of workers' or state *kontrol'*.

This point may be illustrated by a telling episode that occurred during a conference in September 1918 to discuss how factory *kontrol'* should be organized. Present were representatives of the Moscow Council of Trade Unions, VSNKh, the Moscow *oblast'* economic council, and state *kontrol'*; the controllers were in the majority. The conference discussed a proposal from a representative of state *kontrol'* that would have made the state *kontrol'* commissariat the sole center for statewide control. In the factories elected workers, subject to the approval of state *kontrol'*, would work together with the state controllers to carry out *kontrol'*. The state controllers would examine the books; the workers would inspect stocks of materials, fuel and products.

The proposal was opposed from two sides. The trade union and VNSKh representatives denounced the scheme for restoring the old bureaucratic spirit, for seeking to intrude into the sphere which trade union control commissions were perfectly capable of handling, and for ignoring the fact that neither state *kontrol'* nor the working class could provide a sufficient number of trained controllers to make it work. Eventually, in fact, they refused to take any further part in the deliberations. But when the question of whether state *kontrol'* should have at least some role in the auditing of enterprise records was put to a vote—a question reduced to Shakespearian simplicity as "is state *kontrol'* to be or not to be in the factories" ("byt' na fabrikakh Gosudarstvennomu Kontroliu ili ne byt'?")—the proposition passed unanimously. Yet the state controllers at the meeting were no happier with the scheme, since it delegated responsibility for inspections to the workers, while the specialists from state *kontrol'* would have a secondary role, "a division of roles insulting to intelligent officials" ("obidnoe dlia intelligentnykh rabotnikov raspredelenie rolei"). These controllers believed that workers were unready for the work of *kontrol'* and that *kontrol'* should be concerned strictly with monitoring records, not with raising productivity and discipline. Blocked by the combined opposition of the old specialists and the VSNKh–trade union alliance, the scheme failed.[33]

Criticism from the Red Army may have been the catalyst that resulted in the reorganization of 1919. N. I. Podvoiskii, who headed the army's Supreme Military Inspectorate, proposed in October 1918 to Iakov Sverdlov, as chairman of the Central Executive Committee, that all *kontrol'* activity be comprehended under a single authority.[34] Late in December the VTsIK Presidium agreed to consider this, charging Sverdlov with creating such a body. Sverdlov chaired a commission, which included representatives of state *kontrol'*, the soviets, and the railroad and food inspectorates, to formulate a new plan of organization. The primary aim of the commission seems to have been to pry state *kontrol'* away from its preoccupation with audits and budget reviews and to focus it on "factual" review—particularly supervision of the severely strained food and fuel supply and distribution systems. Beyond auditing, *kontrol'* should see to it that all activity of a given institution was in order, giving advice as needed on how to remedy problems. These tasks, Sverdlov observed at the commissions' first meeting, were currently beyond the powers of state *kontrol'*. The commission decided, nonetheless, to build the new body on the basis of the old.[35]

As the commission worked on devising a new body, one that would unite the existing state *kontrol'* organs with the military and perhaps the workers' inspectorates, Stalin and Dzerzhinskii weighed in with further advice. In a report of January 31, 1918, to Lenin from the field explaining the reasons for the fall of Perm' to the Whites, they recommended the formation of an audit-review commission under the Defense Council that would investigate deficiencies in the work of commissariats and departments of local government.[36] The party Central Committee then instructed Sverdlov to add Stalin and Dzerzhinskii to the commission.[37] The pressure of war had already, in early December 1918, led the Defense Council to discuss the need for state *kontrol'* to raise the productivity and military preparedness of the economy and to help fight sabotage.[38] When Sverdlov suddenly died on the eve of the Eighth Party Congress, Stalin replaced him as chairman of the *kontrol'* commission. Otherwise Sverdlov rather than Stalin would surely have become the new commissar, although neither had the time to make *kontrol'* into an effectively functioning organization. Since state *kontrol'* never enjoyed the priority that more pressing tasks, such as war, foreign policy, internal security, party and state organization, and economic administration, did, it constantly suffered from the shortage of capable and loyal cadres that hampered all units of the young state and it was also deprived of the competence, attention, and energy that senior Bolsheviks brought to more important fields.

The resolution on *kontrol'* adopted by the party's eighth congress called in general terms for "radical reorganization" "so as to create genuine *kontrol'* of a socialist character." The resolution provided little guidance about how this function should be organized, however, demanding only that the party and trade unions must assume the leading role in carrying it out.[39]

As against the widespread desire to make *kontrol'* both socialist and genuine, which presumably referred to the need to make *kontrol'* in whatever form an effective arm of the government in monitoring bureaucratic behavior so as to improve economic and governmental performance, Lenin, when he reviewed the work of the Sverdlov commission, offered yet another desideratum: the proposed reorganization should ensure that *kontrol'* recruit workers at the central and local levels, and, moreover, that at least two-thirds of the controllers be women.[40] Lenin saw a somewhat different set of tasks as demanding the attention of this broadly participatory movement: it would conduct surprise raids in response to citizens' complaints, fight red tape and bureaucratic abuses, increase the availability of foodstuffs, and simultaneously raise labor productivity.

The commission now sought to combine several conceptions. Sovnarkom and VTsIK finally issued their decree on the reorganization of state *kontrol'* on April 9, 1919. Stalin had already been named commissar of state *kontrol'*, on March 30, and as commissar he signed the April 9 decree. Under its terms, a major part of the reformed commissariat's duties consisted in receiving and investigating complaints, and in this work it was to avail itself as much as possible of the popular masses. The decree formally established a reorganized Complaints Bureau, naming M. M. Litvinov its head.[41] The formalistic methods of work of the old state *kontrol'* commissariat were to be replaced by methods of "factual *kontrol'* " carried out by the broad strata of workers and peasants, who would ensure the prompt and expedient execution of decrees and orders in all spheres of economy and state administration.[42] The commissariat was also to unite all the internal control offices of other agencies under its authority.

Outgoing commissar Lander greeted the decree for bringing about an "October Revolution" in *kontrol'*, because it directed the commissariat's activity to "factual control," which he termed *political* control of the broadest kind.[43] Factual control did broaden the scope of control. Under the reorganization, the commissariat could bring violators of the law to court; it was to find ways to simplify overcomplicated organizational structures and eliminate redundancy, inefficiency, and red tape throughout the state apparatus. Expanding the mandate of the commissariat could not, nevertheless, improve the quality of its activity, both because of its limited resources and reluctance to abandon familiar auditing methods and because of the mistrust and hostility felt toward it by many of the heads of institutions it inspected. The shift of attention to "factual" control may have exacerbated the view that state controllers had no right to intrude into the internal affairs of Soviet organizations, since so few controllers were communists.[44]

The decree also increased frictions by calling for the unification of control under the commissariat and the infusion of workers' control bodies into it. Following the decree, workers' inspectorates did establish working cooperation with state *kontrol'* for various raids and inspections, carried out, for example, in the food distribution network.[45] Some three hundred controllers delegated from the trade unions joined state *kontrol'* for "flying reviews." Lander described the procedure used in Smolensk *guberniia* and several of its *uezds*. A food or timber committee was selected for a review, and state controllers drafted a detailed list of questions to be answered about it. The trade union council or another workers' organization designated between fifteen and forty worker-inspectors, who conducted the actual inspection themselves under the direction of one or two officials from the trade union and a technical director familiar with auditing procedures.[46]

Hundreds of "flying raids"—unannounced inspections of some particular office or facility—were conducted. As demands for inspections were received from central government bodies or prompted by reports from the field, ad hoc on-site reviews were conducted—most in Moscow, some in outlying provinces (in the May-August period, some 85 spot checks were performed, 47 in

Moscow).[47] The commissariat became one of the points of extrabureaucratic authority to which citizens could address petitions and complaints (the largest number of complaints were received from peasants about food requisitions; complaints against the Chekas followed them in number; next most common were complaints against government housing and other agencies).[48] In the month of December 1919 alone, the Central Complaints Bureau examined about 700 cases, its local bureaus another 1,300.[49] The main activity of the commissariat in this period probably consisted of responses to reports of abuses rather than of general oversight of the state bureaucracy, and the main form in which it recruited popular assistance was through its raids and field inspections, which inevitably had a sporadic, ad hoc character.

Field inspections generated so much tension between state *kontrol'* and agencies it investigated that the Complaints Bureau sought independent investigative power. The commissariat sought to escape the jurisdictional authority of local soviets, but the party overruled it. The party's Orgburo issued a ruling on June 26, 1919, that state *kontrol'* must observe the principle of dual subordination— that is, to both the commissariat and the local soviet executive committees.[50] The commissariat even protested this decision, but the Orgburo reconfirmed it.[51] Despite the party's position, however, state *kontrol'* acted independently of local soviets and demanded the right to approve all plans for expenditures.

An article by the chairman of the Moscow *guberniia ispolkom*, T. V. Sapronov, in mid-1919 entitled "Kontrol' as a Superstructure over the Soviets or an Organ of the Soviets?" attacked state *kontrol'* for taking the same independent path as the Cheka. According to Sapronov, despite the party's concern with making *kontrol'* effective and nonbureaucratic, *kontrol'* organs had become self-enclosed and autonomous of local soviet authorities, higher even than the Sovnarkom. The regime had become, Sapronov bitterly observed, not the "power of the soviets" ("vlast' sovetov") but "power of *kontrol'*" ("vlast' kontrolia").[52] From the standpoint of the central political leaders for whom it was axiomatic that the commissariat should be a school of managerial training for the workers, the limited nature of collaboration between state *kontrol'* and workers' control remained the thorniest problem. Both the Eighth Party Conference and Eighth Soviet Congress, at the end of 1919, called for unifying state *kontrol'* with the workers' inspectorates and with the *kontrol'* bodies that continued to function independently in other agencies.

3. The Worker-Peasant Inspectorate

In view of the substantial literature in Soviet and Western sources on workers' control in 1917 and early 1918, it is odd that so little research has been conducted on the worker's inspectorates in the Civil War period. To be sure, relatively few references to them are found even in the trade union and government periodicals, and perhaps state archives contain little more. An interesting topic for subsequent research into the social history of the period would be these and other bodies of workers conducting control "from below."

The institution of worker inspectorates had arisen by October 1918. Very likely they emerged as replacement for the old state factory inspectors and consisted of elected bodies composed of workers and technical specialists charged with checking on safety and other working conditions. The October 1918 issue of *Biulleten' narodnogo komissariata truda* reports that 42 workers and 72 technical inspectors were engaged in this work, with the shortage of qualified cadres a serious hindrance to its expansion.[53] By early December the number had risen from 259 to 655, but the number remained well below the need.[54] In some cases the inspectors were members of the intelligentsia, even former factory inspectors; in others, they were workers who had done a spell of duty in the state *kontrol'* commissariat and started equivalent offices in their own factories.[55] Eventually, local units of factories and districts of Moscow united to form the Moscow Workers' Inspectorate, formal establishment of which dates to March 1919. By joining across factories, the inspectorate could organized special-purpose inspection raids, such as that conducted in June of bread bakeries. Altogether it comprised about 300 factory cells and about 60,000 participants.[56] Responding to issues as they arose, the worker-inspectors operated without reference to state *kontrol'* organs and often duplicated their activity.

Another step in the development of workers' inspectorates occurred when the Central Council of Trade Unions decided to sponsor a specialized workers' inspectorate for railway shipments of military goods and food; apparently parallel to this was formation by Sovnarkom, under a decree of December 5, 1918, of a special inspectorate for the food distribution system.[57] This was intended as a department of the Commissariat of Food Provisions. It worked in tandem with the inspectorate formed under the Military-Food Bureau of the Central Trade Union Council until the two inspectorates agreed to merge in May 1919 to form the Central Bureau of Workers' Food Inspectorate, with branches in each province.[58]

The Food Inspectorate worked under the direction of the Food Commissariat and the Central Trade Union Council and carried out on-site inspections to guard the shipment of provisions from procurement through delivery and distribution. It quickly became apparent that a specialized railroad inspectorate along similar lines was needed.[59] In the spring of 1919 such a body was founded under the Military-Food Bureau of the Central Trade Union Council and engaged in investigation, auditing, oversight of repairs, and eliminating snarls and breakdowns in the transportation system. It organized several hundred workers into small groups (*piaterki*) to ride shotgun on trains.[60] They saw to the unloading of trains, prevention of looting and disorder, the evacuation of goods from cities threatened with White occupation, and similar needs. By a statute of state *kontrol'* of July 25, 1919, in agreement with the inspectorate, the worker-inspectors were to be assigned to state *kontrol'* as fully empowered controllers in carrying out their work while retaining their autonomy as representatives of the Military-Food Bureau of the Central Trade Union Council.[61]

When the military situation improved at the end of 1919, three proposals for merger of state *kontrol'* and the workers' inspectorates circulated, one submitted by the Moscow Workers' Inspectorate, another by the Railroad Inspectorate and the Central Trade Union Council, and the third by the State *Kontrol'* Commissariat. That of the railroad inspectorate would effectively have abolished state *kontrol'* and replaced it with the workers' inspectorates. State *kontrol'*'s proposal would have absorbed the workers' inspectorates into the state apparatus.[62] As a special commission of the Presidium of the Central Executive Committee (with representatives of VTsIK, VTsSPS, state *kontrol'*, the Moscow Workers' Inspectorate, and the Railroad Inspectorate) sought to reconcile these competing conceptions, Lenin, in a note of January 24, 1920, suggested combining them by merging the workers' inspectorates into the state *kontrol'* apparatus. The Politburo examined the question on January 23 and again on January 28, and the Central Committee did so on January 31. The issue evidently provoked a stiff jurisdictional fight. The unpopularity and ineffectiveness of the state *kontrol'* apparatus notwithstanding, the principle of a state-centered and centralized organization for *kontrol'* with extensive worker and peasant and, above all, female participation seems to have been generally favored by the central political leadership.

Finally, Deputy Commissar of State *Kontrol'* Avanesov worked out a compromise, under which, rather than making the workers' inspectorates a department of state *kontrol'*, the state *kontrol'* commissariat would itself be reorganized into the Commissariat of Worker-Peasant Inspection.[63] By a Central Executive Committee decree of February 7, 1920, the new commissariat was founded.

As had so often been the case previously, the February 1920 decree effected reorganization on paper more than in fact. The functions and core organization of state *kontrol'* were not greatly touched by it.[64] On the other hand, although its central offices continued to review the accounts of other state bodies, in the factories, new "cells of assistance" comprising part-time volunteer participants spread and grew to the point that most provinces had cells and some 45,000 persons were enrolled in a total of 12,000 such cells by mid-1921.[65] For various reasons, however, including the pressure of renewed fighting, the inexperience of the members, the resistance of the trade unions to surrendering the autonomy of their inspectorates, and the absence of clear administrative direction, the cells were relatively ineffective.[66]

The RKI Commissariat (Rabkrin) comprised both permanent and temporary controllers, the latter being elected by the factory workforce: a major round of elections were held in September 1920 and was conducted with extensive propaganda around the theme of learning state governance by participation in the inspectorate.[67] A minority—perhaps 10 percent—attended courses on how to conduct inspections and audits. RKI's work included both the familiar "flying inspections" as well as "mass inquiries" (*massovye obsledovaniia*), which comprised large-scale turnouts to check on the work of particular organizations or even entire branches, especially communal services such as laundries, cafeterias, baths, and stores. These might last a week or ten days.[68] One particularly large inspection of the latter sort was directed to childcare facilities: hundreds of inspectors took part and, according to the records, over 3,400 children's institutions were examined. The RKI also continued in the tradition of the old factory committee bodies and took an active role in economic administration, advising, for example, that production of soap be concentrated in a few more efficient enterprises instead of being dispersed among dozens of enterprises.[69] Likewise it carried out audits of stocks and operations in the *glavki* and trusts overseeing the handicrafts enterprises, making various suggestions on how to bring these under more effective coordination and planning.[70] Characteristic of its activity were checks to determine whether agencies claiming certain numbers of employees for food rationing purposes did in fact employ that many people.[71] As can be imagined, these inspections and reports brought RKI into collision with executive agencies, which undermined the cooperation needed to remedy the defects that under the conditions of the day were only too readily apparent.

Most workers who were deputed to work with the RKI stayed for a short period, four months at most.[72] Of the regular staff, only a small proportion was made up of workers and peasants; the RKI was one of the havens for the old intelligentsia and bureaucratic classes.[73] Of the members of cells of assistance, according to one estimate, two-thirds were office employees (*kantseliarskie rabotniki*).[74] The compromise formula embodied in the February 1920 decree sought to dissolve the trade union *kontrol'* commissions and inspectorates and replace them with an expanding network of RKI inspectorates in localities and cells of assistance in factories.[75] Although workers entered the factory cells and the local inspectorates in large numbers, however, the overarching unitary direction that was intended by the decree and that was to be exercised by the central apparatus of the commissariat still was lacking. In the *glavki*, separate *kontrol'* organs continued to monitor management in particular branches. Trade unions continued to direct local inspections; the commissariat the activity from above. Some railway unions resisted holding elections to deputize workers to state *kontrol'* or refused to send those who were elected.[76] The bifurcation between "workers' *kontrol'* " and "state *kontrol'* " remained unresolved.[77]

Discontent with the RKI at the end of 1920 accordingly sounded much like the complaints voiced the previous year. In its annual report for 1920 the RKI itself acknowledged that its subordinate offices often acted in an excessively formalistic and bureaucratic manner and concentrated too often on the purely financial and material side of administration, that too many of its personnel were former *chinovniki* rather than workers, and that its relations with local soviets and soviet departments were often poor.[78] Lenin's criticism was harsher. Speaking at the Moscow *guberniia* party conference on November 21, 1920, Lenin observed that the RKI was "more of a wish" than a reality and that it had failed to exercise the kind of far-reaching proletarian oversight of the state that had been hoped for, mainly because the best workers had been mobilized to the front and the overall cultural level of the rest was low. He also offered a "political cultural" explanation when he characterized Russians as poor organizers. The main thrust of the speech, however, was an attack on the workers' opposition movement for failing to offer constructive remedies to the ills of the RKI.[79] In a similar vein, several days later (November 29), Lenin said of RKI that it had hardly been in evidence (*malo sebia proiavil*) as a school for training workers to govern the state.[80] Lenin seems not to have recognized any insurmountable difficulty in reconciling the twin goals of employing the RKI simultaneously to raise the masses' level of culture and to exert centralized control over the behavior of the state bureaucracy. He may also have underestimated the positive contributions made by the commissariat in its ombudsman role.

A resolution of the implicit war over turf between the state controllers and the trade unions was reached by the Tenth Party Congress. Here a resolution on *kontrol'* and inspection work ("kontrol'no-inspektsionnaia rabota") declared that the RKI must work *through* the trade union factory cells in carrying out reviews and audits of factory accounts and must not create separate units.[81] The Fourth Trade Union Congress (May 17–25, 1921) discussed how to end the redundancy between the RKI and the unions, and resolved that trade union controllers should hold corresponding positions in the RKI apparatus (which seems to assume a some continued parallelism of structure).[82] Trade union officials considered this compromise a victory since it preserved factory-level independence for *kontrol'*.[83] The solution, however, did not improve the effectiveness of *kontrol'* from the standpoint of the central authorities. In the fall of 1921, Lenin still found the RKI severely wanting and urged that its orientation shift from the aim of "exposing" malfeasance to that of "correcting" it; still, Lenin was not ready to abolish it. Only in 1922 did he propose the radical reorganization under which the RKI was to be cut back in size sharply, the party *kontrol'* commission expanded, and the two merged.[84]

The greater influence on the RKI's activity and effectiveness, though, was probably the shift to legal private production and trade. This had the effect of sharply diminishing the size of the full-time and temporary force working in RKI. In the first several months of NEP as many as 70 percent of RKI's staff left.[85] The collapse of RKI was so deep that the VTsIK responded with a new decree, of January 9, 1922, that reaffirmed the former division of labor between the central organs of the commissariat—the complaints bureau and branch offices, which conducted inspections and audits in state organizations—and the local cells of assistance, which oversaw *kontrol'* in the factories and villages, including private and leased-out enterprises.[86] The RKI also continued to serve as a pool of mobilizable manpower for special purposes, as when 1,500 of its employees were diverted to collect the tax-in-kind from the peasants in 1921.[87]

Both as a formal organization and as a set of functions, *kontrol'* was affected at least as much by the adaptation of the bodies claiming supervisory powers to the bureaucratic environment in which they operated as by any policy acts of the government. By the end of the War Communism period, the jurisdictional fight between the state controllers and the trade unions had reached a stalemate, reflecting the roughly equal importance of two competing principles of organization, centralism and mass participation, state control and workers' control. Stalin articulated both principles in an address at the First All-Russian Conference of Executives of RKI, October 15, 1920. He divided the tasks of *kontrol'* into two groups—helping overcome disorder in economic administration and improve recordkeeping and accountability and training workers and peasants as future managers. Noting that the performance of government rests not merely on enactment of laws, but on their implementation as well, he urged RKI to become a repository of oversight power and expertise about bureaucracy. In turn this meant that the RKI must go beyond the role of policeman and must help solve problems and offer guidance. On the other hand, RKI must itself be incorruptible and merciless: in investigating wrong doing it must spare no one.[88]

Both workers' control and state control institutions had evolved from more narrowly conceived agencies verifying the propriety of transactions into organizations with much broader mandates. In 1917 the expansion of workers' control into administration had presented the Bolsheviks with both opportunities and dilemmas. Similarly, as state *kontrol'* moved away from "prior" and "post facto" review and increasingly into "factual" control, its duties became broader and more diffuse. Its inspections and raids lent its work a quasi-procuratorial character. Frequently the commissariat demanded procuratorial powers and had to be satisfied with the right to transfer cases to the slow-moving Commissariat of Justice.[89] When in 1922 a formal procuracy was established, a better delineation of duties could be laid out.[90] The fact that so many of the complaints received concerned abuses by the Cheka raised particularly sharp jurisdictional conflicts, and Dzerzhinskii himself was forced to demand that local units of Cheka cooperate with *kontrol'*'s "Fifth Department," created to follow up on complaints concerning the Cheka.[91]

In both cases, though, the lack of specificity about the tasks of control created problems that the Soviet government sought to solve through statutes intended to centralize, unify and focus control. Both state and workers' control bodies made use of those aspects of Bolshevik edicts that supported their own institutional self-conceptions to legitimate their institutional autonomy. Measured against the demands that state *kontrol'* be an effective tool of central power and a training-ground for the future proletarian administrators, the commissariat was consistently found wanting. Encouraged by the same demands, the commissariat sought commensurate power and collided with both trade union–based *kontrol'* and central and local state bodies. Rationalization of state *kontrol'*, therefore, failed in the Civil War period because it depended less on any decreed elaboration of powers and responsibilities than on the rationalization of state administration overall, so as to reduce the tendency for state *kontrol'* to be drawn into and replace weak executive authority. Simultaneously the enervating jurisdictional competition between sources of state and social or public authority had to be resolved, first, by the legalization of market relations in society and, ultimately, by the Stalin revolution.

NOTES

1. On the interpretation of these events, I differ somewhat from S. A. Smith in his generally excellent study *Red Petrograd*. Smith gives too little attention to the tactical reasons Lenin and his colleagues might have had for supporting the factory committee movement and its aspirations. Smith therefore credits Lenin after October with a "spirit of libertarianism" about the significance of workers' control that cannot be reconciled with the leader's actions. When Smith claims that Lenin, rather than the factory committee leadership, drafted a decree ratifying enterprise-level workers' control because the proposal by the factory committee leaders for a "Supreme Economic Council" omitted a point on workers' control, he is in error. See Smith, *Red Petrograd: Revolution in the Factories, 1917–1918* (Cambridge, 1983). David Mandel's volumes, *The Petrograd Workers and the Fall of the Old Regime: From the February Revolution to the July Days, 1917* (London, 1983) and *The Petrograd Workers and the Soviet Seizure of Power: From the July Days to July 1918* (London, 1984), are also valuable in relating workers' control to the broader social and political movements of the time. Recent Soviet surveys of workers' control and the factory committee movement include L. F. Morozov and V. P. Portnov, *Sotsialisticheskii kontrol' v SSSR: istoricheskii ocherk* (Moscow, 1984) and V. A. Vinogradov, *Rabochii kontrol' nad proizvodstvom: teoriia, istoriia, sovremennost'* (Moscow, 1983). An indispensable source of documents is P. N. Amosov, et al., comp. *Oktiabr'skaia revoliutsiia i fabzavkomy: Materialy po istorii fabrichno-zavodskikh komitetov*, 2 vols. (Moscow, 1927). Additional references will be found in Thomas Remington, "Institution-Building in Bolshevik Russia: The Case of 'State Kontrol','" *Slavic Review*, March 1982, vol. 41, no. 1, pp. 91–103; and idem, *Building Socialism in Bolshevik Russia: Ideology and Industrial Organization, 1917–1921* (Pittsburgh, 1984), chap. 2.

2. *Novyi put'*, 1919, no. 3, p. 26.

3. *Ekonomicheskaia zhizn'*, 1924, no. 95, p. 3.

4. V. Z. Drobizhev and A. B. Medvedev, *Iz istorii sovnarkhozov (1917–1918 gg.)* (Moscow, 1964), pp. 64–65.

5. Smith, p. 213; V. V. Zhuravlev, *Dekrety sovetskoi vlasti 1917–1920 gg. kak istoricheskii istochnik* (Moscow, 1979), pp. 41–46.

6. Smith, p. 211; *Dekrety sovetskoi vlasti* (Moscow, 1957–   ), 1:77–82; V. L. Meller and A. M. Pankratova, *Rabochee dvizhenie v 1917 godu* (Moscow, 1926), pp. 321–22.

7. Amosov, 1:75.

8. A. V. Venediktov, *Organizatsiia gosudarstvennoi promyshlennosti v SSSR*, 2 vols. (Leningrad, 1957), 1:100.

9. Remington, *Building Socialism*, p. 45.

10. Smith, pp. 211–12; Remington, "Institution-Building," p. 93. At the All-Russian Factory Committee Congress in October 1917, the congress resolution also referred to the role of workers' control in establishing "democratic self-management by the workers themselves" (Meller and Pankratova, p. 318). David Mandel tends to interpret the factory committee movement's position as a defensive reaction to impersonal forces,

seeking to rescue its reputation from the odium of "anarcho-syndicalism." This tends to overlook its capacity for independent political vision and action. Mandel is right to point out that after October, the nationalization of industry and the creation of a new administration had the effect of making workers' control "as a form of factory dual power" unnecessary and created objective contradictions between the factory committees and the "overall needs of the economy as perceived by the central economic bodies." We must remember, though, that for the first weeks of Soviet power there were no working "central economic bodies" and how best to deal with the "overall needs of the economy" was a matter of intense political debate. The effort to explain the politics of the "workers"—as if all had similar views and interests—and the actions of the party leadership as "rational" responses to circumstances places an undue burden of explanation on "rationality" (which under the best of circumstances is colored by uncertainty, experience, and normative preferences) and diverts attention from the political arena in which policy demands are voiced (Mandel, *Petrograd Workers*, pp. 274, 284, 366–67, 375). On the concept of rationality in political life, a major restatement of the "bounded rationality" theory is Herbert A. Simon, "Human Nature in Politics: The Dialogue of Psychology with Political Science," *American Political Science Review*, June 1985, vol. 79, no. 2, pp. 293–304.

11. *Ekonomicheskaia zhizn'*, 1924, no. 95 p. 3.

12. P. V'ii, "K voprosu o vedomstvennykh kontroliakh," *Izvestiia gosudarstvennogo kontrolia* (hereafter IGK), 1919, no. 17 p. 3.

13. A. I. Koniaev, "Gosudarstvennyi kontrol' v pervye gody sovetskoi vlasti," *Istoriia SSSR*, 1964, no. 1, pp. 30–31.

14. L. F. Morozov and V. P. Portnov, *Sotsialisticheskii kontrol' v SSSR; Istoricheskii ocherk*, p. 15; also, *Biulleten' izvestii gosudarstvennogo kontrolia*, no. 4 (1918), p. 14.

15. Koniaev, p. 31.

16. Morozov and Portnov, *Sotsialisticheskii kontrol'*, p. 15.

17. A. I. Chugunov, *Organy sotsialisticheskogo kontrolia RSFSR, 1923–1934 gg.* (Moscow, 1972), p. 23.

18. N. A. Voskresenskaia, *V. I. Lenin—Organizator sotsialisticheskogo kontrolia* (Moscow, 1970), p. 99; Koniaev, p. 31.

19. L. S. Gaponenko, et al., eds., *Rabochii klass v oktiabr'skoi revoliutsii i na zashchite ee zavoevanii, 1917–1920 gg.* (Moscow, 1984), 1:156–57.

20. On this, see Remington, *Building Socialism*, pp. 117–31.

21. S. A. Gadziatskii, "Reforma gosudarstvennogo kontrolia," IGK, 1919, no. 6, pp. 6–7.

22. K. Lander, "Bor'ba protiv Kontrolia (otvet tov. Larinu i drugim protivnikam Kontrolia)," IGK, 1919, no. 6, p. 2.

23. K. Lander, "Pod blagovidnym predlogom," IGK, 1919, no. 8 pp. 6–7.

24. K. Lander, "Bor'ba protiv Kontrolia," IGK, 1919, no. 6, p. 1.

25. Voskresenskaia, p. 103.

26. G. A. Dorokhova, *Raboche-krest'ianskaia inspektsiia v 1920–1923 gg.* (Moscow, 1959), p. 9; Morozov and Portnov, *Sotsialisticheskii kontrol'*, p. 16; *Ekonomicheskaia zhizn'*, 1918, no. 31, p. 1; V. Sokolov, "Khronika reorganizatsii i deiatel'nosti Gosudarstvennogo Kontrolia," IGK, 1918, no. 6, p. 186.

27. "Professional'naia zhizn'," IGK, 1918, no. 6, pp. 218–19.

28. Morozov and Portnov, *Sotsialisticheskii kontrol'*, p. 19.

29. *Biulleten' izvestii gosudarstvennogo kontrolia*, July 20, 1918, no. 1, p. 2.

30. S. Engel, "Konstitutsiia RSFSR," IGK, 1918, no. 6, pp. 26–30.

31. *Biulleten' izvestii gosudarstvennogo kontrolia*, August 20, 1918, no. 5, pp. 2–3.

32. Voskresenskaia, p. 114.

33. A. Golopolosov, "Tri techeniia," IGK, 1918, no. 6, pp. 106–31.

34. Koniaev, "Gosudarstvennyi kontrol'," p. 37.

35. Ibid., pp. 37–38.

36. I. V. Stalin, *Sochineniia*, 13 vols., (Moscow: 1947), 4:217.

37. S. N. Ikonnikov, *Organizatsiia i deiatel'nost' RKI v 1920–1925 gg.* (Moscow, 1960), pp. 16–17.

38. Dorokhova, pp. 13–14.

39. *Vos'moi s"ezd RKP(b). Mart 1919: Protokoly* (Moscow, 1959), p. 428.

40. V. I. Lenin, *Polnoe sobranie sochinenii*, 5th ed., (Moscow, 1958–65), 37:541–42.

41. Koniaev, p. 40. See also L. F. Morozov and V. P. Portnov, "Nachal'nyi etap v osushchestvlenii leninskikh idei o gosudarstvennom kontrole," *Voprosy istorii KPSS*, 1979, no. 11 esp. p. 37.

42. Koniaev, pp. 38–39.

43. K. Lander, "Novyi kontrol'," IGK, 1919, no. 8, p. 2.

44. N. N., "Fakticheskii kontrol'," IGK, 1919, no. 9, p. 5.

45. "Zasedanie vremennogo Soveta Gosudarstvennogo Kontrolia," IGK, 1919, no. 10, p. 14.

46. K. Lander, "Letuchaia reviziia sovetskoi raboty na mestakh," IGK, 1919, nos. 13–14, p. 2.

47. Morozov and Portnov, "Osushchestvlenie," p. 39.

48. "Deiatel'nost' Tsentral'nogo Biuro Zhalob i Zaiavlenii," IGK, 1919, no. 16, p. 4–5.

49. Morozov and Portnov, "Osushchestvlenie," p. 39.

50. Ibid., p. 37.

51. Ibid., p. 38.

52. T. V. Sapronov, "Kontrol' kak nadstroika nad sovetami ili organ sovetov?" *Sotsialisticheskoe stroitel'stvo*, 1919, no. 6 pp. 3–5.

53. Kratkii otchet o deiatel'nosti narodnogo komissariata truda," *Biulleten' narodnogo komissariata truda*, October 1918, nos. 5–6 pp. 5–6.

54. Ibid., January 1919, nos. 1–2, p. 67; Voskresenskaia, p. 141.

55. Ibid.

56. Morozov and Portnov, *Sotsialisticheskii kontrol'*, pp. 27–28.

57. K. V. Gusev, *Kratkii ocherk istorii organov partiino-gosudarstvennogo kontrolia v SSSR* (Moscow, 1965), p. 11.

58. Morozov and Portnov, *Sotsialisticheskii kontrol'*, p. 25.

59. Ibid., p. 26.

60. Ibid., p. 27.

61. "Polozhenie o rabochei zheleznodorozhnoi inspektsii," IGK, 1919, no. 16, p. 13. The provisions of the agreement about the relationship between the workers' railroad inspectorate and state *kontrol'* attest to the suspicions the workers bore toward state *kontrol'*: "The union will recruit, supervise and defend them and maintain its own office for current business, and the workers will be free to convene their own conferences to discuss how the work in the localities is going."

62. V. Avanesov, "O rabochei inspektsii," IGK, 1920, no. 1 pp. 2–4; Dorokhova, pp. 24–26; *Obrazovanie i razvitie organov sotsialisticheskogo kontrolia v SSSR (1917–1975): Sbornik dokumentov i materialov* (Moscow, 1975), pp. 579–80.

63. Koniaev, p. 43; Dorokhova, p. 29.

64. Dorokhova, p. 31.

65. Chugunov, *Organy sotsialisticheskgo kontrolia* p. 26; Ikonnikov, pp. 38–39.

66. "O iacheikakh sodeistvii RKI," IGK, 1921, nos. 3–4, pp. 10–11.

67. Ikonnikov, p. 31.

68. Ibid., pp. 39–40. ·

69. Ibid., pp. 46.

70. Ibid., p. 47.

71. Ibid., p. 51.

72. Ibid., p. 31; Morozov and Portnov, *Sotsialisticheskii kontrol'*, p. 39.

73. Ikonnikov, p. 72; Morozov and Portnov, *Sotsialisticheskii kontrol'*, p. 39.

74. "O iacheikakh sodeistvii RKI," IGK, 1921, nos. 3–4, p. 10.

75. B. Bor'ian, "Rabochii kontrol' (1917–1921)," *Vestnik truda*, October/November 1921, nos. 10–11, p. 35.

76. "Profsoiuzy i Raboche-krest'ianskoi Inspektsii," IGK, 1921, nos. 1–2, pp. 13–14.

77. Ibid., pp. 36–37; Chugunov, p. 27.

78. Ikonnikov, pp. 55–56.

79. Lenin, PSS, 42:34–37.

80. Ibid., 42:49.

81. *Desiatyi s"ezd RKP(b). Mart 1921 goda. Stenograficheskii otchet* (Moscow, 1963), p. 588.

82. Ikonnikov, p. 71.

83. Bor'ian, "Rabochii kontrol'," p. 36–37.

84. Ikonnikov, p. 59.

85. Morozov and Portnov, "Osushchestvlenie," p. 42.

86. Ibid., p. 42; Ikonnikov, pp. 59–60.

87. Koniaev, p. 46.

88. Stalin, *Sochineniia*, 4:364–69.

89. Martysevich and Portnov, p. 67, 74, 85.

90. Dorokhova, p. 92.

91. Martysevich and Portnov, pp. 77–78.

COMMENTARY
ADMINISTRATION AND STATE BUILDING

Ronald Grigor Suny

The chapters in this section look beneath the phenomena of political and ideological struggle in search of the transformation that actually occurred in society and institutions. They depict the painstaking conflict between old and new that took place in dingy governmental offices rather than on revolutionary battlefields. During the Civil War, there was another war going on between the political leadership and the social reality, human and institutional, that presumably brought that leadership into power. Here the crucial transformation from revolutionary to state institutions is elaborated by the authors, unadorned by political rhetoric or abstract sociological categories.

Thomas F. Remington shows how the meaning of *kontrol'* changed from workers' control over the management of plant operation to bureaucratic institutions of control representing an extension of the state. Control from above, in the sense of supervision and accountability, replaced control from below in the sense of democratic oversight. Remington describes the manifold difficulties encountered in establishing effective and rational control organs. Bureaucratic control failed to correct abuses, as, in fact, bureaucratic control always fails to realize its goals. Remington's focus on the specific institutional changes occurring step by step during the years of the Civil War takes the form of a chronicle that almost ignores causation and general institutional dynamics. Yet what he describes is not an accidental evolution brought about by immediate necessity but a process of institutional rationalization that aborts owing to the conditions and institutional strategies of this period. The leadership, though sometimes evasive and intentionally ambiguous, presses with consistent determination to centralize direction of control operations, but the confusion of regulations and the overlapping of control and administrative authorities thwart its goals.

Focusing on personnel rather than institutions, Daniel Orlovsky describes the persistence of a group he calls the "lower-middle strata." These white-collar workers and intellectuals in state and public institutions are the unseen actors in the revolution; hiding behind the grand gestures of the leadership, they took control of institutions once the dust of the fray had settled. Despite the proletarian bias of the Bolshevik leadership in the first years of power, the leadership in governmental institutions and membership of the party included a significant component of the "lower-middle strata." Theorists at the time usually described these strata as servants of the working class, but Orlovsky implies that they were the servants of whatever leadership triumphed. And because political leaders, irrespective of ideology, required intellectual and clerical skills, the servants often took over many of the minor, though crucial, tasks from the masters. Again the question of causation is not addressed, but the dynamic suggested is one of a revolutionary ideology submerged in the social reality of Russian institutions, of Lenin's revolutionary dreams transformed by the grey world of the petty intelligentsia that had to comprehend and implement them.

Alexander Rabinowitch shows how centralization came about in the face of what he calls the press of events: the breakdown of the democratic legacy of 1917, the nagging problem of food supplies, the lack of cadres, the collapse of the coalition with the Left SRs, and the military threat. Although in the first months of Bolshevik power the soviet retained considerable autonomy from central control, that autonomy was ultimately undermined by the "economic and military crises of 1919." The major justification for centralization on the part of higher authorities was "invariably that of eliminating organizational chaos and making optimum use of critically scarce resources in a time of dire national emergency." Rather than ideology and human intentions, the exigencies of war and economic breakdown made Soviet Russia dictatorial and undemocratic, thereby thwarting the designs of the leadership.

Mary McAuley corroborates many of the conclusions of the other chapters, bringing into focus the irony of a revolutionary state forced to become something different from what it had anticipated. "Civil War experience could and did influence previously held beliefs, although not in a predictable or straightforward fashion." Ideology seemed to fall away before the chaos of social reality. Concentrating on the problem of trade, she shows that the Bolsheviks opposed free trade and relied on rationing because of their socialist principles, yet "again practice confounded principles of intention." The private sector could not be completely eliminated, and in the end the search went on for bourgeois enemies even within the state apparatus. "Ironically the attempt to introduce centralized state administration in place of the market produced a population of traders, but unwilling traders."

The processes that the authors describe are remarkably similar. Proletarian institutions gave way to the institutions and personnel of bureaucracy, whether because of the scheme of a mobilizing elite, the persistence of old groups and ideas, or the pressures of events. This complex process can be seen in the context of "state building," but in Russia that process is different from similar developments in other parts of the world. State building usually refers to the formation of centralized political power in conditions previously characterized by one form or another of a dispersion of authority. But in a nation such as Russia, ruled by a centralized state for over three hundred years, a country that lacked localistic and pluralistic traditions, the rapid resurgence of old groups and practices speaks more plausible for the rebuilding or, more accurately, the resurrection of the state. The leading groups in this respect may be yielding to history rather than creating it, resorting to traditional responses when confronted by the inevitable necessities of rule.

The Soviet state, of course, was not identical to the tsarist autocracy but a transformation and adaptation of the old structure to new needs. In the example of bureaucratic control, Remington's account of the establishment of such institutions is almost a replay of eighteenth-century sequences beginning during the reign of Peter the Great. Attempting to introduce vast transformations from above, the tsarist government created organ after organ to oversee local officials and ensure that they acted according to the prescriptions of the central authority.

The loss of autonomy by local institutions is also a familiar, almost monotonous theme of tsarist institutional history. Tsarist authorities regarded even the hint of local authority as a challenge to central authority that threatened "the unity of state institutions." The independence of the First City District soviet may be ascribed to the power vacuum of late 1917 and early 1918 and Lenin's tactic of allowing local initiative before the assault on power.

Orlovsky's "lower-middle strata" were the bearers of the official mentality in the new institutions and represent the structural counterpart of the clerks in the prereform tsarist administration. Since the heads of many tsarist offices were either disinclined or unable to involve themselves in the technical work of the chancellery, they left most matters to those with the appropriate institutional habits and skills. The revolution introduced a new leadership group little more disposed to trifle with administrative technicalities. In both cases the institutions of the state, bureaucratic habits and operations overwhelmed the leadership of the state and set the parameters of their effective power.

As exciting and revealing as these chapters are, they raise many questions. Some readers may find the term "lower-middle strata" misleading and reminiscent of an obsolete Marxist sociology. What was the specific consciousness or impact of this group? Was their stranglehold on Soviet institutions reflected also in an implicit transformation of ideology and goals into an ideology of clerical workers, or did they in fact, as the leadership contended, faithfully implement the programs of the new dominant class?

Rabinowitch expresses doubts about the dichotomy between ideology or circumstances, yet he certainly tilts to the side of circumstances. One needs to know how typical or representative of district soviets was the First City District soviet. Was the relative absence of party controls in the central institutions' relations with local organs part of a larger design or was it dictated by necessity? Why were there no expressions of regret or efforts to reverse the process of centralization underway during the Civil War?

McAuley shows that the districts lost to the centralists, each side arguing that it could husband the scarce resources more efficiently. What were the main reasons for this victory? She seems to doubt that the experience of the Civil War was formative: it "was too short and owed too much to a very powerful set of revolutionary ideas to be able to product its 'own' coherent set."

Conclusions about ideology versus circumstances must be tentative, and the ultimate answer to why choices were made to eliminate local authorities and build a centralized state may never be completely answered to the satisfaction of the entire historical community. But these explorations in the social history of politics reveal at one and the same time the rich potential of a social historical approach and the difficulties of relating the problem of state building to chaotic social forces, shifting groups of actors, and conflicting perceptions and ideological rationalizations.

IV

The Bolsheviks and the Intelligentsia

INTRODUCTION
THE BOLSHEVIKS AND THE INTELLIGENTSIA

Peter Kenez

The Bolsheviks in 1917 came to power with a breathtakingly radical program of remaking not only politics and society, but humanity itself. How the Russian intelligentsia, especially its well-known representatives who enjoyed prestige in their own country and abroad, responded to the extraordinary social and political transformation taking place around them and what kind of treatment they received at the hands of the Bolsheviks are interesting and important topics. An examination of them will contribute to our understanding of the mentality and values of both groups.

The essays that make up this section tell us not only about how some segments of the intelligentsia welcomed the Bolshevik victory, but also about how the scholars, scientists, and artists accommodated themselves to life in Lenin's regime. James C. McClelland and Kendall E. Bailes discuss these matters explicitly, but Lynn Mally's article on the Proletkult also sheds considerable light on the attitude of individual artists to the new regime.

We learn that the intelligentsia was a heterogeneous group and that the attitudes of its members varied. Few identified themselves completely with Bolshevik positions. Some saw in the revolution a cleansing experience from which they derived inspiration for their work; the great majority, however, including the best-known figures of the scientific and creative intelligentsia, was to a greater or smaller extent hostile to the new regime. In this respect the artists and scientists were not different from members of other professional groups, such as officers, teachers, and doctors. To the extent that there was a home for liberalism in Imperial Russia, it had been among educated and professional groups. The new rulers now faced the hostility of the intelligentsia, and it was evident from the first moment that cooperation was to be difficult.

The essays in this section emphasize the degree to which the Bolsheviks, Lenin in particular, paid serious attention to cultural matters. Since McClelland and Bailes look at the relationship of the intelligentsia and the Bolsheviks

239

largely from the point of view of the intelligentsia, it might be worthwhile to summarize briefly how matters looked from the Bolshevik point of view and attempt to explain the seeming riddles of Bolshevik behavior.

It is difficult to generalize about Bolshevik attitudes toward culture, for in addition to the dominant, Leninist point of view, there were others. Clearly, those Bolsheviks who were attracted by the ideology of Proletkult and emphasized the class essence of cultures desired a different policy toward artists, and to a lesser extent toward scientists, than the party in fact pursued. Those earnest and radical Communists who were dismayed at the use of "bourgeois" experts in any field did not like the privileges that at least some members of the intelligentsia continued to enjoy. I will limit the following remarks to an examination of the Leninist position.

Even the Leninists, however, did not have a uniform attitude concerning the intelligentsia as a whole. For Lenin, Marxism was a scientific doctrine, and therefore he may have felt a certain kinship with scientists. He regarded them by and large as more valuable than artists. He was also a man of conservative taste who had little appreciation for people engaged in artistic experiments. He was, on the other hand, impressed by fame and reputation. As a result, he paid more attention to Russia's most prominent scientists.

It is striking that after 1917 the immensely practical Lenin became greatly interested in culture and devoted a large portion of his writings to this topic. He, of course, remained a thoroughly political person who looked at culture almost exclusively from a political point of view. Although he obviously could not admit it, he was stung by the Menshevik criticism of his revolution, according to which Russia was too backward for a socialist transformation.

This particular attack hit its target, for on the one hand the criticism was firmly grounded in Marxist theory, and on the other Lenin felt the backwardness of his homeland every bit as keenly as any Menshevik. Following Plekhanov, he considered Russia "Asiatic," and saw nothing admirable in its national traditions. He wrote:

> Our opponents told us repeatedly that we were rash in undertaking to implant socialism in an insufficiently cultured country. They base themselves on theory (the theory of all pedants) in saying that we started at the wrong end. In our country the political and social turnover turned out to be a precondition for that cultural revolution that is ahead of us at the moment.

> This cultural revolution will be sufficient to make our country into a fully socialist one. But it presents immense difficulties in purely cultural terms (for we are illiterate) and also in a material sense (for us to become cultured it is necessary to have a certain material base).[1]

The solution, at least to him, was obvious: proletarian Russia must go through a "cultural revolution" to accomplish in the cultural sphere what capitalism had failed to accomplish: to raise the cultural level of the country to that of Western Europe.[2]

Therefore, to bring "culture" to the Russians was an issue of great political significance, for that alone could guarantee the final success of the revolution, and in retrospect prove Lenin's wisdom in overthrowing the previous political and social order in October 1917.

Lenin did not have anything particularly original to say about the nature of culture or about the interaction of culture and politics. He did not even make it clear what exactly he meant by culture. It would appear that at least most of the time he was not thinking of humanity's highest artistic achievement but, rather, had in mind what we think of as material civilization. To him, as to many of his contemporaries, culture was, above all, the opposite of backwardness.[3] It is in this context that we should understand such striking statements as: "Socialism without postal and telegraph services is the emptiest of phrases" and "Electrification and Soviet power equals communism." It is this understanding of culture that explains Lenin's passionate commitment to overcome illiteracy in the future land of socialism.

Lenin and, for that matter, other major leaders of the Bolshevik state, such as Trotskii or Bukharin, were descendants of the Russian nineteenth-century intelligentsia. Although they had rebelled against some of its traditions, such as interminable discussions and moral scruples, nonetheless, they continued to share many assumptions of the intelligentsia, perhaps to a greater extent than they themselves realized. One of these unquestioned assumptions was that "culture," however defined and understood, was somehow a good thing.

Under the circumstances, most of the Bolshevik leaders simply took it for granted that art and science were the natural helpmates in the struggle to build socialism. With their utopian and in many ways wildly optimistic view of the world, it did not occur to them for some time that the values inherent in some art might be inimical to their political goals. As a consequence, while they allowed one and only one interpretation of political events, namely, their own, at the same time that they permitted a remarkable variety of artists and philosophers to publish unhindered.

The Bolsheviks were not and never pretended to be liberals. Immediately after coming to power they suppressed the free press. The Cheka, established in December 1917, took resolute steps against real and imaginary enemies. The party jealously guarded its organizational monopoly, and Communists were intensely suspicious of any sign of genuine autonomy. The party went so far as to suppress even the boy scout movement. Under the circumstances it is surprising that the universities and the Academy of Sciences continued to enjoy a considerable degree of autonomy that lasted to the end of the period of the New Economic Policy. Reading McClelland's account of the professoriate and Bailes's of the natural scientists during the Civil War, we get the impression that the Bolsheviks treated these people remarkably well. How are we to explain Bolshevik restraint? Obviously, we can only speculate; the Leninists never made their reasons clear, even to themselves.

The first reason must be the simplest one. Lenin possessed extraordinary political sense. He well understood that a persecution of famous artists and scientists would harm the image of his regime not only at home but also abroad. He, after all, restrained his more radical followers from carrying out a frontal attack on the church, an organization that was politically far more powerful and therefore more dangerous than any organization of artists and scientists might be. It is true that during the Civil War churchmen were often abused and persecuted. This happened, however, at the hands of local radicals who disregarded the policies set forth by Moscow. Similarly, the central government invariably treated the intelligentsia better than the local authorities.

Second, the scientists received preferential treatment because the Leninists believed that they needed them and that they had much to contribute to the national recovery. In this respect, the scientists, and, to a lesser extent, even the artists, fell into the category established by the Bolsheviks of "experts." After coming to power the realistic Lenin quickly understood that his regime needed to help of experts in running the country. Bailes gives us several examples of how the new regime intended to utilize the skills of scientists. As far as the Bolsheviks were concerned, scientists were like army officers; they possessed essential skills that the revolutionary government could not do without. Of course, scientists were more likely to benefit from this attitude than artists. In the Bolshevik view of the world, however, artists too were needed, if not as urgently as economists and scientists.

Third, and most important, the artists and scientists were treated well by the new rulers because the most prominent Bolsheviks were interested in cultural life and admired people who were engaged in creative activities.

NOTES

1. V. I. Lenin, "O kooperatsii," *Polnoe sobranie sochinenii*, 5th ed. (Moscow, 1970) 45: 376–77.

2. Since Lenin's time the concept of cultural revolution has been used by many in rather different senses. Lenin, unlike Stalin, or Mao, had nothing more in mind by the use of the phrase than the quick acquisition of "culture" by the common people.

3. Maxim Gorky in May 1918 wrote an amusing article in *Novaia Zhizn'* in which he discussed the various understandings of the term culture. Among others, he quoted Z. G. (Presumably Zinaida Gippius) "I can imagine tens and even hundreds of peasant men and women acquiring culture, but when I think of all the peasants learning to clean their fingernails or blow their noses into handkerchiefs, this picture seems to me a funny utopia" (M. Gorkii, *Nesvoe-vremennye mysli. Statia. 1917*, ed. H. Ermolaev. [Paris, 1971], p. 227. The Bolsheviks were not alone in their condescension toward the common people.

THE PROFESSORIATE IN THE RUSSIAN CIVIL WAR

James C. McClelland

Educated Russia reacted to the Bolshevik seizure of power with undisguised dismay. The prospect of intensifying class conflict, of increased power for the soviets and other forms of mass rule, and of continuing erosion of the army could hardly be appealing to conservatives, liberals, or non-Bolshevik socialists. Most thought that Bolshevik rule would not last long but feared that the threat to their lives, possessions, and values would continue. Even should Lenin and his comrades prove able to ride and control the whirlwind, their prerevolutionary statements provided cold comfort to those with liberal political, social, and educational values to defend or material interests to preserve.

There was little military resistance (except in the south) during the first six months of Soviet rule, but many found ways to make their opposition known. Lunacharskii found the premises of the former Ministry of Education virtually deserted when he arrived to take over, as most employees of the ministry joined other *chinovniki* in refusing to work for the new government. The Provisional Government's State Committee for Public Education decided not to recognize or cooperate with Soviet organs, and its chairman, the pedagogue V. I. Charnoluskii, declined to shake Lunacharskii's hand. Municipal employees in Moscow went on strike. Most damaging of all was a strike call by the All-Russian Union of Teachers, which led to teachers' strikes in Moscow from December 1917 to March 1918, and for shorter periods of time in Petrograd, Ufa, Ekaterinburg, and Astrakhan.[1]

Higher education's reaction was more passive but no less negative. On November 26, shortly after the arrest of two of its teachers who were active in the elections to the Constituent Asssembly, the academic council of Petrograd University voted a strong rhetorical statement condemning the Bolsheviks and supporting the forthcoming Constituent Assembly. "A great calamity has befallen Russia," it began, under the yoke of aggressors who have seized power, the Russian people are losing the consciousness of their personality and their worth, they are selling their soul and at the cost of a shameful and flimsy separate peace, are ready to betray their allies and deliver themselves into the hands of their enemies. What is being prepared for Russia by those who forget about her cultural mission and her public honor?—internal weakness, harsh disillusionment, and contempt from allies and enemies.

Russia does not deserve such a disgrace: the will of all her people has entrusted the determination of her fate to the Constituent Assembly, which will preserve her from internal and external violence, which will guarantee the growth of her culture and will strengthen her position among enlightened states.

In the indissoluble unity of true sons of the Motherland, the servants of *nauka* and enlightenment recognize her might and bow before her will; they are prepared with all of their knowledge and all of their strength to assist in that great creative work which free Russia is entrusting to the Constituent Assembly.[2]

A number of hastily organized academic groups in Petrograd issued declarations opposing recognition of the Soviet government. Among them were a conference of rectors and directors of higher schools in Petrograd, a revived Petrograd section of the academic union, and the Russian Union of Research Institutions and Higher Educational Institutions. The last group was organized by the Presidium of the Academy of Sciences on the initiative of historian-academician A. S. Lappo-Danilevskii.[3] The academic councils of many institutions, including Tomsk, Kazan, and Kharkov universities, voted declarations of nonrecognition.[4] Most student groups (in which SRs, Mensheviks, and Kadets predominated) found themselves in the unaccustomed position of agreeing with their faculty councils.

What was the cause of this widespread antagonism to Bolshevik rule among Russia's academics? After all, hadn't Lunacharskii promised a vast expansion of education, culture, and science under Soviet rule? Why then was there so much resistance among Russia's educated elite, and in particular the professoriate?

Reasons already hinted at—fear of mob rule, support for the war effort, support for and participation in the Provisional Government and forthcoming Constituent Assembly—certainly played a role. But the most basic cause of the antagonism between Bolsheviks and professors lay not in political or social factors but rather in the intellectual and ideological sphere. Bolshevik ideology has been well studied. Less well known is that Russian academics also had a world view that guided their activities in educational and political matters, a view that diverged in important respects from that of Lenin and Lunacharskii. Only after familiarizing ourselves with this world view can we hope to understand the Russian professoriate's response to Bolshevik power and Bolshevik educational reforms.

The Russian professoriate on the eve of revolution had developed over the previous half-century a proud intellectual tradition that included international distinction in some areas of science and scholarship as well as a widely held belief in both the value of pure science (*nauka*) in its own right and the positive role that higher education and the pursuit of *nauka* could play in the anticipated liberalization of the Russian autocratic social and political structures. Russian scientists from Mendeleev to Pavlov had made discoveries of worldwide significance, and the more recent decades in particular had also witnessed considerable creativity in social and humanistic disciplines such as history, sociology, and idealist philosophy. Most Russian academics had great respect for the German university system, with its ideals of fostering pure science and university autonomy. They wholeheartedly agreed with the sentiments expressed by Wilhelm von Humboldt, founder of the University of Berlin in 1810, who had insisted that "the principle of cultivating science and scholarship for their own sake . . . [must be] placed in a dominant position in higher intellectual institutions," and that "the state must understand that intellectual work will go on infinitely better if it does not intrude" in the internal affairs of these institutions.[5]

Although strongly influenced by German academic thought and practice, leading members of the Russian professoriate added a social and political component to their academic calling that was largely absent from the outlook of their generally conservative counterparts in Bismarckian Germany. Many regarded themselves as heirs and executors of the Russian intelligentsia's traditional commitment to popular enlightenment,[6] and indeed the term "academic intelligentsia" is a good designation for the majority of professors who viewed themselves in this way. The study of *nauka*, they insisted, should not be restricted to a small social or intellectual elite but should be made available to as broad a spectrum of the population as possible. They acted on this principle by, in addition to their university duties, participating in adult education activities designed to promote an understanding of the various branches of science and scholarship among the educated public—enlightenment from the top down, so to speak.[7]

Many of their activities, both within and without their teaching institutions, brought the most outspoken academics into conflict with the autocratic government, which periodically seemed bent on restricting the universities it had founded, harassing the teachers that it hired, and obstructing the enlightenment of the people it ruled. As a result the academic intellegentsia was thrust by these arbitrary actions into a mildly oppositional stance toward the autocracy. Its members hoped the autocracy could be reformed to allow the unimpeded spread of *nauka* and enlightenment throughout the population. They regarded *nauka* itself as nonpartisan, as above politics, as above narrow party or class interests, and by and large they did not see themselves as political actors in the conventional sense. But some of their most influential spokesmen were convinced that *nauka* contained the seeds of liberalism and democracy and that the spread of learning and education was the best means of achieving the liberalization of the autocratic system.[8]

During and after the Revolution of 1905 prominent academics played key roles in the leadership of the liberal Constitutional Democratic Party and the Party of Democratic Reforms.[9] There was, to be sure, a range of political opinion within the Russian professoriate, from a significant minority of conservative nationalists on the right to a sprinkling of socialists on the left, as well as many careerists and others with no definite political outlook. Few Russian professors favored immediate political democracy or believed that the Russian people as a whole, still over 60 percent illiterate, would in the foreseeable future be capable of exercising political power—a fact that was to be of great importance in 1917 and after. By the same token, however, few indeed would accept the position of the mainstream of the German academic community, which resisted public intrusion into its academic domain, deliberately highlighted the elitist, esoteric aspects of its subject matter, and after 1918 staunchly resisted the Weimar Republic as a whole and its democratic education reforms in particular.[10] The dominant element in the Russian professoriate, virtually all those who enjoyed the respect and esteem of their colleagues, who tended to act as spokesmen for the profession, and who after 1905 tended to be elected to positions of rector and university representative to the State Council were liberal in both their political and educational views.[11]

The main bone of contention between professoriate and autocracy was not in the arena of politics writ large, however, but concerned the issue of the proper nature of higher educational institutions in the Russian Empire. What should be the goals of the country's universities and institutes, how should they be governed, who should be admitted to them, what should be the rights of professors and students?—these were the bread-and-butter issues that provoked continuing debate, controversy, and conflict between professors and tsarist ministers, and it would be these same issues that shaped and influenced the relations between Bolsheviks and professors during the Civil War era.

The position of the Ministry of Public Education on all of these matters was set forth most clearly in the university charter of 1884, which allowed little autonomy to the universities, placed numerous restrictions on the rights of professors and students, and sought to reserve as much control as possible to officials of the state educational bureaucracy.[12] The charter was deeply resented by most professors, who were nonetheless powerless to reject or alter it. By the turn of the century continued growth in enrollment as well as the development of new academic subjects and subdisciplines had rendered it increasingly out of date, and even some ministry officials became convinced of the need for its revision. Spiraling student activism further increased the urgency for reform, and during the revolutionary tumult of 1905–1906, professors participated in three different efforts to compose a new university charter. One was drawn up by the academic union (a recently formed national organization of professors); one by the academic council of St. Petersburg University; and one by a conference of representatives of the professoriate and Ministry of Education (headed at the time by the liberal, and short-termed, minister I. I. Tolstoi).[13] As it turned out, none of these three drafts was implemented, because by 1907 the autocracy recovered control over the country and reverted to traditional higher education policies. But the three draft charters of 1905–1906 will nonetheless repay a brief analysis at this point. They provide an excellent cross section of the educational views of the professoriate and thereby serve as essential background for our subsequent discussion of the relations between Bolsheviks and professors and, in particular, of their efforts to agree on a new university charter in the summer of 1918.

All three drafts made a sharp break with the 1884 charter by proclaiming the principle of autonomy. There was some disagreement on the precise meaning of the term and on the ways in which it should be implemented in practice. The most commonly accepted definition was that the university had the right independently to regulate its own internal affairs in the areas of research, curriculum, and administration. It would be supervised by the Ministry of Education, but only with regard to finances and to assure that state laws and the charter provisions were not violated.

The key body in exercising institutional autonomy was to be the academic council (*uchenyi sovet*) of each university and institute. Traditionally, all the professors of a given institution had the right to sit on the academic council, whereas private-docents and other junior faculty were excluded. Although the 1884 character had considerably limited the rights of the councils, they continued to serve as the main outlet for professorial opinion and lay at the heart of the 1905 projects under discussion. Whereas the 1884 rules called for the rector and new professorial appointments to be selected by ministry officials, all three drafts stipulated that they should be elected (or confirmed) by the councils. St. Petersburg University and the Tolstoi conference each voted (against some opposition) to allow the state the right of confirming candidates elected by the council, whereas the more liberal project of the academic union did not include such a provision. Also controversial was the question of whether to permit junior faculty to be represented on the council. The Tolstoi draft opposed this principle, whereas the other two accepted and incorporated it.

All three agreed that student discipline should be handled within the institution itself rather than by a government-appointed inspector as in the past. They all sought to loosen significantly the admission restrictions of the ministry, which barred women, set quotas on Jews, and until recently allowed graduates only of the elitist classical gymnasia (not of the *realschulen*) to enter the universities. All three drafts, while granting the right of each institution to set its own admission requirements, specified that all secondary school graduates of both sexes would be eligible. St. Petersburg University proposed in addition a Latin requirement; the Tolstoi and academic union projects specifically outlawed discrimination on the basis of religion and nationality in addition to sex. The academic union added a provision that anyone, even without a secondary school diploma, had the right to audit lectures.

It was during the tenure of the Provisional Government in 1917 that the academic intelligentsia finally received the opportunity to put some of its ideas into practice. Leadership of the Provisional Government's Ministry of Education was entrusted to prominent academics who were active members of the Kadet Party: A. A. Manuilov, whose resignation in protest from his position of rector of Moscow University in 1910 had precipitated a crisis between the university and the tsarist government; S. F. Oldenburg, Orientalist and permanent secretary of the Academy of Sciences; V. I. Vernadskii, geochemist, academician, and founder of the academic union in 1904.[14] For the first time in history, true representatives of the professoriate and its value system were firmly in power, and the higher schools' academic councils did in fact begin to enjoy extensive autonomy. Two of the first acts of Manuilov were to abolish the Jewish quota and reinstate all students and teachers who had been removed for political reasons. A major issue that cropped up immediately in a number of educational institutions involved demands by both junior faculty and students for representation on the faculty assemblies and academic councils. The intensity of the demands varied from one school to another—at Rostov University the revolutionary student committee claimed the right to dismiss the rector, a demand that was gently rebuffed by the council.[15] Professors were willing to make some compromises. The Kazan University council, in a series of close votes, resolved on April 5 to give students voting representation in faculty assemblies but not in the academic council.[16] In June a national conference of higher school representatives was much more cautious, resolving to give qualified junior faculty the right to vote in faculty assemblies and to deliberate but not vote in the councils. Student input was authorized only in specially created commissions of professors and students.[17] On other issues, a Commission on the Reform of the Higher School chaired by M. M. Novikov (chemist, former Kadet Duma representative, and future elected rector of Moscow University) met forty-four times, drawing up a number of specific reforms and supervising the opening of several new higher educational institutions.[18] By the time of the fall of the Kerensky government, these reforms were still partial and incomplete; no new charter or other sweeping measures had as yet been drawn up or implemented. But the Russian professoriate for the first time had had a taste of true autonomy and of genuine political power to shape educational legislation.

Most Russian academics, therefore, did not regard their opposition to Bolshevik power and their support for the Constituent Assembly as in any sense self-serving or even political in nature. They had long viewed a liberalized Russia as the best possible setting for the development of *nauka* and culture. In serving *nauka* they saw themselves as serving the people and the nation, and any infringement on their autonomy in the pursuit of scientific truth they viewed as a blow against *nauka* and the Russian people. They feared (correctly, as it turned out) that the Soviet government would seek to restrict that autonomy. What perhaps they did not foresee at first was how close they and Narkompros would come, in the summer of 1918, to cooperation and agreement on higher education reform, before hostilities arose again and each side reverted to name-calling and bitterness.

Classes, which for the most part had ceased right after the Bolshevik coup, began to resume in most higher educational institutions during the months of December and January and continued throughout the rest of the academic year in more or less traditional form.[19] Meanwhile, the academic councils' refusal to deal with the new government began to lead in early 1918 to increasingly awkward situations. The practice was for the councils, when the need arose for governmental action on some matter or other, to submit their request to the Provisional Government's Ministry of Education for action "when the possibility for this arises."[20] Local soviets at times tried to exert authority over higher schools in their districts,[21] which alarmed professors, whose experience with tsarist curators had led them to prefer central over local control as the lesser of two evils. Financial problems were mounting, and salaries, though paid, were in arrears. Dispersal of the Constituent Assembly in January indicated there would be no quick change of government. One of the first higher schools to enter into official contact with Narkompros was the Petrograd Polytechnic Institute, the academic council of which voted to do so on January 24, "in order to guarantee the continued activity of the institute on the basis of autonomy." Petrograd University in early February resolved to continue its nonrecognition of Narkompros but had to reverse its decision later in the month. Moscow University's council grudgingly agreed on February 28/March 13 "to enter into business relations (*delovye snosheniia*) with the educational authorities to the extent necessary," and most other schools did likewise.[22]

Not all scholars and scientists refused initially to cooperate with the new regime. Two who immediately went out of their way to offer their services were Vladimir N. Ipatiev and Valentin P. Zubov. On the surface they seem to be individuals of a different stripe. Ipatiev was a no-nonsense chemist with a strictly military education who headed the chemical industry during the war; he was a full member of the Academy of Sciences and retained a teaching position at the Artillery Academy. Soon after the October Revolution he was appointed to the chemical division of Vesenkha, and in March 1918 he became chairman of the Technical Section of the War Council. By 1922 he was a member of Vesenkha's presidium and chairman of its *Nauchnotekhnicheskoe upravlenie*. Zubov was an art historian, a self-confessed sybarite as a youth who received his education in Western Europe, then founded and became director of the Institute for the History of Art in Petrograd, and after the February Revolution was sent as a government specialist to the Gatchina imperial palace to help preserve its works of art against a possible German occupation. When the Bolsheviks took power he and other museum officials immediately reported to Lunacharskii, who gratefully appointed them official representatives of the new government. Zubov soon came into conflict with the Gatchina soviet and was briefly arrested, after which he returned to his own institute where he overcame the resistance of his teaching staff to dealing with the new government and, despite the difficult times, was able to maintain and even expand the luxurious premises of his school.[23]

How is it that two men of such differing backgrounds and personalities should have, quite independently of one another, taken the same path of willing cooperation with the new government? The best answer is that despite their many differences, they nonetheless shared a number of traits that helped determine their actions after October. Both were monarchists at heart who hated the weakness of the Provisional Government and who intuitively grasped that Lenin's Bolsheviks, whose principles they abhorred, would nonetheless be strong enough to restore order. Both were ardently devoted to their objectives— the restoration of the chemical industry and the national economy, the preservation of works of art from destruction or dispersal—and both were convinced that the only way to accomplish these goals was to cooperate with the Soviet government. Neither had been educated or employed by the universities or technical institutes that formed the mainstream of Russia's educational life and molded the outlook of its academic intelligentsia. Finally, both were frequently harassed in their work by lower-level Soviet and party officials, pressures that increased during the twenties, and both eventually decided to emigrate to the West.

A third and final figure to be considered in this section is D. F. Sinitsyn. A zoologist who left Moscow University during Kasso's "purge," he was in 1917 a teacher at the Nizhnii-Novgorod Polytechnical Institute (recently evacuated from Warsaw) as well as director of the Nizhnii-Novgorod People's University. He was thus a solid member of the professoriate, though one who would give its ideals an extremely liberal and reformist interpretation. Unlike Zubov or Ipatiev, he did not offer his services to the central government but, rather, convinced the Nizhnii-Novgorod Provincial Soviet to support and finance his plan for creating a new university based on significantly new principles and with himself as the first rector. The most obvious new departure in his university was its inclusion of technical faculties, which greatly outnumbered the traditional university faculties. The idea of adding technical faculties to universities, usually regarded as the exclusive preserve of pure science, had been debated recently, and although traditionalists firmly opposed it, some prominent scientists were beginning to advocate it.[24] Another innovative feature was the close links envisioned between the university and the local population. Although a secondary education was expected for regular study in the various faculties, additional systematic courses were to be offered in all fields for those without such a background. Junior faculty and students would enjoy participation in most administrative organs, as would a few representatives of the local government. Sinitsyn summed up his goal as, "A free-autonomous university, independent of any party and of any government . . . A university in which there is one sovereign—*nauka*, and one god—mankind."[25]

A major problem, however, stemmed from the necessity of closing the three existing higher schools in the city in order to use their facilities for the new university. Sinitsyn was unwilling to hire the displaced teachers for his own institution and seems in general to have acted in a high-handed manner. This behavior and some of the liberal features of his project aroused the hostility of professors in nearby Moscow.[26] Bolshevik authorities smiled on the project, however, and the university was founded in the spring of 1918.

What were the Soviet government's *own* intentions concerning higher education reform? They were slow in being formulated. Rumors circulated about dramatic (and frightening) changes in store for universities and the Academy of Sciences, as iconoclasts from the Proletkult and elsewhere proclaimed the need for the complete transformation of *nauka* and other forms of "bourgeois" culture.[27] One especially radical center within Narkompros was the Scientific Sector of the regional Commissariat of Enlightenment centered in Petrograd, which had alarmed Lunacharskii as early as June 1918. In the fall of 1918 it called for the "revolutionizing" of science by creating a new type of scientific-educational institution and liquidating old institutions such as the academy.[28] The top Narkompros leaders, however, took a more moderate stance, and at first even seemed to embrace the concept of autonomy. Lunacharskii and Krupskaia originally saw their role not as erecting another centralized educational bureaucracy, but as guiding and inspiring the activity of local workers' and peasants' cultural-enlightenment organizations, which should "possess full autonomy, in relation to both the state center and municipal centers." The original name of the Narkompros department that dealt with higher education was Sector of Autonomous Higher Educational Institutions, although by July 1918, the word "autonomous" had disappeared from the title.[29] Throughout the first half of 1918 this sector did not try to interfere in the affairs of the higher schools, which since the fall of the tsar had been enjoying virtually complete autonomy. For example, a circular from the sector to Moscow University in March requested notification of any personnel changes merely for its "information," and indicated that only if a change in expenditures were required, would "confirmation" from the sector be necessary. The sector approved the charter of Sinitsyn's Nizhegorodskii University, which proclaimed its autonomy and, while involving local governmental representatives, made no reference whatever to the central government.[30]

Narkompros's plan for the reform of higher education was first announced in the spring of 1918. Formulators of the policy were M. N. Pokrovskii, P. K. Shternberg, and M. A. Reisner. All had academic backgrounds. Pokrovskii had studied history at the graduate level under Vinogradov and Kliuchevskii, but instead of taking a teaching position he had suddenly become a Bolshevik in 1905 and then emigrated to Western Europe. Shternberg was a professor of astronomy at Moscow University—one of the few from the professorial ranks who joined or even sympathized with the Bolsheviks. He also joined the party in 1905, had been an active participant in street-fighting in both the 1905 and 1917 revolutions, and was subsequently killed at the front in the Civil War. Reisner had been a professor of law at Tomsk University before being removed in 1903 for involvement in student disturbances. In 1907 he obtained a position of private-docent at St. Petersburg University and was known for a legal approach that combined the ideas of Marx and Petrazhitskii. After 1917 he worked for the Commissariat of Justice as well as Narkompros.[31]

The three prepared a long, detailed draft of a charter for universities and specialized institutes that embodied those reforms they considered both desirable and attainable. The plan was to present this draft as the basis for discussion at a specially convoked conference in July of representatives from higher schools throughout the country. It was hoped that at the conference a revised draft, acceptable to both Narkompros and the professoriate, could be agreed on and then immediately implemented, in time for the next academic year. In view of the basic differences between the two groups, this was a bold and optimistic plan but one that, as we shall see, came surprisingly close to success.

The fundamental differences between the moderate Bolsheviks within Narkompros and the liberal professoriate are best highlighted by a liberal university reform project submitted to Narkompros at this time by the well-known chemist L. A. Chugaev of Petrograd University. Chugaev had been active since the spring of 1917 in an association that organized lecture series designed to introduce workers and others with little educational background to scientific concepts.[32] Interested in university reform but unable to attend the 1918 conference, he forwarded his reform proposals to Narkompros in the hope they would be presented for discussion at the conference. Lunacharskii, however, disagreed with them on two major points. He wrote some unfavorable comments in the margin and decided to shelve them rather than make them public.[33]

One of the points at issue concerned admission requirements. Chugaev wanted each higher school to have a division called a "people's university," which would offer popular lectures to all who wished to attend. Admission to the regular classes of the university, however, would require the completion of a course similar to that of the reformed secondary school, although the most successful and outstanding students of the people's university might be admitted without a school diploma. Next to this provision Lunacharskii wrote the word "weak."[34] Indeed, liberal professors and moderate Bolsheviks had different reasons for favoring the dissemination of knowledge among the public. The goal of Chugaev and his liberal colleagues was to ensure that every individual, regardless of class, sex, or religion, had the chance to rise in the educational system according to his or her ability to master the academic material. Lunacharskii and the Bolsheviks, however, regarded the mass infusion of workers and poor peasants into the higher schools as an essential end in itself, both because it would benefit the lower-class students and because it would help reform the tenor of the educational institutions. In his first piece of advice to Lunacharskii on higher educational reform, Lenin had stated, "One thing is clear: we must concentrate on widening access to higher educational institutions to the broad masses, first of all to proletarian youth."[35]

This disagreement reflected a more basic difference concerning the nature of education and science. The Bolsheviks regarded education not as something above politics but, rather, as a weapon inevitably controlled by the ruling class and used to its political advantage. In August 1918, Lenin said, "We openly declare, that to state that the school is above life, above politics, is a lie and hypocrisy . . . these people [educators] consider knowledge to be their own monopoly, and are converting it into a weapon of their rule over the so-called lower elements."[36]

The second major issue dividing Chugaev and Lunacharskii was that of autonomy. Predictably, Chugaev called for full autonomy for the academic councils and faculty assemblies. Lunacharskii's marginal comment was, "Completely unacceptable, if we are speaking of the present composition of the councils."[37] Indeed, Pokrovskii, in a set of theses drawn up at about the same time, allowed for some autonomy, but only after basic structural reforms in the composition of the councils had been enacted.[38] Even this formulation was vehemently rejected by Lenin when Pokrovskii presented his theses to the Central Committee.[39] As we shall see, the Narkompros draft charter contained an interesting approach to the concept of autonomy, but by and large Lenin's opposition in the Central Committee marked the beginning of the end for Narkompros's flirtation with the concept of autonomy in any form.

The Narkompros draft charter contained the following main elements. Each higher school was to be more or less evenly divided into three associations: scientific, for the conduct of research; academic, for university-level education of registered students; and enlightenment, for the dissemination of knowledge among the public. All tuition was to be abolished, and admission to the academic association was to be open to all those aged sixteen and over who "could demonstrate sufficient preparation for successful completion of the course."[40] The individual faculties were to be allowed to devise their own admission requirements and ways of applying them. Professors were to be elected by the faculties on the basis of public competition, but for only a seven-year term (instead of the previous twenty-five years' tenure), after which they would have to undergo a new competition. Concerning autonomy, the role of Narkompros was restricted to the unobjectionable right of confirming annual reports and budgets. But Narkompros did not intend to leave the schools completely in the hands of the highly distrusted "academic corporations" of professors. Instead of bureaucratic control from above, it sought to achieve a new kind of "social control" from below. In the first place, the academic councils were to be composed not just of the professors of the institution, but also of representatives from both junior faculty and students, each in an equal number to that of the professors and each with full voting rights. As a result, professors would exercise only one-third of the vote in the councils, which would be equal in weight to the vote of student representatives. In the second place, a new institution, called a "people's council" was to be established at each higher school. It was to be composed exclusively of representatives of local organizations such as political parties, trade unions, cooperatives, and soviets. Its functions were vaguely described as "discussing" the annual report of the university, "mapping out" the necessary measures, "expressing its opinion" on the budget, and informing the central educational authority of its desires and dissatisfactions.[41]

In many respects this draft charter represented an olive branch extended to the professoriate. The very willingness of the government to convene a conference for mutual discussion of higher education reform conformed to a long-standing academic demand that had but rarely been met under the tsars. Also, the draft contained no Proletkultish calls for the "socializing" or "revolutionizing" of science whatsoever. Although the plan for three different associations appeared to be institutionally and bureaucratically awkward, the scientific association nonetheless seemed to offer full scope for the professorial pursuit of *nauka* in its traditional sense, while the enlightenment association was based on principles that the most liberal professors such as Chugaev had already proposed, and no sweeping curricular changes seemed to be contemplated for the academic association. Nor did the draft particularly emphasize applied research and vocational education, which would soon become a rallying cry for some prominent Bolsheviks outside of Narkompros. Indeed, one disgruntled radical Bolshevik subsequently complained that "it was the most ordinary old bourgeois charter, somewhat retouched."[42]

Yet a comparison of the Narkompros charter with the 1906 draft charters and the education reforms of the Provisional Government indicates that the Narkompros provisions were much more extreme than anything the professoriate as a whole (as opposed to some of its most liberal members) had ever been willing to accept. Still more important, in its denial of tenure, its extreme reduction of professorial influence in the academic councils, and in the nature and membership of the people's council, the Narkompros draft went well beyond the bounds of even the most liberal conception of university administration. That many of the university representatives were nonetheless willing to use it as a basis of discussion and negotiation indicates clearly that the professoriate was interested in higher education reform and was willing to compromise and cooperate with Narkompros in an effort to achieve it.[43]

On the eve of the July conference, therefore, both sides appeared ready and willing to compromise. Meanwhile, however, tensions in the country as a whole were rising ominously. Late May witnessed the beginning of clashes between Czech and Soviet troops in Siberia and the introduction of partial conscription for the Red Army. A White government was established in Omsk on June 8, and an unsuccessful rebellion against the Soviet government flared in Tambov June 17–19. On July 6 the German ambassador Mirbach was assassinated by disaffected Left SRs. Two hours before the conference was scheduled to open on July 8, a group of delegates approached Shternberg and expressed concern that continued street fighting in Moscow might interfere with the work of the conference. Shternberg replied, "Well, if shooting starts again today, then we shall take up rifles and proceed to the street, but if that is not necessary, then why not go ahead and discuss higher education reform?"[44]

Some of the delegates, as well as some professors elsewhere, rejected the Narkompros charter out of hand. Professor Ivanovskii of Kazan University labeled it a doctrinaire monstrosity, and at an academic union meeting held in Moscow before the conference, it was characterized as "the clearly expressed police-enlightenment tendencies of despotic socialism."[45] In general, delegates from Moscow were less willing to cooperate than those from Petrograd. Moscow University's elected rector M. A. Menzbir, an ornithologist whose *Birds of Russia* was a recognized classic, was highly critical of the draft, though not hostile to some of the reform ideas that lay behind it. In his speech at the conference he asked where the requisite funds would come from, a point that, in view of the proposed abolition of tuition, concerned other delegates as well. Menzbir was also concerned about the enlightenment association and the relatively lax admission requirements for the academic association. While stating that he and his colleagues had always favored democratization of higher education "in the best sense of the word" (Menzbir himself had helped organize university extension programs), he feared that opening the schools to "a flood from the street of people thirsting after elementary knowledge" would risk a serious lowering of academic standards.[46]

A majority of the higher schools' representatives at the conference were willing to negotiate, however, and coalesced into the so-called Academic Group, in which the most prominent spokesmen were N. Ia. Marr, F. Iu. Levinson-Lessing, and D. S. Zernov. Marr, a linguist and academician who, as dean of Petrograd University's faculty of Oriental Languages, had signed an extremely bitter protest against the Bolsheviks on November 24, 1917, was now among those most eager to cooperate with Narkompros and in subsequent years would become a Marxist and join the Communist Party. Levinson-Lessing was a well-known geologist and academic spokesman at Leningrad Polytechnical Institute. Zernov was a Kadet, an active figure in municipal government and a popular professor at Petrograd Technological Institute, where he had served as director before the war.[47]

The three most contentious issues at the conference were papered over with vaguely worded compromises that postponed the most crucial decisions. A resolution by Zernov branded the composition and powers of the people's council as an unacceptable violation of autonomy, but when Lunacharskii assured the delegates of the government's willingness to make changes to meet some of the objections, Zernov moved and the conference voted to accept both Zernov's resolution and Lunacharskii's statement.[48] The conference overwhelmingly opposed as too short the principle of seven-year terms for those elected to professorial positions but left open the question of just how long the term should be.[49] Concerning the composition of the academic councils and faculty assemblies, the majority accepted the principle of participation by the upper ranks of the junior faculty. Student representation was regarded as "in some cases necessary and in others permissible," and the resolution "did not object" to student representatives having full voting rights on all questions except the election of professors and the awarding of degrees. What would constitute an acceptable number of student representatives was not specified.[50] This issue reveals an interesting liberalization in the position of the professoriate since 1906. In that year the three draft charters were split on the question of junior faculty participation in administrative bodies but unanimous against student representation. Legislation of 1917 had granted junior faculty full voting rights on the faculty assemblies and nonvoting rights on the academic councils while calling for special student-faculty commissions for the expression of student opinion. Now, under pressure from Narkompros, the majority of delegates accepted full junior faculty rights and even partial student representation on the prestigious academic councils.

The issue of admission requirements also reveals a change through time in the position of the elected representatives of the professoriate. In both 1906 and 1917 professors had called for an end to legal discrimination and the monopolistic hold of the classical gynmasium by specifying that graduates of all secondary schools would be eligible for admission to any higher school. In 1918 the delegates, with relatively little discussion, accepted Narkompros's proposals to remove two further barriers to widespread admission. Thus they accepted the proposal to abolish tuition and the provision that, although a secondary school level of preparation was expected for admission, earning a school diploma was not the only way this requirement could be met.[51]

The conference ended on a harmonious note, with an agreement to establish a commission charged with hammering out the details of a compromise draft that would then be sent to higher schools throughout the country for their comments. A second national conference would then be held to adopt the final version.[52]

The end of the July conference, however, was to mark the high point in relations between Narkompros and the professoriate. The commission met July 15–23 but proved unable to agree on a common draft, so both Narkompros and the representatives of the Academic Group compiled their own drafts.[53] Each filled in the disputed details in accord with its own preferences and made only slight efforts at compromise. Furthermore, Narkompros on one point presented a position much more extreme than its earlier one. The commissariat's new draft stated that admission should be granted to all those sixteen or over who "desire" to attend a higher educational institution, with no requirement at all of preparation equivalent to that of a secondary school. This was followed two weeks later by a legislative bombshell. A Sovnarkom decree signed by Lenin and published August 6 announced the abolition for the forthcoming academic year of all admission requirements other than the attainment of sixteen years of age. Narkompros was instructed to ensure that all desiring to study would be able to do so, and that priority would go to those from the proletariat and poor peasantry, who were to be assured of receiving stipends.[54] This action was contrary both to the provisions of the original Narkompros draft charter and to the implicit assumption of the July conference that reform measures would be enacted only after they had been agreed on or at least discussed in consultation with higher school representatives. Meanwhile, the Civil War continued to spread in the east, the former tsar and his family were executed in Ekaterinburg, and Pokrovskii published a hostile and unconciliatory report on the July conference.[55]

What prompted the Narkompros change? The most likely explanation is that after the July conference Pokrovskii and Lunacharskii reported to Lenin, who immediately insisted on a harder line. Recall that it was Lenin, who overruled Pokrovskii's autonomy formulation in an earlier Central Committee meeting and it was Lenin who signed the August 6 decree on open admissions. To be sure, Lenin wanted the cooperation of the professoriate, but on *his* terms, and he was not prepared to endorse all the compromises proposed by his Narkompros lieutenants.

The two revised drafts of Narkompros and the Academic Group were both sent to the country's higher educational institutions, which held meetings of their councils to discuss them during the first three weeks of August. A survey of the responses yields some interesting information about the attitudes of the rank and file professoriate. First, unsurprisingly the higher schools were virtually unanimous in preferring the draft of the Academic Group to that of Narkompros. Second, whereas many schools criticized individual provisions in the Academic draft, relatively few dismissed it out of hand as too radical to merit discussion, which suggests that the Academic Group was not out of touch with the opinion of the professoriate. Finally, the responses of some of the smaller and medium-sized institutes indicated the great extent to which they shared the rhetoric, the values, and the concerns of professors at the older universities and institutes. Thus, the Moscow Surveying Institute feared a diminution in the purely theoretical or "nauchnyi" methodology in teaching, proclaimed that the history of higher education in Europe had demonstrated that "*nauka* . . . can flourish only on the soil of academic autonomy," and supported the new enlightenment functions as corresponding to the long-standing aspiration of the higher school to spread *nauka* among the masses. The Petrograd Women's Polytechnical Institute objected to the regimentation it found in the Narkompros draft and wished the Academic draft had more explicitly authorized individual schools to give admissions exams if secondary school diplomas were no longer required. The Petrograd Mining Institute, while approving most of the more liberal provisions of both drafts, such as the abolition of tuition and student participation in administration, wanted an additional provision guaranteeing autonomy to be written into the charter.[56] Some of the older schools were more critical. The Academy of Agriculture at Petrovka criticized the provisions institutionalizing enlightenment work and extensively increasing the administrative role of younger faculty.[57] The council of St. Petersburg University was highly critical of the entire Narkompros draft, particularly its assumption of the existence of class conflict between senior and junior faculty and between teachers and students. The university, responded the council, is an "institution outside of and above classes," and its goal of communicating scientific knowledge is "quite unrelated to membership in any given class."[58]

By and large, however, most of the schools' reports were guardedly optimistic about the possibility of acceptable reform. Such was not the case at Moscow University. A committee of the academic council had drawn up a strong memorandum (*zapiska*) sharply criticizing many of the Narkompros principles that had been accepted by the Academic Group at the July conference. The council on August 14 debated the wisdom of forwarding the memorandum, with some

members arguing that it would be better to work at the forthcoming conference
for specific changes rather than risk futility by attacking general principles.
But the historian A. A. Kizevetter carried the day when he charged that the
recently published decree on admissions proved the government was determined to reform on its own terms rather than pay attention to conference
results, and when he concluded by dramatically urging that the uncompro-
mising *zapiska* be dispatched as the "swan song" of Moscow University.[59]

The reaction from Narkompros was bitter. August 1918 was a difficult
month for the Soviet government. British and American troops landed at Arch-
angel on August 2, Czech and White forces captured Kazan on the August 6,
a British force occupied Baku on the August 14, Denikin's Volunteer Army
took Ekaterinodar on the August 15, and Lenin was wounded and Uritskii
killed by SR terrorists on the August 30. This chain of events doubtless contributed to further hardening the *Narkompros* position. In a speech on August
26 Lunacharskii chose to regard the Moscow University *zapiska* as representing
the views of the entire professoriate, which he charged with reneging on its
concessions of July. These claims were false, and the commissar must have
known it. As we have seen, the majority of universities and institutes throughout the country had in fact supported the reforms and concessions of the
Academic Group; it was the Soviet government—not the professoriate—that
had reneged on a major concession by its open admissions decree of August
6, and it was this decree that had provoked the hostile response from Moscow
University. Nonetheless, Lunacharskii threatened that if the professors persisted in their "declaration of war," Narkompros would accept their challenge
and carry out higher education reforms without their participation.[60]

Emotions ran high when the second conference met September 4–8, and it
is not surprising that no agreement on a charter was reached. The attempt of
Narkompros and the professoriate to reach a compromise had broken down.
As a result, for the next two and a half years the Soviet government contented
itself with issuing piecemeal educational legislation on an ad hoc basis. Only
in 1921 did it return to the task of drafting a comprehensive charter. And at
that time, the opposition of the professoriate would not be able to prevent its
implementation.

The period from the fall of 1918 to the spring of 1921 was one of terrible
material deprivation in central Russia and chaos, bloodshed, and fighting on
the periphery. Universities and institutes remained open, but despite an initial
flood of students taking advantage of the new open admissions policy, the
number of those actively attending lectures soon dwindled to an abnormally
low level. Some professors remained at their posts throughout the period, while
many others fled, either in search of warmth and food or out of political
sympathy for the Whites.

The White movement in fact received extensive support from Russian academics. D. D. Grimm, former rector of St. Petersburg University and assistant
minister of education under the Provisional Government, served as an aide to

General Iudenich and drew up a memorandum recommending educational policies for a future White government. (It called for autonomy for all educational institutions and an emphasis on scientific, technical, and vocational training.) Tomsk University's faculty furnished much of Kolchak's government. Former rector V. V. Sapozhnikov was minister of education, his deputies were Professor V. N. Savvin and George Guins (the latter a professor at the new Polytechnical Institute at Omsk), and other Tomsk professors held the ministries of interior, justice, and religion. Denikin's commissar of education in Kiev (Spektorskii) had been rector of Kiev University, and his minister of finance had been on the staff of the Petrograd Polytechnical Institute. The young George Vernadskii briefly served as Wrangel's minister of the press.[61]

White troops were warmly welcomed by the staffs of higher educational institutions in the combat zone. A former student and White supporter testifies that whereas most people in the Novocherkassk area were indifferent to the outcome of the struggle, professors at the polytechnical institute were militant: they risked death by calling for a ruthless struggle against the Bolsheviks and helped recruit a student detachment. When the Bolsheviks were driven out of Kazan, the university council adopted without debate a resolution that welcomed the new government, promised full assistance in the rebuilding of the country, and called for a monetary collection to support the anti-Bolshevik army. The council of Kiev University took a similar action when Denikin's army entered the city.[62] When the Red Army returned to Kazan on September 9, almost half of the professors and a majority of the students fled east with the retreating White troops. But the Bolsheviks turned out to be fairly lenient in this instance. The remaining members of the council were summoned by the Cheka, required to donate to the Red Army ten times what they had contributed to the White cause, and then released, except for the rector, who was imprisoned for a month. When the Kolchak movement collapsed, Pokrovskii guaranteed a safe return for those who had fled with the White army, whereupon, according to a Soviet commentator, the returning "émigrés," like the Bourbons, "having learned nothing and forgotten nothing," immediately resumed their former resistance to Narkompros reforms.[63]

Southern Russia was a natural destination for those who were fleeing Soviet rule without actively enlisting in the White cause. It was made still more attractive by the decision of Kiev University in 1918 to open a new branch of the university at Simferopol on the Crimea, which under the name of Tauride University soon became a haven for academic refugees. George Vernadskii was one of the first professors, along with another young historian from Perm University, B. D. Grekov. When Vladimir Vernadskii arrived in the Crimea in 1919, he was elected rector. The university apparently flourished despite the vicissitudes of occupation by Germans, Whites, the French, Bolsheviks, and then Whites again. On Wrangel's defeat, however, he arranged for the evacuation of those desiring to emigrate. Most of the professors chose to leave, but Vladimir Vernadskii decided at the last minute to remain. When Lenin learned of this decision, he ordered Vernadskii and a few others who remained to be arrested for their own safety and transported under guard to Moscow, where they were freed.[64]

This is probably the most dramatic illustration of the concern of Lenin and the Soviet government to win over and utilize the services of "bourgeois" specialists. But the tolerance of Narkompros, although it extended to many, did not apply to all academics who had sided with the Whites. In January 1921, Lunacharskii and the collegium of Narkompros turned down the request of five out of six academics who wanted to return to the RSFSR from Georgia.[65] During the following year, a large group of well-known writers and humanist scholars were arrested and forcibly exiled from the country.

What was life like for those who stayed behind during the Civil War? Most suffered severe material deprivation, yet enjoyed surprising freedom to teach as they pleased in the desolate but as yet unregimented classrooms.

Death by starvation was in the air, especially in Petrograd, and scientists and scholars at first were no more immune than other members of the population. Ipatiev reports that in one year seven of the forty-five members of the Academy of Sciences died of starvation.[66] The university had a long list of deaths by starvation, disease, and suicide and the rector used grim humor in pleading with his faculty members to stay alive so that their colleagues would not be faced with the considerable trouble of arranging burials.[67] Wooden houses were torn down for fuel in the winter. Professors, like other members of the educated classes, were harassed by being forced to turn out for forced labor projects and by having their apartments requisitioned for others to live in. Lunacharskii sought to have Petrograd University personnel spared from these measures, but in general he had little control over them.[68] Frequently the higher educational institutions had no funds to pay salaries, so survival depended on the stingy rationing system. Sometimes professors were able to find surprising sources of extra employment and hence extra rations. Despite periodic arrests, Kizevetter was able to work at a bookstore, travel regularly to Ivanovo-Voznesensk to lecture at a polytechnical institute, and make trips by horse and carriage to give public lectures at Tula, Vladimir, and villages en route, where he was warmly received and paid in kind. N. O. Losskii was invited to give a series of lectures in philosophy at a people's university (that is, school of adult education) in the Shlissel'burg district of Petrograd, which provided him and his family with an invaluable source of extra rations.[69]

By 1919 the government had begun to institute a series of privileges for professors and academicians by placing them in a higher rationing category than other members of the bourgeoisie and even some workers. In January 1920, the Home for Scholars and Scientists (*Dom uchenykh*), combining a place of work, club, dining hall, and dormitory, was opened in Petrograd, an idea that spread to other university cities. In November 1921, the Central Commission for the Improvement of the Living Conditions of Scientists and Scholars (TseKUBU) was established as a standing committee of the RSFSR Sovnarkom and remained active throughout the twenties. In 1922 Narkompros devised a ranking system of five different categories within the group of scientists and scholars who were receiving supplemental rations from TseKUBU. Criteria for ranking included scientific or scholarly eminence and importance of field of specialization to the Soviet government. Younger academics in the lowest category were expected to demonstrate a knowledge of Marxism before receiving their rations.[70]

Central Russian higher schools had few active students during the Civil War years of 1918–20. The proletarian youth that the Bolsheviks wanted to send into the universities and institutes now had a more urgent assignment with the Red Army. Many former or potential students fled to the borderlands. Most of those who remained spent their time and energy just trying to remain alive. Most of the schools lacked heating and lighting and were in a terrible state of disrepair. Nonetheless classes continued to meet at a reduced rate. Even in Petrograd, which was the hardest hit, hardy bands of students and professors met in cold, candle-lit classrooms for lectures and discussion. Enough supplies were usually found to keep laboratories open.[71]

Under these circumstances, Narkompros's efforts to exert some authority over the schools did not meet with much success. Special commissars were sometimes appointed, with power to attend council meetings and overrule decisions, but this practice had little practical effect.[72] In an effort to reform the teaching of the social sciences, Narkompros ordered the abolition of all the law faculties and the establishment of new faculties of social science, where it was hoped that Marxist methodologies would flourish. The new faculties of social science, however, were staffed primarily by members of the former law faculties and some historians, most of whom were hostile to Marxism and continued to teach their traditional courses. For example, Moscow University's faculty of social science at this time offered several courses on the history of religion but not one on historical materialism.[73]

Numerous memoirs testify to the freedom of teaching that prevailed in this period. Most professors taught their regular courses without interference, and some even added new material that was critical of Marxism. The idealist philosopher Losskii set up a seminar on materialism, which he taught from an antimaterialist perspective. The sociologist Timasheff criticized Marx in his course on the theory of law, and a professor in Kazan University's faculty of social science reportedly called Marx a fool. Nikolai Berdiaev in Moscow and Andrei Belyi in Petrograd established philosophical academies that sponsored public lectures and discussion on theology, philosophy, and ethics. Berdiaev, although he did not have an advanced degree, was elected professor of philosophy at Moscow University in 1920.[74]

Autonomy for the professoriate did not long outlast the Civil War. A new charter was imposed in 1921 that sought to achieve firm administrative control over the higher schools both from above via Narkompros and from below via Communist Party organs and trade unions. The charter did not accomplish its goals all at once, but in the next few years the room for independent maneuver on the part of either the individual teacher or the administrative bodies of the professoriate was sharply reduced. The government did not totally control the universities and institutes in the twenties, but it was considerably closer to that objective in 1928 than it had been in 1921.

To be sure, the blow to academic independence was softened by some positive factors. In a material sense the professoriate was in a privileged position compared to the bulk of the population, and talented or ambitious individuals had opportunities to rise still higher. The Soviet government, compared to the tsarist, promised to be more consistent, more sincere, and more generous in its support for research and education, especially in the areas of science.

But the establishment of Soviet government control over higher education was a blow nonetheless. For most professors, the government's ideology was wrong, its use of coercion was wrong, and its sponsorship of lower-class rule was insulting and at times frightening. And now their beloved autonomy, will-o'-the-wisp that it may have been, was being taken away once and for all.

NOTES

1. A. V. Lunacharskii o narodnom obrazovanii (M, 1958), pp. 365–66; M. B. Keirim-Markus, "Gosudarstvennaia komissiia po prosveshcheniiu (1917–1918)," Istoriia SSSR, 1969, no. 6, pp. 126–27; I. S. Smirnov, Lenin i sovetskaia kul'tura (M, 1960), pp. 197–200, 215–16; S. A. Fediukin, Velikii Oktiabr' i intelligentsiia (M, 1972), pp. 42–43, 51. (Throughout, Moscow is abbreviated as "M," Leningrad as "L," St. Petersburg as "SP," and Petrograd as "P.")

2. Leningradskii gosudarstvennyi istoricheskii arkhiv (hereafter, LGIA), fond 14, opis' 27, delo 62, pp. 59–60.

3. G. V. Burtsev, "Politekhnicheskii institut v pervye gody Sovetskoi vlasti (1918–1922)," Trudy Leningradskogo politekhnicheskogo instituta, 1957, no. 190, p. 92; G. D. Alekseeva, Oktiabr'skaia revoliutsiia i istoricheskaia nauka v Rossii (1917–1923 gg.) (M, 1968), pp. 202–3 (citing Griadushchii den', Nov. 28, 1917); Tekhnologicheskii institut imeni Leningradskogo Soveta: Sto let, 1828–1928, 2 vols. (L, 1928), 1:211–12.

4. P. A. Zaichenko, Tomskii gosudarstvennyi universitet imeni B. B. Kuibysheva (Tomsk, 1960), p. 209; Arkhiv Moskovskogo gosudarstvennogo universiteta (hereafter, Arkhiv MGU), Sovet 1918, p. 7; M. K. Korbut, Kazanskii gosudarstvennyi universitet im. V. I. Ulianova-Lenina za 125 let, 2 vols. (Kazan, 1930), 2:300.

5. Wilhelm von Humboldt, "On the Spirit and the Organizational Framework of Intellectual Institutions in Berlin," (1809–1810), trans. in Minerva, April 1970, vol. 8, pp. 245, 244.

6. Typical was the statement by the eminent historian P. G. Vinogradov, "If there is anything incontrovertible in Russia, it is the truth that enlightenment opens the way to the well-being and power of the people." Vinogradov, "Uchebnoe delo v nashikh universitetov," Vestnik Evropy, October 1901, vol. 5, p. 537.

7. For a discussion of the efforts of Paul Miliukov, M. A. Menzbir, P. G. Vinogradov, A. A. Kizevetter, and others to establish a university extension system in the 1890s, see A. A. Kizevetter, Na rubezhe dvukh stoletii (Prague, 1929), pp. 286–305. Professors were also active in establishing and teaching at the higher courses for women and a number of other innovative institutions, such as the Shaniavskii University in

Moscow. See Elena Likhacheva, *Materialy dlia istorii zhenskago obrazovaniia v Rossii, 1856–1880* (SP, 1901), esp. pp. 493–535; and N. V. Speranskii, *Krizis Russkoi shkoly* (M, 1914), pp. 160–63.

8. See, for example, V. I. Vernadskii, *Pis'ma o vyshem obrazovanii v Rossii* (Moscow, 1913), *passim*; and K. A. Timiriazev, *Nauka i demokratiia* (Moscow, 1963), *passim*.

9. William G. Rosenberg, *Liberals in the Russian Revolution* (Princeton, 1974), pp. 20–21, 24; B. N. Menshutkin, *Zhizn' i deiatel'nost' Nikolaia Aleksandrovicha Menshutkina* (SP, 1908), pp. 293–95. The academic conception of *nauka* as standing above all partisan interests corresponded to the Kadets' proclamation of "nadpartinost' "—their belief that their party stood for the interests of all the people, not just certain classes or groups (Rosenberg, p. 13). Thus, even the most politically active professors did not, as a rule, view their activity as furthering partisan interests.

10. Paulsen, writing soon after the turn of the century, thought that this traditional attitude of German academics was undergoing a decisive change (Friedrich Paulsen, *The German Universities and University Study*, trans. F. Thilly and W. Elwang [London, 1906], pp. 117–19). Ringer, however, shows that aside from an important minority of German professors, this position was vigorously maintained by the majority into the 1930s (Fritz K. Ringer, *The Decline of the German Mandarins: The German Academic Community, 1890–1933* [Cambridge, Mass., 1969], pp. 128–43, 200–27, 269–95).

11. See my *Autocrats and Academics: Education, Culture, and Society in Tsarist Russia* (Chicago, 1979), pp. 57–113, for a more extended summary and analysis of the Russian academic ideology, which I refer to, somewhat critically, as "the mystique of nauka." It goes almost without saying that the cultural and intellectual significance of Russia's higher education teaching staff was out of all proportion to its tiny numerical size, which on the eve of World War I was about five thousand individuals. Estimating this number with any precision is a difficult task. The Ministry of Public Education published fairly reliable figures for university teachers. As of January 1, 1912, there were 612 professors, somewhat over 600 private-docents, and a total of 2,212 teaching personnel, including lecturers and assistants. Ministerstvo Narodnago Prosveshcheniia, *Vsepoddaneishii otchet Ministra Narodnago Prosveshcheniia za 1911* (SP, 1913), appendix, pp. 2–3. But university enrollments comprised only about one-third of total higher education enrollments before the war. Data on the teaching staffs of institutes administered by other ministries are highly scattered, do not always indicate whether they refer just to professors and private-docents or to all engaged in teaching, and are sometimes missing altogether. The best estimate for all teaching personnel at all higher educational institutions is provided by Leikina-Svirskaia, who came up with an approximate total of 6,400. V. R. Leikina-Svirskaia, *Russkaia intelligentsiia v 1900–1917 godakh* (M, 1981), pp. 96–97. As she herself grants, however, this number must be exaggerated, for she counted the total number of teaching *positions* at various institutions, without taking into consideration that a number of professors or private-docents held positions at two, or sometimes even three, institutions. We are left to agree with Vernadskii, who in 1914 estimated the number as "more than 5,000." V. I. Vernadskii, "Vysshaia shkola v Rossii," *Ezhegodnik gazety Rech' na 1914 god* (SP, 1914), p. 314.

12. The 1884 charter can be found in "Svod ustavov uchenykh uchrezhdenii i uchebnykh zavedenii vedomstva Ministerstva Narodnago Prosveshcheniia," in *Polnyi svod zakonov rossiiskoi imperii*, vol. 11, pt. 1 (SP, 1911), arts. 402–559.

13. For the academic union draft, see "Proekt glavnykh osnovanii obshchago ustava vysshikh uchebnykh zavedenii," *Pravo*, October 9, 1905, no. 40, cols. 3349–3356; for the St. Petersburg University draft, see St. Petersburg University, *Proekt glavnykh polozhenii ustava universiteta vyrabotannyi sovetom imperatorskago S-Peterburgskago Universiteta* (SP, 1905); for the Tolstoi conference and its draft charter, see Silke Spieler, *Autonomie oder Reglementierung: Die russische Universität am Vorabend des Ersten Weltkrieges* (Cologne, 1981), pp. 124–57; and Samuel D Kassow, "The Russian Uni-

versity in Crisis: 1899–1911," Ph.D. dissertation, Princeton University, 1976, pp. 447–61.

14. Vladimir Vernadsky, "The First Year of the Ukrainian Academy of Sciences," *The Annals of the Ukrainian Academy of Arts and Sciences in the U.S., Inc.*, 1964–68, vol. 11, nos. 1–2 (31–32), pp. 13–14.

15. S. E. Belozerov, *Ocherki istorii Rostovskogo universiteta* (Rostov, 1959), pp. 54–55; *Rostovskii gosudarstvennyi universitet, 1915–1965: Stat'i, vospominaniia, dokumenty* (Rostov, 1965), pp. 285–87.

16. Korbut, 2:294–95.

17. P. N. Ignatiev, D. M. Odinetz, and P. J. Novgorotsev, *Russian Schools and Universities in the World War* (New Haven, 1929), p. 233; Robert P. Browder and Alexander F. Kerensky, eds., *The Russian Provisional Government, 1917: Documents*, 3 vols. (Stanford, 1961), 2:796–99.

18. F. F. Korolev, "Iz istorii narodnogo obrazovaniia v Sovetskoi Rossii: Srednie professional'nye shkoly i vysshee obrazovanie v 1917–1920 gg.," *Izvestiia Akademii pedagogicheskikh nauk RSFSR*, vol. 102, 1959, pp. 88–90.

19. Smirnov, p. 236.

20. L. A. Shilov, "Deiatel'nost' Kommunisticheskoi partii po perestroike vysshei shkoly v pervye gody sovetskoi vlasti (1917–1921 gg.)," Candidate's dissertation, Leningrad State University, 1965, p. 33; Korbut, 2:301.

21. *Arkhiv MGU*, Sovet 1918, p. 35rev.; Shilov, p. 35.

22. Burtsev, p. 93; *Istoriia Leningradskogo universiteta* (L, 1969), pp. 182–83; *Arkhiv MGU*, Sovet 1918, pp. 16rev.–17rev.; Shilov, p. 34.

23. Vladimir N. Ipatieff, *The Life of a Chemist: Memoirs of Vladimir N. Ipatieff*, ed. by X. J. Eudin, H. D. Fisher, and H. H. Fisher, trans. V. Haensel and R. Lusher (Stanford, 1946), esp. pp. 243ff.; V. P. Zubov, *Stradnye gody Rossii: Vospominaniia o Revoliutsii (1917–1925)* (Munich, 1968), pp. 8–10, 30–68, 80–98.

24. F. Iu. Levinson-Lessing, *I. Edinaia vysshaia shkola, II. Dal'neishee razvitie Politekhnicheskogo instituta* (P, 1915), pp. 1–10; M. M. Novikov, *Ot Moskvy do N'iu-Iorka: Moia zhizn' v nauke i politike* (New York, 1952), pp. 198–99.

25. *Vestnik Nizhegorodskogo universiteta*, April 10, 1918, no. 1, pp. 2 (quotation), 5–6, and appendix. The charter is reprinted in *Izvestiia Nizhegorodskogo gosudarstvennogo universiteta*, 1928, vol. 2, pp. 85–88.

26. For professorial criticism of Sinitsyn and his project, see *Novoe Slovo*, March 31 (18), 1918, no. 43, p. 1; and *Svoboda Rossii*, April 26 (13), 1918, no. 13, p. 1; ibid., April 28 (15), 1918, no. 15, p. 1; ibid., May 14 (1), 1918, no. 24, p. 3; ibid., May 30 (17), 1918, no. 38, p. 4.

27. *Svoboda Rossii*, May 16 (3), 1918, no. 26, p. 1; A. V. Kol'tsov, *Lenin i stanovlenie Akademii nauk kak tsentr sovetskoi nauki* (L, 1969), pp. 59–60.

28. *Literaturnoe nasledstvo*, vol. 80, 1971, p. 72; *Tsentral'nyi gosudarstvennyi arkhiv RSFSR* (hereafter *TsGA RSFSR*), f. 2306, op. 18, d. 24, pp. 44–49, 59–60.

29. *Sobranie uzakonenii i rasporiazhenii rabochego i krestianskogo pravitel'stva RSFSR* (hereafter, *SU*), 1917–18, no. 2, art. 16; ibid., 1917–18, no. 12, art. 183; *TsGA RSFSR*, f. 2306, op. 18, d. 92, p. 28; ibid., f. 2306, op. 18, d. 384.

30. *Arkhiv MGU*, Sovet 1918, pp. 13–13rev.; *Svoboda Rossii*, April 25 (12), 1918, no. 12, p. 4; Shilov, pp. 42–45.

31. On Pokrovskii, see George M. Enteen, *The Soviet Scholar-Bureaucrat* (University Park and London, 1978), pp. 11–29; on Shternberg, K. V. Ostrovitianov, *Dumy o proshlom* (M, 1967), pp. 240–43, 285–98; on Reisner, "M. A. Reisner (nekrolog)," *Vestnik Kommunisticheskoi akademii*, vol. 28, 1928, pp. 3–6.

32. S. Z. Mandel', "Kul'turno-prosvetitel'naia deiatel'nost' uchenykh Petrogradskogo universiteta v pervye gody sovetskoi vlasti," in *Ocherki po istorii Leningradskogo universiteta*, v. 1 (L, 1962), pp. 143–44.

33. Chugaev's handwritten theses, with Lunacharskii's comments written in the margin, are in *TsGA RSFSR*, f. 2906, op. 2, d. 12, pp. 213–26.

34. Ibid., p. 217.

35. A. V. *Lunacharskii o narodnom obrazovanii*, p. 18.

36. V. I. Lenin, *Lenin o narodnom obrazovanii* (M, 1957), p. 251.

37. *TsGA*, f. 2306, op. 2, d. 12, p. 216.

38. Ibid., f. 2306, op. 18, d. 28, p. 18.

39. M. N. Pokrovskii, *Izbrannye proizvedeniia*, 4 vols. (M, 1965–67), 4:9–10. See also Sh. Kh. Chanbarisov, *Formirovanie sovetskoi universitetskoi sistemy (1917–1938 gg.)* (Ufa, 1973), pp. 98–99.

40. *TsGA*, f. 2306, op. 18, d. 28, p. 14. The charter as a whole is on pp. 13–17.

41. Ibid., pp. 15–15rev.

42. V. I. Nevskii, quoted by Shilov, p. 48.

43. The charge subsequently made by *Narkompros* and endorsed by Sheila Fitzpatrick that the universities were totally hostile and unreceptive to reform is quite incorrect. Fitzpatrick, *The Commissariat of Enlightenment* (Cambridge, 1970), p. 68.

44. A. K. Timiriazev, "Kak zarozhdalsia sovetskii universitet," *Sovetskoe studenchestvo*, 1937, no. 8, p. 49.

45. *TsGA*, f. 2306, op. 18, d. 28, pp. 93–94; *Svoboda Rossii*, June 12, 1918, no. 45, p. 4.

46. *TsGA*, f. 2306, op. 18, d. 28, pp. 79–82. Quote on p. 79rev.

47. *LGIA*, f. 14, op. 27, d. 62, pp. 62–63; *TsGA*, f. 2306, op. 18, d. 28, pp. 85–86; Ibid., f. 2306, op. 2, d. 12, p. 229rev.; *Tekhnologicheskii institut imeni Leningradskogo soveta*, 1:292–93.

48. *TsGA*, f. 2306, op. 2, d. 12, pp. 244–50, 261–62.

49. Ibid., f. 2306, op. 18, d. 28, pp. 164, 170.

50. Ibid., f. 2306, op. 2, d. 12, pp. 249rev.–50; ibid., f. 2306, op. 18, d. 28, p. 196.

51. Ibid., f. 2306, op. 18, d. 28, pp. 14, 18, 75, 145.

52. Ibid., f. 2306, op. 18, d. 65, p. 2.

53. The revised *Narkompros* draft is in ibid., f. 2306, op. 18, d. 65, pp. 52–64. The Academic Group's draft is in ibid., f. 2306, op. 18, d. 64, pp. 50–57.

54. *Dekrety sovetskoi vlasti*, 4 vols. (M, 1957–68), 3:137–38, 141.

55. *Narodnoe Prosveshchenie: Ezhenedel'noe prilozhenie k Izvestiiam VTsIK*, July 20, 1918, no. 9.

56. Respectively, *TsGA*, f. 2306, op. 18, d. 64, pp. 14–14rev; pp. 34–35; pp. 24–24rev.

57. Ibid., pp. 124–124rev.

58. *Tsentral'nyi gosudarstvennyi arkhiv Oktiabr'skoi revoliutsii i sotsialisticheskogo stroitel'stva Leningrada (TsGAOR Len.)*, f. 7240, op. 14, d. 20, pp. 15–17. Quote on pp. 16rev.–17.

59. *Arkhiv MGU*, Sovet 1918, pp. 136rev.–150.

60. A. V. *Lunacharskii o narodnom obrazovanii*, pp. 43–44.

61. Respectively, D. D. Grimm, *Hoover Institution Archives*, Box 3, "Russian Civil War—Education;" Zaichenko, p. 219; University of California Bancroft Library, Regional Oral History Office, George C. Guins, "Professor and Government Official: Russia, China, and California," interview conducted by Boris Raymond, Berkeley, 1966, p. 177; S. P. Timoshenko, *As I Remember*, trans. Robert Addis (Princeton, 1968), pp. 173–74; G. V. Vernadskii, "Iz vospominanii," *Novyi zhurnal*, 1971, no. 105, pp. 219–20.

62. Respectively, B. P. Proshchanov, "Zhizn' i rabota professorov v SSSR," *Bakhmeteff Archive of the Rare Book and Manuscript Library of Columbia University*, pp. 1–3; Korbut, 2:303; *Stoletie Kievskogo universiteta cv. Vladimira* (Belgrad, 1935), p. 79.

63. Korbut, 2:303, 313–14; Chanbarisov, pp. 324–25. Quote in Korbut, 2: 313.

64. G. V. Vernadskii, "Iz vospominanii," *Novyi zhurnal*, 1971, no. 104, p. 187; ibid., 1971, no. 105, pp. 203–20; G. V. Vernadskii, "Bratstvo 'Priiutino,' " *Novyi zhurnal*, 1969, no. 97, pp. 229–30.

65. *TsGA*, f. 2306, op. 1, d. 634, p. 9rev. Those turned down included the economist and Provisional Government minister A. A. Manuilov and the engineer and Kadet D. S. Zernov. The one admitted was M. I. Rostovtsev, because (according to Lunacharskii) of his great expertise as an archaeologist. As it turned out, however, Rostovtsev decided to emigrate and Zernov managed to return anyway.

66. Ipatieff, p. 271.

67. Pitirim A. Sorokin, *Leaves from a Russian Diary* (NY, 1924), pp. 229–34.

68. Ibid., pp. 224–25; *Svoboda Rossii*, July 4, 1918, no. 63; *Istoriia Leningradskogo gosudarstvennogo universiteta*, pp. 188–89.

69. *Segodnia*, Riga, Sept. 20, 1931, no. 260, p. 4; ibid., Oct. 31, 1931, no. 301, p. 2; N. O. Losskii, *Vospominaniia: Zhizn' i filosofskii put'* (Munich, 1969), pp. 209–11.

70. *Piat' let raboty Tsentral'noi komissii po uluchsheniiu byta uchenykh* (M, 1927), pp. 3–7; Chanbarisov, pp. 329–34; *Rostovskii gosudarstvennyi universitet, 1915–1965*, pp. 291–92; Sorokin, *Leaves*, pp. 245–46; *TsGA*, f. 298, op. 1, d. 21, pp. 34–35, 51, 55–56rev.

71. *Tekhnologicheskii institut imeni Leningradskogo soveta*, 1: 212; Losskii, p. 206; Sorokin, *Leaves*, pp. 223–24.

72. Korbut, 2:308; Ipatieff, pp. 277–78.

73. Korolev, p. 132.

74. Losskii, p. 212; N. S. Timashev, "1915–1921," *S-Peterburgskii politekhnicheskii institut Imperatora Petra Velikogo, 1902–1952*, sbornik no. 2 (Paris-New York, 1958), p. 120; Korbut, 2:330; N. A. Berdiaev, *Dream and Reality: An Essay in Autobiography*, trans. Katherine Lampert (New York, 1951), pp. 232–36.

NATURAL SCIENTISTS AND THE SOVIET SYSTEM

Kendall E. Bailes

Historians have traditionally stressed the weakness of the middle class in late Imperial Russia. What they have largely overlooked is that the Russian middle class, admittedly small, was also not homogeneous. It was as much a professional class, perhaps more so, as an entrepreneurial class (to use a distinction developed more fully in Harold Perkin's book *The Origins of Modern English Society, 1780–1884*). The evidence in Alfred Rieber's recent book, which documents considerable conflict between entrepreneurial, merchant, and professional groups in late tsarist Russia, strongly suggests that the already small Russian middle class was further weakened by such conflicts and by the relative size and prominence of the professionals in comparison with merchants entrepreneurs.[1]

Tension between the ideals and aims of Russian professionals and those of businessmen, including industrialists and commercial farmers, is evident in the late tsarist period and received different political expression after the legalization of parties following the 1905 revolution. The Russian middle class was weak not simply because it was small in numbers, but also because it lacked homogeneity and cohesion in its values and outlook. There were, however, growing intermediate occupational groups that were increasingly conscious of their common interests, as well as the conflicts among them, whether one chooses to call them a middle class, the middle classes, or use some other label, like entrepreneurial and professional groups. Lenin and the Bolshevik leadership, well aware of this divide within the Russian middle class between the professional occupations and entrepreneurial and mercantile groups attempted to exploit it after the October Revolution.

A study of one professional group, natural scientists, in the years from 1917 to 1921 is instructive, both in demonstrating a high degree of continuity with the prerevolutionary era in the attitudes and behavior of this professional group and its need to adapt to a rapidly changing political, social, and economic situation. The material below should demonstrate the degree to which scientists themselves played a leading role in shaping Soviet research institutions and professional culture in the early years of the Soviet system and why they were able to maintain considerable autonomy from the state.

Natural Scientists and the Soviet State

Most natural scientists, like the large majority of other professional groups, greeted the October Revolution with either hostility or scepticism about its aims and viability. There were few Marxists among the natural scientists, let alone members or sympathizers of the Bolsheviks. In the first few weeks after the October Revolution, the General Assembly of the Academy of Sciences, the most authoritative scientific institution in Russia, passed a resolution condemning the Bolshevik seizure of power and supporting the election of a constituent assembly to create a parliamentary system. In their opposition to the October Revolution, the Academy of Sciences joined many other prominent professional organizations such as the Union of Engineers, the Teachers' Union, the Academic Union, and the Pirogov Society of Physicians, all of which passed resolutions condemning the Bolshevik seizure of power and calling for a boycott of the new government.[2] Only a handful of natural scientists, in the first few months after the October Revolution, approached the new Soviet government and offered their help.[3] Most waited for the Bolsheviks to approach them, and such overtures were not generally made until the first part of 1918.

Unlike the municipal unions and unions of government workers, however, most scientists stayed on the job and did not join the picket lines of civil servants who took strike action in front of government buildings for a time after the October Revolution. Most adopted a "wait-and-see" attitude. For the most part, their approach, expressed in N. I. Vavilov's directive to R. E. Regel at the end of 1917, was to "Act as if nothing has happened."[4] Many scientists undoubtedly hoped that, if ignored, the Bolsheviks would simply go away: their government was not considered viable, and they would not, it was believed, be able to hold onto power. Others, like the prominent geochemist and academician V. I. Vernadskii, took a longer, more evolutionary point of view. Even if the Bolsheviks did not disappear, their government would evolve into a form less radical and more suited to the realities of Russia. As Vernadskii wrote on February 9, 1918, to his former student, the mineralogist Alexander Fersman (who was to play an important role in talks between the Soviet government and the Academy of Sciences during 1918 to 1921):

> For me, one thing alone is clear. We must use all our strength to insure that scientific (and all cultural work) in Russia is not interrupted but strengthened. . . . In the final analysis, I do not doubt [our] eventual triumph and I look upon the forms of new governmental structures with equanimity: the masses are simply too great and there is too much talent in them. It is necessary to use

all our effort to insure that the new generation makes a break with the past of its fathers . . . and here our chief strength lies in scientific work.[5]

There were even fewer Bolsheviks among natural scientists than among engineers and physicians, where there existed a small nucleus of party members who were to play an important organizational role in the early years of the Soviet government. The few professional scientists who were also Marxists tended to be young and lacked prestige or influence in their profession. Natural science was dominated politically by Russian liberals who were either active members of the Kadet Party or sympathized with many of its aims. Those scientists who were not political liberals tended either to be apolitical, immersed in their scientific work, or quietly conservative.

Most politically active natural scientists wanted parliamentary government, civil liberties, and local self-government, as well as economic development, the spread of education and "enlightened" ideas, and greater corporate autonomy. Curiously enough, however, there seem to have been few spokesmen for the development of capitalism per se, among those Russian scientists who did make public their views both before and after the 1917 revolution.[6] In searching for a hint of economic views in prerevolutionary writings of prominent Russian scientists one finds, if anything, that they generally stressed the need for state direction and regulation of the economy. They were probably comfortable with a mixed economy in which the state, particularly in Russia, played a leading role in economic development. Natural scientists were sympathetic toward diversification of the network of scientific research, which before 1917 was largely concentrated in the state universities and higher technical schools. They favored decentralization of its control, with a variety of sources of support, private and public, and with self-administration by autonomous groups of scientists.[7]

Many scientists had therefore pinned their hopes on the Provisional Government and its replacement by a liberal democracy allied with the democratic countries of the West, a government that would be more decentralized than its predecessor, that would encourage more initiative from its citizens, and that would permit more self-rule by public and professional bodies. The Ministry of Education of the Provisional Government had formed several commissions to prepare a reorganization of the scientific research network and to propose legal guarantees of academic freedom and increased corporate autonomy for scientific institutions.[8] The work of these commissions, which were composed of prominent scientists such as Vernadskii, the chemist N. S. Kurnakov, the physicist D. S. Rozhdestvenskii and the permanent secretary of the Academy of Sciences, Sergei F. Oldenburg, was interrupted by the October Revolution. (Before the October Revolution, Oldenburg had been minister of education in Kerenskii's cabinet; he had appointed his lifelong friend from university days, Vernadskii, asistant minister of education, in charge of higher education and scientific research institutions.)

It is therefore not surprising that the Academy of Sciences, which had felt so powerless under the tsarist regime, would be less than enthusiastic about the overthrow of the Provisional Government, in which some of its most prominent members had become influential. Oldenburg, for example, expressed his indignation and pessimism about the Bolshevik takeover at a general meeting of the academy held on December 29, 1917: "It would be cowardly not to look truth straight in the eye and recognize now that the Russian people have failed a great historical test and not stood their ground in a great world conflict: the dark ignorant masses have succumbed to a deceptive temptation and to superficial and criminal promises, and Russia stands on the edge of destruction."[9] It is also not surprising that in one of the first official communications between the academy and the Soviet government, during early 1918, the academy's president, the geologist A. P. Karpinskii, called on the soviets to revive the work of these commissions and bemoaned the break in continuity that had become "one of the misfortunes of Russian life."[10]

What perhaps is surprising is the great caution and tact with which the Soviet government, especially the central authorities, such as Lenin and his minister of education, A. V. Lunacharskii, treated the scientific community, beginning with the Academy of Sciences. The large majority of scientists were treated with great circumspection in the early months of Soviet rule. The permanent secretary of the academy, Oldenburg, was not arrested as a former minister of the Provisional Government nor apparently even harrassed for published statements such as the one quoted above. In fact, he remained the chief administrator of the academy until his removal by Stalin's government in 1929. Oldenburg, in turn, was greatly impressed by Lenin when he made a courtesy call to see the new Soviet leaders soon after the Bolshevik takeover. Although there was a great divide beween this Kadet scholar and Lenin, the radical intellectual, Oldenburg seems to have come partially under Lenin's spell.[11] What particularly impressed him was Lenin's passionate interest in education and science and his skills as a politician. For an establishment intellectual like Oldenburg, the contrast between Lenin and the last tsar, Nicholas II—surrounded as he was by people whom the educated classes considered charlatans and ignoramuses—could not have been sharper. Although Soviet sources no doubt exaggerate the ease with which scientists like Oldenburg were won over and the degree to which they enthusiastically supported the government, many prominent members of the academy were willing to judge the situation for themselves as it developed rather than actively seeking to oppose the new government. Their modus operandi for decades had been one of working within the established governmental system for peaceful change rather than taking to the streets in order to force change more rapidly. Thus, the development of their relations with the Soviet government was consistent with their previous behavior.

Several weeks after the October Revolution, at a meeting of the newly established Commission on Education (which later became the Commissariat of Education, Narkompros), a special commissar for the academy was appointed, I. V. Yegorov.[12] His role appears to have been more to protect the academy from mob attacks and the chaotic conditions of the time than to interfere in its work, and by early 1918 he had faded from the scene. Within a month of the October Revolution, the president of the academy, Karpinskii, its vice president, the mathematician Steklov, and Oldenburg, its secretary, paid a visit to the new commissar of education, Lunacharskii. No record of their conversation has been found, and it is unclear whether this represented more than a courtesy call. Substantive talks between the academy and the Soviet government began in January 1918.

The academy was the first Russian scientific institution that the Soviet government attemped to win over to active cooperation. Although small in size, with only 44 full members and some 220 employees in 1917 (109 of them qualified specialists), in prestige and authority the academy represented the acme of Russian scholarly life. Fewer than half of its full members in 1917 were in the natural sciences, but, in contrast to earlier periods of its history, the natural scientists had begun to dominate its activity by 1917.[13] Karpinskii and Steklov, both natural scientists, became its first freely elected officers after the fall of the tsarist government in 1917. Its permanent secretary, Oldenburg, though a specialist on Eastern religions and cultures, got along well with natural scientists and numbered among his closest friends the most prominent spokesman for the liberal scientific community during the previous decade, V. I. Vernadskii, founder and chairman of the academy's Commission for the Study of Natural Productive Forces (KEPS). He was also close to Vernadskii's former student Alexander Fersman, the scientific secretary of KEPS who was elected a full member of the academy in 1918. (The Soviet government was to foster this trend toward dominance of the natural scientists in the academy by its policy of budget appropriations after 1917.)

Although the size of the Academy of Sciences in 1917–18 is known, the exact number of natural scientists who did research professionally in Russia during this period is not. In fact, one of the complaints of the scientific intelligentsia during the late tsarist period was that no survey of scientists or scientific insitutions had ever been undertaken by the government, a situation the Academy of Sciences set out to rectify in 1918. Until that time, the academy complained, Russian scientists had to turn to a German yearbook, *Minerva*, for up-to-date surveys and information about developments in Russian science. This German source was neither comprehensive nor necessarily accurate. The academy's survey of scientists and scientific institutions in Russia was, however, interrupted by the 1917 revolutions and Civil War. The first volume, *Nauka v Rossii*, was not published until the 1920s.[14] The best estimate is that in 1914 there were approximately 12,000 professional research scholars in Imperial Russia, but this number includes scholars in the humanities, including theology, the social sciences, engineering, and agronomy as well as the natural sciences.[15]

To estimate the number of professionals in the natural sciences (physics, mathematics, chemistry, the earth sciences and biology primarily) is much more difficult. We do know that in the period between 1904 and 1913, only about one-sixth of all the higher degrees (*magister* and doctoral degrees) granted by Russian universities were in the physical and mathematical sciences.[16] Because most Russian natural scientists received their higher degrees from a Russian university by this time, the proportion provides some guide to the percentage of scholars who worked in the natural sciences, albeit an unreliable one. According to figures compiled by the Soviet government, by 1918 there were 7,326 professional scholars in the RSFSR (excluding the Ukraine and border areas.)[17] Again, however, the data is not broken down by disciplines, and these figures include those in the humanities, social sciences, and technology.

By 1928, according to Soviet data, these numbers had grown to 14,805 for the RSFSR, with more than half in the "exact and applied sciences," but this larger proportion no doubt owed to the Soviet government's active policy of favoring natural science and technology over other areas of research.[18] My best guess is that beween one-sixth and one-third of the professional researchers in Russia by 1914 were natural scientists, that is, between 2,000 and 4,000. They were employed mostly in higher education, although increasing numbers worked as consultants to government and industry and an unknown number worked full-time in government ministries or in government technical services such as the Geological Committee (which employed 114 scientists by 1916).[19] Few worked full time in private industry, in the Academy of Sciences, or in the tiny number of private science institutes that existed by 1917. Their numbers are unlikely to have grown much by 1917–18, given the war and the fact that many university students were drafted or volunteered for military service.

In other words, the group we are considering here is unlikely by 1918 to have represented more than a few thousand active researchers, a minuscule part of Soviet Russia's population of well over one hundred million persons (excluding Poland, the Ukraine, Finland, the Caucasus, and Central Asia). Although the cooperation of this group was certainly not necessary for the Bolsheviks to take power and perhaps not even necessary for them to hold power in the short run, over the long term Bolsheviks such as Lenin and Lunacharskii could not conceive of building the Soviet state or a communist society without their help. The Russian scientific community, though small, represented for a significant part of the Bolshevik leadership an essential element of the future that they had seized power to build.

In January 1918, a special section of the Commission of Education was created for the "mobilization of scientific forces" to aid the Soviet government. It was headed by a former Menshevik who joined the Communist Party in 1918, L. G. Shapiro. Shapiro promptly met with Sergei Oldenburg and presented him with a request that the academy aid the Soviet government in matters requiring scientific expertise, particularly in areas related to the economy and social policy. Shapiro's written proposal was that the academy create a special commission for this purpose that would draw on the talents of all scientists in the country, not just those associated with the academy.[20] Shortly after Shapiro submitted this proposal, he also approached one of the officers of the Moscow Society of Agriculture, a group of biologists and agricultural scientists, as well as the Petrograd Association for the Development and Dissemination of the Positive Sciences and asked for their cooperation with the new government. The vice president of the Moscow Agricultural Society immediately turned to the Academy of Sciences to ask its opinion of such cooperation. He told Shapiro that the society would probably not oppose such cooperation with the Soviet government, especially if it could be conducted under the general supervision of the Academy of Sciences.[21]

According to the mathematician Steklov's diary entry for January 24, 1918, Oldenburg reported to a general meeting of the academy that Shapiro had promised the academy "full preservation of its independence."[22] On January 29, the commissar of education, Lunacharskii, reported to the Education Commission (Narkompros) that the academy was ready to aid it and that VSNKh and had agreed to enter into talks about reform of the academy.[23] Lunacharskii mentioned nothing about a promise to preserve the independence of the academy, and the published report of the academy's discussions of this first approach from the government for cooperation makes no mention of the academy's willingness to consider reform of its structure. Thus, from the beginning of formal talks between the Soviet government and the Academy of Sciences, two issues surfaced that were to become points of friction between the Soviet authorities and members of the academy. Nonetheless, other factors drove the two groups together as well: the academy, traditionally a state-supported institution, needed money to operate and protection from popular forces among the radical intelligentsia and working class (such as the Proletkult movement and the Education Department of the Petrograd regional government [Sevpros]) that wanted to abolish it altogether.

A general meeting of the academy discussed Shapiro's proposal on February 16(3) and formed a commission to prepare a reply. Alexander Fersman, the academic secretary of KEPS, wrote this commission a long memorandum in which he objected to giving the Soviet government advice on particular, specialized segments of the economy. The academy, he believed, should continue to concern itself with broad scientific questions. He added, "In these grave moments of Russian reality, the task of conserving what we have must take precedence over the idea of new tasks."[24] A few days later, the academy formulated its reply to Shapiro. It was couched in vague and general terms. The academy, in essence, indicated that it would judge each request for help from the government on its own merits and would help if equipped to do so. The main task of the academy, the reply emphasized, was to foster scientific creativity, but it would assist the government where possible "for the good of Russia." The academy's reply was followed a few days later by a request from Oldenburg for an advance to the academy of 65,000 rubles. On March 5, Lunacharskii wrote the academy disagreeing with the implication that it was not properly equipped to aid the government on economic and technical problems and urging cooperation. On March 9, Oldenburg again wrote Lunacharskii, asking for money for the academy. This time Narkompros came forward with a generous appropriation and also intervened with the local

Petrograd authorities to prevent some of the academy's space from being re-quisitioned as living quarters for outsiders. Lunacharskii also assured the aca-demy that its press would not be seized or closed down, a fear that may have been provoked by the actions of the Soviet government in closing opposition newspapers in this period.[25]

By March 24, Fersman apparently had a change of heart and sent a memo-randum from KEPS outlining the concrete ways in which it was willing to help the Soviet economy. That same day, the president of the academy, Karpinskii, sent a letter to Lunacharskii indicating that the academy had not ceased work-ing a single day since the October Revolution. At the same time he complained of the popular view in Soviet circles that intellectual workers were somehow privileged and undemocratic. A week later (April 2) Oldenburg again wrote Lunacharskii asking for money, this time specifically to support KEPS, which he indicated had never had a regular budget under the tsarist government. By early April, Lunacharskii reported to Lenin and to the Council of People's Commissars (Sovnarkom) the academy's readiness to cooperate with the gov-ernment. On April 5, 1918, Luncharskii announced this publicly with a news-paper article about the academy, and on April 19, the Soviet government issued its first public decree in the area of science and announced that it was financing the work of the academy to study the natural productive resources of Russia.[26]

Although Lenin apparently took no direct role in these early negotiations with the academy, he was pleased with the initial results. As Lunacharskii remembered Lenin's reaction during the April Sovnarkom meeting, "Vladimir Il'ich responded to my report about the Academy of Sciences that it was nec-essary to support it financially, to motivate it to take those steps which would link its work with our tasks, that it was necessary to find support there among the more progressive scientists."[27] Lenin advised Lunacharskii to publicize widely the academy's agreement to cooperate with the Soviet government. "The fact that they wish to help us is good," he reportedly told Lunacharskii. "Tell the whole world that the Academy of Sciences has recognized our govern-ment."[28]

Soviet historians consider Lenin's desire to attract "bourgeois specialists" such as scientists as part of his general strategy of proletarian class struggle, in this case to detach professionals from support of the bourgeoisie in an effort to weaken and divide the opposition. This may be true for the later Civil War period (1919–20), but one should be cautious in drawing such a conclusion about these early months of Soviet rule. The negotiations between the Soviet government and scientists during this early period took place primarily at the level of Narkompros. Lenin and most other party and government leaders were preoccupied with much more pressing matters in the early months of Soviet rule, such as ending the strikes of public employees and conducting peace negotiations with Germany. No documentary evidence has come to light in-dicating that Lenin paid a great deal of attention to the academy prior to April. One should be careful about reading back into the record arguments that Lenin made during the party debates of 1919 over the use of "bourgeois specialists," arguments justifying their use as a form of "class struggle," giving "experts" higher pay and other privileges. To note this is not to deny that securing the cooperation of the academy and other members of the scientific and technical intelligentsia did, in fact, objectively weaken the middle-class opposition to the Bolsheviks and aided the process of detaching a large part of the professional middle class from possible attempts to create a more unified opposition to Bolshevik rule. This doubtless was a consequence, but that it was among the original intentions of early Bolshevik talks with the Academy of Sciences is unclear.

In March and April 1918, the Soviet government also began to formulate more general principles as the basis of a science policy. In the March 1918 issue of the journal *The National Economy [Narodnoe khoziaistvo]*, an article appeared under the title "The Mobilization of Science." Because it was signed with the initials L. Sh. and Lev Shapiro was the head of Narkompros's section for the mobilization of scientific forces, it likely represented an official view from within Narkompros. It emphasized several points that were to become shibboleths of Soviet science: the need to bring science closer to production, the need for more collective forms of scientific research, and the requirement for centralized state regulation and direction of scientific research. The latter was especially acute in a country such as Russia, where qualified scientists were few in number and dispersed in their concerns and in their institutional affiliations.[29] Although no direct reaction by scientists to this article has been found, a close reading of their articles and statements over the next several years indicate that leading spokesmen for the scientific community had strong reservations about these principles.[30] Many, if not most, favored increased application of science to problems of the economy, but those in scientific research feared a neglect of more fundamental questions. The trend in world science toward more collective forms of research in large institutes and laboratories was undeniable, but prominent spokesmen like Alexander Fersman qualified the desirability of trend by indicating that much of the work of synthesis in science was still the task of individuals. Their creativity depended on fostering an environment that encouraged individuality, openness to debate, and critical thinking by individuals.[31] Regarding the third point in the article, state direction and planning of science, organized groups of scientists throughout this early period reiterated the need for scientists themselves to determine the direction of science, the need for freedom to organize autonomous groups that would work closely with the government but would not be subsumed within it.[32]

In April 1918, Lenin outlined some of his preliminary thinking about science and the needs of the economy. His notes were sketchy but constituted his first written attempt at a plan for the reorganization of industry and the economy of Russia. He wanted VSNKh to ask the Academy of Sciences to appoint scientific and technical specialists to a series of commissions that would develop detailed plans for the more rational distribution of industry, closer to sources of raw materials. With the lessons of World War I acutely in mind, particularly the consequences of the blockade that cut Russia off from Germany and from easy access to the allies, Lenin also outlined the need to develop more self-sufficiency in raw materials and manufactures that had earlier been imported. Lenin also highlighted a plan for the rapid electrification of Russia.[33] The academy and other scientists quickly picked up on these general points and in response began proposing research programs and new scientific institutes. Already in April, KEPS began to organize new sections that later evolved into institutes in the applied sciences: sections to find and study rare elements, new sources of fuel and raw materials like iron; a section on optical technology (an area in which Russia had been dependent on the German industry); and so on.[34]

By April the Academy of Sciences was eager to show the government its interest in conducting work in such areas of applied science, now that the government had demonstrated its willingness to provide funds and encouragement. Despite this rapprochement between scientists and the Soviet state, evidence of conflict is also abundant in the years 1918–19. Between April and July 1918, the secretary of the Sovnarkom, N. P. Gorbunov, began to conduct talks with large numbers of scientists about the needs of the economy and Russian science. In June alone Gorbunov turned to the academy twice to express Lenin's desire for their views about the tasks of Russian science, in response to which KEPS drafted a memorandum, "On the Tasks of Scientific Construction." While Lenin and Gorbunov were following a technocratic model in seeking to involve scientists and other specialists in government commissions and as consultants on a variety of practical problems, Narkompros and the local education department of the Petrograd regional government in April began to take a different direction, an approach aimed at changing the institutional structure of science. Narkompros's direction increasingly alarmed not only scientists, but Gorbunov and Lenin as well. Narkompros began to work out plans and pressure for the reform and democratization of scientific institutions. (The head of the Education Department of Petrograd, M. P. Kristi, even went so far as to propose in this period the abolition of the Academy of Sciences as a "completely unnecessary survival of a false class epoch and class society."[35]) In March 1918, Narkompros abolished the section for the mobilization of science and replaced it with the Scientific Section (NO), which had two responsible workers: L. G. Shapiro and its new head, a young astronomer, V. T. Ter-Oganesov, who began to work on a reform plan for Russian science.

Until August, the Scientific Section of Narkompros was the only government bureau whose primary responsibility was the supervision of Russian scientific institutions and the development of science policy. It was created by Narkompros with the specific charge to make the reform of scientific institutions its first priority. The assistant commissar of education, M. P. Pokrovskii, who took a dim view of academics and professors from the old regime,[36] was apparently one of the first to suggest, at a meeting of the collegium of Narkompros on April 24, 1918, that this reform take the general direction of creating an association of Russian science, to which the Academy of Sciences would be transferred.[37] According to the diary of the vice president of the academy, Steklov, by late March and early April 1918, Ter-Oganesov began to talk to academy members about the creation of a "federation of scientific societies."[38] By June 1918, L. G. Shapiro was already discussing the details of such a reform project with Sergei Oldenburg.[39] Ter-Oganesov reported to Narkompros that the association would include "representatives of scientific societies and institutions and would be a body to which the government could turn for the solution of problems in all branches of knowledge."[40] Although the advocates of this plan spoke of it as creating a kind of "parliament of scientific opinion," they also intended it to be directed and coordinated by the government and closely linked to the tasks of economic development.

Members of the Academy of Sciences at first treated this plan cautiously. They began to propose their own plans. For example, in June 1918 Fersman sent Narkompros a plan that called for the creation of a "Union of Scientific Organizations." Bastrakova denies that this was a counterplan, but her own analysis of differences between the Narkompros project and academy project suggests otherwise. The plans differed both in terms of internal organization and, most significantly, in terms of the new body's relationship to the state. The Narkompros project made it clear that its association would be subordinate to the government. The academy project, however, foresaw that the Union of Scientific Institutions, would receive financial support from the state but remain independent and self-governing; only science and its workers were considered competent to establish the form and direction of their work and their relationship to the government.[41]

Beyond the assertion of independence, there is a further hint that scientists, particularly in the academy, were disturbed by the Narkompros plan and concerned about the fate of the academy should it be subsumed in the proposed association. Gorbunov, who had been conducting extensive talks with scientists since April, wrote a letter to the Central Committee of the Communist Party in July protesting that the Narkompros reform plan "would harm an institution of worldwide prestige and hinder active cooperation between scientists and the Soviet government."[42] What provoked this sharp reaction and apparently also hardened the opposition of the academy was a new variant of the Narkompros plan produced in the summer of 1918 that clearly threatened the existence of the academy and the continuance of its traditions. In January 1919, the president of the academy, Karpinskii, wrote directly to Narkompros warning of the dangers contained in its reform plan. In this same period, Lenin apparently had several conversations with Lunacharskii, telling him that reform of the academy must await a "quieter time" and warning him against breaking any "valuable china" in the academy. Members of the academy, Lenin indicated, had shown a cooperative attitude toward the Soviet government, and Narkompros's plans threatened to disrupt that relationship. What probably happened is that prominent members of the academy, increasingly alarmed by what they were hearing from officials in Narkompros, attempted to find patrons for their interests by appealing to prominent Bolsheviks outside Lunacharskii's bailiwick. Gorbunov was readily available and was close to Lenin. He was also a young chemical engineer (who received his degree in 1917), someone who was impressed by the authority of scientific greybeards, with whom he established good working relations in subsequent years.[43] The concern of academy members may have been what motivated Gorbunov's offer to the party's Central Committee, judging from another instance in which scientists sought to reach Lenin's ear.

On August 15, 1919, Sergei Oldenburg wrote to the well-known physicist P. P. Lazarev, who at that time was conducting field studies in the Ukraine. He pleaded with Lazarev to use his influence with the prominent Bolshevik engineer L. B. Krasin to gain Lenin's help. (Krasin headed the state's Commission for Supply of the Red Army and used this important position to aid Lazarev's research with supplies and other forms of assistance.) Krasin, a long-time associate of Lenin, was in frequent contact with the Soviet leader during the Civil War, and Oldenburg hoped that he might intervene on the academy's behalf. As Oldenburg wrote Lazarev,

> A black cloud from Moscow, they say, is hanging over the Academy: Artem'ev and Ter-Oganesov [officials of Narkompros] have some kind of plan for the complete liquidation of the Academy simply by decree. No one and nothing, of course, can abolish science while even one person is still alive, but it is easy to disorganize it. Talk with Krasin, ask him to speak with Lenin, who is an intelligent man and understands that the liquidation of the Academy of Sciences would bring shame on any government.[44]

Whether Krasin spoke directly with Lenin about this issue is unclear from the record, but in 1919 Lenin intervened to stop the Narkompros plan. He called in Lunacharskii several times to express his concern, telling him, according to Lunacharskii's account published in 1925, "It is not necessary to let the Academy be devoured by a few Communist-fanatics." Lunacharskii says that he defended the need to adapt the academy to existing governmental institutions and prevent it from remaining "a state within a state" but agreed with Lenin that the Narkompros plan was not appropriate or timely.[45]

Lenin obviously was not opposed to an eventual reform of the academy that would bring it more tightly under Soviet control, but he opposed such attempts in the middle of a civil war when he considered the cooperation of the academy important to Soviet goals. Beyond that, Lenin did not fully trust former "left Bolsheviks" like Lunacharskii and Pokrovskii because of their longtime association with the radical cultural policies of the Proletkult movement, and this probably heightened his concern about their aims regarding the academy.[46] For their part, the leaders of the academy proposed a different reform plan to Narkompros in 1919. Their plan was based on the recommendations of a commission created within the academy to reexamine its charter and propose changes. In creating such a commission, the Academy of Sciences had responded to pressure from Narkompros, but in July 1919, Narkompros rejected the academy's plan as too mild and "not conforming with the spirit of the times."[47]

In general, by 1920 the Academy of Sciences had become a more open and democratic institution than the old Imperial Academy of Sciences, and it remained relatively autonomous from the Soviet government, although completely dependent on it financially. By 1920 ten full members were elected under the new rules to replace twelve academicians who had died since 1917, most of them at an advanced age. Many of the new members were young; Fersman, for example, was only thirty-five when he was elected a full member in 1918, and A. F. Ioffe was not yet forty, when elected in 1920. (Ioffe, who was elected unanimously by the academy, was its first Jewish member, and his election, proposed by more than twenty scientists within and without the academy, would have been impossible in late Imperial Russia.) A number of these new members were proposed by universities and scientific institutions outside the academy, but one recent Soviet historian believes that the scientific community as a whole, although it gained the right to do so, generally did not participate in the affairs of the academy, even in the election of new members.[48]

While making compromises with the Soviet government, the scientific community was able to defend effectively many of its interests during this period. This was in part because of divisions within the Soviet leadership over how to deal with the scientific-technical intelligentsia, in part because of the government's preoccupation with the Civil War, and in part because the system of scientific research became more diversified and decentralized during this period, despite official rhetoric about the need for centralized direction and coordination. The mixed public-private system of scientific research that replaced its predecessor allowed scientists a good deal of self-governance and flexibility for promoting and protecting their interests. The small size of the scientific community meant that the government's expansion of the scientific network created many opportunities for ambitious entrepreneurs among established scientists to organize their own institutes and play an important role as consultants and advisors to the government. Most of the established scientists who chose to be active organizers in this period remained prominent leaders in their respective fields for the remainder of their lives. In that sense, the Civil War period was formative for the history of Soviet science for many decades to come, and it was the Civil War cohort of scientists that dominated Soviet science for the next three decades.

One of the first steps toward the diversification and decentralization of the network of scientific research was taken during the fall of 1918 when Narkompros lost its monopoly of supervision over scientific institutions. In June of 1918, N. P. Gorbunov, after several months of talks with the scientific community, wrote a letter to the Bolshevik Central Committee severely criticizing Narkompros for its lack of accomplishment in mobilizing science for Soviet goals. He was particularly critical of its inability to organize effectively a system of scientific advisors for industry. Gorbunov sent forward a plan of his own: that a special section of VSNKh be created to organize a scientific network to serve industry. He proposed taking away from Narkompros a whole series of scientific institutions, including the Academy of Sciences, and placing them under this special section of VSNKh. The essence of Gorbunov's proposal was accepted by the Soviet government although his suggestion that the academy be transferred to this new body was not included in the project's final form. On August 16, 1918, the new Scientific-Technical Section of VSNKh (NTO) was created by a Sovnarkom decree. Gorbunov was appointed its head.[49]

The Soviet historian Bastrakova believes that such an institution as the NTO met not only the needs of Soviet industry, but also the desires of many prominent Soviet scientists. She cites a similar proposal made at about the same time for an All-Russian Association of Experimental Research that would create a network to aid the economy. This proposal was sponsored by the mathematician A. N. Krylov, who had been a prominent advisor to the tsarist military and then to the Red Army, and by the geologist F. Iu. Levinson-Lessing, a well-known Petrograd scientist. Because the proposal has not been published, it is difficult to judge how similar it was in all details to the proposal for the NTO. One difference, however, which has been noted by the Soviet historian Kol'tsov, is significant. The association proposed by scientists was an independent organization of scientists that would advise VSNKh but would remain autonomous from the government.[50]

Once created, the NTO moved much more quickly than Narkompros to directly involve prominent Russian scientists in its work. In contrast, the scientific section of Narkompros was run by a small staff of young Soviet bureaucrats who had some scientific training but who kept the bulk of the scientific community at arm's length, refusing to approve any kind of representative organization of scientists to advise them.[51] Gorbunov, on the other hand, moved quickly to create within the NTO two commissions of scientists with which he worked closely, one centered in Petrograd, headed by the prominent chemist N. S. Kurnakov, and the other located in Moscow, headed by M. M. Novikov, the rector of Moscow University (later expelled from the USSR for his role in the academic strikes of 1922). By 1919, over two hundred prominent scientists and technical specialists were involved in the work of the NTO.[52]

This is not to imply that scientists were able to dictate terms to the leadership of the NTO. For example, in the summer of 1919 the Petrograd Scientific Commission sent the NTO a list of proposed research topics for the NTO to fund. Gorbunov refused, telling the scientists that their topics were too theoretical and did not meet the needs of Soviet industry. At the present time, he indicated, resources were too scarce to sponsor such topics, although he did not rule out their funding in more peaceful times. One Soviet historian indicates that by the end of 1918, the NTO had begun to function virtually as an independent commissariat of science. It acquired the former tsarist laboratory for military research, the former Bureau of Weights and Measures, the Committee on Inventions, the laboratories that once belonged to the Ledentsov Society, the industrial labs that had belonged to private industry, and so on. It was also responsive to proposals from scientists and other experts to organize new institutes, as long as they were in the area of applied science or technology. By 1920, the NTO supervised some sixteen specialized institutes and labs, most of them organized over the previous two years. These included the Central Aerodynamic-Hydrological Institute (TsAGI), which became the main research center for the aviation industry; the automotive lab that developed into the principal research body for the development of an indigenous truck and automobile industry; an Institute for Food Research, another for fertilizers, one for chemical preparations, and so on. During the Civil War period, most of these institutes were small (with an average size of twenty to twenty-five employees), but they provided a nucleus for future expansion.[53]

During the Civil War period more than forty new scientific research institutes were created, more than half of the seventy that existed by 1922. Besides those under the jurisdiction of the NTO, a number were organized in various commissariats, such as the Commissariats of Agriculture and Health. The former palaces of the Romanovs, the mansions of the nobility and the upper bourgeoisie were often turned over to such research complexes. Although severe shortages of virtually everything needed for research greatly hampered work, many scientists were clearly impressed by the rapidity with which so many of their proposals were accepted and instituted by various branches of the government. Applied research became centered in the NTO and in commissariats that supervised branches of the economy outside of industry. Institutes in areas of more fundamental research generally remained under the Academy of Sciences or were created by Narkompros and placed under its jurisdiction. (For example, the X-ray Institute and the Optical Institute, in which much fundamental research on the structure of matter was conducted under the auspices of A. F. Ioffe, were created in this period and placed under Narkompros.)[54]

Thus, for scientists the period of War Communism did not see the creation of a monolithic or highly centralized system of scientific research, but one that remained flexible and largely decentralized. While the opportunities grew for scientists to display initiative and realize a number of projects that they had only dreamed about before 1917, the leaders of the scientific community remained, with good reason, concerned about long-range Soviet plans for science, and they were determined to keep as much corporate autonomy and room for maneuver as possible. Most projects put forward by scientists during this period contained a demand for autonomy, demands that were always rejected in principle by Soviet authorities.[55] Scientific workers were also the last major professional group to be organized into a Soviet-controlled union, something that did not occur until 1923. Throughout the Civil War period, a significant element of the scientific community included members of an independent union that lobbied for their interests and attempted to improve living and working conditions.

Living and Working Conditions, 1918–21

The independent union referred to above was initiated by prominent members of the Academy of Sciences during 1917, before the Bolshevik takeover. At the time, the president of the academy, Karpinskii, headed up something called the Permanent Conference of Representatives of Scientific Institutions and Higher Education, which was intended as a kind of lobby with the Provisional Government for the professional interest of scholars. This body appears to have been quiescent during the first year after the Bolshevik takeover but was reactivated by a conference held in October-November of 1918. (It is probably not coincidental, in light of its later activity, that its reinvigoration came within a month or so after the beginning of the Red Terror. The terror, which was often directed indiscriminately at middle-class elements, as well as remnants of the old regime, led to the arrest and detention of many professional people.)[56] This conference created an organization known as the Union of Scientific Institutions and Higher Education, with an elected directorate that included Karpinskii, Oldenburg, the prominent engineer Osadchii, Steklov, Fersman, and other important scientists. It enjoyed the patronage and strong support of the writer Maxim Gorkii, a critic of the Bolsheviks who soon after the February 1917 revolution had begun to work with prominent Petrograd scientists on a number of projects for the popularization of science. Gorkii remained close to the scientific intelligentsia until he left the Soviet Union for Italy in the early 1920s.[57]

The union's primary activity as the Civil War gained momentum in late 1918 through 1920 appears to have been measures to protect scholars from hunger and from arbitrary arrest by the Soviet government. For example, in 1919 the union asked the Commissariat of Food for ration cards for its members; it also organized the purchase of food on the free market in the Ukraine for shipment to Moscow and Petrograd; and it requested all member institutions to send lists of their members to protect them from arbitrary searches and arrests. When members of these institutions were arrested, the union asked member institutions to send detailed information about the circumstances of arrest so that it could intervene with the Cheka or other appropriate Soviet bodies.[58] A recent Soviet historian has characterized the union as oppositional in mood, though not openly anti-Soviet;[59] it appears, however, to have been tolerated during the Civil War period, perhaps in large part because of the prominence of its leaders and Lenin's policy of appeasing the scientific community, as long as its members did not work against the Soviet government.

The controversy over the existence of this independent union came to a head only after the Civil War, when in 1921–22 it opposed Narkompros's plan to reform higher education and severely restrict the autonomy of the universities. In a letter to Lenin of June 8, 1921, the assistant commissar of education, Pokrovskii, asked for the immediate liquidation of this independent body, maintaining that it was "trying to extend university autonomy to limits which it has never before enjoyed in Russia."[60] Here he differed with the commissar of education, Lunacharskii, who conceded the oppositional nature of the union but counseled a more patient approach of negotiation and conciliation. The standard Soviet policy in this period was to abolish independent unions of professional groups such as engineers, physicians, and scientists and incorporate them in separate subsections of Soviet-controlled, mass unions that included all workers in a particular branch of the economy, such as health workers, engineering-technical workers, and cultural-education-scientific workers. Such a mass union for the latter group, the All-Russian Union of Cultural-Educational Workers (*Vserabotpros*) had been created in 1919–20 but held little attraction for prominent professors and scientists. In 1921, Vserabotpros created a separate section for scientific workers (SNR), but it was another two years before the independent Union of Scientific Institutions and Higher Education ceased to exist and, under pressure from Soviet authorities, part of its leadership agreed to join the directorate of SNR.

Partly because of the Red Terror, partly because of the increasing deterioration of the economic situation, living and working conditions for scientists began to worsen in the fall of 1918. The Soviet government reacted slowly to their complaints. Lenin and the central government waited well over a year after September 1918 before responding with firm measures of support, and even then, frequent personal intervention by Lenin was required to prevent abuses by local officials. To be more specific, on September 25, 1918, the permanent secretary of the Academy of Sciences first wrote Narkompros about deteriorating conditions for members of the research community. Oldenburg asked for prompt measures to improve their food, to free them from being drafted for compulsory physical labor, and to protect their apartments from being requisitioned by local authorities.[61] The same month Maksim Gorkii whose newspaper *Novaia zhizn'* had opposed the October Revolution and had continued to criticize the Soviet government until it was closed down in the summer of 1918, traveled from his home in Petrograd to meet personally with Lenin. One of his purposes was to discuss the role of the scientific intelligenstia in the revolution. Gorkii had strong doubts about the ability of the proletariat to create a civilized society on its own. Lenin at that time made no concessions but pointed out the hostile attitude of the scientific intelligentsia to the Bolshevik revolution and simply asked Gorkii to convince them to cooperate more. Given Gorkii's past and future record of active intervention for arrested intellectuals and professional people, it seems likely that this flurry of complaints in September and October 1918 was linked to the Red Terror and it effects on the scientific intelligentsia. Soviet secondary works, however, do not spell out the link explicitly or detail the effects of terror on scientists.[62]

On October 4, 1918, Lunacharskii met with Oldenburg to discuss the concerns of scientists, and they talked at that time about the creation of a special commission "to ease the situation of intellectual workers."[63] Such a commission was not actually created until early 1920, toward the end of the Civil War. Hunger, however, reached its height in Petrograd during the winter of 1918–19. In place of bread many residents of the city were reduced to eating oats intended for horses. The use of terror by the regime was particularly unrestrained in Petrograd in the year between the fall of 1918 and the fall of 1919 as the Civil War gained momentum. At this time, some scientists, especially the more elderly and sickly, began to die of exhaustion and starvation. How many scientists were arrested or executed is more difficult to establish, but this year was undoubtedly the most difficult for members of the scientific intelligentsia living under Soviet rule.[64] In Petrograd, Gorkii and his companion Maria Andreeva organized an unofficial committee to aid the intelligentsia. They organized a cafeteria for the hungry, and under their direction a volunteer group of nurses visited the elderly and ill among the intelligentsia, bringing food and medicine. This unofficial committee was viewed with great suspicion by Dzerzhinskii and the Cheka, which periodically harassed it and arrested individuals whom the authorities viewed as anti-Soviet. Gorkii's unofficial committee, which included a number of prominent natural scientists, became the basis for the Petrograd Commission for Improving the Living Conditions of Scholars, given official status by the Soviet government in early 1920.[65]

On February 19, 1919, at the urging of Lunacharskii, the local Petrograd government wrote the president of the academy offering him Red Army rations sufficient for one hundred scholars. Considering that by the end of 1920 some six thousand rations were being distributed to the scientific community of Petrograd, this first offer seems woefully inadequate. One of the problems, of course, was strong opposition within the Communist Party to giving preferential treatment to such "bourgeois specialists." This issue came to a head at the Eighth Party Congress, held in March 1919, when Lenin's policy of preferential treatment for "bourgeois specialists" who worked loyally for the Soviet regime was officially adopted as party policy.[66] It took many more months for that policy to be instituted.

The trend during much of 1918 and early 1919 was in the opposite direction. For example, a policy of wage leveling is reflected in Soviet wage scales published in this period. That policy aroused strong opposition from the scholarly community, since it reduced the pay of professors and other professional researchers close to the level of ordinary workers.[67] The Sovnarkom and the Council on Labor and Defense began to discuss pay scales for specialists, including scientists, beginning January 2, 1919, and continued to do so through much of the spring and summer of 1919. On May 22, 1919, the Sovnarkom created a special commission headed by Lenin that was charged with revising such pay scales upward, to raise the material status of specialists above that of other occupational groups. By August these revised pay scales were being promulgated not only in the RSFSR but in the Ukraine and other Soviet-controlled areas.[68] Yet in a period when money had lost much or all of its value, such reforms were more symbolic than real.

Besides pay scales, scientists and other scholars had a number of additional complaints. Some scientists and scholars were drafted for physical labor and their apartments commandeered by local authorities. In March 1919, Karpinskii wrote Narkompros to complain about attempts by the commandant of the building in which most members of the Academy of Sciences lived to requisition their apartments. This remained a problem as late as October 1920, when Gorkii complained that scholars in Petrograd were still being deprived of part of their living quarters. On October 21, 1920, Lenin wrote a letter to a department of the Petrograd regional government. He stated that to allow a scholar an extra room for a study or laboratory was scarcely a sin and urged more leniency in this regard.[69] The documentary record does not show whether Lenin's letter, which was a politely worded request rather than an order, was honored or disregarded.

For scientists in Petrograd, as for other middle-class professionals, one of the most dangerous periods during the Civil War came in 1919 when the White general Iudenich approached Petrograd with his army. The first period of approach by Iudenich's army occurred between May and August; the second between the end of October and the end of November. On June 4, the Cheka began general searches of the middle-class districts in Petrograd with the help of workers' detachments, comprising some 20,000 men. Large caches of arms and documents were reportedly uncovered and many arrests of "bourgeois elements" took place. Those arrested, according to a recent Soviet source, included a large number of professors, engineers, artists, and other professionals who were held as hostages. Gorkii wrote a letter to Lenin protesting these arrests, but Lenin defended their necessity and indicated that those members of the intelligentsia who were working loyally for the Soviets were being treated generously and had nothing to fear.[70]

Large numbers of middle- and upper-class families had already fled Petrograd by the spring of 1919, either emigrating or searching for some quiet corner in the countryside where food would be more plentiful and the risk of being caught in the fighting less. Other large cities like Moscow were also affected by this exodus, although Petrograd seems to have suffered the greatest depopulation. Where did professionals such as natural scientists tend to congregate if they left Petrograd or Moscow? Large numbers went to three places in particular: the Ukraine, where food was thought to be easier to find; the Crimea, where many prosperous scientists had summer dachas and where the dangers of Civil War seemed less; and Siberia, particularly Tomsk, the site of Siberia's only university and its one technological institute. Some also ended up on other Siberian towns like Omsk, Irkutsk, and Vladivostok. Although the Civil War soon reached these regions, all three experienced a kind of cultural renaissance. In Siberia, a new university was created in Irkutsk, a new privately supported polytechnic in Vladivostok, an Institute of Agriculture and

Industry in Omsk, and an Institute for the Study of Siberia in Tomsk. The latter institution had been discussed in 1917 but was only created in 1919 with the influx of intelligentsia from European Russia to the region.[71] It began with sixty members and was intended to study the natural history, geography, industry, ethnography, history, and economy of Siberia; in other words, it was to function as a kind of Siberian academy of sciences. The Siberian Institute was short-lived; it was closed down in 1920 with the establishment of Soviet rule in Tomsk. Some of the institutions created in this period, however, did survive, particularly the new higher educational institutions. A Siberian geological committee, also created during the Civil War, carried out important field explorations of coal, iron, and other mineral deposits despite the dangers from partisan detachments and banditry. At the end of the Civil War, this body remained, but as a branch of the Soviet-controlled Geological Committee in Petrograd.[72]

The Ukraine and the Crimea experienced similar cultural growth, despite often chaotic conditions. During 1918 a group of Ukrainian intellectuals, together with the geochemist V. I. Vernadskii, a member of the Imperial Academy of Sciences, founded the Ukrainian Academy of Sciences in Kiev. Vernadskii, who had moved from Petrograd to Ukraine in 1917 at his doctor's orders (he was diagnosed as suffering from tuberculosis), was named the first president of the Ukrainian academy and spent a great deal of effort trying to raise money for this new institution from the many governments that came and went in the Ukraine during 1919 and 1920.[73] One of his associates, the engineering professor S. P. Timoshenko (who later emigrated to the United States and taught for many years at Stanford), recalled that the Bolshevik government was more forthcoming with aid for the new academy than either the Petliura government or the Volunteer Army when they were in power in Kiev.[74] Vernadskii's own memoir about these years, however, indicates that, after traveling to the headquarters of the White government in Rostov and talking with its officials, they recognized the need for the academy and gave it financial support.[75] How much money actually reached the academy in Kiev from the Volunteer Army is uncertain, since lines of communication were frequently cut during the Civil War in the Ukraine. The academy lived largely on whatever handouts it could get from any of the existing governments.

The memoirs of Vernadskii and Timoshenko agree on one important point: the alienation they felt from all sides fighting in the Civil War. As much as both men disliked the Bolsheviks, they felt little attraction toward the Whites. Vernadskii wrote in his unpublished diary on December 29, 1919, "Both the Volunteer Army and the Bolsheviks did a mass of unclean deeds; and in the final analysis one was no better than the other."[76] Vernadskii argued with other scientists in the Ukrainian academy about whether or not the Bolsheviks would last. Vernadskii's view was that the popularity of Bolshevism was fading and their government would not last.[77] Yet he wavered on this question, noting at another point in his diary that if the Bolsheviks would stop their use of terror, the population would support them in large numbers.[78] A month earlier, he had already noted a loss of support for the Volunteer Army, which he criticized in his diary for being too selfish and class oriented, not thinking about the good of Russia as a whole.[79]

Fewer prominent natural scientists actively cooperated with the various White armies and governments than cooperated with the Soviets. Those who fled Bolshevik-controlled areas associated themselves primarily with cultural and educational activities rather than with active support of the White cause. Vernadskii, however, notes in his diary that he personally felt safer under the Volunteer Army than under the Bolsheviks or Petliura's Ukrainian nationalist regime because of his connections with the former tsarist government (strained though his relationship with that regime had been) and his high position in the Provisional Government.[80]

For scientists the Civil War was not an entirely unproductive period, although conditions tended to be somewhat better for theoreticians than for experimentalists, who suffered more from the shortages of supplies and equipment. Many who had been politically active before the war retreated into their scientific work. The winters in particular were difficult. A number of institutes simply closed down for a period of months. In other institutions the top floors were sealed off, and the staff huddled in a single room on the ground floor around small pot-bellied stoves that were dubbed "little bourgeois" (*burzhuyky*), drinking tea made from carrots and other vegetables or eating a thin gruel made from oats, trying to conserve their energy.[81] Finally, in December 1919, the central government issued a decree aimed at dealing with many of the complaints of the scientific intelligentsia. Based on a draft written by the assistant commissar of education, Pokrovskii, the decree ("On Improving the Situation of Scientific Specialists") was approved by the Sovnarkom on December 23, 1919. Yet at first it only applied to 500 scholars and 50 "literati," whose place on the list was to decided by a three-man commission composed of Pokrovskii, the Bolshevik engineer L. Ia. Karpov from VSNKh, and V. N. Iakovlev, a representative of the Commissariat of Supply. Those lucky enough to be placed on the list were exempted from compulsory military service and labor service not connected with their scientific work. They were also made eligible for a special ration, the so-called academic ration.[82]

Gradually, over the next year or so, the list of persons eligible for these rations was extended. Early in January 1920, a special Petrograd Commission for Improving the Living Conditions of Scholars (Petrokubu) was established, headed by Maksim Gorkii. It was based, as earlier noted, on the unofficial committee that Gorkii had organized as early as 1918 but that had suffered from the harassment of the Cheka and Petrograd regional government and party. In March 1920, Gorkii asked Lenin for 1,800 daily rations for scholars in Petrograd alone. Two weeks later, Lenin granted this request. In August, Gorkii asked the Sovnarkom to increase the allocation of academic rations in Petrograd to 2,000, and by 1921 over 6,000 daily rations were being distributed to Petrograd scholars and their families. But the continued flow of such supplies required frequent intervention by Lenin and the central authorities. For example, in October 1920, acting on a complaint of Gorkii, Lenin wrote the Petrograd authorities, demanding that they stop requisitioning supplies intended for Petrokubu. "This means that Petrograd has no right to requisition and appropriate, *without the permission of the center!*"[83] Lenin's intervention was requested several more times during 1920, in order to secure sufficient fuel for the Academy of Sciences' building and to stop the continued requisitioning of scientists' apartments by local authorities. Lenin's personal intervention was even required to obtain heated and guarded railway cars to take the academy's invaluable manuscript collections back to Petrograd from Saratov where they had been evacuated earlier in the Civil War.[84] One recent Soviet historian sees this as evidence of Lenin's concern for the well-being of the scientific community. Although Lenin's involvement becomes increasingly evident toward the end of the Civil War, it also reveals the degree to which the head of the Soviet state had to intervene directly to prevent abuses by local officials and see that the decrees of the central government were properly enforced.

Lenin and the Sovnarkom began to give more attention to the needs of the scientific intelligentsia toward the end of 1919 and the beginning of 1920 than they had for the preceding year or so. The memoir by Lenin's secretary, V. D. Bonch-Bruevich, suggests that his increased concern was sparked by I. P. Pavlov's request to leave the country.[85] Some time toward the end of 1919, the Noble prize–winning physiologist wrote the Soviet government asking permission to leave Russia so that he could continue his scientific work abroad. Bonch-Bruevich and Lenin thought this would be a serious blow to Soviet prestige abroad, where hostile propaganda emphasized the uncivilized nature of the Bolshevik regime and the decline of science and education under its rule. When Lenin saw the letter he blamed the Petrograd regional government for not looking after the needs of such eminent scientists. Bonch-Bruevich was instructed to write Pavlov, assuring him that the Soviet government would provide everything he needed to continue his work. Then Lenin told his secretary to telephone the chairman of the Petrograd soviet and inform him that he would be held personally responsible for Pavlov's safety and the well-being of his laboratory, his helpers, and his lab animals. Pavlov's answer to Bonch-Bruevich's letter was a detailed description of the difficult conditions in which Petrograd scientists were forced to live and work. Lenin instructed his secretary to reply that the government would take prompt measures to improve the situation of scientists. Bonch-Bruevich again wrote Pavlov requesting that he postpone his emigration from Russia, promising that the government would move rapidly to help scientists.

Lenin's secretary also advised the head of state to summon Gorkii to Moscow as soon as possible and place him at the head of a special society to help scholars and literati. Bonch-Bruevich knew of Gorkii's private efforts to provide help, and despite past differences with Gorkii, Lenin accepted his secretary's proposal. Thus, according to this account, Petrokubu was born in January 1920.[86] Yet as far as Pavlov was concerned, working and living conditions did not improve sufficiently. Although Pavlov remained in Petrograd, Lenin was required to sign a special decree a year after the events described above that established a commission of the Petrograd soviet "to create in the shortest possible time the most favorable conditions for assuring the scientific work of Academician Pavlov and his coworkers."[87] Gorkii was made head of this special three-man commission, which included M. P. Kristi from the Petrograd education department and another official of the Petrograd soviet.

By 1921, with the end of the Civil War, the scientific community began to survey the state of science in Soviet Russia. In a memorandum from the Academy of Sciences to the Sovnarkom and in articles and letters to their friends, prominent scientists saw reason for both hope and pessimism. In a protocol approved by the General Assembly of the Academy of Sciences in November 1920, the Academy warned of the grave situation in which Russian scientists found themselves. This protocol was sent to Lenin and the Sovnarkom in early December and resulted in a meeting between Lenin and prominent members of the scientific community in January 1921. There he assured them that measures would be taken to improve their living and working conditions. But on May 17, 1921, the academy again complained that little had been done:

> In the beginning of December 1920 the Russian Academy of Sciences turned to the Sovnarkom with a memorandum, referring to the critical situation in which Russian science and Russian scientists find themselves and pointing out those measures which must be taken without delay to avoid the destruction of science and scientists in Russia. A conference chaired by the Commissar of Education, with representatives from the Sovnarkom and various bureaus, acknowledged the correctness of suggestions made by the Academy; the Chairman of the Sovnarkom, meeting with representatives of the Academy and other scientific institutions, acknowledged the urgency of this whole business and instructed the Small Sovnarkom to examine it immediately. It seemed that government decisions and measures would be forthcoming when, for unknown reasons, everything came to a standstill. In the meantime, the situation has become more difficult, new developments, new sufferings among scientists and a sharp deterioration in their condition demonstrates convincingly how critical the situation is. The Russian Academy of Sciences considers its duty before the people and the nation to point out the destruction which threatens science and culture in Russia in the near furture if the immediate measures which it has pointed out, the importance of which have already been acknowledged by the government, are not taken.[88]

If immediate measures were not taken, the letter continued, Russian scientists and their families should be allowed to go abroad "where their health and lives will be preserved for scientific work." Thus the academy accompanied its demands with a veiled threat of a large-scale emigration of Russian scientists. They probably knew from Pavlov's experience that Soviet leaders would want to avoid such an embarrassment, especially as they sought diplomatic recognition and respectibility in Western Europe and America. Although the full protocol sent by the academy to the government has not been published, it is clear from published excerpts that the measures demanded by scientists included such things as an improvement in food, fuel, and other supplies. publication of a large backlog of scientific books and papers, reestablishment of scientific exchanges of information and personnel with the West, and so on.

Despite the tone of imminent peril of the academy's protocol, Russian scientists had a good deal to be proud of in their accomplishments over the previous four years. On the positive side was the growth of scientific institutions: since 1917 a number of new universities had been founded, mostly on the initiative of local intelligentsia; dozens of new research institutes, although mostly small, had also been founded with the help of various branches of the Soviet government, creating a system for supporting science that had existed only in nucleus form before 1917. For natural scientists who disliked the proletarianization of Soviet universities, the new network of research institutes provided a refuge into which they could withdraw in the years to come and devote their time exclusively to research, a possibility that was largely absent under the tsarist regime.

Prominent natural scientists like Alexander Fersman, while hailing the creation of such institutes, also believed that they might contain some dangers. Fersman, for example, warned against overspecialization, fearing that institutes composed exclusively of specialists in a single field could lose the broader view of a problem. He therefore recommended that such scientific organizations be composed of a variety of scientists who could communicate their differing knowledge and points of view to each other. Fersman also feared that too much emphasis on collective research might work to the disadvantage of individual creativity. "I see the future of scientific creativity in the harmonious combination of these two paths [individual and collective research]; and it will be destructive if either one of them triumphs by itself. . . . For different natures, for different minds there cannot be and must not be identical forms of creativity, and woe to that organization which would wish to impose such," Fersman warned. "Let collective creativity develop and let the individual mind work freely."[89]

The Academy of Sciences was heartened by the dispersion of scientific institutions and societies away from Moscow and Petrograd, the centers of science before the revolution, into provincial areas. The new universities were mostly in such areas, as was the new Ukrainian Academy of Sciences, which set the precedent for other provincial academies that were eventually established in various Soviet republics. Further aiding the spread and popularization of science was the creation of dozens of new societies for regional studies during the revolutionary and Civil War periods. Such groups dated back to the nineteenth century and had usually been centers for the local intelligentsia to study the ethnography, archaeology, and natural and human history of a particular region.[90] Not only did the number of such societies grow after 1917, but their emphasis shifted more toward the study of natural productive resources and local demography and economy, including statistical studies of such subjects.

Although these *kraeved* organizations were composed mostly of amateurs, the Academy of Sciences saw them as bases for the spread of scientific research and a scientific worldview. In 1919, the academy created the Central Bureau for Regional Studies to provide assistance to such local groups, which often established museums, study circles, lecture series, and so on. The first National Congress of Scientific Societies for the Study of Local Life was held in Moscow in 1921, and by 1922, the membership of such organizations was estimated at forty thousand.[91]

Besides the creation of many new institutions, scientists were heartened by their ability to protect the autonomy of such a venerable organization as the Academy of Sciences. For example, V. I. Vernadskii, who went abroad in 1922 to work at the Radium Institute in Paris, wrote in March of 1923 to his longtime friend I. I. Petrunkevich, the former zemstvo activist:

> Let me touch on the state of science in Russia. It seems to me that here [in the West] they do not recognize the huge cultural task that has been accomplished, accomplished in the face of sufferings, humiliations, destruction. Scientific work in Russia has not perished, but on the contrary is developing . . . scientific work in Russia has been preserved and lives a *vast* life thanks to a conscious act of the will. It has been necessary and will be necessary to fight for it every day, every step . . . I tell people [here] how this has been accomplished and how much has perished. People have died. . . . but not a single scientific organization has perished in these years. They have suffered much—and in the Ukraine, perhaps in connection with the chauvinistic policy of the Ukrainian Bolsheviks, the universities in particular [have suffered], but their scientific life has been preserved. The Russian Academy of Sciences is the single institution in which *nothing* has been touched. It remains as before, with full internal freedom. Of course, in a police state this freedom is relative and it is necessary to defend it continually. Much new has been created in Moscow and Petersburg, *de facto* much, although by comparison with the plans of 1915–17, little. And curiously enough, much has been created in the provinces.[92]

Vernadskii, no friend of Bolshevism, gave credit for what had been accomplished primarily to the scientific intelligentsia itself, and although it is clear that much of the initiative and effort to preserve and develop science did come from scientists, such accomplishments could not have taken place without the active support and cooperation of the central Bolshevik authorities. This was particularly true of Lenin and the Sovnarkom, Lunacharskii and Narkompros, Gorbunov and VSNKh, and the heads of many other central commissariats, such as the commissar of health, Semashko, who needed science and who protected the natural scientific community against their more zealous colleagues in the Communist Party and local soviets. In fact, one of the major conflicts that surfaced during the revolution and Civil War and remained an important issue in later years was the tension between egalitarianism and a technocratic approach. One was a popular movement to do away with privilege, among whose representatives scientists were frequently counted by the masses and more by local party and Soviet activists. The other was the more technocratic approach favored by central Bolshevik authorities like Lenin, who believed in the necessity of expertise and who established institutional means for consulting experts, providing in return protection and certain privileges. The community of natural scientists proved to be cohesive in exploiting to their own advantage such conflicts within the Soviet government and Bolshevik Party to prevent the centralization of science and protect the relative autonomy of many of their institutions.

When one compares the aims and accomplishments of the Soviet government toward science and the aims and accomplishments of scientists themselves, scientists appear to have had the advantage by 1921. As early as 1918, the Soviet government aimed at creating a centralized system of scientific research, planned and controlled by the government, not by scientists. Scientists preferred a diversified and decentralized system controlled by their own autonomous organizations. Although they did not achieve such control, by 1921 scientists enjoyed considerable influence in a diversified and decentralized system of government research organizations, in which there was little planning or central coordination, a system that was much more the product of institutional conflicts (for example, between Narkompros and VSNKh) than it was of Marxist-Leninist ideology. In terms of the historiographical debate over the relative importance of ideology versus pragmatism during the period of War Communism, this case study provides much evidence for those who argue the pragmatism of Soviet decisions. If ideology had an influence, it was primarily the ideology of the leaders of the scientific community, not Bolshevik ideology.

NOTES

1. Alfred J. Rieber, *Merchants and Entrepreneurs in Imperial Russia* (Chapel Hill, N.C., 1982).

2. S. Fediukin, *Velikii Oktiabr' i intelligentsiia* (Moscow, 1972); M. S. Bastrakova, *Stanovlenie sovetskoi sistemy organizatsii nauki, 1917–1922* (Moscow, 1972), p. 156.

3. Bastrakova, p. 124.

4. S. Reznik, *Nikolai Vavilov* (Moscow, 1968), p. 104.

5. Letter of Vernadskii to Fersman, dated Feb. 9, 1918, in *Aleksandr Fersman. Zhizn' i deiatel'nost* (Moscow, 1965), pp. 419–20.

6. A. K. Kol'tsov, *Lenin i stanovlenie akademii nauk kak tsentra sovetskoi nauki* (Moscow, 1969), p. 44. In 1918 the prominent engineer and Moscow professor Grinevetskii authored a pamphlet that expressed similar views, but here I am concerned with the views of natural scientists rather than engineers.

7. V. P. Leikina-Svirskaia, *Russkaia intelligentsiia v 1900–1917 gg.* (Moscow, 1981), p. 95.

8. TsGA RSFSR, f. 2306, op. 19, ed. khr. 220, 1.27, cited in Bastrakova, p. 59.

9. I. I. Mochalov, *Vladimir Ivanovich Vernadskii, 1863–1945* (Moscow, 1982), p. 187.

10. Letter of A. P. Karpinskii to A. V. Lunacharskii March 24, 1918. The text of

this letter is published in *Organizatsiia nauki v pervye gody Sovetskoi vlasti, 1917–1925. Sbornik dokumentov* (Leningrad, 1968), pp. 113–15.

11. "Vospominaniia akademika S. F. Oldenburga o vstrechakh s V. I. Leninym v 1887 i 1921 godakh," in *Lenin i Akademiia nauk*, pp. 88–94. The great impression Lenin made on Oldenburg is corroborated by the memoirs of his friend V. I. Vernadskii and by Lenin's secretary, V. D. Bonch-Bruevich. Vernadskii's comment is to be found in Arkhiv Akademiia nauk, f. 518, op. 4, ed. khr. 45, 1. 12 and Bonch-Bruevich's in *Lenin i Akademiia nauk*, pp. 25–26.

12. Kol'tsov, p. 34.

13. Seven were in the physical and mathematical sciences, four in chemistry, four in the earth sciences, and five in biological sciences. AAN SSR, f. 410, op. 1, ed. khr. no. 94, 1. 4, cited in N. M. Mistriakova, "Struktura, nauchnye uchrezhdeniia i kadry AN SSR (1917–1940 gg.)," in *Organizatsiia nauchnoi deiatel'nosti* (Moscow, 1968), p. 214.

14. Bastrakova, p. 22.

15. L. V. Ivanova, *Formirovanie sovetskoi nauchnoi intelligentsii 1917–1927* (Moscow, 1980), p. 273.

16. A. Sinetskii, *Professorsko-prepodavatel'skie kadry vysshei shkoly SSSR* (Moscow, 1950), p. 30–35.

17. *Nauchnye kadry RSFSR* (Moscow, 1930), p. 7.

18. Ibid.

19. Leikina-Svirskaia, pp. 90–91.

20. Ivanova, p. 39.

21. See the letter of A. Stebut to S. F. Oldenburg, dated Feb. 19, 1918, and published in *Organizatsiia nauki v pervye gody Sovetskoi vlasti (1917–1925)* (Moscow, 1968), p. 106.

22. *Vestnik Akademii nauk*, 1967, no. 8, pp. 69–70.

23. The report of this meeting is contained in TSGA RSFSR, f. 2306, op. 19, ed. khr. 3, 1. 86, cited in Ivanova, p. 37.

24. Kol'tsov, p. 41.

25. George Leggett, *The Cheka: Lenin's Political Police* (Oxford, 1981), pp. 306–8.

26. See the article by Lunacharskii in *Novosti dni*, April 5, 1918, p. 1, and a more detailed account of Narkompros's negotiations with the academy in *Izvestiia*, April 12, 1918, p. 3. The Sovnarkom decree, signed April 12, 1918, was first published in *Izvestiia*, April 19, 1918.

27. *Ekonomicheskaia gazeta*, July 21, 1931, p. 3.

28. V. A. Ulianovskaia, *Formirovanie nauchnoi intelligentsii v SSSR, 1917–1927* (Moscow, 1966), p. 59.

29. *Narodnoe khoziaistvo*, 1918, no. 1, pp. 3–6.

30. See, for example, Alexander Fersman in *Nauka i ee rabotniki*, 1921, no. 1, p. 3ff.

31. Ibid.

32. Kol'tsov, pp. 99, 111, 123–24, 133.

33. "Nabrosok plana nauchno-tekhnicheskikh rabot," April 18–25, 1918, reprinted in *Lenin i Akademiia nauk*, pp. 44–47.

34. See the documents in *Organizatsiia nauki v pervye gody*, pp. 113–23.

35. Published in *Vestnik proveshcheniia soiuza kommun Severnoi oblasti*, 1919, nos. 6–8, pp. 15–23, cited in Bastrakova, pp. 97–98 and Kol'tsov, p. 61.

36. Sheila Fitzpatrick, *The Commissariat of Enlightenment: Soviet Organization of Education and the Arts under Lunacharsky* (Cambridge, 1970), p. 75.

37. Bastrakova, p. 212, cited TsGA RSFSR, f 2306, op. 1, ed. khr. 35, 11. 95–96.

38. AAN SSSR, f. 162, op. 3, ed. khr. 171, 11. 41, 51–51 ob., st. 56, cited in Bastrakova, p. 100.

39. TSGA RSFSR, f. 2306, op. 19, ed. khr. 18, 1. 198, cited in Bastrakova, pp. 100–1.

40. Bastrakova, pp. 100–101.

41. Ibid., pp. 104–8.

42. TsGABKh SSSR, f. 3429, op. 60, ed. khr 20, 11. 207, 207 ob., cited in Bastrakova, p. 213.

43. See, for example, Fitzpatrick, pp. 71–72.

44. This letter is published in *Lenin i Akademiia nauk. Sbornik dokumentov*, p. 61.

45. *Novyi mir*, 1925, no. 10, p. 110; Kol'tsov, p. 63.

46. On the Proletkult during this period, see, for example, V. V. Gorbunov, "Iz istorii bor'by Kommunisticheskoi partii s sektanstvom Proletkul'ta," in *Ocherki po istorii sovetskoi nauki i kul'tury* (Moscow, 1968), pp. 29–68, and Fitzpatrick, pp. 89–109, 178–80, 185–87, 238–41, 269–70.

47. Kol'tsov, p. 177.

48. Ibid., p. 181.

49. Bastrakova, p. 166–67.

50. Kol'tsov, p. 158.

51. Bastrakova, p. 158.

52. Ibid., p. 158; *Organizatsiia nauki v pervye gody*, pp. 78–96.

53. *Organizatsiia nauki v pervye gody*, pp. 93–94.

54. Ivanova, p. 360; Bastrakova, p. 162.

55. See Kol'tsov, pp. 99, 111, 123–24, 133.

56. Leggett, pp. 102–20.

57. See *Gor'kii i nauka. Stat'i, rechi, pis'ma vospominaniia* (Moscow, 1965); and L. V. Zarzhitskaia, "O novykh pis'makh M. Gor'kogo. (K voprosu o sokhranenii kadrov uchenykh v pervye gody Sovetskoi vlast)," in *Ocherki po istorii sovetskoi nauki i kul'tury*. pp. 101–12.

58. Ivanova, pp. 210–11.

59. Ibid., pp. 211–12.

60. Ibid., p. 216.

61. AAN, f. 2, op. 1–1917, no. 41, 11. 306–307 ob., cited in Kol'tsov, p. 138.

62. M. Iunovich. *M. Gor'kii—propagandist nauki* (Moscow, 1968), pp. 77–78.

63. Kol'tsov, p. 139.

64. See V. D. Bonch-Bruevich, "Iz vospominanii," *Lenin i Akademiia nauk*, p. 67; Kol'tsov, p. 138; *Nauka i ee rabotniki*, 1921, no. 3, pp. 34–38.

65. Bonch-Bruevich, p. 67.

66. See Kendall Bailes, *Technology and Society under Lenin and Stalin: Origins of the Soviet Technical Intelligentsia, 1917–1941* (Princeton, 1978), p. 59.

67. Ivanova, pp. 178–79.

68. Ibid.

69. V. I. Lenin, *Polnoe sobranie sochenenii*, 5th ed., pp. 312–13.

70. Fediukin, p. 58.

71. See documents in *Organizatsiia nauki v pervye gody*, p. 191.

72. Most of the information for this section is taken from an article by a Siberian geologist entitled "Scientists in Siberia" and published in a journal edited by Maksim Gorkii, Alexander Fersman, and other Petrograd intellectuals: *Nauki i ee rabotniki*, 1921, no. 1, pp. 7–23.

73. Mochalov, pp. 213–25.

74. Sergei Timoshenko, *As I Remember* (Princeton, 1968), p. 166ff.

75. V. I. Vernadskii, "The First Year of the Ukrainian Academy," in *Annals of the Ukrainian Academy of Arts and Sciences in the U.S., Inc.*, 1964–68, vol. 11, nos 1–2. (31–32), pp. 13–22.

76. Archive AN SSSR. f. 518, op. 2, khr. 11.

77. Diary entry of April 19, 1919, AAn SSSR, f. 518, op. 2, ed. khr. 11.

78. Diary entry of November 30, 1919, AAN SSSR, f. 518, op. 2, ed. khr. 11.

79. Diary entry of October 14, 1919, AAN SSR, f. 518, op. 2, ed. khr. 11.

80. Diary entry of December 29, 1919, AAAN SSR, f. 516, op. 2, ed. khr. 11.

81. Kol'tsov, pp. 134–38.

82. This decree is published in *Organizatsiia nauki v pervye gody Sovetskoi vlasti (1917–1929)*, pp. 339–40.

83. Kol'tsov, p. 144.

84. Ibid., p. 148.

85. Bonch-Bruevich, p. 68–69.

86. This account is partially corroborated by documents in the following collections: *Organizatsiia nauki v pervye gody Sovetskoi vlasti*, p. 340–41; *V. I. Lenin i A. M. Gor'kii (Pis'ma, vospominaniia, dokumenty)* (Moscow, 1961).

87. "Postanovlenie SNK o sozdanii uslovii, obespechivaiushchikh nauchnuiu rabotu akademika I. P. Pavlova i ego sotrudnikov," signed January 24, 1921, and published in *Izvestiia*, on February 11, 1921. See *Lenin i Akademiia nauk*, p. 88.

88. "Pis'mo Rossiiskoi Akademii nauk v SNK s srochnom priniatii mer dlia uluchsheniia polozheniia uchenykh i nauki v Rossii," dated May 17, 1921, and published in *Organizatsiia nauki v pervye gody*, p. 342–44.

89. Fersman, p. 6.

90. Leikina-Svirskaia, pp. 90–91.

91. Alexander Vucinich, *Empire of Knowledge: The Academy of Sciences of the USSR (1917–1970)* (Berkeley, 1984), pp. 80–81; see also N. V. Grave, "Kraevednye uchrezhdeniia SSSR," in *Priroda*, 1926, nos. 1–2, pp. 127–28; B. A. Lindener, "Issledovatel'skaia rabota Akademii nauk SSSR v sovetskoi obstanovke," *Nauchnyi rabotnik*, 1925, no. 3, pp. 9–24; N. Ia Marr, "Kraevedcheskaia rabota," *Nauchnyi rabotnik*, 1925, no. 1, pp. 10–18; and articles about the creation and activity of particular *kraeved* organizations in *Nauki i ee rabotniki*, 1921, no. 2, p. 30; 1921, no. 5, p. 35.

92. V. I. Vernadskii to Ivan Il'ich Petrunkevich, March 10, 1923, Vernadsky collection, Bakhmeteff Archive, Columbia University.

INTELLECTUALS IN THE PROLETKULT

PROBLEMS OF AUTHORITY AND EXPERTISE

Lynn Mally

"Dictatorship in politics, dictatorship in economics, dictatorship in culture—here is the political axiom to build a new socialist Russia."[1] This bold statement by three worker-activists reflected the desire of many revolutionaries to extend proletarian hegemony to all aspects of life. It was also an explicit endorsement of a new revolutionary institution known as the Proletkult, which claimed to embody the proletarian dictatorship in the cultural sphere. Proletkult theorists believed that workers should exert their power through three autonomous yet coordinated institutions. The Communist Party expressed workers' political interests and trade unions aggrandized their economic power. The third member of the triumvirate, the Proletkult, would insure that proletarian philosophy, art, and ideology asserted itself over the alien culture of the bourgeoisie.[2]

The Proletkult quickly won a reputation as a radical advocate of cultural change. Its leaders demanded autonomy from all other institutions, and particularly from the state's educational apparatus, because they believed the state could not adequately represent the interests of the proletariat.[3] Despite its independent stance, the Proletkult initially received generous state funding and in many areas enjoyed the aid and encouragement of local groups, from unions to Communist Party divisions. Participants founded theaters, educational classes, artistic studios, and agitational troupes that set out for the combat zones. By late 1920, the national organization claimed almost half a million followers, 80,000 in specialized workshops, and 300 local chapters throughout Soviet territory.[4]

Despite its success as a mass organization, the Proletkult encountered many obstacles in its efforts to create a proletarian culture. It proved especially difficult to achieve one of its most fundamental goals—to further a proletarian leadership within the organization itself. Although Proletkultists passionately endorsed putting power into workers' hands, intellectuals occupied a prominent place at the national and local levels and exerted a powerful influence over its cultural programs.

During the Civil War years, many revolutionary hopes for the establishment of proletarian leadership in politics, economics, and social life were disappointed. The movement for workers' management in industry faltered, and by the end of the war many workers complained about the domination of specialists and bureaucrats in factories, unions, and the Communist Party. This left segments of the proletariat disaffected and discouraged by the results of the revolution.

This transformation has long been the topic of historical debate, and the discussion shows no sign of ending. Western scholars have traditionally blamed the Bolsheviks, charging that they simply used proletarian enthusiasm to achieve power but never had any intention of offering workers any power themselves.[5] Recently, though, researchers have drawn attention to the disintegrating economy, the changing nature of the proletariat, and the strains of the Civil War.[6] Faced with extraordinary circumstances, workers had to call for the aid of central institutions, bureaucrats, and experts, thus giving up some of the autonomy they had claimed for themselves in 1917.

The Proletkult offers an interesting case to test the limits of proletarian control. During the Civil War, it operated fairly freely and inspired a broad and enthusiastic following. The fact that this organization, despite its many advantages, had difficulty developing a proletarian leadership illuminates the practical and ideological limits to the rapid redistribution of cultural skills and authority during the early Soviet years. The glaring discrepancies between its promise of a proletarian dictatorship in culture and its much more modest accomplishments made the Proletkult vulnerable to outside criticism. Although the Communist Party did not initially hamper the Proletkult's efforts, the organization's shortcomings provided the party a convenient excuse to place it under state control once the Civil War had ended.

Intellectuals' Place in a Proletarian Movement

The Proletkult was inspired by the sophisticated ideas of Alexander Bogdanov and his associates in the "Vpered" (Forward) circle within Russian Bolshevism.[7] In the troubled years after the failure of the 1905 revolution, the Vperedists opposed Lenin's ideas on party organization and political tactics. They believed that a working-class intelligentsia had to take control of the Russian socialist movement in order to prepare itself for a new revolutionary upheaval. This proletarian vanguard had to assume both political and cultural leadership, elaborating its own approach to problems of science, art, and politics in order to construct the ideological foundations for the future socialist society.

To accomplish these ambitious goals, Bogdanov and his allies started special schools for workers in Capri and Bologna in 1909 and 1910.[8] These experiments raised problems that would continue to plague Proletkult. Although workers were the source of the new intelligentsia, they were still dependent on the old one for guidance. The teachers at the Capri and Bologna schools were intellectuals, not workers, and the major proponents of proletarian culture were intellectuals as well. However self-effacing they were, however much they claimed that they had gained their insights into politics and culture from workers themselves, they still enjoyed power and authority based on their superior education.

As the Proletkult movement took shape in the early Soviet years, the influence of Bogdanov and his allies was easily apparent in its expansive cultural platform. The Proletkult's official task was to discover new systems of knowledge and cultural creation shaped by a working-class elite. But the Vperedists were joined by other forces with their own agendas. Activists in workers' cultural circles had formed their own clubs and artistic groups in the years following 1905.[9] They brought to the movement an ambivalent attitude toward "bourgeois culture" and the intellectuals who possessed it. The Proletkult's function as an educational institution also attracted many teachers from the numerous adult education projects that had sprung up in late tsarist Russia.[10] They saw the organization as a way to transmit the classics of Russian culture to the broadest possible audience. Finally, the Proletkult's apparent promise of a new culture inspired those who wanted nothing to do with the cultural baggage of prerevolutionary society.

This coalition was fraught with conflicts over the most basic questions. But participants did share one assumption: the Proletkult's purpose was at least in part to redefine the relationship between the intelligentsia who possessed cultural skills and access to education and the working class (or working masses) who aspired to them. The solutions proposed to achieve these ends were by no means similar, ranging from annihilation to emulation of the old cultural elite. But no matter what path participants devised to change the balance of power between workers and intellectuals, they discovered that it was a much more difficult proposition than anyone had foreseen.

True to its commitment to proletarian dictatorship in culture, the national Proletkult organization made class exclusivity its basic organizing principle. The most important central leaders, including Alexander Bogdanov, Pavel Lebedev-Polianskii, and Fedor Kalinin, were former Vperedists who had a unique understanding of the proletariat's cultural mission. The industrial working class alone possessed collective values, forged in the factory labor process, and only these could form the foundation for a truly socialist society. All other social groups, from the bourgeoisie to the peasantry, were tainted with individualism and were thus unable to understand workers' collectivist consciousness.[11] Lebedev-Polianskii was even willing to push these assumptions to their logical but extreme conclusion; he wanted to exclude not only peasants but also artisans, unskilled workers, and the unemployed.[12] Intellectuals were obviously a suspect group. Like the petty-bourgeoisie and the peasantry, they had an individualistic world-view and thus could not comprehend workers' unique understanding of art, science, and the problems of daily life.

The arguments of central leaders ultimately did little to shape the social composition of the Proletkult. Ignoring central guidelines, local organizations opened their doors to a broadly defined laboring population, including white-collar employees, artisans, and sometimes even peasants.[13] Yet the highly critical language that central leaders directed against intellectuals struck a responsive cord. It evoked the deeply rooted resentment of the laboring masses against the privileged old elite, the plebeian "us" against the patrician "them." In the words of a delegate at the first Proletkult national congress, "I know of only two classes—the oppressed poor and the rich exploiters."[14] Privileged intellectuals could easily be relegated to the external, alien world of "the *burzhui* and their lackeys."[15]

Bitter debates over intellectual-worker relations raged in the Proletkult throughout its history, beginning with the first organizing conference in October 1917.[16] The most extreme opponents of intellectual involvement believed that the revolution was meant to bring about an end to all social hierarchy, including one based on knowledge and creative skills. They were opposed to the old intellectual elite and also to the creation of a new workers' intelligentsia. As one writer from the Tambov Proletkult argued, the new society did not need an intelligentsia at all. By definition, intellectuals were bourgeois no matter what class they came from. As soon as workers left the bench to follow intellectual pursuits, they left the proletariat behind. What the socialist state needed were accomplished workers and not a new intelligentsia.[17]

These radical egalitarians spoke out against any method that would elevate one worker above another, including scholarship programs, auditions, and contests. As one outraged worker wrote when hearing of a competition for the best proletarian poet, "We who were born in the thunder of plants and factories, in the mines and pits and behind the plow, we do not recognize 'kings' or 'best poets.' "[18] These were by no means isolated views. There were heated discussions over whether the Proletkult should educate workers who stayed in the factories or encourage talented individuals to become professional artists and intellectuals. The "professionalism debate," as it was known in the Proletkult press, was eventually won by those who opposed radical egalitarianism.[19]

On the other side were those who believed that the Proletkult was meant to transmit the learning and cultural achievements of prerevolutionary society to a greatly expanded audience. These participants solicited and welcomed intellectuals' involvement with little remorse or ambivalence. Carrying on the prerevolutionary traditions of adult education, they believed it was the intelligentsia's duty to impart its learning to the lower classes. One speaker at a Proletkult conference in Novgorod province insisted that all intellectuals could help the cause of education, regardless of their political views. "Therefore it is necessary to try with all our power to attract intellectuals to take part in the work of the Proletkults."[20]

The national organization's position lay somewhere in the middle of these two extremes. The most visible national leaders, like Fedor Kalinin, made frequent statements against intellectuals, denouncing their alien world-view.[21] Nonetheless, they were pragmatic enough to realize that the Proletkult had to employ intellectuals in some capacity. In the words of the first Proletkult national president, Pavel Lebedev-Polianskii, intellectuals had "cultural experience" [*kul'turnyi stazh*].[22] That was one asset a cultural organization could not forgo.

Rather than barring intellectuals altogether, the central leadership defined precise guidelines to limit their influence. The membership rules drawn up in January 1919 stated that intellectuals could participate, but only in an advisory capacity.[23] They would be the organization's specialists, relegated to the sidelines. Ideally, a workers' collegium would set the direction of study and then call in experts to fulfill predefined tasks.[24] It was an elegant solution that restricted the intellectual elite to the role of outside helpmate in an organization supposedly composed of and led by workers.

During the Civil War years, the Proletkult fulfilled at least part of its commitment to proletarian advancement by attracting an impressive range of working-class leaders to its ranks. From its inception, it included seasoned proletarian cultural activists like Fedor Kalinin, Vasilii Kirillov, and Alexei Samobytnik-Mashirov. A new generation of worker-leaders, like Grigorii Nazarov and Leonid Tsinovskii, moved rapidly through the organizational hierarchy to assume positions of power by the end of the Civil War.[25] Still, the organization could never claim a purely proletarian leadership at any point in its history. The language of class control was stretched and redefined to make way for many talented intellectuals who were sympathetic to the Proletkult's cause.

Intellectual Leaders

Although Proletkult guidelines were meant to discourage nonworkers from assuming positions of power, intellectuals were well represented at both the national and local levels. Participants simply ignored the rules and sought well-educated, artistically gifted individuals at the expense of class purity. There was, however, also a more complicated process at work that allowed some intellectuals to claim the status of "insiders" whose class standing and background did not threaten the proletarian nature of the organization.

Indeed, the term *intelligent* was not used with any precision in the Civil War years. For Proletkultists, it proved to be an even more slippery social category than worker, which was also given an elastic definition. *Intelligent* was not a class-based description. It was applied to a wide variety of people who possessed some educational training and did not hold working-class jobs. What the term did convey was a sense of approbation. During the revolutionary years, it was a derogatory label almost synonymous with the word *burzhui* and liberally applied to those with suspect political and economic views.[26] Since the very word for intellectual became an insult, standing for unfeeling class selfishness, Proletkult participants invented new social categories for those who gave generously of their time and energy.

This confusion of class terms is immediately apparent in Proletkult publications. The angry attacks on intellectuals, so common in the Proletkult press, were not consistent in their targets. They were usually directed at those who saw the Proletkult primarily as a source of employment. Intellectuals who had proven their commitment through longstanding involvement in projects to aid the lower classes could be exempted from criticism. This "socialist," "revolutionary," or "communist" intelligentsia had shown that it did not intend to sabotage the Proletkult or stand in the way of workers' creativity.[27] They escaped condemnation through a transformation from outsider to insider. This redefinition of friend and foe based on attitude and function, rather than on class standing, allowed Proletkult participants to entrust intellectuals with important positions without appearing to abandon the organization's principles.

The Proletkult's most visible theorists and leaders, many of whom did not come from working-class backgrounds, contributed to this complicated use of social categories. Pavel Lebedev-Polianskii, the first national president, was the university-educated son of a minor tsarist official. As one of the most outspoken advocates of class purity, he frequently warned of the dangers of intellectual involvement. They came to us, he said, and they have skills we need, but we should place them under strict controls.[28] Obviously, he did not consider himself to be a suspect outsider. Bogdanov, another intellectual, argued for the integrity of the proletarian world-view, unsullied and unaltered by the manipulations of class-alien elements. But he certainly did not question his own ability to articulate proletarian attitudes.[29] Although Fedor Kalinin was skeptical about intellectuals' abilities to comprehend the world of workers, he shared the national leadership with his friends and mentors, Bogdanov and Lebedev-Polianskii.

The integral involvement of nonproletarian leaders was already apparent in the composition of the central committee of the national organization. This body, elected at periodic national conventions, was responsible for crucial policy decisions. It distributed staff, funding, and supplies to local organizations and decided whether or not to recognize new groups. It could also reorganize or close organizations that did not fulfill the Proletkult's goals.[30]

Many intellectuals found their way onto this vitally important board. In 1918, the five officers and eleven central committee members included Lebedev-Polianskii; Bogdanov; Anna Dodonova, an intellectual and Moscow Party leader who would soon become president of the Moscow Proletkult; and Vladimir Faidysh, another Moscow intellectual. Among the candidate-members were Fedor Blagonravov, E. P. Khersonskaia, and Olga Vladimirova, all of whom came from the socialist intelligentsia.[31] By late 1920, thirteen out of thirty members of the central committee did not come from the working class.[32] In 1921, the former worker Valerian Pletnev replaced Lebedev-

Polianskii as national president, giving the organization a more proletarian appearance. But his closest advisors were evenly divided between workers and intellectuals.[33]

At the local level, intellectuals also held powerful and responsible positions. In Petrograd worker-artists occupied the highest posts, but there were many intellectuals on the governing board, including the old Bolshevik Praskovia Kudelli, who initially headed the club division, and Alexander Mgebrov, who led theater work.[34] Olga Vladimirova, an intellectual party member, was Proletkult president in the staunchly proletarian town of Ivanovo-Voznesensk.[35] The Tver Proletkult was led by Vladislava Lie, a teacher who traced her social roots to the nobility.[36]

The first Proletkult in the Urals was started by the Moscow party member V. D. Buzin. When he died of typhus in 1922, the head of the local Communist Party division called him "one of those strong links which tied the working-class masses to the Communist Party. Comrade Buzin was not a worker but [he] lived and breathed in a working-class milieu."[37] His class background did not prevent him from becoming a member of the Ekaterinburg Proletkult presidium. In the town of Belev, Tula province, Valentin Nikolaitsev was elected president at the end of the Civil War. Nikolaitsev, who had joined the Proletkult in 1919, was a party member, son of a school teacher and a forester, and had been educated at Moscow University.[38]

For the most part, these leaders did not alter the "proworker" stance of their organizations. The Petrograd Proletkult under the leadership of the former worker Alexei Samobytnik-Mashirov was not more sympathetic to the proletariat than the Tver Proletkult headed by the former noble Vladislava Lie. Indeed, in some cases intellectuals could be the most vociferous defenders of working-class influence and proletarian control. The apparent paradox of their position as intellectuals in a sphere reserved for workers was resolved by their good intentions. By working for the proletariat, they somehow became part of the proletariat and thus were entitled to speak on its behalf.

Nonetheless, good intentions alone did not prevent intellectuals from making full use of the power inherent in their position. Lebedev-Polianskii employed the central Proletkult journal *Proletarian Culture* (*Proletarskaia kul'tura*) to dictate the form and content of workers' writing. In numerous articles he bemoaned the state of proletarian literature, claiming that it lacked style, talent, and was devoid of "real" class consciousness. He then took it on himself to show the proper path.[39] Platon Kerzhentsev, a party intellectual and theater expert, gave graphic instructions on how workers should organize their creative circles to emphasize proletarian collectivism.[40] Bogdanov moved to shut off funds for a division of socialist education in the Petrograd Proletkult because he believed its educational programs, which were mainly technical training courses, were not socialist at all.[41] Through their offices intellectuals could influence Proletkult activities in the way they thought was best, which sometimes meant telling workers what was best for them.

Intellectuals on the Proletkult Staff

The lowest rung in the Proletkult hierarchy was occupied by teachers, lecturers, and studio instructors. These staff members were the Proletkult's experts brought in primarily because of their knowledge and skills in particular artistic or academic pursuits. Not even the central organization tried to bar nonproletarians from these positions, although it tried to limit their influence.

Despite its often abrasively stated class-based ideology, the Proletkult was in a strong position to attract educators and artists to staff its programs. Some were drawn in by the Proletkult's antiintellectual rhetoric and saw their participation as proof of their loyalty to the victorious working class. Others perceived the Proletkult as an educational institution similar to prerevolutionary programs in which they could put their talents to work in order to "serve the people." Finally, many came just to find employment, wages, and rations. During the Civil War, when inflation was rampant and many cultural institutions closed down, that alone was a compelling motivation.

Intellectual staff members participated in Proletkult activities on many different levels. Most gave lectures or taught workshops in their particular areas of expertise, such as piano or voice. Some took on more responsibility, helping plan artistic and educational programs for the membership. For the latter group, there was only a semantic distinction between their role and the job of someone who had an official post on the governing board. In fact, for those participants who came to the Proletkult to learn a specific skill, studio instructors exerted much greater influence than did the local president.

The list of intellectuals who taught in Proletkult programs is long and impressive, including some of Russia's finest artists. Andrei Belyi, Nikolai Gumilev, and Vladislav Khodasevich all taught literature classes.[42] In music, the Proletkult had the services of Alexander Kastal'skii, Reinhold Glière, and Dmitrii Vasilev-Buglai.[43] Art courses were devised by avant-gardists like Olga Rozanova and Boris Arvatov, along with more traditional figures like the academician Timofei Katurkin.[44] The theater was particularly well endowed. "Who didn't teach in the Proletkult?" asked the Moscow drama student and future national artist of the Soviet Union Maxim Shtraukh. "Starting with Stanislavskii himself who sometimes gave lectures, Prince Volkonskii, artists from the Moscow Art Theater, the Adel'geim brothers, followers of Isadora Duncan, and many, many others."[45] Even small town organizations could often boast a highly qualified staff.[46]

Some instructors did not conceal their doubts about the theoretical premises of the organization. Prince Sergei Volkonskii, for example, had been the director of the imperial theaters before the revolution. After 1917, he lost not only his position, but all his property as well. He took numerous small jobs to try to survive, one as a lecturer on theater in the Moscow Proletkult. In his memoirs, written after he emigrated to the West, Volkonskii admitted quite frankly that he had no sympathy with (or even any understanding of) the ideas behind the Proletkult. Although he was very impressed with his eager working-class students, he never believed that there could be a uniquely proletarian art form.[47] In the words of the actor Igor Il'inskii, who was briefly a participant in the Moscow provincial organization, "Only a very small group of theater people went to the workers, to their uncomfortable, poor and cold clubs out of a conscious commitment . . . [T]he majority went there only to get rations to supplement their paltry wages which were shrinking due to the inflation."[48]

It would be unfair, however, to assign merely mercenary motives to all of these cultural experts. Many artists, writers, and teachers came with the express purpose of serving the working class and the revolution. As a music teacher from the small town of Kologriv explained, the Proletkult gave the intelligentsia a chance to pay off a "centuries-old debt" to the people by opening up the doors of art to them.[49] The same tone pervades the memoirs of Alexander Mgebrov, who headed the theater division in Petrograd. For Mgebrov, the Proletkult ended "long ordeals and a dissatisfying separation from the masses." With romantic enthusiasm he wrote, "Once again, as in 1905 when I stood with the workers on the barricades, I found myself side by side with the working class in its grandiose struggle for the future."[50] The Proletkult offered a dual advantage to sympathetic intellectuals like Mgebrov; they could settle past accounts and also feel as though they were helping build the future.

It was simply not possible to limit these skilled artists and intellectuals to advisory roles. Like all early Soviet institutions, the Proletkult was chronically understaffed. Local organizations continually sent pleas to the center for more aid and more instructors. Although a few asked that their helpers be familiar with the problems of proletarian culture, none made any stipulations about their social origins.[51] Even if local organizations had wanted to, they hardly had the resources to insure that specialists did not overstep the narrow bounds of creative control allowed in the national guidelines.

Proletkult experts had considerable freedom to shape their offerings according to their own understandings of proletarian culture. As a consequence, artistic and educational programs differed radically from one organization to the next, and even from one workshop to the next. In Moscow, the music department was largely controlled by Alexander Kastal'skii and Grigorii Liubimov, who had long histories in workers' artistic programs. Both of these men believed in folk music as a way to interest the masses in musical training. Thus, the Moscow Proletkult had a large folk music section and classes for instruments like the balalaika.[52] In Petrograd, by contrast, the music division was in the hands of a young Latvian composer, Ia. Ozolin, who thought the organization should create revolutionary songs. He and his supporters took a dim view of Moscow's programs, finding them too conservative.[53] In Kologriv, where the music studio was headed by a Petrograd conservatory graduate, Maria Shipova, the approach was entirely conventional. She taught her students piano, violin, and songs by classic Russian composers.[54]

This broad range of offerings was not unique to music. The Petrograd Proletkult theater, headed by Alexander Mgebrov, took a symbolist approach, while in Ivanovo-Voznesensk it tended toward realism.[55] In Saratov, the art studio was led by an avant-garde painter who advocated abstract art.[56] Moscow art studios were split acrimoniously between instructors who taught portrait painting and still-life, and the aggressive advocates of production art who believed that "easel art" should be abandoned for techniques tied more closely to industrial production.[57]

The phenomenon of sympathetic experts presented yet another conceptual and linguistic problem for Proletkult participants. In Civil War Russia, the term "specialist," just like the word *intelligent*, conjured up all sorts of negative connotations. In this case, the central Proletkult organization devised its own terminology to circumvent the problem by creating a new name for those who had moved from the outer to the inner circle. In questionnaires sent out to the provinces in 1921, the central organization asked its local affiliates who was in charge of studio activities—"Proletkultists" (*Proletkul'tovtsy*) or "specialists."

The answers sent back to Moscow indicated that local organizations tried to put "Proletkultists" in control. Still, they do not give any clues about the class background of those who governed studio work.[58] The Proletkult in Belev reported that its drama, literature, and art sections were led by Proletkultists, while the others were led by specialists. But this placed the intellectual Timofei Katurkin, who was in charge of art, into the Proletkult camp. The Samara leadership insisted that its specialists were closely supervised by a Proletkultist, when the supervisor in question was a twenty-one-year-old school teacher who described herself as an *intelligent*.[59]

This flexible use of social categories clearly helped mask the power of intellectuals within the Proletkult hierarchy, but that was not its primary function. It was a creative solution to a social and cultural dilemma. The simplest way to acknowledge intellectuals' contributions without relinquishing proletarian control was to rename them as part of the Proletkult.

Proletkult or Intelligentkult?

The Proletkult's aggressive stance on proletarian leadership, combined with its sobering record on intellectual involvement, inevitably produced strains and conflicts. According to one report in the central journal *Proletarian Culture*, the predominance of intellectuals in local Proletkults was a frequent complaint at union meetings. Disputes emerged over whether the new culture would be made "from above," by intellectuals, or "from below," by the workers themselves.[60] At a Moscow conference in 1919, a critic complained that the Proletkult was ineffective because it was led by representatives of the bourgeoisie, people without ties to a proletarian milieu and therefore without any understanding of proletarian creativity. As a result, some had branded the Proletkult "Intelligentkult."[61] These tensions could lead to bitter power struggles. In the

town of Brasovo, Orel province, participants threatened to expel all intellectuals because they wanted too much power. The vice president of the Kologriv
Proletkult was ousted when a rival candidate exposed him as an intellectual
careerist who had worked his way into proletarian organizations under false
pretenses.[62]

Yet some of the battles within the Proletkult that appeared to center around
workers' control were in fact conflicts between different groups of intellectuals
who claimed to represent workers' interests. A fight developed in Petrograd
between two factions that advocated different theatrical programs. The young
director Dmitrii Shcheglov, a proponent of realism, was quickly called to task
for departing from the symbolist direction of other Petrograd studios. According to Shcheglov's memoirs, the working-class leader of the Petrograd
organization criticized him for the independent direction of his classes, and
then berated himself for giving an intellectual so much control. Shcheglov did
not respond to these charges. "Why? Because I really never had worked in a
factory and did not have the merits that my Proletkult comrades had."[63]

Shcheglov was bitter, though, when Lebedev-Polianskii visited Petrograd and
chided participants there for the undue influence intellectuals had gained. The
Proletkult president singled out Shcheglov for criticism and told him that he
should emulate the proletarian methods of the head theater director, Alexander
Mgebrov. Shcheglov noted with sarcasm that not only was Mgebrov an intellectual, but Lebedev-Polianskii was one as well.[64] This incident shows the
malleability and the inadequacy of the Proletkult's class-based language. When
Shcheglov opposed the Petrograd leadership, he was singled out as a suspect
intellectual. But the social origins of intellectual friends went unnoticed. This
was a struggle over aesthetics hidden under the guise of workers' control.

The Proletkult's practice during the Russian Civil War indicates that it was
simply not possible to pursue the task of cultural transformation without granting prestige and power to the bearers of cultural expertise. Indeed, intellectuals'
influential role leads one to question just what proletarian culture meant to
the organization's participants. Did they aspire to create a distinctive approach
to science, art, and learning, as many central leaders claimed? Or did they
hope that the fruits of culture—the "high" culture that intellectuals held the
keys to—would finally be made accessible to them? These questions were
fervently argued within the Proletkult, and there is no single answer that applies
to the organization as a whole. But at least part of the Proletkult's following
pursued the simpler goal. As one participant wrote, intellectuals had a responsibility to disseminate the knowledge they had gained at the cost of workers and peasants before the revolution.[65] Such a project unavoidably placed
considerable power in intellectuals' hands.

The demographic shifts and social dislocations caused by the Civil War
weakened the Proletkult's ability to attract a proletarian leadership. Factory
closures and the exodus of workers to the countryside depleted the ranks of
the experienced proletariat, the intended clientele of Proletkult work. Educated
workers, particularly those who were party members, had many other re-

sponsibilities and opportunities during the war, and this also held true for Proletkultists. Local organizations frequently complained that proletarian activists did not have enough time to devote to their cultural work.[66] Mobilizations decimated many local memberships and governing boards, and they also affected the central Proletkult. Two of the best known proletarian leaders, Pavel Bessal'ko and Fedor Kalinin, died at the front during the war.[67]

At the same time, the war created conditions that attracted intellectuals and artists to the Proletkult. It offered them employment, often in areas completely familiar to those who had been involved in adult education projects before the revolution. It gave the socially conscious a chance to "serve the people" and allowed them to shape educational and artistic programs according to their tastes. As Proletkult critics charged, some intellectuals might well have come to the organization because it claimed independence from all institutions, including the Bolshevik Party, thus giving them a chance to earn a living without lending direct support to the new regime.[68]

These intellectuals were not forced on an unwilling and resentful audience. Local working-class leaders openly solicited the help of outside experts, and they were seriously concerned when intellectuals did not respond. Proletkult students could receive a level of education and training from intellectuals that would not have been possible had their organizations indeed eschewed outside aid. As scattered memoirs suggest, Proletkult participants sincerely appreciated the training they received.[69]

The Proletkult never altered its ideological commitment to proletarian leadership. Class exclusivity and class control defined the organization and, in the opinion of Proletkult theorists, justified its independent status. Clearly, though, these principles were reshaped to integrate intellectuals sympathetic to the workers' cause. Proletkult practice displays the flexibility of class terms in the midst of radical social upheaval. Rather than give up the principle of workers' control, or adjust the slogan to describe a much more complicated power-sharing relationship, Proletkult participants reformulated their social categories, allowing some nonworkers entry into the inner proletarian circle.

The Proletkult was not an organization where intellectuals led and workers followed; the interactions were much more complicated. Nonetheless nonproletarians exerted a problematic influence. They had the power to impose their own vision of proper proletarian behavior, thus limiting workers' ability to find their own solutions to the problems of cultural transformation. Through their knowledge and expertise, they also shaped participants' perceptions of what the new culture should be. Perhaps most important, intellectuals' integral role made the Proletkult an easy target for its critics. All they had to do was point to the actual structure of the Proletkult leadership in order to charge the organization with hypocrisy and undermine the theoretical justification for its autonomy within the state.

In the fall of 1920, just as the worst of the Civil War was coming to a close, Lenin began to scrutinize carefully the theory and practice of the Proletkult movement. He found much to alarm him, including its adamantly independent stance, its claims to a large proletarian following, and its inspiration in the theories of his old opponent Bogdanov.[70] With the Central Committee of the Communist Party behind him, Lenin moved swiftly. He took away the Proletkult's autonomy, subordinating it to the state's educational bureaucracy. Then he helped write and publish a devastating critique of the Proletkult's work.

The Central Committee's public letter "On the Proletkults," published in *Pravda* in December 1920, cleverly exploited the organization's internal inconsistencies. The letter charged that the Proletkult's autonomous pretensions toward the Soviet state had turned it into a haven for petty-bourgeois and socially alien elements. The organization was dominated from top to bottom with dissatisfied intellectuals who tried to pass off their reactionary politics and decadent artistic tastes under the label of proletarian culture.[71]

These were not legitimate criticisms, and they were energetically rejected by the Proletkult central leadership.[72] But the discrepancies between Proletkult ideals and practice gave party leaders a chance to declare themselves to be the true advocates of proletarian culture. As the Central Committee's letter proudly proclaimed, the Communist Party had nothing against workers who wanted to devote themselves to artistic pursuits. It simply wanted to make sure that these activities were not controlled by class-alien elements but, rather, by the proletariat's own intelligentsia.[73] In an ironic twist, they used the Proletkult's own arguments to discredit the organization.

NOTES

1. A. M. Knizhnik, Karl Ozol'-Prednek, "God bor'by za proletarskuiu kul'turu," *Griadushchee*, 1918, no. 8, p. 18.

2. For the most comprehensive works on the Proletkult movement, see V. V. Gorbunov, *V. I. Lenin i Proletkul't* (Moscow, 1974); Peter Gorsen and Eberhard Knödler-Bunte, *Proletkult. System einer proletarischen Kultur*, 2 vols. (Stuttgart, 1974); Gabriele Gorzka, *A. Bogdanov und der russische Proletkult* (Frankfurt am Main, 1980); Lynn Mally, *Culture of the Future: The Proletkult Movement in Revolutionary Russia* (Berkeley, 1990); L. A. Pinegina, *Sovetskii rabochii klass i khudozhestvennaia kul'tura* (Moscow, 1984); Zenovia A. Sochor, *Revolution and Culture: The Bogdanov-Lenin Controversy* (Ithaca, N.Y., 1988).

3. On the relationship between the Proletkult and the state's educational commissariat, see Sheila Fitzpatrick, *The Commissariat of Enlightenment: Soviet Organization of Education and the Arts under Lunacharsky* (Cambridge, 1970), esp. pp. 89–109.

4. *Proletarskaia kul'tura* (henceforth cited as PK), 1920, no. 19/20 p. 74.

5. The clearest statement of this position is in John L. H. Keep, *The Russian Revolution: A Study in Mass Mobilization* (New York, 1976), especially parts 4 and 5. For factory committees, see Paul Avrich, "The Bolshevik Revolution and Workers' Control in Russian Industry," *Slavic Review*, 1963, vol. 22, pp. 47–63.

6. See William J. Chase, *Workers, Society, and the Soviet State: Labor and Life in Moscow, 1918–1929* (Urbana, 1987), pp. 11–72; William Husband, "Workers' Control and Centralization in the Russian Revolution: The Textile Industry of the Central

Industrial Region, 1917–1920," *Carl Beck Papers in Russian and East European Studies*, 1985, no. 403; William G. Rosenberg, "Russian Labor and Bolshevik Power after October," *Slavic Review*, 1985, vol. 44, no. 2, pp. 213–38; Robert Service, *The Bolshevik Party in Revolution, 1917–1923: A Study in Organizational Change* (London, 1979); S. A. Smith, *Red Petrograd: Revolution in the Factories, 1917–1918* (Cambridge, 1983).

7. On Bogdanov and Vpered see John Biggart, " 'Anti-Leninist Bolshevism': The Forward Group of the RSDRP," *Canadian Slavonic Papers*, 1981, vol. 23, no. 2, pp. 134–53; and Robert C. Williams, *The Other Bolsheviks: Lenin and His Critics, 1904–1914* (Bloomington, Ind., 1986), esp. pp. 49–65; 144–61.

8. See Jutta Scherrer, "Les écoles du parti de Capri et de Bologne: La formation de l'intelligentsia du parti," *Cahiers du monde russe et soviétique*, 1978, no. 19, pp. 259–84.

9. Victoria E. Bonnell, *Roots of Rebellion: Workers' Politics and Organizations in St. Petersburg and Moscow, 1900–1914*, (Berkeley, 1984), pp. 328–34.

10. On adult education in prerevolutionary Russia, see E. N. Medynskii, *Vneshkol'noe obrazovanie; ego znachenie, organizatsiia i tekhnika* (Moscow, 1918).

11. A. Bogdanov, "Nasha kritika," PK, 1918, no. 3, p. 13.

12. V. Polianskii, "Pod znamia Proletkul'ta," PK, 1918, no. 1, p. 6.

13. For an analysis of Proletkult membership, see Mally, *Culture of the Future*, chap. 3.

14. *Protokoly pervoi Vserossiiskoi konferentsii proletarskikh kul'turno-prosvetitel'nykh organizatsii, 15–20 sentiabria 1918 g.* (Moscow, 1918) p. 22 (henceforth cited as *Protokoly pervoi konferentsii*.)

15. *Vneshkol'noe obrazovanie*, 1919, no. 1, p. 96.

16. *Rabochii put'*, October 26, 1917; *Rabochaia gazeta*, October 17, 1917.

17. R., "Sushchnost' intelligentsii," *Griadushchaia kul'tura*, 1918, no. l, p. 20.

18. F. Kiselev, "Otvet Pkh-voi na ee statiiu 'Konkurs poetov,' " *Gudki*, 1918, no. 2, p. 15.

19. A. V. Lunacharskii, "O professionalizme rabochikh v iskusstve," PK, 1920, no. 17/19, p. 80.

20. A. P., "Kholmskii s"ezd rabotnikov po vneshkol'nomu obrazovaniiu," *Vneshkol'noe obrazovanie* (Petrograd), 1919, no. 4/5 p. 95. See also N. Kuz'min, "Intelligentsiia i proletariat," *Griadushchee*, 1920, no. 5/6, p. 16.

21. See, for example, F. I. Kalinin, "Proletariat i iskusstvo," PK, 1918, no. 3, p. 13.

22. "Revoliutsiia i kul'turnye zadachi proletariata," *Protokoly pervoi konferentsii*, p. 2.

23. "Plan organizatsii Proletkul'ta," PK, 1919, no. 6, p. 27.

24. See the suggestions made by the leaders of the Moscow Proletkult's theater and music studios in *Gorn*, 1918, no. 1, pp. 53, 59–60.

25. The careers of Kalinin, Kirillov, and Samobytnik-Mashirov are documented in numerous studies. On Nazarov and Tsinovskii, see A. A. Mgebrov, *Zhizn' v teatre* (Moscow, 1933), 2: 304, 373; and Tsentral'nyi gosudarstvennyi arkhiv literatury i iskusstv (henceforth, TsGALI), f. 1230 (Proletkul't), op. 1, d. 118, ll. 27 ob, 28; 60–61 ob.

26. These views were certainly not limited to the Proletkult. On general attitudes toward intellectuals in the revolutionary period, see Charles Rougle, "The Intelligentsia in Russia, 1917–1918," in *Art, Society, Revolution. Russia, 1917–1921*, ed. Nils A. Nilsson (Stockholm, 1979); and David Mandel, "The Intelligentsia and the Working Class in 1917," *Critique*, 1981, no. 14, pp. 67–87.

27. See I. Fuks, "Intelligentsiia i kollektivnoe tvorchestvo," *Griadushchaia kul'tura*, 1919, no. 4/5, p. 20; S. Krivtsov, "Konferentsiia Proletkul'tov," *Rabochii mir*, 1919, no. 14, p. 32.

28. P. I. Lebedev-Polianskii, *Protokoly pervoi konferentsii*, p. 26.
29. See, for example, A. A. Bogdanov, "Proletarskii universitet," PK, 1918, no. 5, pp. 9–13.
30. See the minutes of Proletkult central committee meetings for 1918–20 in TsGALI f. 1230, op. l, dd. 2, 3, 4 and 6.
31. For a list of Proletkul't officers and central committee members, see *Protokoly pervoi konferentsii*, p. 55. On their social backgrounds, see questionnaires for the 1921 Proletkult congress, TsGALI f. 1230, op. l, d. 144 and d. 118.
32. "Neobkhodimoe ob"iasnenie," TsGALI f. 1230, op. 1. d. 51, l. 6.
33. *Biulleten' vtorogo s"ezda Proletkul'tov*, 1921, no. 2, p. 93.
34. *Griadushchee*, 1919, no. 4, p. 12; T. A. Khavina, "Bor'ba Kommunisticheskoi partii za Proletkul't i rukovodstvo ego deiatel'nostiu, 1917–1932 gg." (Candidate Dissertation, Leningrad, 1978), p. 40.
35. TsGALI f. 1230, op. 1, d. 1245, ll. 8–9; d. 118, ll. 31–31 ob.
36. TsGALI f. 1230, op. 1, d. 144, l. 128.
37. S. Korniakov, "Otkliki na smert' tov. Buzina," TsGALI f. 1230, op. 1, d. 1220, 1. 14.
38. "Lichnaia anketa," TsGALI f. 1230, op. 1, d. 118, ll. 5–6.
39. See, for example, V. Polianskii, "Motivy rabochei poezii," PK, 1919, no. 3, pp. 1–12; idem, "Poeziia sovetskoi provintsii," PK, 1919, no. 7/8, pp. 43–57.
40. V. Kerzhentsev, " 'Proletkul't'—organizatsiia proletarskoi samodeiatel'nosti," PK, 1918, no. 1, pp. 7–8; idem, "Organizatsiia literaturnogo tvorchestva," PK, 1918, no. 5, pp. 23–26.
41. On the classes, see *Griadushchee*, 1919, no. 5/6, p. 31. On Bogdanov's objections, see TsGALI f. 1230, op. 1, d. 3, l.
42. Belyi—*Gudki*, 1919, no. 2, pp. 30–31; Gumilev—*Griadushchee*, 1919, no. 7/8, p. 30; V. Khodasevich, *Literaturnye stati i vospominaniia* (New York, 1954), pp. 325–31.
43. *Muzykal'naia entsiklopediia*, ed. Iu. V. Keldysh et al., (Moscow, 1973–81); Boris Schwarz, *Music and Musical Life in Soviet Russia, 1917–1981*, 2nd ed. (Bloomington, Ind., 1983), pp. 20–22.
44. On avant-gardists, see Christina Lodder, *Russian Constructivism* (New Haven, 1983), pp. 255, 239; on Katurkin, N. A. Milonov, "O deiatel'nosti Tul'skogo Proletkul'ta," in *Aktual'nye voprosy istorii literatury* (Tula, 1969), pp. 148–49.
45. M. Shtraukh, "Dva Sergeia Mikhailovicha," *Teatr*, 1966, no. 12, p. 69.
46. See the instructors registered in Moscow province theater studios, "Svedeniia teatral'nogo otdela Moskovskogo gubernskogo Proletkul'ta," in N. B. Vol'kova, "Teatral'naia deiatel'nost' Proletkul'ta," *Russkii sovetskii teatr, 1917–1921* (Leningrad, 1968), pp. 334–36, 341.
47. Prince Sergei Wolkonsky, *My Reminiscences*, trans. A. E. Chamat (London, 1924), 2: 220–23, 227.
48. Igor Il'inskii, *Sam o sebe* (Moscow, 1961), pp. 96–97.
49. TsGALI f. 1230, op. 1, d. 1278, l. 13.
50. Mgebrov, *Zhizn' v teatre*, 2:301.
51. See, for example, requests from the Rybinsk, Ivanovo-Voznesensk, and Samara organizations in 1920, TsGALI f. 1230, op. 1, d. 117, ll. 5 ob., 47 ob., 6 ob.
52. G. Liubimov, "Narodnye orkestry i ikh znachenie v muzykal'nom prosveshchenii mass," *Gorn*, 1919, no. 2/3, pp. 99–105; A. D. Kastal'skii, "K voprosu ob organizatsii muzukal'nykh zaniatii v tsentral'noi studii Moskovskogo Proletkul'ta," *Muzykal'naia zhizn' Moskvy v pervye gody posle Oktiabria*, ed. S. R. Stepanova (Moscow, 1972), pp. 283–84.
53. For a critique of Moscow's approach by a Petrograd Proletkult member, see TsGALI f. 1230, op. 1, d. 3, ll. 71–72.
54. TsGALI, f. 1230, op. 1, d. 1278, ll. 13, 22 ob.

55. D. Zolotnitskii, "Teatral'nye studii Proletkul'ta," in *Teatr i dramaturgiia. Trudy Leningradskogo gosudarstvennogo instituta teatra, muzyki i kinematografii*, 1971, vyp. 3, pp. 134–45.

56. *Vzmakhi*, 1920, no. 2, p. 81.

57. TsGALI, f. 1230, op. 1, d. 3, ll. 52–53 ob. On production art, see Lodder, *Constuctivism*, pp. 75–76, 103.

58. Questionnaires for provincial Proletkult organizations, 1921–22, TsGALI f. 1230, op. 1, dd. 117 and 118 *passim*.

59. TsGALI, f. 1230, op. 1, d. 118, l. 7 ob.; d. 1581, ll. 28–28 ob.; d. 117, l. 98; d. 144, l. 124.

60. "Khronika Proletkul'ta," PK, 1919, no. 6, p. 30.

61. V. A. Razumov, "Rol' rabochego klassa v stroitel'stve sotsialisticheskoi kul'tury v nachale revoliutsii i v gody grazhdanskoi voiny," in *Rol' rabochego klassa v razvitii sotsialisticheskoi kul'tury* (Moscow, 1967), pp. 18–19.

62. PK, 1919, no. 9/10, p. 31; TsGALI f. 1230, op. 1, d. 1278.

63. D. Shcheglov, "U istokov," in *U istokov. Sbornik*, ed. I. P. Skachkov (Moscow, 1975), p. 70.

64. Ibid., p. 75.

65. N. Kuz'min, "Intelligentsia i proletariat," *Griadushchee*, 1920, no. 5/6, p. 16.

66. See a December 6, 1919, letter from the Orsha Proletkult, TsGALI f. 1230, op. 1, d. 1211, l. 10; a 1919 report from the Tver Proletkult, d. 1527, l. 14 ob; "O rabote Arkhangel'skogo Proletkul'ta," *Griadushchee*, 1920, no. 11, p. 17.

67. PK, 1920, no. 13/14, pp. 1–10.

68. This was N. K. Krupskaia's view. See her assessment of Proletkult activities in 1918, "K istorii Proletkul'ta," *Voprosy literatury*, 1968, no. 1, pp. 122, 124.

69. See L. A. Pinegina, "Organizatsii proletarskoi kul'tury 1920-kh godov i kul'turnoe nasledie," *Voprosy istorii*, 1981, no. 7 pp. 89–90; the memoirs of Shtraukh, "Dva Sergeia Mikhailovicha," pp. 69–72; P. N. Zubova, "Vospominaniia o Proletkul'te," TsGALI f. 1230, op. 2, d. 14; L. Granat and N. Varzin, *Aktery-agitatory, boitsy* (Moscow, 1970), pp. 112–76.

70. On Lenin's move against the Proletkult, see John Biggart, "Bukharin and the Origins of the 'Proletarian Culture' Debate," *Soviet Studies*, April 1987, vol. 39, no. 2, pp. 231–35; Fitzpatrick, *Commissariat*, pp. 176–87; *V.I. Lenin o literature i iskusstve*, 7th ed., ed. N. Krutikov (Moscow, 1985), pp. 286–313; 408–23.

71. "O Proletkul'takh. Pis'mo Tsk RKP," *Pravda*, December 1, 1920.

72. The central Proletkult's unpublished response, "Neobkhodimoe ob"iasnenie," is in TsGALI, f. 1230, op. 1, d. 51, l. 6.

73. "O Proletkul'takh."

COMMENTARY
THE REVOLUTION AND THE INTELLECTUALS

Diane P. Koenker

Inasmuch as "traditional" historians view history from the perspective of the elite and social historians from the vantage point of mass society, from either perspective intellectuals receive short shrift. As the preceding essays point out, the intellectuals were a small group of people, certainly not the masses, who were relatively, but not supremely, privileged before the revolution. Like other liberals in tsarist society, they wanted more professional autonomy, more respect, more freedom. Along came the revolution, and once again, intellectuals found themselves less privileged than the newly enfranchised class elite, although still better off than their former social betters. The intellectuals therefore constituted neither a pillar of the new regime nor a bastion of the old: their position in the developing society was thus ambiguous, undefined, problematic. Defining their position became one of the tasks during the Civil War both for the new regime and for the intellectuals themselves. Appropriately for a forum in social history, these chapters look for this definition from the perspective of the social group, the intellectuals.

Two themes characterize the social history of intellectuals during the Civil War. One is the attempt of intellectuals, particularly scientists and academics, to continue their revolution against the old order, to achieve their revolutionary dream of professional identity and autonomy. The Bolsheviks may have disliked this autonomy, but they did relatively little during the Civil War to deny it. A second theme is the efforts of intellectuals seeking to define their place in the new society turned upside down, individually and collectively, intellectually and materially.

James C. McClelland clearly establishes the dissatisfaction of professors with their position under the old regime. Theirs was not an elitist world-view: science and enlightenment could benefit all mankind, not just the privileged few. Above all, professors sought from the revolution the freedom to define their tasks and to serve mankind as they thought appropriate, given their intellectual

312

qualifications for this assignment. Nonetheless, although the new regime also valued science and knowledge, it did not acknowledge the professoriate's right to professional autonomy.

The actual implementation of this point of view, as McClelland documents, was uneven, and the story of university professors echoes that in other areas of life during the Civil War years, the complicated relationship between policy and reality. We are by now attuned to the divisions over basic policies that existed among the Bolsheviks, but here even Narkompros itself did not follow a consistent line regarding university autonomy. Its draft charter in early 1918 sought to democratize the university and to make it more responsive to the society as a whole—hence the "people's council" of representatives of local organizations (not too different from elected boards of trustees that govern state universities in the United States). But then, suddenly, Narkompros took a harder line. Here is where the events of the Civil War interacted with the slower process of policy formation and social change. McClelland does not say explicitly why, but Lenin intervened to insist on a harsher attitude toward university professors.

The intensification of military activities and of attacks in the capital seems to have discouraged any further spirit of compromise. The negotiations between Narkompros and the universities in 1918 illustrate not only the absence of firm social revolutionary policies on the part of the Bolshevik regime, but also the Bolsheviks' predilection for hard-line measures when threatened by political emergencies. If the universities retained some measure of autonomy up to the end of the Civil War, and if professors' privileges gradually returned, this was not because of any single policy decision but, rather, a consensus that the social question of the role of intellectuals could be deferred until the consolidation of the revolution after the Civil War.

The few thousand members of the Academy of Sciences, as Kendall E. Bailes points out, also managed to achieve a de facto autonomy during the Civil War without resolving the longer-term issue of their position as professionals under the dictatorship of the proletariat. They, too, shared a goal of corporate autonomy within the new system, an autonomy that Narkompros sought to curtail from the outset. But whereas Narkompros never gave up its ultimate goal of placing universities under its control, the scientists could appeal to other patrons in economic circles and thus resist subordination to the Commissariat of the People's Enlightenment. The scientists' ability to appeal to more than one master helped preserve more autonomy for them than for their colleagues in the classrooms.

Lenin's response to the two groups (or just as likely to their respective partisans within his regime) also illustrates the differences between them. Universities were part of the educational system, an important component of the regime's future mobilizational plans (however undefined they remained for the duration of the Civil War). But it was the natural scientists who best illustrated the educators' claims for the benevolent neutrality of *nauka*. Lenin appeared to acknowledge that science was too independent, and especially too important for future development, to bludgeon into subservience to the state. This was one factor in his decision to override Narkompros's plan to place the Academy of Sciences under its tutelage.

The role of Lenin is important in another way. Bailes stresses the dynamic element in the evolution of Soviet policy toward science. Lenin's views also changed, and his argument about the need to detach bourgeois specialists from the ranks of a potentially unified middle-class opposition, stated forcefully in 1919, did not necessarily reflect his position in early 1918. Before the beginning of armed hostilities, state science policy had to compete for attention with many other issues, and the threat of armed opposition to Bolshevik rule backed by the support of scientists and intellectuals did not yet appear as immediate as it would in 1919, that most critical year of the Civil War. Likewise, the attitude of scientists toward the state cannot be considered unchanging. The informal scientists' lobby, the Permanent Conference of Representatives of Scientific Institutions and Higher Education, intensified its activities only after the onset of the Red Terror; in other words, they assumed a more activist position in response to a change in their collective status in the new society.

Additionally, one must factor in the dismal economic conditions faced by urban Russian society as an element in the intellectuals' political and social choices. In his comments at the seminar, Gregory Freiden remarked on the role played by the "burzhuika" stoves and on the ironic symbolism of their name, "the little bourgeois," which provided so much warmth and sustenance. The regime came to acknowledge the importance of bourgeois professionals in the survival of the revolution, and scientists and professors achieved some success in surviving themselves, both individually and collectively. But individual survival must have come at the expense of attention to political issues of professional status and autonomy. And insofar as these professionals eked out a living in unheated classrooms and underequipped laboratories, their professional autonomy survived on borrowed time, because the revolutionary programmers were otherwise engaged.

Lynn Mally offers a more direct view of the process of revolutionary programming among intellectuals as well as a different view of intellectuals in their relationship to the revolution. Proletkult experts had no wish to preserve their autonomy outside the revolution: they sought to be part of the revolution and its working class. Whereas the university professors held up an ideal of culture and science as standing above and outside class distinctions, Proletkult intellectuals sought to merge intellectuals with workers and intellectual activity with the social needs of the working class. This amalgamation was itself a problematic task, for it involved the transformation of social identities, complicated, as Mally points out, by the inadequacy of the Proletkult's class-based language. What did it *mean* to be an intellectual? A worker? Even those committed to the Proletkult ideal did not share common answers to these questions.

In surveying the Civil War experience of the three sets of intellectuals discussed in these chapters, Mary McAuley remarked that it was only the artists, the cultural intelligentsia, who identified their struggle with the Civil War around them, who appropriated the language of class struggle for their own endeavors. Their contest was not between "intellectuals" who stood outside the political process and the "proletarian dictatorship," but among intellectuals, between those who "truly" represented the working class and those who betrayed that class through their attitude of intellectual superiority and condescension. Mally's study emphasizes the difficulty of the position of intellectuals, the poignancy of their efforts to become part of the revolution and not remain on the outside. Professors and scientists, on the other hand, preferred to remain outside, united and autonomous. "This was not their Civil War," argued McAuley. Theirs would come later.

Taken together, these three chapters offer important perspectives on the relationship of intellectuals to the new society. Mally identifies three types of Proletkult participants: idealists, pragmatists, and cynics. Surely these designations apply to professors and natural scientists as well, although the community of scientists and professors seemed able to coalesce around the pragmatist position and, in this unity, to defend their interests in the face of an ambiguous and uncertain state policy. These chapters also emphasize the importance of assessing the balance between policies and the response of the actors involved, between ideology and the specific historical context. If the Bolsheviks' socialist ideology sought to subordinate all social groups to the needs of the state, the intellectuals' ideology contained a powerful urge for autonomy. The victory of one ideology over the other, during the Civil War and later, was by no means predetermined, as these essays reveal. The ultimate place of intellectuals in the new society was contingent on many factors, including political rivalries, economic and military exigencies, and personality, as well as on ideas themselves.

V
Workers and Socialists

INTRODUCTION
WORKERS AND SOCIALISTS

Allan K. Wildman

In the works of Victoria E. Bonnell, Robert Johnson, Leopold H. Haimson, Rose L. Glickman, Henry Reichman, and Laura Engelstein,[1] a rich literature is now available on Russian labor history. Although no one work covers every dimension and large sectors remain untouched (particularly regions and types of labor), as a body it yields a fairly comprehensive view of "the working class" of late Imperial Russia. Moreover, the relationship of labor to general social and political history has been fairly well established so that many of the old shop-worn clichés have been, or should have been, discarded (for example, ascribing politics and "conscious" activity exclusively to revolutionary intellectuals or party organizations). Despite its late appearance and relatively small number of participants, the labor movement in Russia emerges from these studies as equal in importance to that of European countries, and of cardinal importance in the revolutions of 1905 and 1917. Studies of 1917 by John L. H. Keep, Diane Koenker, Alexander Rabinowitch, S. A. Smith, Rex A. Wade, and David Mandel now make it impossible to see Bolshevism as the exclusive prime mover of events or the surrogate of working-class involvement.[2] The workers developed their own self-awareness, definition of goals, and intensity of action, which, reversing the conventional equation, reshaped the Bolshevism of 1917. The Bolshevik Party succeeded in forging firm links to the working class in 1917 because it articulated and promoted this "consciousness" more vigorously than its rivals, and in the process it reabsorbed something of the "proletarian" ethos.

If the latter proposition remains controversial, the importance of working-class support for the October Revolution and the establishment of Soviet power can no longer be denied. Both the short-term and long-term parameters of working-class consciousness have been thoroughly explored and identified. A firm core of revolutionary tradition, to which the Bolsheviks made their specific contribution, endured the post-1905 repression, revived in the years

319

1912–14, survived the wartime turnover, and revealed itself at once in the February days. But events mobilized and radicalized ever new layers of workers in the course of 1917, and by September alienated them definitively from coalition politics and the old Soviet leadership of Mensheviks and Socialist Revolutionaries. That workers arrived at the characteristic slogans of Soviet power, workers' control, and peace as a rational, comprehensible defensive reaction against real or perceived threats from the "bourgeoisie" and counter revolution has, through research established its validity as opposed to the view that workers' were the victim of irrational outbursts stimulated by Bolshevik demagoguery. The dramatic shift toward identification with Bolshevism, first in Petrograd and subsequently in Moscow and the rest of the country, and the virtual collapse of support for the Mensheviks and orthodox SRs simply registered what the respective parties were saying and doing.

The important new social reality was that by October backward female textile workers and confectioners were as engaged and committed as skilled, literate male metalists, and in by-elections to the Soviet and every other opportunity chose Bolsheviks or other leftists to represent them, a reality on which the Bolsheviks could now reckon, whether or not they supported Lenin's call for an armed insurrection (and we now know many did not). Although the quality and durability of the workers' mood requires careful evaluation, it may with certitude be characterized as "revolutionary class consciousness," that is, as a clear perception of the opposition of their own interests to those of the "counterrevolutionary bourgeoisie," that demanded immediate revolutionary solution. Whether any part of it can be qualified as "socialist" or even "anarcho-syndicalist," particularly for the short-term perspective (socialist ideas had long been implanted among a certain cohort of skilled workers) is more questionable; recent investigations have stressed the more immediate, visceral issues that nourished it—the economic deterioration, the threat of unemployment, inflation, and fear of a new *kornilovshchina*.[3] But that Soviet power was now broadly perceived as the only possible alternative to the thoroughly discredited coalition arrangements is now beyond dispute. On the other hand, the same evidence suggests that workers varied considerably in how firmly they adhered to the notion that an armed struggle or force was necessary in view of the convocation of the Soviet Congress, as anxiety over the "isolation of the proletariat," "division within the democracy," and civil war remained a legacy of the July days. Only when the chips were down on October 27 with the junker uprising in Petrograd and the advance of Kerenskii's expedition from the front did most workers rally around the "legitimate" Soviet government and respond to the call to arms. It was not so much that they acknowledged the Bolsheviks as their standardbearers as that the moderate socialists had ruled themselves out by opposing Soviet power. Despite Lenin's concealed intransigence, the prolonged Vikzhel crisis is proof of continuing anxiety over "division within the democracy"; again the open intransigence of the Mensheviks and SRs destroyed the possibility of a compromise.

Elections to the Constituent Assembly confirm the high degree of support for the Bolsheviks in the urban working-class areas despite their poor showing nationwide. Thus, the October Revolution represented the strongest working-class cohesion behind the idea of Soviet power, ratifying the Bolshevik initiative. In a short time, however, well before the onset of the Civil War, the elements of that cohesion began to give way. The economic problems that had heightened class polarization and the sense of helplessness resisted solution: unemployment, plant closings, and the food shortage escalated relentlessly, while spontaneous seizures and attempts at self-management through factory committees likewise failed. On most of the issues that had shaped the workers' 1917 experience the new Bolshevik-dominated organs of authority took an increasingly different line (hierarchical management, piece work, reimportation of "bourgeois specialists"), which led to chronic conflicts. In short, the high expectations generated by the advent of Soviet power soon began to fade, and by summer the catastrophe that had been miraculously avoided in 1917, full-scale civil war, became a cruel reality. With the massive exodus from the cities, the drastic decline of production and the work force, the removal of the seat of government to Moscow (which workers stubbornly resisted in 1917), the siphoning off of the most "conscious" working-class elements, above all the zealous youth of the Red Guards, into the Red Army and Soviet institutions, the solidity of the class basis of the new regime fast eroded. On some of these developments we are well informed, on others far less so, but certainly the configurations of class consciousness, degree of mobilization, infraorganization, party, state, and class relationships were drastically changing, and a new polarization not unlike 1917 was taking place: state and party organs monopolized authority, preempting or subduing working-class organs, while the "class" itself was left largely to its own devices, ironically throwing up new representative organizations (for example, *sobraniia upolnomochennykh*) and responding to the agitation of the parties they rejected in 1917, the Mensheviks and SRs. Indeed, by the outset of the Civil War all the various interrelationships had become so altered that the ideology of 1917 seemed anomalous.

Sheila Fitzpatrick argued in *The Russian Revolution* that the workers nevertheless remained the class basis of the new regime, that through new recruitments into the party and state apparatus, workers became the new ruling class, and that therefore the Soviet experience should be viewed as a "revolution fulfilled" rather than as a "revolution betrayed."[4] Although the conceptualization is refreshingly unorthodox, is "the working class" still the same? Or had it become so transformed and disfigured in the process that its "consciousness" was now qualitatively different? Could the class by any stretch of the imagination any longer perceive the party-state as the embodiment of "its own" dictatorship? Certainly the chronic workers' oppositions of the early 1920s cast a pall of doubt. Furthermore, does the selective recruitment of workers into the party and state apparatus necessarily impart a class character to the state, or are the interests of those individuals refined by their new status? Does not bureaucratization itself generate a new sort of consciousness resting on its own socioeconomic base alien to and distinct from the rest of Soviet society? Although these problems are not new, most attempts to apply Marxian analysis, beginning with Trotskii, have become mired in contradictions and call into question the validity of conventional Marxist notions of class and class consciousness. Other types of analysis have been equally unsatisfactory, as they tend to ignore the empirical facts of class and class consciousness. Before the theoretical issues can be resolved there is a mountainous agenda of historical research to be done, simply to define what in fact the working class in the postrevolutionary era had become within the overall patterns of society. For this the Civil War period is critical.

Research in this area has scarcely begun. The only large-scale work remains that of E. H. Carr, a remarkable effort for its time but restricted to a particular range of questions and type of sources.[5] His approach was essentially teleological and institutional, measuring the degree to which advances were made toward a rational planned socialist economy. Hence, it was not conceptualized as social history, and, for all the invaluable information on structures, did not greatly help illuminate class relationships and textures. Thus, a clear set of tasks faces the current generation of researchers. They boil down to carrying forward with clarity and consistency the types of research that have so successfully illuminated the prerevolutionary period and 1917, applying similar concepts and tools to the new institutions and economic realities without wasting energy in a fruitless campaign against the "old historiography." Much of the old research of Leonard Schapiro, E. H. Carr, Robert V. Daniels, Isaac Deutscher, and Stephen F. Cohen,[6] which perhaps overemphasized ideology and politics, still has great value and should be recombined and integrated into the new findings of social history rather than discarded. After all, the theoretical and factional struggles often reflected the very real dilemmas of a ruling elite in coping with an ever-changing socioeconomic landscape. The fact that not one of the major figures, Lenin included, maintained a consistent ideological posture over time is a lesson in itself and cannot simply be ascribed to the vagaries of ideology. The changes in working-class make-up, its living conditions, institutions, infrastructure, the quality of its self-awareness, its attitudes toward the new state and social superstructure all bear serious examination. The Civil War era, as Sheila Fitzpatrick so cogently argues in the introductory essay to this volume, was the most intense period of gestation and restructuring, laying the foundations for a new system and social configuration. Civil War research on workers is indeed timely, and the contributions here of William G. Rosenberg and Ronald Grigor Suny are a welcome beginning.

NOTES

1. Victoria E. Bonnell, *Roots of Rebellion: Workers' Politics and Organizations in St. Petersburg and Moscow, 1900–1914* (Berkeley, 1983); Robert Eugene Johnson,

Peasant and Proletarian: The Working Class of Moscow in the Late Nineteenth Century (New Brunswick, N.J., 1979); Leopold H. Haimson, "The Problem of Social Stability in Urban Russia, 1905–1914," *Slavic Review*, 1964, no. 4; 1965, no. 1; and Leopold H. Haimson with Eric Brian, "Changements demographiques et grèves ouvrières á St. Petersbourg, 1905–1914," *Annales: economies, sociétés, civilisations*, 1985, no. 4, pp. 781–803; Rose L. Glickman, *Russian Factory Women: Workplace and Society, 1880–1914* (Berkeley, 1984); Henry Reichman, *Railwaymen and Revolution: Russia, 1905* (Berkeley, 1987); Laura Engelstein, *Moscow, 1905: Working-Class Organization and Political Conflict* (Stanford, 1982).

2. John L. H. Keep, *The Russian Revolution: A Study in Mass Mobilization* (New York, 1976); Diane Koenker, *Moscow Workers and the 1917 Revolution* (Princeton, 1981); Alexander Rabinowitch, *Prelude to Revolution: The Petrograd Bolsheviks and the July 1917 Uprising* (Bloomington, Ind., 1968) and *The Bolsheviks Come To Power: The Revolution of 1917 in Petrograd* (New York, 1976); S. A. Smith, *Red Petrograd: Revolution in the Factories, 1917–18* (Cambridge, 1983); Rex A. Wade, *Red Guards and Workers' Militias in the Russian Revolution* (Stanford, 1984); David Mandel, *The Petrograd Workers and the Fall of the Old Regime: From the February Revolution to the July Days, 1917* (London, 1983) and *The Petrograd Workers and the Soviet Seizure of Power: From the July Days 1917 to July 1918* (London, 1984).

3. See, for example, the works by Smith and Mandel cited above.

4. Sheila Fitzpatrick, *The Russian Revolution* (Oxford, 1982).

5. E. H. Carr, *The Bolshevik Revolution, 1917–1923*, 3 vols. (London, 1950–53).

6. Leonard Schapiro, *The Origin of the Communist Autocracy: Political Opposition in the Soviet State, First Phase, 1917–1922*, 2nd ed. (Cambridge, Mass., 1977); Carr, *Bolshevik Revolution*; Robert V. Daniels, *The Conscience of the Revolution: Communist Opposition in Soviet Russia* (Cambridge, Mass., 1960); Isaac Deutscher's three-part biography of Trotsky, *The Prophet Armed: Trotsky: 1879–1921* (Oxford, 1954), *The Prophet Unarmed: Trotsky: 1921–1929* (Oxford, 1959), *The Prophet Outcast: Trotsky: 1929–1940* (Oxford, 1963); Deutscher, *Stalin: A Political Biography*, rev. ed. (Harmondsworth, Eng., 1966); and Stephen F. Cohen, *Bukharin and the Bolshevik Revolution: A Political Biography, 1888–1938* (New York, 1973).

SOCIAL DEMOCRATS IN POWER
MENSHEVIK GEORGIA AND
THE RUSSIAN CIVIL WAR

Ronald Grigor Suny

The curious relationship between the violent upheaval of revolution and the forms and practices of a democratic order have at times led pessimists to contend that the two are incompatible. Democracy of a Western European type has seldom survived the trauma of revolution (the American case is an exceptional example), and certainly in the twentieth century the more likely outcome of social revolution seems to be a single party state willing (or compelled) to use political terror to maintain itself in power. Since revolutions are usually the product of social crisis and the mere change in the political elite is often insufficient to bring an end to the breakdown of normal order, continued compulsion by the new rulers may be required in the absence of traditional legitimacy to create a firm authority. If one accepts the arguments of successful revolutionaries in power, it is not just the breaking of eggs that is necessary for the omelet of social revolution but also the ability to institutionalize the egg-smashing instruments.

The Russian revolution and the establishment of the Soviet state appear to confirm the general proposition that democracy and violent social revolution cannot coexist. Whether one attributes the demise of democracy in Russia to the extraordinary social backwardness and the prolonged crisis of scarcity or to the ideological and personal propensities of Lenin and his comrades, so ready to seize power and so unwilling to surrender it, it is not unreasonable to see the Bolsheviks' failure to realize their own project for socialist democracy as the result both of the circumstances in which they found themselves and the political choices they made. Rather than deciding between a fatalistic view that the context of the Civil War itself (economic breakdown, foreign intervention, erosion of working-class support) made the drift toward dictatorship inevitable or the more voluntarist one that Lenin had a number of alternatives but given his ideological and personal preferences consistently chose those that enhanced his party's power, a more integrated analysis that relates ideology and political practice to circumstances in a reciprocal way appears more helpful.

The contrast between context and ideology found in many writers on the Soviet experience is far too stark. Rather than setting environment and agents, ideas and circumstances, against one another, this approach sees ideology as both shaped by the political and social context in which it emerges and operates and shaping that context in some way, at least in the perceptions of the actors. As Michael Burowoy puts it, "It is lived experience that produces ideology, not the other way around. Ideology is rooted in and expresses the activities out of which it emerges."[1] At the same time political circumstances are changed by the interventions of particular people, well-positioned individuals or multitudes, that are affected in particular ways by theoretical perspectives, biases, preferences, or expectations. Once certain actions are taken for whatever personal, ideological, or expedient reason, these interventions help determine the further development of circumstances. Once the Constituent Assembly was dissolved by the Bolsheviks, for example, the political context was irrevocably altered. Certain options were eliminated, others became acceptable or possible. The situation had been changed, and particular aspects of ideology had been reinforced while others had become irrelevant. In looking at the question of the descent from democracy to dictatorship in Russia, the complex interplay of environment, personality, ideology, and available choices must be considered, and neither circumstances, personality nor ideology should be given a privileged place in the overall explanation.

One way to consider possible alternatives in historical outcomes is through comparative studies. Although they are suggestive rather than conclusive, investigations of the Russian revolutionary process in a variety of localities can illuminate the available choices and the results of decisions made. When one looks at the attempts of moderate socialists during the Russian Civil War to maintain democratic forms, the picture is often bleak, but in the southern borderland of Georgia a successful experiment in socialist democracy was carried on for almost four years. Here representative institutions, periodic elections, and relative civil freedom managed to survive the violence of revolution and the need to construct a firm state authority. By investigating the experience of the Georgian Mensheviks the relationship between revolution and democracy might be better understood, and the descent into dictatorship of Bolshevik Russia be viewed, not as a necessary model for all postrevolutionary states, but as a particular outcome in a specific situation.

The Georgian Context

The one hundred–odd years of tsarist rule in Georgia had transformed the separate kingdoms, principalities, and dynastic regions into an interconnected national territorial unit. From the variety of tribal and local loyalties, a concept of Georgia as a nation had been forged by the political unification imposed by Russia, the consequent social and economic development that broke down local autarchy and expanded the market economy, and the intellectual and cultural awakening stimulated by the Georgian intelligentsia. By 1917, Georgians not only had a sense of their own history and national character, but as an emerging nation they had also developed their own national leadership in the Social Democrats, a cohesive and confident group of national Marxist intellectuals who enjoyed support among the peasants as well as their original constituents, the workers.

Yet for all their cultural, social, and ethnic developments by the second decade of the twentieth century, the Georgians had not held political and economic power in their own country. Russian bureaucracy and Armenian and foreign capital had rendered Georgians the least potent ethnic group in western Transcaucasia, despite their demographic dominance. Under tsarist autocracy with its protected capitalism, the Georgians had been unable to make significant inroads into the dominant political and economic circles. The Revolution of 1917 provided the Georgians with the first important political institutions (the soviets) they controlled since the 1870s. The Social Democrats so easily dominated Georgian politics through 1917 that there was no particular urgency about the implementation of political autonomy. The conjuncture of events that led to independence was in no sense the controlled result of Social Democratic aspirations or planning. Despite the hopes of the small number of Georgian nationalists, independence was not the goal of the leading political movement among Georgians. Rather, the physical and political separation from Bolshevik Russia created by incipient civil war and the immediate threat of a Turkish invasion forced the Georgians (as well as the Azerbaijanis and Armenians) to break officially with Russia.

Socially and politically Transcaucasia differed significantly from central Russia. Even more peasant in composition than Russia, the region was marked by an underdeveloped agriculture, overcrowding on the land, and legal restrictions on peasant mobility. As a Soviet historian wrote:

> Great feudal-serfowning remnants strongly inhibited the process here of the social disintegration of the peasantry. In Azerbaijan, Armenia, and Georgia the princes, nobles, and beks, as a rule, did not carry on their own (seigneurial) economy but existed almost entirely on the basis of natural payments of dues [obrok] which they received from the temporarily-obligated peasants. For this reason almost all agricultural production was in fact concentrated in the hands of the petty producers, the peasants.[2]

The peasant emancipation had been incomplete in Transcaucasia. As P. A. Zaionchkovskii put it: "As a result of the abolition of serfdom in Georgia feudal-serfowning remnants were preserved to a greater degree than the central regions of Russia."[3] Georgian peasants remained "temporarily obligated" until 1912, more than two decades after their Russian counterparts had been freed from this status, and the great power that traditionally minded nobles held over the rural economy retarded the creation of a significant pool of free workers.

Social cleavages in Georgia were far less extreme than in the countryside and towns of Russia proper. Georgian nobles were in general small landholders who often lived in villages alongside their peasants and operated in time-sanctioned ways. They were not disposed to reorganize agriculture along commercial lines. Although conflicts existed between peasants and landlords, they were mediated by the paternalistic ideology of the nobles, and Georgian villages remained cohesive. The nobles were simply too weak economically and politically to take on the peasantry directly, and by 1905 peasants had been organized and mobilized by the Social Democrats to resist any encroachments on their customary prerogatives.

The more intense social conflicts were, on the one hand, between Georgians as a whole and tsarist officialdom, and, on the other, between Georgian workers (and to some extent peasants) and the Armenian middle class. Georgia suffered from a dual colonialism: the political dominance of the Russian state and the economic hegemony of foreign, primarily Armenian, businessmen. The power of Social Democracy stemmed directly from its ability in the early part of the twentieth century to convince large numbers of Georgian workers, peasants, and intellectuals that the Marxist strategy of a class-based struggle against both autocracy and the bourgeoisie was the only effective means to achieve Georgia's full emancipation. Rather than promoting ethnic conflicts, the Social Democrats sublimated national tensions into a political-class conflict in which the Armenians were transmogrified into "bourgeoisie" and the Russians into "bureaucracy." The appeal of the Georgian Mensheviks eliminated the Bolsheviks as serious rivals well before the Revolution of 1917. The central political fact of Georgian life by the end of the first decade of the twentieth century was the absolute and almost unchallenged dominance of the Mensheviks. Their leader, Noe Zhordania, was recognized as the head of the nation, and Social Democracy had become the expression of an all-class national liberation movement of the Georgian people.

The remarkable political achievement of the Mensheviks in Georgia made their task during the years of revolution and Civil War far easier than that of their Bolshevik opponents in Russia. Yet the relative cohesiveness of Georgian society and the political potency of the Mensheviks were still severely tested when the older forms of political authority and social deference were swept away by the revolution. Georgia was faced with foreign threats (primarily from Ottoman Turkey up to November 1918) and domestic opponents (Denikin's army, local Bolsheviks, and peasant rebels). Yet the responses of the Mensheviks to the pressures of war and revolution were different from those of the Russian Bolsheviks. Instead of establishing a one-party dictatorship, for both ideology and practical reasons they maintained a multiparty parliamentary system. Instead of resorting to terror as an instrument of control, they usually devised less brutal solutions. Although the People's Guards were used to suppress rebellion, and although censorship and and limitations on political organization were imposed at times, the Mensheviks maintained a far more tolerant and open political environment than was common in Bolshevik Russia.

The Mensheviks of Georgia were undeniably more successful in establishing democratic practices and institutions than the Bolsheviks of Russia, but the question remains: was democracy possible only because of the less threatening political circumstances that the party found itself in, or was it also related to the Social Democratic view of the revolution? Any exploration of the context in which the Mensheviks of Georgia operated requires an appreciation both of social environment and ideology. In order to understand the range of their responses, four problems will be investigated: the creation of a new political order after the February Revolution; the challenge of the Bolshevik soldiery after October; Menshevik-peasant relations; and the treatment of opposition.

The February Regime

Just as in central Russia, so in Transcaucasia, the February Revolution gave birth, not to a single political authority, but to what contemporaries referred to as *dvoevlastie*. Even before the new Provisional Government in Petrograd could designate its local agency in Transcaucasia (the Osobyi Zakavkazskii Komitet or OZAKOM), the workers of Tiflis and Baku had elected their own representatives to local soviets. At first the soldiers met separately, and the old city dumas continued to function, but soon after the tsarist authorities abdicated their power, the workers' soviets emerged as the principal centers of power in Caucasian cities. In Tiflis the Georgian Social Democrats under Zhordania took control of the soviet, and within weeks they had established their authority over other competing organs. The Tiflis Executive Committee, which was made up of spokesmen of various social and political groups, rapidly came under the influence of the soviet, and with the democratization of the bourgeois-dominated municipal duma later in the year the power of the Armenian middle class, which had run the city in tsarist times, came to an end. The OZAKOM, as Zhordania pointed out to the soviet leadership, was made up of nationalists who did not have the confidence of the "democracy."[4] In the spring of 1917 authorities sanctioned by the Provisional Government had only as much power as they had support from the soviet and the populace. The soviet alone could bring crowds into the streets, order the soldiers to fire, and compel obedience to its decrees.

The Tiflis soviet adopted the basic view of the revolution outlined by its chairman, Zhordania. Three main forces, he argued, had made the revolution: the working class, the revolutionary army, and the progressive bourgeoisie. Unity among these three groups was imperative for victory. This meant that the proletariat should curb its demands for the immediate future in order not to frighten the bourgeoisie and drive it into alliance with the right. The errors of 1905 that had led to the isolation of the working class should not be repeated.[5] In concert with this line, the soviet resolved to support the Provisional Government "in so far as" (*postol'ku, poskol'ku*) it would support the interests of the democratic republic.[6] And it came out in favor of the Petrograd soviet's position on the war, refusing to support the war effort unconditionally "to a victorious conclusion" but, rather, advocating the pursuit of a "democratic peace without annexations or contributions."[7] The soviet of the Tiflis garrison also backed the March 14 declaration of the Petrograd Soviet on the war.[8]

The unity of the revolutionary front in Georgia was breached in the second month of revolution. The soldiers, the great majority of whom were Russian and, in so far as they had developed any party sympathies, were closest to the Socialist Revolutionaries, became agitated in April over Georgian nationalist efforts to establish autonomy for Georgia. The soldiers opposed any movement toward separation from Russia, and the Social Democratic leaders of the soviet assured the garrison that "extraordinary measures" would be taken against the nationalists.[9] Discussion of autonomy was curtailed in the press, and armed units formed by the various nationalities were disbanded. When the First Congress of the Caucasian Army met in late April, the soldiers made clear their opposition to separatism by urging postponement of the "national question" until the Constituent Assembly.[10]

In the stratified ethnic conglomerate of Tiflis, Zhordania's three major revolutionary forces were at one and the same time three different social classes made up predominantly of three different ethnic groups and influenced primarily by three different political parties. The workers, as noted before, were largely Georgian and Menshevik, the soldiers were Russian peasants and SR, and the "progressive bourgeoisie" was largely Armenian and politically divided between the Dashnaks and the liberal parties (the Kadets and their local Armenian ally, the Armenian People's Party). Every issue that arose in 1917—the introduction of the eight-hour day, the question of the war, the Coalition Government, Georgian national autonomy, or Soviet Power—was debated and decided by balancing and satisfying the competing interests and suspicions of these contending political actors.

The fragile alliance of the Tiflis soviet parties was sorely tested by the successive political crises in Petrograd. The inability of the Provisional Government to maintain credibility without active participation within it of prominent members of the Petrograd soviet forced the Mensheviks and the SRs of the capital to agree reluctantly at the end of April to the formation of a coalition government. But the Mensheviks in Tiflis vigorously opposed socialists sitting in the same government with representatives of the propertied classes. Zhordania argued for a purely bourgeois government without Kadet leader Pavel Miliukov and those like him who favored an "annexationist" peace. For the Georgian Mensheviks, like their comrades in Russia, the issue of the nature of the government was crucial, for it not only would establish which social class would have its interests promoted by the state but also whether the revolution would continue as a "bourgeois-democratic" revolution or be transformed into a "socialist" one. Sharing the Menshevik view that the essential preconditions for a socialist revolution simply did not exist in Russia, Zhordania concluded that representatives of the "democracy" should neither form their own government nor join an essentially bourgeois coalition. As his Menshevik comrade Evgenii Gegechkori told the Tiflis soviet: "If the socialist wing of the Provisional Government acts in the interests of the democracy but without a socialist outlook, then it will deserve the just protests of the proletariat; if it acts in the interests of the proletariat, then this will alienate the bourgeoisie from the other revolutionary strata of society, and this will be the beginning of the end."[11]

Once the "April Crisis" over foreign policy brought down the first Provisional Government, the tensions in the democratic front of workers and soldiers in Tiflis began to intensify. While the Menshevik-led workers' soviet opposed formation of a coalition government (April 29) and promised it only conditional support (postol'ku, poskol'ku) (May 6), the soldiers' soviet, led by the Socialist Revolutionaries, came out for unconditional support of the new government (May 16), defeating a motion by Zhordania.[12] The Mensheviks tried to hold the front together by merging the two soviets (May 26), and Bolsheviks who agitated among the soldiers against the war were arrested.[13] The Mensheviks tried to keep local Bolsheviks within the common SD organization, but in early June the Bolsheviks decided to form their own party, drawing a sharp line between the position of the moderate socialists who supported, however tentatively, the coalition government and their own advocacy of "All Power to the Soviets!"

What support the Bolsheviks of Tiflis had came largely from the soldiers and, to some extent, from Russian workers. For the first two months of revolution the only Social Democratic newspaper in the Russian language was Kavkazskii rabochii, the organ of the Bolshevik faction. The Menshevik equivalent, Bor'ba (which complemented ertoba [unity]) did not appear until May. Bolsheviks began to make serious inroads among the soldiers once it became clear that the government, instead of bringing the war to a speedy conclusion, was planning a major campaign in the summer. Embarrassed by the so-called Kerenskii Offensive, the Tiflis soviet on June 23 adopted a lukewarm resolution that considered the offensive "one of the military episodes in the world war which in no way changes our aims in it."[14] The next day four thousand soldiers gathered in the Aleksandr Garden and adopted a Bolshevik resolution calling for the end of the offensive.[15] Following the lead of their comrades in Petrograd, the Tiflis Bolsheviks organized a protest march for June 25. As in the capital the moderate socialists tried to coopt the demonstration by rescheduling it and providing their own slogans and orators, but the demonstrators, some ten thousand soldiers, shouted down the Menshevik speakers and applauded only the Bolsheviks. This meeting too adopted a Bolshevik resolution opposing the Kerenskii Offensive and added a call for a government dominated by the soviet.

The sudden radicalization of the Tiflis garrison was a great victory for the Caucasian Bolsheviks and a serious threat to the Mensheviks. The army, the most potent force in the revolution, had moved from patriotic support for the war effort to an active opposition to any offensive action. Their enthusiasm for the Provisional Government on which they had based their hopes for an end to the war had evaporated with the June offensive. The Mensheviks feared civil war in the city and acted resolutely to head off a crisis. Refusing to have the soviet reelected as demanded by the left, they decided instead to organize a reliable military force and carry on their own agitation in the army. Mensheviks and Bolsheviks now began an intensive campaign for the loyalty of the Tiflis garrison. It was simultaneously a struggle for power in the city, the outcome of which would determine if the representatives of the Georgian working class or the Russian soldiery would decide the political fate of central Transcaucasia.

Events in Petrograd in July—the ill-fated uprising of radical military units with the tentative support of the Bolshevik Party, the subsequent suppression of the Bolsheviks, and the formation of a new government under Aleksandr Kerenskii—marked a temporary halt in the leftward drift of the revolution both in the capital and in Tiflis. For the first time the Tiflis soviet approved the coalition government and warned of the danger of counterrevolution from the left. Rallying behind the Central Executive Committee of the Petrograd soviet, the Tiflis soviet prohibited any further meetings of soldiers in the Aleksandr Garden, where Bolshevik agitators had daily been addressing them.[16] As the danger from radical Russian soldiers grew, the Mensheviks demonstrated that they were prepared to use their control of political institutions to curb the Bolsheviks and limit the propagation of maximalist views.

The October Crisis

The effect of the *Kornilovshchina* was not only to radicalize the urban lower classes, but also to push moderate leaders into actions that further compromised the authority of the Provisional Government. In Tiflis Gegechkori announced, "For everyone it is now clear that the counterrevolutionaries have declared civil war."[17] The Caucasian Territorial Center of Soviets decided to form a revolutionary committee that would have supreme power in the region. Unauthorized demonstrations were prohibited; Kornilov sympathizers arrested; and the Kadet party was declared counterrevolutionary.[18] Although some Mensheviks, like Chkhenkeli, opposed the formation of the Revolutionary Committee (REVKOM) and the Provisional Government ordered its liquidation, the local soviets refused to comply. The soviets, which had always been suspicious of the OZAKOM, attempted to reorganize that body by adding Social Democrats and Socialist Revolutionaries and declared that it would work with the "confidence of the Territorial Center of Soviets."[19] The Provisional Government rejected the new composition of OZAKOM, and a stand-off occurred between the local REVKOM, which had the confidence of the soviets, and the powerless OZAKOM, which had its legitimacy conferred by a government that the soviets nominally recognized. For all intents and purposes the actual sovereign body in Transcaucasia by the early fall of 1917 was the Territorial Center of Soviets. Soviet power existed except in name.

Although to an outsider Tiflis may have looked calmer and less savage than Petrograd or Moscow, the Menshevik leaders were aware of a broadening social disintegration. Early in October it was reported that 128,000 soldiers had deserted from the Caucasian Army.[20] A bread shortage in Tiflis had created a "dangerous mood" in the city. Georgian bakers shut off their *tonirebi* (clay ovens) and went on strike.[21] In Kutaisi soldiers, supported by townspeople who hated the merchants, began looting shops. The local soviet requested help from Tiflis and Batumi, and Gegechkori rushed to the scene and tried speaking to the crowd. But only Cossacks and cadets from Tiflis stopped the looting.[22] Although some blamed the Bolsheviks for the soldiers' lack of discipline, Gegechkori pointed out that there were few Bolsheviks in Kutaisi. The real problem was the need to establish a strong political authority to stave off chaos and to create a reliable military force based on "the more trustworthy elements in the population, among them the workers."[23]

Conflict between the leaders of the soviets and the army came to a head in late September–early October. The REVKOM dismissed certain officers on the commanding staff and replaced them with men loyal to the soviets. The Territorial Council of the Army voted on September 21 to have the REVKOM dispersed. The REVKOM found it could not act in the face of army opposition. When it tried to purge the postal-telegraph service, which was restricting socialist propaganda among soldiers, the Territorial Council defended the postal employees.[24] The REVKOM was reorganized by the soviets as a Committee of Public Safety on the eve of the October Revolution. Given full power to prevent anarchy and pogroms, the committee was able to arrest suspected counterrevolutionaries. But the army's leaders refused to go along with this new arrangement, and the very day that the Bolsheviks overthrew the Provisional Government in Petrograd the Territorial Council of the Caucasian Army rejected the REVKOM and recognized only the Kerenskii government.[25]

The Mensheviks were placed in an unenviable dilemma by the Bolshevik insurrection. They wanted neither the triumph nor the defeat of the Leninists, neither the unity of Russia under a Bolshevik government nor separation of Transcaucasia from Russia. In the soviet they called for the "peaceful liquidation" of the uprising and the creation of a homogeneous democratic government. Bolsheviks and SRs, both of whom had great support among soldiers who feared separation from Russia, abstained from voting for the Social Democrats' motion.[26] The Bolsheviks wanted soviet power; the SRs preferred using force against the Bolsheviks. On October 28, representatives of thirty-six military units in the Tiflis garrison organized a delegates assembly and came out in support of the October Revolution. The assembly was opposed to the existing soldiers' soviet and the Territorial Council of the Army and declared itself the sole representative of the soldiers until new elections were held to those bodies. The soviets ordered the dispersal of the assembly, and in response the Bolsheviks walked out of the Executive Committee of the Soviets (IKS).

Within days of the October Revolution the worst fears of the Mensheviks had been realized—a complete schism occurred in the revolutionary democracy.

Bolshevik strength in the garrison increased daily. Even Georgian national regiments were sympathetic to the party that seemed most dedicated to ending the war.[27] Most important, Bolshevized soldiers controlled the arsenal and refused to give arms to people authorized by the IKS. On November 11 the soviets decided to give all administrative direction (*upravlenie*) to a new government of Transcaucasia responsible to the soviets.[28] This government, the Transcaucasian Commissariat (ZAVKOM), was to be the kind of authoritative democratic government that, it was hoped, could win over support from the more radical elements in the population. The Bolsheviks, however, refused to join the government, but when promises to organize new elections to the soviets were made, the Bolsheviks decided to reenter the IKS and disband the Delegates Assembly.[29] For reasons that remain obscure (and are still debated in the Soviet literature) the Transcaucasian Bolsheviks did not seize the opportunity that their support in the garrison and the relative weakness of the Mensheviks presented. Instead they decided to work within the soviet structure and await the outcome of the elections. Since ZAVKOM was responsible to IKS, it was in a sense a "soviet government," though more broadly conceived than its counterparts in Russia to include the lower middle-class elements of the "democracy."

The peculiar political allegiances in the city of Tiflis were reflected in the elections to the Constituent Assembly in November. Of 103,777 votes cast, the Mensheviks won 32,000, the Dashnaks 20,000, the Bolsheviks 19,000, the SRs 11,500, and the Kadets 9,600.[30] A slightly less complete total from a local newspaper gives a revealing breakdown of votes from city residents and the garrison:[31]

Party	City Residents	Garrison	Total
Mensheviks	27,125	4,267	31,392
Dashnaks	18,218	1,689	19,907
Bolsheviks	6,023	13,134	19,157
SRs	3,750	7,633	11,383
Kadets	7,794	1,765	9,559

Far more radical than the city population, the garrison, as the only source of significant support for the Bolsheviks, was a threat to the Menshevik hegemony over the city. But just as the Bolsheviks hesitated to act, the Mensheviks took the initiative into their own hands. The newly formed Red Guards, made up of city workers and under the command of former Bolshevik Valiko Jugeli, asked the arsenal for arms. When they were refused, the guards disarmed the soldiers at the arsenal and arrested the Bolsheviks Kote Tsintsadze and Kuznetsov. Soldiers protested the seizure, as did the SR Party, but the protest remained unpublished and the arsenal in the hands of the Mensheviks. The demobilization of the garrison followed, and, with the soldiers leaving the city and the front, the last bases of Bolshevik support outside of Baku evaporated.[32]

In order to justify the military action against the arsenal, Zhordania revealed intercepted Bolshevik telegrams from Shahumian to Stalin. Jugeli told the soviet: "Until the last moment I believed in the possibility of an agreement with the Bolsheviks, but Shahumian's telegram proved to me that the Bolsheviks, completely ignoring the workers, want to decide the matter by means of bayonets. Bayonets must be opposed by bayonets."[33] Shahumian attempted in vain to explain the telegrams, denying that his comrades were preparing an uprising, but his arguments fell on deaf ears. The damage had been done by publication of the telegrams. Prepared to employ demagogy and even create a degree of hysteria to combat Bolshevism, Zhordania then pushed through a motion to declare martial law.

In fact the Bolsheviks of Caucasia were undecided about direct action against the ZAVKOM. The moderate Territorial Committee of the party (KRAIKOM) did not want bloody confrontation or civil war and insisted on a strategy of working through the promised elections to the soviets. The Mensheviks, however, argued that soviet elections would have to wait until after the elections to the Constituent Assembly. In the famous telegram to Stalin, which was interpreted to have called for a coup against the Transcaucasian government, Shahumian had actually limited Bolshevik action to pressure. It is worth quoting that telegram in full.

> A Transcaucasian government has been formed from defensists and nationalists, headed by Gegechkori and not recognizing the power of the People's Commissars. We have declared war on them recognizing this government as counterrevolutionary. The troops look on it as an action of separation from revolutionary Russia. Turkey has agreed to an armistice. The presence of your representatives to participate in the negotiations for an armistace is essential. You can depend on the soldiers and the Baku soviet to force the local government to recognize your government.[34]

The circumstances surrounding Bolshevik actions (or inaction) are murky, but it is known that Shahumian and the KRAIKOM were not in complete agreement as to strategy. What is clear is that the Mensheviks were not prepared to wait for the Bolsheviks to act or for the soldiers to position themselves for a coup against the soviets. Long before October, governmental authority in Tiflis had ceased to be a matter of legitimation by a superordinate authority, whether it be the Provisional Government or the Petrograd Soviet. Power was the product of the effectiveness an institution had in commanding people into the streets. Authority, in a sense, followed power and had to be acquired over time. By acting decisively, by mobilizing their worker constituency against the arsenal, the Mensheviks changed the entire political balance in Tiflis and at a single blow began the process of demobilization that doomed the local Bolsheviks to impotence. The Mensheviks were able to use their genuine social support, political manipulation by the institutions they controlled (delaying elections, declaring martial law), and even physical force to maintain their rule in the city. Principled advocates of political democracy, the Georgian Mensheviks were nevertheless prepared to act decisively to prevent their rivals from gaining military advantage in the city. As they saw it, their political survival (and indeed the fate of the revolution) required the bold use of power against the Bolshevik threat. At this moment and in the future the Mensheviks did not hesitate to use force in order to create the conditions for the continuation of the revolution as they conceived it.

Independent Georgia and the Peasants

The long years of Menshevik political hegemony among workers and peasants in Georgia, stretching back into the first years of the century, gave the Georgian Social Democrats distinct advantages over their Bolshevik opponents in Petrograd. The challenge to the Social Democratic Party in Transcaucasia came primarily from Russian soldiers, an alien (and as it turned out, temporary) element, which was quickly eliminated. Other parties were far too weak to resist Menshevik persuasion or pressure. The local bourgeoisie lost its political clout after the February Revolution, and with the declaration of Georgian independence in May 1918 the appeal of the Georgian nationalist parties was in part surrendered to the Social Democrats, who had actually achieved the nationalists' goal. The only major social force inside the country that potentially could thwart the measured policies of the Mensheviks was the peasant majority in the countryside. But here Menshevik policy differed most sharply with Bolshevik practice in Russia. Instead of initiating class divisions in the villages and extracting surpluses by force, a far more conciliatory approach was adopted, one that did not set the state in opposition to its majority constituents and require an authoritarian political structure.

Of all the classes in Georgian society the peasantry appeared in 1917 to be the one most unwilling to submit to new authorities. Caucasian peasants almost immediately ceased paying their redemption payments and taxes to the state and either refused altogether to pay dues to the landlords or demanded that they be reduced. When in the first days of revolution Zhordania had set forth his analysis that its moving forces were the workers, army, and liberal bourgeoisie, he had not mentioned the peasantry, though his party did have much support in the villages. The ostensibly peasant party, the SRs, had support in the army ("peasants in uniform"), not in the countryside, and the First Congress of the Caucasian Army (April-May 1917) had voted overwhelmingly for the SR resolution calling for socialization of all land. The Menshevik program, which asked only for confiscation of state and church lands, had been rejected, though all parties agreed that full implementation of the land reform should await the Constituent Assembly.[35] A few weeks later, the Mensheviks won the crucial vote at the Transcaucasian Congress of Soviets of Workers' and Peas-

ants' Deputies (in which peasants were poorly represented), where it was decided the *otrezki* (the lands cut off from peasant holdings and given to nobles
in the Emancipation settlement) would be returned to peasants and lands confiscated from the state and church could be rented by peasants.[36]

By late spring 1917 the Mensheviks had been impressed sufficiently by the
activity of the peasantry to include them in their formulation as one of the
"moving forces" of the revolution.[37] But they consistently opposed the more
radical stand of the Bolsheviks and the SRs, which favored abolishing private
property in land. Their prerevolutionary efforts in the countryside made them
nearly invulnerable in rural Georgia, as was evidenced by the nearly two-to-
one margin by which the June Congress of Peasant Deputies of Transcaucasia
adopted the moderate Social Democratic agrarian program. Georgian and
Azerbaijani deputies voted for the Menshevik proposal, while most Armenians
followed the Dashnaks and the Russians followed the SRs, both parties having
come out for nationalization.[38] Given that all parties except the Bolsheviks
were committed to delaying a final solution of the land question until the
Constituent Assembly, no further action was taken by the leaders of the Caucasian soviets or party organizations until the October Revolution.

Faced with the Bolshevik "Decree on Land," which had essentially adopted
the SR principle of socialization, and the signs of growing impatience on the
part of Caucasian peasants, the Mensheviks of Tiflis decided to implement
their own local land reform. The ZAVKOM, which from November 1917
acted as a fully empowered government, had to contend with opposition to
nationalization from the Muslim leaders and decided to avoid confrontation
by excluding *vaqf* (endowment for clergy) lands from the reforms. The attempt
by the Armenian Catholics to exempt church lands as well was rejected, however.[39] On December 16, 1917, the ZAVKOM decreed that state, church, and
private land above a certain norm be transferred to a national land fund to
be directed by land committees.[40] Three months later the Seim established the
norms: seven *desiatiny* for plots producing valuable cash crops, fifteen for
grain-producing land, and forty for pasture land.[41] Exceptions were later made
for larger holdings that were deemed to have economic value for the national
economy.[42] The laws of December 16, 1917, and March 20, 1918, took the
bulk of noble land away from the nobles without compensation, leaving them
significantly smaller plots in most cases. Poor peasants whose land fell below
the norms were able to lease land from the state land fund, but the private
market in land was eliminated. The status of *khizani* (landless peasant) was
abolished, and those peasants were given the land they had cultivated. Later
it was decided that peasants who used land that had been left in noble hands
were required to pay dues on that land and were retroactively responsible for
a proportionate amount of dues for 1917.[43] The reform had relevance only
for Georgia, for the Muslim landlords who controlled much of the land in the
Azerbaijani and Armenian areas opposed these laws. Ironically the decrees of
1917–18 passed by the all-Transcaucasian governments marked the highwater
mark of a leftist agrarian policy in the region. With the establishment of the

independent Georgian republic in May 1918, the Social Democratic leaders took another look at the land question.

The first months of the new republic were not only occupied with the crucial problems of forming ties with the Germans and fending off the Turks but also with serious internal threats to the establishment of order and authority. In the northern mountainous regions of Georgia, first in Dusheti and later in Racha, Tianeti, and Lechkhumi districts, peasant dissatisfaction with the terms of the land reform and the activity of the land committees created conditions for open rebellion. The smallholders of Dusheti were incensed that large estates were being transferred to state control rather than turned over to the nearest village.[44] Bolsheviks, many of them former soldiers, began agitating in these areas and organized armed detachments of peasants, one of which attacked (but failed to take) the town of Zugdidi on June 27. In Racha, Shamshe Lezhava led a guerrilla band, and in Lechkhumi, Sasha Gegechkori commanded three hundred men. The Osetins of Sachkeri as well worked with the Bolsheviks, who were in close touch with the Territorial Center of the Communist Party in the North Caucasus and the Soviet government in the Terek region.[45] With little hesitation the Mensheviks sent Jugeli's People's Guards (formerly the Red Guards) to the north where they carried out a brutal campaign against the rebels. Villages were burned; the death penalty was reinstated, as was censorship, and one by one the insurrections were put down.[46]

Minister of Agriculture Noe Khomeriki realized early that the land reforms of 1917–18 did not go far enough for the peasants, who opposed leaving the land in the control of local government and having it rented to the peasantry. They looked on the lands leased to them as their own private property and wanted to buy the remaining land from the noble landlords. Buying and selling went on despite the legal prohibitions. Khomeriki was convinced that the government had no choice but to deal with this strong tendency toward private property by transferring much of the state land fund into private hands.[47] Both at conferences of the land committees and at the Menshevik Party Congress in November the view prevailed that land should pass to the peasantry as private property. The congress resolved that most land should go to landless peasants, other land could be sold at low prices, and only land with "broad social significance" would be held by the state or transferred to *zemstva* (local governing bodies).[48] Finally, by the law of January 28, 1919, the peasants were given the land as private property with the right to buy and sell. The Socialist Revolutionaries, Socialist Federalists, and National Democrats voted against the bill, but Khomeriki answered those among his critics who opposed turning confiscated land over to private smallholders: "Our agrarian reform destroyed the principle of feudal property. In general we neither establish nor reject bourgeois private property; this is a fact of life with which, of course, the law has to deal."[49]

Inevitably complaints and resentments about the redistribution surfaced. In some districts where there were few large estates to be confiscated, the land shortages could not be alleviated locally; elsewhere the dense population received only tiny supplements to their small plots. In no district of Kutaisi province, for example, did the average peasant farm exceed 1.6 hectares; the situation was considerably better in Tiflis province where the average plot ran from 4 to 7 hectares. To alleviate shortages, from the second half of 1918 the ministry moved more than eight thousand families to free lands in other districts.[50] Besides the evident economic motivations, there were political considerations in some of these transfers. Georgian peasants were installed in the district of Gagra, for instance, a border region contested with the Volunteer Army of General Denikin, and in Akhalkalaki and Akhaltsikhe, areas with Armenian populations that had been the source of considerable conflict between the Armenian and Georgian republics.[51]

The effects of the Georgian land reforms remain difficult to assess, but their basic contours can be discerned. A year and a half after the final reform law, Khomeriki confidently told the Congress of Georgian Social Democrats that confiscation of noble lands above the set norms had been completed over almost all the territory of the republic and that nine-tenths of that confiscated land had been turned over to peasants with little or no land.[52] Nearly five thousand estates had been affected by the reform. Over 660,000 hectares of land had been taken from noble landlords who were left with about 37,000 hectares. A noble on the average ended up with a holding of about 10 hectares, a plot that was usually larger than that of his peasant neighbor.[53] The least fortunate peasants received the most land from the reform, and the state held on to the forests, much of the pasture land, and the waterways. The extent to which the confiscation and redistribution was actually carried out was quite extraordinary given the fact that the Georgian lands had not been surveyed, that the ministry had few qualified people to carry out the technical aspects of the reform, and that the whole operation was largely completed in two years while the government was fighting off external enemies and internal rebellions.

The smallholding agricultural system that had always existed in Georgia was sanctified by the reform, though at long last the greater part of the nobles' lands (which peasants had always worked) was now in peasant hands. Since Georgia had had little large-scale production, the economy lost little in output as a result of confiscation, but more of the surplus was now consumed by the direct producers. The ultimate rationale of the Mensheviks for abandoning their 1906 program of municipalization of confiscated lands for outright grants to private property holders was simple expedience. There was no desire to thwart peasant desires and risk more unrest and economic dislocation. The socialists were content to oversee the abolition of "feudal vestiges," to live with private farming, and to leave a portion of the land to the nobles in order to maintain social peace.[54]

Both critics and sympathizers of the land reform have pointed out that turning the confiscated land over to private smallholders neither alleviated the problem of land shortage—there were still too many people on the land for the amount of cultivated land available—nor worked to increase output. The Russian Menshevik M. Liadov argued that the only solution was formation of larger farms and intensification of agriculture.[55] In his generally supportive account of Social Democratic Georgia, Kautsky worried about the small surplus produced by small-scale agriculture and hoped that in the future the Georgian form of cooperative agriculture (*nadi*) would evolve into a widespread system of cultivation by the village communes.[56] But a much more telling critique came from Bolsheviks like Pilipe Makharadze, who condemned the reform for preserving noble property. The norms set by law (7–40 *desiatiny*) gave nobles allotments large enough to be worked by hired labor. Moreover, in the absence of cadastral surveys, nobles fictitiously divided their families in order to receive additional allotments.[57] The peasantry was aware that land that could have been turned over to them had been left by the government in the hands of a privileged class that had never itself worked the land.[58] The legalization of buying and selling land rendered the norms established by law for size of holding meaningless and eventually would work to the benefit of the wealthy.[59] In another early Soviet work, Ia. Shafir, writing about the peasant uprising in Guria in 1919, reproduced a dialogue between a peasant and a Bolshevik agitator found in a report to the Menshevik government:

> "If the Menshevik government is not a noble [government], why does it leave the land to the nobles?" asked the peasants. They were answered by the agitators: "The Mensheviks promised the land, but they do not want to give it because they themselves are nobles."[60]

The effect of the land reforms of 1917–20 was to abridge the privileged status on the land of the Georgian nobility but not to eliminate that nobility as a class of landowners. Fifty years after the Emancipation, Georgia's peasants finally held full title to their plots, the large estates had either been broken up or taken over by the state, and nobles had been reduced to petty proprietors like their peasant neighbors. The last vestiges of the seigneurial system had been removed, but, unlike Bolshevik Russia, Menshevik Georgia did not take all the land away from the nobility. To the Mensheviks the "bourgeois transformation" that had taken place with the establishment of private property in land conformed to the wishes of the majority of the peasantry and was consistent with the Mensheviks' understanding of the nature of the revolution at hand. By neither accepting the prerevolutionary status quo in the village nor promoting a more radical land reform (which was never seriously considered by the Social Democrats) and by maintaining market relations with the smallholding peasantry (no forced requisitioning here), the Mensheviks reduced the potential alienation of the peasantry from their urban-based regime.

Opposition and the Institution of Democracy

Recalling the dichotomy between social circumstances and political ideology mentioned early in this chapter as causative factors in moving from democracy to dictatorship, the Menshevik experience in Georgia, it can be argued, indicates that ideology and related political action shape the context in which a party operates while being shaped by it. Exacerbating existing conflicts provides opportunities for certain kinds of political maneuvres but limits other choices. Initial decisions to prevent workers' demonstrations or to force grain from peasants may have allowed Bolsheviks to avoid consulting with their natural constituents but also created the "necessity" of establishing an increasingly authoritarian political structure.

Consciously and deliberately the Georgian Mensheviks worked to avoid exacerbating class and ethnic tensions in their small country. Although they were able and at times willing to use force against opponents, they used it discretely rather than systematically. By adopting a style of conciliatory and consultative politics, the Mensheviks prevented certain kinds of opposition from developing. The National Democrats on the right and the SRs on the left voiced their protests and objections inside the existing institutions, the Georgian parliament (later the Constituent Assembly), the soviets, and the city duma, as well as in the relatively open press. Having limited their program to the goals of the February Revolution, the Mensheviks were able to work with the middle and upper classes, as well as with the ethnic minorities that demographically dominated their capital city. Collaboration rather than class or ethnic warfare marked the Menshevik approach, in clear contrast to that of the Bolsheviks.

There were failures and limits on the democratic approach. Between November 1917 and May 1918 the Mensheviks and their anti-Bolshevik allies, the Armenian Dashnaks and the Muslim parties, attempted to create a representative government for the whole of Transcaucasia. ZAVKOM contained members of all major parties, nationalities, and social classes and was intended to surrender power once the Constituent Assembly convened. When the Bolsheviks dispersed the assembly in January 1918, the delegates elected from Transcaucasia were reconstituted into a local Seim, which operated from February to May 1918. On April 26, 1918, Chkhenkeli formed the first government of the independent Democratic Federative Republic of Transcaucasia. This experiment in multinational parliamentary government failed miserably. As the Turks moved across the frontier on their way to Baku, the Azerbaijani leadership could scarcely conceal its sympathy with Turkish aims. The Armenians, on the other hand, mortal enemies of the Young Turk government, which had organized the deportations and genocidal massacres of 1915, resisted Turkish advances. The Armenians and Russians of Baku, a city administered since early April by a Bolshevik-led soviet, rejected altogether the authority of the independent republic. The Georgian Mensheviks realized that keeping the new republic united and defended in the face of the Turkish threat was impossible, and they accepted a German offer of protection. On May 26, 1918, the Georgians abandoned the Azerbaijanis and Armenians and declared themselves independent.

Independence did not end the divisions and conflicts within Georgia. Not only were the Bolsheviks active in opposing Georgian separatism, but even within the Social Democratic party there were opponents to independence. Zhordania himself was at first unreconciled to independence and decided not to serve in the first government. The day after the *Oblastnoi komitet* and the Tiflis Menshevik Committee resolved that Georgia must be declared independent, one of the founders of Caucasian Social Democracy, S. T. Arkomed (Gevork Gharajian), made a symbolic, though politically impotent, gesture by resigning from the *Obkom* "because of the impossibility for me to go along with the policy of Chkhenkelism, which had sustained victory over revolutionary Social Democracy."[61] The Menshevik movement had in the eyes of its socialist critics moved closer to those parties whose advocacy of Georgian autonomy or independence had made them the bitterest enemies of the socialists. A small group of "internationalist" Social Democrats, most of them Armenian and Russian, began issuing their own newspaper, *Sotsial-Demokrat*, directed against the "nationalism" of their former Georgian comrades.[62] A bitter conflict developed between the two wings of Social Democracy, but the ruling party allowed the antiindependence fraction a degree of freedom to propogate its views.

Once independence had been established, the leading Mensheviks defended it as the only practical choice and were prepared to use whatever means were necessary to prevent the Bolsheviks from exploiting economic or political difficulties faced by the republic. Bolshevik demonstrations were broken up by workers or by the police. A constant barrage of anti-Bolshevik propaganda appeared in the press, and Bolshevik activists were periodically arrested. Though the potential danger from the Bolsheviks increased once the Germans and the British left Georgia, it was always an external danger rather than one generated by sources of Bolshevik strength within the country. Now at the head of an independent state, the Mensheviks enjoyed the luxury of having no major social groups able to compromise their political decisions. At the same time they trimmed their aims in order to keep the country from splintering along class or ethnic lines.

Whatever enthusiasm many Georgian Social Democrats may have felt for Georgian independence was tempered by the dilemma posed for socialists as the ruling party in a "bourgeois" republic. At the first general session of the Tiflis soviet after independence (June 1, 1918), Irakli Tsereteli defended the party's actions as the only alternative to total destruction, and the soviet accepted the necessity of the act. Following the same instincts that had led him to take a hard line against Bolshevik opposition in Petrograd, Tsereteli advocated strong measures against the opponents of independence. The government closed down *Znamia truda* (Banner of Labor), the local organ of the Socialist Revolutionaries, for editorializing against independence.[64] A week later Tsereteli told the joint meeting of the Transcaucasian Center of Soviets and the Tiflis Executive Committee that the mistakes of the moderates in central Russia should not be repeated in the Caucasus: there should be no duality of power.

> The cause of our defeat was the absence of one, fully empowered democratic state authority. The democracy ought to create one. The revolutionary organizations of one class must refuse to take on state functions and return to their true role, to the leadership of their class.[65]

The meeting voted to back a strong government and to limit the activity of the soviets to the defense of working-class interests. This policy of reducing the role of the mass organizations was adopted the next day by the Tiflis soviet and the staff of the Red Guards, both of which repudiated any pretensions to governmental power. All power was delegated to a "united democratic government" to be headed by Noe Zhordania.[66]

As prime minister in a socialist government, Zhordania understood the paradox of his administration of a "bourgeois" state. A year earlier he had strongly condemned Tsereteli's policy of participation in the Coalition Government in Petrograd. But rather than surrender power to the feeble Georgian bourgeoisie, represented ostensibly by the National Democratic Party, Zhordania now implemented his notion of a government of the "democracy," a government representing the lower classes but carrying out the reforms appropriate to the bourgeois stage. Borrowing from the German socialist theorist Karl Kautsky, Zhordania argued that "the first steps of the victorious proletariat will be, not social reforms, but the introduction of democratic institutions, the realization of the party's minimum program, and only afterwards the gradual transition to the socialist maximum program.[67] The Georgian state, limited as it had to be by the level of social development, "cannot avoid serving in one way or another . . . the interests of the bourgeoisie."[68] Social Democracy was compelled to "play the principal role in building a modern state. . . . The question arises: how to reconcile our Social Democratic ideology with the work of creating bourgeois institutions; how to do this so that in the process the party does not go off the track of Social Democracy and turn into a petty-bourgeois party." At the same time there was no reason to fear opposition to socialist rule from the upper and middle classes. Given the weakness of the Georgian aristocracy and bourgeoisie, Zhordania concluded that there was "no social base for reaction here, for restoration or constitutional monarchy." The major danger to democracy in a primarily peasant country like Georgia comes from the village, but the government can guarantee "support for the revolution and the rule of democracy" by satisfying the peasants' foremost demand and promulgating a land reform.[69]

Given their position at the helm of a "bourgeois" state, their broad base among the peasantry, and the fact that they were now a party of the whole nation, the Social Democrats of Georgia were nevertheless careful to maintain and nurture their special relationship with the small and variegated working class. While the Bolsheviks managed at various times to find sympathizers among soldiers, mountaineers, and national minorities, seldom were they able to make inroads into the Georgian working class. Workers not only made up the most active elements within the Menshevik party but were the backbone of the People's Guards, the weapon on which the government depended to disarm the Bolshevized soldiers of 1917, to disperse the rebel peasants of 1918–19, and to defend the shifting frontiers of the republic against Armenians (1918), Denikin's Volunteer Army (1919), and finally the invading Red Army (1921).

The isolation of Georgia from Russia, Azerbaijan, and the West in the years of independence had a devastating effect on her industrial economy. Though not nearly as miserable and helpless as the tiny Armenian republic, Georgia suffered from the disruption of trade with the other parts of the former tsarist empire and a general breakdown of internal economic relationships. Estimates by Soviet scholars hold that coal production fell nearly 50 percent from 1913 to 1919; the extraction of manganese ore diminished to about 13 percent of prewar production by 1920.[70] The shortages of raw material caused reductions in industrial output; only about 60 percent of Georgia's largest plants managed to operate steadily.[71] The total number of workers fell. Inflation, the resultant fall in real wages, and unemployment increased labor unrest and presented the Mensheviks with one of their most vexing dilemmas: how to reconcile their role as the traditional representatives of working-class interests and their new position as head of a government representing the interests of the whole nation.

The two decades of Social Democratic activity among Georgian workers had established a trust in the Menshevik intelligentsia that served the government well. When workers began to question the wisdom of Georgia's separation from Russia and Bolsheviks argued that the shortages of goods were a direct result of that break, the minister of labor, Giorgi Eradze, was able to convince a mass meeting that independence had in fact saved Georgia from the ravages of the Russian Civil War and the harsh policies of forced requisitioning of foodstuffs from the peasantry that the Bolsheviks had imposed on Russia.[72] When Tiflis city workers went on strike to protest the municipality's failure to pay them, a united front of Menshevik-led institutions condemned the walkout. Not only the Tiflis Soviet but even the Council of Trade Unions opposed the strike and demanded sacrifices in the national interest.[73] In general workers showed restraint in their protests, though strike activity was widespread. In order to stop the cycle of inflation and rising wages, the Ministry of Labor set up a *tarifnaya palata* (wage board) in May 1919 to set wage rates.[74] Representatives of the trade unions (over 56,000 workers were organized in Georgia) sat down with representatives of industry, the banks, and the government in an official arbitration process expected to bring some order into the highly individualized negotiations between workers and employers. The Mensheviks preferred policies such as state mediation of economic disputes rather than the outright nationalization eventually favored by the Bolsheviks. Their success testifies to their skills in labor relations. It may also be that class antagonisms in Georgia were not as deep as they were in central Russian cities or even in Baku. But this whole area of economic problems, food shortages, and living standards remains to be investigated.

Georgian Social Democratic leaders frequently contrasted their more mod-

erate and democratic system of government and economy with the more centralized and dictatorial system in Soviet Russia. Based on their conviction that
the preconditions did not exist for socialism, the Mensheviks held back from
assaults on the capitalist mode of production. In August 1919, a state monopoly
on manganese export to Europe was established, the forerunner of a general
state monopoly on foreign trade.[75] But such state intervention was exceptional,
and the opposition parties called for more radical measures. While the Bolsheviks demanded an end to capitalism, the Socialist Revolutionaries and Socialist Federalists more modestly argued for a "deepening of the revolution"
and more radical economic policies as an alternative to political repression in
the struggle against Bolshevism.[76] The Mensheviks' hegemony over the urban
workers of Georgia was so complete that they made few concessions to the
left. The major representative body of workers, the Tiflis soviet, had given up
its prerogatives to the government, and the Georgian Constituent Assembly
and was rarely called into session except to sanction positions taken by the
government. In a real sense Georgia exemplified the Social Democratic ideal—
a working class deferring to its socialist intelligentsia, prepared to follow its
lead in building a democratic nation-state and willing to wait for the distant
victory of socialism.

Georgian democracy was far from perfect. The government was willing to
shut down newspapers that opposed independence. The minister of the interior,
Noe Ramishvili, organized the Special Detachment to Fight Speculation and
Counterrevolution to deal with the internal enemies of the republic. This
Cheka-like organization was opposed by the representatives of the Armenian
minority and the Georgian bourgeoisie, but the SD Lomtatidze mocked their
fears that the detachment might be used against them: "There is a Georgian
saying, if you did not eat a hot pepper, why is your mouth burning?"[77] In fact
the detachment, like the People's Guard, was used primarily aginst the Bolsheviks. The Armenians of Tiflis found themselves in an unenviable position
when open conflict broke out late in 1918 between the republic of Armenia
and Georgia. Prominent political figures were detained by the police. Yet the
parliamentary institutions were opened to non-Georgians by the fall of 1918,
and elections continued through the period of the republic with special representation of minorities.

Given that Georgia faced external threats from Denikin in the north and
from Armenia and the Turks in the south, as well as the activities of Bolsheviks
and other opponents within the country, the record of democratic practice is
extraordinary. It is not surprising that Georgia became a model for Second
International socialists of a successful experiment in social democracy. Part of
the explanation for the success may be related to relatively favorable social
and political circumstances in which the Georgians found themselves. The long
period of Menshevik hegemony among workers and peasants provided the
party with a firm social base on which it could build. The Mensheviks, unlike
the Russian Bolsheviks, were a majority party. Democratic elections did not
threaten their continued rule as it might have the Bolsheviks.

But equally important were the political choices made by the Social Democrats—to mediate rather than intensify social conflicts, to keep as open as possible a political forum, both in the press and in elected institutions, and to use force minimally. The ability to eliminate the threat posed by Russian soldiers in 1917–18 and to neutralize potential peasant opposition by the moderate land reform made it easier to maintain a fairly tolerant political system through the years of the republic. Zhordania and the Mensheviks rejected the idea that the working class, particularly in backward countries like Russia or Georgia, could act alone through its own class institutions. Rather than soviet power they preferred a broader representative system of the parliamentary type. They feared that the proletariat, cut off from the democracy, would create a climate of civil war, and looking from Tiflis northward they believed that their expectations had been cruelly confirmed by the Bolsheviks' attempts, however sincerely motivated, to rule in the name of the soviets. Perhaps circumstances were far less favorable to the Russian Bolsheviks, but the repeated reliance on compulsion rather than compromise by the Leninists drew the Bolshevik Party away from their democratic impulses of 1917 and toward an authoritarian political practice that soon became part of a new and brutal political culture.

NOTES

1. Michael Burowoy, *Manufacturing Consent* (Chicago, 1979), p. 18.

2. V. D. Mochalov, *Krest'ianskoe khoziaistvo v Zakavkaz'e k kontsu XIX v.* (Moscow, 1958), p. 5.

3. P. A. Zaionchkovskii, *Otmena krepostnogo prava v Rossii*, 3rd ed. (Moscow, 1968), p. 333.

4. Ia. Shafir, *Ocherki gruzinskoi zhirondy* (Moscow, 1925), p. 8.

5. N. N. Zhordaniia, *Za dva goda. (S marta 1917 po 1 marta 1919 g.) Doklady i rechi* (Tiflis, 1919), pp. 5–6.

6. *Protokoly zakavkazskikh revoliutsionnykh sovetskikh organizatsii, I* (Tiflis, 1920), pp. 125–26.

7. Ibid.

8. *Izvestiia* (of the Tiflis soviet), March 28, 1917, no. 2.

9. Ibid., April 7, 1917, no. 8.

10. *Bor'ba*, May 14, 1917, no. 8.

11. Ibid., May 11, 1917, no. 6.

12. *Protokoly*, pp. 145–58; *Izvestiia*, May 9, 1917, no. 34; May 19, 1917, no. 41; May 20, 1917, no. 42.

13. *Protokoly*, pp. 41–44; *Izvestiia*, May 31, 1917, no. 50.

14. *Izvestiia*, June 25, 1917, no. 72.

15. *Kavkazskii rabochii*, June 28, 1917, no. 86.

16. *Izvestiia*, July 25, 1917, no. 96; July 26, 1917, no. 97; S. E. Sef, *Revoliutsiia 1917 goda v Zakavkaz'i* (Tiflis, 1927), pp. 192–93.

17. Sef, *Revoliutsiia 1917 goda*, p. 211.

18. Ibid., pp. 211–15.

19. *Izvestiia*, September 8, 1917, no. 133.

20. *Golos kraevogo soveta*, October 3, 1917, no. 90.

21. *Bor'ba*, October 20, 1917, no. 136.

22. Ibid., October 5, 1917, no. 123.

23. Georgian Archive (Houghton Library, Harvard University), Boxes 1, 2, no. 3 (film 76–4545, reel 2), p. 905.

24. *Izvestiia*, October 19, 1917, no. 165; October 20, 1917, no. 166.

25. A. L. Popov, "Iz istorii revoliutsii v Vostochnom Zakavkaz'e," *Proletarskaia revoliutsiia*, 1924, no. 5 (28), p. 14.

26. *Izvestiia*, October 27, 1917, no. 172.

27. Noi Zhordania, *Moia zhizn'* (Stanford, 1968), p. 79.

28. *Izvestiia*, November 7, 1917, no. 181.

29. Sef argues that the disbanding of the Delegates Assembly and the Bolshevik reentry into the IKS were both "serious tactical mistakes" by the Tiflis Bolsheviks (Sef, *Revoliutsiia 1917 goda*, pp. 46–47).

30. *Bor'ba*, December 12, 1917, no. 176.

31. *Molot*, November 19, 1917, no. 39.

32. *Bor'ba*, December 12, 1918, no. 241; Zhordania, *Za dva goda*, p. 95; Zhordania, *Moia zhizn'*, pp. 80–81.

33. *Bor'ba*, December 12, 1918, no. 241.

34. *Izvestiia*, December 8, 1917, no. 206. This text is taken from the stenographic report of the session of the Tiflis soviet of December 4, 1917. Interestingly enough, a recent Soviet collection of Shahumian's writings reproduces a text of a telegram to Lenin of November 23, 1917, which it translates from the Georgian newspaper *brdzola*, December 9, 1917, no. 51: "We have declared battle against the Transcaucasian Commissariat as it is counterrevolutionary. The greater part of the garrison is on our side. We can with the help of the army force the Commissariat to recognize the power of the Council of People's Commissars. We request that you immediately communicate to us what is to be. St. Shaumian" (S. G. Shaumian, *Izbrannye proizvedeniia v dvukh tomakh, II [1915–1918 gg.]* [Moscow, 1978], p. 152).

35. *Bor'ba*, May 13, 1917, no. 7; *Izvestiia*, May 16, 1917, no. 38.

36. *Izvestiia*, June 2, 1917, no. 52.

37. *Izveshchenie o shestoi oblastnoi s"ezde Zakavkaszskikh rabochikh organizatsii RSDRP* (Tiflis, 1917), p. 3.

38. *Delo naroda* (Petrograd), August 15, 1917, no. 127.

39. Georgian Archive (Harvard University), Boxes 1, 2, no. 3 (film 76–4545, reel 2), pp. 1309–16.

40. The text of this law can be found in *Sbornik izdannykh s nachala revoliutsii po 1 noiabria 1918 goda zakonov, instrutsii i raz'iasnenii po ministerstvu zemledeliia (Polozhenie o zemel'nykh komitetakh, o konfiskatsii zemel' i pr.)*, comp. L. G. Asatiani (Tiflis, 1918), pp. 42–45.

41. Ibid., pp. 45–48.

42. The supplementary law of May 2, 1918, can be found in ibid., pp. 43–44. This law left larger holdings in the hands of noble and other proprietors.

43. Ibid., pp. 27–28.

44. *Bor'ba*, July 2, 1918, no. 106.

45. The Terek People's Soviet Socialist Republic, centered at Vladikavkaz, was established in March 1918 and headed by the Georgian Bolshevik Noe Buachidze. A month later it recognized the sovereignty of the RSFSR. In August local Cossacks drove the Bolsheviks from Vladikavkaz briefly, but in alliance with Ingush tribesmen the Bolsheviks retook the city a few weeks later. In 1919 Denikin's Volunteer Army moved into the area. It was not until late March 1920 that the Whites were driven out of Vladikavkaz.

46. Firuz Kazemzadeh, *The Struggle for Transcaucasia (1:17–1921)* (New York, 1951), pp. 189–93.

47. Interview with N. G. Komeriki in *Bor'ba*, July 5, 1918, no. 109.

48. Ibid., November 17, 1918, no. 221.

49. *Zakavkazskoe slovo*, January 24, 1919, no. 5. In a contemporary study of the Georgian land reform, S. Avaliani presents the following figures to illustrate the decline in the nobles' economic position by 1918:

NOBLES' LANDHOLDINGS

(in *desiatiny*)

	Tiflis Province	Kutaisi Province
1860s	961,502	815,321
c. 1900	992,216	495,125
Jan. 1, 1918	511,538	110,157

(From S. Avaliani, *Mitsismplobeloba sakartveloshi* (Kutaisi, 1920), p. 12)

50. M. Khomeriki, *La réforme agraire et l'économie rurale en Géorgia. Rapport au Congrès du Parti Social-Democrate de Géorgie, en juillet 1920* (Paris, 1921), pp. 28–30.

51. Ibid., pp. 30–31.

52. Ibid., p. 23.

53. Ibid., p. 19.

54. Ibid., pp. 36–37.

55. *Bor'ba*, January 16, 1919, no. 11 (267).

56. Karl Kautsky, *Georgia, a Social-Democratic Peasant Republic: Impressions and Observations* (London, 1921), pp. 54–55.

57. Filipp Makharadze, *Diktatura men'shevistskoi partii v Gruzii* (Moscow, 1921), p. 39.

58. Ibid., p. 44.

59. Ibid., p. 45.

60. Shafir, *Ocherki gruzinskoi girondy*, p. 46.

61. S. T. Arkomed, *Rabochee dvizhenie i sotsial-demokratiia na Kavkaze (s 80-kh godov po 1903 g.)* (2nd ed., Moscow-Petrograd, 1923), pp. 12–13n.

62. *Sotsial-Demokrat* appeared in Tiflis from June 10, 1918, as the organ of a group of Mensheviks who opposed the creation of independent republics in Transcaucasia and the separation from "Russian democracy." Of the eighteen members of the editorial collective only one was clearly a Georgian; the others were Armenian, Russian, and Jewish.

63. *Bor'ba*, June 4, 1918, no. 84.

64. Ibid.

65. *Sotsial-Demokrat*, June 10, 1918, no. 1; *Bor'ba*, June 11, 1918, no. 90; no. 91, June 12, 1918.

66. *Bor'ba*, June 11, 1918, no. 90; June 12, 1918, no. 91.

67. Ibid., August 28, 1918, no. 153; August 29, 1918, no. 154; August 30, 1918, no. 155; August 31, 1918, no. 156.

68. This speech was reprinted in Zhordaniia, *Za dva goda*, pp. 109–135.

69. "Social relationships in Georgia," Zhordania argued, "have given rise to three democratic classes—the workers, the peasants, and the petty bourgeoisie—which constitute the social basis for the building of the Georgian state. In such circumstances the state can only be democratic or it cannot exist at all" (ibid., p. 113).

70. M. V. Natmeladze and N. N. Sturua, *Iz istorii rabochego klassa Gruzii (1921–1958 gg.)* (Tbilisi, 1961), p. 10.

71. Ibid.

72. Interview with Giorgi Eradze conducted by Leopold H. Haimson (Menshevik Project, Columbia University), no. 17, pp. 95–102.

73. *Bor'ba*, March 28, 1919, no. 70 (326); March 29, 1919, no. 71 (327).

74. Ibid., May 14, 1919, no. 104 (360).

75. Grigorii Uratadze, *Obrazovanie i konsolidatsiia Gruzinskoi Demokraticheskoi Respubliki* (Munich, 1956), p. 106.

76. *Bor'ba*, November 2, 1919, no. 250 (508); November 4, 1919, no. 251 (509).

77. Ibid., July 28, 1918, no. 129.

THE SOCIAL BACKGROUND
TO TSEKTRAN

William G. Rosenberg

In the late spring of 1920, as the pressures of civil war and the policies of War Communism brought Soviet Russia to the verge of collapse, Trotskii embarked on a series of drastic measures designed to improve Russia's transport system. The most controversial soon proved to be his reorganization of the transport union leadership, and its amalgamation into a new Central Committee, Tsektran, under conditions of strict military discipline. Tsektran was to serve as a transport "high command," controlling a militarized railway labor force and forcefully implementing party policy. As such it represented an amalgamation of state, party, and trade union functions as well as their institutional coalescence, and it soon raised sharp cries of protest from those who believed in trade union autonomy and who objected strongly to its methods. The controversy broke into the open at the Fifth Trade Union Congress in November. It raged in the party's highest circles for most of the winter, following a course of angry debate through a labyrinth of open and secret party meetings, oppositional caucuses, platforms, and resolutions to the eventual reorganization of Tsektran at the Tenth Party Congress in April 1921, and the famous ban, at the same time, of all factionalism and oppositional groupings.[1]

The controversy has been treated almost exclusively in the literature as a conflict over the nature and function of Communist political dictatorship. The party's leadership is thought to have split over two equally possible courses of political action, one tending in the direction of greater proletarian democracy, one "repudiating democracy," as Deutscher put it, in favor of the dictatorial controls we have come to label "Stalinist." Arrayed behind Trotskii in the controversy were the partisans of labor militarization, the centralization of power, and "merciless jackboot discipline," to use the unfortunate phrase attributed to A. Z. Gol'tsman (a metalist on the Central Trade Union Council and one of Trotskii's supporters). Opposed were "democratic centralists" like Osinskii and Sapronov, the "workers' opposition" led by Shliapnikov and

Kollontai, and those leaders of the trade union movement like Tomskii, who fought for union autonomy, resisted authoritarianism, and hoped to "overthrow Tsektran" in their effort to prevent the dictatorial centralization of party authority.[2] A "buffer" group stood between the two, organized by the cautious and manipulative Zinoviev, who hoped to quiet the conflict in the interest of maintaining party authority, and, of course, Lenin himself, who skillfully crafted the Platform of the Ten, the "compromise" solution that leaned first in one way, then another, and became the basis of party policy toward labor and the trade unions at the Tenth Party Congress. As Schapiro writes,

> [the controversy] was one part of the struggle for power which was taking place inside the Central Committee during 1920 and 1921. This struggle was waged primarily around the whole question of the centralization of authority within the party, and those who professed to oppose centralization emerged victorious, only to introduce a greater degree of centralization than had existed before . . . [The downfall of men lacking] the calibre or temperament to carry out ruthless measures . . . and the rise of men who replaced them, heralded a new era in the political history of Russia."[3]

The problem with this perspective is not, of course, that it is wrong, but that it largely conceptualizes political conflict in this critical period independently of its relationship to social reality and constructs the "origin of communist autocracy" out of ruthless personalities and the political machinations of the Bolshevik Central Committee, rather than by investigating carefully the ways in which social conditions and processes shaped political positions, or at least limited the range of viable political responses. The issue obviously is not one of straight line determinism, as if social structures or conditions obviate the role of personal temperament and force particular policies on party leaders, but concerns the interaction between social circumstances and political actions; and while the Tsektran controversy in the last months of the Civil War was of course a political one, concerning the very nature of the party, it was also, and more importantly, a dispute that stemmed from the interrelationships between Bolshevik authoritarianism, socioeconomic conditions, and the actual functioning of political bodies on both a local and national level, as well as the influence of these groups—local soviets, trade union groups, local party organizations—on social developments. The most important issues for historical analysis in the Tsektran controversy, in other words, concern not so much the ideological or political commitments of men like Trotskii or Lenin, their temperaments, or even the "struggle for power" itself within the Central Committee (although these all deserve careful attention), but what might be called the social foundations of authoritarian politics and, by implication, of Stalinist dictatorship itself.

These issues, so readily susceptible to ahistorical generalization, are not easily addressed in a short essay. They require close attention to social context, with all of its complexity and nuance; the sifting of factual detail, which in this period is extremely difficult to come by; and an effort to weigh the effect of powerful anxieties and tensions (rarely evidenced in any explicit way) that gripped ordinary men and women struggling for their lives in a world where survival was becoming the exception rather than the norm. What I will attempt to do here, rather, is lay the issues out in their broadest contours, focusing first, but only briefly, on the Tsektran controversy itself, and then on several of the larger patterns of social change in the Civil War as they affected workers (and, consequently, economic administration) in an effort to situate the controversy in its proper social context. I will then examine in some detail one "slice" of this context, the work life of railroaders and the operation of transport, since it was here that Tsektran was expected to bring major changes. Against this background we might be able, in the end, to reconsider the meanings of "dictatorship" and "democracy" as they emerged in the Tsektran dispute, and see the controversy itself in a somewhat different light.

The chain of events leading to the open split within the party over the Tsektran issue began in the mid-winter of 1919–20, when the Bolshevik leadership, under Lenin's direction, confronted two pressing and related problems. One was the task of maintaining the now sizable Red Army as an active fighting force after the defeats of Wrangel and Denikin; the other was the need to stave off the immediate threat of new and even deeper shortages of food, particularly in Moscow and Petrograd, caused in part by the exhausted state of Russia's pillaged and increasingly resistant countryside, in part by the near cessation of all foreign trade, and most importantly by the virtual collapse of Russian transport, which made it nearly impossible to distribute even available supplies in an orderly manner. The need to maintain the army required no argument. Wrangel remained a threat in the Crimea, and peasant bands under Antonov and others posed a constant danger almost everywhere, especially in the Tambov region. There was also the fact that any massive demobilization would cause enormous strains on social relations and an already devastated economy, strains that had greatly troubled the Bolshevik regime in the first months after October 1917. That Soviet transport had collapsed seemed equally self-evident, whether measured by declining freight traffic in the capitals or the apparent indifference and apathy of transport workers. Every day brought a spate of grim statistics.

Many believed these conditions mandated a relaxation of the party's confiscatory policies toward the peasantry and the resumption of at least some degree of private trade, a course of action Lenin and others considered ideologically unacceptable. In early 1920, however, in contrast to the spring of 1921 when these central elements of the NEP were actually set in motion, the military danger facing Soviet Russia still remained serious, requiring the maintenance of substantial forces, and the need for food was so widespread and urgent, particularly in the cities, that hungry workers and soldiers in armed special detachments would undoubtedly have continued in the short term to take what they could from the countryside, regardless of party directives to the contrary. Social circumstances and military need thus reinforced Bolshevik ideological dispositions, at least for many: until some semblance of recovery in the transport system allowed greater state control over trade relations and the movement of goods, and until the party could risk the potentially cata- strophic hardships of demobilization in conditions of relative military security and a relaxation of international trade restrictions, as was the case in 1921 after the defeat of Wrangel and the Greens, other "solutions" had to be sought and applied.

Hence the logic, at least in part, of the decisions taken in January and February 1920 to create "labor armies" out of idle military units in the Urals, Caucasus, and the Ukraine and to "militarize" civilian labor itself through the mobilization of workers for compulsory labor service under the Council of Defense and Glavkomtrud (*Glavnyi Komitet po Vseobshei Trudovoi Povin- nosti*), organized on January 29.[4] On January 30, Russia's railways themselves were "mobilized" by special decree. Shortly afterward a shock force of some five thousand railroad workers was organized to assist in major line repairs. To a considerable extent, these measures reflected Trotskii's views on the tasks of economic reconstruction, submitted to the Central Committee as a series of "Theses" in December 1919, and largely adopted by the Central Committee on January 22, 1920.[5] In early March, Trotskii himself became commissar of transport, in addition to his duties as head of the Red Army and the Revo- lutionary War Council.

Trotskii approached his new post not only with the energy and disposition he showed in building the Red Army and the determination to apply military methods to transport, as Deutscher and others have pointed out, but also with an evident prejudice against railroad workers generally, whom he regarded as untrustworthy and "backward." He also had little confidence in the railroad union, Tsekprofsozh. As he charged around the country in 1918 and 1919 he often found himself desperate over delays and incompetence on the lines, in- cluding once the derailment of his own train in snow and freezing temperatures that apparently went unnoticed for more than a day and a half. Rather than draw railroad union leaders into his efforts to revitalize transport by increasing their authority, Trotskii set out instead to use the party arm of the Commis- sariat of Transport, Glavpolitput, which had been formed in the spring of 1919 for organizational and propaganda work within the commissariat bureaucracy. With Central Committee support, and armed with a new decree imposing strict sanctions for the least malfeasance, special plenipotentiaries from Glavpolitput were soon traveling along the lines with military escorts, replacing local of- ficials, arresting others, and issuing rafts of new instructions and orders. Not surprisingly their appearance was instantly objectionable to scores of rail- roaders and local officials, inside the party and out.

Trotskii had several goals in mind in reorganizing Glavpolitput into a "fight- ing party and soviet organ," as the process was officially described.[6] He hoped to shake what he regarded as the complacency of union leaders, and attack the bureaucratic "nesting," which he felt was infecting party and state structures everywhere. He also wanted to mold the railroad union into an organization of talented, competent administrators, capable of assuming direct control over management and production, and committed primarily to the tasks of economic administration. In the process, the union would be drawn closer to the state commissariats, and the party would be used to thwart what Trotskii regarded as the increasing danger of its independence and the development of parallel (and competitive) institutions. "The last step in this process" was to be the "complete statization (*ogosudarstvlenie*) of the trade union, that is, the transfer of the entire administration of transport into its hands."[7]

Trotskii also hoped to rationalize transport administration itself, a task he believed required both the centralization of decision making and planning and the implementation throughout the system of one man rule (*edinolichnost'*). Above all was the need for discipline and order. Daily absenteeism among railroaders was reported to be close to 30 percent. Work stoppages were commonplace. In January 1920 the vital repair shops of the Moscow-Kursk line had been shut down briefly by a strike. All this clearly had to change, and change rapidly in Trotskii's view, if new disasters were to be avoided.[8]

Despite later polemics, each of these objectives was strongly supported by party members in and outside the trade union movement, as well as within the Central Committee, the Commissariat of Transport, and even the railroad union itself. The official formulation of the Ninth Party Congress was that trade unions were to serve as the "link tying the most backward . . . masses of the proletariat with its vanguard, the Communist party," but their development as "production unions"—that is, organizations capable of directly managing the economy—was not only a tenet of the party's program, but also assumed to be an element that would naturally emerge with the development of a healthy socialist order, as the unions "more and more became the fundamental base of the soviet economic apparatus."[9] The railroad union itself was formally reorganized into a production union early in 1919, along with other groups; and its vice president, Amosov, presented the Communist fraction report himself to the Third All-Russian Trade Union Congress, repudiating the call of Dallin, Ratner, and other non-Bolsheviks for union independence.[10] Whether this meant unions would "fuse" with state commissariats and whether, more importantly in the view of many, Soviet Russia was ready in 1920 to move as rapidly in this direction as Trotskii, Kossior, Gol'tsman, and others insisted, seemed at first a question of historical timing and the pace of socialist development rather than a matter of principle—a question to be resolved by determining the most effective, practical ways to organize and manage a socialist economic system.[11]

The use of a revitalized Glavpolitput to "shake up" transport from the "outside" also had the official endorsement of the Ninth Party Congress, which resolved in early April 1920 that the "weakness" of the railroad union was a "fundamental impediment to the task of improving transport."[12] So did the merger of water and rail transport administration into a single apparatus (a process approved by the Central Committee on March 13 to expedite goods shipments of all kinds, particularly grain), as well as the restructuring of all administrative procedures in rail and water transport along well-defined military lines: relations top to bottom strictly "through channels" (*po instantsiiam*); the immediate execution of orders; "strict accountability" to higher units; and collective (collegial) leadership on the basis of a "precise division of labor," with each official bearing "personal responsibility for the fulfillment of his tasks."[13] It soon became clear that this meant as well the end of the so-called district system of transport union organization, in which the country's 800,000 or so railroad workers and twenty-eight lines were divided into thirteen districts, each headed by a Raikom, and further subdivided, regardless of line or occupational divisions, into a number of subordinate territorial sections headed by individual Uchkoms. The district system had been developed in 1917 and early 1918 as a way of combatting the syndicalist tendencies of individual railroad lines and "shop separatism" (*tsekhovshchina*) among different occupational groups. Trotskii and his assistants in the Transport Commissariat now proposed to align a single national transport union with the actual units of rail and water management, which remained largely organized by individual lines.[14] The purpose here, again, was to meld union officials more closely into the actual tasks of transport management, a goal that became even more explicit with the promulgation in May of Trotskii's Order 1042, a "five-year plan" for railroad repair and reconstruction work based on the active participation (and responsibility) of local union figures.[15]

The principal difficulties here soon became apparent. In the midst of a continuing national crisis, aggravated in the late spring and summer of 1920 by Wrangel's offensive and the Polish campaigns, Trotskii was pressing extraordinary tasks on rail and water transport union leaders while simultaneously insisting their own past failures had much to do with current transport problems. He was also implementing a fundamental reorganization of their union's structure, which involved for many the loss of their positions and the dissolution of their regional and district committees. In July 1920, a national congress of railroad workers convened to discuss and approve these changes. A new central committee was elected after the congress felt impelled to blame the union itself for past failures. Shortly afterward, when a plenary session of the Central Trade Union Council voted on September 3 to merge the rail and water unions into a single organization, the new committee took on the designation of "Provisional Central Committee for Transport," or Tsektran, and began immediately, in the most heavy-handed way, to "root out" additional numbers of those "responsible" for the transport mess. A centralized union administration would now rationalize all transport operations, rail and water, and impose strict discipline and efficiency.

Many inside the party had serious doubts whether any administrative changes of this sort would actually improve transport. There were also doubts as to whether Order 1042 articulated realistic goals and serious questions about the value of even highly centralized trade unions taking on the tasks of managing this or other sectors of the economy at this particular juncture, with their grave responsibilities and the obvious consequences of failure. Two things, however, were clear. The transport unions were indeed being roundly "shaken up," as Glavpolitput and other commissariat officials dissolved important union committees, reassigned officials, and attempted to mobilize the unions to meet new goals, and this arbitrary use of state power, "categorically forbidden" earlier in the year by a circular letter of the Central Committee published in *Pravda*, was now being used on rail and water lines to pursue tasks of economic revitalization that union leaders themselves openly admitted were extremely urgent. Thus they found themselves increasingly agonized over the use by Trotskii and others of objectionable methods for desirable ends, a familiar contradiction.

The various participants in the developing "Tsektran controversy" did not generally express the conflict in these terms, of course, but raised the debate to abstractions of principle, particularly those concerning "democratic centralism," "trade union democracy," and the issues of "state," "party," and "worker" (union) relations in conditions of "proletarian dictatorship." The inverted commas are important here because with rare exception, the increasingly angry attacks on Tsektran failed to touch seriously the social and political realities of 1920, either in broad or narrow terms: what "trade union democracy" had actually become in practice on the railroads, or how party-worker relations generally had developed under War Communism. The dispute raged, in other words, over the ways in which Trotskii and others were responsible through Tsektran for the "degeneration of centralization and of militarized forms of work into bureaucracy, self-conceit, and officiousness which interferes with the unions," as one Central Committee resolution put it.[16] Yet perhaps the most important issue facing the party, and one that needed to be addressed in both theoretical and practical terms in charting Soviet Russia's future, was how both the nature and fate of the forms of dictatorship reflected in Tsektran turned on their relationship to social conditions.

What can one say in a few pages about the broader social context in which the Tsektran dispute emerged. Socioeconomic development during the Civil War was, of course, enormously complex, and we can only highlight here those aspects of this development that impinged most on Russian transport, and hence on the issues of Tsektran. These were essentially of two sorts, inextricably related in reality but analytically distinct. On one hand were the staggering objective indices of economic decline and social dislocation. These included overwhelming losses in industrial and agrarian output, sharp declines in productivity, a near collapse in the official mechanisms of commodity exchange, and such phenomena as the "de-urbanization" of Petrograd and other major industrial centers, which lost more than 50 percent of their populations. On the other were the unmeasurable subjective elements of this process, the fear produced by hunger and unemployment, the emotional tension of revolutionary enthusiasm tempered by disillusion, the sheer agony of physical deprivation and loss, the conflicts associated with dependency on officals who seemed increasingly unable to manage affairs or control their own agencies. "We must protest against the Center's policies," workers describing themselves as "conscious" and "patiently starving revolutionaries" telegraphed from Ivanovo-Voznesensk late in 1918, for example. "Everything is taken from us, nothing is provided . . . We have not a pound of reserves . . . We can accept no responsibility for what happens if our needs are not met."[17] More than five thousand similar complaints were received by party authorities in the course of 1919, according to official records, even from such loyal groups as the Central Committee of the Metallists' Union.[18] They found expression as well in workers' protests and demonstrations affecting such vital enterprises as the Putilov works, the Tula armament factories, and the Moscow railroad shops,[19] and they infused virtually every objective indication of economic crisis with a complex and powerful emotional content: "unemployment" also meant anxiety and, for many, a new, humiliating sense of dependency on those who led the revolution. "De-urbanization" often involved the breakup of families; "fuel shortages" meant a numbing cold and the discomfort of daily life often stressed in memoirs; transport "difficulties" meant hunger, malnutrition, and illness.

If one bears these subjective elements in mind when examining more objective patterns and processes of Soviet Russia's Civil War experience, one can begin to perceive as well the historical importance of what might be called the "adaptive" responses on the part of both ordinary workers and party officials, responses that often appear at first to be directive policies or, as one historian of the period puts it, "the extreme socialist doctrines" that dedicated, utopian revolutionaries "put into practice."[20] Consider the near total breakdown in traditional methods of financing both industrial and agrarian production, which occurred within the first six months of Bolshevik rule, and the simultaneous collapse of industrial production, which reached its nadir in the first four months of 1920.

The quick withdrawal of both foreign and private domestic capital from Russia's credit markets in the fall and winter of 1917–18 is both well known and eminently understandable, considering the lack of credit-worthiness among Russian enterprises generally and the Bolsheviks' ideological posture. Whether the nationalization of banks and other financial institutions was essentially a defensive maneuver on the Bolsheviks' part or an aggressive aspect of revolutionary policy is an interesting question that has yet to be studied in detail, but the result in either case is well known. Money rapidly lost its meaning as a stable medium of exchange. Under pressure, the Bolsheviks moved to a system of wages in kind and other elements of a "natural" economy, a policy whose wisdom was hotly debated but made sense for many in both practical and ideological terms.

For large industrial enterprises, however, managed in one form or another during most of 1918 by factory committees, this meant a loss of established means of credit, as well as an inability to collect on receivable accounts or rely on new or outstanding orders to purchase materials, pay wages, or finance production. The Commissariat of Finance, having taken over the banking system, became, in effect, a universal underwriter of industrial production. This was not only bureaucratically cumbersome, but involved mountainous accounting problems, most easily resolved in conditions of day-to-day emergencies with "special" outlays of funds and "extraordinary" collections of taxes and receipts, frequently accomplished simply by sending emissaries to the factories themselves. Enterprises soon began to operate on the basis of "estimates" (*po smetam*). While these were adequate to secure state support in the case of the largest producers, particularly in essential branches like metals production, they hardly served small producers and brought with them a range of new problems, many of which were insoluble.

For one, there was a natural tendency for estimates to be inflated—even a pressing need, from the standpoint of beleaguered factory workers, whose welfare depended on factories staying open. There was also an impetus to conceal receipts, hoard supplies, and press new demands on party and state officials, particularly for higher wages in kind. Documents also had to be presented to those special branches of the Sovnarkhoz apparatus charged with fuel and food distribution to justify plant allocations, a process that induced dissimulation along with traditional forms of competition between plants, despite simultaneous efforts to develop psychological and institutional forms of "socialist legality" and collectivism. And with the various offices of the Sovnarkhoz and commissariat structure literally swamped with "urgent" delegations and submerged in paperwork, even the most committed supporters of the revolution—perhaps one should say *especially* the most committed—felt impelled to act independently to get what workers and factories needed, even if this circumvented party directives.

It was, of course, a losing battle from early 1918 until well into 1920. Factories pressed to be nationalized (or "nationalized" themselves), creating the rudiments of a "socialist" economy, and detachments of workers scavenging for food or factory supplies were given such names as "Committees of the Poor" and absorbed into the party's official program of action, as if according to Communist doctrine and Bolshevik plan. The impelling reality, of course, was economic failure and deep social deprivation on all levels, even as the new regime successfully defended itself militarily. By mid-1920 the industrial labor force was less than half of what it had been in 1917. Overall production was at one-seventh prewar levels.[21]

As the crisis deepened, these changes began to affect larger enterprises more than smaller ones, leading to one of the most important (and paradoxical) shifts in the pattern of industrial production during the Civil War period. The logic of this is clear, even if the statistics are murky. Many of Russia's largest enterprises, like Lessner, Baranovskii, and Parviainen in Petrograd, Dinamo in Moscow, and such firms as the Singer (Zinger) works, which had branches throughout the country, were former joint-stock corporations, making the transition to state financing difficult even as their very size and importance commanded top commissariat priority. The sheer burden of adjusting large enterprises of this sort to socialist management and the "estimate" system of accounting also made the plants particularly vulnerable. As *Ekonomicheskaia Zhizn'* reported more than once in 1918, local Sovnarkhozy, usually at the *uezd* level, often seized the books and revenues of what they regarded as private local enterprises but which in fact were parts of much larger, integrated operations, causing administrative chaos.[22]

Smaller enterprises also began to benefit from their obscurity, at least in relative terms. Denied official allocations of fuel or raw materials, or given reduced allotments, they naturally began to compensate by procuring necessary goods illegally, enormously stimulating the burgeoning black and grey markets out of sheer necessity. There was also a genuine advantage to workers' control in small enterprises as opposed to large, as the issue of who controlled hiring and firing, and hence individual welfare and even the chances of survival, were more easily susceptible to personal pressures and relations in small shops, particularly after "bourgeois" owners had been driven off. Again, objective evidence is thin, but according to one estimate, as many as 30,000 small enterprises (with less than twenty to twenty-five employees) may have been functioning in Soviet Russia in 1920 completely outside the administrative controls of the the Sovnarkhoz system, despite their official "nationalized" status. Methods, values, and even patterns of industrial organization directly contrary to those formally supported and promoted by the Soviet regime, in other words, were encouraged by the very socioeconomic structures lying ostensibly at the foundation of the new Communist order.

A similar development occurred with the crisis of goods distribution, particularly food and fuel, and the changes in levels of workers' productivity. Even incomplete statistics on goods shipments and internal trade show appalling deficiencies throughout the Civil War period, but the social significance of these figures becomes clear only if one evaluates them in light of the party's monopolization of trade (by a series of decrees, including two comprehensive statutes on April 2 and November 21, 1918, "On the Organization of Supplies") and its shift to natural wages as a result, largely, of financial collapse. The monopolization of trade, the introduction of rationing, and the concurrent, brutal campaign against "bagmen" may well have been necessary from the standpoint of scarcity, and certainly preserved control for the party over at least a minimal supply of foodstuffs and essential goods, but it also impelled many enterprises, particularly smaller ones, to circumvent the system in order to "provide adequately for their own."[23] Most workers, also, were hardly passive about these matters. According to *Vestnik Statistiki*, a competent publication in this period, natural wages at best never provided more than 75 percent of a worker's essential needs, and this only in major plants favored as "shock" enterprises. As much as 60 percent of all grain in Soviet Russia may have been distributed illegally on "free trade" markets during this period, official rhetoric and "the most strict and severe penalties" for black marketeering notwithstanding.[24] The situation was similar with fuel, clothing, and other commodities. In effect, virtually all enterprises, large and small, were manufacturing "currency" during these months since almost any item could be used for wages or as a medium of exchange. One had only to avoid having output confiscated entirely by the authorities (or compensate by doing a little confiscating on one's own), a precondition for survival during the Civil War that turned concealment into an art form among workers and peasants alike, and that simultaneously reinforced some of the worst social impulses of pre-revolutionary society. In conditions of great scarcity, welfare for many depended as much on the "primitive capitalist" adaptations of a "second economy" as on the "primitive socialist" mechanisms of the party/state.

Productivity of course declined further in such circumstances, but again what is especially interesting for our purposes is not so much the objective data as the less clear subjective conditions, and the ways in which these conditions undermined important party objectives. According to available data, output per worker fell precipitously in 1918 and 1919. Strumilin estimates figures of 44 percent and 22 percent for these years relative to 1913, and 52 percent and 25 percent relative to 1917.[25] Huge declines occurred in particular in the food processing sector and in all branches of the metal industry, particularly machine construction. In the mines, many of which had been flooded in the Donbas area during the Whites' retreat, output per worker in 1920 was as low as 9 percent of the prewar figure.[26]

Obviously these figures reflect the relationship between the horrendous fall in gross industrial output and the somewhat less steep decline in levels of employment during the Civil War, a point we will return to in a moment. They also represent an inability to maintain and repair equipment (caused in part by the shop floor purge of engineers and other technical personnel in the months after October), as well as the inability of plants to secure adequate supplies of raw materials and fuel and the changing mix of the factory labor force, which saw large numbers of skilled and energetic workers move into various administrative positions in the Soviet regime.

But the data also shows productivity declining because of escalating absenteeism, a phenomenon that caused enormous problems for those attempting to manage the economy, and one that was not primarily the result of workers in power yielding to their lazy instincts, as many have charged. According to a careful survey of Moscow and five other provinces of the Central Industrial Region between September and December 1919, for example, workers on the whole were absent approximately one day for every three they worked.[27] Related data gathered from the Moscow court system suggest that absentee rates were highest in the metal industry, tailoring, chemicals, and communications, and almost nonexistent in the food processing sector, where workers reported consistently for work but had the highest percentage by far of individuals convicted for "failing to obey directives."[28]

Proguly occurred for the most part, however, precisely because workers had to obtain food on their own, procure goods, "requisition" fuel and raw materials, and perform independently (and anarchically) the tasks ordinarily fulfilled by state authorities, the tasks that the fledgling Soviet regime was insisting it *could* perform. Illness explained approximately 25 percent of the absentee rate, and many workers left to participate in congresses, meetings, or other "social organizational" work. But more than half of all lost workdays were because of efforts of one sort or another to circumvent inadequacies in the official networks of goods procurement and distribution, and, according to some estimates, the figure may be as high as 65 percent.[29] The paradox here, of course, is that absenteeism in the service of survival had to be treated by factory or state officials in the same way as absenteeism for any other reason, even if the plant's own welfare was at stake. This clearly engendered a poisonous mix of collusion on one hand and antagonism on the other, even though most offenders in the Moscow area, at least, were not treated with special brutality if caught (as often happened elsewhere) but given formal reprimands or sentenced by disciplinary courts to compulsory overtime work. Some were, however, sent demonstratively to concentration camps, and in virtually all cases, the contradiction between the need simultaneously for order and for flexibility in developing Russia's new "socialist" society was apparent even to party workers in the state control apparatus, who frequently experienced the familiar attraction of *krugovaia poruka*, and sometimes even complained about it.[30]

In these circumstances as well, the problem of unemployment took on special political implications in addition to becoming a particularly heavy social, economic, and administrative burden. Census data collected in the summer of 1920 from the same enterprises that had provided data two years earlier, in August 1918, showed a decline of more than 30 percent, and these figures excluded plants that had ceased operations entirely.[31] The biggest declines by far were in the textile industry, and while many other branches had a higher demand for some categories of workers than the labor exchanges could supply, the more important point is that considerations of political and social welfare impelled the Bolsheviks to maintain as high a level of employment as possible, however contrary to the new state's economic interests and, hence, its chances for survival. The relatively less rapid decline in employment compared to the fall in industrial output (which led statistically to the high declines in worker productivity we have just referred to) represented, in effect, a mode of compromise with mutually unacceptable and potentially destructive socioeconomic circumstances, each of which pressed centrifugally to tear Soviet society apart.

It is hardly surprising that Bolsheviks relied on heavy-handed "agitation and propaganda" to reinforce "proletarian solidarity" in these circumstances or resorted to repression like other Civil War regimes, thereby generating further dissidence and opposition. More germane for our purposes, however, is the way many of the bureaucratic processes of state administration can also be seen as a response to social conditions, while creating additional tensions. By the fall of 1918, for example, the collapse of Russian finance and the emergence of the new accounting and exchange mechanisms of a "natural" economy led to the development of what was called "glavkism," since state and soviet offices both were needed to process accounts, distribute capital and other essential resources, and generally substitute for the ruined mechanism of capitalist exchange. The complex hierarchy of Sovnarkhozy set up during 1918 on the local (*uezd*), provincial, regional (*oblast*), and national level included more than seventy different *otdely* and *glavnye upravleniia* by the end of the year, many of which overlapped comparable organs in the hierarchy of soviets.[32] Yet even as these offices were required to process the production estimates and accounts of hundreds of nationalized enterprises and to coordinate the distribution of goods and materials, the task itself became totally unmanageable, as most observers soon realized. The new regime lacked the capacity to plan, the resources to capitalize production, the administrative capability to control markets efficiently, or even the information necessary to make appropriate decisions—even as these decisions were logically its to make. What emerged instead of a socialist (or Communist) system of economic control was a proliferate, ineffective bureaucracy, unable to make necessary economic decisions rationally in the new state's best interests and vested instead only with an official "authority," which, if it could be exercised at all, could only be done so in an arbitrary way.

At least three sets of tensions emerged as a consequence, each of which reinforced the broader centrifugal pressures wearing at Bolshevik control: a persistent conflict between central and local organs, even within the same administrative system; a tension between the need for collegial administration and decisionmaking, required because of the multiplicity of institutions and the amount of information that had to be coordinated even in the allocation of essential goods and materials, and the pressure for quick decisions and their rapid implementation; and, third, increasing antagonism associated simply with the bureaucracy's official control over manifestly inadequate resources. No enterprise or group of workers could easily be satisfied during the Civil War, whatever pride one had in revolutionary achievements. In this respect, maintaining the distinction between "state" and "party" institutions was a protective device for the Bolsheviks even when the difference was more theoretical than real. So, too, was the manner in which party figures turned local soviets into scapegoats for failure, especially those with substantial non-Bolshevik memberships.

The party's decision to maintain piece rates and wage premiums in the factories was also not without problems. As *Ekonomicheskaia Zhizn'* insisted repeatedly in the spring of 1919, premiums in kind were a particularly strong incentive to increasing productivity. By April 1919 it was obligatory for all trade unions to apply them within limits established by the Commissariat of Labor.[33] Piece rates were also extensively used. In the metal industry, workers earned as much as 50 percent more from piece rate payments than they did from basic wages; fairly elaborate scales were worked out to reward different professions differentially, according to their overall value to the production process.[34] In the Putilov plant, for example, the so-called Rouen system was applied, in which each worker was assigned a definite time to perform a given task; if he or she completed it more quickly, a bonus was awarded proportionate to the time saved. By one account, certain types of assembly in the plant were being completed under the new system in some 60 percent of the time previously required; the cleaning of furnaces and flues in 40 percent.[35]

Yet premiums required surplus goods be available for distribution, and piece rates, particularly those differentiated by craft, required that raw materials be available to keep production going. Otherwise both incentives could only multiply labor dissidence, particularly if ordinary wages were reduced (as they were in real terms) and if workers consequently depended on premiums and piece work to survive. Such wage incentives, while perhaps resulting in some increased productivity,[36] also increased worker dependency on the new regime when it was least able to meet legitimate needs. The contradiction involved in applying "capitalist" incentives was thus not only one of compromising socialist values, but also of engendering the very real antagonism and resistance on the part of workers characteristic of capitalist societies.

Hence, above all, these social circumstances prompted many Bolsheviks to accept the necessity, simultaneously, of massive agitation and brutal repression. *Subbotnik* campaigns and similar efforts to reinforce the "heroic" and "volunteerist" aspects of revolutionary struggle simply had to be pressed to deflect the selfish "shop-oriented individualism" that socioeconomic conditions (and Russia's cultural heritage) were producing. And tendencies toward brutality were reinforced everywhere in conditions of enormous scarcity, political weakness, personal danger, and with the breakdown of the ordinary social mechanisms of production and exchange that usually kept people alive. Workers or peasants defending from confiscation the goods they produced had no less cause for brutality than those whose survival required the goods be seized.

Most important, however, is not so much the wantonness of repression as its chaotic and destructive character in economic terms. This is not to dehumanize the terrors of Civil War existence but to recognize, as the editors of *Ekonomicheskaia Zhizn'* themselves pointed out, that when local Cheka agents began "arresting workers and administrators and throwing them in prison for rightist tendencies and compromising attitudes even though there had not been any active demonstrations against the regime or efforts to arouse the population," enterprises simply could not function. Soviet plants had to be "liberated from the burden of providing hostages to local Cheka authorities"; the operation of the economy as a whole had to be freed from the *tsentrorazrukha* that hordes of state and party officials, each armed with urgent orders and "extraordinary" authority, were visiting on the enterprises they were dispatched to control.[37]

The steady extension of *edinolichnost'* throughout this period, while clearly compromising both the party's commitment to workers' control and the more democratic forms of industrial management that workers' themselves had created after October, served as a means of protecting many workers and administrators during these months, even as it concentrated power and undermined Communist values. A single forceful plant official could deter Cheka agents or others much more readily than could an employees' committee, particularly if the committee was composed of engineers or other socially suspect professional personnel and if the plant official, in contrast, carried relatively sound party credentials. Here again, we see the contradictions of civil war existence and the broad social context underlying the paradoxical pursuit of socialist objectives through antisocialist means.

From all this, finally, we can begin to appreciate why Russian transport emerged during the Civil War period as one of the most pressing problems confronting the new revolutionary regime and seemed increasingly to be the one industrial sector on whose performance the very fate of Bolshevik Russia might rest. Food and fuel supplies, the procurement of raw materials, the distribution of goods, even the success of requisitioning and procurement teams sent out by enterprises to round up needed materials, all depended on transport operations, not to mention the movement of troops and other obvious military needs. Here, too, consequently, absenteeism and *proguly*, the question of worker productivity, the effect of wage premiums and other incentives, the role of specialists, and such issues as the organization of line or shop administration and the effectiveness of trade unions were not questions about which the Bolsheviks had the luxury of prolonged theoretical debate. The slogan "All for Transport!" which emerged in early 1920 as a rhetorical keystone to Trotskii's plans for the radical reorganization of railroad and water transport operations, was as much an index of socioeconomic crisis and political desperation as it was of practical need.

What was the real state of transport operations during 1918–19, and what light can this particular "slice" of social reality shed on the ensuing Tsektran controversy? The easiest (and most superficial) answer can be deduced from data on locomotives and cars in service, quantity of goods carried, and output of repair shops, labor statistics, and the like, all of which show a disaster of monumental proportions. When the Bolsheviks came to power in October 1917, they took over a rail net of approximately 50,000 versts. They also assumed control over some 360,000 operational freight cars and approximately 15,000 locomotives, and, according to data assembled by the Commissariat of Transport in 1920, approximately 35,000 cars were still being loaded and unloaded in November 1917, although that number fell precipitously, to a little more than 15,000 by the end of the year. A loaded freight car traveled an average of 42 versts in a twenty-four-hour period; a locomotive, 88 versts.[38]

By the end of 1918, the Bolsheviks controlled only 27,000 versts of track, yet the amount of freight carried on these lines had fallen almost 70 percent. In August 1918, only some 9,000 freight cars were loaded or unloaded. Eighteen months later, in January 1920, the figure had barely risen to 12,000. The quantity of goods carried on the lines fell accordingly, from 37 million tons in 1918 to some 30 million in 1919, in contrast to more than 132 million carried in 1913, adjusted for the changing amount of track in service.[39]

Even these dismal figures, however, overstate the ability of Soviet lines to function effectively in 1919 and early 1920. They neglect the effect of some

4,000 bridges that had been destroyed as the railroads themselves became the focal point of much fighting in the Civil War, and the consequent bottlenecks of goods at important river crossings that piled up while authorities sought alternative routings. Track conditions almost everywhere were precarious, leading to an enormous increase in the number of accidents and derailments. Some 86,000 versts of telegraph line and more than 3,500 locomotives were also destroyed in 1918 and 1919, and by January 1920, only some 6,700 locomotives were still operational (in contrast to the more than 20,000 in 1913). Some 9,000 or more were in yards or shops, awaiting repair. The situation with rolling stock was similar. The number of freight cars in service fell to less than 18,000 in early 1919, while production of new equipment dropped from approximately 5,400 cars (and 420 locomotives) in 1917 to only 712 cars (and 74 locomotives) in 1919, and only 129 cars in 1920, when not a single new locomotive was constructed.[40] Meanwhile, the number of workers employed on the railroads increased dramatically, from 815,000 at the end of 1916 to more than 1,200,000 in early 1920, according to Commissariat of Transport (NKPS) figures, even though major lines like the Moscow-Kursk, Moscow-Kazan, Riazan-Uralsk, and Northern all notified the commissariat of serious shortages of skilled personnel, especially machinists (locomotive engineers) and conductors.[41] According to one careful analysis, the wage costs alone required to maintain this relatively unproductive "labor army" increased to more than 75 percent of all line expenses by the end of 1919, helping boost the ratio of expenditures over receipts from approximately 2:1 in 1917 to 3:1 in 1918, 6:1 in 1919, and a figure of almost 7:1 in 1920.[42] By any accounting system, and with ample allowance for inadequate statistics, Soviet Russia's railroads were pulling the new regime headlong toward bankruptcy at the time Trotskii became Commissar of Transport, however alien such a "capitalist" concept might have been at the time.

Again, however, it is not so much these physical indices of Soviet Russia's transport crisis that interest us as what might be called the "infrastructural" elements of the process, and the ways in which both ordinary railroaders and officials adapted to the enormous subjective pressures and tensions they experienced during the Civil War. We can distinguish at least three such further dimensions of the problem to examine briefly: the actual administration of railroad operations, the operational processes themselves, and the social consequences for railroaders of a revolutionary state system that increasingly looked to them for survival and that impelled them, like other workers, to find special ways to adapt to crisis conditions.

The central element of railroad administration during 1918–19 was its effort to be democratically responsive to the needs and interests of railroad workers themselves and to adjust the highly centralized and impersonal procedures of prerevolutionary administration to meet local conditions. The impetus for this came from several sources. Tsarist railroad officials had recognized already during the war that administrative decentralization was necessary to improve line efficiency, and important steps had been taken in that direction by the

Ministry of Transport during the Provisional Government, which was headed by the left Kadet Nekrasov. Russia's railroads had traditionally been divided administratively by different service divisions (*sluzhby*) and geographically by districts (*uchastki*). Administrators at the district level were given substantial new authority in 1917, while workers in the different service divisions, grouped on the basis of occupational specialties, were encouraged to organize themselves professionally and take responsibility for setting more equitable and efficient working conditions and wage rates on individual lines.

These changes corresponded with other elements of railroad democratization in 1917, particularly the development of workers' participation in line operations and the eventual assumption of control over the lines in the fall of 1917 by various "Line Committees," generally elected, at large representative line congresses. Both the professional divisions and the geographical sections of individual railroads developed logically in this process as the basic representational units of the railroads' overall democratic structure. Divisions and sections both held local congresses, elected delegates to broader gatherings, and sought to place representatives on the various committees and boards that were assuming administrative responsibilities. The professional divisions gave many party leaders pause, however, because they emphasized occupational distinctions and competitive interests (*tsekhovshchina*) at the expense of proletarian solidarity. As part of the general reorganization of the railroad union in early 1918, consequently, various professional unions were integrated as "sections" into the all-Russian union (Vseprofzhel) and lost much of their autonomy. The geographical divisions remained, however, and were even strengthened, both within the all-Russian union and in the administrative offices of railroads themselves. Whereas lines were previously administered through individual company headquarters, with orders and directives dispatched down the line to particular sections and divisions, the new districts that emerged in 1918 essentially administered all roads within a given locality, with little distinction between individual lines.

The Bolsheviks themselves encouraged this process, at least indirectly. During 1917, local party committees had formed powerful "district railroad soviets," designed in part to weaken the Provisional Government's control over line operations. The strongest of these was in Moscow and played an important role in undermining the authority of Vikzhel in the crucial period around the party's seizure of power. In the course of the party's consolidation of control over the railroads in late 1917 and early 1918, these district railroad soviets naturally emerged as a state (or party) counterpart to the railroaders' own administrative divisions. The bureaucratic foundations were laid during these early months, in other words, for a powerful, decentralized administrative system, rationalized and supported by considerations of operational efficiency, proletarian democracy, and Bolshevik party control.

Thus, by May 1919 there were some twenty different raion administrations controlling railroad operations throughout Soviet Russia, run by collegial boards of trade union leaders, elected rank-and-file workers, and professional administrators. The most powerful was in Moscow, governing seven major railroads and covering more than 227,000 workers, although similar groups governed local operations all over Soviet Russia, having worked with great energy throughout 1918 to amalgamate various individual line committees and thwart the anarcho-syndicalist tendencies they seemed to represent.[43] The fact that the day-to-day administration of a major railroad line like the Moscow-Kursk or Nikolaevskaia (which ran between Moscow and Petrograd) was now divided between two or more regional organizations was regarded by many, especially in the railroad trade union hierarchy, as an important political and economic safeguard for the Bolshevik regime.[44]

With increasing scarcities of food, fuel, and other essential goods, however, one can readily understand how these same administrative divisions gave rise to a new wave of competition and antagonism on the lines and engendered the type of *krugovaia poruka* historians generally associate with the 1930s. As a special commission of Rabkrin determined during a detailed investigation of railroad operations in the spring of 1919, there was increasingly less necessity for local organizations to be responsive to central directives. On the contrary, invested with "revolutionary authority" of their own, which allowed them to act with near dictatorial power over their own transport operations, and staffed with "elected, independent leaders" thoroughly familiar with the particularities of their own regions, these administrative units were naturally inclined instead to "defend" themselves from any sort of outside interference, whatever their own, simultaneous, commitments to Bolshevik state power. When administrators in one district needed additional specialists or technical personnel, for example, it was far easier simply to go out and hire them away from other places with special bonuses or perquisites rather than seek assistance from the state commissariats.[45] Special commissions or delegations coming from these offices were also frequently shunted aside, sometimes literally, as their trains took unexpected detours, or they were buried with paperwork, often containing inaccurate information.[46] Commissions and commissars were spoken of as part of the "disease of parallelism" and soon acquired the derogatory appelation *naznachentsy*, a term connoting both ignorance and arrogance.[47]

These patterns on the railroads mirrored those of other industrial sectors in 1919, yet the fact that railroads were responsible for transporting scarce and precious commodities engendered enormous temptations, along with heavy responsibilities. Such circumstances obviously warranted strict discipline. District railroad Cheka units operated with great ruthlessness throughout 1918 and 1919, and district trade union organizations also set up fairly extensive disciplinary court systems, trying in some areas as many as several hundred cases a month.[48]

As disciplinary pressures increased, however, in direct relation (although not *caused* by) economic deterioration, a new set of protective "adaptations" began to emerge in day-to-day railroad operations. District dispatchers, for example, fearful of being disciplined if they could not provide necessary equipment, began to prevent locomotives from leaving their districts (and their control).

Instead they reverted to a system of "turning points," where locomotives were uncoupled from trains and returned to depots by their own crews, a clearly inefficient system but one that allowed local personnel to keep a close hold on their "own" essential equipment.[49]

Such was the case in other railroad operations. Squeezed between the threat of harsh discipline and arguments "settled with revolvers," as *Zheleznyi Put'* put it, railroaders at all levels of service sought to conceal information, hide equipment, lie about available supplies. Central authorities demanded more cars be put in service, but in many places idle cars were "rented out" as housing, and rather than risk trouble by evicting hundreds of squatters (as well as whatever they may have personally gained from the arrangement), local personnel listed the equipment as "in use." When loading goods onto cars meant throwing people out, it was far easier to channel goods onto the black market, and far more lucrative, despite the risk; if unloading arriving trains meant risking a gun battle between different groups fighting for the consignments, it was easier not to unload the material at all and simply keep it under guard until local authorities could straighten matters out. This led, of course, to long delays, and central authorities complained bitterly about hundreds of loaded freight cars being left on sidings for weeks. But from the railroaders' viewpoint it was relatively safe and far preferable to being arrested for having surrendered the goods to the wrong party.[50]

The same sort of "adaptive mechanisms" emerged in virtually every area of transport operations in 1919, each having a rationale of its own, but all contributing to the crisis facing Soviet Russia rather than alleviating it. Trains were often stalled by signals blocking the line, but since engine personnel could not know if they were stopped because of malfunctioning equipment, dereliction on the part of signalmen, or actual traffic on the line ahead, the best (and safest) course was simply to wait for the signal to change and not risk harsh sanctions for violating regulations or taking unauthorized personal initiative. Depots and repair shops were often unable to repair equipment because they lacked material, but discharging idle personnel exposed shop managers both to the anger of their employees and to the risk of not having enough personnel available to do the work if "requisition committees" actually secured the needed parts. Again it was far less risky to await proper orders. Similarly with the use of fuel. Idle engines under steam obviously wasted fuel, but if drivers shut them down and went off, they could either be punished for leaving their work or risk even harsher sanctions if the equipment was suddenly needed and not ready to run. It was simply safer to burn the fuel.

Yet these "adaptive" responses led themselves to charges of sabotage and to the emergence, finally, of what might be called a sullen "siege mentality" among railroaders in 1919—a psychological disposition to regard Soviet power with an equal mix of apprehension and disdain, not dissimilar from the way tsarist authorities and managers were regarded earlier: apprehension, of course, because authorities now were so unpredictable and repressive; disdain because it seemed increasingly the case that those in charge did not know what they were doing. Mentalities are as difficult to measure as they are important. From the countless complaints in periodicals and newspapers in this period, there can be little doubt that railroaders felt themselves abused, as the "pariahs" of the Soviet labor force, and unjustly, even senselessly repressed. So great were abuses along the lines that in July 1919, Trotskii's predecessor as commissar of transport, Krasin, ordered full wages paid to all railroad personnel who were improperly or "falsely" arrested.[51] It was precisely such wanton repression that was "destroying Soviet transport," *Ekonomicheskaia Zhizn'* editorialized, and generating great hostility among even the most loyal transport workers.[52]

Yet overt hostility was not as characteristic of railroader mentality in 1919 as passivity and *vialos'*—a more or less intractible psychological adaptation to what was perceived as a hopeless condition. And since little more could apparently be done by railroaders themselves, their union representatives, or even their local technical and professional personnel to improve matters, simply to "protect oneself" made sense.[53] Plundering soon began to spread, despite the greater risks. (In one incident, for example, all the lamps in a major depot were stolen and resold on the black market when the electrical supply failed.) Absenteeism increased. At the same time, party cells along the lines began to lose members. Even Bolshevik railroaders formerly active in revolutionary line committees apparently began to give up their posts, sometimes by way of demonstrative protest against unjust abuse. At a major gathering of railroads in the Moscow district in July 1919, for example, attended by more than five hundred elected delegates, resignations from the party were said to have reached "huge" proportions, leading one militant faction to propose a whole-sale purge of party members as a means of weeding out "waverers and shirkers." Although a sizable minority argued that individuals should be al-lowed to leave the party "freely, without risking any repressive sanctions," the conference majority voted instead to make "unauthorized resignations" equiva-lent to "desertion" and punishable by "forced labor or concentration camps."[54] Meanwhile, as we have seen, Glavpolitput was formed in the summer of 1919 as part of the Commissariat of Transport and began its propaganda activi-ties. The first Subbotnik was held with much fanfare on the Moscow-Kursk line. Political agitators were dispatched in large numbers up and down the lines. There was little indication by autumn, however, that these measures would change things. Indeed, despite battlefield successes against both Kolchak and Denikin, there were increasing signs that even more difficult conditions lay ahead.

The overwhelming horrors of the Stalinist period and the catastrophic cir-cumstances that followed the collapse of all vestiges of political democracy in Soviet Russia understandably obscure every humane observer's perspective on the revolution and its aftermath, yet without a firm grasp of Soviet social reality in this period, the relationship between Bolshevism and the end of revolutionary democracy cannot be fully understood. It was undoubtedly the case, as many have argued, that a disposition toward totalistic authoritarianism was present from the outset in the psychologies and ideological commitments of most Bolshevik leaders. Such tendencies exist everywhere, even in the advanced political democracies of the West, and they certainly characterized a broad spectrum of European and Russian political activism in the first decades of this century. In my view, however, the vital historical questions of this epoch concern not only the various origins of this tendency but also the nature of the social reality that allowed it to flourish—indeed, nourished it both by giving credence to its utopian visions and the view that alternative possibilities would prove ineffective (and were hence "illegitimate"). Such possibilities, of course, clearly existed. Social historians must be as wary of assuming rigid causal relationships between Russia's desperate circumstances and the party's policies in the Civil War period as they are about ideological determinism. Yet social conditions always circumscribe the range of possible responses, and in Civil War Russia, this range was narrow indeed.

If one attempts from this perspective to focus on those few crucial months in 1920 when the Tsektran controversy gave broad avenues to democratically inclined factions within the Bolshevik movement, what impresses one as much as the vitality of the groups themselves is the near hopelessness of *all* "solutions" to Russia's socioeconomic crisis and the realization that the Tenth Party Congress and the start of NEP was as much a decision to let social and economic catastrophe fall where it might as a recognition of past failures and an effort to chart a new course. By relaxing harsh discipline and loosening tight controls, the party retreated from both responsibility and blame. It survived the ensuing horrors of 1921 and 1922, of course, but one tends to forget that despite the end of Russia's political crisis, hundreds of thousands of those who struggled heroically through the revolution and Civil War did not.

If improving transport was the key to economic recovery at the beginning of 1920, as almost everyone thought it was, and if this prompted Trotskii to assume control over the Commissariat of Transport, it is also true that each of the contradictions besetting economic policy in other sectors also applied to transport. Administrative centralization reflected elsewhere in the *glavki* and on the railroads with the introduction of *edinolichnost'*, formally decreed in the spring of 1919, led more to the ignorance of distance and the inability to respond properly to local circumstances than to the end of collegial turpitude. "I have no instructions" became all the more effective as a defensive and self-protective rationalization as party officials vested with unilateral power insisted all their orders be strictly obeyed. Cheka ruthlessness instilled fear, but repression could hardly improve a transport apparatus desperately short of qualified personnel and, in fact, only impaired the very exercise of initiative that daily operations required. Even the implementation of wage premiums, bonuses, and other material incentives worked only as well as the availability of supplies.[55] Absenteeism increased (as workers struggled to supply themselves with necessities); so did the number of work stoppages, against which, in the end, the authorities were virtually helpless.[56] The result, as I have tried to argue, was the natural emergence of psychological and social "adaptations" at once antithetical to Bolshevik revolutionary principles and inevitable as mechanisms for survival.

In the face of this, it is not surprising that Trotskii and others in the spring of 1920 began to squeeze the trade union movement in an effort to turn Soviet Russia around. While alternative courses of action clearly existed, and while social conditions themselves did not determine policy, they nonetheless encouraged the authoritarian tendencies that Tsektran reflected. Lacking a well-reasoned economic or political model, ideologically biased in favor of centralization and hierarchical discipline, and without either sufficient resources or an adequate technical-administrative structure to implement economic policy effectively, energetic and impatient Bolshevik activists naturally found fault with the broad stratum of trade union personnel, which was unwittingly becoming, in effect, the buffer between workers struggling with the practical difficulties of production and those wielding political power. In effect, Trotskii and others sought to compensate with human commitment what the unstable Soviet order lacked in clarity of thought, material resources, and technical competence. The intensification of labor and, indeed, the reconstruction of the whole trade union apparatus from top to bottom into an instrument of economic compulsion was an effort to induce artificially the "heroic" efforts Soviet Russia needed to survive, and that neither the party nor the state apparatus themselves could readily provide or cultivate.

The formal resolutions passed at the Ninth Party Congress in early April gave broad party sanction to this approach. Trade unions were recognized as "one of the primary structures of the Soviet state." They were to "fulfill the most vital function, that of economic administration, entering Soviet organizations, saturating (*propityvaia*) them, and turning themselves in the process more and more into the fundamental base (*osnovnyi baz*) of the Soviet economic system." As the "most competent organizations" directly involved in production, and the only ones that united all workers within a production branch, unions also constituted "the primary base of the economic organization managing industry." Moreover, since politics was "the most concentrated expression of economics and its generalization and extension (*obshchenie i zavershenie*)," it was "altogether senseless and a deviation from Marxism toward bourgeois, and in particular, bourgeois-trade-union dispositions, for trade unions, as the economic organization of the working class, to set themselves up against the soviets," its political organization:

> Particularly absurd and harmful is such a contraposition in the epoch of the proletarian dicatatorship, when all its struggle and all its activities, economic and political, must more than ever be unified, concentrated, directed by a single will, and held together by an iron unity.[57]

These resolutions, it might also be emphasized, were neither particularly new, nor were they pressed on the trade union leadership itself against its will. They corresponded rather closely, at least in principle, to the ambitions even of trade union democrats and to a whole series of past resolutions of both individual and joint trade union congresses. Tsektran carried them through, albeit in the intensified and exaggerated way one might have expected from a man of Trotskii's temperament.

What is important about them, however, as I hope by now is reasonably clear, is that they represented tasks that neither the railroad trade union nor trade unions in other industrial branches were capable of fulfilling adequately in 1920. Hence it should also be clear why the policies of Glavpolitput and Tsektran in the summer and fall were bound to be deeply resented as practically unworkable and morally unjust. They also could not help but generate great bitterness, some of which was soon cloaked in a new-found appreciation of democratic procedures, since by implication, Tsektran identified specific faults for what was, in fact, a massive and generalized crisis. In one sense the controversy over its methods "hung on air" as it related to social conditions (to use an idiom of the times), insofar as it addressed as matters of political principle issues of economic administration whose viability really depended on their effectiveness. And if an admirable, even heroic, opposition emerged against Tsektran in the early winter of 1920, and if Trotskii's approach was soon officially discredited, this may not have reflected so much the strengthening of new, more democratic commitments on the party's part, or a new confidence in the workability of more democratic alternatives, but a reflection for many of the political need, finally, to abandon almost entirely, at least for a time, serious efforts at managing and controlling essentially intractable socioeconomic conditions.

NOTES

1. A brief review of the principal events in the Tsektran controversy can be found in Robert Daniels, *The Conscience of the Revolution* (Cambridge, Mass., 1965), pp. 129–32; and James Bunyan, *The Origin of Forced Labor in the Soviet State, 1917–1921* (Baltimore, 1967), pp. 181–212, which includes some document excerpts. An important collection of primary materials on the crisis, edited by Zinoviev, is *Partiia i Soiuzy* (Petrograd, 1921).

2. L. Schapiro, *The Origin of the Communist Autocracy* (Cambridge, Mass., 1956), p. 274; Bunyan, *Origin*, pp. 189–91.

3. Schapiro, *Communist Autocracy*, pp. 261, 272.

4. See Bunyan, *Origin*, pp. 110–12.

5. *Pravda*, December 17, 1919; L. Trotskii, *Sochineniia*, vol. 15 (*Khoziaistvennoe stroitel'stvo sovetskoi respubliki*) (Moscow-Leningrad, 1927), pp. 107–14. See also the translation in Bunyan, pp. 95–101.

6. *Otchet tsektrana* (Moscow, 1920), p. 11.

7. Ibid., pp. 10–11.

8. See esp. Trotskii's proposal to the Ninth Party Congress, "Ocherednye zadachi khoziaistvennogo stroitel'stva," in *Deviatyi s"ezd RKP(b). Protokoly* (Moscow, 1960),

pp. 533–39; *Otchet tsektrana*, pp. 10–12; and *Zheleznodorozhnik*, 1920, nos. 15–16.

9. *Deviatyi S"ezd*, p. 418.

10. *Tretii Vserossiiskii s"ezd professional'nykh soiuzov*, pt. 1 (Moscow, 1921), p. 74. See also, pp. 107–8.

11. See the report on the Third Trade Union Congress in *Zheleznodorozhnik*, 1920, nos. 17–19, and the discussion in A. Khain, *Proidennyi put'. Soiuz masterovykh i rabochikh zh.d. Petrogradskogo uzla 1917–1919 gg.* (Moscow-Leningrad, 1925), pp. 36–37.

12. *Deviatyi s"ezd*, pp. 412–13.

13. *Otchet tsektrana*, p. 14.

14. See *Zheleznodorozhnik*, 1920, nos. 12–14; P. Vompe, *Tri goda revoliutsionnogo dvizheniia na zheleznykh dorogakh Rossiiskoi sovetskoi respubliki* (Moscow, 1920).

15. *Otchet tsektrana*, pp. 20–21.

16. *Otchety o deiatel'nosti tsentral'nogo komiteta R.K.P. (b) s VIII do X s"ezda* (Moscow, 1921), p. 47.

17. *Ekonomicheskaia Zhizn'*, November 16, 1918.

18. Ibid., January 1, 1919; *Izvestiia Gosudarstvennago Kontrolia*, nos. 20–21, November 1, 1919.

19. See, for example, *Piat' let vlast' sovetov* (Moscow, 1922), pp. 480–81; E. G. Gimpel'son, *Sovetskoi rabochii klass* (Moscow, 1974), pp. 124–26.

20. Schapiro, *Origins*, p. 211.

21. Thus, the number of workers employed by large (*tsenzovaia*) industrial enterprises declined from approximately 2.6 million in 1913 to less than 1.6 million in early 1920, while the gross value of production (in 1913 rubles) fell from 5.6 billion to approximately 1 billion. Using 1913 as a base year (100, in other words), the index of industrial output in 1917 stood at 77, 1918 at 35, 1919 at 26, and 1920 at 18. See the discussion by N. Vorob'ev, "Izmeneniia v russkoi promyshlennosti v period voiny i revoliutsii," *Vestnik Statistiki*, 1923, no. 46, pp. 115–54.

22. See, for example, *Ekonomicheskaia Zhizn'*, November 14, 1918.

23. L. Kritsman, *Geroicheskii period velikoi russkoi revoliutsii* (Moscow, n.d. [1924]), p. 116.

24. *Vestnik Statistiki*, 1920, nos. 1–4, p. 70.

25. S. G. Strumilin, *Zarabotnaia plata i proizvoditel'nost' truda v russkoi promyshlennosti v 1913–1922 gg.* (Moscow, 1923), p. 56.

26. *Izvestiia Gosudarstvennago Kontrolia*, April 15, 1919, no. 8, pp. 12–13. See also, Kritsman, *Geroicheskii period*, pp. 186–87.

27. "Rabota i proguly v fabrichno-zavodskikh predpriiatiakh," *Biulleten' Tsentral'nago Statisticheskago Upravleniia*, 1920, no. 25.

28. K. Egorov, *Moskovskie tovarishcheskie distsiplinarnye sudy za 1920* (Moscow, 1921), p. 13.

29. A. I. Rabinovich, *Trud i byt rabochego* (Moscow, 1923), p. 36.

30. See esp. *Izvestiia gosudarstvennago kontrolia*, April 15, 1919, no. 8, and May 15, 1919, no. 10.

31. TsSU, *Trudy*, vol. 8, vyp. 2, p. 355 (tables 3 and 4).

32. Sarabianov, *Ekonomika*, pp. 109–11.

33. *Ekonomicheskaia Zhizn'*, April 1, 1919. See also Gimpel'son, *Sovetskii rabochii klass*, pp. 166–67.

34. *Ekonomicheskaia Zhizn'*, July 4, 1919.

35. Ibid., May 27, 1919.

36. See the discussion in *Ekonomicheskaia Zhizn'*, March 27, 1919, no. 66.

37. Ibid., November 12, 1918, no. 4; *Izvestiia Gosudarstvennago Kontrolia*, March 15, 1919, no. 6.

38. V. Klemenchich, *Itogi raboty zheleznykh dorog za 3 goda (1917–1920)* (Moscow, 1920), p. 5.

39. P. B. Orlov, *Razvitie transporta SSSR, 1917–1962. Istoriko-ekonomicheskii ocherk* (Moscow, 1963), p. 48.

40. A. I. Golopolosov, *Obzor zheleznodorozhnogo transporta (po dannym chrezvychainoi revizii 1919 g.)* (Moscow, 1920), p. 29.

41. Orlov, *Razvitie*, p. 40.

42. M. M. Shmukker, *Ocherki finansov i ekonomiki zheleznodorozhnogo transporta Rossii za 1913–1922 gg.* (Moscow, n.d. [1923]), p. 139.

43. See, for example, *Zheleznodorozhnik*, 1919, no. 2(18).

44. *Krasnyi Put' Zheleznodorozhnika*, 1919, no. 23, esp. pp. 20ff.

45. *Volia i Dumy Zheleznodorozhnika*, 1918, no. 77.

46. *Zheleznodorozhnik*, 1919, nos. 5–6.

47. *Krasnyi Put' Zheleznodorozhnika*, 1919, no. 17.

48. See esp. *Zheleznodorozhnik*, 1919, nos. 7–8; Golopolsov, *Obzor*, pp. 44ff.; *Gudok*, September 9, 1920. Offenders were generally sentenced by these courts to compulsory work assignments rather than to prison or concentration camps, although these were also used.

49. *Zheleznodorozhnik*, 1919, no. 2(18).

50. See, for example, Golopolosov, *Obzor*, pp. 89–95.

51. *Zheleznodorozhnik*, 1919, nos. 7–8.

52. *Ekonomicheskaia Zhizn'*, November 23, 1918. Such hostility emerged clearly in the Aleksandrovsk railroad shops in Moscow toward the end of winter 1919 and led to a series of angry strikes. Precisely when locomotives and rolling stock were most urgently in need of repair, the Bolshevik authorities locked out some 2,500 shop workers to control their discontent, rehiring them after careful screening when the shops reopened, just as Putilov and other industrial magnates had done before 1917 (see *Zheleznodorozhnik*, May 2, 1919). Similar situations occurred elsewhere, most importantly at the Moscow-Kursk shops in December 1919 and early in January 1920.

53. See esp. *Krasnyi Put' Zheleznodorozhnika*, no. 18, pp. 13ff.; *Zheleznodorozhnik*, 1919, nos. 7–8.

54. *Krasnyi Put' Zheleznodorozhnika*, 1919, no. 27.

55. An extensive premium system was introduced in the railroads in the spring of 1919, for example, closely tailored to time-saving efficiencies and to maximizing the use of available equipment. But while extensive savings were realized, particularly in locomotive and freight car use time, the failure of authorities to have ample supplies of supplementary foodstuffs and the consequent delay in premium payments was a significant source of unrest, particularly in the railroad shops.

56. See the discussion in *Ekonomicheskaia Zhizn'*, September 16, 1919.

57. *Deviatyi s"ezd RKP(b). Mart-Aprel' 1920. Protokoly* (Moscow, 1960), p. 418.

COMMENTARY
CIRCUMSTANCE AND POLITICAL WILL IN THE RUSSIAN CIVIL WAR

Reginald E. Zelnik

It is hardly an exaggeration to say that the history of the Russian working class under Soviet rule reads more and more like a sad tale of tragic disappointment, ineffectual resistance, and effective repression. The word "disappointment" is meant to have a double poignancy here, for it refers not only to the attitudes of the thousands of workers whose great October expectations were so swiftly dashed, and dashed again, but also to the tone of several authors—including some contributors to this volume—who have recently made important contributions to the study of post-October Russia. Even an article on the relatively benign period that immediately preceded the Civil War, written by William G. Rosenberg, tells us that although "workers entered their plants in early November [1917] with a new sense of commitment and enthusiasm . . . ," and with high expectations that their situation would improve once the new Bolshevik regime began to employ "the full resources of the state" in support of their class interests, "[i]rreversible forces were already working to pulverize these hopes. . . . [T]he Bolsheviks were simply not able to provide the relief that the workers expected and which their coming to power had promised."[1]

Much of the rest of that important article is devoted to describing and explaining the widening rift between workers and the party in the ensuing months, a rift that eventually led to "open conflict, repression, and the consolidation of Bolshevik dictatorship over the proletariat in place of proletarian dictatorship itself."[2] It is noteworthy that in the spirited debate between Rosenberg and Vladimir Brovkin that follows the article, one of the issues joined is not whether this dismal picture is accurate—its general accuracy is not contested—but whether the failure of the widespread "workers' opposition" of 1918 to evolve into an effective anti-Bolshevik political movement should

374

be attributed mainly to repressive measures (Brovkin) or to the self-imposed limits of the workers' deeply felt but ultimately nonideological hostility (Rosenberg).[3]

Rosenberg's essay in the present volume moves the clock ahead a year or two, plunging us into the turmoil of the Civil War. Although it is now 1919–20, Rosenberg tells the story in evocative terms that recall his earlier article. We read of "the fear produced [among many workers] by hunger and unemployment," "the emotional tension of [their] revolutionary enthusiasm tempered by disillusion," and their "new, humiliating sense of dependency on those who led the revolution," just to sample a few key phrases that occur within a single paragraph. Railroad workers (the main subject of the essay), who "felt themselves abused as the 'pariahs' of the Soviet labor force, and unjustly, even senselessly repressed," were so discouraged "even the most loyal" among them were hostile to the Bolshevik authorities by the final phase of War Communism.

Although our hopes are somewhat raised by the closing paragraph of Rosenberg's essay, what we mainly have here is a story of painful disappointment, one of the low points in an unhappy cyclical pattern experienced by Soviet workers from the spring of 1918 through the Civil War, even into the period of "relaxation" presumably heralded by the NEP.[4] This rapid transformation of what in October 1917 appeared to be a triumphant working class into what soon looked more like a victimized proletariat has been so clearly established by now that the most interesting issues addressed in this section of the seminar—hardly a hotbed of Cold War historiography—were not whether or even when the transformation occurred but *why* it occurred and why workers resisted it so ineffectually. These are much the same issues engaged in the earlier Rosenberg-Brovkin debate, except that now Brovkin's key explanation of the workers' subjugation, the Bolsheviks' successful use of military force against them, fades from view. For the Civil War period the burden of explanation falls instead on the workers' fear of the White menace, which helped forestall their showdown with the Bolsheviks.

Why did the Bolsheviks resort to policies and actions that threatened to erode the support of their original working-class constituency? Rosenberg seeks the answer primarily in what appears to be a descriptive, objective concept: the importance of *circumstance*, particularly circumstances of a social and economic character that lay beyond the Bolsheviks' control.

In his illuminating analysis of the background to the Tsektran controversy, Rosenberg, always sensitive to historical complexity, states the problem cautiously. He is interested in "the ways in which social conditions and processes shaped political positions, or at least limited the range of viable political responses." His is not a reductionist position, for he readily acknowledges that Bolshevik ideology and political temperament are important areas for scholarly investigation, and he is sometimes able to draw analytical strength from his own doubts about purely circumstantial explanations. Nevertheless, the social and economic conditions that accompanied the Civil War occupy a privileged position in Rosenberg's analysis. It is surely noteworthy that, despite his firm grip on the importance of "interactions" in historical explanation, his choice of metaphors gives pride of place, at the *bottom* of things, to what he thinks of as social reality, however that elusive concept may be defined. It is the "social *foundations* of authoritarian politics" that Rosenberg is seeking (my italics), and he conveys the impression that the relevant social circumstances are *out there*, waiting for the political actors to respond to *them*.

The kind of circumstances he has in mind (though not necessarily why they qualify as "social") is abundantly clear throughout the paper. Most important were the extreme shortages of food, particularly in the cities, and the collapse of the transportation system (which intensified the food problem). He offers nuanced explanations of the disruptive impact of changing economic circumstances on conditions in the factories and links these developments to the intensification of bureaucratic interference.

Almost from the outset, however, Rosenberg implicitly recognizes the difficulties entailed in trying to isolate such "social circumstances" from their political context. Both the food shortage and the transport problem, for example, were matters of life and death for the regime primarily because of the political-military situation, the need to feed, supply, and move the beleaguered Red Army; the food shortage was caused in part by a "resistant countryside" (that is, resistant peasants); and the transport crisis was closely connected to "the apparent indifference and apathy" of railroad workers whose organizational and professional autonomy had been undermined by the Bolsheviks since early 1918 and who by 1919 were disposed to view the authorities who abused and "senselessly repressed" them with "an equal mix of apprehension and disdain." The examples could be multiplied.

It may simply be the case that a meaningful line between the social and the political is impossible to draw under conditions of civil war—indeed, that it was precisely the fusion of the social and the political that characterized the situation itself. And by no means would I argue that Rosenberg is wrong to see such developments as the food and transportation crises as in some way accounting for, circumscribing, or "shaping" policies such as the creation of "labor armies," the militarization of civilian labor, or the Tsektran dictatorship. It is necessary, however, to probe more deeply into the policies and attitudes that "shaped" or "accounted" for those crises to begin with. If Bolshevik policies hastened the alienation of peasants and railroad workers (including worker-Bolsheviks) from a regime that would obviously have preferred their voluntary compliance, we must be willing to entertain the notion that some of these ominous social circumstances were themselves the products of earlier political decisions, the unwelcome and perhaps even unforeseen consequences of specific Bolshevik actions (and not merely of some vague authoritarian tendency of the early twentieth century).

Since many leading Bolsheviks arrived on the scene with preconceived biases against "petty bourgeois" peasants and "anarcho-syndicalist" railroad workers, some of the political-ideological determinants of the policies in question should be fairly close at hand. Rosenberg's account is by no means insensitive to such considerations, but his attention to them seems to flag whenever "social reality" can be called on to supplant them. This social reality is generally presented not exactly as an autonomous sphere, but as a sort of independent variable whose relative impact on Bolshevik policy, the dependent variable, can be measured against other factors. It is rarely presented as an outcome, a situation itself in need of explanation, including explanation based on the government's political decisions. If Rosenberg is justified in reminding us that "social conditions always circumscribe the range of possible responses," and that this range was narrow during the Civil War, we should also recognize that social circumstances do not have the structural durability of geography or even grammar. They are highly sensitive to the pressures of political action, and Rosenberg's pioneering work in this area demonstrates as well as any other just how powerful those pressures could be.

The subject of Ronald Grigor Suny's excellent essay is only loosely related to that of Rosenberg's. To be sure, both essays address one of the fundamental themes of this volume: the rapid disintegration of the revolution's democratic impulse. But Suny's essay has other interesting dimensions—related mainly to nationality—that widen the scope of the discussion. And because it examines one of Russia's borderlands rather than its Muscovite core, it offers a unique opportunity for fruitful comparative analysis. To compare the Russian heart-land of the Civil War period with the Caucasus (or, say, with the Ukraine or the Baltic) is to compare two regions where many conditions were similar but political outcomes were significantly different, a situation that may help us isolate the variables that were most decisive.

Among the more or less evident points of similarity between the Georgian and Russian cases were: a history of exposure to Imperial Russian institutions; an agrarian-based social structure with pockets of developing urbanization and industrialization; a branch of Orthodox Christianity as the majority faith (not discussed in the paper); the presence of a serious foreign menace (perhaps even more serious in the Georgian case); the extreme devastation of the economy; and, last but by no means least, the Marxist (Social Democratic) political heritage of the dominant party. (Thus it would be less illuminating—or illu-minating in a different way—to compare the territory of Lenin with that of Denikin.)

Among the more obvious points of contrast, apart from the thorny but critical distinction between Bolshevism and Menshevism, were: Georgia's pe-ripheral location; the prior experience of the Georgians—though now the majority nationality within their own territory—as an ethnic minority within the empire; and the relative weakness and even semipeasant character of the Georgian nobility.

Although a fuller examination of these similarities and differences is needed before we can draw definitive conclusions, Suny's paper makes a convincing preliminary case that Menshevik hegemony is the best explanation for the course the revolution took in Georgia. His apparent point of departure is the depth of Menshevik roots among the ethnic Georgian (but not the non-Georgian) lower classes, both urban and rural, in effect transforming whatever pro-Bolshevik sentiment existed in the region into something resembling foreign subversion in the eyes of much of the population. Pushing his argument a little further than he may appreciate, I would argue that in Georgia, Menshevism had become the genuine political expression of the *narod*, a statement that obviously could not be made for any other part of the old empire.

Of course in recognizing the importance of Menshevism's sway among the Georgian people, we are forced to confront a more fundamental issue, the historical origins of its popularity. I have in mind not only the early successes in Georgia of Marxism as such, a question explored by Suny elsewhere,[5] but more specifically the continuous success of its Menshevik variant after 1903. This phenomenon not only contradicts conventional sociological explanations of political allegiances on the Russian left, it even seems to defy common sense, unless, of course, one links Menshevism's appeal to Georgians with its transformation into a *national* movement. Through the mediation of Menshevism, it would seem, Marxism and Georgian nationalism intermingled and merged to become, in Suny's apt phrase, "the national liberation movement of the Georgian people."[6] Their merger, in turn, reduced the intensity of internal conflict and, as a consequence, lessened the Menshevik government's need to rely on coercion during the Civil War while heightening the popular tendency to identify the few local Bolsheviks as agents of foreign (that is, Russian) intervention. (A close examination of the language of anti-Bolshevik polemics in Georgia—how anti-*Russian*? how purely political?—would shed more light on these questions.)

A closely related point—particularly with regard to Tiflis, but relevant to other parts of Georgia as well—is the degree of identification in the public mind between Bolshevik and soldier (or garrison member) and between soldier and Russian. If the reasons for the soldier-Russian equation are rather obvious, the soldier-Bolshevik equation—which was evidently stronger in Georgia than in Russia proper—requires further explanation. To simply assert that many of the Russian soldiers in Georgia were Bolsheviks is not enough. As non-workers, with what aspects of Bolshevism were the soldiers identifying? What was on their minds when they first chose to think of themselves as Bolsheviks? Ending the war and getting the land? Combating Georgian separatism? And if the latter (briefly mentioned in the essay), does this not suggest that ethnic self-identification contributed mightily to the Bolsheviks' appeal to Russians garrisoned in the borderlands? Were Red Army and Red Russia replacing class as sources of popular identification with the Bolshevik Revolution?

The comparison between Georgian Menshevik and Russian Bolshevik performance implicit in Suny's paper (it becomes explicit mainly in the last pages) recalls us to our earlier remarks about the relationship between circumstances and political action. Suny, like Rosenberg, is certainly no stranger to the use of circumstantial explanation. He stresses, for example, that in Menshevik Georgia the absence of any need for the forced requisitioning of grain helped avert the alienation of the peasantry from the regime that occurred in Soviet Russia. In effect, he is joining Rosenberg in citing the relative scarcity of resources as an objective "material" constraint that explains diverse political actions (for example, recourse to coercion versus use of persuasion) more or less independently of political or ideological considerations.

But Suny's essay can also be read as shifting the balance of explanation in the other direction, of implicitly subordinating circumstantial determinism to political intent, and I would carry his implicit argument a step further. For even some of the conditions favorable to democratic practice, the "circumstances" that he highlights in order to balance his argument, were circumstances of the Mensheviks' own making, hence not independent or external factors, as the term might suggest. In other words, the "long period of Menshevik hegemony among workers and peasants" in Georgia was itself a manifestation of their successful political practice, and the policies of 1918–20, with their deliberate emphasis on "social peace," are more comprehensible as a continuation of that practice than as a response to some kind of preexisting objective conditions. Democratic elections were never that threatening to the Georgian Mensheviks precisely because of the Mensheviks' hard-earned and relatively long-lived political popularity, a "circumstance" that can hardly be counterposed to the political strategy of which it was the desired fruit.

Conversely, the Bolsheviks' failure to sustain the sort of dynamic majority they briefly enjoyed in the fall of 1917, let alone the formal majority that would have obviated the need to disperse the Constituent Assembly, was a threatening "circumstance" that at the very least was conditioned by their own vanguard politics, their own political choices and predispositions. Surely it cannot be portrayed as if it were an external situation or circumstance—like a hurricane or an earthquake—to which the Bolsheviks were suddenly compelled to react.

The above remarks should not be taken as an attempt to turn the argument from circumstance on its head, reverting to the jaded ideological determinism that Rosenberg, Suny, and other contributors to this volume have been challenging so effectively. What these informative and thought-provoking essays succeed in doing is to instruct us on the need for historians to be constantly engaged in working their way through a complex dialectic of ideology and circumstance, consciousness and experience, reality and will, a dialectic that can never be reduced to a catchy formula, and certainly not to a formula that awards a golden certificate of causal primacy. Perhaps the problem is not so much to balance one term against another, but to recognize that although the notion of "circumstance" may be indispensable, some of the most interesting historical circumstances are themselves engendered and shaped by politically and ideologically inspired decisions, decisions that restrict the subsequent range of alternatives, precluding some and enhancing the attractiveness of others.

And even when circumstances can be taken as a given, it is hard to conceive of ways of perceiving and reacting to them that are not ideologically mediated, the more so when we are talking about deeply committed political actors.

Happily, simplistic images of canonical Marxist-Leninist texts that contained the genetic code for the Communist future, or of a single fountainhead of unbending Bolshevik ideology that can be held accountable for the range of Bolshevisms that emerged over time, are losing their power to convince. But that there was a powerful Bolshevik political culture, however broad, diverse, and difficult to define, can hardly be denied. Whether or not it was an "organizational weapon," the Bolshevik Party was surely a social institution, with its own internal coherence, structure, values, and sense of purpose. One of its salient characteristics, sometimes visible even on the Bolshevik left, was a low level of tolerance for working-class autonomy from the vanguard party, coupled with a powerful commitment to productivity as an incontrovertible revolutionary goal. Another characteristic, sometimes visible even on the Bolshevik right, was a low level of tolerance for cooperation, let alone for power sharing, with other political groups and orientations. To varying degrees, several essays in this volume suggest the way in which each of these attitudes repeatedly contributed to the shaping of the "circumstances" of the Civil War period, to the party's interpretation of their meaning, and to its definition of its range of options, making certain choices seem "necessary," including some that proved to be ineffective or even counterproductive.[7] And such was the case whether the circumstances obtained before, during, or following the Civil War.

NOTES

I am most grateful to Laura Engelstein, Diane Koenker, Nicholas Riasanovsky, and Irwin Scheiner for their valuable comments on an earlier draft of this commentary.

1. William G. Rosenberg, "Russian Labor and Bolshevik Power After October," *Slavic Review*, 1985, 44, no. 2, p. 222.

2. Ibid., p. 228.

3. Brovkin, "Politics, Not Economics Was the Key," ibid., pp. 244–50; Rosenberg, "Reply," ibid., pp. 251–56. See also the relevant remarks of Moshe Lewin, ibid., pp. 239–43.

4. On the difficulties of Soviet workers during NEP, see William J. Chase, *Workers, Society, and the Soviet State: Labor and Life in Moscow, 1918–1929* (Urbana, Ill., 1987). Chase emphasizes the workers' resentment in the early 1920s that improvements brought about by the NEP had passed them by. Having described in some detail how the government's labor policies and other hardships of the Civil War years had shattered the workers' revolutionary dreams and given rise to labor unrest (chap. 1), he goes on to show that workers "bore the brunt" of the sacrifices demanded under early NEP: "In only one major area did NEP labor policies differ from those of high War Communism: they sanctioned and contributed to high unemployment" (p. 56). Between late 1920 and 1924, he writes, Moscow workers "seethed with discontent" (p. 231).

5. "The Emergence of Political Society in Georgia," in Ronald Grigor Suny, ed.,

Transcaucasia: Nationalism and Social Change (Ann Arbor, Mich., 1983), pp. 139–40.

6. On page 249 of *Transcaucasia: Nationalism and Social Change*, Suny writes that "the Georgian Mensheviks were to all intents and purposes the leaders of the national liberation movement of the Georgian people." In light of subsequent developments in the Third World, one might add, this combination of Marxism and national liberation in a dependent agrarian society is not entirely surprising.

7. A case in point is the policy of militarization of labor. William Chase has written: "Given the draconian nature of labor militarization, one wonders about the extent to which it was successful," and he cites the high desertion rate among militarized workers as an indication of the policy's "limited effectiveness" (Chase, *Workers, Society, and the Soviet State*, p. 46; see also pp. 47–48).

VI

The Legacy of the
Civil War

THE LEGACY OF THE CIVIL WAR

Sheila Fitzpatrick

In his classic work on the Civil War,[1] Lev Kritsman called it "the heroic period" of the Russian Revolution. That has remained its image in Soviet historiography. But for many years Western scholars paid little attention to the Civil War (except in studies of foreign intervention and the White Armies, which flourished partly because they could be written from archival and other sources available outside the Soviet Union), and this comparative neglect reflected their judgement that it was not a turning point or crucial phase in Soviet development. The crucial phases, in the standard Western view, were the pre-revolutionary development of the Bolshevik Party and Leninist ideology, the Bolshevik seizure of power in 1917, and the Stalin period.

This chronology was an important part of the "totalitarian" interpretation of the Soviet system that dominated Western Sovietology after the Second World War. For scholars of this generation, the two key questions were how did the totalitarian system work and what were the origins of totalitarianism. The origins were found, in the first place, in Leninist ideology and the organizational pattern laid down for the Bolshevik Party in Lenin's *What Is To Be Done?* (1902) and, in the second place, in the Bolsheviks' seizure of power in October 1917 and establishment of a party dictatorship. In this view, the Bolsheviks' professions of soviet democracy were a sham, and their claim to be a proletarian party acting with popular support in October equally fraudulent.[2] It was inevitable that they would emasculate the soviets, suppress all other political parties, and use terror to intimidate their opponents and compensate for their lack of popular support. Their rule had no legitimacy or basis in the society, and their objectives were political power and the use of that power to control society and transform it according to their ideological blueprint. Lenin achieved the first objective and laid the groundwork for Stalin's accomplishment of the second and consolidation of totalitarian rule.

In recent years, the totalitarian model has been criticized on many counts, including its inappropriateness to the pre-Stalin period and the biased perspective it imposed on study of the prerevolutionary Bolshevik Party, 1917, and the early years of Soviet power. In his article "Bolshevism and Stalinism",[3] Stephen Cohen forcefully challenged the idea of historically inevitable progression from Lenin to Stalin, arguing that Bolshevism was not monolithic and contained seeds of democratic as well as Stalinist-totalitarian development. To assume the inevitability of the Stalinist outcome, Cohen argued, was to impose a "Whig interpretation" of history, the Whigs in this case being Cold War anti-Communists whose hatred of Stalinist totalitarianism colored their view of its revolutionary antecedents. Some years earlier, Moshe Lewin had offered a reinterpretation of the late Lenin that questioned assumptions of ideological continuity between Lenin and Stalin,[4] and both he and Cohen investigated the possibility that in the political conflicts of the late 1920s it was Bukharin rather than Stalin who could legitimately claim to be Lenin's heir.[5] Robert C. Tucker took a more qualified revisionist position when he argued that historically there were at least two Leninisms—one associated with War Communism, the Civil War experience, and coercive dictatorship; the other associated with NEP and its more pragmatic, gradualist, and socially conciliatory policies.[6] In this scheme, Bukharin was the heir of NEP Leninism, and Stalin of the Leninism of the Civil War.

The idea that the origins of Stalinism might be found in the Civil War period interested a number of scholars in the 1970s. Cohen and Lewin both touched on this question in several works,[7] and a similar interpretation was implied in my treatment of Cultural Revolution.[8] Roger Pethybridge's pioneering essays on the social history of the Civil War appeared under the title *The Social Prelude to Stalinism*,[9] and Robert Service's book on the Bolshevik Party's organizational experiences in the first years after the October Revolution reinforced the hypothesis that the Civil War was a turning point in the direction of Stalinism.[10]

At the same time, social historians were entering the Soviet field for the first time, almost invariably repudiating the totalitarian model (in which society was little more than an object of manipulation by the political leadership) and rejecting its "Cold War" premises. The 1917 revolution was the first subject of reappraisal, and the conventional picture began to change under the impact of detailed studies by historians like Rabinowitch (whose two monographs challenged the premise of a monolithic Bolshevik Party without popular support),[11] Koenker, Mandel, and Smith.[12] It no longer seemed plausible to depict the Bolsheviks in 1917 as hard-eyed elitist conspirators bound by tight party discipline. The new work showed them in the midst of a radical working-class movement, swayed by grass-roots pressure, often disorganized and disputing amongst themselves, and swept forward by events and tides of popular opinion over which they had little control.

While this work undercut the totalitarian interpretation of 1917, it also raised new questions about the dynamics of Soviet development after the October Revolution. The revised picture of the Bolshevik Party in 1917 showed it to be unlike the later Stalinist Communist Party. What could have caused such a drastic change? What happened to the soviets and the factory committees, the Bolsheviks' contact with the grass roots, their base of working-class support and the lively disputatiousness of party life? The answers to these questions, many scholars surmised, must lie in the Civil War.

The Revisionist Approach

In current Sovietological usage, "revisionist" is a term used for scholarship that is explicitly abandoning the totalitarian model. Most recent social history falls under this heading, as do many recent studies in political history that emphasize the social context. The characteristic perspective is "from below" rather than "from above". In relation to the Civil War, revisionist scholars are often interested in the hypothesis that the origins of Stalinism may lie in the Civil War experience rather than in earlier Bolshevik organization and ideology or the Bolsheviks' assumption of power in the October Revolution. In this volume, the articles by Rosenberg, Rabinowitch, and Suny are most clearly revisionist in tendency. But my comments on the revisionist approach are not only or even primarily directed at these articles, which to my mind exemplify the virtues of revisionist scholarship rather than its potential problems.

The problems—which might arise in the future if, as seems possible, the revisionist approach becomes a new orthodoxy for young historians—are of three kinds. First, there is the possibility of rejecting too much of the old totalitarian orthodoxy, and specifically of forgetting that Bolshevik ideology and the October seizure of power had something to do with the outbreak of Civil War and the lessons the Bolsheviks drew from their Civil War experiences. Second, there is a danger of replacing the biases of totalitarian scholarship with a new set of biases of opposite tendency.[13] Third, there is a question to be considered about the relationship between social history methodology and revisionist conclusions. It may be that our new methodology and sources tend to produce revisionist conclusions, just as the old methodology and sources tended to reinforce the totalitarian interpretation.

With regard to the first problem, the revisionist approach sometimes offers the Civil War as an alternative to traditional explanations of the origins of Stalinism, implying that without this experience the Bolsheviks might not have followed the path of coercion, one-party dictatorship, and suppression of internal debate in the name of party unity.[14] Of course we cannot say for certain what would have happened had there been no Civil War. But it is surely misleading to suggest that the Bolsheviks were likely under any circumstances to have followed a democratic, pluralist and nonconfrontational path. The old emphasis on ideology (or, to use a newer term, political culture) was not entirely misplaced, for the Bolsheviks had always been the tough guys of the Russian Social Democratic movement, and in 1917 they were still the intransigents who denounced compromises and coalitions with other parties and called for class war. To labor an obvious point, Bolsheviks were not Mensheviks. When they took power in Russia, as Suny's article reminds us, they behaved differently from the Mensheviks in power in Georgia. This was not just because the external circumstances were different, but also because the Bolsheviks had different ideas about politics and a different approach to government.

Although Cohen's version of the "traditional" interpretation stressed Bolshevik ideology,[15] that interpretation also emphasized the significance of the Bolsheviks' seizure of power in October 1917. Perhaps, as Rabinowitch suggested in his book on October,[16] that characterization of their actions is too harsh and implies a denial that the Bolsheviks had substantial popular support from the urban working class and in the armed forces. Yet granting the popular support, it is still the case that the Bolsheviks preempted any decision by the Second Congress of Soviets by their actions and then, in a totally unexpected and provocative move, set up a *Bolshevik* cabinet (Sovnarkom) as the successor to the Provisional Government. This was not likely to produce a democratic, pluralist, or nonconfrontational outcome. In fact, as many external and internal critics suggested, it was likely to produce both a Bolshevik dictatorship and a civil war.

The Bolshevik leaders were clearly willing to take that risk. Furthermore, they anticipated a "dictatorship of the proletariat," and that concept was a good deal closer to a party dictatorship in Lenin's 1917 usage[17] than revisionist scholars sometimes suggest. As for the possibility of civil war, this did not frighten the Bolsheviks and to some degree attracted them, since they sensed that only violent confrontation with the class enemy would guarantee a true revolutionary victory. In these circumstances, it is hard to see the Civil War as a turning point for the Bolsheviks, or the basis for an alternative explanation of the origins of Stalinism. It was not a new direction but, rather, another step in the direction indicated by the October Revolution.

The problem of interpretative bias is always a complicated one. Yet as Cohen and others (including myself) have pointed out, the traditional totalitarian interpretation often reads like an indictment of the Bolsheviks and the Soviet regime rather than an objective explanation of historical processes. In a revisionist essay like Rosenberg's in this volume, we see a scholar explaining the processes that led the Bolsheviks toward coercive solutions while avoiding both the old tone of indictment and its opposite, the tone of exculpation. But not all revisionist argument is so successful in maintaining objectivity and detachment. Western revisionists are sometimes tempted to follow the example of Soviet "de-Stalinizing" historians, whose aim is not just to restore objectivity and accuracy to discussion of the Stalin period but also to save Lenin and the revolution from the taint of association with Stalin's "mistakes." There is, however, a difference between rehabilitating the pre-Stalin period and treating it objectively. The old Russian question of "who is to blame?" is still hovering in the background, particularly on the issue of the origins of Stalinism. Thus, there is a danger in tying our new study of Civil War social history to this sensitive issue. The danger is that we may unconsciously be looking for a new culprit—the Civil War—to exonerate Lenin and the revolution from responsibility for Stalinism. This approach would be unsatisfactory in intellectual terms because the Civil War was so much a product of the Bolshevik Revolution. It would also be unsatisfactory because the allocation of blame is a task for political revisionists, not historical ones.

The third problem to be considered has to do with methodology and sources. In the 1950s, when access to Soviet libraries and archives was limited or nonexistent for Western scholars, Sovietologists often depended heavily on *Pravda*, the resolutions of the CPSU, and Lenin's and Stalin's *Works* for their data. This research base may have been narrow even in terms of the resources available, but it was in a sense appropriate for totalitarian-model scholarship, which postulated that all significant impulses came from the top. On this premise, the history of a totalitarian society could be understood by reading the instructions and pronouncements of its political leaders.

Social historians prefer the perspective "from below" and are also conditioned by the more rigorous research requirements that are normal in the historical profession. The new generation therefore uses a much greater variety of sources than most of its predecessors and consequently has much richer and more detailed data at its disposal. It is clear that the introduction of data from lower-level sources is likely to change the historical picture substantially. Rabinowitch, for example, draws on a Petrograd local newspaper (*Vestnik pervogo gorodskogo raiona*), whose existence was probably not even known to earlier Sovietologists. His picture of Petrograd's political life in 1918 could not possibly have been deduced from central newspapers and materials of the Bolshevik Central Committee. Indeed, it is incompatible in many ways with the conventional wisdom about the party and its relationship to the soviets after the October Revolution and requires us to reconsider many familiar generalizations.

We should bear in mind, however, that sources may influence conclusions. The use of lower-level sources almost inevitably highlights lower-level initiatives, just as the use of high-policy sources emphasizes the initiatives taken at the top. Similarly, the use of archives of government bureaucracies leads scholars to think in terms of bureaucratic conflict. Both types of sources tend to undermine the totalitarian model: indeed, it is hard to imagine such a model gaining the ascendancy it did in the postwar period if historians at that time had access to local newspapers and state bureaucratic archives. This suggests significant weaknesses in the model, but it does not mean that lower-level initiatives were necessarily more important than central ones or that the bureaucratic conflicts of Soviet politics were its most singular feature. We need only imagine the impact on scholarship of a sudden opening of Central Committee and Politburo archives to see how sharply perspectives can shift in response to new types of accessible data.

Another caveat, or reminder of the relativity of revisionist truth, has to do with the recent entry of historians into the field of early Soviet studies and the departure of political scientists. Detailed historical research always tends to undermine the sense of general purpose, direction, or overarching framework. Historians often see this as an absolute good, and certainly in the Soviet case the simplicity and clarity of the old explanatory models and their strong overtones of historical determinism owed something to sheer ignorance and inaccessibility of data. There is always, however, a danger of missing the wood for the trees, or reducing everything to the meaningless chaos of Tolstoii's battlefield in *War and Peace*. Most historians do not share Tolstoii's view of history or they would have gone into another profession. Which means that they still have the task of explaining historical processes.

At present, on every major issue of Soviet history, historians seem to be submerging themselves in data and periodically surfacing with a single astonished cry: "Improvisation!" Chaos is almost becoming the dominant principle of Soviet development as the old explanatory structures disintegrate. Nothing is planned in advance; no policy is implemented in the manner intended; results are always unpremeditated and responses unpredicted. Political leaders stagger from one unexpected crisis to another, pragmatically muddling through. Their minds are empty of ideology, they are incapable of planning, and only circumstances govern their actions.

This is certainly a healthy corrective to the previous emphasis on overarching plans and totalitarian control, and in some ways it is appropriate to see the Civil War, for example, as a Tolstoiian battlefield. All the same, it is surely possible to carry improvisational arguments too far. The Bolsheviks may have improvised War Communism and provided a post hoc theoretical justification. But the Georgian Mensheviks, who presumably also improvised, found different solutions. People make choices even on a battlefield; politicans act pragmatically, but within a context of their particular assumptions and instincts and those of their political and social constituencies.

In traditional Sovietology, the context was labeled "ideology" and often described simplistically in terms of political theories and published party platforms. We may prefer to use another shorthand like "political culture" and cast the net more broadly. But it should not be forgotten that the Bolsheviks *had* a distinctive political culture that shaped their policy decisions and behavior in power; that there were central policy decisions as well as local improvisation; that, despite the chaos of the Civil War battlefields, there was a real Civil War with winners, losers and an identifiable outcome.

The Legacy of the Civil War

Great events leave many kinds of legacy. The Civil War had, first of all, an immediate practical outcome: it left the Bolsheviks victory, power, and a daunting array of economic, social, and political problems. But the Civil War also left a legacy of heroic myth, contributing to the legitimacy of the new regime and its supporters' sense of solidarity and identity. That legacy was recalled at the end of the 1920s as a means of mobilizing the party and society for Stalins's "revolution from above," creating a relationship (though not necessarily a causal connection) between the Civil War and the Stalinism of the 1920s. These different aspects of the legacy all need to be considered.

The immediate practical legacy of the Civil War included industrial collapse, disintegration of the working class, alienation of the peasantry by requisitions, and emigration of a large part of the old upper classes. But perhaps the most interesting Civil War creation and legacy was the Civil War Red Army—five million strong at the end of the war, rapidly demobilized (for the most part) in 1921, and sending millions of veterans "tempered by the struggle" back into the civilian society of NEP.

In an immediate sense, demobilization was part of the Bolshevik political and psychological trauma of 1921, along with the Kronstadt revolt and the recognition of economic breakdown that prompted the abandonment of War Communism and the introduction of NEP. The message of Kronstadt and the Petrograd strikes was that the new regime had lost the confidence of at least a part of its old revolutionary constituency of workers, soldiers, and sailors. But this was only one component of the Bolsheviks' traumatic sense of isolation and abandonment. Almost more threatening was their simultaneous realization that the revolutionary constituency—the proletariat, in whose name the Bolsheviks had taken power—had largely disintegrated, making the Bolshevik Party "the vanguard of a nonexistent class," as one critic of the leadership expressed it.[18]

In the strict sense, "the proletariat" meant the industrial working class. But the Bolsheviks were also accustomed to regarding soldiers and sailors as "proletarian" and the Red Army as a base of social as well as military support.[19] Demobilization drastically diminished that base; moreover, the erstwhile "proletarian" veterans suddenly appeared in a different light to the Bolshevik leaders when some of the demobilized men turned to banditry on their way back to the villages and others, congregating without employment in the towns, contributed to urban crime and social disorder. The disillusionment with the industrial proletariat, freely expressed by Lenin and other party leaders in the early 1920s, was matched by disillusionment with the demobilized Red Army men.

In the longer term, however, this was not the most important aspect of the Civil War Red Army's legacy. While the Bolsheviks may have strained Marxist theory by regarding the Red Army men as proletarian, there was a lot of practical sense in their view that Red Army service and the experience of the Civil War instilled "proletarian consciousness"—urban mores, identification with the revolution, and loyalty to the Soviet regime—in peasant and other non–working-class recruits. This consciousness persisted after demobilization as part of the esprit de corps of Red Army veterans of the Civil War cohort. After the initial disruption, the veterans' return to civilian life meant dissemination of Soviet and revolutionary values throughout the country and in all strata of society.

In the villages, Civil War veterans had the authority of men who had seen the world as well as the restlessness that goes with it and often challenged peasant conservatism and clashed with the elders of the *mir*. In the factories, veterans provided a nucleus for the revival of working-class solidarity and a sense of proprietary commitment to the Soviet regime. In technical schools and universities, the returned soldiers kept aloof from the younger "bourgeois" students but, as the new "proletarian" element, often took positions of leadership and kept a wary eye on the potentially anti-Soviet professors. Even the literary world felt the impact of the veterans' return, since a particularly aggressive group—young Communists of intelligentsia background who had served as political commissars during the Civil War—created the proletarian writers' association (RAPP) that sent literary vigilantes to harrass the old "bourgeois" writers throughout the 1920s.

Red Army veterans, moreover, formed the backbone of Soviet administration after the Civil War. Indeed, they should probably be regarded as the formative cohort, since it was only after the Civil War, as the Red Army withdrew from its substantial wartime administrative role, that a coherent civilian administrative structure took shape. The veterans' style of organization and leadership reflected their experience in the military, and "civilian" Communists often complained that they were given to command rather than consultation and had little appreciation of the participatory aspects of soviet democracy. On the vexed question of the collapse of soviet democracy, the emergence of an authoritarian-bureaucratic administrative style and the relationship of these processes to the Civil War,[20] we should perhaps look not only at the Civil War period itself but also at the aftermath. In the most literal sense, civilian administration was not "militarized" during the Civil War but *after* it, when the demobilized veterans moved in and, according to some contemporary reports, transformed the mores of local administration.

As to the Bolshevik Party, its literal "militarization" occurred during the Civil War, when a high proportion of all party members were mobilized for service in the Red Army and the Red Army was the major channel of party recruitment. The dichotomy between "military" and "civilian" Bolsheviks was an immediate product of the war, and the deference of "civilians" to their Red Army comrades—based on the Red Army's status as defender of the revolution and the danger, heroism, and sacrifice associated with military service—also developed during the Civil War. It should not be forgotten, however, that "civilian" Bolsheviks actually ran the party and government at this period while the "military" Bolsheviks were away at the front and out in the provinces.

With regard to the central party and government leadership, any actual "militarization" had to be a postwar phenomenon—the product of the military Bolsheviks' return and assumption of civilian leadership roles. While this process has yet to be thoroughly investigated, it is likely that some of the travails that the Bolshevik leadership went through in 1920–21 were related to the return of Red Army Bolsheviks and their clashes with entrenched "civilians." For example, the military cohort may well have been particularly insistent on party unity and intolerant of the faction fighting that had become endemic in the basically civilian party leadership during the Civil War. Lenin, an unabashedly "civilian" Bolshevik while the fighting was in progress, switched abruptly into belligerent "military" rhetoric once the war was over in 1921–22.[21] This is hard to explain satisfactorily except in terms of response to the Red Army Bolsheviks' return and a consequent "militarization" of mood and ethos in the central party organization, which Lenin found it necessary to match.

In the 1920s, Russia differed from all other First World War belligerent nations in that it had no mass veterans' associations. This was reportedly because the Bolshevik leadership made a decision in principle against them. Yet the Civil War veterans, in particular, retained so strong a sense of common identity that the apparent lack of an organizational focus—and the absence of forcefully expressed grievance on the part of the veterans—should arouse historians' curiosity. One possible explanation is that the Bolshevik Party itself took the place and performed the functions of a veterans' organization.

This hypothesis opens up many lines of inquiry about the legacy of the Civil War. It throws a new light on the question of social support, since the veterans as a group might then be considered a base of social support for the Bolshevik Party and the Soviet regime. It helps explain some striking departures from prerevolutionary Bolshevik tradition in the 1920s, such as the abrupt descent of women to a kind of second-class citizenship in the Bolshevik Party. Certainly the Bolsheviks of the 1920s behaved like veterans (whether or not they had actually fought), wearing Army tunics and boots, cultivating a macho image, and treating the party like a fighting brotherhood. In this regard—though they would strongly have denied it—they resembled the contemporary European paramilitary political organizations based on veterans' solidarity and grievances more than they resembled the prewar Bolshevik Party or any other social democratic group.

This last analogy may seem far-fetched, since the Bolsheviks were in power and not radical outsiders with a grievance against their society and its rulers. Yet in a sense theirs *was* an outsider's psychology in the 1920s, particularly in the case of the Bolshevik veterans, whose problems of postwar (and postrevolutionary) adjustment were exacerbated by NEP and the spectacle of a reviving bourgeoisie. Red Army men had been a privileged group during the Civil War, protected by their ration priority from the worst consequences of War Communism and probably much less disposed than the civilian population to criticize it as a system. Demobilization removed their economic privileges, and the simultaneous introduction of NEP left them to make their own way in a peacetime world where privation and unemployment were common and the prevailing social mores often seemed alien.

It is interesting to speculate how far the "military" Bolsheviks initially accepted NEP and to what extent they regarded it as a policy of civilians, introduced in their absence. "Voennyi kommunizm" (War Communism) was often used pejoratively in the public discourse of NEP. But the Bolshevik "voennye" of the Civil War cohort seem more likely to have resented the pejorative overtones and responded positively to the new term. They were probably more likely than other party members to doubt the wisdom of such NEP policies as conciliation of the middle peasantry and tolerance of urban Nepmen. In at least one case, a group of young Communist veterans—the leaders of RAPP—challenged the party's official NEP policy of coexistence in literature and declared themselves "on guard" for the revolution.[22]

This brings us to the question of the viability of NEP, given the veterans' numerical strength within the party and the broader diffusion of an heroic myth of the Civil War that made NEP seem drab, uncongenial, and even Thermidorian to many Communists. If the veterans were a base of social support, their attitudes and grievances had to be taken seriously by the party leadership. Can it be plausibly argued that they made NEP unviable and pushed the party into the more aggressive and confrontational policies of "revolution from above"?

In considering this argument, two points must be borne in mind. First, it is necessary to distinguish between sentiment, a potential constituency for hard-line policies, and an irresistible pressure from the grass roots for radical action. Nostalgic veterans may have belligerent sentiments and approve hard-line policies without necessarily wanting to go off and personally fight another war. Their sentiments may have encouraged politicians to use hard-line rhetoric, or even persuaded them that there was a political constituency for confrontational policies, without actually forcing the politicians to adopt such policies. Second, any argument for the nonviability of NEP must explain why it was possible to introduce NEP at the beginning of the 1920s but not possible to sustain it beyond the end of the decade. In other words, the argument must show that pressures against NEP had a tendency to increase, not just that such pressures existed.

To this author, it seems doubtful that the argument on Bolshevik veterans meets these criteria. However belligerent their sentiments, many Civil War veterans were in responsible administrative jobs by the mid-1920s and were in no apparent danger of losing them. The party leaders could always have bought them off by higher salaries and privileges if necessary. Moreover, the veterans were getting older and more settled in civilian life: it is hard to see why, if they had swallowed NEP (however unwillingly) in 1921, they should suddenly have found it intolerable seven or eight years later. Their proportional weight in the party probably declined as a result of the Lenin levy (though it is not clear how many worker-veterans came into the party between 1924 and 1928) and was certainly likely to decline in the future. If the party resembled a veterans' organization in the first half of NEP, its tendency from 1924 was to rebuild the working-class base and revive the older image of a workers' party.

A more plausible contention is that, rather than forcing Stalin and the party leadership into "revolution from above," the veterans offered a potential constituency to support such policies and cadres to implement them. If this is so, the question of timing is crucial. Veterans in their early thirties—their average age when "revolution from above" was launched—might be relied on to respond to a call for action. But this would surely not have been the case ten or even five years later. For policies requiring vigor, zeal, and self-sacrifice from the party cadres, the Civil War veterans were an asset whose value diminished with each passing year.

The Civil War and Stalinism

The striking similarities between the periods of the Civil War and "revolution from above" at the end of the 1920s have intrigued historians and constitute the main support for the hypothesis that the origins of Stalinism lie in the Civil War. With regard to policy and methods of implementation, the connections between War Communism and Stalin's revolution are obvious. In both periods, the regime pushed for full nationalization of production, elimination of private manufacturing and private trade, and (albeit on a smaller scale under War Communism) collectivization of agriculture. Grain requisitioning was practiced (though not acknowledged as state policy) in 1928–29, as it had been during the Civil War. Social confrontation was charcteristic of both periods, with kulaks and urban traders taking the brunt of the regime's class-war policies and the bourgeois intelligentsia also subject to suspicion and attack. "Class enemies" were terrorized by the Cheka during the Civil War and the OGPU at the end of the 1920s, and the courts followed principles of "class justice" that effectively deprived such persons of protection by law.

The similarities were atmospheric as well as substantive. Utopian dreaming and apocalyptic fears were prevalent in both periods. Communist enthusiasm ran high, and the revolutionary spirit made incremental gains seem paltry and prudence or legalistic scruples discreditable for a Communist. Foreign threats, sabotage, and counterrevolutionary conspiracy loomed large, making Communist vigilance imperative. In the "revolution from above," the militant rhetoric—"storming the fortresses," "fighting on the front of collectivization," and so on—often explicitly recalled the Civil War, and the struggle for the First Five-Year Plan was treated as if it were a war for national survival. The sense of wartime emergency, initially generated by the 1927 war scare, provided justification for the material sacrifices required of the population, which were of similar magnitude to those of the Civil War period. For the urban population, the reintroduction of rationing, levying of state loans, closing of markets, and other disruptions of everyday life reinforced the parallel. For Communists and workers, liable to mobilization for service in the countryside during collectivization and for other state purposes, the parallel with the Civil War was even closer.

We should be wary, however, of jumping to the conclusion that these similarities imply a causal relationship or demonstrate that Stalinism was an outcome of the Civil War. At the level of policy and goals, "revolution from above" may be seen as (in part) a repetition of War Communism, but one obvious explanation for this is that these were basic policies and goals of the

Bolshevik Party, whose implementation was merely delayed during the interlude of NEP. To be sure, this is not a full explanation, especially if one sees substantial elements of improvisation and response to Civil War emergency in the policies of War Communism. But it seems perverse to deny that the Bolsheviks had goals and some notion of the policies appropriate for their achievement when they took power in October 1917, or that their predisposition at that date was toward revolutionary rather than incremental change.

The atmospheric similarities may be attributed in part to the important contribution of Civil War veterans in implementing Stalin's revolution, and perhaps also to the gusto with which younger Communists and Komsomols compensated for their disappointment at missing the earlier "heroic period" of the revolution. But there is another dimension to the story. If "revolution from above" strikes historians as a reenactment of Civil War themes, this is partly because, in a literal sense, it was. There was a strong element of political theater—agitdrama, to use a Civil War term—in the regime's presentation of its new policies to the public, and the message of the agitdrama was that the revolution was once again in danger from internal class enemies and foreign interventionists. The Shakhty trial and other subsequent show trials made this point in overtly theatrical form,[23] and it was reinforced by the highly stylized Civil War imagery in the agitational rhetoric of the period and the media's insistent coverage of foreign interventionist designs and the (largely imaginary) danger of war.[24]

If the Civil War theme was a mobilization device for Stalin's revolution, we should perhaps credit Stalin and his agitprop men with being the first to suggest that "revolution from above" was a logical and necessary continuation of the revolutionary Civil War. Of course, this does not in itself discredit the hypothesis, though it may suggest that historians should approach it with caution. But there are further difficulties ahead if we try to extend the hypothesis to cover "Stalinism" and not just Stalinist "revolution from above."

Virtually any characterization of Stalinism will include Stalin's personal dictatorship and the cult that surrounded it in the 1930s and 1940s, the Great Purges, routine police controls over the population, and the party's mobilizing and organizational role as it evolved in the pre- and postwar period. Unlike the First Five-Year Plan "revolution from above," none of these phenomena has any indisputable or self-evident connection with the Civil War. The personal dictatorship and the cult have no overt connection with the Civil War or the Civil War myth. The routine functions of the police under high Stalinism were different from those of the Cheka in the Civil War, and the party's role owed less to the Civil War experience than to that of the First Five-Year Plan. In the case of the Great Purges, the absence of obvious precedents—at least since the reign of Ivan the Terrible—has notoriously baffled historians, and their occasional references to the 1920–21 party purge should be dismissed as mere tokens of desperation. To be sure, there were elements of reenactment of Cultural Revolution in the Great Purges and elements of reenactment of the Civil War in Cultural Revolution, but this is a rather distant family connection.

Moreover, the Civil War veterans as a group were victims rather than imple-menters of the Great Purges.

We are left, then, with a complex but basically noncausal relationship be-tween the Civil War and the "revolution from above" that inaugurated the era of Stalinism. In assessing the legacy of the Civil War, we should surely focus primarily on NEP, which may be regarded as a premature Thermidor that failed to thrive because of Civil War passions and, perhaps, the influence of Civil War veterans in the party and secondarily on the "revolution from above," which was both a second try at War Communism and a staged but still serious reenactment of the heroic Civil War myth.

After this point, connections with the Civil War become tenuous. We speak of the Civil War as a "formative experience" for Soviet society and the Soviet regime, but, even accepting Freudian premises on the importance of early child-hood experiences, it is doubtful that societies and regimes follow human de-velopmental principles or that revolution can be equated with birth. Soviet society has had many formative experiences, each tending to supersede its predecessor. Perhaps in a more peaceful history the trauma of the Civil War would have cast a longer shadow, but it was followed by other traumas in swift succession. By the mid-1920s, the Civil War was already a distant memory, overshadowed by the bitter struggles of collectivization. By the late 1930s, the party had gone through another trauma in the Great Purges. Within a few years, the nation plunged into the Second World War, which created its own myth of heroic struggle for survival. Red Army troops sang Civil War songs in the Second World War, and Khrushchev still recalled those songs (in their original version) nostalgically in the 1960s. After 1945, however, "the war" meant the Second World War, not the Civil War. The Civil War had become a part, not a participant, of history.

NOTES

1. L. Kritsman, *Geroicheskii period velikoi russkoi revoliutsii*, 2d ed. (Moscow-Leningrad, 1926).

2. See, for example, Leonard Schapiro, *The Origin of the Communist Autocracy* (Cambridge, Mass., 1955).

3. In Robert C. Tucker, ed., *Stalinism: An Essay in Historical Interpretation* (New York, 1977).

4. Moshe Lewin, *Lenin's Last Struggle* (New York, 1970).

5. See Moshe Lewin, *Political Undercurrents in Soviet Economic Debates: From Bukharin to the Modern Reformers* (Princeton, 1974); and Stephen F. Cohen, *Bukharin and the Bolshevik Revolution* (New York, 1973).

6. Robert C. Tucker, "Stalinism as Revolution from Above," in Tucker, ed., *Stalinism*, pp. 80–82, 89–92.

7. Cohen, *Bukharin*, p. 60; and "Bolshevism and Stalinism," in Tucker ed., *Stalinism*, p. 12; Lewin, *Lenin's Last Struggle*, p. 12; and "The Social Background of Stalinism," in Tucker, ed., *Stalinism*, p. 113.

8. Sheila Fitzpatrick, "Cultural Revolution as Class War," in Sheila Fitzpatrick, ed., *Cultural Revolution in Russia, 1928–1931* (Bloomington, Ind., 1978), pp. 18–19, 25.

9. Roger Pethybridge, *The Social Prelude to Stalinism* (London, 1974).

10. Robert Service, *The Bolshevik Party in Revolution, 1917–1923: A Study in Organisational Change* (New York, 1979).

11. Alexander Rabinowitch, *Prelude to Revolution: The Petrograd Bolsheviks and the July 1917 Uprising* (Bloomington, Ind., 1968) and *The Bolsheviks Come to Power: The Revolution of 1917 in Petrograd* (New York, 1976).

12. Diane Koenker, *Moscow Workers and the 1917 Revolution* (Princeton, 1981); David Mandel, *The Petrograd Workers and the Fall of the Old Regime: From the February Revolution to the July Days, 1917* (New York, 1983) and *The Petrograd Workers and the Soviet Seizure of Power* (New York, 1984); and S. A. Smith, *Red Petrograd: Revolution in the Factories, 1917–1918* (Cambridge and New York, 1983).

13. The argument is developed in Sheila Fitzpatrick, "Origins of Stalinism: How Important Was the Civil War?" *Acta Slavica Iaponica*, 1984, 2, pp. 105–16.

14. See, for example, Cohen, *Bukharin*, p. 60; Service, p. 110; Roy A. Medvedev, *The October Revolution* (New York, 1979), p. 152; Jean Elleinstein, *The Stalin Phenomenon* (London, 1976), p. 14.

15. Cohen, "Bolshevism and Stalinism," pp. 3–11.

16. Rabinowitch, *The Bolsheviks Come To Power*. The title indicates Rabinowitch's rejection of the idea of a Bolshevik "seizure" of power.

17. For example, in his article "Can the Bolsheviks Retain State Power?" as well as the better known *State and Revolution*.

18. Shliapnikov, in *XI s"ezd RKP (b), Mart-aprel' 1922 g. Stenograficheskii otchet* (Moscow, 1961), pp. 103–4.

19. At the Tenth Party Congress, when a Workers' Opposition speaker suggested that to preserve the party from degeneration in power all cadres should periodically return to work in the factories a voice from the floor interjected, "And in the Army!" (*Desiatyi s"ezd RKP[b], Mart 1921 g. Stenograficheskii otchet* [Moscow, 1963], p. 239). In his organizational report to the Twelfth Party Congress in 1923, Stalin dwelled on the importance of the Red Army in transmitting Communist influence and bringing peasants into contact with workers (I. V. Stalin, *Sochineniia* [Moscow, 1952], 5: 204–5).

20. Discussed from different standpoints in, for example, Service; John L. H. Keep, *The Russian Revolution: A Study in Mass Mobilization* (New York, 1976); Marc Ferro, *October 1917: A Social History of the Russian Revolution* (London, 1980), pp. 179–214.

21. See, for example, his political report to the Eleventh Party Congress (March 1922), in V. I. Lenin, *Collected Works*, (Moscow, 1966), 33: 282.

22. Described in Sheila Fitzpatrick, "The 'Soft' Line on Culture and Its Enemies: Soviet Cultural Policy, 1922–1927," *Slavic Review*, June 1974, vol. 33, no 2, pp. 278–85.

23. On the Shakhty trial and its successors, see Kendall E. Bailes, *Technology and Society under Lenin and Stalin* (Princeton, 1978), chaps. 3–5.

24. See Sheila Fitzpatrick, "The Foreign Threat during the First Five-Year Plan," *Soviet Union/Union soviétique*, 1978, vol. 5, pt. 1.

THE CIVIL WAR
DYNAMICS AND LEGACY

Moshe Lewin

While this concluding chapter builds on the foregoing chapters to produce a tentative summary of the Civil War and its impact on the subsequent development of the Soviet system, it also introduces some new themes and raises questions for future debate.

The Civil War was, no doubt, a crucial period in the history of the new Soviet regime. The demarcation of this period is a matter for debate. It may be argued that it began in November 1917 and ended in the middle of 1922. These dates encompass all the most important trends and traits that produced the flavor and substance of the period, the particular ways of acting, and the specific culture of the emerging system and its leaders. By mid-1922, almost all the military operations of importance, including those directed against the widespread bands of guerrillas and bandits, had ceased; the first reasonably abundant harvest had begun to supply enough food to start healing the country's terrible wounds, particularly the consequences of the atrocious famine of 1921; and the war economy was returning to more normal, peacetime functioning.

We are dealing therefore with a time-span of about four years, marked by upheavals, battles, slaughter—a protracted national agony during which the new system was created and took shape. For historians and for other students of social and political systems, it was not simply an important period but also a very exciting one. It seems easier to grasp the essential features of a regime at its inception rather than to try to extract them from the numerous accretions that accumulated at later stages of development.

The system we are studying was not built methodically according to some preestablished blueprint. It was, rather, improvised under the pressure of constant emergencies, although ideologies and programs of the previous era did play their role. This is visible, notably, in some policy preferences such as distaste for markets and a special relation with the working class, to take just

399

a few examples. But these ideological preferences produced more than just facts. They also engendered illusions which are best illustrated by the policies subsumed under the term "War Communism." An "illusion in action" or, to use a better term, "utopia" is a powerful mobilizer and yet its results can be—and were—quite different from what was hoped for. In any case, utopias of different kinds are often an important part of historical events and present an intricate subject for study.

We can state further that although improvised, the key institution of the new system, the party—its only preexisting feature—was created or re-created in the course of the events under consideration, in a new garb, quite different from what it had been at the start. Party cadres, during their short history before October, had trained themselves to be leaders in a revolution that was not even supposed to be socialist. During this period they produced an ideology and a small number of dedicated cadres who, after October, engaged in activities and events, notably a bloody Civil War, during which they organized and ran armies, built a state apparatus, and presided over a new state. As they became rulers of the improvised regime, they re-created themselves and acquired a new identity, even if initially this process was not self-apparent. Nevertheless, the transformation went on speedily in all facets of party life and in many of its principles, such as ties with the masses, organizational structure, modus operandi, social composition, ways of ruling, and style of life.

All this was not the main concern of the participants in the events, proponents or foes of the new regime. They, and observers abroad, were still absorbed by the novelties introduced by this newcomer into the family of world systems. Whether a separate peace with Germany, land to the peasants, workers' control, nationalization of banks and key industries, or less formalized but sharper and more frightening notions such as "rob from the robbers" [*grab' nagrablennoe*]—all of these developments were an outrage to domestic opponents and an insult to the Western world. Forced labor for the bourgeoisie did not improve matters. Under these conditions a civil war was inevitable. What was puzzling was the considerable calm that prevailed during the regime's first months in power. Some would explain it as a power vacuum that the Bolsheviks skillfully filled. But with the crumbling of the Provisional Government the power vacuum was filled, at least partly, by the networks of soviets that had helped the Bolsheviks into power and given them strong initial backing. As for the forces of the old regime and many who were undecided, they needed some time to regroup, to recover from the initial shock, and to reap the benefits of the new regime's predictable difficulties and errors—errors that did not fail to appear.

That civil war was likely can be hypothesized on grounds other than the sole challenge of the Bolshevik program. We know how deeply the Whites hated the forces that stood behind the Kerenskii government. SRs, Mensheviks, and later also the Liberals, were considered by monarchists and nationalists, especially by the officers, to have been the main culprits of the Bolshevik takeover. It is therefore not an idle speculation to contend that a Constituent

Assembly dominated by the SRs would have been dispersed; indeed, the SRs gave ample proof that they were incapable of mounting an effective defense. They did little when told to disperse by the Bolshevik sailors, and later, in their Samara stronghold, they failed again to produce a military force capable of sustaining them. They depended fully on the Czechoslovak units. Their own forces were commanded by White officers who were just waiting for the chance to eliminate them,[1] which is what happened somewhat later in Siberia, where White officers eliminated SR leaders, making clear how unwelcome they were in the White camp.

The basic reality of those years was that the battle was being waged not between democracy and authoritarianism but between two different authoritarian political camps that could field big armies and fight it out. Supporters of the Constituent Assembly could not do the same—and they were eliminated from the historical arena.

We are next faced with another riddle: why did the Bolsheviks, whom we just described as unprepared for the job of ruling a huge country, nevertheless become victors in the Civil War? An easy answer comes to mind—which has a grain of truth to it: their success owed mainly to the ineptitude of their opponents. Victor Shklovskii, in his riveting *Sentimental Journey*, said that it was not a matter of who was the stronger but, rather, who was less weak.[2]

But such an explanation will not do. The Bolsheviks worked feverishly to create a central government as well as important civilian services and local authorities; at the same time they organized a war machine, complete with an armament industry. To sum it all up, they created a state. This achievement testified to a dynamism that the other side clearly lacked. Neither of the main White territories—the Siberian or the southern—managed to produce a credible state administration, despite their claim to superior experience in "statehood" (*gosudarstvennost'*). Numerous documents, notably memoirs of White officers, written during and after the events, testified to the sad state of affairs in the different central and local administrations of the White areas.[3] One officer described the administration of the Stavropol region under the Whites as the rule of *pompadury*, corrupt and arbitrary little despots.[4] The evidence from Kolchak country was not more cheerful. In the battle between the *pompadury* and the *komissary*, the latter certainly deserved to win. They turned out to have had a knack for state building that representatives of previously privileged classes lacked or lost. The deeper cause of this deficiency lay in their inability to convince their previously faithful subjects, especially the peasants, that they still had something to offer them. Their demise in October was not really an accident.

It is worth noting that the Bolsheviks were entrenched in the very heart of historical Muscovy, where they drew most of their support. Russia's heartland, and the resources of the nation and the state accumulated by history in this area, served them well in winning the war and, later, in reuniting the country. The huge border areas (*okrainy*) where the Whites operated, although well provided with raw materials, grain, and an excellent military resource—the

Cossacks—did not give them the hoped for chance to surround and take Moscow. The *okrainy* proved, on the contrary, too diversified, too distant from each other. Instead of being a base for victory, they turned into a morass that engulfed them.

The sociohistorical study of this period, focusing on classes, nationalities, bureaucracies, and parties, as well as on the social composition of the armies, is an indispensable tool, although this kind of study is still in its infancy. Yet, it is particularly satisfying to the historian to learn that not just the Bolsheviks but also the key figures of the opposite camp, notably Paul Miliukov and General Denikin, looked to the social factors, including the class composition of the contending camps and of the country as a whole, in order to explain the victories and defeats. The nefarious role of backward-looking *pomeshchiki*, the actions of the bourgeoisie, their policies in relation to the peasantry, the behavior and attitudes of workers—such were the factors Miliukov cited in his post-mortem analysis of the Whites. And Denikin, although he denied that his side had a class character, admitted and regretted that it never managed to shed its class image in the eyes of the population, a derogatory image at that. Denikin also resented the duplicity and stinginess of the bourgeoisie who did not want to come up with the necessary means to save what they themselves declared to be their cause.[5]

Such explanations are, in fact, indispensable, provided they are used flexibly and are based on good research. Both camps were coalitions, not neat, clear-cut classes. Each side had an obvious, although not entirely monolithic, core, around which coalesced broader layers of the population that often hesitated, changed sides, returned to the fold again, or created a camp of their own. It was this flux that made the Civil War so unpredictable for its participants at the time and so complicated for the analyst today. Such a fluid state of affairs applied equally to both sides. We can cite many examples of military or partisan units, armed with red banners and commissars, turning against the Communists, even killing them, and going over to the other side, continuing on their own—or even staying . . . with the Reds.[6]

We know that there was a nucleus of workers, poor peasants, and *raznochintsy* on the side of the Reds and a core of members of the former privileged classes, richer peasants, and, especially, military officers on the side of the Whites. The problem was who would emerge as the better social and political strategist, who could mobilize the support of large circles of the urban population and, more importantly, the small scale peasant farmers. In this crucial task of social strategy the Bolsheviks proved superior. The Whites, on the other hand, who much of the time were stronger militarily, found themselves in trouble the moment they turned to the forceful drafting of peasants. According to Lenin, that was their undoing.[7] Their basic force became hopelessly diluted.

But social analysis makes us aware of yet another complexity and strain in the social environment of each side. The heat generated by the Civil War was such that the nucleus of both sides showed cracks at different moments, especially in the later stages of war. Dissension and decomposition settled into the White camp first, but neither were the Bolsheviks spared. Confusion, exhaustion, and signs of fragmentation finally hit the party—the tool that the Whites could not match—but luckily for the Reds this occurred after the Whites' defeat.

What it all means is that the Reds were tested in the crucible as cruelly as anybody. The Civil War marked them as deeply as it marked the whole nation.

This was a time of incredible suffering, cruelty, and destruction. Terms like "time on the cross" and "via dolorosa" were evocative of the age for many deeply religious people. Writers used such terms in their works about the period. The symbolists even posed the question of whose side Christ was on. The church, though, was quite firmly on the side of the Whites.

The human suffering resulted not only from the direct cruelties of the Civil War but also from its broader aspect: the widespread dislocation; destruction; decomposition of groups, classes, and parties—briefly a deeply morbid state of the whole social fabric. Shklovskii, again, in his strangely titled work written soon after the events, was particularly impressed, even fascinated, by the phenomena of morbidity—cruelty, the dissolution of social and human bonds, the sickening sight of a society in a state of disaggregation.

These important—and fatal—characteristics of the period have to be studied attentively. Without them, the problem of the aftermath and the legacy of the Civil War will remain unintelligible. We have emphasized that social strategy was a key aspect in the outcome of the war. But we have also mentioned one other aspect of the big game in which the Bolsheviks bested the Whites, namely, the domain of state building. Once the tsarist state collapsed and the Provisional Government was unable to shore it up or build a new one, the stage was set for the social forces in attendance to try their hand at recreating a new political organization. There is no need to repeat the well-known story about who tried and failed. The country was going to be reunited and the sociopolitical system would be established by the camp that could produce a state. In abstract terms, one can imagine situations where a large movement of the masses could win and could subsequently create a state. Historically, such seems to have been the case during "the time of troubles" (*smutnoe vremia*) in Russia at the beginning of the seventeenth century. During the no less tragic *smuta* of the twentieth century the (Bolshevik-run) state was produced, at first, hand-in-hand with a social movement, and soon ever more independently of it, or at least independently of the shifting moods of the sympathetic, neutral, or even hostile masses. An important feature of this process, to which we will return, was that the new state was being erected amidst a disintegrating economy and a decomposing social fabric, at a catastrophic time for the whole country. Indeed, the state was emerging on the basis of a social development in reverse. The Bolsheviks were little aware at that time of this aspect of their achievement, but at the very moment of their triumph, the shadow of Pyrrhus, was certainly present.

The Ordeal

Studying the demographic trends, cities, social classes, economy, and parties will allow us to distinguish such shadowy aspects of the emerging regime. These factors are "system makers" in any conditions, and we shall try to pull together these themes, after a survey of the different components. The chapters of this book quite eloquently describe the hunger, breakdown of communications, and demographic losses endured by the population. I would like to draw attention, in particular, to the collapse of the two capitals. The capitals were the centers and main bases of the revolutionary movements, in particular for the Bolsheviks. But both Petrograd and Moscow suffered the biggest losses. Neither was ever conquered, but the enemy was at times nearby, and the social and economic situation was particularly severe in the capitals. In 1917 the two cities had a combined population of 4 million inhabitants. In 1920 only 1,674,000 remained. Almost the entire industrial workforce of Petrograd was lost through migration, mobilization, and death. Existing data show that 380,000 industrial workers left production, and only some 80,000 remained.[8] Calamity is certainly an appropriate characterization.

But the weakening of the social mainstay of the regime was occurring not just in the capitals. The population of all the big cities shrank to different degrees: the more developed and dynamic the city, the more it suffered. Smaller and less industrialized cities declined less, and some might even have grown. Branches of large-scale industry that did not come to a full standstill declined drastically. Finally, the national industrial labor force decreased by half and was strongly "diluted" or "declassed" by black market activities, idleness, and flight to the villages.[9] The term "deindustrialization" is fully legitimate here. Only armament industries working for the Red Army were kept alive. By the end of the Civil War many key industries, absolutely vital for the functioning of the country, had reverted to their pre-1861 levels.[10] Cities and industries became parasites on the rural economy, not unlike the armies of those days that lived "off the land." As long as such a situation prevailed, an ever-deepening economic crisis, coupled with the continued tearing apart of the social fabric, was inevitable. There were in addition, other corrosive and destructive factors, such as the onerous duty of raising and equipping, let alone enduring, so many armies, their activities, iniquities, and casualties.

The Reds alone had an army of about 5 million toward the end of the Civil War and suffered some 1.2 casualties. Kolchak, at his peak, mobilized some half-a-million people. Denikin began his dashing northbound drive in mid-1919 with some 300,000 under his banners, but as his offensive developed, he mobilized several hundred thousand more, mainly peasants.[11] His army seemed to have stumbled badly with these draftees.

The casualties of the Whites are not known, but we have different assessments of the general population losses from war, epidemics, and famine.[12] A figure of 8 million people, including the unborn, is sometimes quoted in Soviet sources as the sum total of direct losses from the Civil War. But all assessments must be tentative. On the other hand, the whole problem of mobilizations and of armies and their numbers urgently needs further study. Let us take, for example, the problem of deserters. The figures quoted for the Red camp alone are staggering. Some talk about 1.5 million, others of 1 million. With such disparate figures no data on the size of the armies can be reliable. Many joined at the induction centers, even enrolled in units, and then melted away. Many others, who did not present themselves at all, stayed in their villages or headed immediately for the forests. They also, at some stage, returned in considerable numbers,[13] an event of great significance for the outcome of the war. The riffraff quality of the Red Army, especially in the early stages, was predictable in these conditions, and the shiftiness and unreliability of the recruits instilled considerable paranoia in the Red camp. So many of those recruits could easily find their way to and swell the ranks of all kinds of "greens"—Makhno, Grigoriev, Antonov—and of the opposite camp. But the other side faced a similar problem.

The story of the deserters is, of course, a story of peasants. It does reflect, quite faithfully, their moods and attitudes toward both camps. The figures given for the numbers of deserters who began to return in mid-1919 and later are significant not only for their impact on the rout of the Whites in the autumn of the same year but also for the hint they give us about the predominantly peasant character of the Red Army. When the Reds were recruiting volunteers only, the majority of the soldiers were workers. After compulsory drafting was instituted, the Red Army became 80 percent peasant. Its NCOs were at this time 60 percent peasant, but the peasant component diminished drastically in the middle and higher ranks.[14]

Such a huge peasant participation in the ranks of the army at a time when the peasantry was not only supporting but also deserting, "hesitating," and changing sides underscores both the complexity of the tasks the Reds were facing and the degree of their achievement in transforming rather unruly bands into something resembling an army and in learning to execute serious strategic and tactical moves amidst the chaotic conditions of those years. All this testified to the talent of the leadership and their growing military know how.

Until recently, modern Soviet writers still stuck, officially, to the version that all the achievements were due to the leadership of Lenin and the party. Trotskii was mentioned mainly for his real or imaginary errors, although some writings in the mid eighties managed not to mention him at all, or to mention him occasionally but without the usual virulence. Finally, the days of *glasnost'* saw the beginning of a reassessment and "creeping rehabilitation" of Trotskii that is still inconclusive.[15]

Memoirs of the Whites, among others, are an inestimable source for the assessment of the Red Army, the Whites themselves, and the behavior of different groups in the population toward them. We read often in generals' memoirs about how industrial settlements or even quite peaceful-looking villages could suddenly open fire at the approaching Whites. They prided themselves that their hundreds could easily rout thousands of Reds, but they also noticed, with growing disillusionment, that the Reds kept coming at them as their supporters never dried up. The quality of the Red Army kept improving and the memoirists consoled themselves that it all was because of the good work of their own kind who deserted to the Reds or were forced to serve them.

In fact the Reds had their own problems with numbers, especially when "bayonets and sabers" were concerned. When it came to fielding armies, they were often outnumbered by the Whites, who almost always had a superior cavalry—the Cossacks—at their disposal. A measure of the difficulty of wrenching out fighting units from the mobilized mass of recruits is that in an army about five million strong [by the end of 1920], no more than 400,000 "bayonets and sabers" could be fielded. But the same figures (see note 13) make clear why the Whites believed the Reds were "inexhaustible." The latter managed to build up reserves that the Whites could not even dream of. Support for the Reds—enthusiastic, lukewarm, or even nonhostile neutrality—is confirmed by these figures. But this is certainly not the whole story. The picture of social decomposition we are sketching suggests convincingly why the support for the Reds was weakening and had actually begun drying up toward the end of the war.

In our inventory of destructive and decomposing forces we next should mention terror. For some, of course, this was an indispensable tool of war, notably as a means of paralyzing actual and potential enemies by spreading fear among them. But at the same time terror is a physical and psychological source of all kinds of pathologies and an important factor of demoralization for all involved. The existing literature in the West has paid attention mainly to the Cheka. In fact, even on the Red side alone there were all kinds of other security units, as well as a special security army to deal with security problems in the rear of the fighting forces.

But the depth and scope of the destructive effects of terror cannot be understood without realizing that terror was not a monopoly of the Reds. It is less known that the different White armies had intelligence and security units of all kinds, special antisubversive squads and punitive squads. All of them applied individual and mass terror against the population, chased after Communists or members of soviets, engaged in executions or mass flogging of whole villages. All this is well described, sometimes with glee, sometimes with disgust, by White memoirists. There were so many armies, each with its own *karateli*, that villages, or cities, were not always sure who was marching in, assembling the population, and engaging in exactions and executions. Such killings and atrocities were widespread—and the existence of illegal networks of sympathizers, spies, and saboteurs on both sides of enemy lines made sure that a "rationale" for terror and counterterror was not lacking. In the conditions of moral decay, so ripe in those days, terror easily gained its own momentum and acquired a special attraction for psychological perverts of all kinds. The chaos and arbitrariness of those times offered considerable scope for destructive urges in the human psyche.

Among the casualties the country suffered—through terror, starvation, migration, demoralization, or death—we should mention the loss of a considerable number of professionals and intellectuals. This important pool of talent—Kendall E. Bailes shows that it was not that big in the first place—was greatly diminished by the ordeals of the war. The damage caused by casualties of this type has been directly acknowledged in Soviet writings only recently. No quantitative assessment has been offered as yet, to my knowledge. What was never acknowledged as constituting a regrettable loss was the dispersal or destruction of the cadres and leaders of the multiparty system that emerged at the time of the Revolution of 1905. Only Bolsheviks and some remnants from other parties were preserved by either joining the Bolsheviks or being employed by them as "bourgeois specialists."[16] It is worth discussing whether, how, and to what extent the loss of at least certain parts of the political class contributed to the political and intellectual impoverishment of the country.

Whatever the cost, presumed unavoidable, of a revolutionary upheaval, Lenin must have known the extent of such damage. We have an indirect inkling of his thinking from Lunacharskii's *Revolutionary Silhouettes*, written in 1919 and published just after Lenin's death. Lunacharskii reveals, among many other important things, that Lenin did regret that it was not possible to attract a man like Martov to the Bolshevik party. He might have made, Lenin said, an excellent leader for the party's right wing.[17]

If the problem of a political class is sufficiently tricky, the loss of a different group of opponents—the owners and captains of industry—most of the country's entrepreneurial talent—is certainly an obvious and straightforward debit. Such a "commodity" takes time and effort to be re-created. After all, if there were parasitic sectors in the Russian economy and society that had to be removed, the dynamic capitalist sector was not one of them. Lenin's awareness of this problem is reflected in his hope that the country would become "state capitalist," albeit under the aegis of a socialist government. This meant not just employment of bourgeois technicians and specialists but cooperation with big and smaller owners of capitalist enterprises in a regime of coownership. Whatever the merits and realism of this idea, it proves our point that the loss of the entrepreneurs was a deep tear in the social fabric that has to be included here in the "decomposition" column.

Demographic losses and other forms of social decay struck all the classes, groups, and caucuses, in different ways and degrees—except, probably, the criminal underworld, which should have actually thrived in such conditions. The peasantry, the sturdiest and least vulnerable of all classes because of its closeness to the essential means of biological survival, also endured its share of calamities, deaths, casualties, and loss, at least temporarily, of a great mass of able-bodied men through mobilizations, desertions and participation in guerrilla groups.[18] The worst disasters struck millions of peasants just after the Whites were defeated: the famine that resulted from a poor crop in 1920 was followed by an even worse crop and famine in 1921. These same years saw the most furious and widespread uprisings of peasants against the Reds, under the slogans, "down with the *prodrazverstka*" (compulsory grain requisitions) and "Soviets without Bolsheviks." Finally, workers in industrial centers—or what was left of them—engaged in waves of strikes, making it clear that they, too, had had enough. The whole system looked like a phantom. A rickety state faced emaciated masses who seethed with unrest but were so enfeebled that even the rickety state could put them down.

The turmoil and general exhaustion finally caught up with the ruling—and now victorious—party, until now almost indefatigable. Leaders and the rank and file in different ways showed symptoms of strain. This was most obvious at the moment of transition to the NEP, when the "trade union debate" revealed a party splintering into groups and grouplets, disoriented and, according to Lenin, "shivering" badly. "Partiiu likhoradit," he declared, and decided to take drastic measures.

But even before the decision to forbid factions, which effected a fundamental change in the party's inner life, keeping the party in a state of permanent alert and high morale was not easy. Even in the highest echelons of leadership, cliques and personal infighting were rife. Intrigue reached particularly dangerous proportions in mid-1919, when it began to weaken the very top, until then the party's main asset. It revolved around the powerful, yet vulnerable figure of Trotskii, whose strength derived in part from his talents but also from the crucial support of Lenin. The cooperation and mutual trust between these two leaders was an important source of strength for the Reds, but the intriguers, whatever their reasons, were working hard to breakup this duumvirate, as the party, the country, and the world conceived it.

During these years, Lenin, working at a superhuman pace, suffered debilitating headaches. One can surmise that some of his chief lieutenants' relentless efforts to discredit Trotskii must have made him waver. A crisis was reached in early July 1919. During a meeting of the Politburo on July 3–4, Lenin abandoned Trotskii and voted with his critics on all points in dispute. Outraged, Trotskii resigned from all his posts and stormed out of the room. Members of the Politburo, first among them Stalin, ran after him and implored him to stay on, notably in his capacity of war overlord. The vote was reversed, and Trotskii was, officially, given satisfaction on points of interest to him.[19]

It would be interesting to see whether the protocols verify this story. But it is clear that at this point the intriguers overplayed their hand. They would be back at work later. Relations between Lenin and Trotskii remained strained during the next year and a half. Another crisis was the trade-union debate, when the two fought each other over issues that would soon become irrelevant. In 1922, however, there were signs of a new rapprochement.

These events illustrate, among other things, the ravages and the difficult legacies of the Civil War. The war certainly undermined Lenin's health and soon removed him from effective leadership. Iakov Sverdlov died from an illness in early 1919. Trotskii emerged from the war apparently basking in glory but was in fact isolated within the party, having provoked an alliance against him that would bring about his undoing. In short, not all was well with the victorious party and its leaders at the end of the Civil War.

The Intelligentsia

The complicated and tortured saga of the new regime's relations with the intelligentsia, related to the crisis and dislocation of the Civil War, also illuminates the problems of state building, with many important implications for the future. Although both sides had good reasons to distrust each other, they had equally good reasons to cooperate. But the intelligentsia, along with the mass of elementary school teachers, responded to the new government with a wave of strikes and hostility. This attitude, widespread among intellectuals of all kinds, was shared by yet another large literate group—the state officials.

The strikes, though of short duration, taught Bolsheviks a bitter and unexpected lesson: the professional segments of the population, however small their relative numbers, were strategically important. It was impossible to build and run a state and an economy without them. Even the army could not be built and run without ex-tsarist officers. Communism, intended as the creation of the liberated popular masses and a revolutionary party, had to be constructed, as Lenin said, "with foreign hands." But restoring members of the previous ruling class to positions of privilege and power smacked of treason. Even if flanked by commissars, the presence of "bourgeois specialists" in the government, and especially in the army, was offensive to most party members and to many working people.

The new regime's policy of enlisting the services of experts tended to reinforce antibourgeois and antiintellectual feelings among the popular classes that supported the revolution. Uncontrolled, such attitudes could cause a reaction against the party, especially against many of its leaders, themselves intellectuals. Keeping an alien body in sensitive positions was a dangerous strategy that did not augur well for the smooth functioning of the new system. Distaste for the privileged bourgeois experts, expressed in "specialist baiting" (*spetseedstvo*), was widespread not only among the rank and file but also among activists in the middle and upper levels of the party and the state. A powerful "military opposition," for example, resented and fought bitterly against the employment of such experts in high places.

With the end of the Civil War, the situation became calmer, but nothing was simple as yet in this vexed domain. The expert, even if ready now to shed some or most of his previous hostility, remained at best skeptical and eager, in any case, to end his subservience to politically appointed superiors. Party bosses in commissariats and factories resented their own dependence on the "bourgeois," with his expertise and accompanying air of superiority. The regime defended the bourgeois experts but proclaimed that its aim was to produce, as soon as feasible, "its own" experts endowed with the right ideology and class origin.

But soon a new dimension entered—imperceptibly at the start, ever more visible later—into the complicated partnership. As long as revolution was the aim, the party's orientation toward the masses took precedence. This was true, as well, during the Civil War, when the moods, interests, and reactions of the masses were decisive for the outcome of the struggle. But as the task of ruling began to assume the first priority, the party's emphasis switched to "the cadres." This tendency was to blossom a decade later, but many militants or just attentive observers perceived the buds with increasing anxiety. To assuage such anxieties, the party argued, often quite sincerely, that there was no danger involved in cadres of popular extraction. As for the experts of alien origin, their expertise was being used without conceding any power to them. Such arguments sounded plausible as long as the experts were openly hostile, making clear that they remained on the job just because there was no other employer.

The situation began to change when, during the NEP, many specialists got used to and accepted the regime and even found more positive reasons for continuing to work for it. Their party bosses also learned to live and work with them, came to trust many of them, and defended them from detractors. During the NEP a partnership, and here and there even a co-rulership, began to emerge. This, though, was just a beginning. A status revolution would take place in the thirties and would then involve a larger sector than just those old specialists. Although this process would be marred by tragic setbacks, it would not be reversed. The co-rulership, in conditions of the dictatorship of those days, would turn out to be easier to preserve than the wholehearted loyalty of the popular masses—and that much could already be perceived by perspicacious observers during the NEP and even during the Civil War.[20]

It should become clear to the reader how many problems, lessons, and legacies were rooted in the party's relations with the professional classes that were trained in the tsarist period. Out of this maze emerged a certain "Bolshevik art of governing" that the leaders presented often, especially in the 1930s, as the quintessential wisdom for governing and motivating cadres. When charging people to do what was asked of them they were to be told, "If you do not know how, we will teach you; if you refuse, we will force you." This prescription seems to have emerged during the Civil War. The first part of the slogan applied to those who were not professionally prepared for the jobs to which they were being promoted. It sounded paternalistic and was certainly a mass phenomenon in those years. The other half of the slogan was applied to those who did not wish to serve, notably the professionals of the previous regime. The term "art" implied some fine balancing between persuasion and coercion, but in fact the whole prescription was sternly dictatorial. The fact that so many experts helped build the Soviet system was not the result of coercion alone. A relaxed interpretation of the "art" was possible, but in the absence of clear rules for restraint, the ingredient of force had ominous implications. The force aspect prevailed during the Civil War, subsided during the NEP, and prevailed again, full blast, under Stalin. Yet, during the Great Purges, the "art" was applied much more leniently to the "bourgeois" intelligentsia than to the huge numbers of newly created cadres of immaculate social origin and ideology. This is one of the enigmas of Stalinism.

The Party

It is time to turn our attention to the ruling party—an agency without precedent in the history of political systems before 1917. The opponents of the regime during the Civil War did not have at their disposal any equivalent to it.

The party certainly was a versatile agency. It helped produce a central and local government, raised and organized an army, sustained the fighting military by an influx of dedicated party members, responded to mobilizations for all kind of tasks and, finally, effectively carried out clandestine activities behind enemy lines.

Not unexpectedly, a tendency appeared among party leaders, with the exception of Lenin, to glorify, later even to "mythologize," the party. This certainly did not testify to its continuing good health. A political party has to be submitted to all the stringencies of socio-historical and political analysis—and the tendency to turn the Bolshevik Party into some sort of superhistorical tool hindered analysis from early in the party's development. We know that the party went through rough times and acted in ever more complicated and changing situations. The impression given by Soviet and many Western presentations of an immutable "essence" called "the Communist Party" has to be dispelled. First, as we know, the party consisted of a network of clandestine committees, not more than 24,000 strong, at the beginning of 1917. During its short history, the number of its adherents had fluctuated widely. It was led, from abroad mostly, by its founder Lenin. There also was leadership inside Russia, but it was often decimated by arrests.

Was the party before 1917 really the disciplined and centralized squad of "professional revolutionaries" who did as told by the top leader? Would this "classical" Leninist model withstand the scrutiny of a good monograph? The party represented more than just professional revolutionaries. There were elections, conferences, congresses, debates. As is often the case, a closer look may change many preconceived ideas. It is clear, though, that the Bolshevik Party was an unusual organization. It was not bracing itself to take power directly because its leaders did not expect the coming revolution to be immediately socialist. At least they were not at all sure what its character would be.

Dramatic changes occurred in this party in 1917. It became at least a different genus of the same species, if not an entirely different species. It was now a legal organization operating in a multiparty system; it grew in size to perhaps more than 250,000 members and it operated as a democratic political party, under a strong authoritative leadership. Lenin was at the helm, but he was flanked at the apex by a group of leaders, below whom were influential networks of lower cadres who participated actively in policymaking. If his col-

The Legacy of the Civil War

leagues accepted Lenin's line, it was mostly after lively debates and having sounded out the moods and opinions of the rank and file. Factions existed and were fully acknowledged as the party's normal way of doing business. At this stage, under Lenin's proddings, the party was aiming at power, but, again, not without serious differences of opinion about the modalities of taking and exercising it.

Once in power, in conditions of a civil war, another, deep transformation took place: the party became militarized and highly centralized, in a state of almost permanent mobilization and disciplined action. Its cadres were moved around where necessary by a newly created department, the *uchraspred*. Elections to secretarial positions ended, not to reappear in any meaningful way until Gorbachev's recent efforts to reintroduce them. The center became all powerful, even if this development was often regretted as an unavoidable evil in the circumstances of war. The situation did, in fact, demand it. Still, factions and intraparty debates continued, and conferences and congresses were regularly convened.

During the Civil War there was no sign of any "religious" reverence toward Lenin in the party caucuses. His prestige was enormous, but criticisms of party policies and of Lenin personally were often sharp. This aspect of the party tradition was unextinguished. There was hardly a leader or activist of any standing who did not engage in a polemic or even a serious challenge to Lenin's policies at one time or another.

Another important factor for change in the party was the fluctuating membership and shifting social composition characteristic of those years. We learn from one good source that there were 350,000 members between October 1917 and mid-1918; this figure subsequently dropped to 150,000 and then began to climb again, reaching 600,000 in the spring of 1921.[21] Whatever the accuracy of such figures, one interesting phenomenon becomes obvious: the party entered a period of hectic growth at a time when mass support for the regime was at its lowest—in 1920 and 1921. Was this an aberration? Probably not.

By the end of the Civil War many would-be members and cadres perceived that the regime was here to stay. The growth of the party reflected the fact that no alternative was visible or possible anymore, despite the incredible furies of the uprisings. It also indicated the party's growing concern with the needs of ruling and running things. Nobody spoke seriously anymore about "every cook" being able to run the state. Hence the influx into the party, including numbers of careerists and crooks, who would soon be removed by a powerful purge of unsavory elements, if such a feat was at all possible.

Toward the spring of 1921, party statistics showed that 90 percent of the membership was now of Civil War vintage.[22] Prerevolutionary cadres, even those who joined in 1917, were drowned in a mass of new entrants, many of them active participants in military and security operations and, quite naturally, imbued with a military, if not militaristic, political culture. The new recruits carried this attitude into the party, where it persisted, in different forms, for decades.

After the 1921 purge that discarded, probably, one-third of the membership, a new, powerful influx occurred and during the next five years the membership reached the one million mark. The majority would now be made up of entrants who joined during NEP, bringing to the party their own political culture and culture *tout court*. In the wake of these massive changes in social composition the "old guard" was still at the top and running the show, but their numbers, stamina, even their health, were slackening. Could they assimilate, reeducate in their own image, the enormous mass of "crude" newcomers? If not, what would stop this mass from having a pervasive impact on the party and from transforming it in *its* own image?

There is evidence that many of "old guard" despaired, overwhelmed and besieged as they were by huge numbers of people whose culture and mentality differed from their own. The Civil War entrants had brought to the party a military culture, whereas the culture of the newer entrants reflected the values of the NEP society. At the same time, the top layer, continuing an earlier Bolshevik tradition, still fought among themselves using terms and arguments that the bulk of the rank and file did not understand. It can be said that the "old guard" came to constitute a separate party within the larger party being formed around them. Finally the new membership created a new model of a party run differently and politically and ideologically transformed.

The Peasant Revolution

The role of the peasantry in these events was multifaceted, and relations between them, the Reds, and the Whites were rich in momentous meanders and turns. Always a heavy factor in Russian history, the peasants' weight, if anything, increased considerably during the Civil War. For one thing, in 1917–18 they produced a genuine agrarian revolution of their own with its own aims and methods. In addition, whether they realized it or not, they became the underwriters of the Bolshevik revolution and the regime it engendered. Without their concurrence, the Bolshevik revolution would not have been possible. A good witness on this score was Trotskii the presumed antimuzhik accused of "underestimating the peasantry".[23] Yet the peasants not only made Bolshevik power possible but they also saddled themselves and the new regime with endless problems.

The support given by the peasants was unpredictable, extended here, withdrawn there, given back again here. Each time the peasants hesitated, as one Soviet author suggested, armies swept to and from Moscow, over the endless stretches of Russian territory.[24] The peasants' support was no more than a marriage of convenience related to the possession of land. This aspect of the revolution—the redistribution among themselves of privately owned land—

was irreversible in the eyes of the peasants. The Whites were blind to this crucial point and paid the price for it. Once they were defeated, the peasants turned against the Bolsheviks, to repay them, in turn, for their iniquities and errors.[25]

The threat of the landlords' returning was gone, but the Bolsheviks were enforcing the policy of *prodrazverstka*, forceful requisitions of grain from the peasants, with the help of a special "food army." The rationale for this policy is still debatable. On one hand, there were ideological motivations, namely, the elimination of the markets that had provided the underpinning for the policies of "War Communism." On the other hand, it cannot be denied that in the prevailing conditions, it was necessary for the regime to acquire some grain from the peasants in ways other than through market transactions. But from this combination of utopia and perceived necessity grew a policy that virtually swept clean the peasants' granaries.[26] The claim that there was no alternative is dubious. It is also reasonable to ask whether a change of strategy similar to the NEP should not have been tried earlier than in the spring of 1921. Some Soviet authors have, cautiously, raised this question themselves.[27]

Two other policies, less often described in the literature, were straightforward blunders that whipped up the ire of the peasants. First, a policy of collectivization proclaimed in 1919, was, at least initially, implemented with considerable zeal and coercive pressure. Although Lenin soon realized the trouble it was causing and tried to apply the brakes, the responsibility for this policy was his. Peasants hated the *kommuniia*, as they called it, as much as they hated the *prodrazverstka*, and it was doubly offensive that the collectivization policy was launched just at a time when the agrarian revolution had whetted their aspirations to become independent farmers on their own land. This was true for the peasants who were better off as well as the poorer ones. It is puzzling that such a policy could have been launched right after the disbanding of the *Kombedy* and the official adoption of a new pro–middle-peasant line.[28]

The collectivization policy failed and was abandoned, only to be replaced by another grand scheme, also of "war communist" inspiration, namely, the "statization" (*ogosudarstvlenie*) of agricultural production. The aim of this plan, of course, was to cope somehow with the desperate food situation.[29] According to this scheme, the peasant household and land were to be left alone but would be subject to a state plan—a sowing plan, to begin with—in which every household would receive its prescribed target of what, how much, even where and how to sow. A national network of "sowing committees" was decreed, to supervise the implementation of the whole scheme and to enforce the quotas. The work of the peasants, well in line with the ideology of the day, was declared to constitute "a state duty" (*gosudarstvennaia povinnost'*) and penalties were to be meted out for noncompliance.

Soviet authors today write about this episode with barely concealed embarrassment and point to the fact that this policy was no more than the last gasp of War Communism. NEP was, in fact, only a few months away. But for the peasants this plan was just the last drop in a bucketful of exactions—labor duties, grain requisitions, collectivization—and they erupted like a chain of volcanos in numerous uprisings and guerrilla movements. They fought against a force they now perceived as a foreign conqueror. Antonov-Ovseenko, in his report to Lenin about the causes of the dangerous uprising in the Tambov area, used the term "military-confiscatory raiders" to describe Soviet officials and the military as seen by the peasants. In this remarkable document Antonov-Ovseenko, himself one of those "raiders" (*naezdniki*), talks with great lucidity about the Soviet power as "military occupants." His opinion may have been instrumental in deepening the NEP policies that were being tried out, initially timidly, from March 1921.[30]

Shedding this kind of image was certainly on Lenin's mind when, two years later, he wrote, "Better Less But Better." His "testament" condemned "war communist" policies, past and future, and offered an alternative strategy. But other, earlier texts of Lenin's supported quite different policies. The "testament" would be entirely forgotten when, some years later, policies were launched that would surpass what "war communism" only adumbrated. This time the collectivization and statization of agriculture would be applied simultaneously.

But the problem is not in the ideological aspects of these precedents for Stalin's policies. It is more important to point out that the seeds of the future fateful turn were sown, to a large extent, by the agrarian revolution of 1918. By forcefully taking and redistributing the land of the *pomeshchiki*, the peasants initiated important changes in their own economy and society. Many poor peasants got land, while many of the richer lost not a little of theirs. Social stratification and differentiation in the countryside were narrowed considerably, and it is legitimate to speak about a certain "equalization" (*poravnenie*) among the peasants. It expressed itself in a new predominance of the middle peasants—the *seredniaki*—in rural society. The peasants' revolution transformed Russia into an ocean of small family farms, mostly oriented toward family consumption, with little left for marketing. Before this equalization there existed sectors of petty bourgeois producers and large-scale entrepreneurs in agriculture. The term "petite bourgeoisie," used in relation to most peasants, did not make much sense at this stage. A petty bourgeois by definition, worked for the market. This not being the case, the term did not apply to the peasants of the early NEP, in a situation where the landlords' estates and the larger-scale peasant producers—that is, any remnants of capitalism—were gone.

There was not too much capitalism in Russian agriculture even before the revolution; otherwise the events we are studying would not have happened. The Stolypin reforms would have been pointless, too, as there would have been no need to turn the countryside upside down in order to create a class of "sturdy producers." One can legitimately expect that debates on such points, never too far from the surface in the Soviet Union, will soon flare up in full limelight.

In the meantime it can be stated that the agrarian revolution wiped out almost all the effects of the Stolypin reforms. Most of the consolidated home-steads (*khutora*), Stolypin's main plank, were reintegrated into the villages except in the western region, which had not had much of a peasant commune (*obshchina*) in the first place. After the revolution, the (*obshchina*) itself—the traditional agrarian community that was the main target of the reforms—reemerged, on a larger scale than before, to become the prevailing form of land use in most of the country. Property rights within the household, which the Stolypin reform had declared the household elder's private property, re-verted to the former, ambiguous collective family ownership.

The Russian peasant now became not just more "traditional," more *muzhik*, than before. Because of the widespread ruin, agriculture and the peasantry now loomed larger in Russian society than ever before in modern times. Along with this "ruralization" of a rural country, the peasant even "ruralized" himself by retreating economically and culturally, at least for some time to come, into his age-old shell, characteristic of much more primitive times. The whole country, willy nilly, was drawn backward to a considerable extent by this retreat. The agrarian revolution in Russia—an event of great consequence and drama—turned out to be sterile, if not actually wasted, at least from the vantage point of its immediate results.[31]

Conclusion

This idea of "a wasted agrarian revolution," a subject for further thought, brings us to our conclusion. It is extremely important to keep in mind phe-nomena of social disintegration discussed above as we now try to pull the threads together. The sufferings endured by the peasant population did not lead it to the same state of decomposition that afflicted other social groups. Peasant society survived much better, but it re-created or reacquired traits that had been on the wane in the prerevolutionary period and that ran counter to the developmental path of the times. The post–Civil-War village hardened into a sturdy system that did not respond easily to change, in particular as long as the urban sectors were still recovering from their own misfortunes. What we described as the "archaization" of the rural world was paralleled by the de-struction or weakening of vulnerable modern sectors of society. We can there-fore speak of a more generalized "primitivization" of the whole social system.[32] The main legacy of the Civil War can be stated simply: When the new regime finally got the chance to lead the country toward its declared goals, the point of departure turned out to be more backward than it would have been in 1917, let alone 1914.[33]

As the peasantry loomed larger and urban society grew weaker, the other side of the legacy became clearer, too. The democratic components of the revolutionary regime that were initially important in this system—trade unions, workers' committees, soviets—were all weakened, atrophied, or eliminated. The bureaucratic and coercive features of the state became, on the contrary, much more potent and, finally, predominant. The democratic aspects of the party itself underwent a metamorphosis in the same direction. Although the militarization of the Civil War subsided, the party was well on its way toward becoming an administrative machine dominated by its top leaders and, increasingly, by its *apparaty*, with little or no say left for the rank and file.

The interaction of the two processes engendered by the Civil War—"archaization" and deep "statization"—created, in due course, most of the sequels that are part of the "legacy" we are trying to establish. The second of the two processes warrants some further remarks. The strain and decomposition caused by the ordeals of the Civil Way made the extensive use of administrative and coercive methods look almost natural, and, often, they were the only ones available. The fact that state agencies were staffed, to a large extent, by revolutionaries and people of popular origin helped mask the ever-deepening trend toward a pervasive authoritarianism: the revolutionary masses were being eased out as meaningful actors and partners in power, whereas bureaucrats and commissars of the new, still rudimentary state were becoming the mainstay of the system. More ominously, the coercive measures that were initially devised mainly for the bourgeoisie—labor conscription and forced labor—soon began to be applied to other groups and, finally, to the main backers of the regime themselves. The militarization drive was all consuming, whereas the shiftiness of social support, including that of the industrial workers, especially in the later stages of the war, instilled a profound anxiety in the system, which required an ever-present vigilance. And again, the decay of any autonomous social activity—the sources inform us[34]—along with the pressures of the prevailing methods of *udarnost'* (shock methods), mobilizational by definition, all worked in the same direction. The constant exactions of "state duties," the unceremonious shuffling of cadres by the *uchraspred*, were all features that had come to stay and later, even, to flourish.

The Civil War dealt a severe blow to the libertarian aspirations of the makers of the 1917 revolutions. By causing an enormous "geological" shift backward in society, it made the historical process change rails, as it were. It created parameters in the social system and political environment that narrowed severely the available choices and made some of the nastier prospects still ahead look more like an inevitable outcome than an alternative. Because of the destruction of so many previous cultural, political, and economic advances, the country and the new state became more open and vulnerable to some of the more archaic features of the Russian historico-political tradition and less open to the deployment of its forward-looking and progressive features.

The peasantry and the state, although shaped by the same circumstances, were, nevertheless, moving in different directions. They lived on different historical floors; that was yet another legacy for the future, portending clashes and crises still to come. The mentality of the rural mass, reared in the communal, relatively isolated, and mostly small villages, was deeply patriarchal, and the culture, naturally, was parochial. The state, however, was authoritarian. It was a dictatorship by its own definition, and its vistas and horizons were of a grand scale. The complicated crisscrossing of these traditions and cultures contributed to the mixture of attitudes and outlooks of the people entering the ruling party in great numbers and of the bureaucracies in party and state that were composed of such heterogenous elements. Authoritarianism was an unavoidable feature in these conditions—the question was, what type of authoritarianism was it going to be. What kind of socialism, if any, there would be was, obviously, a related question. It would be a backward socialism, said Bukharin sometime during the NEP.

In this context it may be appropriate to single out the readiness during the Civil War, among leaders and cadres alike, because of ideology and circumstances, to believe in the instant feasibility of socialism, even communism, despite the prevailing massive disruptions. The well-known caveats that a transitional period would be necessary, especially in a backward country, could be disregarded all too easily. It was understood by some, then and later, that without the creation of indispensable preconditions "instant communism" could not be attempted without massive coercion. In fact, as we know, such coercion was already as characteristic of War Communism as its other trait—extreme egalitarianism—or the aversion to markets and the preference for a "natural," planned economy. Lenin himself spread enough of the War Communist illusions, and maybe he came to believe in some of them himself. Trotskii, as is well known, stumbled on the War Communist identification of militarization with socialism, and many party cadres accepted the practices of the Civil War as the right policies leading directly to the final goal.[35]

All these developments have a direct bearing on our quest for the legacy of the Civil War. Notwithstanding the unpopularity, during the NEP, of terms like "War Communist methods" or "spirit," and the dying Lenin's warnings against such methods, one trait of the temporarily discarded policy proved durable, namely, the identification of statization with socialism—a longstanding Soviet ideological plank that has now begun to lose some of its potency, hesitantly, in the most recent *perestroika*. One of the upshots of this kind of legacy was excessive centralization of power and the stifling of the autonomous initiatives and actions that are indispensable for the healthy development of any modern system. For a time, such action became deeply suspect and was castigated as "spontaneity," the enemy, supposedly, of planning. Instead, there were to be endless agencies of control and others to control the controllers—all embodying the germs of stagnation, at least in the longer run, and in some walks of life, almost immediately.

The way the Civil War evolved and was won carried some concrete, albeit not necessarily openly acknowledged or even consciously perceived, lessons that supported, nevertheless, the future version of Stalinist despotism.

Any proponent of *Realpolitik*—and there were some among the party leaders—could not but have been impressed by the following facts about the recent past:

(1) That there is no class that can be fully trusted in conditions of adversity;

(2) That alliances, on the contrary, can be struck with social groups that

are not necessarily friendly and that support can be gained from such unreliable forces or even from past or potential foes;

(3) That stick-and-carrot policies can be applied successfully to whole social groups, even large ones;

(4) That when popular support is waning or absent, the state, if it wields its power ruthlessly enough, can hold out in relative isolation;

(5) That the condition for holding out in such circumstances is the absence of any real political alternative in the social system;

(6) That, finally, the bureaucracy, even when of alien social origin and ideologically inimical, can become a reliable and even massive social base—not to mention the more favorable situation that occurs when it is staffed by socially more reliable cadres. In this case, such cadres can offer, at least, a surrogate of social support.

All these situations actually did occur during the Civil War, and appropriate policies were implemented, although without much grounding in any experience. They became a legacy, even if dormant for a short period, but certainly remained available for future use.

In brief, the Civil War legated a whole tradition—a knot of problems to handle and some rather grim advice for handling them. It is fascinating to observe, in this context, the current efforts of reform in the Soviet Union under the leadership of Gorbachev. It does not take long to realize that what is being questioned and, slowly, discarded nowadays is not just Stalinism but also this older legacy, stemming from the "archaization cum statization" with which the Civil War saddled the Soviet system.

NOTES

1. Cf. David Footman, *Civil War in Russia* (London, 1961), pp. 85–135, for a description of the ineptitude and full dependence of the Samara government on the Czechoslovaks. There is enough evidence to confirm the statement that the White officers that commanded Samara's own forces were more a threat than a shield to the SRs.

2. Victor Shklovsky, *Sentimental Journey* (Ithaca, N.Y. 1970), p. 187.

3. References to memoirs by White officers are to the useful multivolume collection of excerpts and unabridged texts in S. A. Alekseev, comp., *Revoliutsiia i grazhdanskaia voina v opisaniiakh belogvardeitsev* (Moscow-Leningrad, 1925–27).

4. V. M. Krasnov, "Dobrovol'tsy na Severnom Kavkaze," *Arkhiv russkoi revoliutsii*, vol. 11, reprinted in N. M. Meshcheriakov, *Nachalo grazhdanskoi voiny* (Moscow, 1927), pp. 248–74.

5. Paul N. Miliukov, *Russia Today and Tomorrow* (London, 1922). These were lectures given in the United States soon after the Civil War. For examples of A. I. Denikin's assessments, see his "Kak nachalas' bor'ba s bol'shevikami . . . ," in *Nachalo grazhdanskoi voiny*, p. 31, and passim.

6. For an example of a partisan unit from Antonov-Ovseenko's Red army in the Ukraine that called themselves "Soviet" but that persecuted Communists, or, at best,

prevented them from organizing cells in the unit, see V. I. Nevskii, ed., *Za sem' let* (Leningrad, 1921). There were many partisan, even regular, military units of this kind.

7. V. I. Lenin, in *Deviataia konferentsiia VKP(b), sentiabr' 1920, protokoly* (Moscow, 1972), p. 12. He stated: "We defeated Kolchak and Denikin only . . . after their main, solid cadres were diluted in the mobilized mass of peasants."

8. V. P. Naumov, *Letopis' geroicheskoi bor'by. Sovetskaia istoriografiia grazhdanskoi voiny* (Moscow, 1972), p. 424. According to his data, Leningrad had 2.3 million inhabitants in 1917. In 1919 only 900,000 remained. Industrial workers, 418,700 strong in 1917, numbered only 87,900 in 1920.

The figures on the combined losses of inhabitants in both capitals are from V. Z. Drobizhev et al., *Izmeneniia sotsial'noi struktury sovetskogo obshchestva, 1917–1920* (Moscow, 1976), p. 62. Iu. A. Poliakov's *Sovetskaia strana posle okonchaniia grazhdanskoi voiny: territoriia i naselenie* (Moscow, 1986), which contains a mass of data relevant to our theme, was not available to me when writing this article.

9. I. A. Gladkov, ed., *Istoriia sotsialisticheskoi ekonomiki*, 7 vols. (Moscow, 1976–1981), vol. 1, *1917–1920 gg.* (Moscow, 1976), p. 354.

10. An overall statistical evaluation shows a decline, for 1919–20, to just 13.4 percent of the base year. See I. A. Gladkov ed., pp. 262–63. More revealing data can be found in *Istoriia Kommunisticheskoi Partii Sovetskogo Soiuza*, vol. 4, book 1 (Moscow, 1970), p. 10, where it is stated that in terms of industrial development "Russia was thrown back by whole decades." The so-called census industry produced five times less than in 1913. The output of iron was half of the 1862 output, and output of cotton fabrics stood at the level of 1857.

11. For the overall losses of Russia during the Civil War see V. Z. Drobizhev, p. 333.

12. V. Z. Drobizhev, p. 332, quotes an official Soviet publication that assessed the loss of population during the years 1913–19 at 5.1 million, excluding the unborn. But it is known that the following two years, 1920 and 1921, were particularly devastating for the population. Nevertheless, even 5.1 million looks too small. In his most recent book Iu. A. Poliakov assesses at about 13 million the direct loss of population through war, revolution, and civil war, while another 12 million were indirect losses (unborn) (Iu. A. Poliakov, *Sovetskaia strana posle okonchaniia grazhdanskoi voiny*, pp. 127–28).

13. L. M. Spirin, *Klassy i partii v grazhdanskoi voine* (Moscow, 1968), p. 347, maintains that between June and the end of December 1919, 775,000 deserters returned to the ranks of the Red Army. It is believable that a movement of this magnitude did result from a change of attitude among the peasants and helped clinch the victory. But the basis of this figure is not known.

The number of soldiers in the Red Army is often given as 5 million toward the end of military operations against the Whites. See G. V. Sharapov, ed., *Istoriia sovetskogo krest'ianstva*, vol. 1, 1917–1927 (Moscow, 1986), p. 81. But Iu. A. Poliakov in *Perekhod k Nepu i sovetskoe krest'ianstvo* (Moscow, 1967), quoting different sources, speaks of about 4 million Reds and up to 2 million Whites.

The social composition of the Red Army is given by G. V. Sharapov, ed., *Istoriia sovetskogo krestianstva*: peasants, 77 percent; workers, 14.8 percent; others, 8.2 percent. The commanders of all ranks were: peasant, 67 percent; intelligentsia, 20.7 percent; workers, 12 percent; 20 percent of all commanders were party members. It is obvious that the peasants constituted the majority of the lower ranks, especially of the NCOs. The higher ranks had a majority of ex-tsarist officers (see note 14).

It is highly significant that the units in the field, the actual fighters, had at the same time just 337,879 infantry (bayonets) and 72,374 cavalry (sabers). The figures are from N. N. Azovtsev, ed., *Istoriia grazhdanskoi voiny v SSSR, v dvukh tomakh*, vol. 2 (Moscow, 1986), p. 46. This book by military historians and the one edited by Sharapov contain a wealth of data that allow us to reconstitute the making and composition of the Red Army through consecutive mobilizations. N. N. Azovtsev also includes detailed figures of the field units facing each other on the different fronts during the main battles of the Civil War.

14. The number of ex-tsarist officers who volunteered or were, mostly, drafted into the Red Army reached 48,000; this is the figure most often cited. It is less well known that the number of NCOs from the tsarist army who fought with the Reds, also mostly drafted, reached the substantial figure of 200,000. This was, no doubt, an important factor leading to victory. See also note 13.

15. S. S. Khromov, ed., *Grazhdanskaia voina i inostrannaia interventsiia v SSSR: Entsiklopediia* (Moscow, 1983). For an example of rethinking Trotskii in conditions of *glasnost'*, see V. P. Danilov in "Kruglyi stol," *Voprosy istorii*, 1988, no. 9, pp. 5, 8. Danilov calls the expulsion of the Left from the party in 1928 "a tragic error."

16. By 1921 about 7 percent of all party members came from other parties. *Istoriia KPSS*, vol. 4, p. 85. During the NEP this percentage increased considerably.

17. A. Lunacharskii, *Revoliutsionnye siluety* (Kiev, 1924).

18. Rykov maintained that during the Civil War the countryside lost 30 percent of its able-bodied men; see *Vtoraia sessiia TsIK 4-go sozyva, stenograficheskii otchet* (Leningrad, 1925), p. 24. He did not specify in what way these losses occurred. A similar figures is quoted by N. Oganovskii, *Ekonomicheskoe obozrenie*, 12, p. 60. Many of them are temporarily absent.

19. Some of these events are described briefly by Jan M. Meijer, ed., *The Trotsky Papers, 1917–1922* (The Hague, 1964), 1:592–594. The Politburo decision is on pp. 590–92.

20. N. N. Azovtsev, ed., vol. 2, p. 397, shows that by mid-1919 the Peoples' Commissariats of the RSFSR alone employed 28,000 experienced staffers who had worked for the tsarist regime. In the factories 35 percent of the administrators and technicians were also from the same category.

21. L. M. Spirin, *Klassy i partii*, pp. 29–30. Somewhat different figures are in N. N. Azovtsev, vol. 1 (Moscow, 1986), p. 397, who shows just 4,000 peasants in the party at the beginning of 1918 and 12,000 at the end of the same year. From G. V. Sharapov, p. 176, we get the figure of 55,000 peasants in the party by January 1918 in 40 gubernias of European Russia, followed by a big increase toward the end of the year. Yet another source gives the figure of 16,700 peasant members in 1918, increasing to 165,000 in 1921. All this shows that exact figures were difficult to come by in those years and that, whatever they were, the number of peasants in the party was small. In addition, in 1921 there were 138,000 members classified as "officials" (*sluzhashchie*), only slightly less than the number of peasants.

For the global numbers of party membership we can turn to the computations of S. G. Strumilin based on the 1922 party census, quoted in *Rabochii klass v Oktiabr'skoi revoliutsii i na zashchite ee zavoevanii* (Moscow, 1984), p. 348: in 1918, 115,000; 1919, 251,000; 1920, 431,400; 1921, 585,600. A serious purge followed in 1921 that expelled almost one-third of the total, but during the next few years hundreds of thousands of new members were recruited.

22. *Istoriia KPSS*, vol. 4, no. 2, p. 70, states that 90 percent of the membership at the beginning of 1921 joined in 1918–20. Thus, it is plausible to hypothesize that the party was built anew in those years and from different human material.

23. L. Trotskii, *Istoriia russkoi revoliutsii*, vol. 1 (Berlin, 1931), p. 73: "Had the bourgeoisie solved the agrarian problem, had it been possible to solve it, the Russian proletariat could not have conquered power in 1917." And, "The agrarian problem constituted the subsoil of the revolution" (p. 429)—we do not know whether the pun was intended.

24. L. Kritsman, *Geroicheskii period russkoi revoliutsii* (Moscow, 1925), p. 226.

25. On the widespread and massive peasant uprisings and guerrilla movements, see

Iu. A. Poliakov, p. 194, and more details in Sharapov, pp. 214–17, and Azovtsev, 2:322–27.

26. Iu. A. Poliakov, *Oktiabr' i grazhdanskaia voiny* (Moscow, 1966), p. 367, quoting a letter to Lenin from a rural party member.

27. Iu. A. Poliakov, *Perekhod k Nepu*, pp. 198–99 and 235–36. Although Poliakov dismissed this possibility, he nevertheless raised it.

28. Ibid., pp. 73–74, stated: "the party's programmatic orientation on transition to collectivization was immediately perceived as an orientation on a broad, large-scale forced movement." A noted agrarian specialist and participant in the events of those years, P. Pershin, remarked in his article in *O zemle*, vyp. 1 (Moscow, 1921), pp. 73–74, that collectivization was launched (in the beginning of 1919) just when the peasants aspired predominantly to family farming on their own land. The authorities were blocking initiatives of peasants to move onto separate (*uchastkovye*) lots, and numerous troubles with the peasants followed. V. Osinskii, the chief architect of the new agricultural policy of "statization," stated unambiguously: "The countryside turned out to be indifferent toward socialism. It rejected the *kommuniia* categorically." The quote is from Osinskii's brochure published in 1920 and reproduced in O. S. Rozenblium, *Zemel'nyyi kodeks RSFSR*, 3rd ed. (Moscow, 1929), p. 96.

29. E. G. Gimpelson, *Voennyi kommunizm* (Moscow, 1973), pp. 84–85, describes how the policy of collectivization was rejected and replaced by the one of "statization" (*ogosudarstvlenie*). A contemporary author, I. A. Kirillov, *Ocherki zemleustroistva za tri goda revoliutsii* (Petrograd, 1922), p. 10, stated that it was the catastrophic situation in agriculture that caused the switch to a new policy toward the end of 1920. This policy, as explained by V. Osinskii in *Pravda*, Sept. 5, 1920, p. 2, consisted in essence in "a decisive, coercive intervention of the government" in running the agricultural sector.

For a good brief survey of Soviet agricultural policies during the Civil War see the speech by Sviderskii, *XI Vserossiiskii s"ezd sovetov, stenograficheskii otchet* (Moscow, 1924), pp. 17–19.

30. Antonov-Ovseenko's memorandum to Lenin is in Jan M. Meijer, ed., *The Trotsky Papers*, Vol. 2 (The Hague, 1971), pp. 494–95.

31. The problem needs a special treatment, but we can point to the opinion of a number of Bolsheviks for whom the agrarian revolution was a political success because it enabled the party to conquer power but also constituted a serious economic setback for the country. In fact, the 32 or 35 million *desiatins* the peasants received in the RSFSR at the expense of the *pomeshchiki* diminished the number of *bedniaki* (without eliminating them altogether) but did not raise sufficiently the average size of the farms, did not absorb the notorious overpopulation of the countryside, and did worsen considerably the supply of agricultural output to the markets.

For a contemporary evaluation see B. Knipovich, *O zemle*, vol. 1 (Moscow, 1921); also two leading Narkomzem officials, Latsis and Sviderskii, in *XI Vserossiiskii*, pp. 63, 80.

Seen from the peasants' side, there certainly were important advantages for many of them in reaching the status of independent *khoziaeva* and in some improvement in the economic situation of many of them, except for the richer ones. But for such a stormy and shattering revolution that was not followed by any serious advance in productivity and way of life, the achievement is problematic whereas the negative consequences were quite palpable, especially on the national scale.

32. I raised the problem briefly in my *The Making of the Soviet System* (New York, 1985). See the introduction and the last chapter. The whole subject still needs to be explored in greater depth.

33. The opinion that the countryside moved some centuries backward was expressed by the noted ethnographer Tan-Bogoraz, *Revoliutsiia v derevne* (Moscow-Leningrad,

1924), p. 7. During the Civil War he said: "The Russian village looked as if it was reliving again in the seventeenth and eighteenth centuries." It seemed to be sliding back "a century per year."

34. "Local life came to a full standstill (*sovershenno zamerla*)," wrote V. S. Nemchinov about the Civil War years in his *Izbrannye proizvedeniia*, vol. 3 (Moscow, 1967), p. 31. The quote is from a text written in 1926.

35. We do not know of any serious testimony that Lenin did *not* share some or most of War Communism's illusions. The quotes we are offering here do not exclude Lenin from the general assessment. War Communist policies found a deep response among cadres in the highest positions and this was the reason Lenin, once he went over to a different strategy, had to devote a lot of energy to prove to the party that he was not reneging on principles.

"Things moved at such speed," reminisced Pokrovskii in 1922, "that we imagined we really were near to Communism, a Communism being produced by our own means without awaiting the victory of a proletarian revolution in the West."

Lunacharskii, in the mid-twenties, concurred. It was necessary, he said, to adopt the War Communist road, but "we got used to it, we almost came to like it, and when the times demanded to reject it, we hesitated and stalled." Both quotes are in E. G. Gimpelson, *Voennyi kommunizm*, pp. 196 and 220, respectively. Lunacharskii's statement can be applied to the year 1920, not just to the first months of 1921.

GUIDE TO FURTHER READING

Although this volume focuses on the social history of the Civil War—"the history of society and not just of individuals, events, and ideas"—this guide is designed to introduce the reader to the full range of sources for this period. The following listing, therefore, includes political and military analyses as well as many works that fit comfortably under the rubric of social history. For convenience, the works listed below are arranged topically. Because a full bibliography of the Civil War would be immense, the following suggestions should be regarded as only an introduction to some of the more influential works. This guide emphasizes works available in English but also includes important Russian-language publications. Those wishing to pursue detailed study of a particular topic will find that the bibliographies and notes in the works listed below identify additional primary works and secondary sources. Readers will also find important and interesting work in periodicals, especially *Russian Review*, *Slavic Review*, and *Soviet Studies*. Those who read Russian should also consult the Soviet journals *Istoriia SSSR*, *Istoricheskie Zapiski*, and *Voprosy Istorii*.

The Revolutions of 1917

The essays in this volume demonstrate that it is neither possible nor appropriate to disassociate the events of 1917 from the Civil War that followed. The two most comprehensive general accounts of the revolutions and Civil War are William H. Chamberlin, *The Russian Revolution*, 2 vols. (New York, 1935); and E. H. Carr's more interpretive *The Bolshevik Revolution, 1917–1923*, 3 vols. (New York, 1951–53). Sheila Fitzpatrick's *The Russian Revolution, 1917–1932* (Oxford, 1984), a broad and stimulating interpretive essay, extends analysis through the 1920s.

The February Revolution is examined in detail in T. Hasegawa, *The February Revolution: Petrograd, 1917* (Seattle, 1981); Allan Wildman, *The End of the Russian Imperial Army* (Princeton, 1980); and E. N. Burdzhalov, *Russia's Second Revolution: The February 1917 Uprising in Petrograd*, trans. and ed.

Donald J. Raleigh (Bloomington, Ind., 1987). John L. H. Keep, *The Russian Revolution: A Study in Mass Mobilization* (New York, 1976), offers a broad history of the October Revolution, emphasizing political mobilization. On the roles of political parties in 1917, see Alexander Rabinowitch, *The Bolsheviks Come to Power: The Revolution of 1917 in Petrograd* (New York, 1976); William G. Rosenberg, *Liberals in the Russian Revolution: The Constitutional Democratic Party, 1917–1921* (Princeton, 1974); Ziva Galili, *The Menshevik Leaders in the Russian Revolution* (Princeton, 1989); Leopold H. Haimson, ed., *The Mensheviks: From the October Revolution to World War II* (Chicago, 1974); and Oliver Radkey's two studies of the Socialist Revolutionaries, *The Agrarian Foes of Bolshevism: The Promise and Default of the Russian Socialist Revolutionaries, February to October, 1917* (New York, 1958); and *The Sickle under the Hammer: The Russian Socialist Revolutionaries in the Early Months of Soviet Rule* (New York, 1963). Important studies of workers and the revolution include Diane Koenker, *Moscow Workers and the 1917 Revolution* (Princeton, 1981); Steven Smith, *Red Petrograd: Revolution in the Factories, 1917–1918* (Cambridge, 1983); and Rex A. Wade, *Red Guards and Workers' Militias in the Russian Revolution* (Stanford, 1984). A new study of labor activism in the revolutionary period is Diane P. Koenker and William G. Rosenberg, *Strikes and Revolution in Russia, 1917* (Princeton, 1989). Graeme Gill discusses peasants in 1917 with *Peasant and Government in the Russian Revolution* (London, 1979). An interesting Soviet work taking a social historical approach to the period is the collectively written *Izmeneniia sotsial'noi struktury sovetskogo obshchestva oktiabr' 1917–1920* (Moscow, 1976).

Civil War: Military History

Two competent surveys of the Civil War period emphasizing military, political, and diplomatic developments are Evan Mawdsley, *The Russian Civil War* (Boston, 1987), which contains an excellent bibliography; and John F. Bradley, *Civil War in Russia, 1917–1920* (London, 1975). The most comprehensive account of the Civil War's southern front is Peter Kenez's two-volume study, *Civil War in South Russia, 1918: The First Year of the Volunteer Army* and *Civil War in South Russia, 1919–1920: The Defeat of the Whites* (Berkeley, 1971 and 1977). Richard Luckett's *The White Generals: An Account of the White Movement and the Russian Civil War* (London, 1971) focuses on the White military forces.

The issue of Allied intervention and support for the Whites is examined in W. P. Coates and Z. Coates, *Armed Intervention in Russia, 1918–1922* (London, 1935); George Stewart, *The White Armies of Russia: A Chronicle of Counter-Revolution and Allied Intervention* (New York, 1933); and George A. Brinkley, *The Volunteer Army and Allied Intervention in South Russia, 1917–1921: A Study in the Politics and Diplomacy of the Russian Civil War* (Notre Dame, Ind., 1966). Michael J. Carley examines the activities of the

French in *Revolution and Intervention: The French Government and the Russian Civil War 1917–1919* (Montreal, 1983); and Lloyd C. Gardner focuses on British and American activities in *Safe for Democracy: The Anglo-American Response to Revolution, 1913–1923* (Oxford, 1984). The humanitarian aspect of America's role in the Civil War is chronicled in H. H. Fisher, *The Famine in Soviet Russia 1919–1923: The Operations of the American Relief Administration* (New York, 1927).

The definitive account of Kronstadt, which many consider the final battle of the Civil War, is Paul Avrich, *Kronstadt 1921* (New York, 1970). Israel Getzler traces Kronstadt's political development in *Kronstadt 1917–1921: The Fate of a Soviet Democracy* (Cambridge, 1983). The best Soviet account remains A. S. Pukhov, *Kronshtadtskii miatezh v 1921 g.* (Leningrad, 1931).

The writings of many White generals are available in translation. See, for example, A. I. Denikin, *The Russian Turmoil* and *The White Army* (London, 1930 and 1937); P. N. Wrangel, *The Memoirs of General Wrangel* (London, 1930); and Hoover War Library Publications, no. 10, *The Testimony of Kolchak and Other Siberian Materials* (Stanford, 1935). For the thoughts of leading Red commanders, see V. A. Antonov-Ovseenko, *Zapiski o grazhdanskoi voine*, 4 vols. (Moscow, 1924–33); and L. Trotsky, *The History of the Russian Revolution*, 3 vols. (New York, 1932–57). A recent and comprehensive Soviet-oriented bibliography of the Civil War is S. S. Khromov et al., eds., *Grazhdanskaia voina i voennaia interventsiia v SSSR: Entsiklopediia* (Moscow, 1983).

Civil War: Social and Demographic Impact

Sheila Fitzpatrick's "The Civil War as a Formative Experience," in Abbott Gleason, Peter Kenez, and Richard Stites, eds., *Bolshevik Culture: Experiment and Order in the Russian Revolution* (Bloomington, Ind., 1985), is a good introduction to the Civil War's possible generational impact. A number of informative and more detailed demographic studies are also available. The reader may wish to consult the work of two of the Soviet Union's leading demographers: S. G. Strumilin, especially *Izbranniye proizvedeniia* (Moscow, 1963); and B. Ts. Urlanis, especially *Rozhdaemost' i prodolzhitnost' zhizni v SSSR* (Moscow, 1963). Other important works include F. Lorimer, *Population of the Soviet Union* (Geneva, 1946); S. N. Prokopovich, *Narodnoe khoziaistvo SSSR* (New York, 1957); and A. E. Lossitskii's study of the famine, *Na putem vosstanovlennia selskogo-khoziaistva* (Moscow, 1925). The reader should be warned that because of the difficulty of compiling data in the war years, the figures in these works tend to vary from author to author.

Studies focusing on the working class in the Civil War years include David Mandel, *The Petrograd Workers and the Soviet Seizure of Power: From the July Days 1917 to July 1918* (London, 1984); Carmen Sirianni, *Workers' Control and Socialist Democracy: The Soviet Experience* (London, 1982); and

William G. Rosenberg, "Russian Labor and Bolshevik Power after October," *Slavic Review*, Summer 1985, 44, 2. Two important works by E. F. Gimpel'son, *Sovetskii rabochii klass, 1918–1920 gg.* (Moscow, 1974) and *Rabochii klass v upravlenii Sovetskim gosudarstvom: Noiabr' 1919–1920 gg.* (Moscow, 1982), focus on sociopolitical changes and the working class. See also *Izmenenia v chislennosti i sostave sovetskogo rabochego klassa* (Moscow, 1961), which contains a number of interesting articles; and E. Kabo's early work, *Pitanie russkogo rabochego do i posle voiny* (Moscow, 1926), which remains an important source. The effects of the revolution and Civil War on the Russian peasantry are examined in Dorothy Atkinson, *The End of the Russian Land Commune, 1905–1930* (Stanford, 1983); Graeme Gill, *Peasant and Government in the Russian Revolution*; and Teodor Shanin, *The Awkward Class: Political Sociology of Peasantry in a Developing Society; Russia 1910–1925* (Oxford, 1972). The peasant Green movement and the Anarchists are covered in Paul Avrich, ed. *The Anarchists in the Russian Revolution* (London, 1973); and Oliver Radkey, *The Unknown Civil War in Soviet Russia: A Study of the Green Movement in the Tambov Region 1920–1921* (Stanford, 1976). Additional materials on the Green Movement in Tambov are available in *Antonovshchina* (Tambov, 1923).

There are several excellent studies of women's issues that discuss the Civil War period. Richard Stites's *The Women's Liberation Movement in Russia: Feminism, Nihilism and Bolshevism, 1860–1930* (Princeton, 1978) is the standard work in the field and contains a good bibliography. The reader may also wish to examine two important works by Barbara Evans Clements: *Bolshevik Feminist: The Life of Alexandra Kollontai* (Bloomington, Ind., 1979) and "Working-Class and Peasant Women in the Russian Revolution, 1917–1923," *Signs*, 1982, 8, no. 2. The authoritative history of the family in Soviet Russia is Kent Geiger, *The Family in Soviet Russia* (Cambridge, Mass., 1968). Other article-length studies worth consulting include Beatrice Farnsworth, "Bolshevism, the Woman Question, and Alexandra Kollontai," *American Historical Review*, Summer 1976; and Anne Bobroff, "The Bolsheviks and Working Women, 1905–1920," *Soviet Studies*, October 1974, 26, 4. For an important study of population trends in Russia, see Ansley J. Coale, Barbara Anderson, and Erma Harm, *Human Fertility in Russia since the Nineteenth Century* (Princeton, 1979).

Nationalities and the Civil War

While there are a number of national histories for the peoples in and around the Soviet Union and a rapidly growing body of literature on Soviet nationality policies, the role of nationality in the social history of the Civil War remains little studied. Richard Pipe's *The Formation of the Soviet Union: Communism and Nationalism, 1917–1923* (New York, 1954) addresses the central political issues and contains a thorough bibliography. The complexities of the Ukrainian national movement, German invasion, and Bolshevik revolution are explored in Oleh S. Fedyshyn, *Germany's Drive to the East and the Ukrainian Revolution, 1917–1918* (New Brunswick, N.J., 1977). Arthur Adams's *Bolsheviks in the Ukraine: The Second Campaign, 1918–1919* (New Haven, 1963) emphasizes military matters in the Ukraine. Issues of nationalism and social revolution in the Caucasus are considered in Ronald G. Suny, *The Baku Commune, 1917–1918: Class and Nationality in the Russian Revolution* (Princeton, 1972), and Firuz Kazemzadeh, *The Struggle for Transcaucasia, 1917–1921* (New York, 1951).

Administration and State Building, 1917–1921

Western political histories of this period have tended to emphasize the formation of a one-party dictatorship. Leonard Schapiro's *The Origins of the Communist Autocracy: Political Opposition in the Soviet State: First Phase, 1917–1922* (Cambridge, Mass., 1955), stresses the increasingly repressive nature of the Bolshevik regime and remains one of the more forceful arguments for the "totalitarian" school of Soviet historiography. Peter Kenez's recent study of propaganda and methods of manipulation adds an important dimension to the theme of establishing dictatorial control: see *The Birth of the Propaganda State: Soviet Methods of Mass Mobilization, 1917–1929* (New York, 1985). For a consideration of the role of the political police, see George Leggett, *The Cheka: Lenin's Political Police* (Oxford, 1981). Vladimir Brovkin has studied the Mensheviks in *The Mensheviks after October: Socialist Opposition and the Rise of the Bolshevik Dictatorship* (Ithaca, N.Y., 1988).

In recent years administrative history has become a common method for exploring the formation of the Soviet state. An important English-language administrative history is T. H. Rigby, *Lenin's Government: Sovnarkom, 1917–1922* (Cambridge, 1979). Robert Service focuses on Party administration in the provinces in *The Bolshevik Party in Revolution: A Study in Organisational Change, 1917–1923* (London, 1979). For an understanding of the soviets' changing role, see Oskar Anweiler, *The Soviets: The Russian Workers, Peasants and Soldiers Councils, 1905–1921* (New York, 1974); and E. G. Gimpel'son, *Sovety v gody interventsii i grazhdanskoi voiny*, 2 vols. (Moscow, 1968). Other good Soviet works on this subject include M. P. Iroshnikov, *Sozdanie sovetskogo tsentral'nogo gosudarstvennogo apparata: Sovet narodnykh komissarov i narodnye komissariaty, oktiabr' 1917 g.–ianvar' 1918 g.* (Moscow-Leningrad, 1966); V. Z. Drobizhev and A. B. Medvedev, *Iz istorii Sovnarkhozov, 1917–1918 gg.* (Moscow, 1964); and Iu. K. Avdakov, *Organizatsionnokhoziaistvannaia deiatel'nost' VSNKh v pervye gody sovetskoi vlasti, 1917–1921 gg.* (Moscow, 1971).

Because Soviet state building and economic policy are so closely related, the reader may wish to consult Alec Nove's *An Economic History of the USSR* (London, 1969), especially chapter 3, for a concise but excellent treatment of

War Communism. The most comprehensive study of War Communism is found in Sylvana Malle, *The Economic Organization of War Communism, 1918–1921* (Cambridge, 1985). Other important economic histories of the period include Thomas F. Remington, *Building Socialism in Bolshevik Russia: Ideology and Industrial Organization, 1917–1921* (Pittsburgh, 1984); and E. F. Gimpel'son, *Voennyi kommunizm: Politika, praktika, ideologiia* (Moscow, 1973). For a discussion of forced labor, see James Bunyan, *The Origin of Forced Labor in the Soviet State, 1917–1921* (Baltimore, 1967).

Political Leaders, Intelligentsia, and Culture

Efforts of the prerevolutionary intelligentsia to interpret the Revolution and Civil War are presented in Jane Burbank, *Intelligentsia and Revolution: Russian Views of Bolshevism, 1917–1922* (New York, 1986). Much has been written on the lives and thought of leading Bolsheviks; among the more prominent studies are: Alfred G. Meyer, *Leninism* (Cambridge, Mass., 1957); Adam B. Ulam, *The Bolsheviks: The Intellectual and Political History of the Triumph of Communism in Russia* (New York, 1965); Robert C. Tucker, *Stalin as Revolutionary, 1879–1929* (New York, 1973); Isaac Deutscher, *The Prophet Armed: Trotsky 1879–1921* (New York, 1954), the first of a three-volume chronological biography; and Stephen F. Cohen, *Bukharin and the Bolshevik Revolution: A Political Biography, 1888–1938* (New York, 1973). The reader may also wish to consult the writings of the Bolshevik leaders themselves, many of which are available in translation. See, for example, V. I. Lenin, *Collected Works* (London, 1964–70), especially vols. 26–44; I. V. Stalin, *Works* (Moscow, 1953), especially vols. 4 and 6; L. D. Trotsky, *My Life: An Attempt at an Autobiography* (Harmondsworth, Eng., 1972); and Aleksandra Kollontai, *Selected Writings* (Westport, Conn., 1977).

To further develop an understanding of Civil War culture, the reader may wish to begin with an important biography: Sheila Fitzpatrick, *The Commisariat of Enlightenment* (Cambridge, 1970). For an excellent collection of essays covering many facets of cultural life in this period, see Abbott Gleason, Peter Kenez, and Richard Stites, eds., *Bolshevik Culture: Experiment and Order in the Russian Revolution* (Bloomington, Ind., 1985). Those interested in exploring the period's literature and the interaction between the state and the artistic community might best begin with one of these general surveys: Edward J. Brown, *Russian Literature since the Revolution* (New York, 1963), which has a good bibliography; Marc Slonim, *Soviet Russian Literature: Writers and Problems, 1917–1967*, rev. ed. (New York, 1967); Robert Maguire, *Red Virgin Soil: Soviet Literature in the 1920's* (Princeton, 1968); and Gleb Struve, *Russian Literature under Lenin and Stalin, 1917–1953* (Norman, Ok., 1971). Works of fiction vividly capturing the Civil War's upheaval are Mikhail Sholokhov, *And Quiet Flows the Don* (Harmondsworth, Eng., 1967); and Isaac Babel, *Collected Stories* (Harmondsworth, Eng., 1973). A thorough study of the Russian avant-gardists is available in Christina Lodder, *Russian Constructivism* (New Haven, 1983); and a survey of musical life in the Civil War years can be found in the relevant chapters of Boris Schwarz, *Music and Musical Life in Soviet Russia, 1917–1981*, 2d ed. (Bloomington, Ind., 1983). Good studies of theater and art in this period include K. Rudnitsky, *Meyerhold: The Director* (Ann Arbor, Mich., 1981), and Robert C. Williams, *Artists in Revolution* (Bloomington, Ind., 1977). The thoughts of many leading Bolsheviks on cultural matters are compiled in William G. Rosenberg, ed., *Bolshevik Visions: First Phase of the Cultural Revolution in Soviet Russia* (Ann Arbor, Mich., 1984). See also Maxim Gorky, *Untimely Thoughts: Essays on Revolution, Culture and the Bolsheviks*, trans. Herman Ermolaev (New York, 1968); and I. Ehrenburg, *First Years of the Revolution, 1918–1921* (London, 1962).

The Civil War's Legacy

Debates over the Civil War's impact on Soviet history may never be resolved, but the reader may wish to become familiar with some of the more thoughtful and thought-provoking works assessing the Civil War. See; Walter Laqueur, *The Fate of the Revolution: Interpretations of Soviet History* (London, 1967); Roger Pethybridge, *The Social Prelude to Stalinism* (London, 1974); Victor Serge, *Year One of the Russian Revolution*, trans. and ed. Peter Sedgwick (Chicago, 1972); E. H. Carr, *The October Revolution: Before and After* (New York, 1969); and Roy Medvedev, *The October Revolution*, trans. George Saunders (New York, 1979).

CONTRIBUTORS

Kendall E. Bailes was Professor of History at the University of California, Los Angeles, prior to his death in 1988. He is author of *Technology and Society under Lenin and Stalin: Origins of the Soviet Technical Intelligentsia, 1917–1941* and *Science and Russian Culture in an Age of Revolutions: V. I. Vernadsky and His Scientific School, 1865–1945*.

Victoria E. Bonnell is Associate Professor of Sociology at the University of California at Berkeley. She is the author of *Roots of Rebellion: Workers' Politics and Organizations in St. Petersburg and Moscow, 1900–1917* and *The Russian Worker: Life and Labor under the Tsarist Regime* and is currently completing a book entitled *Iconography of Power: Political Art in Soviet Russia, 1917–1953*.

Daniel R. Brower is Professor of History at the University of California, Davis. His publications include *Training the Nihilists: Education and Radicalism in Tsarist Russia*. He is completing a book entitled *The Russian City between Tradition and Modernity, 1850–1900*.

Barbara Evans Clements is Professor of History at the University of Akron, author of *Bolshevik Feminist: The Life of Aleksandra Kollontai* and coeditor of *Russia's Women: Accommodation, Resistance, Transformation*.

Sheila Fitzpatrick is Professor of History at the University of Texas, Austin. Among her publications are *Education and Social Mobility in the Soviet Union, 1921–1934* and *The Russian Revolution*. She is editor of *Cultural Revolution in Russia, 1928–1931*.

Leopold H. Haimson is Professor of History at Columbia University. He is author of *The Russian Marxists and the Origins of Bolshevism*, coauthor of *The Making of Three Russian Revolutionaries: Voices from the Menshevik Past*, and editor of *The Politics of Rural Russia, 1905–1914*.

Peter Kenez is Professor of History at the University of California, Santa Cruz. His publications include a two-volume work, *Civil War in South Russia*, and *The Birth of the Propaganda State: Soviet Methods of Mass Mobilization, 1917–1929*. He is completing a book entitled *Cinema and Soviet Society*.

Diane P. Koenker, Professor of History at the University of Illinois at Urbana-Champaign, is author of *Moscow Workers and the 1917 Revolution* and co-author of *Strikes and Revolution in Russia, 1917*.

Moshe Lewin is Professor of History at the University of Pennsylvania. He is author of *Russian Peasants and Soviet Power, Lenin's Last Struggle, Political*

Undercurrents in Soviet Economic Debates, The Making of the Soviet System, and, most recently, *The Gorbachev Phenomenon.*

Lynn Mally is Assistant Professor of History at the University of California, Irvine. She is author of *Culture of the Future: The Proletkult Movement in Revolutionary Russia.*

Mary McAuley is Fellow and Tutor in Politics at St. Hilda's College, Oxford. She is author of *Politics and the Soviet Union* and is currently completing a social and political study of Petrograd, 1917–1922.

James C. McClelland is Associate Professor of History at the University of Nebraska-Lincoln. He is author of *Autocrats and Academics: Education, Culture, and Society in Tsarist Russia* and is completing a study of higher education in revolutionary Russia.

Daniel T. Orlovsky is Professor of History at Southern Methodist University and is author of *The Limits of Reform: The Ministry of Internal Affairs in Imperial Russia, 1802–1881* and *Russia's Democratic Revolution.*

Alexander Rabinowitch is Professor of History and Dean for International Programs at Indiana University, Bloomington. He is author of *Prelude to Revolution: The Petrograd Bolsheviks and the July 1917 Uprising* and *The Bolsheviks Come to Power: The Revolution of 1917 in Petrograd* and is completing a study of Petrograd society and politics during the Civil War.

Thomas F. Remington is Associate Professor of Political Science at Emory University. Among his publications are *The Truth of Authority: Ideology and Communication in the Soviet Union, Politics and the Soviet System,* and *Building Socialism in Bolshevik Russia: Ideology and Industrial Organization, 1917–1921.*

William G. Rosenberg is Professor of History at the University of Michigan, author of *Liberals in the Russian Revolution: The Constitutional Democratic Party, 1919–1921,* and coauthor of *Transforming Russia and China: Revolutionary Struggle in the Twentieth Century* and *Strikes and Revolution in Russia, 1917.*

Ronald Grigor Suny is the Alex Manoogian Professor of Modern Armenian History at the University of Michigan. He is the author of *The Baku Commune, 1917–1918: Class and Nationality in the Russian Revolution, Armenia in the Twentieth Century,* and *The Making of the Georgian Nation,* and editor of *Transcaucasia, Nationalism, and Social Change.*

Allan K. Wildman is Professor of History at the Ohio State University and editor of the *Russian Review.* He is author of a two-volume work, *The End of the Russian Imperial Army.*

Reginald E. Zelnik is Professor of History at the University of California, Berkeley. His publications include *Labor and Society in Tsarist Russia* and numerous articles on Russian labor history. He is the translator and editor of *A Radical Worker in Tsarist Russia: The Autobiography of Semen Ivanovich Kanatchikov.*

INDEX

Abortion, legalization of, 116
Absenteeism, 359–60, 363; among railroad workers, 368, 369
Academic association: as part of higher school in Narkompros's plan, 253
Academic councils, 243–44, 248, 249, 257–58; in Narkompros's higher education reform plan, 253, 255–56; replacement draft for 1884 university charter, 246–47
Academic Group, 255, 256–58
Academics. *See* Professoriate
Academic Union, 246–47, 268
Academy of Agriculture, 257
Academy of Sciences, 251, 271, 293 n.13, 313–14; under the Bolsheviks, 270–71, 272–79, 281, 282, 283–85, 288, 289–91; opposition to October Revolution, 268, 269–70
Administrators, 17, 166
Admission requirements for higher education, 247, 256, 258; as issue in Narkompros's reform plans, 252, 253, 255, 256–57
Adult education, 245, 298, 299, 307
Age, 52, 90, 95, 188
Aged in Moscow, 91, 92
Agitation: use to reinforce proletarian solidarity, 360–61, 362
Agitdrama, 396
Agrarian production/agriculture, 60, 77, 107, 181, 355–56, 421 n.23; collectivization and statization of, 395, 414–15, 422 nn.28, 29
Agrarian reform. *See* Land reform
Agrarian revolution of 1917–18, 413–16, 422 n.31
Agronomists as village intelligentsia, 185–86
Aleksandrovskii market, 170
Alexander Nevskii subdistrict (Petrograd), 134, 154 n.9
Allotment, soldier's: as incentive to marry, 110
"All Power to the Soviets," 31, 330
All-Russian Association of Experimental Research, proposal for, 280
All-Russian Conference of Executives of RKI, First: Stalin's address to, 227
All-Russian Congress of Soviets of Peasants' Deputies, 186
All-Russian Council on Workers' Control, 213–14
All-Russian Factory Committee Congress, 228–29 n.10
All-Russian Industrial and Professional Census of 1918, 200–201
All-Russian Peasant Union, 186

All-Russian Union of Cultural-Educational Workers (*Vserabotpros*), 283
All-Russian Union of Teachers, 243, 268
"All-Russian Workers' Council," 215
Amosov (railroad vice-president), 353
Andreeva, Maria, 284
Anti-intellectualism, 13
Antisemitism, 13, 247, 248
Antonov (Bolshevik delegate), 180
Antonov-Ovseenko, V. A., 415, 419–20 n.6
Apartment buildings: management by residents, 96
ARA, 69, 72, 75
A ration categories, 165
Archaization and statization: as legacy of Civil War, 417–19
Aristocracy, 14, 112–13, 173
Arkomed, S. T. (Gevork Gharajian), 341
Armand, Inessa, 97, 105
Armenia, 326, 336, 340, 343, 344
Armenian People's Party, 329
Armenians: in Georgia, 326, 327, 328, 329, 344
Army. *See* Red Army; Soldiers; Tsarist army; White armies
Art courses: in Proletkult program, 303, 305
Artisanry, 76–77
Artists, 166, 239–42, 314–15; on Proletkult staff, 303, 304, 305, 307
Audits, 210, 211, 212, 217–20
Authoritarianism, 350–51, 368–69, 417–18
Autocracy. *See* Tsarist autocracy
Autonomy, 83, 248, 261–62, 312–13, 314; demanded by Proletkult, 296, 308; role in plans to reform higher education, 251, 252, 253; scientists' support for, 248, 269, 281–82; university, 237, 245, 250, 257, 313
Avaliani, S., 347 n.49
Avanesov, V., 224
Avant-garde art, 303, 305
Aver'ev, V. I., 208 n.67
Avrich, Paul, 59
Awkward Class, The (Shanin), 120 n.6, 121 n.25
Azerbaijan, 326, 336, 340, 343
Azovtsev, N. N., 420–21 n.13, 421 n.20

Badaev, A. E., 162, 163
Bagmen, 71, 169, 358
Bailes, Kenneth E., 16, 18, 239–40, 267–95, 313–14, 407
Bakeries, 160, 223

435